SHUNT
The story of James Hunt

The Myrtle Press
London

TOM RUBYTHON

SHUNT
The story of James Hunt

FOREWORD BY JODY SCHECKTER
PROLOGUE BY STIRLING MOSS

also by Tom Rubython

Life of O'Reilly
– the biography of Tony O'Reilly

The Rich 500
– the 500 Richest people in Britain

The Life of Senna
– the biography of Ayrton Senna

Dog Story – An Anthology
– the life and death of our best friends

For Harriet

First published in Great Britain in 2010
by The Myrtle Press

1 3 5 7 9 10 8 6 4 2

A CIP catalogue record for this book is available
from the British Library.

ISBN: 978-0-9565656-0-0

Typeset in Bembo by CBA Harlestone
Reproduction by Fresh Vision, London

Printed and bound in the UK by
CPI Clowes, Ellough, Beccles, Suffolk,
NR34 7TL, United Kingdom

The Myrtle Press
Kemp House
152-160 City Road
London
EC1V 2NX
Tel: 020 7566 1196

Contents

Contents

Contents

Contents

Appendices

If you can meet with Triumph and Disaster
And treat those two impostors just the same...
Or walk with Kings – nor lose the common touch
...Yours is the Earth and everything that's in it,
And – which is more – you'll be a Man, my son!

Rudyard Kipling (1865-1936),
Read on 29th September 1993 by
Innes Ireland (1930-1993)

ACKNOWLEDGMENTS

A book like this owes a great deal to many people.

ACKNOWLEDGMENTS

A book like this owes so many things to so many people. But I must first thank John Hogan for all his help in preparing this new account of James Hunt's life. John was a constant presence throughout the entire process, putting me right so to speak. And there is no one better qualified. Without John, there would have been no James Hunt; and it is just as fair to say that without John, this book wouldn't have happened either. Not only did he provide the basic framework for the book, he also verified and discredited all accounts that had come before. Right from the start, John was a wellspring of information as I went back to him time and time again to get the facts, check the facts and, finally, to verify the facts. John helped me blow away many of the myths surrounding James and urged me to retell the story as it really happened. John felt strongly that previous biographers had been misled by people who had over-exaggerated their roles in James' life. As ever, he was right.

Then there was Gerald Donaldson, who wrote the first significant biography of James Hunt, published shortly after James' death. I have worked closely with Gerald in the past, notably on *Formula 1 Magazine* and my biography of Ayrton Senna. Gerry gave me free rein to dive into his book, which was very kind of him.

Gerry's book was 'approved of' by the Hunt family and was thereby an 'authorised' biography, which mine clearly has not been. Such access made Gerry's book the greater, especially as a result of the illuminating conversations he must have had with James' father, Wallis, before he died in 2001. My book is all the better for access to Gerry's material. The critics' plaudits heaped upon Gerry's book at time of its publication were, I found, very well deserved.

My gratefulness also extends to Christopher Hilton, prolific as ever with his books *Portrait of a Champion* and *Memories* books on James. *Memories* was significant because so many of the people who knew James well have subsequently died, and Chris' book is the only historical record of what they thought about him. Chris is a deeply honourable man and Formula One's most prolific author, and therefore by default also its leading historian. My respect for him just grew and grew during the writing of this book. As it did for the late David Benson, the *Daily Express* motoring editor during the time James was racing. David is quite frankly one of the best car writers of all time and his writings on James and Niki Lauda in that era were remarkable for the depth of their content. 35 years later, David's posthumous contribution to this book should not be underestimated.

Here I must pay tribute also to James' parents, Wallis and Sue. Over time, I became so impressed with their parenting abilities and qualities as people that, quite late into the book, I decided to give them their own chapter. They are clearly outstanding people. Immediately upon speaking with James' 86-year-old mother, it became obvious to me where much of James' charm and sheer goodness came from. All of the Hunt children were exceedingly lucky to have been raised by such fine parents. But whether they all fully appreciate that, I am not sure.

Some of Hunt's family decided not to speak to me about James, and I respected that and worked round it. David Hunt was an exception but, unfortunately, he was a youngster when James was racing. David didn't really see much of James from when he retired to when he died, and naturally has limited recollection of key events. Freddie Hunt also helped me, for which I am grateful.

Inevitably, people's memories vary and are inaccurate when discussing events that took place as long ago as 40 years. Grahame White, part of the fabric of British motor sport, was absolutely delightful and didn't blink an eyelid when my dog Doris joined us for the interview, sitting beside me on the spare chair in front of his desk. Even though he upset Doris when he offered me tea and failed to bring her a cup, they clearly hit it off and, in his subsequent emails, he unfailingly asked me how Doris was.

I extend my thanks also to April Tod, the brilliant tennis journalist who also dabbles in Formula One. She spent an entire Saturday at Silverstone in the British Grand Prix paddock guiding me to people who knew James in his Formula Ford and Formula 3 days. There were some amusing moments when April decided to heavily censor and rewrite some of her own quotes that were to appear in the book. Having had some time to think about it, and perhaps out of sheer modesty, she turned the "long, hot, sweaty, bristled, sloppy, kiss on the lips" that James planted on her on the podium at Rouen in 1971 into a "quick kiss on both cheeks". But that, as everyone knows, was not James at all.

Peter Rieck was one of the few men who got the better of James Hunt over a girl. He wooed and won his wife, Taormina, away from James in 1970. As ever, James took it all in stride and the three of them became great friends. Peter told me two stories, neither of which were fit to be printed in this book, but I thank him anyway.

ACKNOWLEDGEMENTS

Andrew Frankl, the co-founder of *Car* magazine, gave me a brilliant account of what happened at the 1976 British Grand Prix at Brands Hatch from the point of view of the man in the grandstand. It was illuminating.

Philippe Gurdjian buttonholed me in the Silverstone paddock when he heard about my book. It turned out that he and James had a lot of history, all of the social kind, and he kindly recreated some events for me to tell in the book. Obviously, they all occurred many years ago and long before he was married. Thanks to Philippe, the high jinks at Monaco over 37 years ago are much more vividly retold.

Overhearing our conversation, Stirling Moss also began telling me his own stories of James painting Monte Carlo red. But as he began recalling the details, he also began limiting his *exposé,* realising that much of what had happened actually took place after he had married his lovely wife, Suzy – who was standing nearby, taking it all in her stride, and smiling at me knowingly. Suzy Moss remembered James with tremendous affection but wasn't afraid to tell me the negative sides to his character. This was also true of John Surtees, who had immense affection for James although he disliked his lack of respect for the conventions of life.

David Gray was brilliant in giving me a wholly different view of James' days in Formula One from the point of view of the hangers-on. He also took me behind the scenes of some of James' sponsorship deals. Andrew Marriott filled me in on the details of James' commercial deals and put me in touch with his former staff, who checked much of the minutiae that Andrew and David couldn't remember. David was also very helpful to me with all sorts of odd information that I could not have obtained elsewhere. I am deeply indebted to them all.

Of James' broadcasting days at the BBC, Mark Wilkin and Jonathan Martin could not have been more helpful. Mark endured a long interview, and the only question on which he demurred was when I asked him how much James earned. I was immensely grateful for his candour. Jonathan, who launched James' career in television, and without whom it definitely would not have happened, meticulously examined my narrative and made sure it was correct. Jonathan is a broadcasting legend and is responsible for the cult of former sports men and women becoming pundits; the whole of television sport today has reason to be grateful to him. Murray Walker, an immensely important personage in this story, told me the truth about the man he loved and hated, it seemed, in almost equal measure. We have Murray to thank for so much of the story after James Hunt finished racing. Mike Doodson also told me blow-by-blow, sometimes literally, what it was like to sit in the middle of James and Murray in the BBC commentary booth for 13 years.

John Watson was my principal guide to James' Formula One career. At one point during the writing of chapters 14 to 21, I was on the telephone to John every hour, on the hour, and he never once displayed any sign of being fed up with me. John was right there with James for virtually every lap he raced in Formula One, and, when I wanted it unvarnished, I went to John and he delivered. It is not often that someone in his position will take so much time to help an author with a story. Thank you, John, you are a true friend.

Jackie Stewart also chipped in from time to time with his observations. Jackie only raced against James in 1973 and had less to say, but I was nonetheless astonished at his absolute recall and candour. Of all the memories I tested for the writing of this book, Jackie's was the clearest.

Max Mosley was also very helpful about James' early days in Formula 3 and early Formula One. Max and James had the most unusual of relationships and were clearly very close despite their public differences in 1972. Most of Max's stories of that time have made it into the book. Max gave me the unvarnished truth about James, and it was clear he loved the man dearly.

Ian Phillips sat down with me for a long discussion about James and told me everything that went on in those days, leaving nothing to my imagination. James' off-track antics were truly remarkable and do not need any embellishment when told. Alan Henry confirmed the truth of every word Ian told me and added a few more 'truths.' Howden Ganley gave me some very useful insights into James' crossover from Formula Ford to Formula 3, which he personally witnessed and remembered. Bill Brown and Mike Costin, formerly of Cosworth, also furnished historical information and some enlightening stories about Bubbles Horsley and Lord Hesketh.

Peter Collins, the former Lotus team principal, was a passionate admirer of James Hunt. I rank Peter's opinion about all things motor racing incredibly highly, and when I got into difficulty, Peter Collins found out what I needed to know. Peter spent a lot of time with James discussing the deep intricacies of motor racing, and he provided me with a word-for-word account of many of those discussions, as much as he could remember.

Eddie Jordan also chipped in with a few stories about how much James disliked the idea of his brother David entering into motor racing. According to Eddie, James simply didn't think it safe enough and actively tried to sabotage

David's would-be career. Eddie and James ran a mutual appreciation society in the early nineties.

My thanks goes also to Nicky Samengo-Turner who got to the bottom of the Lloyds saga for me but, alas, whose information was too hot even for this book. Nevertheless, we made the point, and Nicky's story will be told at some time, in some place in the future; I feel sure.

Tony Dron's verbal pastiche of his Formula Ford days with James Hunt could have made a book in itself. Tony's detached office, set in his remarkable garden, is a treasure trove of motor racing history. I found I had to be very careful when asking Tony for any additional information because the answers that came back were so detailed I felt embarrassed about taking up so much of his time. Men like him are part of the fabric of motor racing in this country, and they should be treasured. It was easy to see why James liked him so much. Of all the people I met outside Hunt's family, Tony was the person most visibly affected by his friend's death.

Also affected was Patrick McNally. Discussing James with Paddy, I saw tears come into his eyes, making it clear how close both men had been to each other.

In the latter stages of my research, I wasn't surprised to learn that Professor Sid Watkins had also been a good friend to James and to his two boys, Freddie and Tom. Like attracts like, and Sid regaled me with his many stories about James – from the racetrack to the many fishing visits in Scotland at Sid's home.

Many photographers helped me with photos for the book and I hope I have credited them correctly. The process was watched over by Sophia Doe, my picture editor. Keith Sutton and his team at Sutton images were a staple. The late David Phipps, whose photographs now reside in Keith's archive, was responsible for many of the images in this book. David was a man of the seventies, and his presence was sorely missed in the writing of this book. Rainer Schlegelmilch, an artist with the camera, is undoubtedly Formula One's top photographer and has been for four decades. Peter Nygaard is Scandanavia's top sports photographer and helped me a great deal in going through his library, as did Ted Walker of Ferret Photography. Ted's archive is unique in going far back into British club racing in the sixties and seventies. It is thanks to Ted that a photograph of James in his earliest racing car, the gold-coloured Mini, is being seen for the first time ever. Also thanks to James' mother, Sue, who kindly said I could use a few early photos of her son. And lastly, a big acknowledgement to the picture desks of the *Daily Mirror*, the Press Association and the *Daily Mail*, searches of which threw up some very entertaining images – many of which have never before been published.

There are many racing statistics in this book, both in the narrative and the appendices. David Hayhoe did the brunt of the work, and David is now the first port of call for Formula One authors needing to verify their stats. He also pursues the task of resolutely poring over the text to make sure it matches the information in his tables. David was also immensely helpful, especially in digging into the very earliest days of James' career. David runs the Grand Prix Data Book, which specialises in this sort of thing, and was invaluable in helping us get the stats as accurate as they could be.

I can't finish here without thanking my own staff. In the end, there were nearly a dozen of us working on this book as we moved closer to the deadline. Special thanks must go to Carly, for when there were just the two of us in the office. My gratitude extends also to David Peett and Mary Hynes who sold the book to the 2,000 bookshops of Britain and beyond, and to Ania Grzesik who designed it. Kiran Toor, our chief sub editor, knew little about motor racing when we started but quickly became captivated by the subject matter. She ensured that the motor racing chapters were accessible. Kiran is quietly dedicated to her job and, in the end, had read each chapter at least five times.

I can't end without thanking John Blunsden, easily Britain's most experienced motor racing publisher. Whenever I had a sticky problem to solve, John was there to unstick it.

Lastly, a huge thank you to Harry Boggis-Rolfe, our libel reader. Harry, before he retired, was a top libel barrister. In the past, he has accompanied this author many times to Court 13 at the High Court in The Strand in London – thankfully always on the winning side. Harry has an understated but very effective style, and was invaluable in ensuring that this book was libel proof but still got its message through about its wonderful subject.

Also to our dedicated team of printers in Beccles, Suffolk: Ian Foyster, David Brown and Jo Buck did not bat an eyelid when, on the eve of printing, I rang to tell them the book was no longer 650 pages, but 800.

But, above all, my most sincere thanks and deepest gratitude is to James Hunt, whom I had the privilege of meeting only once at a dusty Brands Hatch paddock in 1970. James had an extraordinary wild side and a personality that was immune to embarrassment, and it allowed him to do

ACKNOWLEDGEMENTS

what other humans wouldn't even contemplate. But scratch even a few millimetres below the surface and you expose a very decent man. It has been impossible to write this book without forming a deep bond with James even though he has been dead for 17 years. He was a great human being who, despite his unruly behaviour, brought much joy to the world. Thank you, Wallis and Sue, for that.

Finally, a huge thanks to the people who spoke to me anonymously. I was desperate for information and many of you came through with it. I'm only sorry I can't thank you by name.

The efforts of the people involved in this book were unstinting and I thank you all, although the words that follow – and any errors or omissions – are naturally my responsibility alone.

Tom Rubython
Castle Ashby
Northamptonshire
12th September 2010

PROLOGUE

A very complete sort of person
by Sir Stirling Moss

J ames Hunt was a truly unique personality, and, as Bernie Ecclestone once
said, he had "more facets than a diamond." He was a total non-conformist
and a curious mix of wit, intelligence and unparalleled stubbornness. He
was always a very determined person and someone who stood firmly behind
his actions and beliefs, whether they were right or wrong. Whatever else
he may have been, James was not a hypocrite and he was never ever boring. He
was a very complete sort of person. On many occasions, he was his own
worst enemy: his complex personality, combined with his stubbornness,
often meant trouble. But he was so talented in so many ways. And it was
because of this talent and because he was such a lovely person and so hugely
loyal, that so many people turned out for his memorial service.

I never raced against James, but over the years he was a man that I grew to
know, to like, to trust and to respect; a man whose opinions and friendship
I valued greatly. Although it is now almost 18 years since I saw him last, I
can vividly remember all the facets of James' character: James with the big,
gorgeous German Shepherd; James the snooker player; James the mickey
taker; James the budgerigar and parrot guy; James the fabulous journalist; and
James the loving father. It was only at the end of his life that he really settled
down to being truly what he was: a lovely person who loved his family.

I believe that the contribution he made to our sport, through his television
commentating and his writing, was enormous. He brought to televised
motor racing a dimension that previously had not existed. His explanations
and pithy comments, often controversial, brought to the general public an
interest and understanding that raised the level of Formula One far above
that of mere spectacle. He turned moderately interested viewers into well-
informed enthusiasts. He brought in thousands of extra followers and fans to
our sport. He actually created something rather than following something.

That was the good side. For one of my generation, James' behaviour could
also be quite appalling. I was proud to be his friend, but at other times I
wished he never knew who I was. I was pretty appalled at the way he would

present himself at important events. I never condoned nor saw the funny side of it, but felt it was insulting – particularly, insulting and demeaning to our sport. So that, certainly, was one of his down sides. But somehow, because it was James, one could overlook it.

Undoubtedly, James was outrageous; he did what nobody else did back then, and it was entirely inappropriate. But even when he was misbehaving at his worst, you were only frightened for him, not of him. Underneath it all, he was a lovely person.

He used to come round to my house in Mayfair on his bicycle to sit with me and talk, and I remember him above all else as a great man, full of heart. He was just a lovely person to be with.

Sir Stirling Moss
Mayfair
London
22nd August 2010

PROLOGUE

This friend of mine
by Jody Scheckter

James Hunt was not the sort of racing driver you could ever forget. Despite the years since his premature death and the end of my own racing career thirty years ago, my memories of James are as vivid now as they were back then, a time when James was flat out moulding the legend that still lives on today.

The first time I ever heard his name was back in my fledgling years when James was racing F3, although I don't remember actually racing against him until we were both in Formula One. "He crashes a lot," I was told. They called him 'Hunt the Shunt' back then, but that was a nick-name that could apply to a lot of us in those early days.

James' unique style probably wouldn't have made it in today's strictly clinical approach to Grand Prix racing – not just his driving style, but his approach to life in general, a life in which he lived as hard off the track as he did on it.

Winning the world championship was important to James, not only as a confirmation of his stature as a racing driver and for the financial benefits it brought him, but also for the notoriety. It opened more doors to the high-living playboy life that he enjoyed as a Grand Prix star living in the then tax haven of Marbella in Spain.

For a time, we lived just down the road from each other and it was then that we first became friends, even though I was the poor neighbour compared to the luxurious surroundings in which James lived, amongst Europe's jet-set 'A' list.

Compared to James, I was just the simple South African "okey" from the country, but he worked hard after several races, including a particularly memorable German Grand Prix and United States Grand Prix, to show me that there was more to going out in the evening than simply having a good meal in one of my favourite restaurants, the way I usually did.

I returned the courtesy by showing him a few moves on the track, and he actually came up to me after one noteworthy battle at Paul Ricard to tell me that he had learned a great deal as I kept him behind me by the skin of my teeth. We had a respect for each other on and off the track, and when he was battling for the world championship at Watkins Glen, I had agreed not to block him and let him by a lot sooner than I could have done.

James was a formidable opponent on the track. I think he could have been even stronger had he not lived such a wild life off it. Racing frequently made him tense and testy, yet the pop star, barefoot hippie lifestyle out of the cockpit probably balanced his scales against the often deadly and more weighty, serious side of being a professional racing driver back in the 1970s.

I have dozens of memories of James, most of which probably didn't get past the libel lawyer of this book. Perhaps amongst those that best illustrate his special character is the time he arrived to speak at a very formal Japanese party in his jeans and a t-shirt, and no shoes. On another occasion, soon after our retirement, we were invited to a demonstration event in Dubai. When we arrived, one of the Princes was waiting at the foot of the stairs, but James was too drunk to get down the steps.

Being world champion, he could usually get away with such bad manners, but more to the point he was usually excused his mannerisms simply because he was James, somebody who lived his life to the full and by his own rules.

The more you knew James, the more you liked him. I never really knew why we got on so well together, as we were both very opposite in character. Perhaps that was the secret of our friendship.

There have been few drivers who have left such an impression on our sport as James did, not only as a driver and a person but also in retirement as a popular and often controversial TV co-commentator with Murray Walker until James' tragic death. He certainly would not fit the image of today's modern Formula One driver – but then he probably wouldn't have wanted to.

Jody Scheckter
Laverstoke Park
Hampshire
7th September 2010

SHUNT

SHUNT

PREFACE

A nonfiction book that reads like a novel

There are two most important decisions to be made when you decide to write a book, assuming you already have the subject sorted out. These are the title of the book and the dust jacket photo. Without these, a nonfiction book will not be truly successful, however well it is researched and written. When I was discussing titles for this book with my immediate colleagues, David, Kiran, Ania, Mary, Sophia, Rebecca and Chris, one name kept cropping up, and that was 'Shunt.' To that, we added: 'The Story of James Hunt' and felt very pleased with ourselves.

John Hogan and Max Mosley were the two people most helpful with my research and both were close friends of James. But I hit a snag when neither of them liked the title of the book. They both gave exactly the same reason, saying they found it slightly "derogatory." As our intention was that at least 80 per cent of the sales of the book would come from people purchasing it as gifts for their friends and family, a derogatory title was certainly not what we wanted.

I suppose I was most surprised by Max's reaction, as it was he who originally coined the nickname 'Hunt the Shunt' back in 1969. Then, as now, he had meant it in a humorous rather than a derogatory sense. And so did we. But how would others perceive it? Luckily, everybody liked the photograph we had chosen.

We produced mock up covers of half a dozen alternative names just in case – but none of them jingled in quite the same way. So, last March, I decided to leave it there and to ponder.

Later, when another of James' close friends, Jody Scheckter, wrote his foreword for this book and suggested that the nickname 'Shunt' could just as easily have been to himself as to James, I realised that it wasn't derogatory at all. That was just the way it was in the earliest, rough and tough world of Formula Ford and Formula 3.

So my apologies to John and Max, without whose help this book would not be half as good, but Jody's view won out in the end.

But in reality, as soon as we all sat down to the serious business of the desk research prior to the interviewing and writing process, I soon realised it was the only title to have and, when used in reference to James, was not derogatory at all. In fact, bizarrely, his crashing or 'shunting' is what eventually resulted in him getting into Formula One.

Lord Hesketh, the man who made all of James' success possible, almost confirms it: "I knew he had this tremendous reputation for crashing cars. The first race I saw him drive for me was at Silverstone in the wet. He actually took the lead, which we'd never done before, indeed we'd never even been near the front of the grid. But although he was leading, it was backwards – because he'd spun – he must have travelled about 40 yards in this way, and then he crashed into the pit wall right in front of me, which I wasn't very impressed by."

That was his first race for Lord Hesketh in 1972. At James' next and final Formula 3 foray at Brands Hatch, in the support race for the British Grand Prix, he didn't even make the race and ended up in mid air looping the loop before landing upside down on top of an Armco steel barrier. It's fair to say the Lord was even less impressed than he had been the first time. In truth, the second accident was in no way James' fault, but nevertheless he had an uncanny knack of involving himself even in other peoples' accidents. He defied death twice that weekend, later having a shunt in his road car that put him, his teammate and his girlfriend in hospital for a week.

In fact, we can easily count seven accidents where James Hunt should have been killed and wasn't. No other driver of the time defied such odds. The fact that he was able to die peacefully of natural causes shows just what a lottery Formula One racing really is when it comes to life and death. Frankly, when James died at the age of 45 in 1993, he really had no business being alive – no business at all.

When he had completed his debut, literally wrecking Lord Hesketh's Formula 3 team, the Lord promoted him to Formula 2. It was something James had been trying to achieve for five years and he had finally achieved it by shunting two cars in quick succession He was promoted to Formula One and left Formula 2 behind when he wrecked his Formula 2 car; a car which went back to John Surtees' factory for repairs and never emerged again until only recently.

The following season in 1973, in a new Surtees TS15, Hunt did three races and had two crashes. He failed to start at Pau after destroying the front end in qualifying. With that, the Lord had had enough and decided to enter Formula One.

Without all the Formula 3 crashes, Lord Hesketh would have undoubtedly stayed in that formula. Without the Formula Two crashes disabling the car, the Lord may never have entered Formula One seriously at all, and certainly not as early as 1973 – by which time it might have been too late for James.

So, as it turned out, James Hunt literally shunted his way into Formula One, more than living up to the moniker thrust upon him by Max Mosley all those years earlier.

And when he finally arrived at Formula One, Hunt suddenly cast off the moniker in the finest possible way. No longer was he an inveterate crasher of cars; he had well and truly lost his knack of getting in the way of other peoples' accidents.

But despite the title of this book, crashing race cars is not James Hunt's legacy. Because of the complicated nature of the man, his legacy is also inevitably a multi-faceted one. Multi-faceted is the best description I can give for James Hunt. Indeed, can there ever have been a more multi-faceted sportsman? I doubt it. Leaving aside his character and personality (such inadequate words when talking about James), he could easily have been a world class competitor at tennis, squash or golf had he decided that motor racing was not for him. Can there ever have been a man in the history of sport who was genuinely good enough to play at the top of such varied sports? Well if there was, I don't know of him.

James was also very good-looking, highly personable and immensely charming. He also possessed huge energy levels and extraordinary enthusiasm. He had every good character facet available to a human being. Oh, and don't forget he was also a highly intelligent and thoughtful man, equal to anyone in the brains department.

So that's the good side, but, as everyone knows, there was a bad side. If he hadn't also had the bad side it's impossible to estimate what he could have achieved in his life. Could he have been the first retired sportsman to move into politics and become Prime Minister (something Sebastian Coe tried and failed to do)? Yes, he could have. Without his bad side, he could have achieved anything he wanted to, so endowed was he with the natural talents of life.

But God chose to put some barriers in his path, and they were pretty substantial ones.

Hunt was a hard-drinking, serial-womanising, heavily-smoking man, who also liked taking recreational drugs in large quantities. Because he possessed these defects, he was never destined to achieve all that he could have. The defects stopped him in his tracks and made some 12 years of his life after retirement a pure misery. Although their removal meant that his last three years were happy beyond anything he could have expected.

In truth, I have to admit I did not believe Helen Dyson's account of how James proposed to her over the telephone the evening before he died. It seemed too much like a fairytale. But it was true and, by luck, it was confirmed to me by an unimpeachable third party. So it would seem that by the final night of his life, he had achieved true happiness – until a few hours later when he was struck down by the heart attack or whatever it was that killed him.

Fate intervened in Hunt's life, just as it had so many times before, but this time to end it. He could have no complaints about fate. The fates that had led him directly to John Hogan and Lord Hesketh were as equally kind as they were cruel to James Hunt.

I only met James once. At Brands Hatch in 1970 at the British Grand Prix, where he was competing in the supporting F3 race. I was 15 and still at school and he was 22 and an obscure race driver. He was leaning on a lamp post in the paddock with the inevitable cigarette in his hand. He was looking straight ahead but talking to someone on his left.

No one recognised him at that moment. He was in dirty light blue denims, naked from the waist up with no shoes on. Although he looked like a tramp, the look on his face said it all. He was in deep thought about something, so much so that he didn't notice me. I had my blue autograph book in hand, which Jochen Rindt had just signed, but I didn't even think of asking Hunt for his autograph – who wanted that? He was a driver of no particular distinction. So why was I standing there staring at him? I really can't answer that. Eventually, he said 'hello' to me and I mumbled something back to him.

I can only remember two other images from that weekend: Frank Williams leaning on his awning with his foot on the front tyre of his De Tomaso car, eating an apple; and Mario Andretti in his day-glo orange March 701, looking rather overawed but still fascinated by the strange world of Formula One. It would take Frank Williams another ten years to win his first championship, Andretti another eight, and Hunt just six.

This, then, is the story of James Hunt. As I wrote the last chapter, 'Life After James', I found tears were running down may face straight into the keyboard. It's that sort of book, and he was that sort of man.

PREFACE

I sold this work to the book trade on the basis that it was a non-fiction book that read like a novel. It truly is.

Hunt's story is that of an icon of the 1970s; he was without doubt Britain's most iconic sportsman of that age. It is a truly remarkable story of a most remarkable man – and it is what is says on the tin: the non-fiction book that reads like a novel.

CHAPTER 1

Death – the unexpected

"Dadda's gone to heaven."

As the morning of Friday 11th June 1993 dawned, all was well at the sprawling Wimbledon house, owned by the 1976 Formula One world champion James Hunt. The house, situated next to the All England Club in west London, was quiet by normal standards. Earlier in the week, Hunt had packed off his live-in girlfriend, Helen Dyson, to Lesbos in Greece, leaving him free to enjoy a week of bachelorhood with his friend Mike Dennett.

Dennett was a seemingly ever-present house guest in the Wimbledon house, especially when he was down on his luck – which appears to have been almost always. John Hogan explains it succinctly: "Eccentrics always have a permanent house guest."

Despite having been a loner in his youth, James Hunt now craved company and couldn't bear to be alone. With Helen away, Dennett was on hand. His two sons, Tom and Freddie, were also due to come and stay with him that weekend, which would mean fun and games for all.

Although he missed Helen, James was enjoying her absence. It was the first time in three years that they had been apart. He found he liked the taste of his brief freedom more than he cared to admit. He loved Helen, of course, but then he had loved a lot of women.

The backdrop for her trip to Greece had not been straightforward. In early 1993, they had decided they would try to start a family together. With motherhood apparently imminent, 28-year-old Helen decided to spend a week in Greece with her closest friend, Christina, who was also planning to start a family with her boyfriend. It was to be the two girls' last fling together, and they were determined to enjoy it. Hunt had agreed to pay for the holiday, which his rapidly improving finances could now afford.

So after Helen's return, Hunt was anticipating that she would soon become pregnant and yet another new chapter in his life would commence. As with all his major life decisions, however, Hunt was not entirely convinced this was what he truly wanted. After all, he already had Tom and Freddie. While he thought he wanted children with Helen, in the back of his mind was a nagging thought to the contrary. But in the few days in which she had already been away, he missed her deeply. And by Friday afternoon, he resolved to finally ask her to marry him.

But that weekend, Hunt also had some work to attend to. As it was a Grand Prix weekend, he was due to commentate on the Canadian Grand Prix with Murray Walker on Sunday. His responsibilities to the BBC were important to him. They paid him US$200,000 a year and he needed the money. Although he had recovered from his financial meltdown of two years prior, he still owed the banks UK£800,000.

He made his regular Friday afternoon phone call to Mark Wilkin, a sports producer at the BBC. Hunt always called on Friday afternoons to discuss the upcoming race and his syndicated newspaper column, as Wilkin remembers: "He used to write a column for the *Daily Telegraph* and he'd read his column out to me and say: 'What do you think of this? Is it alright? Can I say that? Is it okay?' I would always reply: 'Well, if it's your opinion James, then it's okay.'"

Wilkin had been a close friend ever since he became producer of the Grand Prix programme five years earlier. Coincidentally, they had both attended Wellington College, although not at the same time. Hunt always found it easy to confide in Wilkin, and that day he wanted to talk about more than just the column.

Wilkin was the first person he informed about his decision to marry Helen. Looking back, Wilkin now refers to it as the 'my life starts from here' conversation. As Wilkin recalls, Hunt told him that he had decided to propose to Helen: "James told me that everything was finalised. 'I'm going to ask Helen to marry me,' he said, 'I really feel that my life starts today and that a weight has been lifted from my shoulders. Everything has to go forward from here."' Wilkin was very pleased for his friend, having witnessed the extraordinarily tough times he had been through over the previous four years. He and Hunt agreed to meet for lunch the following Tuesday to discuss it properly.

When he put down the phone, Hunt couldn't have been happier, and the scene was set for a brilliant weekend. A few hours later, his sons arrived in Wimbledon just in time to go to bed. Together, they thoroughly enjoyed the bedtime rituals of baths, stories, prayers and lights-out. His ex-wife Sarah may have had limitations as a wife, but Hunt had never failed to acknowledge, even in the darkest days of their relationship, that she was an excellent mother and that he couldn't have wished for better for his boys.

When the boys were safely asleep, Hunt and Dennett began playing snooker into the early hours of Saturday morning. Snooker had recently become Hunt's major obsession and he played it at every opportunity. They went to bed at around 2am.

On Saturday, it was a day of fun and games with his boys, seven-year-old Tom and five-year-old Freddie. In the afternoon, they all settled in front of the television and watched the rugby match between the British Lions and the New Zealand All Blacks. That evening, after the boys were safely tucked in and Winston, Hunt's Jamaican houseman, was babysitting, he and Dennett attended a party at the house of their friend Chris Jones. The event was a reunion of old friends and had been arranged by Jones' wife, Suzy.

It was not a late night, and Hunt and Dennett returned to the house at around 11:30pm. According to those present, Hunt had not consumed any alcohol.

On the morning of Sunday 13th June, Hunt woke up and cooked the children's breakfast. As on most Sundays when his sons were in residence, they all then went down to Wimbledon Common to walk the dogs, Jackson and Muffy, and to feed the ducks in the pond.

After that, he made lunch for his sons and got himself ready for the trip into London to meet up with Murray Walker to do the commentary for the Canadian Grand Prix in Montreal. According to Mike Dennett, Hunt was in excellent spirits. The time away from Helen had been reinvigorating. For the first time, Hunt could see his life story unfolding in front of him, and he liked what he saw.

So it was with a very happy heart that he readied himself that Sunday afternoon. As usual, he was bare-chested but had decided to wear jeans

3

rather than shorts for the bicycle ride into London. He strapped a haversack to his back, and cycled the six miles to the BBC Television Centre. He left Wimbledon at around half past two and was at the studio an hour and a half later, in plenty of time for the start of the race at five o'clock. On the way, he stopped off at McDonald's, as he always did, to buy three Big Macs.

As he rode past the barriers at the front of the building and into the BBC Television Centre, Hunt waved to the gateman as he flew past. He stopped right in front of the main doors and leaned his bicycle on the wall, where it would be guarded by the BBC doorman until he returned a few hours later. No one else was allowed to park their bicycles by the front door, and there was a bicycle rack at the back of the building. As Wilkin remembers: "Nobody else ever parked a bicycle there, but that's just what James did."

Before he went inside, James pulled a dirty, old, crumpled, red polo shirt from his haversack and put it on. He went through the front doors and walked around the corridor of the circular building until he arrived at Studio 5, which was permanently occupied by BBC Sport.

Immediately, he sat down, put his brown McDonald's paper bag on the table and lit up a cigarette. The BBC floor manager came up to him and, as usual, said: "You can't smoke in here James," and then placed an ashtray down on the table in front of him.

Hunt had special rules at the BBC pertaining to his bicycle, his dog and his cigarettes.

Murray Walker, who was already at work, turned round to him and said: "I hope you're not going to talk to your public dressed like that."

"No, I'm not, Murray," he said, and changed into a fresh set of clothes.

Seeing that Hunt had arrived, Wilkin descended the spiral iron staircase leading to the gallery in Studio 5 and sat with him. He remembers: "James picked the gherkins out of the Big Macs and wolfed them all down in seconds."

There wasn't much time for chitchat as Hunt and Walker moved into the studio, where the race was being fed in live via satellite feed and projected onto a big screen in front of them. Mike Doodson was on the telephone from the press room in Montreal providing live information, and a lap chart was being kept in the studio.

Remarkably, Hunt and Walker rarely attended races outside Europe and tended to do all their commentary from within the studio. Long haul trips were sometimes funded by the host broadcasters, but the Canadian broadcaster, CBC, preferred to use retired drivers Jackie Stewart and Brett Lunger for the Montreal Grand Prix.

But providing a commentary from the studio that day proved to be just as good, and viewers were never made aware that they were in London instead of Montreal.

Up in the gallery sat Wilkin, who, with his eye on the lap chart, fed instructions through to Walker and Hunt on headphones. As always, Walker stood up for his commentary while Hunt sat down. The scene was very intense as the race started, with both men absolutely concentrating, with no distractions, exerting every sinew in their brains to bring the viewer the best possible commentary. As Wilkin says: "Murray described what happened and James interpreted it; James told you why, Murray told you what." After two hours of racing, Alain Prost's Williams-Renault had beaten Michael Schumacher's Benetton-Ford by 14 seconds, with Damon Hill's Williams-Renault third.

Both Hunt and Walker were mentally exhausted by the end. They turned round, looked at each other and smiled. They were very good at their job and right at the top of their form. Long gone were the days when Hunt didn't take the job seriously. They were now arguably the best sports commentary pair in the world, and Mark Wilkin knew it.

When the race was finished, Walker moved on to record opening and closing sequences for the BBC2 highlights show later that evening. As Hunt changed back into his scruffy clothes, Wilkin descended the stairs to bid him farewell. As he recalls: "I can remember I was in the gallery, which is upstairs, and it's like an iron fire escape that comes down into the studio. I remember clearly walking down the stairs and James walking round the side. I shook his hand and said: 'See you next Tuesday' and that was it. I never saw him again."

By the time Hunt returned to Wimbledon, at around nine o'clock, Sarah had arrived to collect Tom and Freddie. It was getting late but the two had coffee and chatted. Hunt confided in his ex-wife that he was going to marry Helen. The relationship with Sarah was still close, and she told him she was delighted by the news. And she genuinely was. There were no recriminations; they had settled any differences long ago. As they said 'goodbye', Hunt cuddled his children for the last time and waved to them as they went down the road. Dennett recalled the mood to Hunt's biographer, Gerald Donaldson: "I can't remember James being as happy as he was that whole weekend. He was in such a good mood."

SHUNT

With the house quiet and the boys gone, Hunt and Dennett settled down to watch the highlights of the Canadian Grand Prix on television and, as always, they discussed the whys and wherefores of the commentary. After that, they resumed their snooker match and went to bed at around midnight. Hunt was physically and mentally exhausted from his exertions that day. Jackson and Muffy trundled up the stairs after him. They were all soon soundly asleep. There was no hint or sense of pending trouble.

Indeed, Monday could not have been a more normal day. Hunt's good mood continued and he was ecstatic with his decision finally to make an honest woman of Helen. He spent most of the day working on his syndicated post-race column, to appear in newspapers around the world, and he spoke throughout the day to his collaborator Gerald Donaldson, who was at his home in Toronto. Donaldson recalls: "We did the columns on the Monday. They were due on the Tuesday. We would compare notes, and he loved to gossip." Although an excellent verbal communicator, Hunt wasn't a natural writer, so he worked very hard to get the job done. But when they were finished, the columns were of a very high standard indeed. Donaldson concedes: "His columns were, dare I say, extraordinarily well written because he worked really hard on them, and, if he wanted, he could be as articulate in print as he was when he spoke."

As soon as the work was finished, James telephoned Helen Dyson, who was back in her hotel room in Lesbos. It was an extraordinary conversation, with him proposing to her over the telephone. In truth, he was only confirming what they had discussed often but had never finalised. Although Helen had been expecting a formal proposal, she had no idea of the timing and was ecstatic when he finally uttered the words: 'Will you marry me?' She recalls shrieking with joy. As she said later: "He proposed to me and I accepted. It was the last time I ever spoke to him."

With that decided, Hunt once again started up the snooker with Dennett, and other friends popped round to hear his good news. At around ten o'clock, the activity subsided and Hunt cooked spaghetti for his guests. Afterwards, he and Dennett resumed their match.

But suddenly, Hunt started to feel pains in his arms and chest. They were pains he had never before experienced but which are now easily recognisable as the classic early symptoms of a pending heart attack. Hunt was concerned enough to telephone Chris Jones to ask him what he thought. Jones told him it was probably indigestion and not to worry. Dennett agreed. And while

6

he was on the phone to Jones, the pain subsided, virtually confirming the diagnosis.

Hunt and Dennett resumed the match, but Hunt started to feel ill and, at around midnight, he said to Dennett: "I feel really shitty." Dennett recalls: "He sat down, sort of huffing and puffing." At that precise moment, they should have jumped into the car and gone to nearby Wimbledon hospital, but, instead, Dennett suggested they all go to bed. Hunt went off to the kitchen to make coffee, which he always drank before turning in. Dennett's bedroom was above the kitchen, and he could hear Hunt clattering around.

No one really knows what happened next, but it appears Hunt climbed the stairs to his bedroom and was about to get into bed when he suffered a heart attack and collapsed on the floor, unconscious.

Understandably, neither Hunt's family nor his friends wish to relive that night, but the following is what Mike Dennett told Gerald Donaldson 17 years ago: "In the morning, I got up very late, about 10:30am. When he had not come down to breakfast, I went up to wake him. I found him lying there on the floor by the side of his bed. He was in his dressing gown but he hadn't even got into bed. The dogs, Jackson and Muffy, were with him. I called an ambulance but it was too late. And then I started calling out to people. It was awful. Just awful." Straightaway, Dennett called Peter Hunt, who raced around to the house along with Chris Jones.

Murray Walker says: "They found him dead on the bed with the telephone in his hand. It was climbing the stairs that killed him; if you've got a pain in the chest, the first thing you should do is lie down."

After discovering the body, Dennett called an ambulance, which arrived within minutes. A doctor, who had followed, went through the standard procedure of trying to revive the inert body. But it was clearly hopeless, and James Hunt was dead at 45 years old. The ambulance took him away to hospital where he was pronounced dead on arrival, and they took his body to the mortuary. There was nothing suspicious about the death and it was clear that Hunt had died as he had been about to get into bed. The time of death was estimated at around 1:30am on the morning of Tuesday 15th June 1993.

At half past ten, Wilkin dialled Hunt's number at Wimbledon to confirm he was coming up for lunch at 12:30pm. Peter Hunt picked up the phone and Wilkin asked him why he was there. Peter said to him: "Listen I've got bad news. James has had a heart attack and he's dead." Wilkin put the phone down in total shock. A repeat of the Canadian highlights programme was due to be broadcast that afternoon and Wilkin's first thought was to stop it from going out. He now faced the difficult task of telling his boss, Jonathan Martin, the BBC's head of sport, what had happened. Martin had recruited Hunt to the BBC 13 years before and Wilkin knew he would be very upset.

Wilkin recalls: "Normally, you couldn't get in to see him and his secretary would usually stop me and say: 'I'll make an appointment, how about next Thursday?' But he was great friends with James."

Wilkin went straight up to Martin's office and, predictably, found his PA, Rosey Stern, in his way. Wilkin said to her: "I have to see Jonathan now," to which she replied: "You can't go in."

"I have to", he insisted.

"But you can't."

Martin was sitting around the table with seven other BBC execs in an important meeting, but Wilkin couldn't wait. He brushed past an astonished Stern, banged on the door and simultaneously knocked it open. He said to a surprised Martin: "Jonathan, I'm sorry. I've got some news I have to tell you right now." Martin took one look at Wilkin's face and followed him out of the room. Wilkin said simply: "James has died." Stern burst into tears and Martin stood in shock as Wilkin recounted to him what little details he knew. Martin authorised Wilkin to halt the broadcast of the repeat that afternoon and then went back into his office and told his colleagues he would have to reschedule the meeting. He didn't tell them why. With his office emptied, Martin sat behind his desk. He says: "It was an absolutely shattering shock as James had just put his life to rights."

Wilkin came back later and the two discussed what to do next. They quickly decided that ex driver and current pit lane pundit Jonathan Palmer was to be Hunt's replacement and that they would hire Tony Jardine to replace Palmer in the pit lane. Wilkin says that both he and Martin "felt really awful to be discussing their friend's replacement just a few hours after his death." Back at Hunt's mansion, Peter Hunt began the wrenching task of calling the people he thought should hear the news first. He had two particularly difficult calls to make: the first to his parents in Wiltshire and the second to Hunt's ex wife, Sarah, in Sussex. He tackled the call to his parents first – the most difficult of his life. Wallis and Sue Hunt couldn't believe what they were hearing and immediately made preparations to drive up to Wimbledon. The call to Sarah was almost as difficult. As she took in the news, she faced up to what she knew she had to do next. But first, she needed to gather her own thoughts.

One of the first non-family calls was to David Gray, the advertising executive, who had been close to Peter's brother since 1973. Gray remembers: "It was about 8:30 in the morning. I had just got out of the shower and I was just getting dressed at my house in Wandsworth. I answered the call on my mobile and I couldn't believe it. I think I was one of the first he called."

The calls continued. At around nine in the morning in Toronto, one o'clock in London, Gerald Donaldson answered the telephone in his kitchen and Peter told him what had happened. Donaldson recalls: "It was just very difficult to comprehend."

By then it was nearly the middle of the afternoon, and Peter Hunt and his friends gathered in Hunt's sitting room and discussed what to do. A press release was prepared to go out to the Press Association announcing his death.

When Ron Dennis heard the news at the McLaren factory, in Woking, he immediately rang Peter Hunt and offered the services of his private plane. Hunt snapped up the offer and asked him if he could send it to Lesbos to pick up Helen Dyson. Dennis readily agreed and ordered the jet to take off from Farnborough airport just as quickly as the pilots could be at the airport.

But Peter had not even spoken to Helen at that stage. When he called her, the hotel receptionist told him she was out for the day. When Helen finally returned that afternoon, the receptionist told her there had been a number of calls from London. Helen went to her room and called the house, and Peter finally spoke to her at around half past three in the afternoon. When he told her what had happened, she just broke down and couldn't speak through all the tears and the distress. Her friend Christina took the phone to speak to Peter and asked him what had happened. Peter told Christina that a plane was on the way and instructed her to get Helen to the airport as quickly as possible. By this time, Helen was in such shock that she could hardly move. The hotel manager came up to the room and made all the arrangements to get them to the airport. Meanwhile, a grief stricken Helen went out onto the hotel balcony and just stared out at the scene in front of her, not really comprehending what was happening.

With all phone calls attended to, Peter Hunt went outside to address the 50-odd journalists and TV crews who had gathered outside the house. He managed to keep his composure and said as few words as possible to satisfy them: "He had had no indication of any problems, no heart problems in the past, and we're all in shock, really, I am afraid." With that, he went back inside. By then, radio news bulletins were carrying the story of Hunt's death and, almost as soon as he had uttered the words, Peter heard his own voice on the radio repeating back to him what he had just said.

Meanwhile, as soon as Sarah Hunt put down the telephone, she knew she had to suspend any personal feelings for the sake of her children. She went up to her bedroom and quickly prepared herself to tell her sons that their father had died. She glanced down at her children playing in the garden and prepared herself for the most difficult moment of her life.

Leading her two sons out into the middle of the lawn, she sat them down. The father whom they had seen only two days before was now gone forever, and it was no easy truth to explain to a five- and a seven-year-old. With Freddie on her knee and Tom sitting on the grass, she said simply: "Dadda's gone to Heaven." Tom burst into tears, but the younger Freddie remained dry-eyed as he took in the news. Even now, Freddie recalls the precise moment: "I remember the exact time and place I learned of it."

When they realised what their mother was saying, they all cried, and Sarah then repeated to them what James had so often said: 'God is everywhere and everyone's spirit is part of God.' Tom Hunt assured his mother: "Well, his spirit will still be with us." Sarah later told Gerald Donaldson that she was grateful to have her two boys by which to remember her ex husband, and felt sorry for Helen Dyson who only had memories. But, at the time, she admits she was absolutely devastated in a way that perhaps an ex-wife has no right to be. In fact, friends and family who rushed over when they heard the news couldn't understand why she was so upset at the loss of her ex-husband. But, as she explained, she was grieving for her children: "It wasn't only my grief at losing him, it was the grief of my children losing their father."

Murray Walker was out doing some promotional work when he took a call from his wife, Elizabeth, who said to him: "Brace yourself, dear. I've got some very bad news." Walker recalls: "My first thought was for my mother, who was then 95. 'Oh God, is it mother?' 'No, it's James. He's died.' I said: 'James who?' and she said: 'James Hunt'. And human reaction can be quite illogical, as mine was then, as I said to her: 'But I was with him on Sunday night', as though being with him meant he couldn't be dead now."

Meanwhile, in Greece, Helen Dyson and her friend arrived at the airport and were flown to Farnborough aboard the plane belonging to Tag Aviation. There, Helen's brother was waiting for her. As she recalls: "My brother met me at the airport, poor thing, and I looked at him, wanting him to tell me it wasn't true; that it was all a ridiculous nightmare.'

They raced back to Wimbledon from Farnborough. She arrived at around nine o'clock and collapsed into Peter Hunt's arms as he helped her though the door. By then, Hunt's parents had also arrived and they sat in the sitting room with Helen's parents, Mike and Molly, trying to come to terms with the future. Witnessing so many familiar faces all distraught with similar feelings, Helen was overcome with grief. She knew his death was just fate, as she said later to *Daily Mail* reporter Mary Greene: "I feel fate works in funny ways. In all the time we'd been together, I'd never been away without James – until then. Maybe it was just meant to be like that, maybe I was being protected."

Professor Sid Watkins was in South Carolina, in the United States, with his wife Susan, and had just popped into a liquor store to buy a bottle of whisky when the news came over the car radio.

Watkins recalls: "We immediately telephoned our son Matthew, who was in Scotland. All the kids were very upset. They were extremely fond of James."

Tony Dron had been at the Black Bull, Moulton, a famous pub/restaurant in North Yorkshire, for the annual reunion of the Geordie Cresta Club. This involved a very long and splendid lunch for some 16 people, followed by a further session in a remote village pub some miles away – ostensibly to watch a cricket match. Few people had mobiles in those days but somehow his then wife, Karen, tracked him down to the village pub shortly after 5pm. As he recalls: "Somebody said there was a call for me, which seemed absurd as I was in the middle of nowhere, 250 miles from home and even I didn't know the name of the village I was in. When the landlord took me through to his family's private room in the back of his little pub and handed me the old-fashioned telephone, I was utterly baffled. When Karen told me the news, I thanked her and sat down. I didn't move for ages. Tears just ran down my face. I was completely shocked."

Gathered in Hunt's sitting room, his family resolved to hold the funeral as soon as possible. Peter Hunt and Chris Jones began making arrangements. As the evening news bulletins began, they all sat round the television set, many of them in tears, as both the BBC and ITN news led with the story of Hunt's death. By the late evening, bulletins appeared and it was still a big story, with John Humphrys on the BBC and Peter Sissons and Trevor McDonald on ITN telling the story of Hunt's life and death.

The following morning, Nigel Roebuck, the *Autosport* journalist, who had been away at the Grand Prix in Montreal, got a shock. Roebuck was devastated upon hearing the news and immediately set out to write Hunt's obituary for that week's *Autosport*.

He could not be bothered to listen to the phone messages that had built up after three weeks away in North America. As he recalls: "It was not until the next morning that I got around to playing back the messages on my answering machine. There were many, but the last one set me trembling: 'Nigel, J. Hunt speaking. Six twenty-five, Monday evening. Just calling for a gossip. If you're back tonight, give me a shout – failing that, tomorrow perhaps.'"

Roebuck broke down as he came to terms with the enormity of what had happened. He was not alone.

DEATH THE UNEXPECTED

SHUNT

CHAPTER 2

Earliest Life 1947 to 1955
A very precocious child

There might have been a clue that James Hunt would turn out to be a difficult character when he nearly knocked over his mother, Sue, whilst he was still in her womb. She recalls how one day, a few weeks before he was born, he kicked her so hard in the stomach that she feared for her balance and almost fell over. She remembers the incident vividly because, coincidentally, it was the very same day that India was granted its independence.

Needless to say, Sue Hunt was mightily relieved when James Simon Wallis Hunt finally came into the world a few weeks later, on Friday 29th August 1947. So too was his father, Wallis. Mrs Hunt told Gerald Donaldson, one of her son's biographers, her recollections of that moment: "He was an odd little fellow, a rebel right from the moment he was born."

He was born in a small house at Cheam, which was all the family could afford at the time, as Wallis had just come out of the army.

When James arrived, he became the second child in the Hunt family, born two years after his sister Sally. When he was followed by Peter, two years later, Sue thought that her family of three was complete. But James was to be the eldest son in what would become an oversized family, common for the times, ultimately consisting of four brothers and two sisters.

The Hunts eventually moved to a bigger house in nearby Sutton to accommodate the expanding family, and lived there happily for over ten years before finally moving to Belmont.

When Peter arrived, Sue Hunt had no plans to have any more children, even though she was still only 25 years old. But when the youngest was old enough to go off to boarding school at Westerleigh in 1955, she felt a big gap open up in her life. So, in 1958, ten years after the birth of her firstborn, she decided to have more children. By then in her mid thirties, Sue gave birth to her second lot of children, which arrived every two years to balance the first half perfectly with two more boys and a girl. Tim was born in 1958, David in 1960 and, finally, Georgina in 1962. And, with that, Sue's childbearing days were over, just prior to her fortieth birthday, and she settled down to integrate her two-part family together as a unit. She couldn't have been happier.

Large families were fashionable immediately after the Second World War and actively encouraged by Clement Attlee's Labour government to replenish all the good Britons lost. With their six children, Wallis and Sue Hunt had done their bit for the country, although they certainly hadn't ever voted for Attlee.

According to their mother, all of her six children were "active and independently minded and quickly developed strong personalities." But unquestionably, James was the most difficult of the six, as he cried continually. His mother remembers: "He screamed all night as a baby for no apparent reason, and he was a rebellious, unhappy child prone to tantrums."

He may have been a horrible child but he bristled with inquisitiveness and intelligence, and soon began to dominate his parents. Of the six young Hunts, he learned to talk the fastest and had by far the keenest intellect. His determination was also legendary; if he wanted something, there was no question he would eventually get it.

He was always a single-minded boy, with what has been described as a "relentless quest." His mother recalls: "If James wanted something, he'd have it. He'd grind away, figure out how to outflank you and seemed always to win out in the end." It's hard to believe that, at the time, she was talking about a four-year-old.

The young James felt some kind of inner compulsion to continually assert himself, and was obstinate and persistent in that aim. He often dominated his parents and would not accept normal discipline. As he became older, there were continuing battles against his parents' authority. Staggeringly, they admit to having lost many of those battles of will to their precocious son.

He developed a hugely competitive streak at a young age. It was this competitiveness that led to his persistence. At first, there were tearful tantrums. Then, as soon as he learned to talk, he used his growing vocabulary to grind away his parents' resolve.

When he set his heart on something, he was full of determination to get it – be it a banana or a new teddy bear. The more his parents resisted his demands, the more persistent he became. As Sue Hunt puts it: "His relentless quest to get what he wanted was like a steady drip, drip, drip, which eventually wore you down."

Assessing James' childhood, early biographer Christopher Hilton called him: "A difficult child; a loner who actively disliked not winning at anything he did." He was also very aggressive. At four years of age, he whacked his two-year-old brother, Peter, over the head with a shovel. Peter required hospital treatment and stitches. There were several other violent incidents with Peter.

According to Gerald Donaldson, both Sue and Wallis Hunt were concerned about the hyperactivity of their eldest son. At times, he was by all accounts simply "unmanageable."

His parents were brought up in the post Victorian era and were by no means permissive, nor were they naturally strict disciplinarians. But they worked hard at disciplining James, whom Donaldson refers to as their "peculiar and unruly son." Wallis Hunt said before he died: "[James] was against all authority, but authority felt it had to draw the line somewhere."

His mother often became frustrated by James' particular tendency, upon winning a battle, to reject straightaway whatever he had been battling for. But she had some respite: her eldest son may have been ultra competitive, but he was never vengeful. Vengefulness is a very common trait in competitive children, but James showed no sign of it.

As he grew older, he displayed the characteristics of a loner. And yet he didn't seem to enjoy his own company either. He always seemed troubled by one thing or another.

Despite all evidence to the contrary, his mother has no hesitation in describing him as an "exceptional child." His mother is a very remarkable woman and, although she may be criticised for failing to take her eldest son in hand, it is clear she gave her six children the best possible childhood. Although she provided a very loving home, Sue Hunt admits the family was never fully at ease with showing their feelings for each other. Confessing to Donaldson years later, she admitted to "unshared feelings", saying: "private emotions were seldom expressed." There was no lack of love and affection in the Hunt household, it was just that Wallis and Sue were not particularly demonstrative – it seemed to embarrass them.

Years later, amateur psychologists would cite this as a reason for Hunt's strange character.

Chris Witty, a former journalist and sponsorship agent, who often visited the family home in Belmont, says: "I didn't see a lot of – how can I put it? – tactile love there in that respect. It was the way families were brought up. And that's not a criticism; just the way it was."

This was also reflected in Hunt's relationship with his siblings. He was naturally closest to the siblings nearest him in age: Sally and Peter. But as James grew up, he matured and adopted a parental attitude towards the three younger ones.

As he grew older and as school beckoned, another problem loomed. He absolutely hated school. Both his parents were mystified when James treated the beginning of every school term, as they described it, as "a full-fledged catastrophe." There is no other way to say it than he simply loathed school, and the thought of returning to school after a blissful holiday repulsed him.

His first introduction to formal education came on his fifth birthday, when Sue enrolled him in nursery class. He attended the nursery section of Ambleside, a pre-prep school in Cheam. Sue had attended the school herself and Sally Hunt was also enrolled there.

Sue remembers James becoming very agitated when he arrived at the school gates. She recalls how, every morning, he would get dressed in his uniform and happily walk to school with her. But as soon as they arrived at the gates, he would start a tantrum. Many times, his sister had to be summoned from class to comfort him.

According to his mother, the young James detested the confinement for the day, hated the rules and the conformity. He was also uncomfortable with the other children, and carried on his defiance of authority in the classroom.

Thinking it might be the school itself that was troubling him, James' parents placed him in Northlace Prep School, in nearby Sutton. Northlace was less academic and more focused on sports. Even then, at such an early age, it was clear that God had endowed James Hunt with great talent in three areas: running, racket sports and driving. His lean physique had much to do with it. He matched his father Wallis, who was also highly athletic. In fact, his physique had been inherited from both his parents, both of whom were tall with hunched shoulders. From the age of six, he was constantly playing racquet sports. Such sports undoubtedly overdeveloped the muscles in his upper body, which became elongated and contorted. It was this ability to contort his body that would later, and repeatedly, save his life in a racing car, as he was able to thrust his body out of harm's way down into the chassis.

Somehow, he got through his two years at Northlace, by which time he was nearly eight and old enough to be sent away to boarding school for the first time.

SHUNT

CHAPTER 3

The perfect parents 1942
No greater love

Wallis Hunt was the eldest of four children, born to a headmaster in Sussex in 1923. His father had waited to start a family and was already 54 when his son was born. By the time Wallis went to Wellington College, at the age of 13, his father was 67. Wallis continued the long tradition of male Hunts attending Wellington College.

Wallis excelled at Wellington and was a very bright pupil, good with numbers. He was also good at sports. So it was no surprise when he won a scholarship to attend Jesus College, Oxford, in 1940. But that privilege was denied to him when the Second World War intervened, and, in 1941, at the age of 19, he joined the army instead, as a private soldier ready to fight for his country.

However, Wallis was quickly singled out as officer material and enrolled at Sandhurst in 1942. A year later, he was commissioned as a lieutenant into the 11th Hussars, an armoured car unit.

Then, shortly afterwards, romance intervened and Wallis met the woman who would become his wife and lifelong partner.

Wallis and Sue met on a blind date on 5th November 1942. He was 20 and she was 17. A mutual friend, doing some wartime matchmaking, had arranged for them to meet in London at exit five of Piccadilly underground rail station. It was tremendously exciting for both of them, and neither was disappointed when their eyes met for the first time by the polished brickwork of Piccadilly station.

Sue Hunt was a classic beauty of her age and already, at 17, irresistible to most men. She also possessed an unparalleled charm that immediately put Wallis at ease. Equally, he too was quite a catch: tall, blonde and very handsome. Within five minutes, it felt as though they had known each other all their lives. By all accounts, Wallis was startled by Sue's warmth and overwhelming charm. Equally, she couldn't quite believe her luck that a blind date could turn out to be such a handsome army officer, and a hussar at that. It was the start of a remarkable union, and an even more remarkable family would emerge from it.

Sue came from a well-to-do family and had lived in Surrey all her life. She held traditional views, admired consistency in a man and had a strong sense of history. She had been privately educated, and Wallis was effectively the first man she seriously dated. Feeling tremendously blessed to have met someone so perfect so quickly, her thoughts turned immediately to marriage.

On their second date, Wallis took Sue to the ballet – quite an experience in war-ravaged London. If it wasn't love at first sight, it was certainly love after that magical evening. For both of them, there was never to be anyone else again.

They became fixated by the fifth of the month: having met on the fifth, they became engaged on the fifth, and married on the fifth. It was precisely two months after they met, on 5th January 1943, that they announced their engagement. And three months after that, on the 5th April 1943, they were married – some five months after they had first set eyes on each other. From that moment on, anything significant in their lives they planned for the fifth of the month. It served them well for 57 years.

In normal circumstances, the courtship might not have progressed so quickly, but both of them knew the opportunity might not come again. Lieutenant Hunt was a front line officer who went into battle leading his troops. His chances of surviving the war were little better than 50-50. Sue knew that, and the couple lived their lives accordingly. Every time they said 'goodbye', both knew it might be for the last time.

So marriage was no bed of roses and, immediately after the ceremony, Wallis went back to his army post while Sue joined the wrens and worked as an electrical engineer maintaining aircraft radios.

Meanwhile, Wallis prepared for the invasion of France.

After the D-Day breakout in early July 1944, the allies rushed across France in a bid to end the war by Christmas. However, as the Germans eventually regrouped, aided by the discord between British commander General Montgomery and American General George Patton, the allies met fiercer resistance and became bogged down. The Germans fought hard for each and every inch of ground, as French villages along the path were turned into armed fortresses.

In August 1944, Wallis' armoured car unit was attacking just such an occupied French village. The village, which was surrounded and bristling with German howitzers, was in no mood to surrender quietly. General Rommel, who was in overall charge of the defence of France, had ordered every village commander to fight to the last man. Meanwhile, Montgomery was anxious to beat Patton to Berlin, and was in a hurry. Montgomery, with little regard for likely causalities, ordered his British forces to attack aggressively. And the result was predictable. The fierce attacks and equally fierce defence meant only one thing: very high casualties.

Lieutenant Hunt was leading the attack on the village when his armoured vehicle was hit by a shell fired from a German howitzer. It was a direct hit on the vehicle but, somehow, Wallis was thrown clear of the burning car, which was completely destroyed. The other two occupants were not so lucky and were killed outright.

That Wallis survived was a miracle; he had been blown out of a hole in the car caused by the blast. The German shell had literally opened up the vehicle and, as air had rushed in, he had been ejected. No one who was there could quite understand how he had survived.

As it was, he was critically injured and covered in shrapnel, which had pierced his body. Half of his hand was missing. But luckily, British army medics quickly found him and stemmed the blood loss. They immediately shipped him behind the lines to a field hospital, where the nursing care was second to none. The allies had taken the time to set up excellent supply lines after D-Day, and the field medical facilities were the best of their day. There was also an excellent system for shipping home the wounded. As an officer, Wallis was given priority and was quickly sent back to a military hospital in England. As soon as she learned what happened, Sue rushed to his side, thankful her husband was still alive.

After eight months, Wallis made a full recovery. During the period of convalescence, he saw Sue almost every day and they conceived their first child, Sally. He rejoined his regiment in 1945, just in time for the end of the war. But his injuries meant he was assigned a headquarters desk job and appointed adjutant to the regiment's commander, General Robertson. He stayed with the general for the duration. His job was fascinating, as the British and American armies sought to make sense of post-war Germany. As the rebuilding process began, he was right in the thick of it and learned many lessons that were to serve him well in later life.

On one of his rare leaves, he and Sue were told she was expecting again. And James was born in a Sutton nursing home on 29th August 1947.

After he was de-mobbed at the end of 1947, Wallis joined an import-export trading company and worked in both South and North America for more than 20 years. Just as she had been during the war, Sue was often left alone with their growing family, but Wallis' job paid extremely well and some of his income was tax free due to his time out of the country. Wallis was determined that his children had the best education that money could buy. For his four boys, that meant enrolment at Wellington College. At one point, Wallis spent almost two-thirds of his income on school fees. But it was his mission in life, and nothing had a greater priority.

When his eldest son turned 15, and with his family extended to six children, Wallis purchased the main family home in Belmont for approximately UK£65,000. It was a grand, sprawling house, standing in an acre of ground in the most affluent area of Surrey and adjacent to a golf course. Built in the post-Victorian era, it was approached by its own private road. It had seven bedrooms, enough for each child to have their own, and enough garages for their sons to indulge their hobbies. The reception rooms were decorated by Sue in a restrained fashion, perfectly suited to the character of the house's new owners. Sue also took charge of the gardens, which in summer bloomed as perfectly as any in a neighbourhood full of proud gardeners. Tony Dron remembers it fondly: "It was just a big, busy house with everyone getting on with it and being happy. James' mother was a serious, decent woman with very high energy levels."

As soon as her youngest, Georgina, was no longer dependent on her, Sue Hunt threw herself into charity and voluntary work. With the strains of bringing up six young children suddenly behind her, she needed somewhere to channel her enormous energy. The community embraced her, and she embraced it. She was appointed a magistrate and did voluntary work in a local hospital. She also chaired a committee to look after unmarried mothers and took the post of a local school governor. She got involved with every community charity she could and suddenly found, at the age of 50, that she was enjoying life again. It was 20 years of nonstop activity.

When he turned 50, Wallis returned home and joined a stockbroking firm called Hedderwick, Stirling, Grumbar & Co. where he eventually rose through the ranks to become a partner and chairman. He became a respected member of the city of London community, joining Cripplegate and, in 1962, becoming a member of the Court of Common Council. He remained a member of the Court and crowned his service by becoming the Chief Commoner in 1975. He remained a member and most loyal supporter of the Club even after leaving London, and finally resigned due to ill health in 1999. During that period, he was also chairman of the City Police Committee, the Guildhall School of Music and Drama, the Association of British Orchestras and the London Oriana Choir.

The job entailed a commute into London every day and a return to Belmont every night. The routine allowed Sue to enjoy a regular family life with her husband for the first time since they were married.

Wallis also kept fit and ran long distances well into his early sixties. He particularly enjoyed running with his eldest son and, as Peter Hunt remembers: "He played sport into his fifties, running the first of three full marathons when he was 62." Given that one of his knees was locked into position, a legacy from his war wounds, it was an extraordinary achievement.

But in 1981, Wallis suffered a personal financial disaster. At Hedderwick, Stirling, Grumbar & Co., he had risen to partner and then chairman of the board of directors. But the firm was not a limited company; it was a partnership, which meant all the partners were liable for all debts – even down to the window cleaning bill. While that was the downside of the partnership, the upside was that they also shared all the profits. And every year, there were huge profits; profits that had enabled Wallis and Sue to buy their house in Belmont, which, if valued today, would be worth in the region of UK£3 million to UK£4 million.

The 1981 disaster was preceded by elation as Wallis was appointed chairman of the firm. His elevation coincided almost exactly with his downfall.

It was a fairly ordinary day at the office when stock exchange investigators suddenly descended on the firm and started removing files. Word quickly spread around the city about the raid.

When the news got out, a director from the National Westminster Bank rang Wallis and told him that the bank was cancelling the firm's overdraft facility and bouncing UK£3 million worth of cheques and payments going through the account that day.

It turned out that stock exchange investigators, examining an unrelated matter, had learned of a fraud perpetrated by an employee at the firm, but of which the partners were unaware. Once the bank had been alerted, it lost confidence in the firm and decided to take precipitative action. When the stock exchange learned of the bounced payments, the firm was 'hammered' and lost its seat on the exchange. It was all about confidence that suddenly had been lost.

Undoubtedly, the fact that everybody – from the stock exchange to the bank – panicked was what caused the rupture. It was the last ever stockbroking firm to be hammered by the stock exchange, and, afterwards, valuable lessons were learned on how to handle fraud by employees. Today, such situations are dealt with behind closed doors, and solutions are announced before the problem, enabling confidence to be maintained and troubled smaller firms almost always to be absorbed by larger firms. But there was no such understanding in those days.

There was nothing wrong with Hedderwick, it was a very well run organisation and certainly wasn't insolvent. But it relied on confidence to trade, and, when that went, it had to close its doors immediately. If it had been a limited company or a limited liability partnership (LLP), which didn't exist in those days, the partners would not have been liable. Wallis and his partners had no choice but to buckle down and sort out the situation and collect and settle debts. There was no question of calling in a receiver.

Suddenly, Wallis had no income and was getting demands for cash every day. It was a nightmare for the 58-year-old, at a period when he was thinking only of retirement. Undoubtedly, Wallis and Sue would have lost their house and been reduced to penury had not their eldest son come to the rescue. No one besides James and Wallis knew the details of the arrangement and, certainly, no one has ever spoken of it. However, those who were aware of the situation at the time say that James Hunt lent his father a sum not far from UK£500,000 to tide him over.

Barring his war injuries, it was the worst experience of Wallis Hunt's life and deeply humbling for a proud man like him to have to go to his son for money.

But he was made of sterner stuff than most, and he and his partners refused to give up. The inescapable fact was that the firm was solvent when it had been closed down. Wallis and his partners worked hard to rescue the firm and eventually to restore its solvency. It is believed that his son's loan was re-paid in full relatively quickly. Tony Dron is full of admiration for how Hunt helped his father: "No one knew, but I was vaguely aware that James was in a position to help out his father."

Peter Hunt remembers the recovery proudly: "Sadly, his career ended on a less than happy note when the stockbroking firm he was running was brought down, through no fault of his, by fraud. Typically, Wallis toughed it out and was instrumental in ensuring that all the creditors of the firm were paid in full."

But Wallis' heart had gone out of the stockbroking business, and he took up salaried work at an accountancy firm until he retired. Peter says: "Although he never complained, there is no question that this chapter of his life had a big impact on him. He did not work in the city again."

By the time he was 73 and Sue was turning 70, Wallis decided to retire and move to Wiltshire. In order to make a clean break, they decided to sell the family home in Belmont. Wallis' sense of timing proved to be brilliant; he sold his house in Belmont at the very top of the property market and bought in Wiltshire as the market was starting to decline. He was a much bigger fish in the smaller county of Wiltshire than he had been in Surrey, and quickly became one of that county's great and good.

In retirement, he served as governor of Wellington College and chaired the Old Wellingtonians Society and presided over the deanery of his church synod. He also worked tirelessly for charity.

Peter Hunt remembers: "Retirement is a bit of a misnomer because they both found umpteen things to keep themselves out of mischief."

In retirement, they made up for the years they had been apart and did everything together. Wallis quickly became involved with Clouds House, which was an addiction rehabilitation charity. Peter Hunt described it as "probably the most rewarding work he had ever done." Wallis worked closely with Nick Barton, the director of the charity. Sue was also not entirely inactive, serving as a church warden and organising the local meals-on-wheels service.

But there was also plenty of time for leisure, as Peter Hunt recalls: "Wallis sang in several choirs, developed new hobbies, such as bird watching and travelling to remote and exciting countries on what can only be described as 'intrepid holidays.'"

Eventually, Wallis had to slow down, and, after a long illness, he died in the spring of 2001. Wallis and Sue had been married for almost 58 years and had enjoyed every moment together. Sue had hoped he would hang on to celebrate their 58th wedding anniversary, but it was not to be.

He was 78 and dealt with his last illness with great forbearance. Peter Hunt says: "Wallis remained a rock to Sue and his children, grandchildren and great grandchildren until his death. He bore his last illness with remarkable but typical stoicism and strength, never complaining, and was always far more interested in other people than in his own problems."

Announcing his death in *The Times*, Sue Hunt described Wallis as "her best mate." That was surely true. In his eulogy at the memorial service, held at Wellington College, Peter said: "He was, quite simply, a bloody nice bloke and we all miss him terribly." Carolyn Chadwick and the Wellington Choir sang a Mozart anthem and some contemporary Wellingtonians played their trumpets in tribute. Afterwards, there was lunch in the Great School and the Hunts and their friends watched Wellington College 1st XV rugby team play Radley College. As Peter Hunt said: "Wallis would have loved to have been here to watch that."

Indeed, he would have.

THE PERFECT PARENTS

SHUNT

CHAPTER 4

Less than perfect schooldays 1955 to 1964

His heart was never in it

In 1955, James Hunt was sent to Westerleigh Prep School at Hastings, in Sussex. The object was that, five years later, he would pass his common entrance examination and get into Wellington College. Both Wallis and Sue knew it would not be easy. Although fiercely intelligent, James was no student.

Westerleigh was the start of a new tradition for the Hunts, and came about because its headmaster, James Wheeler, knew Wallis from when they had served together with the 11th Hussars in North Africa. Wheeler admired Wallis greatly, and called him "a tough and go-ahead man." He was delighted to welcome James to his school.

But convincing James to attend was a problem for his parents; boarding school was the last thing he wanted. In fact, he didn't want to go to school at all and it was a struggle to get him into the car for the hour and a half journey to Hastings. It was their first experience of the true reluctance of their eldest son to attend school. But once he was there, James appears to have made the best of it, although straightaway he began looking forward to the holidays.

Sue and Wallis were mystified by their son's lack of academic achievement, especially when all his brothers and sisters enjoyed their education and achieved excellent results. They didn't understand what made him so different.

His eccentricity also came to light for the first time when he took up knitting. He knitted a pair of bright green shorts for his younger brother Tim and some socks for his sister Sally. Wheeler told Hunt biographer Christopher Hilton that James actually enjoyed knitting: "He didn't mind in the slightest anyone making silly remarks about the knitting. That sort of thing didn't bother him at all." But he was not particularly gifted with the needles and suffice it to say that none of his garments were ever worn by their recipients; although years later, Tim Hunt swore he had worn his green pants with pride.

The knitting was perhaps a symbol of his rebellious streak and his way of telling his parents he didn't want to be at Westerleigh. He further demonstrated his disinterest by failing to befriend any of his schoolmates. A loner at school, Hunt made no lasting friends.

Useless in class, he threw all his energy into sport. He had incredible energy and tremendous stamina, which, combined with his competitive spirit, determination and tenacity, meant he dominated Westerleigh's sports days. If anyone was up against him in any sort of sporting endeavour, they were destined to lose. His sheer will to win was vastly different from the attitudes of fellow pupils. He was good at virtually every sport on the curriculum, and exceptionally good at any sport that demanded high levels of energy or good hand-eye coordination.

His tennis was easily early-round Wimbledon standard. He could also have been a county-class cricketer had he so desired. He was an all rounder and exceptionally good at bowling and batting in a way that Westerleigh had never before seen in a pupil. He apparently opened up both the batting order and the bowling line for the Westerleigh cricket team. There was one memorable match, still remembered today, when he almost took all ten of the opposing team's wickets. In the end, he settled for nine. He was also a good goalkeeper, playing in that position for Westerleigh's soccer first team.

And then something happened that was to blight his performance, and that may well have contributed to his early death. He began surreptitiously smoking cigarettes at Westerleigh Prep.

Even then, he was an obsessive character and the habit simply grew and grew. It's hard to know how much he was smoking as the habit peaked, but some say it was around 60 cigarettes a day. He started smoking the Embassy brand and, later, Rothmans. He enjoyed smoking and, from the age of 12, was rarely seen without one in his hand. If ever there was a moment for his parents to act, it was when they found out about this new habit. But they could not stop him, and it was to become a pivotal part in his life.

After five years at Westerleigh, he predictably failed his common entrance. But his entry through Wellington's hallowed portals was never in doubt. The common entrance exam in those days was highly subjective in its assessment and in many ways purely symbolic – used by public schools to reject pupils they didn't want. And Wellington badly wanted James Hunt because of his sporting prowess.

Wellington is a magnificent school. Built in between the rolling plains of Berkshire, it is permanent memorial to the Duke of Wellington, and was named after him. It occupies a magnificent ivy-covered, red-brick building that dominates the vista for a mile around.

Wellington College was originally conceived to supply the nearby Sandhurst military college with army officers for training. Consequently, the teaching staff have always adopted a strict, military-style discipline. Hunt hated it, but years later said: "I didn't like it, but it was good for me."

Combined with that, there was an air of benevolence around Wellington that reminded one of the novel *Goodbye Mr Chips*, written in 1933 by James Hilton. *Goodbye Mr Chips* was a seminal work and was turned into countless films and televisions dramas. Wellington could have been 'Brookfield' and any particular master in Hunt's time could easily have been 'Chipping'.

Carved over the doorway at Wellington was the latin motto: 'Sons of heroes'. It was certainly an apt description of Wallis Hunt and his son, James. But in 1960, when he walked through the front gates, Hunt had little appreciation of the privilege being bestowed upon him or of the history of the establishment. He simply didn't want to be there.

Hunt was put into Combermere House, a red-brick extension off the main building. He lived in a dormitory with partitioned cubicles, which allowed some privacy. His cubicle contained only a bed and a bedside cabinet. He was to spend five years there, from age 12 to 17. His parents hoped that entry to Wellington would mark a change in him, but there was simply no hiding the fact that he was useless academically. He simply had no aptitude for it – sport dominated his being.

Wellington was an all boys college with 750 pupils, and it was very difficult for boys who were not academically minded to function there. They existed under a shadow. Hunt continually struggled and simply could not apply himself to conventional studies unless it was a subject that interested him. He did not have the disciplinary capacity; it was just one of those things.

He was saved by his ability at sports and was protected by the sports masters who wanted him to stay the course. Had he dropped out, it is likely he would have been sent to the local grammar school, which is what normally happened to such students. Hunt actually found the latter option more desirable and tried to manipulate the situation. But his parents would have none of it. They told their son that he was to remain at Wellington for the duration, and any thought he had of transferring to the local grammar school was to be a nonstarter. Hunt briefly tried and failed to get himself expelled, but thought better of it afterwards as he realised just how much it would have disappointed his parents.

Instead, he spent long hours arguing with his father, telling him how much money he could save if he sent him to the local state-funded grammar school, but Wallis wouldn't listen. He was determined to do the best for his son.

The public school system required pupils to choose their potential careers very early so that the academic curriculum could be geared around it. Hunt didn't like any of his choices and initially thought that he might follow his father into an army career. It took him all of 30 seconds to reject that notion and he plumped for becoming a doctor, simply because he had to put something on the form in order to choose a curriculum. He noted that becoming 'Dr Hunt' was "the least of the evils in the unimaginative list of careers" presented to him by Wellington's careers department. But by opting for a medical career, he had *de facto* chosen to complete the physics, chemistry and biology courses at Wellington, and they were the most difficult subjects possible.

When Wallis and Sue learned of his chosen career path, they could have been forgiven for breaking out the champagne. Needless to say, his parents got right behind his choice and looked forward to their son going into general practice one day. An air of unreality descended on the Hunt home at Sutton — the notion of Dr James Hunt truly was daft.

Inevitably, it was soon revealed to be a hopeless choice. Hunt had an inbuilt dislike of studying for anything, and he was not able to apply himself to physics and chemistry at all, although he quite liked biology for reasons that were nothing to do with learning. Predictably, he ended up with the minimum number of O-levels and only one A-level when he left Wellington. His parents made him attend a special school in London so that he could at least attempt to qualify for medical school.

But his entire life at college was devoted to avoiding academia. He joined the school orchestra to avoid homework in the evenings. A side effect of that notion was that he became rather an accomplished trumpet player and often played solo at public events. He said later that he found it "oddly relaxing."

Interestingly, upon hearing him play during the school holidays, all three of his brothers – Peter, Tim and David – also took up playing wind instruments when they attended Wellington.

At Wellington, Hunt had the good fortune to have as his music teacher the great Nigel Davison. Davison was a living legend and musical director of Wellington between 1957 and 1967. Davison, who undoubtedly knew his stuff, was extremely complimentary about Hunt's musical prowess: "If James had decided to give trumpet playing the single-minded concentration that he lavished on his sporting activities, I have no doubt that he could have become a professional, perhaps a virtuoso, trumpeter." His former teacher took charge of the music for both of James' weddings and was an important mentor throughout this life; so much so that Davison spoke at his memorial service after his death. The two formed a strong bond. Through his life, Hunt was to have the good fortune to meet remarkable people like Davison. Each one contributed something good to him. Davison died on 26th October 2009, aged 79, and, in his obituary, *The Times* called him: "One of Europe's most distinguished musical scholars and editors of Renaissance polyphony."

After a year at Wellington, Hunt started dating his first girlfriend, Taormina Rich. They were both 15. As they gradually became close, romance eventually ensued. The relationship would last beyond his schooldays. Taormina's presence during the school holidays made James' return to school at the beginning of each term even more fraught.

Aside from his obvious learning difficulties, there is no question that Wellington College brought out the best in James, as it enabled him to pursue sport every day for the five years he was there. Every afternoon, the pupils were required to participate in sports; but Hunt never needed to be 'required.' He represented Wellington's first teams in squash, tennis and cross-country running. Soccer and cricket fell by the wayside as he simply did not like team games; they didn't bring out the best in him.

Davison was also in charge of the Wellington cross-country running team. Hunt's strongly individualistic nature meant he preferred to train on his own, at his own pace.

Davison wrote of Hunt's performance in the team: "With one notable, if successful, exception, the team threw themselves wholeheartedly into the rigorous training programme. James, the notable exception, studiously avoided training with the team because it probably wasn't rigorous enough. For he either won or came first equal in every race of that year, including a particularly gruesome and arduous inter-house match, whose finish involved wading through a large lake."

But Hunt was potentially a county-class athlete and possibly a national-class performer. Although he was also an exceptional tennis player, Wellington was not really a tennis school. That was a shame as, just before he went to Wellington, at the age of 12, he had entered a tennis tournament for boys of up to 16 years. He made it to the final, but was beaten by a 16-year-old. Despite the four year age difference with his competitor, his mother says he was "inconsolable". Showing an early tendency for emotions when things didn't go his way, he cried for hours. As Sue Hunt told biographer Gerald Donaldson: "Only victory would do for James. He always had to win. If he didn't, it was the greatest possible calamity as far as he was concerned." His habit of crying like a baby when things went against him manifested itself time and again in his career, and should perhaps have been extinguished when he was a child. Occasionally, he exhibited a selfishness that was not attractive.

His time at Wellington only honed his competitiveness. But, despite all that, any impression that he enjoyed his time at Wellington was wholly wrong – he didn't, and his vacation time couldn't come soon enough.

When he finally left the college at the age of 17, he felt he had gained nothing from his five years there. As he said: "When I left college, I had nothing going for me. My heart was never in it." It was a tremendous insult to his parents, who had lavished thousands of pounds on his education, as well as to his school, where the devotion of his masters was way beyond the salary they were paid.

Perhaps it was because he felt so oppressed by the Wellington atmosphere that James never formed lasting relationships with any of his school acquaintances. In fact, he only ever had about half a dozen close male friendships in his lifetime, and only a couple of them ever came close to even beginning to understand James Hunt.

But when he finally departed Wellington in July of 1966, he realised he would miss it as much as he had initially hated it. In an open air concert to mark the end of the summer term at Wellington, he performed one of Mozart's horn concertos for the assembled crowd. That September, he played in the Junior Championships of Great Britain, at Wimbledon. No records exist of how he did.

CHAPTER 5

Metamorphosis – doctor to driver
1965 to 1967
The smell of petrol takes over

B ack in 1965, an 18th birthday was not at all significant – nowhere near as significant as it is now due to changes in the law. Back then, 21 was the big birthday, when all sorts of legal privileges were bestowed upon a young man. Nowadays, the same privileges are bestowed at 18, which shows just how much the world has changed. And it was the 18th that proved to be the most significant birthday in James Hunt's life.

Up until then, James' important birthdays had been when he turned 16, when a boy could ride a motorbike up to 250cc, and when he turned 17, when it was legal to drive a car. Hunt did both, and with relish.

His parents struggled to cope with their eldest son's new-found freedoms, and it was far from easy, after he left Wellington College in July 1965, when he returned to live at home again full-time.

Straightaway, he made it clear he had no intention of going to university. Despite that, a fictional spell of unreality pervaded the Hunt household. It was an air of unreality upheld by his parent's conviction that young James was going to medical school. His parents certainly believed it, and had enrolled him at Bart's medical school in anticipation. As far as they were concerned, he was all set to start there. And that was that.

After having left Wellington, James took special lessons to complete the missing A-levels he needed to qualify for medical school. Their completion proved to his parents that he could focus his mind on academic priorities if he really wanted to.

So, it was clear to both Wallis and Sue Hunt that their eldest son had a destiny, which was to be a doctor. But their son had very different ideas, although it was still unclear to him – at least until 29th August 1965 – exactly what that destiny might be.

Short of ideas on how to celebrate his 18th birthday, James Hunt and Christopher Ridge, a friend with whom he played tennis, decided to go out for the day to a race meeting at Silverstone.

Hunt had never before been to a race and thought it might be fun. He liked driving fast cars and was excited, especially as Ridge's older brother Simon was competing in a club race in a Mini that he had modified himself. So they drove the two hours to Silverstone principally to watch Simon race.

Hunt was totally captivated by what he witnessed at Silverstone that Saturday 21st August 1965. The meeting was for saloon cars and sports cars, which then formed the staple of the British racing scene. 12 races were scheduled, and the makes of competing cars included everything from Bentleys to Minis.

Christopher Hilton, one of Hunt's biographers, described the scene as only he could: "Ham's Aston Martin was in the lead, hotly and resoundingly pursued by Chamberlain's Cooper-Jaguar, although pulling away towards the end. Riley in the Mini-Cooper S was hanging on gamely, fighting off Cox's Mini-Cooper, with Gibson's Jaguar-E fifth, Leo's Lagonda back in sixth place after a spin at Woodcote, and Symondson driving his Bugatti with consummate ease. What a race."

Hilton attempted to describe the effect on Hunt's emotions: "Any race, particularly the first time you see, hear and smell it, can be extremely intoxicating...like a feast, with men and their machinery at the limit. To a first-timer with a receptive mind... [it] would grip the imagination and not let go." Hilton added that, as far as Hunt was concerned, "it never did let go."

Hunt later remembered: "I thought: 'This is bloody good.' I absolutely adored driving fast anyway, and was always trying to organise races with my friends on the roads around home." He was almost completely ignorant of racing up to then, as he admitted: "I'd never known there was such a thing as club racing. As far as I knew, motor racing was something impossibly remote; a thing carried out by Jim Clark and a lot of continentals with long names.

But here was something within reach of a mere mortal."

In fact, Hunt was completely intoxicated and became, in modern parlance, a petrolhead. The word wasn't in use back then, but now describes human beings affected by the smell of petrol to the extent that they become obsessed with cars being driven at high speed in circles in competition with others. That was it, in its simplest sense: Hunt had swapped the smell of ether in a hospital for the smell of petrol at a race track.

But deciding to be a racing driver and actually having the talent to do so are two very different things. And this is where Hunt's intelligence kicked in. His decision to change careers was not as hit-and-miss as many people would like to believe.

As he walked around the paddock that day at Silverstone, and as he chatted to some of the young drivers, he discovered that race driving was all about hand-eye coordination and peripheral vision. If he possessed those two abilities, there was a chance he could succeed.

Apart from that, he also thought racing would quench his thirst for competition. As he explained: "It was the immediate answer to this problem of having my needs to compete satisfied." He had long ago realised that he had an obsession with competing against other human beings, which, he concluded, was why he liked sport so much.

Hunt knew from his tennis, squash, cricket, golf and goalkeeping prowess that he had excellent hand-eye coordination. He wasn't sure about his peripheral vision but tested himself as soon as he got home. He found it was well above average when he compared it to that of his friends.

With that, he decided he would become a race driver.

He had not pursued careers in tennis, squash, cricket, golf or soccer because he didn't feel inspired to. But now, he felt invigorated by what he had witnessed at Silverstone, and it had been enough to make him seriously choose it for a career. As he told Gerald Donaldson years later: "All these guys from perfectly ordinary homes had saved up all their money and gone club racing, which is just about within the range of one's pocket if one works at it and one saves up very hard. I thought: 'Well crikey, if they can do it, so can I. I'm jolly well going to have a go.'"

He was as surprised as anyone by the instincts and desires that had been awakened in him after the visit to Silverstone. It seemed that he had always liked driving cars fast and, when he looked back, he realised he had always been what he called "car crazy". He said: "I was 18 and, for the first time in my life, thought that here was something I might be able to do well."

His first contact with cars had come at the age of 11, when he drove a car during a family holiday at a farm in Pembrokeshire, Wales. Going to farms for their holidays was the sort of thing the Hunt family did; Wallis and Sue thought it educational.

James was bored stiff and had no interest in farming at all – he liked animals, but that was about it. So he sought other pursuits and persuaded one of the young farm workers to let him have a go at driving his tractor. Unthinkable now in an era of strict health and safety regulations, Hunt took the controls and drove round the farm. Afterwards, he was allowed to drive the farm's Land Rover, which he found even more to his liking than the tractor. Finding he had a natural instinct for it, he knew how to drive it straightaway. His only problem was with changing gears, as the clutch was heavy.

Hunt spent an hour driving up and down the two-mile drive to the farm. When Wallis saw how happy his son was at the wheel, he let him drive his car on the same track.

From then on, Wallis periodically let him drive and put him behind the wheel on private roads. Seeing all of this as a perfectly natural part of his eldest son growing up, Wallis had no idea where it would eventually lead.

But car racing was by no means his only obsession. Hunt was also obsessive about music and was always listening to the record player in his room. Like all teenagers, he loved pop music but, even from a very early age, he also enjoyed classical music and was encouraged in his tastes by Nigel Davison. He particularly enjoyed Beethoven. In 1967, his life changed when he was given a Philips cassette recorder for his birthday. The invention of the tape cassette meant he could listen to the music he wanted while on the move. From that moment to the end of his life, he always carried a cassette player with him. As he said: "I love music and it's very important to me in my life. I always take a cassette player when I travel to races and it gives me comfort and relaxation. You spend a lot of time on your own, lurking in hotel rooms in strange places, and it's nice to have music with you."

When he was 16, he started driving a scooter and, as his 17th birthday dawned, he applied for his provisional driver's licence and took his first driving lesson. Folklore says he passed his driving test one week after his 17th birthday but, in reality, it took a little bit longer than that. By Christmas 1964, he had his full driver's licence. For James, it felt as though his life really began that day. He remembered later: "I drove immaculately. My hand signals were perfect and I never exceeded 30 miles an hour in a built up area." But he added: "As soon as the examiner got out of the car and handed me my pink slip, I revved up and roared away like a lunatic."

Wallis Hunt soon became painfully aware of his son's new status, and he had two damaged road cars to show for it. As Wallis told Gerald Donaldson: "He wrote off our minivan, rolling it across a field near Epsom." The minivan belonged to his mother and the crash was serious. Hunt was going too fast round a bend and he clipped the kerb at the outside of the corner. The minivan was launched over a fence and 50 metres into the air. It landed upside down in a farmer's field. Hunt had been very fortunate not to break his neck. When the accident happened, he had crouched down in his seat and braced his head between his knees, and he climbed out of the Mini with just cuts and bruises. It was a survival technique he would use very successfully throughout his racing career, and one that undoubtedly saved his life at least four times.

Wallis decided not to replace the van, which Sue Hunt had used for her charity work. He also banned his son from driving his car. So James bought a moped for himself. But Wallis saw how upset his son was at being grounded.

Six months later, Wallis bought his wife a new Fiat 500 and the ban was lifted. Wallis said: "We thought, with its top speed of about 50 miles per hour and no acceleration, that he can't do much harm in this." Wallis could not have been more wrong. The new Fiat 500, his mother's pride and joy, was quickly written off as Hunt tested the limits of his skill on the public roads. Wallis was furious and decided he would not repair the car; he left it on the drive as a permanent warning to his son.

Wallis Hunt remembered the exact moment when he was told the Fiat 500 had been wrecked: "That very night, there was a knock on the bedroom door at about 2 o'clock in the morning. James stood there, looking rather sheepish, and asked if I could spare a minute to come downstairs. I went down to find a large assembly of his friends, all looking solemn and serious." Hunt explained to his father that he had been driving along at about 15 miles per hour when he came upon a car sitting in the middle of the road with no lights on. He explained that he had swerved into a lamp post in order to avoid hitting the car.

Wallis didn't believe a word of it despite the vast number of friends Hunt had brought along as witnesses and whom he had undoubtedly persuaded to lie for him. The only truth in the entire account was that he had certainly hit a lamp post.

Later, Hunt admitted that he was not a responsible driver on the road: "In those days, I never drove anything except flat out. I had a good feel for the road, but I was very raw and driving with no margin for error. It was incredible luck that I wasn't killed."

With that history in mind, he thought about his future very hard that week and was naturally nervous about breaking the news to his parents that he was going to be a racing driver.

Throwing caution to the wind, James decided he would pitch the idea to his father as a deal. He figured it was going to cost some UK£5,000 in fees to put him through medical school, for which his father had agreed to pay.

On his 18th birthday, he sat down for a cup of tea with his parents – as was typical when he had something important to tell them or, as was more usually the case, when he wanted something.

His mother set great store by the family having tea together in the beautiful sitting room she had created in Belmont. As he sat down, James announced: "All your anxieties about my fecklessness are over. I am going to be a racing driver. And I shall be world champion."

If Wallis spluttered into his tea, he could have been forgiven. His mother, not being familiar with motor racing, was not sure what he was talking about. Donaldson wrote of the occasion: "His parents thought their boy was mad. Perhaps a surfeit of confusing teenage male hormones had short-circuited his reason and caused him to take leave of his senses."

His parents were taken completely by surprise. The only sign that he was ever interested in motor racing had been his childhood obsession with the Scalextric set they had bought him when he was eight.

When Sue Hunt realised what he was saying, she became very cross. She remembers telling him, in so many words, that "instead of dedicating his life to saving others, he would be risking his own in an endeavour which was totally useless and unproductive for society."

There is no question that her analysis of motor racing was entirely correct; indeed, it was an endeavour "totally useless and unproductive for society."

Whereas now it employs tens of thousands of people all over the world and has an annual turnover in excess of US$5 billion globally, back then it was a totally unproductive occupation.

Despite an overwhelmingly negative reaction from his parents, Hunt pitched his father with a financial proposal. Years later, he recalled the moment: "I needed money fast and I offered my old man a deal. It would have cost him about five grand to put me through medical school, but, as I wasn't going, I told him I'd settle for UK£2,500 cash now to get my racing car."

Wallis Hunt thought his son's proposal "preposterous" and told him so. His mother was flabbergasted. Hunt says his father used words to the effect of: "Get stuffed."

Hunt left the family sitting room totally demoralised. He had genuinely expected his father to see the merit of the idea and had not foreseen such a negative reaction to his new career choice. Afterwards, he approached his maternal grandmother for the UK£2,500 he needed, and she sent him packing as well.

Apart from the absurdity of it, the Hunt family simply could not afford to fund his racing career. The medical school fees would have been spread out over at least five years, and, as Wallis Hunt told Donaldson: "At the time I was earning a reasonable income, but we had no surplus to throw around. We weren't poor, but we certainly weren't rich. We were just managing to cover everyone's education and take minimal holidays and that sort of thing. And, taking the view that fair is fair, we had six children to help get started in life and we simply couldn't afford to throw it all at one of them." While his grandmother could have afforded it, she chose not to.

Afterwards, Wallis could see how downcast his eldest son was after they had dismissed his plan. Feeling guilty about it, Wallis decided to speak to some friends who knew about motor racing. He wanted to see if there was any merit in the idea, and they suggested that he speak to Stirling Moss, a friend, on the phone. Moss suggested that the first step would be for James to take some race driving lessons at Brands Hatch to see if he was any good at it.

So Wallis told his son that he would pay for a course of lessons at the famous Jim Russell School at Brands Hatch.

Wallis was surprised when his son failed to show any enthusiasm over the proposal. The course was not cheap, at UK£165, and he had expected more gratitude. The truth was that Hunt felt it was beneath him; he had already decided he wanted to race and that he was good enough to race, and he didn't want to go to race school in the company of some novice no-hopers.

Eventually concluding that it was better than nothing, Hunt went to Brands Hatch and took the course. It emerged later that Wallis had paid for the course on the hope that James would realise he was no good and drop the idea. And, indeed, that almost came to pass.

Inexplicably, Hunt did not do well on the course and failed to distinguish himself. The lack of any form of competition completely floored him, and he was not motivated or enthused by it. Afterwards, he said the UK£165 had been wasted and he would rather have had the money to help him buy a car.

But he had found out enough about himself on the course to know he had what it took, so when he got back home the first thing he did was to write to Bart's hospital and withdraw from medical school. When he told his parents, they were devastated. They effectively told him he was now on his own as far as his motor racing ambitions were concerned. Wallis and Sue told him they would provide shelter and food, but the rest was up to him.

It was probably the low point of his relationship with his parents, and Hunt effectively abandoned his education. He famously said: "I could speak the Queen's English and I knew how to hold a knife and fork properly, that was all I needed."

The line had been drawn in the sand, and Hunt knew he had to get on and pursue his dream himself. He felt his only option was to pay for his motor racing obsession himself. And that meant getting a job and earning serious money.

James' first job was for a local printing company, which employed him as a messenger driving a minivan. He was quickly fired when he was seen doing handbrake turns in the vehicle. His next job was selling ice cream from a van on Epsom Downs for another local firm. But he gave ice cream cones to children who didn't have any money and, on another occasion, loaded up the van and drove off to Epsom without turning on the refrigeration unit. The whole day's stock was ruined and, when he returned to the depot, he was sacked.

He then got a job at his local J. Sainsbury supermarket stacking shelves in the evenings, but it lasted a week and he was sacked when he told his supervisor that he didn't think there was enough money in his first pay packet. He briefly apprenticed at a local garage as a trainee mechanic, but quickly left there as well. Four jobs in 12 weeks was not an auspicious start to working life, as he admitted: "I hated every minute of it."

Hunt was also finding out about himself. He decided he was not a public school type. He may have been to public school, but he did not feel part of it. As one of his friends famously described him: "He came from suburbia like the rest of us and he always preferred to be with his suburban mates."

His friends would prove to be very important to him over the years that followed. He struck up friendships with several key people, which endured for the whole of his life. His three closest friends were John Richardson, Chris Jones and Malcolm Wood. All three grew up locally, near the Hunt family home in Belmont. When he left Wellington, those friendships strengthened. When he entered Formula One in 1973, he trusted them because they had known him before he became famous. Richardson said: "He was a terribly hard person to get really close to, and I don't think many ever did." But after he left Wellington, those carefree days with his three friends became the stuff of his happiest memories.

Whilst he was raising the money to buy his own car, he attended as many race meetings as he could and became one of Simon Ridge's hangers-on. The experience was to prove invaluable when, one day, he finally cast his eye on what was to become his Mini in the classified pages of *Motoring News*. At last, he had found one he could afford.

SHUNT

CHAPTER 6

Mini Racer 1965 to 1967
The unreal becomes real

At the age of 18, James Hunt took his first serious step into motor racing. It was an important transition from merely thinking about it to actually doing it. But he had little idea how to go about it; particularly with no money available to fund such an adventure.

His only clue was that a brother of a friend, someone called Simon Ridge, had bought a Mini and converted it for racing quite successfully. He decided that if his friend's brother could do it, so could he. As he said: "Here was my mate's brother, who was about twenty with very little money but had worked as a garage mechanic and built himself a racing Mini."

Hunt had already separately surmised that the easiest point of entry into motor racing would be amateur saloon car racing, which was not as organised at the time as it was later to become. His only other real choice was to make his start in go-karting. But, at 18, he was already too old for that. He had caught the motor racing bug relatively late and had some catching up to do.

In saloon car racing, cars raced in three classes in the same events. It meant a Chevrolet Camaro and Ford Mustang would race alongside Minis. So Hunt decided to buy a Mini to start his career and began scanning the classified pages of *Motoring News*, the weekly that carried pages upon pages of adverts for second-hand race cars.

Eventually, he found one he could afford; a gold-coloured racing Mini stripped down chassis that had been crashed and needed repairs. As 1965 dawned, he bought the bare chassis and body for less than UK£25. It needed repairing and building up almost from scratch.

His father, Wallis, indulged him and let him convert one of the garages at the family home into a workshop, so he set the Mini on stilts and got to work. Hunt was no mechanic and diligently followed the basics laid out in Haynes manual and whatever else was to hand.

He was forced to buy parts second-hand and from scrap yards, and aimed to rebuild the car as best he could. There was no time frame for James; it was simply a matter of money as he rebuilt the car when he could afford to buy the components. He thought it might take him two years, and it did.

He said later: "I had no money, no knowledge of racing cars or the racing business and nobody near me to give help and encouragement. Even so, at 18, I reasoned that three or four years of total dedication to a project wasn't going to cost me too much, even if it failed, which – viewed objectively – it might have been expected to do." Retrospectively, he may have held such an enlightened view, but, at the time, he was not so sanguine. He fully anticipated success at the outset.

It has to be said that the rest of the family thought he was slightly unhinged, but, like his father, they indulged him. He was certainly a different sort of boy from the average. Hunt's boyhood friends also did not believe in him and thought the 'craze', as they called it, soon would pass.

But James Hunt had a rare confidence, knowledge and other-worldly authority that allowed him to pursue his dream and retain his sanity. Set against that, however, was a strange naïveté which meant he often missed the obvious and direct solutions to problems and ended up doing things the hard way. But, that said, doing it the hard way meant he was learning all the time.

The sacrifices he made to pursue his dream, even at that stage, were extensive. He virtually gave up any form of socialising that involved spending money. Luckily, his girlfriend, Taormina Rich, was very understanding and contentedly spent weekend evenings handing him spanners and sanding down bodywork. Hunt pulled in all his friends at weekends to work on the car, including, legend has it, the family milkman, who had a certain technical knowledge useful in rebuilding a Mini.

His parents were not altogether unhappy with their son spending all his weekends in the garage and eschewing a social life. It meant he was always available for babysitting duties at weekends and evenings, often with Taormina's assistance. Tim, David and Georgina were 10, 8 and 6 respectively, and Hunt became close to them as he watched them grow up. Because of his age, James' role towards them was more that of a very close uncle than a brother and he was, by all accounts, a superb uncle. Taormina remembers babysitting with him one evening. After Hunt had tucked them in, she read them a bedtime story. When Taormina came back downstairs, Hunt surprised her by asking if they had said their prayers. They hadn't, and, as she recalls: "James said to me: 'Right. You've missed out hugely there. Come on, we'd better go and do it.' So we did. His attitude was that he had been taught to do that by his parents, and it simply had to be done."

To fund his new career, James had got his first proper full-time job as a van driver for the Medical Research Council, based at the Royal Marsden Hospital, in Belmont. He earned around UK£14 a week delivering packages all over the local area. More usefully, he effectively had use of the van during the day and could easily stop off at scrap yards to buy spare parts for the Mini. In fact, he soon became a very familiar presence at the local scrap yard in Belmont.

The scale of the task facing him was reflected by the fact that his car had no engine. It was just a lump of unattractive metal on stands in his parents' garage. The biggest expense he faced was buying an engine which then would need to be tuned for racing. He eventually found one he could afford, of doubtful origin, in a yard and paid UK£25 for it, almost two weeks' wages.

To earn even more money, he supplemented his day job as a van driver for the Royal Marsden by becoming a cleaner in the hospital for four hours every evening. Even his sceptical father was impressed by his entrepreneurial zeal, astonished that his son was working so hard to turn his dream into reality.

Throughout, Hunt remained realistic about what he was doing. He had no idea whether he would be any good, as he had never driven a car in anger on a circuit nor had be been benchmarked against anyone. Some inner resolve kept him going, but he didn't know what it was and neither did anyone else. It was, one might say, 'a blind faith in himself' that kept him going, spending insane amounts of money on a dream that had no objective prospect of success at all.

Eventually, his father became concerned about his son's obsession and used family connections to get in touch with former Grand Prix driver Stirling

Moss for advice. Moss, although he can't remember now, actually visited Belmont and met young James and gave him some sound advice. But what he couldn't tell Wallis was what Wallis so desperately wanted to know: whether or not his son was any good.

When he had collected most of the parts he needed, Hunt sought a change of job and became a bus conductor to earn even more money. The inspiration behind the change of jobs was farcical. It was rooted in a new TV sitcom that was first broadcast in early 1969 called 'On the Buses,' which aired on ITV every week. 'On the Buses' took Britain by storm and quickly became the country's most popular comedy sitcom. It was written by Ronald Wolfe and Ronald Chesney, and featured a bus company inspector, a bus driver and the star of the show, a bus conductor called Stan Butler, played by one of Britain's top comedy actors, Reg Varney.

The inspector's name was Cyril Blake, whom everyone called Blakey, and the driver was called Jack Harper. The TV show centred around the Butler family, which consisted of his mother, brother-in-law Arthur, and sister Olive. Hunt was attracted to the position of a bus conductor because of Stan Butler's continual success with women – either those he met on the bus or the conductresses who worked for the bus company.

Together, the three main characters and the Butler family made the nation laugh with smutty scripts, in which the unmarried Butler normally ended up with a girl.

Although the show wasn't serious, it had an enormous impact on Hunt, who loved it. Hunt adapted his whole family and work life to characters in the show, although his own mother, Susan, couldn't have been more different from Stan Butler's working-class and over-sentimental mother.

Having applied for a conductor's job on Green Line buses, James Hunt got it. But his attitude turned out to be all wrong. Treating every day on the job like an episode of the TV show, he was often heard using the catchphrases: "I hate you Butler" and "I'll get you for this Butler." In truth, he was not very popular with his work colleagues, who all actually hated the TV show, which they thought belittled their jobs. But Hunt didn't get it, and found that real life as a bus conductor was as far removed from 'On The Buses' as it could be. When he started calling his inspector "Dracula", Cyril Blake's nickname on the show, it was the last straw. He was called into the inspector's office. As his reason for sacking him, the inspector said that James was simply "too tall" for the post.

When Hunt remonstrated and pointed out that there were several other conductors taller than him, the inspector capitulated and told him the truth; he had "too much chat." As a sop, the inspector allowed him to retrain as a bus driver, knowing full well that the minimum age for a driver was 22. So he was out, and his colleagues at the station were pleased to see the back of him. But 'On The Buses' remained his favourite TV programme for the four years it ran, and, years later, as soon as video tape recorders became popular, James purchased all the VHS tapes and watched them with his friends, reliving his own time on the buses.

Undaunted by his brief sojourn on the buses, his next job was working for Telephone Rentals Plc, a quoted company that rented out telephone systems to companies. Telephone systems were taking off in Britain at the time, and it seemed that every company had to have one. It wasn't possible for a customer to buy a system from Telephone Rentals; it had to rent. Telephone Rentals had placed big orders with most of the manufacturers and, along with British Telecom, monopolised supplies. But BT was still supplying old-fashioned switchboards, and only Telephone Rentals had the new electronic models customers actually wanted.

Once a contract was signed with a customer – and a contract could run for as long as 14 years – the customer was trapped. When upgrades came along, a new contract was signed and the existing contract would be extended for even longer. A deal with the company was for life, and there was no way out. When a salesman made a deal, the commissions could be huge.

So Telephone Rentals was all about sales and that vital signature on a contract. It recruited Hunt as a trainee salesman, and he attended a training course on how to sell the systems.

The new job meant that he would have to wear a suit and tie and sport a rather shorter haircut. But he was prepared to do it because the basic salary was good and the commission he would earn for every signature he received was many times his basic salary.

He did some early deals and his earnings rocketed, but every penny went into the car while his lifestyle did not improve at all.

Recalling those years to his biographer Gerald Donaldson, he said: "I lived a life that totally freaked out my friends. They couldn't believe it. They thought I was mad because I gave up everything that was part of normal life for somebody my age. All I ever did was work to earn money and build my car. I had no social life, never went to the pub, never spent on anything I didn't have to. I could not accept other people's hospitality because I couldn't reciprocate. My only relaxation was squash. The club had a beer kitty so I was able to get drunk once a week. That was it. The club members simply regarded me as a nutter."

Chris Jones, who was arguably Hunt's closest friend over his life, admitted he had no faith in his friend's nascent career as a racing driver. Jones confessed that everyone felt James was wasting his time and they doubted whether he would enter even one race, let alone make a career of it.

John Richardson, another of Hunt's very good friends, called the Mini project "strangely eccentric."

But Hunt was deadly serious. He did everything he could to save money for his racing, including cutting down on smoking 40 cigarettes a day to hardly any.

Sue Hunt remembers the period well, as she told Donaldson: "He despaired from time to time. He was always short of cash, always in debt – mostly to us. But we didn't try to dissuade him from going racing. There was no point. He had made up his mind and he never faltered. He used to fly into tantrums over that Mini, but they were over quickly and all was forgiven."

Once he had bought the engine, the only thing he could think of was the day that the car would be fired up. He imagined the sound of the engine running and, when that milestone was passed, he yearned for the day when the car would run under its own steam and, then, the day it would hit the tracks.

In anticipation of that day, Hunt sent off for this competitions' licence from the Royal Automobile Club and went to his doctor to get the necessary medical certificates.

The blind faith in his own ability confounded everyone, as his mother said: "James had a lot of charm, although at this stage he was always more charming when he was out than when he was at home."

Eventually the day came, in 1967, two years after he had started, when the engine did fire up. And, eventually, the day also came when the car ran under its own steam, albeit up and down the Hunt family driveway before he gingerly ventured it onto the streets, totally illegally. The road trips were very risky, as he chanced being shopped to the police by the Hunt family's very annoyed neighbours. They were less than appreciative of having a would-be racing driver living next door continually revving up his car.

But in reality, although his car certainly moved and made noise, Hunt had no idea what he was doing.

He bought some second-hand race tyres, which were worn out and bald, and he hand-cut some treads in them, thinking he could fool the scrutineers into believing they were new.

He had little choice in the matter, as a set of new racing tyres cost over UK£75; money he simply did not have.

He was desperately short of parts, as everything had to be paid for in cash. As the Mini was Britain's most popular car and highly unreliable, second-hand Mini parts were also very expensive. There wasn't even any glass in his car's windows. Saloon car regulations stated that the car had to have a passenger seat, and Mini seats fetched good prices at the scrap yards, so he bolted in a deckchair. Legend has it that it was actually bolted down with parts from an old meccano set he had played with as a child.

With the car virtually completed, Hunt bought a 22-year-old 1947 Rover T6 for UK£15 to use as his tow car. He also bought a car trailer, which cost considerably more.

With that, he was all set to make his racing debut and chose a saloon car race at Snetterton, in Norfolk, as his inaugural event. He couldn't see anything in the regulations that said his Mini had to have windows, so he didn't bother to try and find any.

For his first race, James intended to compete in the under 1300cc class and sent off the entry forms to the British Automobile Racing Club (BARC) which, in those days, was headquartered in Argyll Street, London, above the offices occupied by the Beatles management company Nems Ltd, run by the legendary Brian Epstein.

Knowing it shouldn't have been made possible, James was amazed when the BARC accepted his entry. The official acceptance was delivered to his parents' home by the postman. It was a big moment as he opened the envelope and read aloud the standard stenciled letter, signed by Grahame White, who was competition secretary and then general secretary of the BARC from 1962 to 1973.

White would later become a close friend of Hunt's but does not remember his debut or his first race entry. In fact, the name 'Hunt' did not register with him until James started racing in Formula Ford and delivering his entry forms by hand to Argyll Street. White says it was common for drivers to begin racing Minis in those days: "Minis had been around a few years by then. It was a very good way of starting racing because it was easy to race, easy to drive and cheap to maintain."

With his entry accepted, all that was left was for James to decide on his helmet colours. He had long ago purchased a helmet in preparation for the big day. He scanned the pages of *Autosport* and *Motoring News* looking for inspiration, which finally came from Graham Hill. Inspired by Hill's black helmet design, with the distinctive insignia of his rowing club, James also chose a black design and, just like Hill, painted on his Wellington College colours: red, blue and yellow bands. Rather ironically, having gone through all the trouble of designing the helmet, he could not actually afford to have it painted and so he raced in a white helmet for the first few years. But barring the helmet, proper windows, seat and tyres, Hunt was now ready for his race debut, and he set out to confound his friends and family, who had never thought the day would come.

But, in truth, he wasn't ready and was actually UK£100 short of finishing the job. But he couldn't wait any longer. The project to rebuild the Mini had cost around £250 and he had run up a UK£50 overdraft.

He travelled to his first race with no mechanic, and was accompanied only by his girlfriend for moral support. No family attended. If he was to make a fool of himself, he didn't want any witnesses. Surprisingly, the old black Rover towed the Mini to Snetterton without any trouble.

It had been precisely two years between buying the damaged Mini chassis to entering his first race.

But the race scrutineers were horrified when Hunt drove his Mini into the scrutineering bay. The chief scrutineer said to him: "You cannot be serious", or words to that effect. But Hunt was deadly serious and didn't get the joke.

The scrutineers ruled the car out of the race, principally because its tyres were worn out. The deckchair did not pass muster and there was effectively no proper exhaust system, which was also illegal. They also ruled that the car must have glass in the windows.

Upon receiving the rejection slip listing four major defects and being told he could not start, Hunt was devastated. He burst into tears and made rather an exhibition of himself, just as he would four years later at Brands Hatch, when he was disqualified for cheating. He said later: "My whole world collapsed around me. I was a broken man."

Hunt was, of course, exaggerating, and it was a minor setback in the grand scheme of things. He was no fool and he had a copy of the rule book; he must have known that passing the Mini would present difficulties to the scrutineers. Some people say it was just a sighting shot to see what there was left to do, and that he portrayed it as a crisis as a ruse to get more money out of his father to finish the car more quickly. Whatever the truth of it, Hunt had no choice but to winch the Mini back onto its trailer, ready for the journey home. But before he left, he stopped off to watch the race in which he had so desperately desired to compete. He walked round the paddock and stared closely at the cars and the preparation methods of many of the teams.

When he pulled back into his parents' driveway that evening, his mother was genuinely delighted to see that he was still alive. As far as his parents were concerned, his non-event at Snetterton had been a success. As Hunt later said: "My mother was flabbergasted when she saw me come back alive. She was convinced I would be killed first time out." And there was some validity in those fears. If he had gone out on the track that day as a novice in his car in the state in which it was, that could well have been the result.

Wallis and Sue Hunt fervently hoped the setback would put him off, but they quickly saw that it hadn't. Although they had not shown their opposition to his racing up until then, reasoning that it might encourage him further, now they changed their tune and were vociferous in their opposition. Whilst James may not have raced at Snetterton, the fact that he had gone off and come back from a race made them face up to the reality of what it all entailed. But their son wasn't discouraged in the least and was now as determined as ever to succeed.

He needed about UK£100 to fix the car for the regulations, and he set out to save it and to return for another go. The money was easily raised when he managed to sell some telephone contracts on behalf of Telephone Rentals. As a trainee sales manager with the company, he was now earning a basic salary of UK£1,000 a year and commission, which was worth half as much again.

But after his treatment at Snetterton, he lost interest in Mini racing and resolved to try Formula Ford instead. His appetite had been whetted by a Formula Ford race he had witnessed on the same day at Snetterton, and he had studied it carefully. For James, a Formula Ford car appeared to be a great deal simpler to prepare than a Mini, and he knew that was where he had to go. After that, he just used the Mini to get experience and resolved to buy himself a Formula Ford car. Simply put, he used the Mini to find his feet in racing but, when race days finally came, he was more interested in preserving his machinery than performing with it.

Dave Morgan, another hopeful British driver with whom Hunt would later clash, was also starting his career in saloon cars around that time. He remembers Hunt's Mini being "a bag of rubbish". He actually called it a "well-shunted car".

Hunt also had no luck with his tow car, which, after one race, expired and forced him to acquire an Austin A90, which cost him another £25. He also bought a Lambretta scooter on which to get around, and rested the tow car as much as he could for its real task.

In the end, Hunt entered just four Mini saloon car races, including the non-start at Snetterton. He pursued the races to gain experience and pootled around at the back of the grid, taking no risks and honing his driving skills. He didn't actually finish any of the races, deciding to rest his machinery before the chequered flag fell and failing to distinguish himself in any of the races. Officially, he retired in all of them. The only known photographs of the racing car at this time were taken at Brands Hatch on 8th October and are now the property of Ted Walker of Ferret Photography.

Hunt quickly realised he had no idea how to set up the car. As there were no Mini race car manufacturers, there were no manuals. All the racing Minis had been converted by all sorts of different people and there was no single reference point. This was one of the reasons he so desperately sought to enter Formula Ford, where there were plenty of manuals as well as advice for novices.

Unusually, one routine he did establish when he was driving the Mini was a ritual of vomiting before a race. The nervousness he felt before getting strapped into a car, be it in practice or in qualifying for a race, stayed with him for the remainder of his life. He found the tension to build up to such an extent in his stomach that he could virtually vomit to order before taking to the track. And his total lack of embarrassment meant he didn't mind who witnessed it either. He never discussed his 'urge to purge' with anyone, and most often put it down to severe nerves and the over-production of adrenalin. In reality, it was a combination of all of these, along with his excessive smoking and drinking, that created a chemical reaction in his body before each race start.

Those four races were his first and last foray into saloon car racing on circuits, and, from then on, he stuck to single seaters. His career had not got off to an auspicious start, but he kept faith in himself – even if no one else did. Later, he never really discussed his Mini days, seeming anxious to forget them as quickly as possible. As far as he was concerned, his racing career began with Formula Ford in 1969.

His saloon car career finally ended when he received a surprise offer of UK£325 for his car; it was about the same amount as it had cost him to put it together. Or so he says. Some doubt his version of events, maintaining that he sold the car for a lot less and was desperate to get rid of it. But, despite the naysayers, it appears to have been the truth. On the spur of the moment, Hunt took the money and decided now was the time to invest it all in a Formula Ford car. He said: "I sold it on the spur of the moment, and all my best decisions have been taken on the spur of the moment."

He was set to turn 21 on 29th August 1968, some ten months later, but he somehow persuaded his father to let him have the money he would be due on that date early. So Wallis Hunt handed his son a cheque for UK£100. Together with his overdraft facilities, the contribution took Hunt's war chest to nearly £500, which was enough to launch a proper career in motor racing.

The dress rehearsal was over and, once more, the timing of his latest career move was to prove absolutely spot-on.

SHUNT

60

CHAPTER 7

Into Formula Ford 1968-1969
It all starts to get rather serious

J ames Hunt had his fair share of good and bad days. But the day that Formula Ford was established, in 1967, was one of his better ones. In many ways, it was a formula tailor-made for him to begin his career proper. It was almost as if it had been created especially for him.

Formula Ford was the original idea of John Webb, the managing director of Motor Circuit Developments Ltd (MCD), which owned Brands Hatch and four other British circuits. Webb wanted a standardised entry formula for new drivers, which would be affordable and therefore popular and provide plenty of cars and drivers for races at his circuits. At the time, Webb was short of content and he wanted to encourage a big rush of new talent into the sport. It was all carefully thought through and, together with Geoff Clarke and Jim Russell, who ran race driving schools at MCD circuits, the formula was devised. Webb persuaded Walter Hayes and Henry Taylor of the Ford Motor Company to sponsor the formula's creation, and it was therefore christened Formula Ford.

Before Formula Ford, Formula Vee had been the entry formula but it had never taken off. Formula Vee cars looked like racing cars but handled like saloon cars. It hadn't succeeded simply because a Formula Vee car did not feel like a racing car. To solve that problem, the Formula Ford car was designed with a full racing suspension setup.

Webb cleverly asked Colin Chapman of Lotus to design and build the prototype car in 1966; it was called the Lotus 51. The 51 was really a Formula 3 Lotus 31 with steel wheels and road tyres to suit the FF regulations. The car was made by Lotus Components Ltd, the race car manufacturing subsidiary of Lotus. But part of the regulations was that a car and engine had to cost only UK£1,000 to keep them affordable. Lotus had difficulty making a profit at that price, and the formula was taken over by a host of smaller manufacturers, amongst them Merlin and Alexis. But Lotus still managed to sell over 1,000 Formula Ford cars in the various 51, 51A and 61 models.

So, in 1968, armed with his UK£500, Hunt focused on entering Formula Ford. Not only were the cars relatively cheap, but John Webb had also tied up with some finance companies to offer hire purchase terms to budding race drivers who were cash poor but credit worthy. Credit-worthy Hunt therefore took full advantage of his status and bought a new Russell–Alexis Mk14 Formula Ford car with a Ford 1600 Kent crossflow engine.

Hunt paid a third deposit on the car, around UK£330, and his repayments worked out at UK£30 per month. He also bought another engine, a special from engine builder Chris Steele, also on hire purchase. But buying a second engine was against the spirit of the rules.

He persuaded his somewhat reluctant father, Wallis, to guarantee the hire purchase agreements. He was also forced to insure the car and persuaded his father that, whatever happened, the car could be sold and he would not lose out. When he did the numbers, Wallis Hunt was surprised to find that this was true and so he signed on the dotted line. But Wallis kept it to himself, especially from Hunt's mother, as, publicly, he was discouraging his son from going into motor racing.

As Wallis reasoned, his son was better off and, more importantly, safer racing with new equipment rather than in the old Mini, which had frightened everyone. Wallis even accompanied his son to Brands Hatch to have a look at one of the cars. He was surprised to find himself impressed with what he saw.

Hunt's latest tow car had expired again so this time he bought something more robust, a two-tone green Austin Cambridge for UK£54. He kept the Mini trailer and had UK£100 left to pay for the season's expenses. Almost all of his Telephone Rentals salary and commissions would be put towards it.

Hunt targeted big races in England and became very good friends with Grahame White, the BARC secretary, during the spring, summer and autumn of 1968, when he raced most weekends. White remembers: "James came in and out of my life on many occasions. He used to come into the office quite a bit to say 'hello' and put in a late entry form. There were certain things about James that you couldn't help but notice. He was tall, good looking and he spoke rather nicely. He was the sort of guy you would like to be friends with if you had the opportunity."

Formula Ford meant everyone had equal cars, so ability could come to the fore. Although Hunt was hampered because he could not afford to carry many spare parts or bodywork.

Formula Ford racing couldn't have been more different from what Hunt was used to, and he found that almost every weekend he was at the front and rarely at the back. Much to his surprise, he was immediately competitive and he made his debut at Snetterton almost one year after the Mini fiasco.

Hunt was both driver and mechanic, but occasionally brought along friends with mechanical knowledge. A constant in those days was Taormina Rich, who attended almost every race with him for moral support. She was also prepared to rough it, sleeping in the back of vans and going hungry when necessary.

Also at the start of his racing career at Snetterton was a young driver called Tony Dron. Dron had also been to public school and, like Hunt, had well-to-do parents who did not support his racing career. It was actually Dron's second race and he would become Hunt's first and closest friend in racing. The two men had much in common, and Dron's parents lived a few miles away from Hunt's in Wentworth. Dron remembers: "In those days, we both had short hair and we spoke the same language, as we both came from Surrey. And I was intrigued to discover that we both had the same birthday." Dron adds: "He was a year younger than me, but we were both very serious, short-haired, skint young men."

Unsurprisingly, they hit it off straightaway and started travelling to races together. Dron had bought a Titan car, as he remembers: "I had started racing in the last weekend of May 1968 and my second race was at Snetterton, where James appeared in Formula Ford for the first time."

The only difference between them was that Dron had managed to scrape enough money together to buy his car outright. Dron had also made a better choice of chassis. Hunt's Alexis proved to be a dog, but the Titan was one of the top cars.

But money rather than motor racing actually dominated their lives, as Dron says: "We had very similar backgrounds: our parents had expensive houses in Surrey, they lived very well but really it was all crap – they were spending the children's inheritance and there was very little money for us apart from our education, being fed properly and clothed properly. We lived from hand to mouth, bumping along on 20 quid a week. We got used to living as very hard-up people although we went back to these very lovely houses where everything was comfortable. It was a very funny way of life, really. We were given a great start in life and then it was all down to us. I thoroughly approve of that policy."

Dron remembers how committed his friend was in those days: "He was absolutely hell-bent on getting to the top. He said to me: 'If I don't get to the top in motor racing, I'll get to the top in something else' and I believed him."

Dron and Hunt began travelling together. Taormina and Dron's girlfriend, Doro Marden, used to get on very well. They shared the same philosophy of life and didn't mind roughing it to save money, as Dron remembers: "We got on very well, we kind of teamed up a bit. We would travel together and support each other. We would camp out in the press office to save 30 bob [UK£1.50], which it would have cost for a bed and breakfast in a pub."

Dron remembers it was not fun at the time: "We were committed to, not playing with, race driving. The objective was to get to the very top and it made our lives a serious struggle."

So James Hunt's pattern of life was established. During the week, he was persuading people to rent out telephone systems and earning good money, and, at weekends, he was a racing driver.

But he was conscious that he was almost a complete novice, having only actually competed in three races prior to his single seater debut. The only saving grace, which constantly rescued his thoughts and reassured him when he got depressed, was that half the field was in exactly the same position as him.

Hunt diligently went about his apprenticeship and attended open tests days at nearby Brands Hatch and other circuits. These open test sessions were the brainchild of John Webb, who opened up his circuits to all comers, who shared the circuit for a very small fee. It meant that all sorts of racing machines were on the track together.

It was on one of those test days at Snetterton circuit that Hunt met the man who would influence his career long before he made it to Formula One – Max Mosley. Although there is no real reason to remember the occasion when he first met James Hunt 42 years ago, Mosley recalls it very clearly. He says: "I remember distinctly, it was 1968 and I was at Snetterton driving my Formula Two Brabham BT23. It was a very fast car, relatively speedy. And he was driving Formula Ford and I followed this person round in a Formula Ford and he was going much too fast – much too fast for a Formula Ford, you just didn't expect it. In those days at testing, everything was mixed up; there were motorbikes out there and other things. So I was really impressed. And then in the paddock, I saw this person get out of the car and he was wearing old clothes and gym shoes. And the wisdom in those days was that you never wore something with a rubber sole because if there was any oil on the pedals, you had a problem. And I just thought it was extraordinary for a scruffy, unequipped person to be going so incredibly quickly."

That image was indelibly planted in Mosley's mind, but little did he know how frequently their paths would cross in the years to come and what great friends they eventually would become.

Although he was doing a lot of running in races and testing, Hunt never crashed the car in that first year. Contrary to his later image, he was very careful about bringing the car home in one piece, and it affected his competitiveness. But it was a necessity, as he simply had no money for accident repairs. He knew that one accident could finish his racing career forever. He really was running his race car on a shoestring.

He was also becoming increasingly aware of the economics of Formula Ford. At UK£1,000 a car, the manufacturers were losing money on every chassis they sold. There was simply no profit from selling a car for UK£1,000. But there was plenty of profit to be had from repairing them after the frequent accidents many of the customers seemed to have. But not James Hunt, who focused perhaps more on bringing his car home undamaged than he did on winning races.

Hunt was eminently sensible and practical in those days. Reasoning that he lacked experience, he decided he was in no hurry to make it to the top. Often, he drove round sedately and, as long as he was qualifying for the finals and in the top half of the field, he was happy. It was an unusually mature approach for such a young man, who would behave totally opposite later in his career.

As confidence came to him and he gained in experience, he began to pass other drivers and found it all rather easy.

By summer's end, James Hunt had won his first race. The very first win came at the Lydden Hill circuit, in Kent. He also set a new lap record on the club circuit at Brands Hatch.

Leaning on his sales experience with Telephone Rentals, Hunt decided unilaterally that he was now successful enough to be sponsored. He declared to his friends and father that he was ready to sell sponsorship and to give big companies the privilege of working with him. He had no idea how hard that would prove to be, nor just how unattractive a proposition sponsoring a budding young Formula Ford driver really was. While Hunt saw the glass as half full, sponsors definitely saw it as half empty. He was totally unprepared for the rejections, as he said: "This was just about the lowest period of my life. I had to go knocking on doors to get sponsorship and the doors were always slammed in my face." Unlike his prospective telephone customers, who at least listened to him make his pitch, most prospective sponsors didn't even speak to him, with the line of communication progressing no further than the receptionist.

It was all to do with his naïveté. What he didn't realise was that, at Telephone Rentals, all his leads were carefully obtained through a sophisticated marketing and filtering operation. With prospective sponsors, he was simply approaching any company in the phone book, starting with 'A'. Most of these companies had already been called repeatedly. Eventually, he realised he was better off starting at the back of the telephone directory, since few companies starting with an 'X' had ever been called.

Taormina Rich had to listen to this sort of stuff every time they got together; her boyfriend talked of nothing else.

But his father, listening to him on the phone, understood better and chipped in with some timely advice and told his frustrated son to be persistent. For once, James took his father's advice and carried on. And then he had a eureka moment. He figured if he couldn't sell them sponsorship, they might be interested in a telephone system, and so he uncovered some useful leads.

As for sponsors, Hunt had most success with companies already in the car business, and quickly focused on them.

Mike Hughes, who ran Hughes of Beaconsfield, an upmarket car dealership, was the first to say 'yes' to him and put its name on the car for the 1968 season, although the deal was worth only UK£50. But Hunt carried on making the rounds and managed to get Gowrings of Reading interested in a much bigger deal.

The dealership asked him to prepare a budget for the 1969 season. He went back with a budget of UK£2,000, which was accepted. For their own tax reasons, Gowrings actually bought him a new car so it could take the depreciation write-off against corporation tax. They ordered a brand new Merlyn Mk11A, which was the car to have in 1968 in order to be really competitive.

But the James Hunt story was very nearly over before the 1969 season started. The new car turned out to be an absolute necessity after his Russell-Alexis was written off in a very serious accident at Oulton Park circuit on 26th October.

Hunt was racing in close proximity to Tony Dron when the accident happened. Dron remembers: "It was the first race I did with [seat]belts, which were coming into the lower levels of racing 1968, and the last race he did without a seatbelt."

In the race, the track was very slippery and Dron was running in third place with Hunt only just behind in fifth place. The race leader was already 100 metres up the road by the end of the second lap. The chasing pack ran down to cascades corner, which was adjacent to the lake in the centre of the picturesque circuit. Dron's car suddenly spun and Hunt was caught unawares at over 100 miles per hour. Dron explains: "I spun the Titan at the exit from cascades in a very big way, going off to the right and then to the left." But the car was intact and the engine was still running. Dron put it into gear to get going again but, before he could, he saw Hunt's car headed straight for him. Hunt took avoiding action but was launched into the air and flew over Dron's head.

Dron recalls: "James hit a bump on the edge of the track and that was enough to launch him. His car flew through a Shell advertising hoarding, breaking off a massive piece of wood that was holding it up." Dron was shocked and thought to himself: "That looks very nasty, indeed. That's not good."

Dron leaped from his car to do what he could: "I got out of my car and found bits of his car all along the way, from both the front and the back, so he'd obviously been cartwheeling along at fantastic speed. Then I found his rollover bar, which he had modified to clear his head because he was taller, so I feared the worst."

Dron thought it was unlikely that anyone could have survived such a violent multiple impact. But he couldn't find the car's chassis, as he remembers: "I got to the edge of the lake and there was nothing to be seen. I looked more closely into the lake and saw his car upside down on the bottom. It was completely submerged in about three feet of water, and I thought: 'Oh shit.'" It struck Dron that, even if Hunt had survived the accident, he could drown. In truth, he thought Hunt was dead, saying: "I was about to go into the water. It was a horrible moment."

But suddenly, Hunt stood up. It was like a scene from John Frankenheimer's movie, *Grand Prix*. There was blood running down the side of his face and he was covered from head to toe in brown mud and green slime. Dron says: "He was concussed and he wasn't making sense but he was talking. His head had obviously had a knock. He was actually trying to tell me a dirty joke, but normally he would have made complete sense."

The marshals took ages to arrive and eventually the circuit ambulance turned up. The doctor gave Hunt a cursory examination and decided he was basically alright but took him off on a stretcher to the circuit's medical centre to be treated for shock and some cuts and bruises. Hunt's girlfriend Taormina was sitting in the pits waiting for news and she also thought, because of the reports of the severity of the accident, he was unlikely to have survived. She prepared herself for the worst, especially when the circuit commentator said over the loudspeakers: "I'm afraid it doesn't look too good."

Taormina remembers people coming up to her in the pits: "Everyone came up to console me and we just had to wait. Eventually, he came back from the medical centre and it was obvious he was terribly shaken. He could hardly move because he was so bruised and battered and his face was white. I think it was the first time it really hit home what could happen to him in a car."

Hunt remembered later: "I was flung clear as the car went over. I remember being on my hands and knees under the water and then suddenly emerging like Neptune. Seatbelts were not yet compulsory and I didn't have them because I couldn't afford them. Had I been wearing them, I might have drowned."

Later, Hunt was more shocked when he saw the remains of his car and realised it was a write-off and could not be repaired. Tony Dron was even more shaken than his friend, as he admits: "The experience very nearly put me off racing for good at the time, but I had got over that completely by the time I got home that night. It did not linger in my mind."

Hunt was in no condition to drive himself home, so they locked his car, trailer and race car in a pit garage for the night. Taormina remembers: "He didn't know whether he was coming or going." Dron drove Hunt and Taormina home that night: "I made arrangements to get his stuff sorted out, as he was obviously in no fit state to drive on the road."

At Mallory Park, Hunt was driving his new Merlyn and duelling with Dron's Titan again when they had another accident. In fact, Dron had predicted it would happen. As he recalls: "The first corner at Mallory Park was doubly dangerous in those days, and I remember complaining a lot to the race organisers and just getting a blank look as if to say: 'Get lost'. They started cars much too close together on the grid. It was just ridiculous."

It was the first corner of the circuit and, duelling for fourth place, Hunt put his back wheel between Dron's front and back wheels. But that was par for the course in Formula Ford in those days of very close racing. Dron remembers: "I'll never forget seeing the underside of his car just above my face, still doing 90 miles per hour. I hit the brakes just in time and he landed back on my left front wheel, puncturing the tyre this time."

During all this, Hunt was hit from the rear and his car was launched into the air off Dron's front wheel. Hunt's Merlyn flew into the air and right over the top of Dron's Titan and landed on Dron's nosecone, chopping it off. Dron, with a punctured tyre, couldn't avoid it and ran straight into him.

Both cars came to rest against the bank, Dron recalls: "With our wrecks neatly parked, we sat up on the bank and he got out his packet of ten Embassy and passed it to me. We said nothing. I just took out a cigarette, he took out a cigarette. He lit mine, he lit his and we sat there and watched the race. The accident wasn't mentioned." On closer inspection, the cars were not badly damaged and it could have much more expensive than it was.

Hunt raced the new car a few times in 1968, preparing for a big push in 1969. Formula Ford carried on racing through much of the winter, although not so frequently, so the changeover to the new season was virtually seamless.

At the end of that season, the two men scraped up enough cash to go on holiday together to Oberndorf, near Salzburg, in Austria. They flew out straight after the boxing day race meeting at Brands Hatch and stayed in a family house which belonged to a friend.

The 1969 season turned to be a totally different proposition to 1968. It was the year Formula Ford really took off and entries doubled. Every event now consisted of two qualifying heats and a final. Counting heats, Hunt was now winning races regularly. Also in 1969, Ford promoted Formula Ford outside of Britain for the first time and organised races in continental Europe. It was called the European Formula Ford Championship. It was being run from London by promoter Nick Brittan, who had hired Tony Dron as his personal assistant.

Dron's Formula Ford career hit the buffers after his deal for 1969 fell apart just before the season started, and he decided to become a professional journalist to give him increased credibility and financial back-up. He managed to compete in four races before temporarily retiring.

Dron admits that Hunt was braver than him when it came to taking financial risks: "He had terrible troubles over the next few years, really desperate financial stuff...but he kept going."

Even when they stopped travelling to races together, Hunt and Dron remained close. Hunt spent as much time at Dron's family's home in Wentworth than he did at his own, as he remembers: "James was probably at my house more, and he would drop in unannounced. I would often return home and there would be James eating bacon and eggs with Jim and Audrey, my father and mother. My mother would often give him a meal and he would say 'thank you very much' and go on his way. He was quite charming and everyone accepted that was just how he was."

Hunt was desperate to race abroad and he couldn't wait to start roaming the continent, towing his race car to exotic foreign tracks. He was one of the first British drivers who started travelling regularly to the continental races. The results were noted far more. But it was with some trepidation that he set off on his first European road trip in early April to take in two races in Holland and Austria. At Zandvoort on 8th April he finished third and, then, a week later, he took second place at Aspern on 14th April. His sponsors, Gowrings, weren't particularly pleased and wanted to know what benefit they were getting from his racing in Europe. Luckily, *Autosport* had printed some photographs of his car with the Gowrings name prominent, which placated them for a while.

One of Hunt's enduring faults was that with success came arrogance. That trait never went away whilst he was racing. There was no better example of it than when a young *Autosport* reporter called Ian Phillips approached Hunt at Brands Hatch on 21st April. Phillips was making his first steps in the profession and Hunt was in the middle of pumping up the tyres on his car. Phillips admits he asked Hunt a "stupid" question but says he wasn't prepared for the stream of rudeness he got in reply. Hunt said to him: "What kind of fucking stupid question is that?" Phillips says: "I remember thinking: 'What an obnoxious sod' and so I told him he was."

But Phillips had caught Hunt at a bad moment, and the driver was full of remorse afterwards. As Phillips remembers: "He phoned me up at the office the following week, we went out and, after that, we clicked." He adds: "It was a defence mechanism with him and he was like that with a lot of people." Hunt and Phillips became firm friends after that shaky start and travelled to many European races together. He says: "In those days, you socialised as often as you could for lots of different reasons – booze and birds, mainly."

Phillips became a Hunt promoter in the pages of *Autosport* after that, and, as his reputation grew, so too did the opportunities.

Hunt's occasional rashness and arrogance showed up again when he went on his second European trip in late May. He was due to compete at Vallelunga in Italy for round three of the 1969 European FF Championship on 1st June. Hunt had started the championship well and was keen to perform. The Ford Motor Company was paying generous start and prize money.

But it all went wrong in Vallelunga, and this was the first big negative incident in Hunt's career.

There were problems with his medical papers. All the drivers were required to have a medical certificate stating their blood group. It apparently hadn't been necessary in the two previous rounds in Holland and Austria, but Italy had different rules.

Hunt didn't have the certificate and the organisers told him he couldn't start. In those days, there were no fax machines or overnight couriers such as DHL or FedEx, and there was no way he could get his medical certificate over from England in time.

Hunt was furious and told the organisers he had not been made aware of the requirements in advance nor had they been stated in the entry conditions.

A row began after they point blank refused to let him start in the event. Tony Dron wasn't there that day, but recalls: "He'd travelled all the way to Vallelunga and he was buggered if he wasn't going to race."

Hunt had a rush of blood to the head and decided to take the law into his own hands. He drove his car out of the paddock, parked it at across the front row of the grid, turned the engine off and walked away.

The race couldn't start until Hunt's car was removed. By that time, he was resigned to not starting and to losing the UK£100 he would have earned as well as his leading championship position.

Hunt had chosen the wrong day to make his protest, as in the grandstands was sitting Stuart Turner, head of motorsport at the Ford Motor Company. He had a lot of important guests witnessing the debut of Formula Ford in Italy.

Turner was furious with Hunt, and turned round to Nick Brittan and said: "Mark my words, that young man is going nowhere in motor racing."

Brittan knew Hunt well and liked him. But Turner's displeasure meant he had to take some action. Brittan, who has since died, said at the time: "I took him to task over his silliness and said to him: 'Hunt, you'll never make a professional racing driver as long as you've got a hole up your arse.'" Brittan would later have cause to regret those words as, in 1976, some seven years later, Hunt would approach him at Brands Hatch and say: "I've still got that hole. How am I doing?"

The Vallelunga incident is now lost in the sands of time, and the following week's *Autosport* report of the race hardly mentioned it.

Halfway through the season, Motor Racing Enterprises (MRE), owned by Mike Ticehurst, made Hunt an offer to run his car for him and to relieve him of his responsibilities.

Motor Racing Enterprises ran Formula Ford and F3 cars for drivers who could pay. It was a professional team, run by Mike Ticehurst and Gerard McCaffrey. Like Hunt, they were both ex public schoolboys. McCaffrey was wealthy and lived in a smart mews house in West London. Ticehurst was the wheeler dealer. The ambition was to become a big second hand racing car dealership.

Ticehurst was a huge Hunt fan and the offer was altruistic, not financial. Hunt met Howden Ganley at MRE. Ganley, one of the top drivers in the formula, who had graduated to Formula 3, remembers the change to MRE as being highly significant for Hunt: "James was a bit of a shambles at running his own team, and Ticehurst picked him up and steered him right. Mike had a real insight into James."

Ganley's assessment was correct, and the difference in having his car prepared by a team of people who knew what they were doing was immediate, as Hunt won his first race out of Lydden Hill as an MRE driver.

Getting Ticehurst and McCaffrey's backing was Hunt's first big break, says Tony Dron: "We could all see it quite clearly. Early in 1969, he had really shown his skills and he had certainly got it. People were starting to believe in his ability."

The link up with MRE soon blossomed into something more, and after just a few races Ticehurst told Hunt that it was time to move up a formula and that he would fund it. The big time beckoned, and James Hunt was on his way.

He told his sponsors the good news, and Gowrings got some of its money back when Hunt sold the Merlyn for them. But he didn't get as much money as he had hoped because the car was in bits in a shed in Reading – as one anonymous and bemused would-be buyer recounted years later: "He tried to sell it to me, so I collected him in central London, drove him all the way down to Reading and, as we walked in, he said: 'Oh, by the way, did I say it was disassembled?' And there, on the floor, was a pile of bits and a chassis. I didn't buy it."

SHUNT

CHAPTER 8

The embarrassment factor
The human gene that he lacked

The story of James Hunt's life can in many ways be summed up as the story of a human being born without the embarrassment gene. There is no question that Hunt was born without the capacity for it; in fact, he was never embarrassed by anything in life. It meant he could do anything; things other humans would not even contemplate. And it was all because he never knew or understood what it was to be embarrassed. In some ways, at its most extreme, it can be thought of as a mental deficiency. Certainly, if he had been born with the gene, then his life would have been somewhat smoother to say the least.

Nowadays, most human conditions are chronicled and analysed ad nauseum. For instance, Hunt's enormous libido is now called a 'sex addiction' but it was something he recognised in himself long before anyone coined the phrase. The lack of an embarrassment gene, however, has never been discussed or analysed, probably because most of the people born with the condition in the 21st century are already in jail. But, as Hunt amply demonstrated, if it is a mental condition, then there should be a treatment for it.

But Hunt got away with being without this gene by the skin of his teeth. By some strange twist of luck (never judgment), he was never imprisoned – although there were a few times he perhaps should have been. He certainly would have been had he lived thirty years later. There is no question that, in this century, Hunt never could have been world champion without that gene.

Sarah Lomax, Hunt's second wife, despite every indication to the contrary, was actually the person who understood Hunt's character imperfections better than anyone else. She also passed on that understanding to her sons, Tom and Freddie. Freddie, in particular, understands precisely what his father was and wasn't. As for Sarah, she reacts strongly to people who mistook the lack of embarrassment for arrogance: "There was no arrogance in James as I knew him. Maybe it came across as arrogance, but deep down it wasn't that. It was just his manner or his reactions." Admitting he was stubborn but never arrogant, she insists poignantly: "He was very humble inside – very." That resonates with former Lotus team principal, Peter Collins, who was close to Hunt in his later years: "James was just a terribly decent man with certain defects he could not always control. I'd even go so far as to say he was one of the most genuinely decent men I ever met." None of this of course resonates with what is printed next. But it does go some way to demonstrating just how disadvantaged it is in life to be born without an 'embarrassment gene'.

The truth is that Sarah's description of "humble" does not match what actually defined Hunt. Hunt himself believed he suffered from something he called "arrested emotional development".

It must also be said that Hunt was not a particularly truthful person in private. Although he never told what are best described as 'evil lies', although some could be hurtful if repeated, he frequently told lies to ease his passage in life.

In one instance, he wrote to his last girlfriend, Helen Dyson, and told her that his parents had never loved him. Astonishingly, he used that as an excuse for infidelity throughout his life, and it almost became a private joke in its absurdity. Years later, the comedian Larry David would pick up on the same theme for his hit US cult series called 'Curb Your Enthusiasm', but with comedic treatment. Hunt particularly tended to use this fib on his girlfriends when they caught him out. He found it worked most of the time and, privately, it was just as funny to him as it was to Larry David 30 years later. Hunt demonstrated no insight into the pain it would inevitably cause his parents when the stories got back to them. Nor, indeed, for the hurt it would eventually inflict upon them when it was published in Gerald Donaldson's biography after he died. For Hunt, the prospect of being caught for being unfaithful – be it by Dyson, Birbeck or whomever he was with at the time – simply necessitated an excuse. That was just the way he was.

But Peter Collins points out that his propensity for being economical with the truth mustn't be read as a mark of his dishonesty. Collins says he was a scrupulously honest individual: "James was a very correct man, but seemed to feel that convention did not have to be applied to everybody. And when he felt convention was being forced on him, he may have had a tendency to rebel. James was definitely a little eccentric, very individual and he did not suffer fools." But as Collins ruefully admits, sometimes his rebelliousness against convention may have gone too far.

That rebelliousness often manifested itself in Hunt's choice of attire. There were always issues with his wardrobe, or lack of it. Whenever possible, and with little excuse, Hunt would strip off the top half of his clothing and his jeans, and often get down to the skimpiest underwear or swimming trunks. He would often walk around the Formula One paddock in his trunks, showing not the slightest discomfiture. Sometimes, he might as well have been naked. But most times, he would be in a sleeveless vest-type shirt with shorts, no shoes and no socks – sometimes even on live television as he walked around the starting grid.

There was one very embarrassing moment for Brabham-Ford driver Nelson Piquet on the starting grid at the Monaco Grand Prix in 1981, which Piquet found highly amusing. Piquet was on pole, and Hunt, wearing his shorts, leaned over the car to say something to Piquet. When the Brazilian looked up, as he recounts, all he could see was: "...a pair of bollocks, hanging out of his shorts, and James' voice."

Aside from his wardrobe and the incidents in his love life, the worst examples of Hunt's lack of the embarrassment gene came in three 'urinating incidents.' Many of his close friends, including Chris Jones, found the incidents amusing when they were witnessed or retold later. But they were far from funny. Jones, in particular, could undoubtedly have done more to correct his friend.

Jones was involved in an early urinating incident when, in his teenage years, he organised a birthday party involving a coach trip. Jones' parents were also on the trip and they allowed a makeshift bar to be set up in the coach, which Hunt naturally made full use of. So much so, that the coach regularly had to be halted mid-journey so that Hunt, who had over indulged, could go to the toilet.

At such stops, James simply jumped out and faced the coach's side windows and, in full view of his friends and Jones' parents, unzipped his trousers and urinated. Unfortunately, Jones thought it was highly amusing, and his amusement set an unfortunate precedent for other such occasions, all of which were far from innocently comedic.

When Jones spoke with Gerald Donaldson 17 years ago, after Hunt's death, he told him he didn't think his friend was an "an exhibitionist by nature", just "unconventional." He said: "He always did exactly what he wanted to do. And you could never argue with him. You might suggest something, but he'd do it his own way." Today, Jones seems embarrassed about it all and won't speak about his friend.

Perhaps the most outrageous urinating incident came at a restaurant in France, during Hunt's Formula 3 days in 1971. Patrons in a bistro at Pau were subject to an awful demonstration from Hunt as he left an establishment in which drivers and mechanics were dining after the race. It began when one of the journalists at Hunt's table bet him 100 francs that he wouldn't relieve himself on the restaurant floor. The challenge, according to driver Brendan McInerney, was met. As he recalls: "It produced two inevitable results. One was that James pissed on the floor as he was leaving the restaurant, reversing out the door and laughing uproariously as he went about his business, and the other was that the guy who bet him wouldn't pay up. James was extremely upset that he didn't get paid."

But the worst example, and the most damaging to his reputation, came in 1987 – a few months after the birth of his second son, Freddie. Hunt was on a British Airways flight to Adelaide for the Australian Grand Prix. He had, as usual, consumed the maximum amount of alcohol he could tolerate. When he could drink no more beer, or the stocks had run out, he slumped in his seat and went straight to sleep.

The sheer volume of beer he had consumed meant he soon needed to go to the toilet urgently. So he got up and wandered down the aisle but, in his stupor, couldn't find the toilets. As he got to the curtain that separates the first and business class sections of a Boeing 747, he simply unzipped his jeans and relieved himself against the curtain until urine ran down the aisle. It lasted a minute or more. His conduct was in full view of the passengers, which included the BBC television presenter Esther Rantzen. He then returned to his seat, leaving bemused passengers and stewards wondering what to do.

Knowing who he was, the crew let him sleep it off. But, as it had been witnessed by so many people, it was not an incident that could be covered up and it was recorded in the plane's incident log. Inevitably, one of the passengers told the story to a newspaper, and it was then written up by Reuters journalists and put out on its news service. Typically, the headlines in the newspapers read: 'Hunt For Relief' and 'Drunken Shame of the Speed Ace.' The story travelled all over the world, doubtless embellished with every telling. One embellishment described how Esther Rantzen's daughter had been "splashed." Rantzen was forced to issue a denial, saying that she had not noticed the incident and that what was described had "not happened." In his book about Hunt, Gerald Donaldson was moved to call it "an act of considerable irresponsibility."

In the end, British Airways was forced to issue a statement, in which it simply confirmed the incident and offered their regret, stating baldly: "Mr Hunt had problems controlling his bodily functions during the flight."

With the story continuing to run in the newspapers, it eventually sparked a national discussion about the yobbish behaviour of celebrities. Back at his home in Wimbledon, Hunt was eagerly anticipated by journalists keeping vigil for his return from Adelaide. There was also talk he would be sent home in disgrace by the BBC and his contract torn up. When Hunt finally returned home a week later, the journalists were still there. It was then that the magnitude of the story and the full ramifications of what he had done finally hit home.

In the end, Hunt was forced to respond to the furore, saying that he had been "sleepwalking", which he said he tended to do, especially when he was drunk. Again, some of his more irresponsible friends, and he had many of them, thought the incident was terribly funny. But not Bubbles Horsley, who was stunned by what had happened. He warned Hunt of the likely consequences and told him that that he had gone too far this time. In so many words, Horsley told him he didn't want to be the godfather to a son of a man who behaved as he had done. They were strong words from a friend, but words Hunt needed to hear. Horsley remembered as much later: "I thought that business on the aeroplane was very sad. He made the rather half-hearted excuse about sleepwalking, but I said: 'Well, you were sleep-walking because you were behaving like an asshole. And you know you do that and you shouldn't have done it on the aeroplane. So don't go making half-baked excuses. If you want to go and piss in the cupboards at home, that's another matter', and James took my point. He was contrite and said: 'You're absolutely right'"

But this time the damage was done could not be offset by a stern talking to from his ex team manager. There were no immediate repercussions but the long terms effects on Hunt were catastrophic and unpredictable. It was an event that ultimately caused his financial demise and one that his second wife's solicitors would later exploit to the fullest in his divorce. They ultimately used it to threaten him with the loss of custody of his children. The extra UK£1 million they squeezed out of him, directly because of that aeroplane incident, eventually broke him.

At the time, Hunt was extremely lucky to get away with what he had done; if it were to happen today, he would undoubtedly have been restrained in his seat by the crew, who would then have radioed ahead to the police to arrest him when the plane landed at Adelaide airport, and he would have served at least three months in a foreign jail. But that was then, and there was no police reception at Adelaide airport. But he did suffer a huge reputational backlash from the incident, which some say he never fully recovered from. Stirling Moss says: "He did create a lot of damage to his own reputation overall. But that was so James and there wasn't anything he seemed to be bitter about."

Hunt never urinated in public again after that, but he carried on drinking. Horsley was never able to tackle the root cause of Hunt's problems; that only came about when Hunt lost all his money and could no longer afford to drink.

And Hunt's propensity for alcohol was, of course, legendary. But Hunt was never an alcoholic. All his drinking was done for leisure purposes; he simply enjoyed it greatly. And it never in itself caused any particular problems, except of course when he needed to urinate urgently. Drink did not change his personality at all, and he was certainly never an unpleasant drunk. In fact, it was quite the opposite – he was in fact a very, very pleasant drunk.

And some of his drinking adventures were admittedly very funny. Professor Sid Watkins often observed Hunt's strange habit of dragging around behind him, one in each hand, two black bin liner-type plastic bags after races. In one bag would be full cans of beer, and in the other, the empties. As Watkins recalls: "I always remember when he finished a race, he used to have two black bags – one was full of tins of beer and one was full of the empties – and he used to drag them round, have one, put one in the bag. I mean he was really enjoying himself."

Watkins remembers another occasion, flying back to London from a race: "We'd fly back and, when the luggage was coming out onto the carousel, instead of the luggage coming out, it was James, sitting crossed legged, going round and round on the carousel."

Away from Formula One and in the world of his second great passion, budgerigars, there was also trouble. There was a potentially serious incident on a visit to a budgerigar show in Doncaster, Yorkshire, in November 1989.

At the show, one of Hunt's budgies won first prize. This was as important to him as winning any Grand Prix, and Hunt went on a binge in Doncaster to celebrate. After a meal at Doncaster's Swallow Hotel, he and his budgerigar enthusiast friends decided to go to a nightclub, one recommended by the hotel manager who had unfortunately forgotten to tell him about the club's dress standards. Hunt, dressed in denim jeans and running shoes, went ahead to smooth the way. But at the nightclub, he came up against a doorman called Ian Butterfield. The doorman informed him of his incorrect attire and told him he would not be admitted. Hunt was having none of it and asked the doorman, quite reasonably, to talk to the manager to see if an exception could be made. Butterfield told him there was no point, as there were no exceptions. Hunt asked him again and he was again refused. Frustrated by the doorman's obtuse attitude, Hunt was angry but polite. Unfortunately, Butterfield was holding a paper cup of hot coffee and, as Hunt turned to leave, he flicked the cup of hot, but not scalding, coffee over the doorman in pure frustration. It could have been an accident or it could have been deliberate, it was not clear. Although it looked like an accident, it certainly did not appear that way to the doorman. A scuffle between Hunt and the club's security staff ensued. They manhandled him to the ground and delivered him over to two nearby policemen on patrol. On the word of the nightclub's security staff, Hunt was immediately arrested and taken to the Doncaster police station.

Officers on duty at Doncaster police station couldn't quite believe what they were seeing and wondered what on earth a former Formula One world champion was doing in Doncaster attending a budgerigar show. There was certainly much scratching of heads that night as Hunt languished in a room at the police station. Two hours later, at around midnight, Hunt was charged with assault on the available evidence and released after two hours on his own recognisance. But the first thing he did was return to the club where the doorman was still on duty and apologise to him. The evidence against Hunt was flimsy, especially when the police examined the nightclub's security camera film footage. The charges were quietly dropped. 25 years later, that security film would be broadcast in a television documentary causing his family all sorts of embarrassment and anguish.

John Hogan says he never found Hunt's lack of embarrassment a problem, but admits it did exist. But in Hunt's defence, he says most of the top drivers had "gaps" in their characters, and points to Niki Lauda's well-known callousness as a prime example of another driver with a character defect. A friend of both drivers once witnessed such an incident, as he explains: "I was with James at Brands Hatch, and it was a practice day and some little kid came up to Niki with a Lauda fan book and asked him to sign a picture. This little kid was wide-eyed and struggling with this book. And Niki said: 'Where's the pen?' so the kid got out a pen and he was trying to keep the rain off the book and Niki grabbed it, signed it and just said: 'Thank you, bye' and looked away. James said to me: 'Well, you see, that's the callousness of the cunt.' James hated it, hated that [sort of thing] – absolutely hated it."

Lauda's attitude, of course, was completely the opposite to Hunt's. Hunt's brilliance in situations like that was the reasons he was so beloved by his British fans. Hunt genuinely loved people and he loved mixing with ordinary folk. He had no embarrassment about that either; something that a person with his background and upbringing might have had. His generosity of spirit went to the absolute core of his character.

Many people who never saw the brighter side of Hunt thought his antics were just 'bad behaviour' stemming from his ten years at boarding school, where he had developed the tremendous self-confidence which enabled him to do anything he felt like doing in public without embarrassment. Certainly, it was there also that he had acquired his unfailing self-belief and determination to triumph over adversity. But, despite any obvious defects, Hunt had a very endearing and sincere side to him, although it was not a side that he revealed to everybody.

Grahame White, now chief executive of the Historic Sports Car Club, recognises the validity of all the arguments regarding his friend's lack of the 'embarrassment gene', but says there were times when Hunt could indeed become embarrassed about his behaviour, especially if it was in front of people he liked and respected. Hunt did like and respect White, who was head of the British Automobile Racing Club (BARC) when Hunt was racing in the junior formulae. BARC was the leading organiser of motorsport championships in those days and White was like a guardian angel to the then young, aspiring racing driver. As White recalls, Hunt did once embarrass himself by his behaviour with a woman: "I remember at one race meeting at Thruxton, he came in to sign on and noticed one of the young girls who was working for me. She just caught his eye. He asked me later in the day: 'Who is that girl, what's her name, does she work for you?' I said: 'Yes, she does.' The following morning, she just didn't turn up for work. We normally get ready about 7am, and she arrived at the circuit, very sheepish, at 10am. She came to me and said: 'Sorry, I didn't feel well.' I guessed what had happened and, when I found James, I said: 'James, were you out last night?' I remember his face being an absolute picture, as he searched for his excuse."

Sometimes it seemed that his entire life was spent searching for excuses for his naughtiness.

SHUNT

84

CHAPTER 9

That fateful meeting
as two paths cross 1971

James Hunt and John Hogan get together

John Hogan was sitting at his desk at Wasey's, one of London's top advertising agencies, when he received a telephone call that would change his life. It was early 1971 and on the line was George Pincus, with whom he had previously worked at Benton & Bowles.

Pincus and Australian-born Hogan were close friends. Hogan was regarded in the agency world as somewhat of a motor racing expert, and Pincus said to him: "You know a bit about motor racing, don't you?" "Yes," replied Hogan. "Well," said Pincus, "there's this bloke called James Hunt who is looking for someone who knows a bit about sponsorship. Can he come talk to you?" Hogan said: "Yeah sure." And that's how it all began.

Hogan didn't think much of it at the time, but that short conversation kick-started a chain of events that, for two decades, would make Hogan the most powerful man in Formula One after Bernie Ecclestone, and ultimately lead to Hunt's world championship in 1976. Hogan was 28 years old, and Hunt just 21.

On the appointed day, Hunt turned up at Wasey's offices in London with a young woman called Annabel Lamb. She introduced herself as the young driver's manager.

Lamb made the introductions and Hunt pitched his proposition to Hogan.

Hunt's keen grasp of things impressed Hogan straightaway. He was also impressed by the young man's supreme confidence that he was going to be Formula One world champion in the not-too-distant future.

When Hogan's demeanour revealed a small degree of scepticism towards Hunt's bold claims, Hunt thrust an article from *Autocar* magazine in front of him. The article substantiated his prediction as well as the year in which it would be achieved.

Hogan remembers Hunt telling him: "I've got an article here from *Autocar*, and it says I'm going to be world champion in 1974." *Autocar* magazine updated its predictions every year and was sometimes accurate and sometimes not. That year, as Hogan remembers, it also listed Mike Beuttler as a future world champion; it could not have been more wrong about that.

Hogan now says: "It's the first thing I remember him saying to me: that he was going to be world champion in 1974. So he missed it by two years, but I've never been confronted with somebody who was so convincingly ultra-confident. I would get phone calls every week from somebody saying they were going to be world champion and 'can't you sponsor me?' But this was the one and only time I actually believed what I was hearing."

Hunt was feeling particularly pleased with himself that day. He had just been given a test drive by the new March Formula 3 team and it had gone very well. He had high hopes of being signed as a works driver by the new team. But first, he had to get some sponsorship together to help pay for the drive. Hogan remembers: "He knew Max Mosley and Alan Rees, and he was very keen on March."

By modern standards, Hunt's needs were very modest: just US$5,000 for a season's motor racing. But even a thousand dollars was a lot of money in those days and it was a tough call for an unproven driver. But Hunt already had some sponsorship vaguely promised to him by a company called Rose Bearings, and he wanted Hogan to help seal the deal. Hunt said: "I need you to help me because I've got to go and see Rose Bearings."

Hogan had received countless requests for help before, but something told him that this young man was different. Although he finally agreed to help put together a professional presentation, Hogan made it very clear that the proposition was much too small for Wasey's and that he would handle it only in his spare time, purely as a favour. It was an unusual outcome for Hogan, but he sensed something in Hunt; although today he has no idea what it was.

Their first meeting lasted around half an hour and, throughout, Annabel

Lamb said nothing. In truth, Lamb had little idea about driver management but was a latent petrolhead and liked hanging around with Hunt. At the end, she was absolutely delighted with the outcome and couldn't quite believe that a man with Hogan's reputation in the agency world was prepared to help her driver.

The next day, Hogan wrote Hunt a note, which read: "I have been thinking about what you were saying and I think it's all achievable. So, if you want to do it, you've gotta do this, this and this." He adds: "I can't remember what 'this, this and this' was, though."

After Hogan had put together the presentation, Hunt asked him to go and see the sponsor alone. Making some excuse, Hunt asked: "Can you go and see him?"

Hunt had worked out that a presentation by a professional adverting executive would make a far greater impression than one by a wet-behind-the-ears young driver. Hunt had surmised that his cause would be enhanced by him not being there. It was a very intelligent assessment and Hogan was impressed by his sound judgement. Finding Hunt to be very determined and dedicated to the event at hand, Hogan remembers being delighted by his attitude.

Hogan recalls: "So I went to see Rose Bearings on his behalf, and the guy I saw – I've no idea what his name was – all I remember is that he was a miserable son of a bitch. I tried to explain the sponsorship to him but he didn't want to know." The chairman of Rose even turned the tables and told Hogan: "I think young people like you should be giving me money to run the car. I shouldn't be paying you; it should be a privilege to be putting our name on it."

Ironically, Hogan could see the chairman's point, as he says: "I must say I learned something from that miserable man – a lesson which I've used time and time again. The funny thing was that, many years later, when Audi was looking for sponsorship for its rally team, I told them they should be paying us. And they nearly did because they wanted a big name on the car. So you always learn something."

Eventually, Hunt did get some money from Rose Bearings thanks to the chairman's young assistant, who had also been at the meeting and who could see the merits of the proposal – and who wasn't as miserable as his boss.

It was less than US$1,000 but it was a crucial US$1,000 because, on that basis, Wallis Hunt gave his son another US$1,000, and it was enough to get the season underway.

Then, Hunt had one of his periodic pieces of luck. Coca-Cola was a client of Wasey's, and the drinks company decided to allocate a small amount of money from its budget for motor racing sponsorship. In those days, Coca-Cola was not a big brand in Britain and was just beginning to establish itself outside of America. Generally, colas weren't popular in England, in a market then dominated by lemonade. Coca-Cola found motor racing to be an ideal way to organise sample tastings and to introduce their product to young people.

With not enough money to partner with Formula One or even Formula Two, Hogan was told to spend it in Formula 3. Hogan remembers it clearly: "Absolutely out of the blue, they said to me one day: 'Why don't we sponsor something in motor racing?' So we sponsored James Hunt and also Gerry Birrell's Formula 3 car."

As Hogan remembers, the deal with Coca-Cola was worth around US$1,000. He says: "A thousand dollars was a fortune in those days, so, between his father and Rose, he sort of scratched through the Formula 3 season."

It may have been messy, but it was the start of a relationship of mutual trust and affection that would stretch over two decades. Enduring many trials and tribulations, it would also ultimately lead to great success and firmly establish the reputations of both men.

Hogan says: "I was doing it as more of a favour. You can't imagine what it was like; these were the primitive days of sponsorship." But deep down, Hogan was enormously impressed with Hunt's confidence: "He was totally self-confident. I have never seen anybody quite like him in my life. Let's put it this way, I reckon I knew a lot about motor racing; you have a feel for it. You immediately knew, even in those days, how hard it was to make progress, and James had absolutely no doubt whatsoever that he was going to make the big time." He adds: "James had that public school veneer, that confidence that you could only imagine during the war of spitfire flyers. He could never see a problem, and always said: 'Why shouldn't I be able to do that?'"

Hogan and Hunt also became close personal friends. Hunt introduced him to a motor racing haunt in West London called 365, as it was situated at number 365 on the King's Road. At the bar and in the restaurant, the two men would frequently share a shepherd's pie, the menu speciality which sold for 10s/6d (55 pence) per portion. In that bar, Hunt introduced Hogan to other motor racing characters, such as fellow Australian Tim Schenken. Schenken subsequently introduced Hogan to Ron Dennis, who, at that time, was running a Formula Two team called Rondel Racing with his partner Neil Trundle. It was to be a fateful meeting, as Dennis handed Hogan his first big motor racing assignment when he appointed Wasey's to find sponsorship for the team.

The introduction eventually led to much bigger things, especially when Philip Morris' Marlboro brand moved into Formula One in a big way in 1973 and hired Hogan to manage it day-to-day.

Hogan never secured any more sponsorship for Hunt after that initial foray. The driver couldn't afford to retain Wasey's and it was difficult for Hogan to do it freelance without creating a conflict and risking his job. As Hogan explains: "I suddenly realised how difficult it was. It was very good education because, whilst I was working for an advertising agency at the time, I could see all the reasons why you shouldn't do it, you know, on a daily basis."

The two men met frequently as friends for the next five years until destiny brought them together again professionally in the most decisive way.

SHUNT

CHAPTER 10

The Formula 3 Years
1969 to 1972

Four dispiriting years of slog begin

James Hunt was impressive enough in Formula Ford for his team, Motor Racing Enterprises (MRE), to want to move him up to Formula 3 midway through 1969. Mike Ticehurst and Gerard McCaffery's belief in him simply grew stronger and stronger, and Hunt also became convinced he was going all the way. McCaffery was prepared to fund the drive as long as he could afford it. Ticehurst's faith in Hunt was incredibly important to the young driver in the early days; Ticehurst used to tell anyone who would listen that Hunt was an up and coming man. Howden Ganley, who drove in F3 at the time, remembers becoming very fed up with hearing it. MRE was running Ganley's car, and Hunt was all Ticehurst wanted to talk about. Ganley says: "I remember him saying: 'This young guy's going to be really good.' Tim [Schenken] and I were already in Formula 3 but we knew Mike and we lived locally, so we used to stop by and chat to him. When he was telling us all about this guy James Hunt, we were like: 'Yeah, yeah', because, at that stage, you don't want to hear about anybody else, do you?" Ganley adds: "But Mike was a total believer."

Ticehurst, who died ten years ago, was genuinely a very pleasant individual, much liked in his racing days. Today, he is not even a footnote in the James Hunt story, and, for some reason, Hunt biographers Gerald Donaldson and

Christopher Hilton fail to give him any mention in their books. Hunt – as he did with Tom Wheatcroft – subsequently wrote Ticehurst out of his story and his contribution to his career. But, without Ticehurst, Hunt may never have left Formula Ford.

As it was, after barely one and a half years in Formula Ford, Hunt made the move to the senior formula. As he lined up on the grid for his first Formula 3 race at Mallory Park, on 11th August 1969, he silently toasted his good fortune. He had arrived at the big time.

In truth, Hunt had never felt right in a Formula Ford car and he was glad to leave the junior formula behind. He was much more comfortable in the larger formulae and found Formula 3 to fit him like a glove. Sitting on the grid, he couldn't wait for the starter's flag to fall that sunny August Sunday.

Hunt found the difference between a Formula 3 car and a Formula Ford car to be like night and day. Whilst Formula Ford cars ran on narrow tyres that looked like road car tyres and had more or less standard road car engines, F3 cars had proper slick race tyres and specially tuned racing engines – albeit, in those days, restricted to one-litre capacity to stop the cars from going too fast.

But what he found somewhat disconcerting was the high standard of the opposition.

Formula 3 that year was riddled with stars of the future, drivers that would one day end up in Formula One. They were scattered everywhere amongst the grids in 1969. His competitors included Ronnie Peterson, Tim Schenken, Howden Ganley, Jody Scheckter and Niki Lauda. In fact, 12 drivers competing that year in Formula 3 would eventually sit in a Formula One car.

But luckily, Hunt had plenty of support. Hunt had caught the eye of Barrie Gill and Andrew Marriott, founders of the CSS sponsorship agency. Then in its infancy as a news agency, CSS would grow over the next five to ten years to become the biggest sports sponsorship agency in Britain. The three men became friends, as Andrew Marriott recalls: "I can't remember exactly the first time we met him but he was obviously a likely lad, and I knew the people that were running him. We thought he was great and he just looked the business. He was an exciting driver; even then, he had a lot about him, a lot of charisma. You could just see it." It was a valuable introduction as, a few years later, CSS would play a significant role in Hunt's life.

Formula 3 was so popular in those days that it was not unusual to have 75 or more drivers entered for a single race. Hunt said: "Formula 3 was the right way to go at that time. For an up-and-coming driver, it was the only serious route into Formula One."

He may have achieved his ambition but his car was a second-hand Brabham BT21 that was well over two years old. His engine was tired and desperately needed a rebuild. The quality and quantity of the field in Formula 3 would make it a tough challenge, and the odds were stacked against him performing well enough to be noticed.

Despite that, Hunt did what he did best and was immediately a front runner and contender for F3 podiums. He wrestled the Brabham round to finish seventh in his first race at Mallory Park. Ticehurst was delighted with his debut and promptly entered him for two Formula Libre races where he won both times out, picking up just enough prize money to pay the bills.

The following weekend, he was at Brands Hatch, where, once again, he easily qualified for the main race and scored his first podium finish, placing third. The next weekend, he was fourth at Brands Hatch again.

That August and September of 1969 were two of the finest and happiest months of Hunt's career, as he raced every weekend. He didn't win anything in F3 but it was clear to everyone that, in an up-to-date car, he would easily have been winning races.

On 29th September 1969, he went to Cadwell Park in Lincolnshire. Set in the Lincolnshire Wolds, racing was restricted because of noise. Nevertheless, it was a popular venue and known as a driver's circuit, with varying fast and slow characteristics.

The Cadwell F3 race was significant in 1969 because it was the worldwide race debut of the new March Engineering company. The launch of March had taken the racing world by storm and the eyes of the motor racing world were on Cadwell Park that weekend.

Ronnie Peterson was debuting March's new F3 car, dubbed the March 693. March cars were named after the year and the formula in which they appeared, and it was the only 69 car produced by the new company. The whole of the March team was there to see its debut, including owners Max Mosley, Alan Rees and Robin Herd. Their presence proffered an opportunity for Hunt to shine in front of some very important people, and shine he did. The March company would subsequently become a very important part of the James Hunt story and it was all the result of what happened on that autumn day in Lincolnshire.

Incredibly, Hunt qualified his two-year-old Brabham car on the front row of the grid for his qualifying heat. He qualified easily, despite a minor accident. When all the times were added up, he was on the front row of the grid for the main race.

By the end of the first lap, Hunt was in third place and battling with Ronnie Peterson, who was driving the brand new March 693 in its first race.

At the head of the field, Tim Schenken raced with Howden Ganley and they passed the chequered flag to finish in that order. But Hunt and Peterson jostled for third place from the very start of the race, swapping places in virtually every lap. In the end, they tied for third place, crossing the finish line with identical times. The stewards, however, judging by eye, said Peterson's longer nose cone was fractionally first to the line. So, officially, Hunt placed fourth.

Nevertheless, the race had been so close that Hunt's new lap record was shared by only two other drivers. Suddenly, everyone was talking about the young Briton. The weeklies *Autosport* and *Motoring News* gushed about him that week.

Hunt had made an immediate impact, and Max Mosley was so impressed that he telephoned Hunt a few weeks later with an offer to drive for March at Brands Hatch on 19th October. In between Cadwell and Brands Hatch, Peterson had crashed the new March and it had turned over and caught fire. He had been rescued from the car, but the injuries he had sustained meant he would be out of racing for a month.

Mosley remembers it well as his first serious encounter with James Hunt. It was also when he first christened him 'Hunt the Shunt', as he says: "When we wanted to replace Ronnie, there were two obvious replacements: one was James and the other was someone called Ian Ashley. And when the press asked: 'Who are you going to put in?' I said: 'It's a choice between Crashley (Ashley) and Shunt (Hunt).' And that's actually where that came from, they called him 'Hunt the Shunt', which was just quite right."

But it didn't work out. Hunt was totally overawed at Brands Hatch and could not get in the groove. In truth, Peterson had driven the skin off the new March 693 at Cadwell Park and made it look a lot better than it was. At that time, Hunt was no Ronnie Peterson. And it showed.

In truth, the new March 693 was a dog, and Hunt hankered to get back in his Brabham. At Brands in the March, he could only manage tenth place – far worse than he would have performed in his Brabham, which he knew was a better car.

Hunt received some bad press and went from hero to zero, whilst March was saved some embarrassment about how bad its new car was. Everyone blamed the driver.

Predictably, nothing came from the drive and Hunt finished off the season in his MRE-entered Brabham BT21. At the end of 1969, Hunt placed 15th in the Lombank British Formula 3 Championship with eight points. In truth, it wasn't much to write home about. But, overall, he had made a notable impact in Formula 3 by doing it all in an old car and only competing in half of the season. For now, it was good enough.

All in all, he had competed in 15 races in Formula 3 and scored two first places, one second and two third places. It was a very capable performance and, despite the March fiasco at Brands Hatch, it had got him noticed as a coming man.

So much so that, at the end of the season, he scooped up a Grovewood Award. The Grovewoods were motor racing's Oscars, and the significance of winning one should not be underestimated in Hunt's career. The Awards were sponsored by a conglomerate called Grovewood Securities Ltd, quoted on the London Stock Exchange and run by John Danny.

Grovewood Securities had been founded in 1914 and was initially called The Lady Workers' Homes Ltd, with the object of building houses for the exclusive occupation of working women, until it was bought by Danny in 1958 with backing from the Eagle Star insurance company.

Grovewood dominated British motor racing by dint of its ownership of a company called Motor Circuit Developments Ltd (MCD), which owned five of Britain's top race tracks, including Brands Hatch, Snetterton, Mallory Park and Oulton Park. MCD was run by a very powerful gentleman called John Webb. Webb, a colossus in British motor sport, was famous for unlocking his office cocktail cabinet at 10 o'clock in the morning and consuming most of its contents, helped by his various visitors and staff, by 6 o'clock in the evening. He became a legend in the business.

Luckily for Hunt, the Grovewood awards were judged by members of the British Guild of Motoring Writers, and not by Webb. The Guild's membership included such luminaries as John Blunsden, the legendary Formula One correspondent of *The Sunday Times*. That year, the judges were Philip Turner, sports editor of *Motor* magazine, Michael Cotton, editor of *Motoring News*, and Alan Brinton, associate editor of *Motor Racing* magazine.

The judges decided that James Hunt was the second most promising young race driver in Britain in 1969. First was Dave Walker and third Tony Trimmer, neither of whom went on to make any real impact in motor racing. The award also carried a cash prize of UK£300, then worth around US$750. The prizes were handed out at a special dinner at the Royal Lancaster Hotel in London by Jackie Stewart, that year's world champion. Webb and Danny looked on, and many of Hunt's family and friends were also in attendance.

It proved to be a sea-change in his life, and was most important in establishing his credibility with his own family. Now, he was not the only one telling his father he was a talented driver. From that moment on, his father's wallet was much easier to prise open.

It is true to say that winning the Grovewood Award kicked off Hunt's career and got him noticed. Without it, things could have been very different. And whatever differences arose between Hunt and John Webb in years to come, he never forgot what Webb's organisation had done for him that night. Webb's boss, John Danny, usually a somewhat remote man, warmed to Hunt straightaway and kept an eye on his career until the day he retired.

The Grovewood money settled all of Hunt's debts, and, by the end of 1969, he was left with just a small overdraft position at his bank. Although MRE had financed his racing that year, he had to pay all his own expenses – and much of the money had been borrowed.

That bank overdraft was a constant running sore between James and his father. In those days, bank overdrafts were readily available for well-educated young men of good families, and Hunt had taken full advantage, much to his parent's chagrin. Wallis Hunt was being continually pressed by the family's bank manager to guarantee his son's mounting debts, something he resolutely refused to do. Hence, the younger Hunt was in possession of a growing file of letters from a not-so-friendly bank manager demanding early repayment, something he very rarely received.

The Grovewood cash was put to good use paying off the overdraft, but Hunt was careful not to pay back so much that the bank manager could withdraw the facility and close the account. He had worked out that whilst he still owed the bank money, they would keep the account open and, because of his father, they would be reluctant to bounce his cheques.

But far more important than the cash it provided was the genuine prestige the award bestowed upon him. Whilst journalists had been persuaded to write glowing articles in the past based on nothing but Hunt's charm, the Grovewood Award was an official recognition of his talents, and it proved most helpful with potential sponsors.

It also came at a significant time. At the start of 1970, James Hunt gave up his regular job to race cars full time; he truly became a professional race driver. It was a significant coming of age for any driver. From now on, he would race at the weekend and look for sponsorship full-time during the week.

To mark the occasion, Hunt started on a door-to-door search for cash from local companies.

The cold calling was to pay real dividends as Molyslip, a UK based company which refined industrial grease from crude oil, agreed to put up UK£1,500 to sponsor him for a season of Formula 3.

Hunt also persuaded Lotus Components Ltd, the race car manufacturing arm of Group Lotus, to give him a free chassis and quasi-works backing to run it. This was a serious coup, and Colin Chapman personally approved the deal with the young driver. It made Hunt officially a works driver, a very important distinction in the cut and thrust of Formula 3. But he would have to run the team himself, independently.

Chapman's deal with Hunt was actually very generous and included the car, an engine, a fixed number of engine rebuilds, although not crash repair facilities. Lotus also gave him UK£1,000 in cash, which, with Molyslip's money, gave Hunt a war chest of UK£2,500 for the season. As large as this was, it still didn't cover his anticipated operating budget of UK£5,000 and left him needing to earn UK£2,500 in start and prize money, a tall order in those days.

Start money was the system whereby promoters invited drivers to race at their circuits and paid them a fixed fee regardless of how they performed. Prize money was then handed out as a bonus depending on where a driver finished in the race. The big danger was crashing in qualifying and not being able to start the race – then no money was paid at all.

The money earned was generally given out in cash after the race, before competitors left for home. At every race day evening across the circuits of Europe, Hunt could be seen with all the other drivers queuing for his cash.

With his new-found fortune, Hunt planned to compete in as many races as he could for the 1970 Formula 3 season, in a mix of championships in Britain and across Europe. At the start of 1970, he genuinely felt it would be his year, and that at the end he would be able to attract the attention of a Formula One team principal.

But first, he had to get properly equipped. With no back up from a team, Hunt spent his early sponsorship installments getting set up with a road car and trailer to tow the car across Europe. Later, he would buy a transit van as his tow vehicle. Balancing the books proved difficult right from the start of the season, as he was getting his sponsorship cash from Molyslip and Lotus in staged payments throughout the year.

In 1970, Formula 3 was at a peak in Britain and there were no less than three separate championships: the Shell Super Oil, the Lombank and the Forward Trust. Hunt resolved to compete in all three, whereas other drivers wisely decided to focus on one or two of the series. Of the top runners, only the very well-funded Dave Walker tackled all three and also did well in all three. It was a scattergun approach and Hunt simply didn't have the resources.

It was going to be a difficult year and Hunt geared himself up for the life of a nomad gypsy.

That spring, summer and autumn, he virtually lived in his tent and, when in England, either stayed with his parents or shared a flat in London with one of his myriad of friends, which were growing by the day.

Money was so tight that his taste in women also became low rent, as he could not afford to invite them to dinner unless they could pay for themselves or, better still, pay for him. So he began searching for ways of sleeping with women without wining and dining them. Finding himself remarkably successful at the venture, he wondered why he hadn't tried it before – although he admitted to friends that the girls weren't quite so pretty. Gerald Donaldson says: "He restricted his evenings to socialising or talking shop with his fellow competitors, many of whom were similarly impecunious."

His girlfriend in England, Taormina Rich, took a back seat during this time. She occasionally came to a European race and he saw her casually when he was in England. She knew about his other women, but the couple would not formally split for another 12 months, when she met her future husband at that year's Monaco Grand Prix.

In fact, it was remarkable just how cheaply a group of people with shared ambitions and destinations could make out. It was an era and a mode of life that today's Formula 3 competitors could neither contemplate nor carry out.

When John Hogan's Coca-Cola money came through, Hunt treated himself to the odd night in a cheap hotel, and all his friends piled in to use the shower and run the various establishments completely out of hot water. This happened time and again. Unsurprisingly, Hunt was only able to book into a hotel once, never twice.

The much wealthier Niki Lauda had a flat in London, which was luxurious by Hunt's standards, and he stayed there for a while. But the two were never particular friends in those days. Being friends with Niki was rather a difficult feat because it was always entirely on his terms. But, for a brief period at least, Lauda seemed to enjoy having a proper English friend. And he particularly liked Hunt because he introduced the then somewhat gawky Austrian to his spare girlfriends. Lauda was astonished by Hunt's capacity to bed women; he couldn't even attempt to keep up. Years later, in an interview with *F1 Magazine*, Lauda demonstrated his dry wit when he joked that he "liked sex as much as the next man – unless of course the next man was James Hunt." Nine years later, British comedian Ricky Gervais seemingly picked up on the joke at the 2010 Golden Globe awards in Hollywood. Gervais made the joke about Mel Gibson, but with reference to alcohol rather than sex. It brought the house down.

The Lotus 59 was moderately competitive in 1970, but, Hunt, although running near the front in races, was by no means the star of the show. Others in the same equipment were faster that year, and he did not get a particularly good start to the season and subsequently didn't earn much prize money.

Hunt's first crisis was not long coming. In early April, he was at Pau in the south west of France. The picturesque street circuit had always been a favourite of his. He managed to crash the Lotus twice in qualifying and, after the second crash, the Lotus 59 couldn't be fixed for lack of spares. He therefore forfeited his right to the vital start monies. He was relying on the francs he would have collected from the organisers to help pay for the trip home.

He literally had no money and couldn't borrow any, as none of his fellow competitors thought him likely to repay them; such was his reputation. But at least he had a full tank of petrol, just enough, with some judicious 56 miles per hour motoring, to get him home. But he neglected to fit a locking fuel cap to his car. The device was essential in France, where petrol thievery was almost fashionable and not really considered a crime. So overnight on Friday, as he lay asleep in his tent nearby, all the fuel in his tank was siphoned off by thieves – believed to be some of his fellow competitors. Hunt was certain he knew who had done it, but he couldn't prove it. So he resolved to steal back his petrol, and a bit more. On Saturday evening, finding a car without a locking cap, he got his fuel back by the same means and set off for home. But with no spare money for food, and the journey, at slow speed, taking two days, he and his mechanic went hungry. He just about got to Le Havre and drove the car off the ferry as the petrol ran out. At Dover, he begged money from friends who lived nearby on the coast. As he said later: "I finally got to Le Havre after two days on the road with no food, and when I got off the ferry, I borrowed some money for food and fuel and just about got home."

Lotus Components repaired his car on credit, and two weeks later he had received a stage payment from Molyslip. The money paid for the long drive across France down to Magny-Cours, where he came fourth and earned some much-needed prize money.

After that, came Monte Carlo and the support race for the famous Monaco Grand Prix. Even qualifying for the race was difficult at Monaco. Inevitably, Hunt put the car into one of the steel barriers that line the narrow streets for the race, and that was that. He stayed on for the weekend to sample the nightlife and he liked what he found. He would return to sample its delights many times over the following 23 years. The race was also significant for providing the backdrop to Taormina's first meeting with her future husband, Peter Rieck.

Then, there followed a long trudge through Europe racing almost every weekend, sometimes with impressive results. Between 17th and 31st May, over successive weekends, Hunt placed second three times in races at Österreichring in Austria, Oulton Park in England and Chimay in Belgium.

His performance at Chimay was extraordinary. He dominated qualifying and was on pole position leading from the start. On the second to last lap, he spun the car trying too hard and four cars passed him. Incredibly, within sight of the chequered flag, he overtook three of them and just failed to get the fourth. The first five cars were covered by less than two seconds and Hunt drove a new lap record for the circuit, five seconds faster than he had posted in qualifying. The adrenalin of close competition had made a huge difference to his performance. After that, no one could possibly have doubted that he would make it to Formula One. It was just a shame he could not do it every weekend.

Those results would be his best run all year, making people sit up and take notice. Unfortunately however, the results went to his head as he started to believe his own press cuttings, which were now getting quite copious. The mild arrogance he developed did him no favours, and he was soon brought back to earth by some more modest results and some hand-to-mouth living.

At the next race at Silverstone, he failed in front of his home crowd and finished a disappointing sixth, well below what he now expected of himself. After Silverstone, he made a long trudge to an obscure circuit called Hämeenlinna in Finland, where he managed to get on the podium.

A fortnight later, on 28th June, he was at Rouen, France, desperately searching for his first win in Europe. It didn't look at all good when he placed only 17th on the grid after a host of problems with his car in qualifying. In the end, he did not get in one fast lap. The situation looked hopeless starting from such a lowly grid position.

The car was sorted out for race day and, amazingly, he managed to drive himself into contention. The trouble was that there were another 14 cars all circulating within a few seconds of each other. Any of the 14 could have won the race. It was very close and very dangerous racing with so many cars competing for the same piece of track. On lap 13, the inevitable happened and there was a very serious accident. A French driver called Denis Dayan went straight on into the Armco steel barriers at over 100 miles per hour. He was rushed to hospital by helicopter. Dayan was badly injured with two broken legs and a broken arm. When news got back to the paddock about his condition, bad as it was, everyone thought he had got off lightly bearing in mind the severity of the accident.

The race went on, with the lead swapping many times a lap. Hunt was involved in an accident which sent another French driver, Bob Wollek, flying off over the Armco barrier and straight into trees lining the circuit. Wollek suffered severe chest injuries and a broken arm. The helicopter was back just in time to make a return journey to Rouen hospital.

In the accident, Hunt's Lotus had been hit by parts flying off Wollek's Brabham, but he continued virtually unaffected. With only five laps to go, Hunt was back in eighth place. On the deciding last lap, he came out of the slipstream of the cars in front and flew past them down the start/finish straight to take the chequered flag first. Hunt had won his first international race by less than one tenth of a second from the next man. He was ecstatic and went wild in the cockpit, gesticulating furiously to the crowd on his slowing down lap.

When he got to the podium, a young British girl called April Tod was waiting to greet him. She was the girlfriend of Grahame White, who had co-opted her to present the winner's garland. As she recalls: "I was about 19 at the time and this was my first motor race and I didn't have a clue what was going on. I was wandering around doing nothing and suddenly there was this kerfuffle because they suddenly realised that a British driver had won. They just grabbed me and asked if I would put this garland round this guy's neck whom I'd never met before. I didn't know what I had to do." She adds: "As James got out of his car, he said: 'Got a fag, love?' I said: 'I'm sorry, I don't smoke.' And then he gave me this really wet, sticky kiss because he was sweaty and had grown this little sort of beard, too."

After that somewhat unconventional introduction, Hunt and Tod became lifelong friends, a friendship that endured through the good and bad times that followed. Tod, now a well-known tennis journalist, used to park her car in Hunt's drive during the Wimbledon tennis championships.

But the celebrations that day were muted by tragedy, as the third major accident of the day took place on the last lap. Another French driver, called Jean-Luc Salomon, was launched into the air. This time, Salomon's car landed upside down on top of another competitor. No one could survive that sort of accident and he died instantly from a broken neck. The news travelled quickly and Hunt's celebrations were soon over as the podium ceremony was curtailed. At the time, France had few Grand Prix stars of its own, and Salomon had been France's biggest young hopeful.

For Hunt, though, the Rouen win was a portent of good things to come, and a string of good results followed, culminating in another win at Zolder in Belgium on 6th September and a fine second place at Brands Hatch on 18th October as the season wound its way to a close. In between, he had his famous altercation with Dave Morgan at Crystal Palace on 3rd October, and, after that, he became a household name amongst motor racing fans.

Hunt had been rescued by a strong performance in the second half of the season and, by season end, he had earned UK£2,000 in start and prize money, leaving a UK£500 shortfall in his budget.

His season had also been notable for the lack of accidents. There had only been two of any significance at Pau and Crystal Palace. Pau had cost UK£200 in repairs and Crystal Palace UK£400. As he recalled years later: "Hunt the Shunt hadn't come into existence then, and in fact I had hardly any accident damage that year. My accident bill was about £600, and the one well-publicised shunt at Crystal Palace accounted for about £400 of that."

But a UK£500 shortfall was a lot of money in those days, and, when the season ended, he was desperately short. That winter, he was totally reliant on cash handouts from his father.

For the record, at the end of the 1970 season, Hunt was placed sixth in the Shell Super Oil British Formula 3 Championship with 24 points. It was a creditable performance but he was beaten by a host of people who would go on to be far less successful. Tony Trimmer was F3 champion, scoring 44 points, with Dave Walker second with 41. In the Lombard championship, which ran alongside the Shell series, Hunt was tenth with ten points. He was even beaten by his old foe Dave Morgan, who managed twelve points. Dave Walker was champion with 48 points and Trimmer second on 43. In the Forward Trust series, he was a lowly 15th, scoring only four points. Carlos Pace focused on this series and romped away with it on 41 points, with Dave Walker second on 37. In truth, Hunt's record did not look very good on paper.

But he thought he had done well enough to get a Formula One offer or, at the very least, the offer of an assisted Formula Two seat. As he said: "I had plodded round, living in a tent and collecting start money. It was always a struggle and it meant that I didn't really have the best equipment or enough spares. But it was good for me because it taught me a lot of things about driving, and it certainly taught me to keep out of trouble."

But no offers were forthcoming. And there were plenty of F1 seats available. Apart from the normal retirements, three additional drives had become available through the deaths that year of Bruce McLaren, Piers Courage and Jochen Rindt. It had been a terrible year of carnage in Formula One, but, despite that, there was still no team principal willing to give Hunt a chance for the 1971 season.

The biggest disappointment was that Colin Chapman had passed on him. Chapman had authorised the gift of the Lotus 59 chassis purely to give him a front row seat to look at Hunt's progress. It had been no altruistic act, and so Hunt's biggest opportunity had passed him by. Chapman's rejection hurt him hard, and for the first time he wondered whether he had what it took to go all the way. There was no Grovewood morale booster that year. He was no longer the coming man.

The truth was that while Hunt had won four Formula 3 races in 1970, he had suffered from too many mechanical retirements. Moreover, after the fiasco at Crystal Palace, he was stuck with the nickname 'Hunt the Shunt'. Although it undoubtedly gave him the publicity he might not otherwise have had, he acidly observed to friends that the moniker was a "double-edged sword of the sharpest kind."

With no alternative offers, he reluctantly concluded that another year in Formula 3 was necessary, if not a necessity. But he resolved that it definitely would be his last. As he said later: "I hoped that by staying in Formula 3, I would be able to get good sponsorship, really get into the racing and clean up, then jump straight into Formula One."

But it was taking too long and everyone seemed to know he had had no offers. Effectively, in that close season, he had three choices: stay as he was in F3; move sideways into Formula 5000, sports car racing or even saloon car racing; or move up to F1.

The latter option didn't exist for him. The option of moving sideways would effectively have been a concession that his dream of Formula One was over. He would have become a driver for hire in classes of racing not considered part of the upward ladder – albeit he would have been well paid to do it. In truth, in those days, a driver rarely graduated to Formula One from sports, saloon or F5000 cars. Moreover, there was then no option to take your career to America and compete in Indy cars or Nascar, as these were the exclusive domains of Americans.

Hunt's main asset was that he was now the best driving talent in Formula 3, and on that basis he succeeded in attracting an offer from Max Mosley of March to drive in its works Formula 3 team. It would be a one car team run by mechanics at weekends who worked in the factory on the production line during the week. Mosley remembers: "I received a long hand-written letter from James saying: 'I will drive, I will win. I will.'"

Mosley had been very impressed by his drive a year before at Cadwell Park and had seen nothing in 1970 to change his mind. He also liked Hunt on a personal level. Mosley sweetened the deal by telling Hunt he would give him a run-out in a Formula Two race sometime during the year.

And on the positive side, he had a works drive for which he didn't have to pay, although once again he would have to fund his own expenses and would not get paid a salary.

Getting a works drive for 1971 was particularly important because it was the year that Formula 3 technical regulations changed. With all-new 1600 engines, all the previous year's cars and equipment were rendered effectively redundant. The new chassis was made safer with deformable sections and honeycomb filled fuel tanks, as used in Formula One. The monocoque chassis also arrived in Formula 3, as it had in Formula One five years earlier.

The engine change was particularly significant. Ever since the birth of

Formula Ford, F3 had had a problem in that it used smaller capacity engines than the lower formulae. The change had resolved that anomaly for good. But it inevitably meant a rise in costs and the demise of some lesser funded teams, who relied on being able to use secondhand cars.

Rose Bearings was brought to the team as a sponsor by Hunt. The money was small however, and the team would not be particularly well-endowed. Hunt was more worried about money than usual, saying: "The change in formula and the increase in costs became heavily inflated, to the point where a driver needed a lot of sponsorship. The income that you could derive from Formula 3 became irrelevant weighed against the costs." But he had no choice but to proceed the best he could.

March provided Hunt with a brand new March 713M chassis. The 713M looked far more purposeful than its predecessor, the 703, which, in truth, had been a dog of a car. It was an important year for March in only its second season making F3 customer race cars for sale. The 713M had to succeed or it might not get a second chance.

Curiously, to hedge its bets, March made a monocoque and a space frame version of the car. The 713M was the monocoque car and the 713 the space frame. It was a curious decision and was never fully explained.

In 1971, there were once again three principal Formula 3 championships in Britain: the Shell Super Oil, the Lombard North Central and the Forward Trust. But this time, Hunt put the most effort into the big European races.

Initially, the strategy looked like it was paying off, as Hunt started by winning at Montlhéry in France on 28th March. There, he beat the cream of the French up and coming drivers. Young talented Frenchmen were being produced in droves thanks to sponsorship by the Elf oil company.

Then, two weeks later, he did the same to the Germans at the Nürburgring, when he won the second big international race of the year. The start to the season could not have been better.

But after that, his season deteriorated somewhat. At the next four big international events at Barcelona, Pau, Silverstone and Zandvoort, he retired after accidents that could probably have been avoided. To crash out at four big international races in succession was pushing coincidence to the maximum. In Barcelona, he was leading by a staggering 90 seconds when he hit the Armco barrier after a cloudburst. At Pau, in France, he was caught up in someone else's accident on the first lap. And at Silverstone, he hit another car in the rear.

But worse was to come. At Zandvoort he suffered the worst accident of his career to date. He had started on the last row of the grid for his heat after blowing up his engine during qualifying. But he easily did well enough to get into the main race. But the March was not handling correctly, as March mechanics had too hastily rebuilt his car after the accident at Silverstone.

On the 15th lap at Zandvoort's Tarzan corner, a 180 degree bend, he touched another car trying to get past and his car flipped upside down. When it touched the tarmac, the steel roll bar which protected the driver's head snapped cleanly off and the car skidded along the tarmac for at least a hundred metres with sparks flying. Hunt went into the catch fencing upside down on the outside of Tarzan corner.

Luckily for the driver, the car did not catch fire thanks to the new honeycomb filler material in the tanks, which stopped the fuel spilling out. With the old cars, it would all have sloshed out, ignited and burned Hunt alive.

It was still a very serious accident, and the marshals did not expect to find the driver alive when they turned the car back over. But Hunt had saved his own life, as he did time and time again, by pushing his head down into the cockpit between his knees. His only outward injuries were severely grazed knuckles on his hand, where he had been clenching the steering wheel as tightly as he could. The bones were exposed and he needed immediate medical treatment. The hidden injuries were torn back muscles and some damaged vertebrae. His back was also blue from bruising.

When the marshals got him out, he sat by the side of the track. Drivers in the race were astonished to see him alive after witnessing the severity of the accident. As soon as the circuit ambulance got to him, he was taken straight to the medical centre for treatment. People remember him being totally unconcerned about his injuries; he was simply worried about the ramifications of his retirement and what all the accidents would do to this career.

Hunt was right to be worried. March was on the point of withdrawing its works team from F3; it could no longer afford to repair his car after all the crashes. As it was, he was faced with a month lay-off to recover from his internal injuries and damaged hands.

Howden Ganley, who was keeping his eye on Hunt's career, recalls it as being his lowest moment: "I'd see James occasionally and I knew he had a lot of problems, the Armco kept reaching out and grabbing him." Well that was one way of putting it, and it made Hunt laugh at a time when there was not much to laugh about. Hunt himself couldn't believe just how many times the "Armco had reached out to grab him" in 1971, as Ganley had put it.

Zandvoort proved to be the last straw, and the rumours were revealed to be correct as March was about to close down its works team. The March 713M had been a big success and other drivers, particularly Roger Williamson, were flying March's flag. March no longer needed Hunt.

But help was at hand. A young Irishman called Brendan McInerney arrived at the March factory with bags of cash and wanted to buy a March, but he had no team to run it for him. Max Mosley decided to run McInerney as a second works driver and he introduced a third party entrant willing to run the team. So Hunt was saved when the running of the team was contracted out to Chris Marshall, who then ran Sloan Marshall Garages in Surrey.

Marshall had been running a private March for a no-hoper driver, and gaining the works March contract was his chance of a lifetime. If he seized the opportunity and did well, he was all set for the future. If he did badly, he would be back to where he started – as a chancer who dabbled in motor racing.

Marshall obtained some new sponsorship from Baty Engineering, precision engineers. The team was renamed Team Rose Bearings/Baty Group. Marshall ran the team from the premises of his garage business in Barnes, Surrey. McInerney had brought with him some UK£8,000 in cash to fund it. McInerney also bought the team a new transporter.

Marshall and Hunt got on well and quickly became firm friends. But Marshall felt rather overawed by Hunt and, as a result, the two men did not have the schoolmaster-pupil relationship a team entrant and his driver usually have. Subsequently, Hunt did not have the discipline which he so clearly needed.

Although popular, Marshall had the reputation of being a somewhat flaky individual, who sometimes appeared to have difficulty making up his mind about things. Some people questioned his judgment, and Hunt perhaps could have wished for more in a team entrant. But the two men had a good, easy rapport and it was a happy team, if not a particularly effective one.

The new team started off well after Hunt returned from injury and won first time out at Crystal Palace on the 18th June. But the season deteriorated from then on. Chris Marshall's standards of preparation were not the best, and the car was far from reliable. There were a series of mechanical failures which frustrated Hunt in what he regarded as his make-or-break season. To be fair to Marshall, his small organisation was unprepared and had had little time to get organised. It was stretched running two cars, and the March factory was too busy to help.

The poor spell was broken in mid–August at Brands Hatch when the car held together for once and Hunt beat Formula 3's current star, Roger Williamson. Williamson was an up and coming Brit in an identical car. He was sponsored by wealthy builder Tom Wheatcroft. At the finish line, the gap between the two cars was not measurable, but the stewards judged Hunt was first across the line.

On 11th September, he led the Crystal Palace race on a damp track, but crashed into another car. At Mallory Park, he had another crash

At Snetterton on the 3rd October, he had another serious accident when he drove head on into an earth bank after a shock absorber broke and the suspension collapsed. He was injured for the second time in the season with torn ligaments in his shoulder. He also had a broken arm and a broken shoulder. But he didn't tell anyone about the breaks and was racing again a few weeks later, finishing second at Thruxton on 17th October.

But then serious disaster struck at Brands Hatch on 24th October, far worse than any accident Hunt had suffered. This time, the injury was not physical but to his reputation.

Hunt and Marshall, frustrated at how the season was going, unbeknownst to anyone else, had begun to seek an unfair advantage. It was a serious lack of judgment from Marshall and a mark of Hunt's desperation, as he knew he had not performed well enough during the season and thought his career might end in 1971.

With the bigger-engined formula cars, speeds were restricted by an air intake, which closely regulated how much air could be sucked into the engine when the throttle was pushed down. The air intakes on every engine were identical and rigorously monitored by the race scrutineers. In mid-September, Hunt and Marshall's team members got their heads together and decided to drill a tiny hole in the manifold to increase the amount of air the engine sucked. They figured they could complete the last few races and that the manifold was unlikely to be checked. Or so they figured.

Somehow, what they were doing leaked out, and Marshall's team was shopped to the stewards. After the Formula 3 race at Brands Hatch on 24th October, scrutineers swarmed all over Hunt's engine and took it apart, examining every part of the manifold and air intake minutely. Inevitably, they found the small hole. The car was immediately disqualified.

The governing body of British motorsport, the Royal Automobile Club (RAC) could easily have banned the team for the rest of the season and thrown Hunt and Marshall's team out of the sport. But it didn't. Immediately after it happened, Hunt became very emotional and started crying like a baby in the Brands paddock in full view of fans and other teams. It was most unedifying, as he shouted out: "I'm finished, that's me finished!" Hunt fully expected himself and the team to be banned for the rest of the season, and he knew his career wouldn't survive it. If that didn't happen, he believed March would withdraw its backing and take back its cars. He was also scared of being branded a cheat for the rest of his life. At that moment, Hunt thought he was staring catastrophe in the face. But he was overreacting. In truth, everyone in motor racing had cheated at some point in their careers, but they had simply been careful enough not to get caught. Some even cheated on a regular basis as a way of life. Chris Marshall had just been stupid and virtually got caught first time out.

Tom Wheatcroft, Roger Williamson's team entrant was horrified when he saw Hunt on the ground crying. Wheatcroft, a no-nonsense individual, dragged Hunt to his feet and marched him off to the back of the pit garages, his hand firmly on the scruff of his overalls, so they could talk privately.

When he got to the privacy of the pits, Wheatcroft pushed Hunt to the ground in disgust and told him to wipe his eyes and not get so emotional. Wheatcroft gave him a dressing down and said, in his own inimitable down-to-earth style: "Look, lad, don't let the public see you like that. You must try not to let your feelings show."

At the time, John Webb was unaware of the paddock outburst, but he was not surprised to learn of it, saying later: "He really caused us nothing but embarrassment. His general behaviour, outside of being a very good racing driver, was quite embarrassing."

Hunt had done himself no favours, and, when he returned to his parents house that night, he was full of regrets and wished he could turn back the clock. He had been complicit with Marshall when the manifold had been drilled and could not blame his team manager.

But Tom Wheatcroft, a natural fixer who had done plenty of his own share of bribing and cheating in the building trade to get vital planning permissions over the years, had a word in the right ears. March was squared away by Wheatcroft, who knew the RAC would not act.

Wheatcroft liked Hunt and had helped him out in the past when he had been down on his luck. And when it had looked as though the works March team would be closed after Zandvoort, he had been ready to buy Hunt a car to be Roger Williamson's teammate.

But Wheatcroft was right: the RAC had no wish to wash the dirty linen of motor sport in public. It was aware that other teams had been doing the same thing. The RAC simply chose to make an example of Hunt and Marshall by disqualifying them, and left it at that.

Hunt never knew what Wheatcroft had done for him, and the builder was not a man to blow his own trumpet. Later, Wheatcroft would lend Hunt an engine and commend him to Lord Hesketh when he was having his doubts.

Hunt never knew this, and, when he got into Formula One, he actually came to resent Wheatcroft, perhaps because he had witnessed him at his weakest and most emotional.

Wheatcroft was sad and disappointed, but not surprised. He had witnessed all sorts of human frailties during his life on the building sites. As he recounts in his autobiography, *Thunder in the Park*, written shortly before his death in 2006: "Once [Hunt] had made a name for himself, his attitude towards me changed completely, and it was as if our friendship had never existed. I would see him in the paddock and he would look straight through me. I didn't have a lot to do with him from then on." He adds: "He was not always the easiest man to get along with, and, as soon as he made a name for himself, it seemed he didn't want to know me anymore."

His treatment of Tom Wheatcroft was not James Hunt's finest hour, as Ian Phillips sadly remembers: "It is true he disliked Tom Wheatcroft. Roger [Williamson] was my best mate and Tom gave Roger everything that James wanted, and there was a bit of jealousy there. There was just something he didn't like about Tom. He tried to get me into an argument once, it was at the Donington Grand Prix in 1983, and I just walked away. He was saying to somebody: 'Wheatcroft's a horrible man, always has been. Ian, isn't that right?' Tom remained a friend. James had this bee in his bonnet that Tom was not a nice person. James just had this thing."

Ian Phillips never understood Hunt's vendettas.

The season concluded, and the stars of Formula 3 that year were the Australian Dave Walker, Jody Scheckter and Roger Williamson.

At the end of the 1971 season, Hunt's results in Britain were only a little better than they had been in 1970, but not by much. Hunt had overdone it again; instead of focusing, he had competed in too many races in too many championships. In the Shell, he was tenth with 12 points as Dave Walker dominated and smashed the opposition with 86 points, beating even Roger Williamson, who managed 56 points. In the Lombard, Williamson focused and dominated on 90 points, whereas Hunt could only manage eighth with 12 points. Only in the Forward trust championship did he shine, coming in third on 19 points, whilst Dave Walker managed 63 points to win it from Roger Williamson, on 35 points.

In *Autosport*'s annual review of the F3 season, Hunt was ranked fifth most talented driver in F3. *Autosport* thought his performance had been "one of the disappointments of the year", and the article was written by one of his admirers, Ian Phillips. Phillips noted: "Hopefully, things will turn out better next season." Analysing Hunt's weaknesses, Phillips would say later: "Unfortunately, his hot-headedness sometimes betrayed his sense of responsibility, which was highly developed. The thing that impressed you most when you got to know him was that he was an extremely intelligent person – probably one of the most intelligent racing drivers I've ever known."

Overall, it had been a disastrous season, but Chris Marshall later rewrote history and told Hunt biographer Christopher Hilton that the season had been an outstanding success. He said: "We had a terrific second half of 1971, I think 18 races and we won seven." No one else remembered it quite like that. In fact, in view of what had happened, there was no way March would renew Marshall's contract and, instead, sold him the 713M cars cheap.

As for Hunt, the cheating episode had damaged him and thrown his talent into doubt. Time was running out and the undeniable promise of James Hunt remained entirely unfulfilled.

In simple terms, Hunt had done too much crashing. Never had his 'Hunt the Shunt' nickname been more apt than at the end of 1971. The run of four serious accidents earlier in the season had been astounding and unprecedented for any one driver in motor racing history. March had spent well over UK£15,000 repairing his cars during the season, which in those days was a small fortune. Looking back on his disastrous record in 1971 and reflecting on his nick-name, Hunt said: "It didn't bother me because, to ease the pain, I told myself it was a natural rhyme and not necessarily an aspersion." His assessment might have been baloney but it undoubtedly made him feel better.

Hunt was adamant that most of his accidents were triggered by other drivers, who had lost control of their cars and hit him. Although he did confess that he might have avoided some of the accidents if it hadn't been for his admitted "over-eagerness and inexperience." To explain away the accidents that were his fault, he said they had been "brought on by not really having a competitive car." He added: "I had to stick my neck out more than most, trying to make up for the deficiencies of my car."

There was plenty of truth in that as he contemplated what 1972 held in store for him.

THE FORMULA THREE YEARS

SHUNT

CHAPTER 11

Flattening David Morgan

He would never be forgotten after that

James Hunt always had a problem with arrogance and cockiness when he was successful. It was a natural part of his character. At the latter end of the 1970 season, he had enjoyed a good run in his works Lotus 59. He had won the big international race at Zolder on 6th September and run to a very impressive third place at Cadwell Park a week later. And before that, he had come second in another big international event at Knutstorp in Sweden.

So when he went to Crystal Palace circuit on the Friday and Saturday 2nd-3rd October 1970, he was in one of those dangerous moods when anything could happen and usually did. Gerald Donaldson called his mood "a finely tuned state of aggressive fighting trim."

Crystal Palace circuit was virtually his home race and, as he was now living full time in London, there was no need for any camping out. So every night of that week, as the Formula 3 circus came to town, Hunt was out with his tribe, drinking himself silly at the 365 club on the King's Road, in Chelsea, with soccer players and his growing circle of hangers-on and ne'er-do-wells who were prevalent even in those days.

The state of constant inebriation added to the dangerous cocktail of emotions that was James Hunt that weekend. "Light fuse and stand clear" was how one anonymous observer described it to *Motoring News* after the weekend had ended.

The Crystal Palace Formula 3 event was an unusual race, as it was being broadcast live on BBC television; unusual because even Formula One wasn't broadcast live in those days. But there was a gap in the schedule, cameras were available and the timing was perfect for a slot in the BBC's prestigious Saturday afternoon 'Grandstand' show, fronted by the legendary sport's presenter David Coleman. The race commentator was Murray Walker, in one of his first television jobs. It was certainly the first time he had commentated on a race in which James Hunt had competed, and the introduction to his future commentating partner was not auspicious.

It was also the first time that author Alan Henry, then writing for *Motoring News*, met Hunt. Henry remembers it only because of Hunt's bone-crusher handshake: "I remember he shook my hand and I thought he'd broken two of my fingers. At a time when some of them were wimps, he was a tough guy. He had a charming manner about him, but a bit of a hair trigger temper."

Henry was to witness plenty of that later.

The presence of television meant there was a huge entry for the late season race, which meant two qualifying heats for the main race. Hunt qualified easily by finishing second in his heat.

The main race got underway on cue on Saturday afternoon. Right from the start, there was no doubt who the winner would be, as Dave Walker dominated. But the battle for second was very different, with five cars, including Hunt's Lotus, swapping places every lap.

Formula 3's reputation for close racing was the reason the television cameras were there, and the BBC producer focused entirely on this battle for second.

In the last few laps, it came down to three drivers, with Hunt, Mike Beuttler and Dave Morgan in the reckoning. Morgan, in particular, was fighting aggressively for the place, determined to do well on television in front of the two million extra people viewing this race. It was the chance of a lifetime to shine, and Morgan knew it.

As Walker took the chequered flag, Beuttler held second place, which Morgan desperately wanted for himself. Hunt actually seemed out of it and in his mind had settled for fourth, determined not to crash his car and ruin what had been a virtually crash-free season.

Morgan, in a March 703 desperately hurled his car at the last corner to get ahead of Beuttler. In the process, he swiped Hunt's Lotus and there was what was later described as an "explosion of debris." Hunt's Lotus 59 had its two right side wheels ripped from the chassis and Morgan's March slammed hard into the concrete pit wall.

Hunt's Lotus came to rest in the middle of the track. Unsure what to do about his car in the middle of the track, straddling the finish line, stunned marshals looked on as cars swerved to avoid Hunt as they rushed for the chequered flag.

A red mist came down over Hunt as he climbed from his car, oblivious to the other cars whizzing past. He developed what in those days was called "a raging fury", after the then popular TV show 'The Incredible Hulk'.

Literally bursting out of his overalls like the hulk, he rubbed his eyes and looked round through the smoke and debris for Morgan. He spotted the white overalled figure hunched over his wrecked car, seemingly speculating what the repair cost might be. Later, Morgan revealed he was indeed pondering what would be the cost of repairing his car. It was the sort of thing drivers thought about in those days, when money was so tight and ambitions raged so hot. But on this occasion, his thoughts were about to be rudely interrupted.

Forgetting that the TV cameras were rolling, Hunt ran over to where Morgan was standing and landed him a single right hook to the jaw. Morgan looked at him and managed to say "whaaaat" as he fell to the ground, out cold. Hunt had flattened him with the single blow. But Hunt, disappointed that Morgan had fallen so easily, wanted more and shouted to Morgan, lying on the ground, to stand up like a man and take his punishment.

The entire incident, from accident to punch, was over in less than a minute. But the TV cameras were perfectly positioned on the start line and were running live close-ups for the nation's TV viewers, who were transfixed by their first glimpse of live motor racing. The cameras caught Hunt prodding Morgan's prone body to wake him up so he could pummel him again. But before that could happen, Hunt was quickly dragged away by marshals. Otherwise, the fight would have continued on live television.

In the mayhem, few noticed that Mike Beuttler had taken second place and Tony Trimmer came through the smoke and avoided the debris to take third. Dave Walker also clinched the British Formula 3 championship that day – but no one was in the least bit interested in him.

Murray Walker, in the commentary box overlooking the start line, couldn't believe what he had witnessed. Appalled, he called Hunt "the archetypical, loud-mouthed, totally irresponsible, hooray henry." He also added, for good measure, that Hunt was "erratic, emotional and violent."

Later, when Hunt had made it into Formula One and recalling what he had witnessed that day at Crystal Palace, Walker said: "It exploded all my theories and beliefs about what ought to happen."

Ian Phillips, then of *Autosport* magazine was called upon to make an instant judgment of what had happened. He was watching at the finish line and, although he made no judgment about blame for the accident, he came out against Hunt's antics after the accident, calling his actions "totally unjustified." Hunt, Phillips determined, had "overreacted."

Hunt had undoubtedly suffered a huge rush of blood to the head. His crashing record in 1970 had been almost exemplary and he had then spent less than UK£200 on accident repairs. He had a huge incentive to keep his car in one piece, as his otherwise generous Lotus contract stipulated that he paid for all accident damage. Colin Chapman was no fool. Now, Hunt was staring at UK£400 worth of damage all thanks to Morgan's insane rashness at the finish and his attempt to look good on television.

If it had been a normal race, without the cameras, hardly anyone would have noticed the encounter and the matter would have ended right there, with Hunt and Morgan inevitably making up in the paddock afterwards.

Hunt was, of course, guilty of ungentlemanly conduct; that much was clear. But his conduct was quickly set aside by the media, who chose instead to focus on the issue of whether or not he had been justified in landing the punch. Everyone wanted to know who was at fault in the accident.

When he got back to the paddock, Hunt immediately gathered his fellow competitors and led an official protest to the stewards about Morgan's driving.

There was a strict time limit on this and the protest form had to be accompanied by a fee of UK£5. Hunt kept a five pound note in the pocket of his race overalls for just such an occasion. With the protest duly lodged and the fiver paid, the stewards were obliged to meet immediately to decide the issue.

The enquiry was convened, and Hunt and the other drivers began vigorously protesting Morgan's driving. The drivers told the stewards that Morgan's behavior had been suspect over the whole weekend. They said his maneuver at the finish line had been irresponsible and the action of a desperate man trying to make a name for himself because of the presence of television cameras.

It looked cut and dried, but, unbeknownst to the drivers, the chief steward had telephoned RAC race boss, Dean Delamont, who had been watching the race on TV at home. Delamont was already angry about the number of accidents in Formula 3 and he knew a fatality was likely just around the corner. Wanting to put a stop to it, he decided this was the moment to act.

Believing that the continual accidents brought bad publicity to the sport – publicity that it could do without – Delamont seems to have decided at that precise moment to make a public example of Dave Morgan.

Delamont told the chief steward to arrange for judgment to be reserved and to refer the matter to him for a tribunal to be convened in London. And that is exactly what they did, ruling that the evidence before them was inconclusive. The stewards should have dealt with the matter there and then but, instead, thanks to Delamont's intervention, the incident turned into a cause célèbre that meant the name of James Hunt would be forever remembered in motor racing, whatever else he did in the future.

The tribunal was to be convened in London at the RAC's portalled head-quarters in London's Pall Mall. Delamont told reporters that the Royal Automobile Club, as the governing body of British motor sport, had no choice but to take action. But, secretly, he knew the incident would have been totally ignored if the TV cameras hadn't been there. As it was, the TV tapes would be vital in apportioning blame.

The following Thursday, the whole incident was covered in a minute-by-minute dissection in the *Autosport* weekly motor racing magazine and the *Motoring News* weekly newspaper. *Autosport* journalist Justin Haler made the mistake of writing that Hunt was "justifiably enraged" at Dave Morgan's driving; the inference being he was right to assault Morgan afterwards.

That comment sparked off a hailstorm of letters to the magazine, which were duly printed in the following and successive weeks. The most interesting response came from none other than Morgan's own mother, one Bunty Morgan. In a letter signed 'Mrs H B Morgan', Bunty said she was "quite incensed" at her son's treatment by *Autosport*'s journalists, whom she believed were biased in favour of Hunt. She said, in an eloquent passage of the letter that was clearly not written by her: "At what stage does pressing on, harrying and holding off turn from a virtue into a vice?"

Bunty's letter triggered of a deluge of correspondence in the weeks before the tribunal. Morgan recalled later: "My mother and various aunties and uncles were writing to the press."

Besides Morgan's family, more mothers got in on the act, including Mike

Beuttler's, who stated that her son was "quite horrified". She for some reason took against Hunt, writing: "The boy Hunt was being extremely beastly to my son, who, as always, drove beautifully, although his father and I do rather wish at times he had chosen a more sedate occupation."

The letters were pretty evenly split in their support of either driver, with many criticising Hunt for his "pugilistic behaviour", which they thought had brought the sport into disrepute. One letter writer accused him of a "complete lack of self control", which wasn't far from the mark.

Meanwhile, the soap opera continued in the national press. Morgan, whom no one had heard of previously, or much less cared about, was becoming a national celebrity and even appeared on some TV chat shows. He maintained that, in fact, Hunt's punch had missed him and that he only fell to the ground because he had become "unbalanced." Morgan said: "He missed" and called Hunt a "silly arse." Morgan would later regret that statement once he saw the TV tapes.

Bunty Morgan revealed to journalists that, before the incident, she had been an admirer of Hunt's. She said: "I'd first met James in the Mini days, and then he was just a nice, quiet, but very eager man. I felt it was a put up job." But she said she had changed her view: "At Crystal Palace, it was announced over the loudspeakers that David was guilty while the stewards' meeting was still going on, and in fact the meeting went on for over an hour after the announcement. It was unfair. Formula 3 is terribly competitive and there were lots of incidents, but my David wasn't the kind to make a fuss."

Morgan himself again attempted to explain his position: "James and I were struggling for second place in the race. Moving into the last corner, I did what you'd normally do if you were going to do another lap and came over to the pit side. I was in front and I had the position. I wasn't chopping him off from the inside, I was just making sure he'd have to think twice about which side he was going to try and pass me on. Normally, he'd have come down the inside but he'd be trapped there, so I wanted him to change his mind and come down the outside. That would give me enough leeway to get across the line. But he kept the hammer down and hit me, and I went sideways and spun round. His car was in the middle of the track minus one wheel, and I was into the pit wall minus one wheel."

The RAC tribunal, which would decide the issue, was extremely powerful and wholly made up of influential gentlemen of motor racing. The general mood of the members was that they believed James Hunt had not been a gentleman, and they were after his blood. As for Morgan, they wanted him thrown overboard as well.

So when both Hunt and Morgan were formally summoned by letter to appear before the tribunal and the date was set, Hunt got into a panic. Although he displayed plenty of bravado amongst his friends, he had a natural public schoolboy's respect for authority, especially when it was convened for judgment. Gone was his rebelliousness, and he called up his friend John Hogan for help.

Nowadays, both drivers would have hired lawyers, but there just wasn't the spare money to do so. Friends and family would have to suffice. So Hunt asked Hogan to help organise his defence for the hearing.

Before the tribunal convened, Morgan, Hunt and Hogan went to the BBC studios at White City to view the film of the incident. Afterwards, neither man recognised their initial version of events from the film. Hunt discovered that what he thought had happened was at total odds with what television pictures showed, as he explained: "It's like a lot of people involved in these sorts of scuffles or whatever: his take on what happened is totally at odds with the television."

After viewing the tapes, Morgan maintained that Hunt should have been charged with dangerous conduct, as he had walked through cars, which were still racing at full speed, to reach him at the side of the pit straight. Morgan said: "I was amazed he wasn't run over."

John Hogan was pleased to be able to help his friend and provide moral support, but he says now that his role in the proceedings was exaggerated. Hogan says he simply accompanied Hunt to the tribunal and gave informal advice. He remembers the hearing itself being the first of its kind and the tribunal panel consisting of the most serious people the RAC could muster, including Jack Sears and Dean Delamont. Hogan recalls: "The tribunal committee were the judge, juror and executioners of the RAC. They all had the black caps on before you walked into the room."

Hunt was in fine form for the hearing, as Hogan remembers: "It was one of the few occasions where I saw James actually use the old school tie to full effect. He used his public school background to influence the old fuddy-duddies on the RAC. Dave Morgan was just a regular guy, but James impressed them with his presence, his accent and his articulation."

Hogan advised Hunt to forget his own version and go with the cameras, which he did. Hogan says: "All I did was to say: 'Listen, look at the television and talk to that, not to your mind because otherwise they're going to screw you.' And that was it really. I just told him to stick to the picture and not to fantasise about it."

Morgan had arrived at the tribunal with a box of papers and a borrowed briefcase, so as to look the part. At the hearing, he found himself on the front bench hunched right up to Hunt. But he could not get the briefcase to open. Either he had the wrong combination for the lock or it was jammed. Morgan asked Hunt for help opening it. It was almost comical, as Morgan remembers: "I couldn't open the thing, and I asked James if he could and he did."

Hogan sat on Hunt's other side but didn't give evidence – expert witnesses were not allowed to be heard then. So Hunt simply followed his mentor's advice to the letter, and Hogan tugged his jacket if he started to wander.

The film of the race was played on special monitors provided by the BBC for the day. The tribunal heard evidence from both drivers and from a spectator witness on behalf of Morgan. Hunt had also gathered together a large number of witnesses who testified on his behalf. The TV recording clearly showed that Morgan had run into him, and three other drivers testified that Morgan had overtaken in a dangerous manner.

Inevitably, the tribunal cleared Hunt of wrongdoing and forgot about the punch he had thrown. Not so with Morgan, who they said was guilty of dangerous driving. They handed him a 12-month ban from racing, the heaviest penalty ever given to a driver, and, almost as an afterthought, he was fined UK£25 for "over-exuberant driving."

Everyone was shocked at the penalty. Morgan may have been at fault, but not to the extent of that sort of penalty, which would effectively mean the end of his career. Even Hunt, who was jubilant at the overall result, conceded that Morgan's 12-month ban was "a total injustice."

At the time, no one agreed with the severity of the sentence of the tribunal and felt that Morgan had been made a scapegoat to discourage the wild driving prevalent in Formula 3 at the time.

Early in 1971, justice was finally done when Morgan appealed the 12-month ban and the RAC agreed that it was too harsh and gave him back his licence. Aside from all the drama, Morgan was a talented and capable driver. But the affair had stalled his career and he never quite recovered from it.

John Hogan has the last word, saying: "When I look back at it, it's quite a lot of fuss over nothing." Indeed it was.

FLATTENING DAVID MORGAN

SHUNT

Above: James Hunt, aged three, with his favourite toy, a junior lawnmower. He was described as a rebellious and headstrong child, but also one bristling with intelligence and inquisitiveness.

Right: Hunt, aged four (bottom left), pictured with his parents, Wallis and Sue Hunt, brother Peter, aged two, and sister Sally, aged six, at a family wedding.

Below: James at ten years old holding baby Tim, with Sally (twelve) and Pete (eight). As he matured, he adopted a parental approach to his youngest siblings.

Kind permission of Mrs Sue Hunt

Right: Vacation time from Wellington College couldn't come too soon for Hunt, who actively avoided academia as much as he possibly could.

Above: James Hunt tailgates a competitor in the first racing car he built himself, a Mini Cooper, at a saloon car race on 8th October 1967 at Brands Hatch.

Below: Formula Ford Action: Syd Fox leads James Hunt in his Gowrings sponsored Formula Ford Merlyn on 26th December 1969 at Brands Hatch.

Above: James Hunt was absolutely on it in only his second ever motor race at Brands Hatch, on 8th October 1967. He competed in only three saloon car races before moving to Formula Ford.

Above: Close action at a Formula Ford race for James Hunt at Brands Hatch on 29th November 1969.

Above: High profile action: Leading the Formula 3 support race in his March 713M before the 1971 Spanish Grand Prix on 18th April at Montjuich Park.

David Phipps / Sutton

Above: James Hunt racing the Lotus 59 in a Formula 3 support race at the British Grand Prix, held at Brands Hatch on 17th July 1970, where he finished third.

Below: Second place James Hunt (right) with race winner Freddy Kottulinsky (centre) and third place Barrie Maskell (left) after the Preis von Steiermark F3 race at the Österreichring on 17th May 1970.

Peter Nygaard

Peter Nygaard

Above: Dicing with Alan Jones (number 69) at Brands Hatch in a Formula 3 race in 1971.

Phipps/Sutton

Above: Dave Morgan, the F3 driver whom James Hunt knocked out with one punch.

Left: A young James Hunt, aged 23, at the Spanish Grand Prix at Montjuich Park on 17th April 1971, where he was competing in a supporting F3 race.

Above: Racing for the STP March Racing Team in the first round of the 1972 British Formula 3 Championship at Brands Hatch on 5th March. Hunt finished fourth in the race.

Left: James Hunt leads Colin Vanderwell and Ian Ashley in the first round of the 1972 British Formula 3 Championship at Brands Hatch on 5th March.

Below: Receiving a bouquet of flowers from journalist April Tod after winning round ten of the Formula 3 Grand Prix at Circuit de Rouen-les-Essarts, France, on 28th June 1970.

Formula 2 proves to be the springboard to Formula One

Above: James Hunt in a March 712M on 16th September 1972 at Oulton Park. James came in third and drove the fastest lap during the race.

Below: At the Rothmans 50,000 race for all types of single seaters, on the 28th August 1972 at Brands Hatch, James Hunt took his March 712M to fifth place and won nearly won $5,000 in prize money.

Formula One debut: The Race of Champions at Brands Hatch, 1973

Phipps/Sutton

Above: Hunt finishes third behind Denny Hulme in an undeniably impressive first race in a Formula One car. Hulme also debuted the McLaren M23 that day, a car that Hunt one day would be driving.

Right: His first ever Formula One race was the Race of Champions at Brands Hatch on Sunday 17th March 1973 in a Surtees-Ford TS9B.

The French Grand Prix at Paul Ricard, 1973

In only his and Hesketh Racing's second Grand Prix race on Sunday 1st July 1973, Hunt drove his March-Ford 731 to a sixth place finish. It was his first points finish in Formula One.

Inset: Relaxing with a drink and cigarette in the pit lane at Paul Ricard.

The Monaco Grand Prix 1973.

Left: Lord Hesketh (left) with Leslie Button at the Hesketh team's debut Grand Prix race. He described James Hunt as "like a new born babe" at the event.

Below: Lord Hesketh's Bell Jet Ranger helicopter, which was used to ferry guests back and forth from Nice airport to Monte Carlo on the weekend of 1st-3rd June 1973. Hesketh's expenditure on entertainment positively dwarfed his spending on the team.

Above: Hunt steers his March-Ford around Monaco before retiring on lap 73.

Right: After a tough two hours racing, Hunt sat in his car and contemplated the trials and tribulations of his first Grand Prix. He admitted he had been frightened and realised he was not as fit as he thought. Standing hand on hip next to the car is designer Harvey Poslethwaite.

Phipps/Sutton

The British Grand Prix at Silverstone in 1973

Above: James Hunt goes past the control tower at Silverstone. He finished in fourth place and earned the Hesketh team another three more world championship points.

Right: A somewhat overawed James Hunt ponders the past and the future as he reflects on his meteoric rise to Grand Prix stardom at Silverstone. He was the centre of media attention all weekend - something he was not at all accustomed to.

Below: Preparations to the March-Ford 731 are made by Hesketh team mechanics Nigel Stroud (left) and Malcolm Bowden (right) as they inspect the internals of the Hewland gearbox prior to the start of the British Grand Prix at Silverstone.

Phipps/Sutton

First podium at the Dutch Grand Prix in Zandvoort, 1973

Hunt drives to his first podium finish in only his fourth ever Grand Prix. He finished third at Zandvoort on Sunday 29th July 1973 earning Hesketh Racing another four points.

Phipps / Sutton

Above left: The Hesketh team's liveried vehicles at Zandvoort.

Above right: Lord Hesketh watches his team's first podium success from the Zandvoort pit wall.

Left: The accident that killed popular young British driver Roger Williamson. He died driving a March-Ford 731, just like James Hunt's car.

James Hunt shows his athletic prowess in Monza, 1973

Above left: James Hunt, along with other drivers and team crew, takes part in a running race around the circuit at Monza. The event was organised by Frank Williams at the Italian Grand Prix on Sunday 9th September 1973. Hunt won the race and earned himself a prize of US$1,500 for doing so.

The United States Grand Prix at Watkins Glen in 1973

Left: An extraordinary second place at the United States Grand Prix in 1973 caps off an amazing debut season for Hesketh racing at Watkins Glen on Sunday 7th October 1973.

Phipps/Sutton

Left: Race winner Ronnie Peterson was constantly harried by Hunt, who appears in the background. Hunt chased him throughout the race and finished just one second behind Peterson at the chequered flag.

Above: A Hesketh team pit board makes it clear that Bubbles Horsley will accept no dissent from his driver on this occasion.

Right: In a scene that would become familiar, Hunt enjoys a post-race cigarette.

Below: The weekend brought mixed emotions as French driver François Cevert died in an accident during qualifying, prompting Jackie Stewart to retire on the spot.

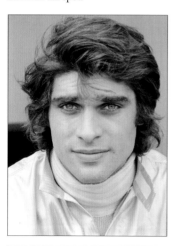

Above: The scene of Francois Cevert's accident, which split the steel Armco barrier. The popular Frenchman died instantly.

Left: James Hunt and Lord Hesketh at Watkins Glen celebrating the end of their first season. The Hesketh team contested seven out of 15 races of the season, scoring two podium finishes and finishing eighth in the world championship with 14 points. Their debut year was nothing short of sensational.

CHAPTER 12

Character building
and no Plan 'B' 1972

The options run out, it's nearly over

J ames Hunt entered Formula 3 in 1969, and it was now the start of 1972. He had already spent three years in a Formula, when he should have done only two. He was now 25 and getting too old. In short, he was going nowhere fast. By now, he should have been an experienced Formula Two campaigner, readying himself for the start of the Formula One season as a new rookie – as was Niki Lauda. Lauda was only 23, yet he was already established in Formula One racing for the works March team alongside Ronnie Peterson. He also had a Formula Two seat with March.

This grated on Hunt, as he considered Lauda an inferior talent. Lauda was also displaying superior sponsorship getting talent whereas Hunt was displaying none. Lauda had managed to raise US$70,000 to pay for his March drive and was being sponsored by a Viennese bank. The sponsorship was by way of a long-term loan in which the interest element was the sponsorship fee, and the bank expected Lauda eventually to pay back the capital. He had also taken out a life insurance policy that would eventually pay back the loan should he be unable. It was an ingenious solution to an age-old problem.

In comparison, a penniless Hunt was staring at a fourth year in Formula 3, which was not a very inviting prospect. The only bright spot on his horizon was that, at least, he had the offer of a drive for which he would not have to pay. Max Mosley had offered him the number one seat at the new works run March F3 team, which was being sponsored by STP, March's Formula One sponsor.

Hunt pitched Mosley for the drive very early on and was surprised when Mosley said 'yes' without asking for any cash. Hunt had written an impassioned letter to Mosley asking for the drive, as Mosley remembers: "It basically said: 'I'll win' and James was always very sure of himself and a very quick driver, though certainly not an obvious candidate for world champion."

Mosley had known Hunt since they had raced together in the junior formulae, and he genuinely liked him. But, like everyone else in motor racing, he was worried about offering him the drive. It was plain to almost everyone that Hunt had great ability, but they disliked his general attitude and his propensity to crash cars. The nickname Mosley had given him of 'Hunt the Shunt' had well and truly stuck. On the plus side, Hunt was, even from a longevity perspective, the undoubted star of Formula 3. He was acknowledged as its fastest driver, notwithstanding the fact that every other driver of note had moved on. On that basis, Mosley decided to take a chance on Hunt.

The relationship with Mosley would be a key one in Hunt's early life, and their paths would cross regularly until the day he died. Mosley was one of the four founders of the phenomenon called March Engineering Ltd which, by 1972, had become an established force in motor sport. March was an acronym of the four founders: Mosley; Alan Rees; (Graham) Coaker; and (Robin) Herd. All four were very clever men in their own right, but they had tried to do the impossible by not only setting up a new two-car Formula One team from scratch with a new car of their own design, but also by becoming manufacturers of F3, F2 and F1 race cars for sale to customers.

They set the company on an industrial estate in the small town of Bicester, in Buckinghamshire, right in the heart of an area of England that would later come to be known as Motorsport Valley. They had hardly any equity capital so were totally reliant from the start on sponsorship and revenue from selling race cars. The cars were designed by Robin Herd, fresh from McLaren and Cosworth, and built by the factory manager, Graham Coaker. Mosley was the salesman and Alan Rees the team manager of the works teams run by March in F3, F2 and F1.

Mosley is an extraordinarily intelligent man which, combined with great charm, can be devastatingly effective. But back then, he had no experience at all of running a business. In fact, he knew literally nothing about business at all. But his instincts were good and, unlike so many of his contemporaries, he knew what he didn't know. There is no question that this combination of talents kept March alive in its early years. His timely interventions also kept James Hunt's career alive.

His parents were Sir Oswald Mosley and Lady Diana Mitford. Whatever one thought of them and their political views, the line of parentage was unrivalled. Mosley received a very loving but disciplined upbringing during the difficult war years, when his parents were interned as dangerous aliens by Winston Churchill's wartime coalition government.

Mosley was educated as a trilingual in England, France and Germany, and gained an honours degree in physics at Oxford. He was secretary of the Oxford Union and called to the bar in 1964. His specialism was patent and trade mark law, which he practiced for three years. During the early to mid sixties, he dabbled in motor racing, reaching Formula 2 in 1968. But like so many others, he may have been a brilliantly fast driver but there were too many others who were faster, and, in 1969, he retired from active driving and started March Engineering with his three friends.

By 1972, March Engineering had been operating for two years. It was being run on a shoestring and clever ideas were needed to bring cash in to pay the wage bill at the end of every month. Hunt knew this when he signed on for the team. He didn't get a salary or expenses, but everything else was paid for. It was a great deal even if Hunt didn't realise it at the time. And no one else wanted him by then.

He was partnered in the STP-March team by his old friend Brendan McInerney, who was paying March around US$10,000 for the seat on an instalment basis race-by-race.

Hunt should have known how lucky he was to have been given the drive by Mosley, but his appreciation often seemed to waver. There was also pressure on him as, after Hunt had been signed, the up and coming German driver Jochen Mass made March a good cash offer for the drive. To Mosley's credit he turned down the offer and honoured the contract with Hunt. Mass was very attractive to March and had backing from Ford of Germany. But Hunt didn't seem to appreciate this either.

Hunt started the season dismally, competing in eight races in the various British F3 championships in March and April. In 1972, there were three championships, the Shell, the Lombard and the Forward Trust, and Hunt raced in all. But the Shell was the dominant championship and Hunt made his biggest effort yet to win it, realising belatedly that he had neglected the British series to his own detriment.

The new March 723 looked good with its low nose and side radiators and red livery, but it was unsorted and slow. The old March 713M of the previous year was clearly a faster car. During that period, Hunt went to Brands Hatch and Silverstone twice, and Snetterton, Oulton Park, Mallory Park once each. He managed to have two accidents, and his best result was a third at Mallory Park. For the so-called star of F3, this was a terrible start to the season and Hunt knew he could not do a fifth year in F3 without becoming a joke, and he soon became very depressed about his future.

Alan Rees and Mosley at March were equally depressed. They did not like Hunt's attitude in adversity. He had been publicly criticising the car. As March relied for its income on selling customer versions of the March 723, his comments had hurt sales. Far from putting his head down and developing the car as March had done to great effect in the previous season – effectively turning the 713 dog into the 713M race winner – Hunt had effectively given up. And as much as Mosley had affection for Hunt, he had given up as well and now wanted him out of the team. Mosley remembers: "James said the 1972 car wasn't as good as the 1971 car, which I think was completely true, but it wasn't good for sales. So I said to him: 'You're a works driver, you can't say things like that. You know, keep quiet.' But he was right and we were right, but I couldn't afford to have people saying that. I didn't design the car, that was down to Robin, but I had to defend it. And James was just saying what he thought. We never actually fell out in any way; we always got on very well."

Ian Phillips remembers it as a dark time: "By the middle of 1971, there was obviously some talent there but he was completely out of control."

And so it came to the annual F3 race supporting the Monaco Grand Prix, ominously scheduled to be run on Saturday 13th May. Mosley's problem was that he had a watertight contract with Hunt, with no get-out clause. It would be difficult to sack him without a pay-off, and March had no cash to do that.

So a stand-off emerged. Mosley hoped Hunt would throw his toys out of the pram and leave, while Hunt hoped Mosley would sack him with a pay-off, enabling him to buy a drive in a more competitive car.

But neither came to pass.

The Monaco Grand Prix support race was a shop window for Formula 3, more important than all the other races combined. Hunt wanted to impress the Formula One team principals and March wanted to sell cars to customers. Prior to Monaco, at Silverstone on 23rd April, Hunt crashed his March 723. The accident removed all its wheels and crumpled the chassis, and it would cost over US$2,000 to repair.

Mosley was furious, especially when Hunt didn't seem to care about what had happened. So the two men had no communication between that Sunday 23rd April and Thursday 10th May, the start of qualifying for Monaco. Hunt said later that Mosley and Rees didn't return his phone calls, but it's not clear whether he ever called them. For the record, he called them "mysteriously uncommunicative."

That Thursday, when Hunt arrived in the makeshift F3 paddock in the car park in Monte Carlo, there was no sign of the March F3 transporter. He watched the first qualifying session in an angry mood. The transporter eventually turned up at midnight, but Hunt's car was still in pieces from its rebuild. The chassis had been repaired but required hours of setting up, and a Monaco car park was not the best place to do it.

The final qualifying session was scheduled for early Friday morning. But there was only one March mechanic and he was exhausted by the long drive from England. He told Hunt he was going to bed and there was nothing Hunt could do to persuade him otherwise. It looked hopeless.

Hunt knew his car would not be ready with his mechanic in bed. He thought quickly and met up with Chris Marshall, his team manager from the previous year. Marshall, down on his luck, was now running a team called L'Équipe La Vie Claire. It had the old March cars from the previous year, with young French drivers and French sponsors. As it happened, one of Marshall's French drivers had had his licence suspended and there was a spare March 713M car available and ready to race.

Bizarrely, the two men decided to break Hunt's contract with March and decided that he would drive that car for the final qualifying session. It was an unbelievably imbecilic decision to leave the works team, especially in view of the fact that it was Hunt's fault that the car wasn't ready after he had crashed it at Silverstone.

Marshall should have told Hunt to pull himself together and helped him to get the March sorted for the race, thereby doing his best for his employer. But he didn't and, with his misguided advice, he nearly derailed Hunt's career.

The F3 race at Monaco was so popular that it was run in two heats and a final on the Saturday before the Grand Prix. Hunt qualified Marshall's car for the second heat.

Mosley and Alan Rees were apoplectic when they heard what Hunt had done. They felt humiliated that their number one driver had defected to another team at the most prestigious race of the year. The two men huddled together that night and decided to give Hunt an ultimatum; he would either drive for them or leave the team.

Hunt was in the car park waiting to take his Marshall-run March down to the grid when a letter was delivered to him from Mosley. It warned him that unless he immediately stepped out of Marshall's car and into his STP-March works car for the heat, he would be sacked from the team.

Hunt got out of his car and briefly conferred with Marshall. They then made another stupid decision: Hunt decided to ignore the letter and race Marshall's old March as planned.

It seems incredible now how two supposedly intelligent men could mess up so badly. Hunt and Marshall, for all their years of experience, seemed to have learned nothing about motor racing in that time. Hunt was ready to toss away an extremely good contract on a whim. With the decision made, he had then to go out and finish high enough in his heat to qualify for the main race. But Hunt was also in no emotional condition to drive – especially around a difficult circuit like Monaco. He went straight out and put the car into the Armco guard rails that lined the circuit, thereby destroying the car's suspension. He was out of the heat and the main race. And he would soon be out of motor racing altogether.

It had been a catastrophic weekend, and the two men returned to England with their tails between their legs. Marshall was left with a crumpled car he had to pay to repair, and Hunt was left with no drive and no prospects of a drive.

By driving for a rival team, Hunt had broken his contract in the most comprehensive way possible. Not only would he now certainly be sacked, March could sue him for breach of contract and would almost certainly win any legal case, thereby making Hunt bankrupt.

A few days later, that is precisely what came to pass. Mosley sent Hunt a letter of termination followed by a press release formally sacking him. He was replaced by Jochen Mass. Mosley wanted a fresh start and Brendan McInerney's contract was also ended. But Mosley, to his credit, did not put the knife into Hunt and was kind in his comments. He admitted March had delivered the car late to the circuit and didn't have time to prepare it properly. Mosley stated that Hunt would probably drive much better without the pressures of being in a works team.

It was not until he returned to England that Hunt realised what a fool he had been. It suddenly dawned on him just how favourably Mosley had treated him and just how stupid he himself had been in his public criticism of the team. But he was still bitter and didn't help himself with a sarky press release written with Chris Marshall's help. Hunt said in the release: "It was only the climax of a situation which had existed all year, and it stemmed from a variety of problems caused basically by a lack of interest and enthusiasm. I made every effort to inject either interest or enthusiasm but without success. Thus I now feel that the interest of my career would be better served by racing on my own." According to his biographer Gerald Donaldson, James told friends privately: "Ford Germany approached them with a bag of gold to put Mass in the car, so they fired me and snatched it." In stark contrast to Hunt, Mosley simply said: "Our Monaco row was only a short affair, and it was soon all amicable and friendly again."

But then, Mosley perhaps could afford to be more magnanimous about the situation; the damage to Hunt was self inflicted, and it had left him dangerously exposed.

And then the recriminations began. Hunt told Marshall the fiasco was all his fault. He had listened to his advice and it was now up to him to help him out of the hole into which he had fallen as a result. Marshall's French driver was still suspended so he agreed Hunt could drive his March 713M at the next F3 race in Chimay in Belgium – but this was only while Marshall's regular driver was suspended. Marshall had no real interest in helping Hunt beyond that. Like many in the paddock, he appeared to believe that Hunt had shot his bolt and was on his way out of motor racing. But Hunt believed Marshall owed him because of the self-evidently poor advice he had given him in Monaco. He felt betrayed by his friend's indifference to his plight. But the one-off race offer was all he had, so he hid his true feelings.

Chris Marshall had always been a minor league player in motor racing hoping to hit the big time. The highlight of his career had been in 1971, when he had effectively run the March works team. But he had failed to seize the opportunity. Now, he rented out his second-hand old cars to drivers who could pay.

With his works drive gone, Hunt was forced to hang about with people like Marshall, desperate for even the crumbs from his table. It was the lowest point of his life, and Marshall wasn't much help.

The humiliation of being fired by Max Mosley only served to increase Hunt's determination to succeed. An inner calling drove him on, and, as he was now so accustomed to setbacks, he told people he used them as inspiration to train his mind to turn every negative into a positive.

In fact, insisting he had a negative psyche, Hunt explained it thus: "Whenever I think I'm going to achieve something, it turns out that I don't. I always have to 'negative think' to get the best out of myself." He added: "I'm a great fatalist." He added the Hunt theory of reverse psychology was to turn negatives into positives. Indeed, many people believed he thrived on adversarial situations, and if they didn't exist, he certainly seemed to go out of his way to create them.

But after his altercation with Mosley at Monaco, there was no need to manufacture any adversity. It had risen and hit him square in the face. Hunt was no fool and he realised that he had to change. He confided in Ian Phillips, who advised him the best he could. As Phillips recalls: "There came a realisation in 1971 that 'I've got to get my act together.' But he couldn't lose the 'Hunt the Shunt' tag, and the world was closing in a little bit."

Hunt was constantly wondering to himself why he was not able to get up and out of Formula 3 as had all his contemporaries. According to David Gray, a lifelong friend, he was hampered by his own attitude to life: "James never outwardly took his racing seriously. To the outside world, he gave a very casual impression of his craft and it appeared it didn't bother him whether he succeeded or not. Of course, this wasn't the case."

Hunt would admit that his approach to racing was not particularly deep. In an interview with *Autosport*'s Nigel Roebuck, he revealed that he believed his approach to be both "good and bad." He readily admitted he did not take the Ayrton Senna or Alain Prost approach to motor racing to "think himself" into a Grand Prix, and he "was never one to allow distractions to get to him."

He also thought it was a fault, as he said: "In bad times, some drivers will get stuck into the root of the problem and regenerate enthusiasm in the team. I was never the man to do that."

Hunt also believed he was an instinctive racer and that this hampered his career by making other people believe he was not serious: "I was never much of a worker, never that much involved with my racing outside of when I got in the car and started to drive it. It's the same with squash, but put me on a court and I give everything. I turn on in a competitive situation."

Hunt also realised he could not easily change; he was what he was. But for now, he was stuck, and looked to Chris Marshall to help him out.

Always at the back of his mind during his row with Mosley was the assurance that Marshall would provide him with a drive if all else failed. He also believed that Marshall's old March 713M was faster than the new March 723, which he regarded as a dog. Armed with the year old car, Hunt believed he could beat Jochen Mass and the works March, and that his performance would persuade someone with deep pockets to give him a Formula One drive.

But when push came to shove, Marshall only offered soothing words. Marshall told him his regular driver would be returning, and that on this occasion, the money had to come first. As one close friend observed: "Chris couldn't give James a regular drive, as he needed the money."

Marshall even had the audacity to suggest that Hunt give up his motor racing dream, retire and get a regular job. Hunt turned round and looked at Marshall as if he had gone out of his mind. The thick-skinned southerner quickly realised that the idea was a non-starter and wished he had never said it. It was not at all what Hunt wanted to hear at that moment, and their friendship, although they remained close, was never quite the same again.

Marshall, of course, puts a different interpretation on it all. He has recounted his own version of events for Hunt's various biographers and, interestingly and perhaps most tellingly, declined to speak to the author of this book about the matter.

After Hunt died, Marshall effectively claimed he was his saviour during this period, maintaining it was he who helped dream up a plan to persuade Max Mosley to give Hunt a March F2 chassis as compensation for sacking him. However, a close member of the Hunt family remains sceptical: "Chris definitely inflated his role in James' story."

But, to his credit, Marshall did admit Hunt was angry with him about the affair. He told Gerald Donaldson: "He jumped up and thumped my desk so hard I thought he was going to break his hand. He said: 'No way, no way, no way. I'm not getting a job.'" Marshall says Hunt yelled at him at the top of his voice, and Marshall told Hunt: "Okay, fine, right. We'll have to find a Plan 'B'."

Now, the cheeky Marshall claims he was the architect of the Plan 'B' that emerged that day. It's an interesting claim since, in reality, there was no Plan 'B'. Hunt was down and out of Formula 3. No one wanted him, and no one cared about him enough to give him a drive.

Only a miracle could save Hunt now, and that is exactly what happened.

SHUNT

CHAPTER 13

The turning point
Meeting Bubbles and Alexander 1972

Hunt's career is saved from oblivion

aught in a bind, Hunt had no Plan 'B' and no get-out-of-jail-free
card to play. He had already used up all his plan Bs earlier in his
career and had already played all his cards. Make no mistake, James
Hunt was down and out of motor racing midway through 1972. He had
literally crashed his way out of the sport and, as one friend sagely observed,
"James was down and out, and without a pot to piss in."

At this point, there can be no doubt that Hunt was finished; he had reached
the point at which he had to give up on motor racing and find another job.

After being sacked by March and temporarily driving for Chris Marshall's
team, Hunt seemed to have learnt nothing. Along with Marshall, Hunt put
out a press release with what appeared to be a veiled attack on his previous
employers, saying: "I am delighted to be driving for a team with so much
enthusiasm." The implicit attack on the powerful March organisation was not
only unjustified, but crazy at a time when Hunt had no hope.

And then, somehow, Hunt was saved. Just at that moment , a miraculous
and most fortuitous event occurred; one that was to save his career and
eventually make him Formula One world champion just four and a half years
later. As Gerald Donaldson sagely put it: "It was as if there was an act of god,
and Alexander Hesketh was put down on earth in front of him." Donaldson's

analysis was absolutely spot-on. The Plan 'B' Hunt didn't have somehow materialised in the unlikely form of a makeshift toilet located in the middle of a Belgian field.

Some months before the fateful meeting, a man called Lord Hesketh had set up a Formula 3 racing team for a friend called Anthony 'Bubbles' Horsley, whom he had met at a wedding. It was a coming together of people with like minds. Hesketh was a latent petrolhead and Horsley was a fully paid-up one.

The Northamptonshire-based baron lived a mile away from Silverstone race track, and as soon as he could afford to indulge in motor racing, he did. He was under no illusions about his own ability. Although he could drive a road car extremely fast and skilfully, he was too rotund to fit in a race car. He weighed 245 pounds and, even if he could get in a car, the extra weight meant he would be seriously uncompetitive.

He also had an early scare when he crashed his road car into a combine harvester. The expensive harvester was so severely damaged that he quickly realised how dangerous and embarrassing the endeavour could be. He also realised how very lucky he was to be alive, and Lord Hesketh very much enjoyed being alive.

With a driving career out of the question, Hesketh chose the next best thing – owning his own race team, which was something he could easily afford to do at the time.

Born Thomas Alexander, he was only the third Baron Hesketh. In 1955, when Thomas Alexander was just five years old, his father, the second baron, died, and his son succeeded to the peerage, but not to the fortune. The third Baron would have to wait another 16 years for that. In 1971, when he finally turned 21, he inherited a large part of the family fortune in cash along with the estate, called Easton Neston, near Towcester, in Northamptonshire. The estate was 9,000 acres of farmland and included the famous Towcester racecourse. The cash element was around US$3 million.

Alexander Hesketh was a true English eccentric in the very best tradition. Always rebellious and unconventional, when he was 15 he ran away from Ampleforth College, in Yorkshire. After leaving school at the earliest opportunity, he sold used cars in Leicestershire and then went to Hong Kong to work as a shipbroker. He quickly moved to Los Angeles and trained as a banker.

As soon as he got his hands on the family money, he splashed out. He took over management of the existing family-owned businesses and set up his own group of companies based in London. To embellish his image, he bought a diamond-encrusted gold Rolex and outfitted himself in monogrammed shirts, with the family crest specially embroidered beside his initials. He also bought a new Bell Jet Ranger helicopter, a lightweight Porsche Carrera RS, a Mercedes SSK and a telephone-equipped Rolls Royce Silver Shadow, each panel of which was outlined in a gold pinstripe. He smoked expensive cigars and drank Cristal champagne.

It was an expensive lifestyle, but one he could well afford. But one character facet would prove very expensive over the years: he had a low boredom threshold.

And that led to the racing team.

The initial catalyst came when Hesketh met Horsley at a wedding in 1967, where they were both guests. Horsley was running his own used car business, wheeling and dealing in luxury motor cars. Realising who he was, Horsley tried to sell Hesketh a second-hand Rolls Royce he had in stock. But instead, Hesketh turned the tables and sold Horsley a Mercedes-Benz car he wanted to get rid of. Hesketh, who was a mere 17 at the time and with no money of his own, had sold Horsley his mother's road car to raise himself some cash. When Horsley found out, he had to hand it back and retrieve his money from the young Lord – which wasn't easy, as he had already spent it. A naturally furious Lady Hesketh packed her son off to America and hoped the time away would instill some sense into him.

Somehow, through this ridiculous saga, the two men became close friends. It seemed that the manner in which Horsley had handled the difficult situation had left an impression on Lord Hesketh, which he was never to forget. He had impressed Hesketh by "understanding his dilemma" and showing forbearance, and it helped forge an incredible bond of loyalty between the two men.

Hesketh proved a good judge of character, as Horsley was a very impressive young man. Born in Newmarket, Suffolk, in 1943, Horsley – like Hesketh – left school as soon as he could. His well-to-do family forced him into an estate management career, but he quickly realised it wasn't for him and, in 1962, when he was 18, he moved to London to wait in restaurants and drive vans in order to make a living.

He got a job in motor racing selling used race cars and fell in with the west London racing set, which included Frank Williams and Piers Courage, both then aspiring racing drivers. Williams and Courage were part of a group that also included Charlie Lucas, Jochen Rindt and Charles Creighton-Stewart, all of whom rented lock-up garages in old railway arches off London's Goldhawk Road. Hesketh remembers: "They used to come and stay with me to go to Silverstone because it was handy." And cheap.

Like them, Horsley bought a second-hand Formula 3 car and went around Europe racing when he could afford it, sleeping in his van and living off the prize and appearance money the rest of the time.

He eventually wrote off his car at the Nürburgring and, without any cash to repair it, retired. With his racing career seemingly over, he departed on a year-long excursion through India and Nepal on foot, earning money along the way.

Returning home, he decided to resume his former career as a car dealer and, finding economic conditions more conducive, attracted enough backing from friends and family to set up a new company he called Horsley's Horseless Carriages. Primarily, he sold secondhand vans and, amazingly, he decided to become an actor in his spare time. Proving quite good at it, he appeared in some lucrative television commercials.

In 1971, when Hesketh returned from America, he renewed his acquaintance with Horsley and, when his inheritance was confirmed, he decided to go racing – with his friend doing the driving.

They decided to run a two car team of Dastles, cars built by a young man called Geoff Rumble. The Dastle was hopelessly slow, but Horsley also suspected that part of the problem might be his lack of driving skills. A driver called Steve Thompson was hired to drive the car at the race supporting the Monaco Grand Prix and, against the odds, qualified for the race.

Halfway through the first season of 1971, Bubbles Horsley found himself with a dilemma. The team had spent substantial sums to get set up and he knew he was wasting his friend's money.

He decided he needed a teammate to find out just how slow he was. Horsley had noticed James Hunt earlier in the season, when he was driving for March, but hadn't dared speak to him. As Horsley admitted: "We were frankly a huge bloody joke as a Formula 3 team. I had stopped driving at the end of 1966 and had come back in, and that had proved a mistake."

By chance, Hunt and Horsley finally met at a most fortuitous time, at a French circuit called Chimay, in Belgium. Hunt was racing the March owned by Marshall, and Horsley was racing Hesketh's Dastle.

Hunt was about to leave the sport when he and Horsley set out from a different directions across a field in a French farm, which served as the circuit's paddock. They suddenly came face-to-face in one of those moments of destiny that was to change both of their lives forever.

Horsley told Hunt biographer Gerald Donaldson: "We met in the middle of a field full of cowpats. We sort of found each other; we sort of needed each other. It was a marriage of convenience." Horsley adds: "No other driver was exactly knocking on our door. Nobody was about to give him a drive either."

Horsley admits he was so naïve at the time that he based his opinion on how Hunt looked: "He looked right. You looked at him and you said to yourself: 'Now that bloke ought to be quick.' You couldn't put your finger on it, it was just a feeling."

The two men found an instant rapport in that Belgian cow field. At first, Hunt didn't want to let on how badly he needed a drive, as he admitted: "For once I kept quiet and let Bubbles talk." But despite that, at the meeting, James Hunt became number one driver for Hesketh Racing, a post he was destined to hold for five years through a quick progression from Formula 3 to Formula One. It was the start of a remarkable journey.

Although Horsley and Hunt quickly agreed terms, the next step was to introduce Hunt to Lord Hesketh, and the first opportunity came as the Lord was relieving himself in the paddock toilets, which consisted of a few buckets and an army surplus tent that had apparently been in service for both the first and second World Wars. Hunt joined him in the latrine and they had their first discussion. Whatever the exact truth of it, this was the venue for the meeting that would decide Hunt's future. Horsley told Hesketh in the presence of Hunt: "I have hired a driver and become team manager."

Hesketh didn't know who Hunt was, but he remembers his first impression of him as a "gangling, blond, long-haired, knock-kneed youth, smiling very nicely and obviously rather pleased with himself."

When they exited the tent, Chris Marshall joined the conversation and even managed to negotiate Hunt a miniscule salary for his driving services. Horsley was not quite sure what he had taken on: "James wasn't your typical up-and-coming racing driver of that time. He was quite tricky and argumentative."

Whatever Hesketh and Horsley's initial reservations, their opinions changed the next day when Hunt, for once, did himself a huge favour and set the second-fastest time in qualifying at Chimay in Marshall's March for his best grid position of the year. He then set out on an eventful race, even by his standards. On the first lap, two cars flipped over and went off the track in front of him. In seventh place by lap five, two other cars nearly crashed into him and he avoided that also. Two laps later, another crash near him ended with the two drivers punching each other at the side of the track. He was up into second place with three laps to go when he suffered a puncture from all the accident debris and struggled home to fifth in a race he probably could have won. Hunt had wrestled his old March 713M through to fifth place, beating the pair of works March 723 cars. All of this unfolded with Lord Hesketh watching from the pit wall. Horsley's Dastle, of course, was nowhere to be seen. As Horsley noted: "Everywhere, he was two seconds a lap quicker than me. That really said it all." Although Hunt had placed only fifth in the end, Lord Hesketh was immensely impressed by his performance.

The die was cast.

SHUNT

CHAPTER 14

Formula 2 proves the springboard to F1

The guardian angel and the promised land

By mid-1972, James Hunt had effectively shot his bolt in Formula 3. His final act had been the virtual destruction of Lord Hesketh's Formula 3 team with a demolition derby at Brands Hatch. His 'Hunt the Shunt' reputation had given him, as one journalist memorably put it, an "accident-about-to-happen" image.

Brands Hatch was extraordinary in its savagery and it followed another fiasco a month earlier at Silverstone, on 11th June. It had been Hunt's first race for Hesketh and he had written off his first Dastle, as Hesketh recalled: "The first race I saw him drive for me was at Silverstone in the wet. He actually took the lead, which we'd never done before. Indeed, we'd never even been near the front of the grid. But when he was leading, it was backwards – because he'd spun, he must have travelled about 40 yards in this way – then he crashed into the pit wall right in front of me, which I wasn't very impressed by."

But much worse was to come at Brands Hatch. It was an important event because it was the support race to the British Grand Prix that weekend. The race weekend began badly when Horsley crashed his car in qualifying. Later that day, Hunt was in his Dastle following another car when it suffered a sudden puncture and spun off. Hunt hit the car and was launched into the air. It somersaulted in mid air and crashed upside down on top of a steel

Armco barrier.

Chris Marshall happened to be standing by and he was certain his friend was dead. Marshall couldn't believe anyone would survive that sort of accident. A few seconds after impact, however, the car fell off the top of the barrier and landed the right side up on the ground. Hunt was inside and moving. He had once again saved himself by putting his head into the cockpit and contorting his body under the protection of the chassis. It was Hunt's second and last race for the Hesketh F3 team, and his last ever race in F3. He had literally crashed his way out of the sport and there were no F3 cars left for him to drive. Worse, his patron Lord Hesketh had been present to witness the wholesale destruction of his racing team at the hands of Hunt. But even worse still, it was followed by an unrelated incident that very nearly saw Lord Hesketh leave the sport altogether.

After qualifying had ended, the Hesketh team packed up to leave and Lord Hesketh got into his helicopter to fly back to Easton Neston for an unscheduled weekend at home.

That day, Brands Hatch was stuffed full of parked helicopters attending the Grand Prix weekend. Hesketh had parked his helicopter in a place convenient for him. As he was leaving, Hesketh was engaged in a row by the operations manager at Brands Hatch. There was a problem with where his helicopter had been parked and, assuming he would be returning for the Grand Prix the next day, Hesketh was told in no uncertain terms not to park there again. He was told his instructions were on the orders of Angela Webb, the operations director of Brands Hatch and the wife of John Webb, managing director. Hesketh wasn't used to being ordered around by the likes of the Webbs, whom he referred to as "ghastly people." As he took off, he resolved it would be the last motor race he attended. Angela Webb says: "I do not remember the incident nor do I recall meeting Lord Hesketh. However, I would be angry with any pilot who parked in a non authorised area, thus negating our aircraft insurance and constituting a danger to the public."

While Hesketh flew off, the crashing action that weekend was not yet over for James Hunt. Hunt stayed on overnight to watch the British Grand Prix the next day. But halfway through the race, he decided to leave for his parent's house to miss the post-race traffic jams and watch the last laps of the race on television.

Hunt was driving a Mini owned by Chris Marshall's secretary and was accompanied by former teammate Brendan McInerney and his new girlfriend Chantal. On the way home, Hunt was steering the Mini rather too fast around a corner when he found a Volvo estate on the wrong side of the road because its driver apparently thought it was a one-way street. Or rather, that was the excuse that Hunt later related to his somewhat dubious father.

There was a head-on collision and a secondary impact as Hunt's Mini hit a tree. Hunt was lucky to survive it and even luckier to be able to walk out of the wreck along with his passengers.

Four of Chantal's ribs were broken and McInerney had chest injuries. Hunt suffered some severe lacerations to his legs. The Volvo occupants were more or less uninjured, protected by the Swedish car's heavy steel chassis as the Mini took the brunt of the impact. For the second time in two days, Hunt had cheated death.

An ambulance transported the passengers of both cars to hospital, but not before Hunt had stood them all a drink in the local pub. The severity of the crash is indicated by the fact that they were all detained in hospital for a week.

Hunt had plenty of time to contemplate life whilst he was in his hospital bed. At the end of 1971, he had thought things couldn't get much worse – but now they had.

Lord Hesketh was aghast when he heard that Hunt had also managed to write off a road car that weekend. But somehow, he wasn't put off. He had quickly forgotten about the helicopter incident and, by the time he landed the Jet Ranger at Easton Neston, he was already making new plans for Hesketh Racing.

For some unfathomable reason, Hesketh kept faith in Hunt and began thinking long and hard about his future. Believing Hunt had spent too long in Formula 3, Hesketh decided that it was now or never for his career. Applying his own unfathomable logic to the situation, Hesketh decided he had failed in Formula 3 and it was now time to enter Formula Two.

It was as though a guardian angel had arrived from god to lead James Hunt to the promised land. Where Gerald Donaldson refers to Hesketh as having employed "skewed logic" to arrive at his decision, others resorted to such phrases for Hesketh as "completely nuts" and "demented." After that weeked, even Bubbles Horsley was doubting the wisdom of employing James Hunt.

It wasn't Hunt's first try at Formula Two. In the late summer of 1971, he had made his Formula Two debut when he was entered by March Engineering in an F2 race at Brands Hatch on 30th August that year. It was a one-off race as part of the contract he had signed with March to drive in its works F3 team in 1971. Hunt drove a March 712M car and it was his first race with some of the big stars of Formula One, who also used to compete in Formula Two in those days. In the field of 26 cars were twice world champion Graham Hill, Ronnie Peterson and Emerson Fittipaldi. Peterson won the race from Hill and Hunt finished in 12th place hampered by a misfiring engine.

Lord Hesketh told Horsley and Hunt to purchase a Formula Two car and gave them a small budget of UK£2,000 to prove themselves all over again. The budget was just enough to buy a new engine, and Hunt would need to find a chassis and some cash to run the car until Hesketh became more certain about him.

Sensing that his career might shortly be over, Hunt knew this was his very last chance.

Despite the huge problems caused by the accident with his secretary's Mini, Hunt roped in Chris Marshall to help. This time, Marshall displayed more savvy. Marshall believed he owed Hunt for some of the terrible advice he had given him, particularly in Monaco earlier in the year, and together they came up with an extraordinary plan to get March Engineering to lend him a Formula Two chassis. He decided to write a letter to Max Mosley saying he was going to sue March for the balance of the money due from his cancelled works Formula 3 contract and for the damage that the sacking had done to his career. None of the other capers cooked up by Marshall and Hunt had ever worked, and there had been many. But there had to be a first time, and this time they enacted their plan with subtlety.

Hunt's letter to Mosley carefully hinted that Hunt would accept an F2 chassis in lieu of payment in order to put right the horrible injustice that had been perpetrated against him. Mosley laughed out loud when he received the letter. But, not one to bear grudges, he immediately picked up the phone and called Hunt, declaring: "I'm the lawyer. You can't go around suing me." It was now Hunt's turn to laugh out loud.

The two men quickly reached an accord. Mosley admitted there was a small amount of merit in Hunt's claim and decided to help. Mosley had an old March 712 chassis lying around at the March factory in Bicester for which he had no use, and he told Hunt it was his. Mosley remembers: "James was sort of fired, but we didn't want to leave him completely high and dry. So he asked if he could borrow free of charge a 1971 Formula Two car, which we agreed to."

Lord Hesketh bought a rebuilt Cosworth BDA engine from Brian Hart and they were in business. Two of Marshall's estate agent friends contributed another £2,000 towards purchasing the advertising space on the car and getting Hunt to turn up to a few parties to glad-hand clients, especially female ones. He was by now reasonably well known in the Brands Hatch area and very popular with the local girls, who treated him like a pop star.

One of Chris Marshall's ideas had come good at last, and Hunt forgave him all his past sins.

But the two men had one last crazy scheme to try out between them. Hunt was in debt and had no money. Hesketh had bought him an engine for the Formula Two car but that was all he had done. To keep going, Hunt tried to pull a fast one on his family. He learned that his grandmother, who was then still alive, had arranged to leave him a fairly large sum of money in her will. Hunt aided and abetted by Marshall, concocted a scheme whereby he would ask his father, Wallis, if he could have the money in advance, albeit ignoring the fact that his grandmother was still very much alive and living.

It was another ludicrous plot and Marshall should have counselled him better.

However, Hunt duly went along to see his father with Marshall in tow, thinking that it somehow added credibility to the request. Marshall attempted to negotiate with Wallis on Hunt's behalf.

Marshall opened the conversation by explaining what they had learned and asked Wallis Hunt if the inheritance process could be speeded up to help his son's motor racing career. He explained that he was short of money to run Hunt's car and could benefit from the inheritance now.

Marshall then stated that his son's sense of propriety stopped him from making such a proposition directly to his grandmother. It was hoped Hunt's father might advance him the money early. Marshall now winces at the memory and the absurdity of it all. It was pure theatre, and history does not record whether Wallis Hunt took the request seriously or just laughed out loud. The latter reaction seems more likely.

Chris Marshall, whose recollection of events is often hazy, told Hunt's biographer Gerald Donaldson that Wallis Hunt took the request very seriously, responding: "I have a simple philosophy. I believe that education is very important and we've given our six children the best education we possibly can. Then we leave them to it. James still has a room here. We have food in the kitchen. There will always be a meal. He'll always be welcome. But there is no money for racing." According to Marshall, Wallis then added: "Would you like some more tea?", as if to make the point that the conversation about money was over.

The two men retreated with their tails between their legs.

Despite the setback, Hunt and Marshall somehow found enough money. Hesketh Racing was painted on the side of the car and the new team went to Brands Hatch on the last weekend of August 1972 for its first F2 race, which happened to be the Rothmans 50,000.

The Rothmans 50,000 was an event created by John Webb for the Rothmans cigarette company. It was so called because the total prize money offered was UK£50,000. The event was open to virtually any type of race car, provided it could qualify. It attracted an entry of Formula One, Formula 5000 as well as Formula Two cars. Eight Formula One cars arrived, led by Emerson Fittipaldi's Lotus-Ford, Jean-Pierre Beltoise's BRM and Brian Redman's McLaren-Ford. One of those three was certain to win and take most of the cash.

The rest were a mixture of cars driven by names that would become famous in the future, including John Watson, Alan Jones, Carlos Reutemann and Jody Scheckter. All saw the chance to make their name and earn some serious money.

Hunt was the second-fastest Formula Two qualifier and drove an absolutely superb, disciplined race for 118 laps, finishing a very impressive fifth. He won UK£2,500 in prize money, which would go toward contesting as many of the remaining Formula Two races as possible. He was second in the F2 category. The race was won easily by Fittipaldi in the Lotus, who walked off with the vast majority of the UK£50,000.

Lord Hesketh was absolutely delighted with the result and agreed to double the prize money the team had won, giving it a budget of UK£5,000 to complete what was left of the Formula Two season.

There then began a non-stop trek across Europe to compete in as many races as possible before the season's end. On 3rd September, a week after Brands Hatch, the car was taken to a round of the European Formula Two Championship in Salzburg, Austria. Hunt qualified the car on the front row and dueled for the lead before he blew up his tired Ford Cosworth BDA engine.

He then travelled back to Britain, to Oulton Park, in Cheshire, on 16th September to contest the final round of the British Formula Two Championship.

FORMULA 2 PROVES THE SPRINGBOARD TO F1

Oulton Park had attracted a top field of F2 drivers, including the likes of Ronnie Peterson, Niki Lauda, Jody Scheckter and Roger Williamson. John Surtees and Graham Hill had also entered. All were driving the latest cars whilst Hunt was driving an early 1971 chassis. He qualified the old March second behind Peterson in the works March 722 car.

Hunt felt he could have taken pole from Peterson, but he was worried about conserving his engine; it was the only one they had. At the end of the first lap, Hunt was fourth behind Peterson and Scheckter and ahead of Lauda. Retirements left Hunt in second, with the works March cars of Peterson and Lauda first and third. Hunt had no business challenging the latest works cars in an old chassis.

But the best was yet to come. Four laps from the end, Hunt overtook Peterson on the longest straight by out-braking him at the end. Hunt was in sight of a great victory in front of Peterson and Lauda. But fate intervened and, with two laps to go, Peterson forced Hunt off the track as he and Lauda went by. Hunt got his car back on the track to finish third.

Hunt was clearly the crowd's favourite; they chanted his name despite the third-place finish. Peterson and Lauda were astounded by what they had seen and were thankful they managed to beat him.

Max Mosley watched all this with wry amusement, saying: "It added insult to injury when he ran round Oulton Park in front of Peterson and Lauda in the works cars."

Chris Marshall was also intrigued by what he saw that day, as Hunt had effectively bested Peterson, who was then regarded as the fastest race driver in the world. He said: "James was never fazed by a bigger talent. He had that tremendous confidence in what he could achieve and an awful lot of talent; but different to Peterson. Peterson's was pure, natural, artistic driving, but he wasn't a great thinker or strategist. But James was an all-rounder – a thinker, and his mental and physical package was very good."

The only downside was that Lord Hesketh had missed the race and had to rely on Bubbles Horsley's third-hand account of it. But it was enough for Hesketh, who had by then very much caught the motor racing bug. He needed only the slightest encouragement to open his cheque book. Summoning Horsley and Hunt to his office at London's Portman Square, he established Hesketh Racing on a proper commercial basis and put Horsley in charge as team manager to run it. The plan was to contest the European Formula Two Championship in 1973 with a new car and a proper, well-funded set-up.

First, though, they had to finish the Formula Two season. Hesketh bought him another engine on 24th September at Albi, France, where Hunt had finished fifth despite having driven much of the race clutch-less. Then it was on to Hockenheim, in Germany, on 1st October for the final race of the season. Hunt finished eighth.

Hesketh was delighted with the results and delighted at the improvement in the discipline of his new driver, something he had severely doubted at the start of the relationship. Ian Phillips witnessed this transformation: "I think mentally he'd worked it out because he was clever enough to do so, but he just needed somebody like Bubbles to come along and impose the discipline and say: 'Look chap, if you don't behave yourself and do this that and the other, you are finished' and that's where it came from. It came from Bubbles."

Hesketh thoroughly enjoyed his sojourns across Europe in his Rolls-Royce, and wanted more.

He provided funds to take the March 712 to a three-race winter series in South America, called the Torneo. The organisers paid for 20 cars to be flown out from Europe, and they included Hunt in their plans after his performance at Oulton Park. The star of the series was Fittipaldi, the new Formula One world champion. Hesketh didn't fly out, but left it to Horsley, Hunt and a couple of mechanics to represent his new team. There were meant to be four races, but the one in Argentina was cancelled. In all three races, each held at Interlagos in São Paulo, Hunt shined; finishing sixth in the final points ranking out of 20 cars.

But the Torneo series became better known for the social high jinks led by Hunt rather than the racing. Lord Hesketh had provided Hunt and Horsley with generous expenses to have a good time. The series was being followed by two well-known British journalists, Ian Phillips and Alan Henry, who witnessed Hunt's escapades at the time and remain impressed by them even to this day. Hunt allegedly made such a nuisance of himself, and his behaviour was so bad, that the organisers considered asking him to return to Britain. Often spending all night drinking and, on more than one occasion, climbing straight into his race car the next day without having gone to bed, Hunt's hell-raising attracted the attention even of the police. He was kept out of jail only after much pleading from the organisers. It was "booze and birds all the way", as Alan Henry remembers it: "Certainly we drank a lot and partied a lot in Brazil." That was something of an understatement, but Henry remembers the following incident particularly well. The incident became part of motor racing folklore and was to be retold many times. It started when Hunt's antics deeply offended one journalist who was also part of the trip. Her name was Priscilla Phipps, wife of the well-known photographer, David Phipps. She was also a well-known author, writing under the pseudonym of Elizabeth Hayward.

Hayward, a not unattractive woman who also liked to drink, enjoyed the company of motor racing people and had enjoyed brief affairs with such notables as Jack Brabham, Denny Hulme and Colin Chapman on previous trips.

The whole of the British group attending the series had gathered for dinner at the hotel. Witnessing Hayward becoming increasingly drunk, Hunt bet Horsley US$100 that he couldn't have his way with her that evening. Horsley took the bet and succeeded. In order to check on the status of his wager, Hunt decided to bang loudly on Horsley's hotel room later that night – while Horsley and Hayward were in the middle of their love-making. When Horsley answered the door, Hunt entered the room in front of a shocked Hayward, who was lying naked on the bed. He proceeded to tell her about the bet and paid Horsley his winnings in front of her. Hayward, who was naturally extremely distraught, screamed at Hunt the memorable line: "My husband and I will ensure that you never, ever get into Formula One."

The outburst was witnessed by many of the people on the trip, who, as it turned out, had followed Hunt up the stairs to Horsley's room. Luckily, none of them could remember much about it the next morning and it was not mentioned again on the trip. There were many more similar antics to follow. So much so that the situation in the Brazilian hotel eventually got completely out of hand, with girls being shuttled in and out of rooms as if on conveyor belts, and furniture being thrown out of the windows onto the street, amidst other high jinks.

The hotel managers were at their wits' end but were in a dilemma as they did not want their guests arrested before they had paid the bill. After all, they had been there for six weeks and the bill was pretty big.

But the real trouble started when some mechanics, aided and abetted by Hunt, stole the number plates from a yellow Ferrari Dino 246 parked outside the hotel. It initiated a chain of events which led eventually to a well-known British journalist being arrested and deported.

Years later, Ian Phillips, who was not at all involved in the pranks, vividly described how he was deported from Brazil in 1972 when he took the rap for Hunt: "All hell had broken loose while I had been out. James had been on his balcony emptying waste baskets full of water over the other hotel guests coming in and some mechanics had been around writing anti-Brazilian slogans on the guest's breakfast cards, hanging outside their doors."

The hotel management decided enough was enough and for some reason made an example of Phillips.

Half an hour after he had gone to bed, six policemen burst into his hotel room and arrested him. He says: "It was always me that opened the door to the porter, it was always me that got caught for stuff that famous racing drivers were up to. Eventually, I was the one thrown into jail and deported. The British consul had to come get me out. I got blamed for everything."

Phillips had trouble denying his role in a litany of incidents in a police report that ran to many sheets of A4 paper. Even São Paulo's chief of police, who was now personally handling the 'situation', was doubtful that one man could have caused so much mayhem in such a short space of time. Phillips says now: "I couldn't deny that I was there and involved, and to get everybody else off the hook I had to take the rap." He eventually got a letter of apology from the Brazilian police over his treatment, but, despite that, São Paulo remains one of his favourite cities in the world.

As for Hunt, he was eventually poured into an aeroplane to go home and he reportedly slept the whole way back. Hunt made a lot of friends during those three weeks in São Paulo; friends that would endure for the whole of his career and to whom he would return time and again.

As the year ended, anyone looking at Hunt's race statistics would not have been impressed. For the record, Hunt was placed 17th with only five points in the 1972 European Formula Two Championship. In the John Player British Formula Two Championship, he was sixth with only eight points. Officially, he was sixth in the Tourneo rankings on five points.

Back in England for the 1973 season, Horsley decided to buy a new Surtees TS15. Mike Hailwood had won the Formula Two Championship the previous year in a Surtees, and Horsley believed it was a better bet than a March. John Surtees had set up his own factory making racing cars when he retired from top line Formula One. Surtees, the only man to have won the world championship on both four and two wheels (as a motorcyclist), also ran his own Formula One team from a factory in Edenbridge, Kent.

The decision was made purely on the basis of what had been the most successful car the previous year. And, as everyone in motor racing knows, that is never the best way to make such a decision.

On paper, however, it looked like a good choice. Surtees sold Horsley a brand new TS15 chassis for US$12,000, and Horsley paid another US$5,000 for two Ford-Cosworth BDA engines.

The first race the team contested was the first round of the British F2 championship at Mallory Park, Leicestershire, on 11th March. The circuit was an hour's drive from Easton Neston. Lord Hesketh decided to have a party weekend and used a Bell Ranger helicopter and Rolls-Royce to ferry his guests to the circuit. He even brought his butler from Easton Neston to serve drinks.

No one was used to this sort of extravagance, not even Hunt. But he took it in his stride, saying: "They were a jolly nice crowd and, after the race, when it was time to stop work, I was able to join the party." In the race, Hunt retired on lap 22 when a wheel fell off the car, and he wasn't classified. The car suffered from a lack of straight line speed and Horsley and the mechanics were unhappy with the TS15's aerodynamics, a disappointment with which Hunt concurred. So Horsley decided to hire the old Goodwood circuit for a test session to see what they could do about it.

The solution was both highly simplistic and highly dangerous. They gradually flattened the wings to give less downforce and, as they did so, the car became faster and faster.

But such changes could be very dangerous when made by people who did not know what they were doing. Horsley seemed completely oblivious to what had happened at the circuit only three years earlier. In June 1970, Bruce McLaren's rear wing had broken on his Can-Am sports car, whereupon he had lost control, hit a marshal's post and been killed.

That day, Horsley seemed flat out determined to kill Hunt in similar circumstances when he finally removed the front and rear wings from the car completely and sent Hunt out. The car was certainly faster, but, without any downforce, it became increasingly unstable and Hunt struggled to keep it on the track. Suddenly and without warning, he felt the front wheels leave the ground. For the mechanics in the pits, the first indication that something was wrong was the complete silence as the engine came to a stop. It was eerily reminiscent of what had happened to Bruce McLaren.

Horsley couldn't see Hunt anywhere on the track. Turning to his two mechanics, he said rather gormlessly: "Where's he gone?"

The situation was serious. The Surtees had taken off at high speed and flown right over an earth bank and landed upside down. Horsley jumped into his road car and drive round the track at high speed looking for the Surtees.

He eventually found the car on its back, but there was no sign of Hunt. He was trapped somewhere in the car, and it was only by chance that the tank had been almost empty and the car hadn't caught fire. As there were no marshals around, Horsley didn't know what to do. Knocking on the side of the chassis to see if there was a response, Horsley heard Hunt swearing at him, telling him to get him out before there was a fire. He eventually managed to turn the car over and Hunt emerged to throw more abuse at the hapless team manager.

At any other time and in any other place, it could have been catastrophic; but Hunt climbed out of the car almost completely unhurt bar a sore neck. The car was wrecked and had to be returned to the Surtees factory at Edenbridge for a complete rebuild.

John Surtees was not impressed when he heard what had happened. Branding the team as irresponsible, he reminded them of the consequences for him if a driver was killed in a Surtees car. The incident and the cavalier behaviour remain etched in Surtees' memory and, unsurprisingly, he does not look back on Hesketh or the crew favourably, saying: "There are things you want to remember in life and things you don't. And Hesketh is one you don't want to remember." Surtees told Horsley never again to remove the wings – with some choice language.

The rebuilt car, with wings firmly in place, was brought to Germany for the first race of the European Formula Two season at Hockenheim on 8th April. Hesketh hired three chauffeur-driven Mercedes–Benz s-class limousines to transport the entourage of friends he had brought with him.

The race was a disaster for the team when the fuel pump failed in qualifying and then again on the warm-up lap of the race. A facetious Horsley gave an extraordinary post-race interview to a German journalist where he blamed a flying buzzard for the retirement. The journalist printed the story verbatim, appearing to take Horsley entirely seriously.

The next race was at Thruxton in Hampshire on 23rd April for the British series. This time, Hunt finished the race in tenth place. The team returned to Germany and Nürburgring on 29th April, when he retired again.

Between the Nürburgring and Pau races, Hunt spent a few days off in Barcelona with Ian Phillips. Phillips, then a journalist on *Autosport* magazine, used to travel with Hunt across Europe in a Ford Granada estate car to save money. In Barcelona, the two men slept on the beach during the day after having spent the entire previous evening in nightclubs.

Phillips remembers Hunt setting up a record player in the back of the Granada, recalling: "The trick was to drive as quickly but as tidily as possible so that the needle didn't jump off the LP record. James didn't regard this as unusual; it was just to keep us amused." In fact, Hunt drove very smoothly and the needle hardly ever left the record.

Phillips was also amused by Hunt's habits as a passenger, saying: "If you drove anywhere with him on a long journey, his brain was like a calculator: average speed, fuel consumption, this, that and the other. Most people would sit in the back and go to sleep, but not him. His brain was whirring, whirring, whirring all the time."

The race at Pau on the weekend of 5th and 6th May was a disaster. Hesketh broke a bone in his foot pushing the car, and then Hunt wrote off the car in qualifying as Phillips remembers: "At Pau, he broke his foot. It wasn't a serious injury, but enough to stop him racing that weekend. He had it in plaster."

Self-evidently, a car that couldn't be repaired would not be able to start, so Hunt found other interests to pursue. Hooking up with a local beauty queen that evening, Hunt wasn't seen again until the team was back in England.

The car was again sent to the Surtees factory in Edenbridge to be repaired, but this time it never came out. It didn't leave the factory again for 35 years. For reasons best known to himself, Horsley refused to pay the repair bill. Hesketh Racing no longer needed the car, as Hunt had driven his last race in Formula Two. The repaired chassis is now in the Barber Museum in California.

Formula Two had been a very unpleasant experience in 1973, and it was all over by the end of April, as Horsley said: "We actually managed to make a bit of a mess. We chose the wrong car for the 1973 season. We did everything that you shouldn't do."

At least he was honest.

After the fiasco, no sane man would give Hunt or Horsley a job nor, indeed, have either of them anywhere near a racing team. But Hesketh saw it all rather differently. He was about to put the two of them in charge of a Formula One team.

But one man who did view Hunt's ascent to Formula One favourably was

John Webb. Despite all of Hunt's shenanigans over the past three seasons, somewhere he saw some good in Hunt – although he told friends he was not sure where.

FORMULA 2 PROVES THE SPRINGBOARD TO F1

SHUNT

CHAPTER 15

Finally Formula One Beckons
1973

Lord Hesketh applies his own logic

Lord Hesketh's decision to enter Formula One was based on a simple premise that appeared to have escaped everyone else involved in Formula Two in 1973. He had worked out that the budgets for a Formula Two team were approximately the same as for Formula One, and he couldn't understand why all the F2 teams weren't competing in F1. In business terms, it was perfectly rational. Upon making the discovery, his next move was fairly obvious. Rather than playing around at the back of Formula Two races, he reasoned, he might as well be running Formula One races for the same money. James Hunt explained it thus: "Alexander suddenly took the rather intelligent view, we all thought, that we might as well do Formula One; his philosophy, very simple, really, being that: 'If we're going to mess around at the back, making fools of ourselves, let's do it in the real thing.'"

The team had had a disastrous start in Formula Two in 1973, writing off its Surtees chassis in a foolhardy aerodynamics experiment at Goodwood during testing. With nothing to lose, therefore, Hesketh became a big believer in the philosophy of "failing upwards."

The truth was that Formula One had become a relatively inexpensive sport in which to participate. The reason was simple: most of the cars were powered by the ubiquitous 3-litre Ford–Cosworth V8 engine.

The engine cost UK£7,500 to buy brand new – the same price it had cost in 1968. High inflation in the years since then had made the engine incredibly cheap. And, as the British currency deteriorated, the dollar price of the engine dropped dramatically.

The reason for that was even simpler. Keith Duckworth and Mike Costin, who owned Cosworth Engineering, were engineers and not business men. They had a profit target of 15 per cent of turnover and they priced the engines accordingly. They charged only UK£3,500 for rebuilds, and a rebuilt engine from Cosworth was effectively the equivalent of a brand new engine. They easily could have charged double or treble. As it stood, Hesketh's total engine bill for its first season of eight races was less than UK£25,000. The low cost and high quality of the engines completely transformed the economics of running a Formula One team.

To Hesketh's further astonishment, it soon became clear that his team was more successful in Formula One than it ever had been in Formula Two. Despite the bizarre results, logic dictated that if the team was more comfortable competing in F1, it should quickly move into that.

Hesketh, like everyone else, had been overawed by Formula One but found the difficulty of competing in the category to be a complete myth. As this became common knowledge, Formula Two eventually came to an end. In fact, it was the main reason why the Formula One grid became so oversubscribed in the mid seventies; and essentially it was all Hesketh's fault: he had shown the way.

But Hesketh, not quite believing his own theory, decided first to test it out. He told Bubbles Horsley to rent a car and engine so they could contest the upcoming Formula One Race of Champions on 18th March. It was a non-championship Formula One race that was held every year at Brands Hatch in the spring.

In a press release, Hesketh announced the foray to the Race of Champions as "an exploratory programme prior to embarking on a full Formula One season in 1974." Sounding rather grand, his news was met with some scepticism, as Gerald Donaldson recounted: "There was amazement at the arrogance and presumption of Hesketh Racing, owned by a zany playboy peer and managed by a failed Formula 3 driver named Bubbles, whose ignorance of the finer points of the sport was confirmed by the choice of driver."

Jackie Stewart, who was a close friend of Hesketh's, was also surprised. He recalls: "Alexander himself was an entertainingly eccentric man, and he still is for that matter, but I thought it was a bit speculative, to say the least, when he announced he was grooming James to be a future champion." Stewart added: "The whole thing seemed to be too outlandish to be a serious consideration for the future."

Soon after the announcement that he was to become an F1 driver, Hunt broke his arm in some high jinks at a country house weekend. He explained: "I was down in the country having lunch, then started playing silly games on the lawn afterwards, like they do in the country, and just fell over." Luckily for Hunt, Hesketh remained resolutely determined to proceed.

Horsley, a consummate wheeler–dealer, was given a tiny budget to find a competitive chassis, engine and some mechanics to run it for a weekend. He tried March, which laughed at his audacity. Max Mosley just didn't take him seriously when he floated the idea of Formula One. In fact, Horsley had a real problem being taken seriously by anyone when he told them he was entering Formula One, especially people who knew him from his Dastle Formula 3 days. So, Horsley was forced to go to John Surtees, who did at least agree to discuss it.

Discovering that Surtees had an old Surtees-Ford TS9B that he used as a reserve chassis, Horsley went down to the factory to take a look. Sure enough, Surtees removed the dust cover and revealed an immaculate TS9B. The TS9B was the 1972 chassis but broadly similar to the 1973 works car, the TS14A being driven that year by Mike Hailwood.

The car hadn't turned a wheel for four months but, after an hour of horse trading with a sceptical Surtees, he finally agreed to hire out the car for the weekend for US$15,000 all in. It included a rebuilt Cosworth engine complete with four mechanics. Surtees says it was a turnkey operation which included repainting the car in Hesketh's simple red and white plain livery. Agreeing to the deal, Surtees practically had to pick himself up off the floor when Horsley produced a blank cheque signed by Hesketh. As Horsley was about to fill in the amount of £8,000, the sterling equivalent, Surtees prodded him with: "plus VAT". "Oh," said Horsley, and meekly added the extra UK£1,500. Surtees remembers: "Bubbles was always out to do a deal; it was our spare car. We had a floating car." Surtees was right to insist on getting his money first, as Hesketh would later refuse to pay him for rebuilding the Formula Two Surtees TS15 when Hunt crashed. Surtees kept the rebuilt chassis and had the last laugh in 2008, 35 years later, when he sold it as one of Hunt's ex chassis for approximately 30 times the rebuild cost for which Horsley had stiffed him.

Surtees couldn't understand the Hesketh set-up at all, and he particularly couldn't understand James Hunt, as he says: "He was a likeable character, but I used to say: 'Stand up, the real James' because there were so many sides."

On Surtees' advice, Hesketh ended up buying Firestone tyres on which to run the car, and Horsley began a relationship with the Firestone that would pay huge dividends over the next two years. Horsley discovered that Firestone's construction design was particularly good, and it perfectly suited Hunt's driving style. Tyre construction design rarely changed, although compounds often did, and, although the Goodyear compounds were often better because they could afford to spend more money on them, the Firestones of the day had superior construction. As Hunt recalled: "That car was a lot better than most people thought it was, and – at Brands Hatch, on Firestones – it was really very good."

The 1973 Race of Champions was open to F1 and Formula 5000 cars. While the Formula 5000 cars were less sophisticated than F1 cars, they were somewhat more powerful, and the established Formula One stars that competed were hard pressed to match their speeds.

The Hesketh team arrived with its full complement of hangers-on, with Hesketh's helicopter ferrying his friends back and forth from his home at Easton Neston. For one hanger-on, it was his very first experience of motor racing. David Gray worked at Collett Dickenson Pearce, London's most creative advertising agency of the era, and he would become an important part of Hunt's commercial future. Gray had a very useful purpose as a link to the agency world. He met Lord Hesketh via Bubbles Horsley's uncle, John Wood, another hanger on. Gray remembers: "Woody became kind of obsessed with the whole thing, the whole racing thing, but I also became a hanger-on without a doubt. Before that, I had never been to a motor race in my life."

Gray says: "I loved it, and we had an extraordinary time. James became a great friend and I loved him dearly. He was irritating quite a lot of the time and also very headstrong. But he was incredibly able." For Hesketh's guests, it was one big party.

The Hesketh team lost time in qualifying while setting up the car for Hunt, and he struggled to adapt to the power of Formula One, which was a big step up from F2. The throttle also kept sticking, which caused Hunt some hairy moments. He said later: "I had to spend the first half of the race getting used to its power and finding out about driving a Formula One car. If we had been able to run a full practice, then there might have been a shock result and we could have won." It was no idle boast. The Surtees-Ford TS9B on its Firestones was very fast round Brands Hatch. Then came crisis. The team's only Cosworth engine blew up and it looked certain Hunt wouldn't be able to start the race. To solve the problem, Lord Hesketh adopted an unusual approach. He gathered the team members in a circle to pray to what Hesketh called the "great white chicken in the sky" to ask for an engine. Amazingly, the unorthodox approach worked. Max Mosley, who happened to be passing by, noticed the curious gathering. He remembers: "I came round the back of the Hesketh transporter and found them all sitting in a circle, and so I said to Hesketh: 'What are you all doing?' And he said: 'We're praying to the great chicken in the sky to give us another engine. We've only got one engine and it's blown up.' And I said: 'Well, maybe the great chicken of Bicester can help you.' So we all started laughing and we lent him an engine; it was the sort of thing one did in those days."

Astonished at Mosley's gesture, Hunt became firm friends with him from that day on. He gave Mosley the nickname the 'great white chicken of Bicester' in recognition of the engine loan. In later life, he modified it to the '*grand poulet*.' Mosley says: "Right to the end of his life, he called me that. If he walked in now, he'd say: 'Oh, there's the *grand poulet*.' It was all very childish, but it kept us amused."

With his new engine, compliments of Mosley, Hunt eventually qualified 13th out of 29 cars in the mixed field of Formula One and Formula 5000 cars. The BRMs of Jean-Pierre Beltoise, Niki Lauda and Vern Schuppan took the first three places on the grid, with Jody Scheckter's McLaren coming in fourth. It appeared that some F1 teams had been clever enough to modify their cars to match the lack of regulations for the race, while established stars such as Emerson Fittipaldi, Ronnie Peterson and Denny Hulme performed surprisingly slower.

Hunt did not find it easy to adapt to the extra power and grip of a Formula One car, as he confessed to journalists at the time: "The car is driving me."

45,000 fans turned up on race day and everything came right for Hunt. The race marked the debut for the new McLaren-Ford M23 model driven by Denny Hulme, and Hunt finished just behind it in third place. Hunt was aided by the fact that all the faster cars, including the two Lotuses of Fittipaldi and Peterson, retired. The race was actually won by ex-F1 driver Peter Gethin in a Formula 5000 Chevron.

The success at Brands Hatch took Lord Hesketh completely by surprise. He wasn't used to any sort of success in motor sport and just couldn't understand the ease of Formula One relative to the trials and tribulations he had undergone in Formula Two and Formula 3. As the light faded at Brands Hatch that evening and the celebrations continued, a light-headed Hesketh told Horsley to turn Hesketh racing into a full-time Formula One team.

Hunt remembered: "Alexander was very encouraged and excited when we came third in the Race of Champions, our first Formula One race. His attitude was that we were doing pretty badly in Formula Two and, for very little additional cost, we could do badly in Formula One."

Hesketh said to Horsley: "Let's go and mess about at the back of Formula One."

Hesketh set Horsley a target of the Monaco Grand Prix on 3rd June for the team's Formula One debut. Horsley had two and a half months to get things together and Hesketh had provided him with a budget of US$100,000 for the year.

Horsley concentrated on Formula One and, in the meantime, the rest of the team got on with its Formula Two programme, competing in four F2 races between then and Monaco.

Horsley hadn't been very impressed with the Surtees experience at Brands Hatch and wanted his team under his own control. He found John Surtees crusty and difficult to get on with, so he approached Mosley and told him he wanted to buy a car. Mosley, again, had great difficulty taking it seriously but he had observed what had gone on at Brands Hatch and instinct told him that it might turn out to be a serious enquiry. Anyway, he had a brand new March-Ford 731 sitting in the factory at Bicester looking for a customer, so he had little to lose and quoted Horsley a price.

The 731 was an upgraded Formula Two chassis with a Ford-Cosworth DFV engine in the back. March had found this combination extremely successful and had abandoned designing expensive, dedicated Formula One chassis. Horsley paid US$35,000 for the chassis. But then he needed a couple of engines, and that meant approaching Cosworth Engineering.

When Horsley phoned Cosworth, however, he couldn't get past the receptionist. Even the store's manager, Jack Field, wouldn't speak to him about buying DFVs. Field wouldn't waste time on him. Cosworth was a very straightforward company and dealt in a very straightforward way. It had a price list and it didn't give discounts or haggle. When it came up against a wheeler dealer character like Horsley it naturally bridled.

When Horsley reported this back to Lord Hesketh, the Lord mistakenly thought that Keith Duckworth might be one of his tenants and told Horsley to go and "sort him out". Duckworth, the brilliant engine designer, was by then a very wealthy man and had no need to rent a house on Hesketh's estate.

By then, Horsley was getting desperate and Cosworth simply would not speak to him. Without Cosworth engines, there was going to be no Formula One team. So Lord Hesketh decided to visit the Cosworth factory at St James Mill Road, in Northampton, which, as it happened, was about 15 minutes by car from Easton Neston.

When Hesketh arrived at the Cosworth reception, he asked to speak to Cosworth director Bill Brown, who was also general manager. Brown's office was upstairs on the mezzanine and his secretary, Valerie Given, buzzed him to say there was someone in reception who wanted to buy two DFV engines and was demanding to see him. But by that time, Hesketh had already mounted the stairs and was standing in Brown's office, uninvited. Brown takes up the story: "One morning, a fat man appeared in my office without warning. 'Who the hell are you?' I asked. 'I am Lord Hesketh', was the reply. 'Well,' I said, 'I am Bill Brown. If you want to see me, go down and clear it with my secretary.'"

Hesketh, not used to being spoken to in such a manner, did as he was told and went down the stairs and politely asked Valerie if he could have an appointment, and, as he was already there, please could it be now. Brown says: "He actually went down and came back up with Valerie, who said: 'This is Lord Hesketh, he wants to buy some engines.' From then on, everything went smoothly, and he bought his engines."

Brown sold him two new Ford-Cosworth engines for another US$30,000. Brown also arranged for one of Cosworth's engine builders, an Irishman called Ray Buckley, to go and work for the team to look after the engines at the track.

With a suitable truck and some spares, the whole package came to US$80,000. This left him US$15,000 to run the car for the season, after paying out the US$5,000 he had agreed to pay Hunt to drive for the team. He had also promised Hunt 45 per cent of any prize money he won, but, in truth, he didn't expect to get any in the first year.

SHUNT

Hesketh took a deep breath and wrote the cheque. He had the cash, some US$3 million in all: the world's economies were booming all around him; his other business interests in London were doing well, at least on paper; and running a Formula One team was really very good value at this time – it was the era of motor racing before the technology and the costs ran out of control. When asked what his motivation was, Hesketh said: "A lot of people want to make a lot of money to store it away. I want to make a lot of money to be able to spend it. I like spending to create something which is entirely my own, and this is why I have the racing team."

Horsley recalls: "Formula One was relatively unsophisticated back then compared to now and there was quite good money to be made. Bernie Ecclestone was beginning to get better appearance money, better travel money and better prize money. And, of course, we were quite quickly running towards the front."

When the car and the two engines arrived at Easton Neston, Hunt was hit with the reality that he was going to be a Formula One driver after all. Finding it hard to cope, his confidence vanished. It seemed that although, in his heart of hearts, he may have always wanted to be a Formula One driver, he had never really thought he would make it. Now, he was scared stiff.

Retreating from his London flat back to his parents' house in Surrey, he tried to prepare for the race and to find some moral support. The nervous tension wore him down. He said: "I had gone home and stayed with my parents in order that I could become really fit before my first Grand Prix." He would say later that he was "fit as a fiddle" otherwise.

But this was not quite true. Five days before he left for Monte Carlo, Hunt started getting terrible headaches. The headaches were a legacy of the accident at Goodwood. He explained: "I'd gone on my head so many times that my neck muscles had sort of seized up from the abuse and the blood supply was restricted. I had been having blinding headaches four or five days a week."

He eventually sought treatment and physiotherapy cured the problem, but he then became reluctant to go to the doctors again for fear that he would be ruled unfit to race. He admitted: "I was frightened to go and get anything done because I thought there might be something seriously wrong and, in truth, I was very worried about my fitness at Monaco."

Meanwhile, the opposite experience was being had by the 23-year-old Lord Hesketh, who was taking it all in his stride and looking forward to the

Monaco Grand Prix, where he was in charge of the social arrangements. His social budget was far bigger than Horsley's; in fact, it was pretty much unlimited, and restricted only by the time he had available to spend. He rented a 162-foot yacht called 'The Southern Breeze', which had originally been owned by John Bloom, the washing machine tycoon who had founded Rolls-Razor. Bloom had sold the yacht when his empire collapsed in the late sixties.

Occupied with the social arrangements, Hesketh wasn't at all worried about challenging the big names of Formula One. Not so the other way around, however. The Formula One world was aghast at Hesketh's entry; the Race of Champions was one thing, but entering the Monaco Grand Prix was quite another. They regarded Hesketh as an upper-class hooray who had no business being in Formula One. There was also the issue of Hunt. With his reputation preceding him, Hunt was labelled by one team principal, who had experienced his antics on Formula 3, as an "overbearing upper-class lout." To most people in Formula One, he was 'Hunt the Shunt.' Universally disliked, Hunt's arrival in Formula One arm-in-arm with Alexander Hesketh didn't serve to increase his popularity.

1973 was the last year Jackie Stewart competed in Formula One. Stewart was arguably the most influential driver ever to race, and a pivotal driver in the history of motor sport. He ushered the sport into the modern era and then quickly retired at the top of his game.

Stewart espoused the importance of preparation. He advocated no smoking, no drinking and no sex in the four or five days before a race. Stewart had established the textbook image of the ideal racing driver. But Hunt was the antithesis of this, positively encouraging smoking, drinking and sex the night before a race; in fact, sometimes five minutes before a race. On more than one occasion, he would have sex with a woman in an empty pit garage just minutes before getting into his cockpit – such was the case at the world championship decider in Mount Fuji in 1976.

To his credit, Jackie Stewart never judged Hunt, but he did look askew at his antics and shrug his shoulders in disbelief. Even today, Stewart is bemused by what Hunt got up to, but refuses to judge him. He says simply: "James was James", and admits that even he enjoyed indulging in the Hesketh hospitality after the race. In fact, Stewart went on to become great friends with Alexander Hesketh at the end of his career.

Although Hesketh's spending on the team was to be dwarfed by his spending on entertainment, this was not so unusual at the time. Most sponsors spent more on hospitality than on racing. Philip Morris's Marlboro hospitality budget, for instance, was three times the amount it spent sponsoring its teams and drivers.

But Hesketh introduced excess to Formula One, as Mosley remembers: "Hesketh would start the day with a glass of champagne to settle his stomach at the beginning of the morning; and on it went."

As well as the yacht bobbing in the harbour, Hesketh flew his Bell Jet Ranger helicopter down to Monte Carlo while his chauffeur drove his Rolls-Royce down to the principality. Hunt drove down in Hesketh's white Porsche Carrera RS and another friend rode his Suzuki superbike across France.

Helicopters were a rarity in Formula One in those days, and the American-built Bell Jet Ranger II was brand-spanking new and had cost close to US$600,000. A makeshift helipad was set up next to Monte Carlo's swimming pool near where the yacht was moored. At night, Lord Hesketh flew the helicopter back to Nice airport so that it would be ready to begin ferrying guests coming in on the first flight the next morning. He then drove back to Monaco in his Rolls-Royce as dusk fell.

The Southern Breeze was one of the biggest private yachts of its day, and it provided a base for the day-long parties indulged in by Lord Hesketh's entourage. The Rolls-Royce was continually ferrying Hesketh's guests from Nice airport, and the helicopter was in and out of the Monte Carlo heliport, transporting his guests back and forth to private villas along the coast.

As the weekend progressed, the pile of empty champagne bottles built up on the quay, and the principality's dust trucks put on an extra lorry to cope.

The only cloud came when the Lord discovered that the yacht next door, chartered by Philip Morris, owners of the Marlboro cigarette brand, was 20 feet longer than his. He told Pete Lyons, the American journalist who was covering Formula One for *Autosport* magazine: "Well, but you can see The Southern Breeze is wider abeam and our guests have a much more comfortable footing in rough seas. And besides, there's our helicopter, and not even those Marlboro people have anything like that."

In the pit lane, the all-white pinstriped March-Ford 731 looked undeniably impressive. Horsley had hired Dr Harvey Postlethwaite to act as the team's chief engineer. Postlethwaite was a designer at March and had been attracted by the notion of working for a race team. Hesketh's was the first offer he received.

Postlethwaite was a sober character who lent the team an air of credibility. Having obtained a PhD in mechanical engineering, he was addressed by Hunt as "Doc Postlethwaite." Postlethwaite had also trained at the feet of the legendary Robin Herd. Given his qualifications, people were often surprised to see him working for Hesketh. When asked how he had been persuaded to take the job, he said: "They got me drunk." It may well have been true. On a more serious note, he admitted that: "The team went from being happy amateurs to a degree of professionalism just because I was the first person they took on who was a motor racing professional."

Horsley said: "Harvey was very good, he knew the car backwards, he was very good at setting up the car." Horsley also hired Nigel Stroud away from March as the team's chief mechanic. Stroud was a talented engineer with a reputation for making cars reliable, as Horsley remembers: "He added a lot of little tweaks and unique things."

The car and the team appeared in the team colours of red, white and blue stripes on a white livery. Choosing the team colours for "reasons of patriotism", Hesketh rejected spraying the car green, which was the official racing colour of Britain. Although Hesketh thought British racing green was magnificent, it was "rather too subtle" he explained: "I'm a great believer in this country. So we ran with the colours of the Union Jack."

The team members also had their names on their shirts and anoraks, a feature which is so common now but was entirely unique back then. Hesketh's shirt had 'Le Patron' emblazoned across it.

All of this rather overshadowed Hunt's Grand Prix debut. The driver became almost peripheral. But Pete Lyons, known for his colourful prose, did notice Hunt at Monaco and described him as follows: "He had the kind of appearance that attracts the eye; once seen, he was remembered."

David Benson, the *Daily Express* motoring editor, also noticed him and wrote: "There was still something of the cavalier in Hunt. An athletic, powerfully-built six-footer, blond with cornflower-blue eyes, he is extremely attractive to women. His handsome looks are reinforced by the self-confidence instilled by his public school education, and he has a swashbuckling personality."

But others were less impressed than Lyons, and most were disbelievers. Peter Windsor, the leading British journalist, said that Hunt lacked the "necessary seriousness of intent ever to become a proper racing driver." It wasn't a very promising prognosis, and many of the British journalists in attendance were similarly disinclined towards Hunt.

But the disbelievers were about to receive a setback.

Hunt's Grand Prix debut was mightily impressive as he qualified the March on the ninth row of the grid. Qualifying, however, was one thing, and racing quite another in the narrow streets of Monaco. Hunt had driven at Monaco in Formula 3 but he found the F3 car like a go-cart compared to his new Formula One car.

Admitting that he was a frightened man, he sat strapped into the cockpit of his March on the Monaco starting grid on Sunday 3rd March 1973, surrounded by all the famous names in motor racing. Jackie Stewart's Tyrrell-Ford and Ronnie Peterson's Lotus-Ford shared the front row. Behind them were Denny Hulme's McLaren and François Cevert's Tyrrell. And behind them were Emerson Fittipaldi's Lotus and Niki Lauda's BRM. Although Hunt had raced against many of these names in F3 and F2, he was totally overawed. He recalled: "Monaco is a pretty tough place to start a Grand Prix career. The track is so narrow and there is absolutely no room for error. Before I got into the car, I was puking all over the place, and on the grid I was just a shaking wreck. I was nervous, very nervous." Lord Hesketh described Hunt's condition as he debuted in the Grand Prix as that of "a new born babe."

As soon as the flag dropped, Hunt forgot about his headaches and his nervousness. He had no choice; he found he couldn't see a thing for all the exhaust fumes and tyre smoke. Pressing the throttle pedal as hard as he could, he simply gripped the steering wheel and prayed. He just about managed to remember to flick up the gear lever to shift the gears.

Hunt somehow got his car up to sixth that day before his brand new engine blew up on the 74th lap. As it was near the end of the race, he was still classified ninth, although it was a tremendous disappointment to be denied a world championship point on his debut. In those days, only the first six places got points, and the points scoring scale was 9,6,4,3,2,1.

Despite missing out on his point, even his severest doubters had to admit that Hunt had driven a fine race. And, as for Hunt, he had learned something about himself as well. It was by far the toughest two hours he had ever spent in a racing car, and he realised he was not as fit as he thought, saying: "I was going well for the first third of the race, then suddenly it hit me. I couldn't drive at that pace any more. I was simply going to drive off the road. The heat plus the physical effort of driving the car had me completely knackered."

At the front, Jackie Stewart went on to win his 25th Grand Prix and was on his way to his third world championship title. He had already made the decision to retire at the end of the season, so, as Hunt's career was beginning, Stewart's was coming to an end.

The rest of the Formula One community was very surprised at the Hesketh's debut. They had expected a shambles but, instead, had witnessed a highly professional set-up going about its business. One man who was not surprised was *Autosport* editor, Ian Philips, who said: "Everybody thought: 'Oh, they're all a joke', but beneath it all was a deadly, deadly, serious operation."

After the race, Hunt threw himself into the celebrations. A party to end all parties began on The Southern Breeze and lasted until the dawn of Monday morning. Hesketh, still in disbelief over how easy and cheap it all was, was pleased most of all by how much fun he was having.

When the dust settled and he was back in England, Hunt immediately threw himself into a fitness programme.

Hunt lived near Stamford Bridge, the Chelsea FC soccer ground, and was friendly with some of the players who drank at his local bar at 365 Kings Road. Some of the players with whom he got drunk there included Peter Osgood, Alan Hudson and John Hollins.

Soon after Monaco, he was discussing his fitness problems with the players and they suggested he joined in some of their training sessions. Hollins, the club captain, said he would ask manager Dave Sexton's permission. Sexton's training regime was known to be the best in British soccer, and he welcomed Hunt to the squad. Most importantly, Sexton taught him a method of strengthening his neck muscles with a medicine ball.

Separately, Hunt also began a punishing jogging routine. He played more tennis and squash, and his fitness philosophy became: "It can't hurt to do something that hurts."

Hunt threw himself into his new career in Formula One and was determined to make the most of it. He also wanted to make some money. Tony Dron remembers how he set about selling himself to supplement his non-existent salary from Hesketh: "He was incredibly busy, he was on the phone all the time, people were always ringing up. He had meetings at breakfast and was then going on to do something , there was action all of the time. It was obvious he was on the way to being a superstar already."

The Hesketh team, exhausted by its efforts in Monaco and short of a spare engine whilst it was being rebuilt, missed the next Grand Prix in Sweden and instead prepared itself for a trip to the south of France.

At least these were the excuses they gave. In reality, their reason for missing the Swedish Grand Prix was much more basic; as Lord Hesketh would later admit: "We forgot to enter."

It was a much more relaxed Hesketh team that pulled into the spacious Paul Ricard paddock for the French Grand Prix on 1st July. In the month between the races, the Hesketh mechanics had taken the car back to Easton Neston and, under Postlethwaite's direction, meticulously rebuilt it, crack testing key components and doing all they could to make it reliable.

Hunt was also much fitter and altogether more relaxed. His headaches had also subsided after some treatment. He had a trouble-free qualifying, placing the March in 14th, and the team learned more about how to make the car go faster. The race was also a trouble-free run, apart from a worrying moment when the top part of his airbox fell off. He brought the car home sixth, aided by the retirements and accidents of others. It was another remarkable race performance and he was still on the same lap as the leader, Ronnie Peterson, who won the race in his Lotus-Ford from François Cevert's Tyrrell-Ford.

After Hunt's exemplary performances in the first two Grand Prix races, the Formula One establishment was baffled. This was not the James Hunt they knew; new teams and rookie drivers didn't just come into Formula One and perform this way.

Hunt's stunning achievements did not go unrecognised in the media either. And although the British motor sport journalists didn't like him, the national newspaper hacks loved his exploits.

Hunt had suddenly come to the British public's attention, and he was instantly famous; so much so that he was invited to drive in the 1975 Tour of Britain being held just before the British Grand Prix. The organisers offered him US$3,000, to which he said 'yes' immediately. Suddenly he was earning big money to participate in his favourite sport.

The Tour was 1,000 miles and a mixture of racing and rallying held over three days on public roads as well as special stages at race tracks. Hunt drove a Chevrolet Camaro and his initial co-driver was to be Richard Lloyd, an experienced driver and team owner. The Camaro was owned by Alan Rivers, a friend of Lloyd's.

On his way to the Monaco Grand Prix, however, Lloyd was injured in a road accident, and *Autosport* magazine's deputy editor, Robert Fearnall, was roped in as Hunt's new co-driver. Fearnall was an old friend of Hunt's from his Formula 3 days.

Hunt didn't take the Tour seriously at all and told Fearnall he was going to thrash the car at Silverstone and blow up the old V8 and retire so he could spend a few days partying with Lord Hesketh at Easton Neston, two miles from Silverstone.

Hunt had tested the Camaro at Brands Hatch prior to the tour and fancied his chances as 83 entry cars took the start at Bath, in Somerset. Other notable competitors entered were Graham Hill and rally champion Roger Clark.

The tour started in farcical circumstances. A few miles down the road from the start, Hunt discovered the fuel tank was empty. Refusing to pay for the fuel, Hunt made Fearnall get out his credit card.

But Hunt found the American V8 engine more difficult to blow up than he had thought and, in the process of trying, managed to set the fastest lap round Silverstone. He soon found himself in line to win the event. As his competitive instincts took over, he suddenly became serious and decided that he wanted to win the event. The outcome of the Tour all rested on a hill climb at Dodington Park in the Cotswolds on the last day. Having had a practice run before anyone else arrived, Hunt managed to win the climb, and the overall event, and garnered plenty of publicity in all the British newspapers.

It was big news, and Hunt scooped all the prize money. As Hesketh remembers: "I think he earned more money winning the Avon Tour of Britain in 1973 than he did driving for me for a whole season." Hunt and Fearnall retired to a Bath hotel to celebrate.

The publicity was far greater than any he had previously received in Britain, and it set him up for his first British Grand Prix appearance on 14th July. But, as ever, the racing seemed almost secondary that weekend. Hesketh set up a hospitality tent in the paddock with lobster on the four-course menu and Dom Pérignon and Taittinger champagne flowing from 8:30am. The tables were laden with silverware, and guests attended with a formality unusual at the dusty airfield. Men in white linen suits and straw hats were arm-in-arm with breathtakingly beautiful young women in flowing summer dresses.

The Hesketh staff was also blue-blooded: the official photographer was Christopher Simon Sykes; team catering was the responsibility of Tom Benson, the top society chef who owned Parkes, a top Knightsbridge restaurant in Beauchamp Place; and the team's logistics chief was Charles Lucas, a schoolboy friend of Hesketh's whose grandfather had built St Pancras railway station and the Royal Albert Hall.

Formula One in Britain had never seen anything like it, as Hesketh's helicopter shuffled his guests in and out of Easton Neston all weekend. Hesketh proclaimed to his guests that Formula One racing was "like a very flat bottle of champagne", explaining: "We intend to give it a vigorous shake."

Jackie Stewart and his wife, Helen, were also enjoying the hospitality at Eaton Neston. He recalls: "Alexander's mother was a Scot, a fantastic lady who wore a patch over one eye and kept a wonderfully eccentric house."

Even Hunt was surprised by the spectacle, and described Hesketh's friends as "a set of extremely keen and committed partiers." For them, he said, it was primarily a weekend in the country with "some motor racing thrown in."

Hunt suffered in qualifying from gearbox problems but still managed his best qualifying position to date with 11th on the grid. Late in qualifying, he had a real scare as the suspension broke at high speed. Fortunately, he wrestled the car to a halt without hitting anything. He said: "I had known that I could be very competitive at Silverstone," and then qualified it by saying: "You do know these things, you see, although you don't tell people about it in case it doesn't come off and you look a bit of a twit."

But the race itself was almost over as soon as it had begun. In only his third start in a Grand Prix, Hunt was almost killed in the first few minutes of the race. Rookie Jody Scheckter lost control of his McLaren on the exit of Woodcote, Silverstone's fastest corner. Scheckter spun into the path of the oncoming cars and the incident involved nine of the 28 starters. The first few cars maneuvered round the wrecked car, which was now parked bang in the middle of the track. But the rest didn't, and piled into each other. The start line resembled a motorway pile-up. The track was blocked and the race stopped.

Hunt arrived on the scene straight after Scheckter's accident and stamped on the brakes to avoid the spinning McLaren. As his car stopped, Hunt ducked down in the cockpit and closed his eyes as he saw Scheckter's rear wing flying straight for his head. If he hadn't ducked, he would undoubtedly have been killed. As it was, the projectile rear wing cut through the March's airbox and sliced it clean off.

That no one was killed or seriously injured was a miracle. After the dust storm created by all the spinning and crashing cars settled down, the only injured driver was Italian Andrea de Adamich, who had suffered a broken ankle. All the other drivers, including Hunt, walked away unscathed.

Apart from bodywork, Hunt's March was undamaged and the restart would be taken by 19 cars.

Hunt admitted: "I had a very lucky escape."

Hunt felt good about the restart and found himself running third in the restarted race. In the process, he set the fastest lap of the race – at an average of 134 miles an hour. The race was won by American Peter Revson, followed by Ronnie Peterson and Denny Hulme; all separated by less than three seconds.

Hunt eventually finished fourth in only his third Grand Prix, and the British fans went wild in recognition of a new star in their midst, whom they had not been expecting. Where Jackie Stewart had been favoured to win, he had an off-day and only managed tenth place behind Hunt. As Hunt lapped Stewart, Stewart actually slowed down to let him pass.

Jackie Stewart was full of praise for Hunt that evening. Listening carefully to every word the world champion had to say, Hunt was touched: "It was enormously encouraging for the team and it was good for the happy atmosphere which we had. I've never been as happy in a racing team before."

At the raucous party at Easton Neston that night, it was Hunt – not Stewart – who was the guest of honour.

With his newly-acquired fame, Hunt found he could earn money effortlessly by making personal appearances. He was paid US$3,000 to co-drive a Chevrolet Camaro in the Spa 24 hour saloon car race at Spa Franchorchamps in Belgium. His co-driver was Richard Lloyd. It was a dangerous circuit and a brutal race that claimed the lives of two drivers and seriously injured several more. Hunt and Lloyd retired early, and Hunt drove back to England.

The next race, and Hunt's fourth Grand Prix, was the Dutch Grand Prix at the Zandvoort circuit, set by the seaside amongst sand dunes. It was a circuit that would later bring Hunt much success and happiness – but not that day.

Hunt qualified his March-Ford in seventh place on the grid alongside Carlos Pace in his Surtees-Ford. Hunt was ahead of Niki Lauda in a BRM. The race turned into a Tyrrell benefit, with Jackie Stewart leading teammate François Cevert home for a 1-2 win. Hunt came in third to score his first podium finish in a Formula One Grand Prix. It was the most success he had had in any category of racing.

Stewart's victory was the 26th win of his career, beating the number of wins by Jim Clark, but it was overshadowed by tragedy. On the eighth lap, Hunt was in fifth place when he passed another car, a March-Ford 731 like his, upside down and in flames. As he circulated, the car carried on burning and became obscured with black smoke. After an age, marshals arrived to put out the fire. All Hunt could see was that a tarpaulin had been thrown over the burnt-out March. What he didn't know was that the driver was still inside the car, hanging upside down by his seat belts. It was the young Englishman Roger Williamson – or what was left of him.

There was no joy on the podium that day as Hunt stood at attention alongside Stewart and Cevert and the British national anthem was played over the circuit's loudspeakers.

Like Hunt, Williamson was a rising star driving a March-Ford paid for by a wealthy mentor; in Williamson's case, the mentor was builder Tom Wheatcroft. Both drivers had been destined for the top, with Williamson considered to be every bit as fast as Hunt.

It transpired that Williamson's car had crashed into a steel guard rail, overturned and caught fire. Another driver, David Purley had stopped his car and tried to get Williamson's car upright to get him out. But he was beaten back by the flames and deeply distressed by the lack of marshals with extinguishers.

Hunt knew Williamson from competing in Formula 3. He remembered his own accident at Zandvoort two years earlier, when his March turned over with fuel leaking around him. The only difference was that his car hadn't caught fire. It was also reminiscent of Piers Courage's accident at Zandvoort three years earlier, when Courage had burned to death.

There were clearly inadequacies in Zandvoort's safety routines. Denny Hulme, president of the Grand Prix Drivers Association, said that unless firefighting was improved at Zandvoort, Formula One would never return to the track.

But as usual, Formula One shrugged its shoulders and carried on. Hesketh didn't enter the next race, the German Grand Prix at Nürburgring on 5th August, as it was only seven days after the race in Holland and they did not have the resources to prepare the car again so quickly.

The team next appeared on 19th August at the Austrian Grand Prix, at the picturesque Österreichring circuit. Hunt qualified ninth but lasted only three laps in the race before retiring with fuel problems. It was the first retirement of his Formula One career.

The race was won by Ronnie Peterson's Lotus, with Jackie Stewart second and Carlos Pace third in his Surtees-Ford.

FINALLY FORMULA ONE BECKONS

The Italian Grand Prix was next, on 9th September. In qualifying on Friday, Hunt had his first Formula One accident. He crashed heavily when his brakes faded and caught him by surprise. The car was badly damaged and the team had no spares with which to repair it. Bubbles Horsley told Hunt he was withdrawing from the race. It was desperately disappointing, but an indication of the shoestring effort on which the team was run. Hunt admitted the accident was his fault: "I made an error and cocked up the whole thing." But he was incensed that Horsley wanted to give up and withdraw. The race witnessed Hunt's first tantrum and a furious row with Horsley.

After the crash, Hunt chased Max Mosley down the paddock and asked his advice on how to repair the car. He wanted the works mechanics to help fix it. According to Mosley, a repair was impossible at the track without a replacement chassis, but he had a spare chassis at the factory which could be flown out to Monza in time for the race. Reporting back to Horsley, Hunt asked him to authorise the cost of air freighting the chassis. The bill for this would have been more than US$7,000, and Horsley refused. He told Hunt there wasn't enough time and he wanted the team to return immediately to England to prepare for the final two races of the season, to be held in North America. Horsley remembers: "James was furious and his short fuse was well and truly lit, and we had a tremendous row." In the end, Horsley got his way and Hunt simmered for an hour before accepting his fate.

After what had been such a good start, it was rather a dejected team that made its first trip outside of Europe. They flew the Atlantic on the Formula One charter to Toronto for the Canadian Grand Prix at Mosport on 23rd September.

But before that, there had been some good news. Hunt had been signed as a client by International Management Group (IMG), the sports agency owned by super agent Mark McCormack. IMG was the leading agency in the world and McCormack, undoubtedly having been prodded by star client Jackie Stewart, recognised Hunt's potential. Hunt was now starting to earn serious money from his outside promotional activities. He was getting a lot of work and earning around US$5,000 to US$10,000 a day for it. As much as he liked to party, he was a different person where work was concerned. He was meticulous with his business arrangements and always on time for events, and rarely failed to please. As a result, he was also starting to pay a lot of tax on his earnings as the incumbent Labour government began putting the squeeze on wealthy people in Britain.

In Canada, suffering from jet lag, which cramped his performance, Hunt qualified 15th. After the crash in Monza, Hunt was also under strict orders from Horsley not to take any risks that might damage the car. The team had hardly any spares, apart from a spare engine, and had to be cautious. If Hunt crashed again, he would have been unable to race in Watkins Glen at the United States Grand Prix a fortnight later. Hunt, who really wanted to go to Watkins Glen, played it safe and trundled in seventh, two laps behind winner Peter Revson and Emerson Fittipaldi, who finished second.

No such rules would apply in Watkins Glen, the last race of the season. Hunt was ordered to go for it by Horsley.

The race would be a significant one, as it was to be Jackie Stewart's last and 100th Grand Prix, as his retirement became official. But no one knew that at the time, and, although Stewart had made the decision in April, some six months earlier, he had informed only Ken Tyrrell and Ford's Walter Hayes. He had not even told his wife, Helen, nor François Cevert, the Tyrrell number two driver.

As it happened, Stewart and Helen had been holidaying with Cevert in the week between Mosport and Watkins Glen. They had borrowed a Ford Galaxy from Ford Motor Company and taken a trip to Niagara Falls and spent a few nights at the Essex House in New York. After that, they had spent a week on the beaches of Bermuda. Cevert was nursing an ankle injury and Stewart remembers having to carry him around.

The holiday was difficult, as Stewart was having to keep his upcoming retirement a secret. This was particularly difficult, as his job as team leader at Tyrrell was to be taken over by Cevert, and Cevert did not have any inkling thereof. But in a cruel twist of fate, it was never to be.

Meanwhile, James Hunt was enjoying the last race of the season. He loved America and said: "It was really good fun, with no pressure and just racing for racing's sake." He was enjoying staying at the Glen Motor Inn, just outside the circuit and mixing with many of the drivers for the first time socially. On Friday, he was 17th fastest from 28 cars. On Saturday morning, he was fifth.

But later that morning, it all became meaningless as François Cevert lost control of his Tyrrell–Ford and had a huge accident which ended with his car lying on top of a steel Armco barrier. The Frenchman died instantly.

Jody Scheckter was first driver to arrive at the scene, and Jackie Stewart was devastated when he saw Cevert's body strapped in the car and the terrible injuries he had sustained. Both he and Scheckter were mentally scarred that day. It was the worst accident they had ever witnessed.

Upon returning to the pits and speaking to Ken Tyrrell, Stewart decided not to take part in the race, thus ending his career. But he did take part in the afternoon qualifying session and explains why: "The reason I did that was because of François' mechanics, and particularly his chief mechanic, Jo Ramirez. Jo was fearful that [the accident] had been a mechanical failure. I was confident that it was not."

Stewart felt he had to show confidence in the car and in the mechanics by going out again. He recalls: "I thought I knew why the accident had occurred and it was not a mechanical failure. François was using one gear lower than I was going through that corner, and there was a very bad bump on the exit of the left hander going up the hill at Turn Two. As the car went over it, the rear end got loose and went into oversteer. The barrier was hard up against the track with no run off area, and when François took his foot off the gas, the car snapped into oversteer. Being a gear lower than me, the car was very reactive [it was small wheelbase car]. The car reacted in such a vicious way that he hit the barrier quite hard and it ricocheted into the double height barrier. During the accident the car somehow turned upside down and landed on top of the barrier, causing the fatal injuries." The guardrail actually split in two but did not kill him. It was the fact that he landed upside down that did that.

Stewart was already world champion and about to compete in his 100th race – it was meant to be a perfect end to his career. Instead, it had ended in tragedy. Cevert was the fourth very close friend he had lost on the track in eight years of racing. The list included the likes of Jim Clark, Piers Courage and Jochen Rindt, but this was the most horrible death he had witnessed.

The piano-playing Cevert was a very cultured man from a very civilized and loving family. Every year from that day on, Stewart sent Cevert's father and mother flowers to mark the anniversary of their son's death. When they both finally passed away, the flowers were put on his grave. And they continue to be placed there on 6th October every year. Stewart wearily went on the well-trodden path of repatriating Cevert's body and effects to his home country, and preparing to fly to his funeral.

Hunt was promoted to fourth on the grid on the second row alongside Emerson Fittipaldi's Lotus. Ronnie Peterson was on pole alongside Carlos Reutemann in his Brabham-Ford.

At the start, Hunt beat Fittipaldi into the first corner and he overtook

Reutemann on lap four. For the next hour and a half, Hunt chased Peterson with Fittipaldi, Hailwood and Scheckter close behind him. To the surprise of everyone, Hunt was able to stay around a second behind Peterson as the race progressed.

Finding that the straight line speed of the March was superior to that of Peterson's Lotus, Hunt made up any time lost in the corners on the straight and decided to bide his time until the final few laps to pass Peterson. But suddenly, the March began to develop oversteer due to its lightening fuel load. However, Hunt maintained the challenge to the flag, and his next to last lap was the race's fastest. They crossed the finish line separated by 0.688 of a second; at that time the second smallest winning margin in Formula One history. The entire Hesketh team jumped the pit wall and embraced a bemused Hunt for at least five minutes.

In his first season, Hunt drove in seven of the 15 events. He scored two podiums and was eighth in the world championship, on 14 points. Jackie Stewart was world champion with 71 points, and Hunt was eighth in the world championship behind Emerson Fittipaldi, Ronnie Peterson, François Cevert, Peter Revson, Denny Hulme and Carlos Reutemann. As Hesketh told Hunt, he was now officially the eighth best driver in the world.

With accident and engine rebuilds, Hesketh had spent US$145,000 in that first season of Formula One and had won back nearly US$80,000 in prize money, keeping Horsley just inside his US$100,000 budget. Hunt received 45 per cent of the prize money and, for the first time in his life, had serious money in the bank. Added to the money he received for his personal appearances, Hunt had earned up to US$50,000 by season end. To celebrate, he bought himself a new 3-litre Ford Capri with a proper stereo system.

Hunt said: "Nobody was prepared to give any sort of chance to a new Formula One team managed by someone called Bubbles Horsley and with a driver named James Hunt, but I have a theory about rich people – and Alexander in particular – that when they touch something, it turns to gold." Hunt's theory was proved correct. The Hesketh team's performance in a customer March was nothing short of sensational.

Jackie Stewart, the retiring world champion was also impressed with Hesketh, especially by its second place at Watkins Glen. As he recalls: "As things developed, it became clear that the team knew what it was doing, and James had great skill as a driver. He had great natural talent. I could see that in the few times I raced against him before I retired. But he became abstract in quite a lot of ways."

Hesketh, pleased that his total expenditure had been less than US$100,000, was blinded by the success of that first season. He signaled a big effort for 1974, which would cost three times as much, including the building of a new car with his name on it. But as he was revealing his plans to journalists, the Arabs and the Israelis were making plans for war – a war which would drive up the price of oil, cut many ties and plunge the world into a harsh economic recession that would jeopardise Hesketh's businesses and his racing team. The world was about to undergo a substantial change.

On his return to England, Hunt was awarded the Campbell Trophy by the British Royal Automobile Club (RAC). It was the same club that had almost banned him from competing in Formula 3. The trophy was to celebrate the 'Best performance in motor sport by a British driver in a British car.' The citation read: 'In his first season of Formula One racing, James Hunt in the Hesketh March consistently showed outstanding ability against established racing stars.'

It was the perfect description of a perfect first season in Formula One. After six years of struggling to succeed in motor racing, the world was suddenly at James Hunt's feet.

Hunt rounded off his season by flying to Johannesburg to compete in the Nine-Hour Endurance sports car race at Kyalami. He had been invited by John Wyer's Gulf Research Racing team to drive a Mirage-Ford M6 for the race, and was persuaded to do it by his friend Mike Hailwood, who was also driving for Gulf in a sister Mirage. Hunt teamed up with sports car specialist Derek Bell as his co-driver. Mike Hailwood retired whilst leading the race, leaving Hunt to come second behind Reinhold Joest's Porsche 908/3. But the main motivation for the South African trip was not racing; it was to hang out with his friend Hailwood, drink himself silly and chase women.

Together, they got through plenty of both.

SHUNT

CHAPTER 16

Established in Formula One 1974

The year of no return

In mid-September 1973, Lord Hesketh held a press conference to announce his plans for 1974. He was in expansive mood and at the top of his game, with no idea of what was just around the corner. As the world's economies were booming, no one suspected that a financial crash was imminent.

Hesketh told journalists he would contest the full Formula One season in 1974; a declaration which came as no surprise. But his next statement shocked them. Hesketh announced that the team would be building its own car, designed by Harvey Postlethwaite. The car, he announced, would be built by the mechanics over the winter in the converted stables at Easton Neston. Feeling that it "demonstrated serious intent", he added: "There's no point in playing amateur heroics at the back of the grid. Our intention is to create an exciting new car and race to win."

Hesketh Racing had been unexpectedly competitive with its March-Ford. Postlethwaite had made it quicker than any of the works March cars on its Firestone tyres. The choice of Firestones had given the car an advantage over its mostly Goodyear shod rivals.

But Formula One insiders believed that attempting to build its own car was a mistake for an independent team with limited resources. One said anonymously: "Now they'll find out how difficult this business is."

Disagreeing with the critics, Postlethwaite said: "It is almost necessary if you want to continue to grow. You have to become a constructor, you have to be masters of your own fate. If you buy a racing car off somebody else, you never have first access to the technology and the goods. To go motor racing properly, you have to build your own car; do your own thing." He would say later, upon reflection: "It was a big moment in my career."

Hesketh wanted people to know it was a serious effort, saying: "James has shown that he's capable of winning Grand Prix races and, to win, I feel that you've got to build your own cars. But we're in this game to entertain just as much as we are to race."

Not content merely with announcing the team's own car, Hesketh also announced that it would be building its own V12 engine. It was not as fanciful as it sounded. Conventional Formula One wisdom at the time held that the Cosworth V8 was no longer powerful enough and that a V12 engine would be essential in the future. But the engine project was abandoned after an initial budget forecast showed it would cost over US$250,000 just to design and build a prototype.

Hesketh also took the opportunity to stress the Britishness of the team. He said: "I am convinced that one of the essential ingredients that makes this team work is that it is decidedly British. I am a completely unashamed jingoist. I am proud to be British, to have a British passport and to paint my car red, white and blue. Our ambition is to win a world championship for Britain – with a British driver."

The Britishness argument was put to the test as a month later, when it became clear that Emerson Fittipaldi would be leaving Lotus at the end of the year. In a strange turn of events, Hesketh offered the Brazilian a drive alongside Hunt in a two-car team. It was a serious offer, in which he tempted Fittipaldi with a US$150,000 retainer. Fittipaldi remembers: "I was interested but the team was too new, so I was not sure. I signed with McLaren and, at that time, it was a good thing to do." He added as an afterthought: "The Hesketh team was very strange."

It was certainly very strange for Hesketh to have entered into serious negotiations with the Brazilian, but the negotiations were done with Hunt's full knowledge; Hunt originally had introduced Fittipaldi to Hesketh.

Hesketh also announced that the team would have a budget of US$400,000 for 1974. However, having released the figure, he then told journalists that it "frightened him" and insisted the budget would be "strict." He then announced that Hunt's retainer to drive the car would increase to US$35,000 from US$5,000 the year before. With prize money and personal appearances, Hunt's income for 1974 looked set to top US$100,000. To announce a driver's salary, normally a very private and sometime contentious matter, for public consumption was certainly a new and novel way of doing things. But Hunt didn't seem to mind.

However, between the press conference in September and the launch of the new car in January, the world began to change and Hesketh probably wished he had not been so expansive. The world's stock markets had been declining since January 1973 as inflation started unsettling investors around the world. But the decline had not been too serious and, as the market was coming off record highs the year before, most reckoned it was a short-term adjustment.

Indeed, it might have been had the situation in the Middle East remained calm. It was later revealed that the Arab nations had begun preparing for war in late August, when President Sadat had secretly visited King Faisal in Riyadh. The Egyptian president and the Saudi Arabian King had agreed that there would be an oil embargo should western countries, primarily the United States, back Israel in the upcoming war. At the time, the idea of using oil as a weapon was an entirely new one.

There wasn't long to wait as, on 6th October 1973, Egypt and Syria attacked Israel on two fronts; in Sinai and on the Golan Heights. The attack was carefully timed for the beginning of the Jewish religious festival of Yom Kippur. As all of Israel prepared for the festival, its army was caught by surprise. The attack marked the beginning of the fourth Arab-Israeli War and the resulting oil embargo destroyed the economies of the western world.

While the Egyptians had successfully attacked across the Suez Canal in Sinai, in the north the Syrians had attacked the Golan Heights. But within a week, upon recovering from the initial surprise, the Israeli army launched a counterattack into Syria. The Israelis also counterattacked the Egyptian armies and crossed the Suez Canal, advancing south and east. Israel encircled Egypt's Third Army and, by the end of the fighting, Israeli forces were 40 kilometres from Damascus and 101 kilometres from Cairo.

As the Arab nations began losing the war, the oil weapon planned by President Sadat and King Faisal was brought into play on 8th October. The Organisation of Petroleum Exporting Countries (OPEC) suddenly informed western oil companies that it wanted to revise the 1971 Tehran Price Agreement. The announcement was intended as a warning, but the United States responded with a massive airlift of arms to Israel on 16th October. Saudi Arabia, Iran, Iraq, Abu Dhabi, Kuwait and Qatar unilaterally raised the price of a barrel of oil to US$3.65 per barrel. It was an increase of 17 per cent overnight. They also announced cuts in production.

The United States refused to be intimidated and, on 19th October, President Nixon offered US$2.2 billion in emergency aid to Israel. That prompted OPEC to announce a complete oil embargo to the United States and other western countries. Oil prices now doubled and then trebled as western countries began bidding sky-high for any oil that had already left the gulf and was being held in storage.

On 26th October, the Arab–Israeli war was ended, with Israel winning. But the economic war waged on as the oil embargoes intensified. The situation escalated dramatically on 5th November when OPEC announced it was cutting overall production by a quarter on top of previous cuts.

By late November, the western world was in a panic, and petrol rationing began in most countries. In January 1974, OPEC cut production by another five per cent.

By this time, the Saudi oil minister Sheikh Yamani had become effective head of OPEC and its chief negotiator. He was a moderate and, on 17th March, the oil embargo was ended and production returned to normal. By then, however, oil prices had spiked to as much as US$14 a barrel; some six times what they had been a year earlier. The Israelis may have won the battle, but the Arab nations had won the economic war. And there was little doubt whose was the greater victory.

The price spike and shortage had caused all the western economies to collapse into recession, and the stock market fell by as much as 70 per cent in several countries. The stock market did not begin to recover until December 1974.

Initially, none of this seemed to trouble Lord Hesketh. Thinking things would quickly return to normal, he carried on with his plans for the Formula One team as if nothing had happened.

On the first working day after the New Year, in January 1974, the new Hesketh 308 emerged from the Easton Neston stable block and the world's press were called into witness it. Postlethwaite presided over the launch of the new car. The Hesketh 308 also had a new colour scheme. White, with thick red and blue stripes on its flanks, the car was described by Hunt as "beautiful", a descriptor usually reserved for his women.

Bizarrely, Hesketh declared that the car's designation, 308, stood for the number of litres (three) and the '08' for the number of cylinders (eight).

Although the car was all-new and had been designed from the ground up by Postlethwaite, it was clearly an adaptation of the March 731. Postlethwaite had designed the new car and then ordered in all the components, including the aluminium monocoque chassis, from outside suppliers. Virtually the entire car was made by small factories in and around Northamptonshire, the area later known as Motorsport Valley. In effect, the Hesketh mechanics took delivery of parts and then assembled them. Provided the original designs were correct, and there was money available to pay and motivate the suppliers to deliver on time, it was not a particularly difficult job. The larger components such as the engine came from Cosworth and the gearbox from a supplier called Hewland.

The plan was to test the new car and then quickly to air freight it to Argentina for the first race. The old March 731 had already been sent on the special FOCA chartered Boeing 747 jumbo jet with the plan for it to act as a spare car if anything went wrong with the new one. FOCA, the Formula One Constructors Association organised by Bernie Ecclestone, chartered special planes on which all Formula One freight travelled to races outside Europe.

Although Lord Hesketh was confined to his bed with the flu at the time, he did make an appearance to watch the new car being wheeled out of the Easton Neston stable block. Quickly forgetting his sniffles, he expounded to the press his philosophy for Formula One. Telling the assembled journalists how inspiring the setting of Easton Neston had been for Postlethwaite and the mechanics, he revealed that he had converted a farmhouse on his estate into residential flats for the mechanics, who had been working long hours.

Calling his team "rule-breakers", Hesketh continued: "We've managed to break many of the unwritten rules of Formula One." He then listed a series of negatives, although they turned out to be rules that no Formula One insider had ever heard of. But the Lord, his mind numbed with medicinal whisky, couldn't resist the sound of his own voice that day. He pontificated about Formula One and praised Bubbles Horsley profusely: "For me, Bubbles is the man who has made Hesketh Racing what it is. He is the guy who revs James up; he's the guy who stops the doctor from falling asleep as he is prone to do, thinking about wings and ride heights and things."

He went on to praise Hesketh Racing's "*esprit de corps*", noting that it didn't exist in any other team. "If you look at it like a football team, all the other teams have played so many games that they have a certain amount of staleness, whereas we're still filled with a childish enthusiasm. And I think one of the essential ingredients of our team is that we have to keep it funny."

The speech was mostly nonsense and "rot" as one journalist called it, but Hesketh clearly enjoyed delivering it.

The Hesketh mechanics, who by then numbered as many as 12, looked on with bleary eyes. This small group of people had produced a miracle getting the new car assembled in time.

Hesketh went on to proclaim that he had adopted a yellow teddy bear as the team's mascot. Having seen a teddy bear illustration on a postcard in an airport, he gave the bear a helmet with a Union Jack flag on the front and the logo 'Super Bear'. The plan was to launch a campaign called 'Back British Bears.' He did later erect a big poster in central London featuring the bear and the words: "Hesketh Racing, the biggest little racing team in the world – racing for Britain and racing for you." Hesketh talked more about the new logo than he did the car itself.

Explaining that he was trying to "sell Britain", Hesketh added: "We want to give the public, to whom the Hesketh Team seems very important, the opportunity to participate and identify their support, both at home and abroad."

The hyperbole continued all morning and, to go with the launch of the new car that day, Bubbles Horsley had had a book printed, entitled *The Heavily Censored History of Hesketh Racing*, which he intended to sell to fans. In it, Lord Hesketh had written: "When I first entered motor sport, most people thought me a buffoon with a lot of money and astonishingly little sense. However, this theory is now totally demolished, not so much through the heroic efforts of a man with a long history of attempted suicide by means of thumping into Armco [steel guardrails] called Hunt, nor by a figure sought by Interpol in every country where loons do speed, known as Bubbles, nor by the invention of the madman Postlethwaite, but by the fact that I have persuaded you to unload 1s/6d [7.5p] for this nonsensical publication. Nothing has given me greater faith in the future of Hesketh Racing than this selfless act of extravagance on your part which indicates that Bears are destined to breed at a rate hitherto unknown in British history."

There has never been a Formula One launch like it before, nor indeed since. It was said by some who witnessed it to have been the most extraordinary product launch they had ever attended.

After the photographs and the speeches, the Hesketh mechanics loaded the new 308 into the transporter and took it to Silverstone for its first run. Hesketh declined to accompany the transporter and returned to his bed fortified with a few more whiskies, evidently very pleased with himself. The following morning, upon reading the newspapers' almost verbatim account of what he had said at the launch, even Hesketh had to admit that much of it had been sheer nonsense.

At Silverstone, Hunt got in the car and did 12 laps in the wet. Although the fact that it ran was in itself a huge achievement, it was immediately obvious that the car was far from race ready, and an immediate decision was made to use the old March-Ford 731 at the first two races in Argentina and Brazil and to save the new car for the European season. It was a sensible decision and immediately took the pressure off Postlethwaite. The new car was shipped to São Paulo a few weeks later to act as an emergency spare car and to participate in a test session planned after the Brazilian Grand Prix as well as in a non-championship race, but the team would not risk it in a Grand Prix.

The Formula One circus gathered in Buenos Aires for the Argentinian Grand Prix on 13th January. There were plenty of team and driver changes but the big news was that Fittipaldi had moved from Lotus to McLaren and that Jacky Ickx had replaced him at Lotus. Niki Lauda and Clay Regazzoni were the new drivers at Ferrari after its new boss, the youthful 26-year-old Luca di Montezemolo, had ejected many of the old staff – including the drivers – and begun the task of rebuilding the team. After Jackie Stewart's retirement and the death of François Cevert, Jody Scheckter and Patrick Depailler were also a new pairing at Tyrrell.

Hunt was in top form in the March, and some members of the team had already begun to ask themselves why it had gone to all the expense of building a new car if the March was so competitive. But much of the competitiveness was due to the fact that it was one of the few cars still racing on Firestone tyres. Firestone was winding down its involvement in Formula One and most teams had moved on to Goodyear tyres in anticipation of it. But the old Firestone tyre construction was as good as ever and the alchemists back in the United States who mixed the secret rubber solutions that made the tyres work were still in place and determined to leave the sport in a blaze of glory.

Combined with the inevitable complacency of Goodyear, which shod all the top teams and was going to win come what may, Hunt's car was left with an incredible one-off advantage to exploit.

Hunt recorded the fastest lap on the Friday qualifying session and ended up fifth on the grid. He even out-qualified the new Ferrari being driven by Lauda, who could only manage eighth. In truth, it was all down to the Firestone tyres which were working superbly on the March chassis; the tyres were perfectly suited to both man and machine. But, amazingly, no one realised this at the time. Everybody credited Postlethwaite's skill for keeping the old March competitive over the winter. But in truth, he had not touched it and it was in exactly the same specification with which it had ended the season a few months earlier in America.

Ronnie Peterson took pole in his Lotus Ford, with Regazzoni's Ferrari coming in second on the grid and Fittipaldi's McLaren third. Peter Revson's Shadow-Ford came in fourth, with Hunt alongside it.

At the start, Peterson got the lead and Hunt was quickly up to second place. Hunt then passed Peterson halfway round the first lap, but Peterson let him go ahead. He thought Hunt was driving wildly, and he was right. Almost as soon as he had passed, Hunt went off the track and the Swede re-took his lead. Hunt was forced to the pit with superficial damage but had to retire ten laps later as the radiator had been damaged when he had gone off the track. In reality, Hunt had been astonished to be leading the Grand Prix and to find himself so much quicker than Peterson.

Horsley however was enraged, telling journalists that Hunt had "lost his head" and thrown away his chances on the first lap of 53. Indeed he had. Hunt's tyre advantage was so pronounced he could have walked it that day.

When Hunt retired, Horsley marched the sheepish looking driver off to an empty office and, as he would later put it, "bawled him out." Denny Hulme went on to win the race for McLaren, eclipsing his new teammate, while Lauda debuted for Ferrari in second and Regazzoni third.

Hunt realised he had got it wrong in a big way, and admitted as much later: "I arrived at the hairpin in the lead and unexpectedly clutchless. Quite frankly, it freaked me into a mistake. I got confused and overshot the hairpin. I looked down for a moment and off I went. It was a mistake of inexperience. I was over-excited at being in the lead. I had never led a Grand Prix before and I was taken by surprise when the clutch went."

Overall, however, the team was pleased with the competitiveness of the car. The Hesketh team celebrated and enjoyed themselves lavishly, as Hesketh continued to allocate far more cash to what Horsley now called the "leisure division" than to the race team. Around US$16,000 was spent on entertainment in a week in South America, as Horsley remembers: "We were actually very, very serious about the racing, but the leisure division – the party division – was run by the Lord." The team was high on its success at the opening race of the year.

Once the partying subsided, the serious racing took over. And it didn't get more serious than when Lord Hesketh arrived at the Interlagos circuit in his chauffeur-driven Rolls, which had been rented for the weekend. Ordering the chauffeur to stop the car, Hesketh got out to inspect one of the flagpoles at the entrance to the circuit. What he saw infuriated him – the British Union Jack flag was flying upside down. He marched up to the organiser's office and demanded to see the circuit manager. After a dressing down from the Lord, the hapless man shouted out something to his minions and immediately the flag was taken down. Hesketh then went into the paddock, gathered up his team of mechanics and, as they stood at the bottom of the flagpole, they raised the flag again; the correct way up. They all saluted. It was a perfectly earnest moment.

Unfortunately, the fortunes of the team were not to be helped by the flag being the right way up. The weather was incredibly hot and the March 731 handled badly on the sticky Interlagos tarmac. The Firestone tyres were useless at the higher temperature levels, which is when the Goodyears really came into their own. The stickier Goodyear tyres reigned supreme on this occasion, and Hunt only qualified 18th and managed to limp home in ninth place. The race was won by Fittipaldi in his McLaren-Ford, with Regazzoni second. Ickx pleased Lotus by finishing third.

It was a necessary wakeup call, although the team still had no idea why it had been so successful in Buenos Aires and so awful at Interlagos.

After the race, the Hesketh team stayed on to test the new 308 car, which had been specially shipped in from England. The weather in England was so poor that any meaningful testing was proving impossible.

It turned out to be a stunning debut. Hunt's best lap in the new car was four seconds faster than his best time in the March a few days earlier. He even beat Fittipaldi's pole position time for the Grand Prix. There were a few other teams also testing that day and they were stunned. The new car easily topped the test times. Horsley recalls: "It was very special when our new car was so quick right out of the box." But it flattered to deceive. The temperature had dropped dramatically after the race and the harder Firestones were brilliant, while the stickier, softer Goodyears were much less effective in the cooler temperatures.

The telephone lines buzzed red hot with reports of the new car's speed, and the news reverberated around the motor sport community in England that night. Horsley would say later that the São Paulo test session was the most satisfying moment in his entire time in the sport.

Unusually, a non-championship race had been arranged for the following weekend at a new 5.5-kilometre circuit in Brasilia, the capital of Brazil. The non-championship race was called the Presidente Medici Grand Prix and was scheduled for 3rd February. The plan was to race the new car, but it was thwarted by a leaking fuel tank that couldn't be fixed so Hunt raced his March instead. He started on the last row of the grid and retired after four laps when his gearbox broke. Fittipaldi won the race; much to the delight of local fans. Although the Brasilia race turned out to be a total disaster, the team did earn decent money for turning up.

The new car was shipped back to England with high hopes. The next race was a month away and there was plenty of time to get it ready for the South African Grand Prix on 30th March. There were, however, plenty of doubts about whether the South African Grand Prix would indeed go ahead. The oil crisis peaked at the end of March and South Africa was suffering more than most from the rise in price; the result being an electricity shortage in a country which relied almost exclusively on oil-fired electricity-generating stations.

As soon as Hunt and the new car were back in London, serious testing began at Silverstone. Hunt hated testing, but he knew it was his big chance. The new car had obvious potential.

The South African Grand Prix did go ahead, although the Hesketh team was soon wishing it hadn't. The new car bombed. Hunt admitted later that its speed was totally dependent on how well the Firestones worked at any given circuit. And in very hot temperatures, they didn't. But the team were simply unaware of this at the time. No one had any idea the Firestone tyres were responsible for Hunt being so fast one weekend and so slow the next.

At Kyalami, the 308 had a bad vibration problem all weekend and the team was ill-equipped to sort it out. As a result, Hunt qualified 14th and retired when the car shook the gearbox to bits and it broke. The race marked

Lauda's first pole position for Ferrari, while the race was won by Carlos Reutemann's Brabham-Ford.

The team rushed back to England to prepare for the Daily Express Silverstone International Trophy scheduled for 7th April, a week after Kyalami. Because of the close proximity to the South African race, it did not attract much of an entry. The only established stars were Ronnie Peterson in a Lotus and Denny Hulme in a McLaren. In order to make up the numbers, the race was opened to Formula 5000 cars. 15 Formula One cars would race alongside ten Formula 5000 cars – 25 cars in all.

Crucially, the typical English weather meant cooler temperatures. The Firestones worked so well in these cool conditions that, at a Silverstone test session before the race, Hunt found he could take Woodcote corner flat out in his new car. This was something no one had managed before, and his confidence was sky high.

When qualifying began, Hunt was in startling form, and it had the rest of the Formula One community seriously worried. His pole position time was 1.7 seconds quicker than Peterson's second-placed Lotus. Lord Hesketh reflected: "That was a very bizarre weekend really. We went up there and the weather was perfect, which was very unusual because the race was always held in April. We went out and we got round in 1 minute 16.7 seconds; we just shattered the lap record."

The news attracted over 35,000 fans to Silverstone for race day.

Hunt knew he could win. While everyone was under the impression that the 308 was wholly superior, he had calculated that its performance was down to the Firestone tyres on which the car was running. On the warm-up lap, Hunt hit a hare running across the track and smashed the front wing. It was a potentially nasty incident but Hunt kept the car under control and brought it back to the pit lane for a replacement.

But the drama was not yet over. At the start, the gear lever knob came off in his hand and the stationary Hesketh-Ford was overtaken by virtually half the grid. 14 cars went past before he could get the car in gear. From then on, he was forced to use the sharp stub of the gear lever shaft to change gear. It was undoubtedly very painful.

But he was so much quicker than the rest of the field that, by lap five, he was in fifth place; by lap 13, he was second; and by lap 28, he had taken the lead.

His daring passing maneuver around Ronnie Peterson on Woodcote corner at over 160 miles per hour is still spoken of by people who were there that day. The two cars were side by side round Woodcote, opposite-locking on the limit of their tyres' adhesion. Hunt's Firestones were stickier than Peterson's Goodyears, but that didn't stop Gerald Donaldson calling it a "breathtaking ballet of high-speed car control."

Hunt passed Peterson with two wheels on the grass, and the crowds in the grandstands erupted with joy. Murray Walker, commentating that day, said: "My goodness, that was a consummate bit of motor racing artistry, the like of which I have seldom seen before."

Peterson had literally worn out his Goodyears trying to keep up, and he retired when his engine expired with the strain. Hunt set the fastest lap of the race, with an average speed of 137.38 miles per hour. Lord Hesketh would say that his finest moment was when Hunt took the chequered flag for his maiden victory. He remembered: "On that beautiful April day, I walked towards Bubbles and Harvey and all the rest of the team. We were hysterical with laughter and tears. James suddenly flung away his helmet and belted out a rendition of the 'Dambusters March', and we all dementedly joined in."

Noticing Hunt's bloody hands after the race, Hesketh was full of admiration for his driver: "He drove a 40-lap race with the top of the gearstick embedded in his hand. And it looked like a mess. He literally crucified his hand to drive the car and to win."

Hunt's average race speed of 133.58 miles per hour made the race the fastest ever held in Britain since the Second World War, at the old banked Brooklands track. Hunt said: "It was just a super day, and it was lovely to win in England. But we had no illusions: we knew the moment we crossed the line that it wasn't a Grand Prix. So we sat back and enjoyed it for what it was – our first win. It was a great day." According to Gerald Donaldson, the whole team went to celebrate at the famous Trader Vic's bar in the basement of the London Hilton in Park Lane. There, they drank Mai Tais until morning. The following day, Hunt was lauded in the British newspapers as a new British hero.

At Silverstone that day Hunt also met Professor Sid Watkins for the first time. The two were later to become truly great friends but their first exchange of words was simple enough, as Watkins recalls: "He'd already acquired the name 'Hunt the Shunt', and I said to him: 'Are you going to have a shunt today, James?' and he said: 'I'm going to do my level best.'" Watkins now calls it his "un-introduced encounter."

Three weeks later, it was the Spanish Grand Prix and, by now, it was clear the new 308 had flattered to deceive at Interlagos and Silverstone. It was only fast in cooler weather on circuits that suited the Firestone tyres, and there weren't many in those days. At the Jarama circuit, Hunt could only qualify tenth and, by the finish of the race, he was three laps behind Niki Lauda, the eventual winner. It was Lauda's maiden win for Ferrari from pole position. Hunt later admitted that it was extremely galling to see Lauda, who was a contemporary in Formula 3, winning races in a top team.

The Belgian Grand Prix was held at Nivelles a fortnight later, on 12th May, and it was more of the same for Hunt as he qualified ninth and became involved in an accident halfway through the race. Fittipaldi took the race from Lauda, and the championship battle shaped up to be a matter of contention between the two of them.

In the weekend in between, Hunt drove to Nürburgring to compete in the 1000-kilometre sports car race for the Gulf-Mirage team. The race was held on 19th May. He shared a car with Vern Schuppan and they were teammates to Mike Hailwood and Derek Bell. He finished fourth and partied hard with Hailwood afterwards.

On 26th May, the Monaco Grand Prix rolled around again. It was the first anniversary of the team's Formula One debut. As ever, Hesketh, remained oblivious to the worldwide recession going on around him.

He rented two yachts for the race: a large one called Nefertiti for himself; and a smaller one, the Henry Morgan, for the Hesketh team. The Hesketh helicopter and the Rolls-Royce had also made the trip down and were busy shuttling guests to and from the airport. The champagne flowed even more freely than it had in 1973.

The race itself was disappointing compared to what was going on in the paddock. Hunt qualified well for seventh, with Lauda on pole next to teammate Regazzoni, and Peterson third. But Hunt was out halfway through the race when his driveshaft broke. Retiring to the yacht, he and the team celebrated regardless. Peterson's Lotus-Ford won it in the end, from Scheckter's Tyrrell-Ford.

The Swedish Grand Prix on 9th June was far more encouraging, and showed that Hunt had not lost his ability to perform at the front of the grid – something which people in the paddock were beginning to doubt. This time, there were no problems with an entry, and in cool conditions, Hunt qualified sixth behind Peterson. But the two Tyrrell-Fords dominated, with

Depailler and Scheckter first and second in qualifying, and first and second in the race the other way around.

Hunt duelled with Lauda for 20 laps before passing him on lap 66. He then began chasing down the Tyrrells at two seconds a lap. He finished third, three seconds short at the end. Another five laps and surely he would have won.

At Zandvoort on 23rd June, it was again cooler and Hunt qualified sixth, mixing it with the McLarens, Ferraris and the Tyrrells in a heartwarming performance. But by lap three, he was out of the race as he collided with the Shadow-Ford being driven by the hard-charging Tom Pryce. Lauda and Regazzoni won the race in a Ferrari 1-2.

Now that the heat of the summer had arrived, Hunt's window of opportunity began to close in on him. In 1974, the French Grand Prix was held at Dijon, one of Hunt's favourite tracks, but he was denied the chance to perform. Although he had qualified tenth, Hunt was taken out at the start for the second race in succession by Tom Pryce's Shadow-Ford, which had qualified an amazing third. Hunt's Hesketh was completely wrecked, and he blamed his friend Fittipaldi for causing the accident. Hunt said the accident had been triggered by Fittipaldi's dangerous driving. He climbed out of his car and performed his fist-waving antics each time Fittipaldi's McLaren-Ford came by. Fittipaldi was smiling behind his helmet, hoping his friend would calm down by the time he got back to the pits. Fittipaldi's engine blew up on lap 28 and the race was won by Peterson's Lotus from Lauda and Regazzoni coming in second and third. Hunt had indeed calmed down, and the two men embraced in the pit lane.

Two weeks later, Hunt was back home with his parents in Surrey preparing for the British Grand Prix at Brands Hatch. Hunt qualified sixth, with Lauda on pole. His new girlfriend, Suzy Miller, also joined him and was introduced to his parents. The meeting was a success and Wallis and Sue really like Suzy. In fact, they bonded straightaway. It was this familial ease that finally convinced Hunt that Suzy was the girl for him.

It was a tricky weekend and little went right. In an unfortunate accident upon leaving the pits prior to the race, Hunt ran over Bob Simpson, a Tyrrell mechanic, and broke both his legs. While others cleared up the mess, Hunt carried on with the race. He made a reasonable start, but it didn't matter because on lap three his suspension broke and his car went off into the barriers.

It had been a thoroughly disappointing weekend, and Hunt immediately left the circuit to pack up. He flew back to Spain with Suzy Miller, to whom he was intending to propose. Scheckter won the race, followed by Fittipaldi, with Jacky Ickx taking another third place in his Lotus.

So the Formula One circus moved to Nürburgring, with all the usual trepidation about safety.

As usual, the race was to claim another victim. Although it wasn't fatal, the accident did mark the last ever race for McLaren driver Mike Hailwood. Hailwood went off the circuit and wrecked his car, suffering leg injuries that effectively finished his career. It also marked the first race for Jacques Laffite in one of Frank Williams' cars, then called the Iso-Marlboro-Fords.

If Jackie Stewart had still been racing, it is unlikely that cars would have continued to race at the Nürburgring. But safety was not paramount for the current crop of drivers, who were too interested in winning and competing. There had been some attempts to make the circuit safer: the main straight had been widened and made smoother where, originally, it was rather narrow and bumpy and flanked by bushes the entire way down; and the organisers had also replaced the bushes that previously lined the track with steel Armco barriers and installed run-off areas filled with sand. But the rest of the 14-mile circuit remained virtually unchanged and highly dangerous, as Hailwood found out.

Lauda got pole and came within a whisker of managing a sub seven-minute lap. Regazzoni's Ferrari was alongside him on the front row. On a hot day, Hunt could only qualify thirteenth.

At the start, accidents abounded. Lauda crashed out in the first lap while trying to pass Scheckter's Tyrrell. Fittipaldi could not select a gear and was passed by everybody on the grid in the process, after which he was side-swiped by teammate Hulme and both were out. Regazzoni went on to win the race from Scheckter. Hunt went out on lap twelve when his gearbox gave up the ghost.

It was clear by then that the team was performing worse than it had in 1973, when it was competing in only half the number of races. The new car was actually a dog flattered by its tyres. There was much soul-searching to be done, especially as the team began to experience the first winds of recession and money suddenly became less plentiful. It was clear that the team would have done just as well and saved itself a lot of money had it simply bought a new March 741. The car, inevitably, was struggling with reliability issues and there had been a depressing sequence of retirements.

Hunt was sanguine about the situation, admitting: "The Hesketh was a pretty good workmanlike car, but it wasn't as competitive (as the March).

Therein lay the differences in results. I had to keep the sharp edges on my driving to do it justice as it was, but, even if it had been quicker, it definitely wasn't a race-winning car." But Hunt was enjoying just being in Formula One and competing. At that stage of his career, being successful was still a bonus: "It was very good training, driving a car that was not too good."

Horsley was less forgiving, saying: "We recognise that if we are to survive, we must turn completely professional."

But just as things were beginning to look their bleakest, the team was rewarded with a good result on 18th August, and morale was boosted accordingly. At the Austrian Grand Prix at Österreichring, another of Hunt's favourite circuits, he qualified seventh and brought the car home third, albeit a minute behind the leader, Carlos Reutemann, and 19 seconds behind second-placed Denny Hulme. On this occasion, Hunt was lucky and only just managed to finish ahead of John Watson, Clay Regazzoni and Vittorio Brambilla, all of whom were on his tail at the finish. Another two laps and he could have been fifth. The cooler weather had worked wonders again.

So the team went to Monza for the Italian Grand Prix on 8th September with high hopes. Hunt easily put the car on the fourth row of the grid. Niki Lauda was dominant on pole and looked set to win the race easily, but he retired with a blown engine in the lead. Hunt only made it to lap three before his engine blew up as well. Peterson won the race in the Lotus, with Fittipaldi second and Scheckter third.

Formula One now crossed the Atlantic Ocean to Toronto, for the Canadian Grand Prix on 22nd September. It was the penultimate round of the world championship, with Fittipaldi and Lauda seemingly battling for the world title – but with Regazzoni and Scheckter also in the hunt.

The race marked the debut of two new American Formula One teams: Penske, owned by Roger Penske; and Vel's Parnelli Racing, owned by Parnelli Jones and Vel Miletich. Both teams had built new cars, suggesting a serious commitment by a country that previously had been uninterested in Formula One. Both cars qualified and finished their first race.

Fittipaldi rose to the occasion of the world championship battle, positioned side-by-side with Lauda on the front row of the starting grid. Lauda retired on lap 68 after crashing the car, and Fittipaldi won. The second retirement in a row was a disaster for Lauda's title hopes and he now had to rely on his rivals retiring as well. Hunt qualified eighth, but lost a very tight battle for second place with Regazzoni and Peterson, who finished third, with only two and a half seconds between each of them.

A fortnight later, on 6th October, the United States Grand Prix saw the final race of the season held at Watkins Glen. Interestingly, only one of three drivers – Fittipaldi, Regazzoni or Scheckter – seemed set to win the championship, as Lauda's retirements in Italy and Canada had ruined his hopes. Fittipaldi and Regazzoni had 52 points each. Scheckter, on 45 points, had a more difficult job to do. There was also a last race battle for the constructors' championship. Either McLaren on 70 points or Ferrari on 65 points would be world champion constructor.

It was also the first anniversary of the dreadful accident that had killed François Cevert, and the Tyrrell team was very sombre all weekend. Unfortunately, the race was to claim a second victim in tragically similar circumstances.

The race was marked by the first installation of pit-to-car two-way radios in the McLaren cars of Fittipaldi and Hulme. Although standard in American racing, the radios were completely new to Formula One.

None of the championship contenders shone in qualifying or the race. Their performances were strangely muted. The three contenders were markedly unimpressive, with Scheckter coming in sixth, Fittipaldi managing only eighth, and Regazzoni ninth.

Qualifying was dominated by the Brabham team, with Carlos Reutemann on pole position ahead of teammate Carlos Pace in fourth. American Mario Andretti shone in front of his home crowd and qualified best of the rest in the new American team, Vel's Parnelli Racing. The home fans also had another American hero to cheer with Mark Donohue, who was driving an American-built car for the Penske team.

But the star of qualifying was James Hunt, who battled Reutemann and was alongside him on the front row of the grid. Firestone engineers made a huge effort on home soil in what would be the American tyre company's last ever Formula One race.

Qualifying was marked by three accidents, involving the cars of Regazzoni, Jean-Pierre Beltoise and Andretti. Watkins Glen was not a safe circuit and the accidents caused concern amongst the drivers; concerns that were to be justified the following day.

The world championship showdown on Sunday was a glorious warm day, as can only be had in New York state in late October. But before it could start, the US organisers demonstrated an inordinate degree of favouritism to local hero Mario Andretti. The start was delayed 25 minutes to allow Andretti's team to solve a technical problem with the car's ignition. The organisers were mindful that at least half of the 100,000-plus crowd had come to see Andretti race, and were determined that they not be disappointed. The other team managers simply shrugged their shoulders, content that the favouritism was at least transparent – unlike in Italy where it was all done under the table.

In those days, races were still started by the drop of a flag, and American eccentric Tex Hopkins traditionally did the honours at Watkins Glen, dropping the green flag. Reutemann led Hunt, Pace, Lauda, Scheckter, Fittipaldi and Regazzoni off the line. Andretti was out straightaway when he was disqualified for a push start on the grid. His two laps, however, were just enough to keep the fans happy.

Gradually, the gap between Reutemann and Hunt widened and, by the end of the third lap, Regazzoni was struggling with suspension problems. His world championship aspirations were over.

On lap ten, the Surtees-Ford of Austrian Helmut Koinigg, in only his second Grand Prix, went off at the hairpin where the cars had crashed in qualifying the previous day. His rear tyre deflated slowly and, not recognising the problem, he eventually lost control of his car and hit the Armco barrier. The bottom rail gave way but the top one held firm. Koinigg went underneath and had no chance of survival. When Lauda pitted on lap 38, the Ferrari mechanics told him his fellow Austrian had died. Out of respect for his countryman, Lauda immediately retired.

With Regazzoni out of the picture, Fittipaldi knew the title was his so long as Scheckter didn't win. Scheckter continued to hold fourth ahead of Fittipaldi, but on the 45th lap his engine suddenly lost fuel pressure when a pipe cracked. When he learned over the radio that Scheckter had retired, and before the race had even ended, Fittipaldi knew he was to be world champion.

At the front, Reutemann was struggling with his brakes and Pace saw his chance. He overtook Hunt, who was also struggling with his Hesketh. But none of it really mattered as Hunt rolled in for his third podium of the season. Fittipaldi's fourth place clinched his second world championship in three years and the first constructors' title for McLaren, barely seven years after Bruce McLaren first entered Formula One.

Koinigg's death created a difficult situation. Since most people didn't know him, it was easy to forget that he had perished only an hour before. He was written out of the history books as the McLaren mechanics mobbed their new world champion. The Brabham team also celebrated its 1-2 finish. A few Brazilians, who had made the trip to support Fittipaldi, occupied the pit lane, waving Brazilian flags. Lost in the melee was news that the race also marked the 100th Grand Prix victory for the Cosworth Ford engine in Formula One. It was probably the biggest achievement of all, and Keith Duckworth and Mike Costin clinked glasses back in Northampton, England. What also went unnoticed was that it was the end to Firestone's time in Formula One and, in particular, to its contribution to James Hunt's first two seasons in Formula One. For next year, Hunt would be on Goodyears like everyone else.

Even with the tyre advantage, though, the season had been a disappointment. Hesketh and Horsley had expected much more. Hunt had scored 15 points, only one more than in 1973, and he was eighth in the world championship. The highlights had been third in Sweden, third in Austria, third in the USA and fourth in Canada. But that was it. There was no second place as in 1973, and, in 11 races, Hunt hadn't scored points at all.

As he wound down his year, with the cool winds of recession fanning his fortunes, Lord Hesketh knew it was no longer good enough and that the money was running out. The Hesketh dream had only one more year to run.

SHUNT

CHAPTER 17

Spain and tax exile 1974
Wilson and Healey force him abroad

On Monday 4th March 1974, Harold Wilson's Labour Party returned to power and took over the government of Britain from incumbent Edward Heath's Conservatives. Although the Conservatives had won more votes, Labour had more seats; although not enough to form a majority.

This was extremely bad news for James Hunt, whose earnings were exploding as he became a successful Formula One driver. Although his Hesketh retainer was still relatively small, he was raking it in from his 45 per cent share of prize money and the US$5,000-10,000 a day he was making from personal appearances. At a minimum, he was set to earn US$200,000 in 1974 alone.

On 18th February 1974, shadow chancellor Denis Healey had made a speech promising that Labour would "tax the rich until the pips squeaked" if it won the general election on 28th February 1974.

Hunt and his advisers at his management company, International Management Group (IMG), were under no illusions about what was coming. Hunt had signed with Mark McCormack and his American IMG organisation in September 1973. Before that, his accountant brother Peter had handled his financial affairs exclusively. Hunt had signed on the direct advice of Jackie Stewart, who had prospered mightily under McCormack's stewardship. Almost as soon as Hunt started performing at the wheel of the Hesketh and earning good money, he joined Stewart and became one of McCormack's clients.

IMG's London office was headed by Ian Todd, IMG's senior vice president. Todd directly managed Hunt's affairs and rang him to warn him that he may have to leave England quickly and start making preparations. Initially, Hunt didn't take it seriously but after Labour was elected and Todd spelled out the repercussions, he quickly changed his mind. Together, they decided Hunt should leave before the start of the new tax year; Todd told him it couldn't be soon enough.

Todd was right. Shortly afterwards, Denis Healey presented his first budget to the House of Commons, and the wealthy people of Britain were the main target. The top rate of tax was increased to 83 per cent on salaries over UK£20,000, together with a 15 per cent surcharge on unearned income, which made the top tax rate on unearned income 98 per cent. It was an extraordinary attack on Britain's wealth creators by one of the worst chancellors ever to hold office.

Under Labour's new tax proposals, Hunt's predicted earnings of US$200,000 would mean a tax bill of US$135,000. Over US$160,000 of his salary would be subject to 85 per cent tax. It was too much to bear.

Eddie Broughton, then a 30-year-old chartered accountant who advised clients, recalls it being an era of very high taxation. He says: "James would probably have been faced with paying a notional rate of 90 per cent on his overall income. From what we know, he was probably earning around US$200,000 a year, so would have been looking at paying half that at least. It was a lot of money in those days, and he really didn't have any choice. I reckon 750,000 people were affected, and probably a third of those left the UK in that period. "

The sudden abruptness with which Hunt left Britain shocked his friends. There one minute, he was gone the next. John Hogan was astonished when Hunt rang him and told him he was now living in Marbella. Apparently, even his brother Peter didn't know until after he had left.

IMG's Todd was worried that Peter, a traditional accountant, would be concerned about the Inland Revenue's reaction to Hunt leaving and might advise him against it. The move, Todd was convinced, should be a *fait accompli*.

Todd, providing Hunt with some very sound advice, ultimately saved him around US$3 million in tax. Hogan says: "I don't think anybody knew a lot about it – especially his brother. I think that was an IMG thing." He adds: "IMG had a cookie-cutter approach to everything and I think they were just pushing everybody abroad."

Peter Hunt soberly described the situation for Hunt biographer Gerald Donaldson: "When James signed with McCormack's organisation in September 1973, the London firm in which I'm a partner was already advising James on tax matters. It was arranged that we would continue to advise on special tax matters and that McCormack's organisation would handle the business side."

But when he found out his brother had left, Peter Hunt was sanguine. As a British accountant, it was difficult for him to maintain a good relationship with the Inland Revenue by advising his clients to move abroad effectively to avoid paying tax. But IMG could do so with impunity. Peter Hunt said: "The British public has come to accept the fact that successful personalities who earn a lot of money often have a relatively short span of peak earning capacity before they either have to go abroad or exert their considerable talents on behalf of the British tax man. It would be different if James was the only sportsman or personality to have left the country for that reason, but it has become pretty much the accepted thing these days."

Accepted thing or not, James Hunt found it an enormous wrench to leave the familiar streets of London for the unfamiliar paths of Marbella. He arrived in Spain with a suitcase and nothing else. It was very inconvenient, as he had just taken a new lease on a swish apartment near London's Park Lane and it had cost him plenty to cancel it. With hardly any notice, he packed all his bags into Lord Hesketh's Porsche Carrera RS and drove down to Portsmouth on his own and caught the ferry. On Todd's instructions, he was careful to retain all his ticket stubs and customs documentation for the car so he could prove to the Inland Revenue that he had left the country for good and was not coming back.

A day later, he was driving up the coast road to Marbella wondering what to do with himself.

When he arrived, he described himself as "absolutely homeless" and checked into the first hotel he came to. One night was enough, and he checked into a different hotel every night until he found one that he liked and that would do a deal with him for a long stay.

He made a half-hearted attempt to find a permanent home but wasn't suited to the task, resigning himself to a long stay in a hotel. Initially, he wasn't sure he could stomach such a long stay in Spain and didn't want to put down any permanent roots. But, once he got details of Denis Healey's first budget, he couldn't stomach paying the tax either. He was grateful to Ian Todd for having packed him off so quickly and was thankful for the 'cookie-cutter' approach, although he would later change his mind about IMG as a management agency.

In Spain, no one knew who he was, and there were plenty of young, handsome, blonde Brits with whom he had to compete for women. In fact, he found suitable women few and far between in early spring in Spain, so he took to playing tennis at the Lew Hoad Club to wile away his time.

He soon found he was lonely. None of his friends would come over as they couldn't afford the hotel prices. They were all freeloaders and told him blatantly they would wait until he got a house so that they could stay for free.

He told biographer Gerald Donaldson: "One day, sitting in a strange hotel bedroom in Torremolinos, I suddenly realised that I was totally alone. I knew nobody. I could barely speak the language. Thus, stricken by loneliness in a strange country, and with no home, no chance of even trying to make new friends because of my constant coming and going to races throughout the world, instead of following my heart and instincts, I began to think."

Hunt found himself a real fish out of water and experienced an attack of shyness, something he had not felt for years. Donaldson, who spent many hours with Hunt before he died working on his stillborn autobiography, said: "Despite his gregariousness in his own milieu, James was essentially a shy person in unfamiliar social circumstances and found it difficult to make new friends. His feelings of isolation made him begin to realise that the strong sense of independence and self-confidence which had so far served him so well had always been reinforced by the knowledge that his family and close friends, and especially his girlfriends, were close by. Perhaps he was not naturally a loner after all."

That thinking process brought about the end of his singleton status. It proved to be some of the worst thinking he had done in his life and led to his marriage to Suzy Miller, whom he met at the Lew Hoad Club a few weeks after he arrived in Spain, later that year.

When he first met Suzy Miller, she was living in a small rented apartment with a sea view of the Costa del Sol. After they became engaged, she found a villa to rent in the mountain village of Mijas, five miles inland from the coast.

Hunt found the conditions ideal for his fitness regime and started running up and down the hill roads in the morning and playing tennis in the afternoon.

With Suzy Miller on his arm, his social circle widened and soon the two of them were socialising every night amongst the large British expatriate community, which had exploded in size after Denis Healey's new tax regime took effect. Marbella proved to be the favourite destination for Brits leaving Britain in a hurry. Hunt named it the 'gringo community.'

Hunt and Miller had a wonderful first summer in Marbella once they had found a house to live in. Hunt was away for at least half the time racing. When he came home that autumn, they went to England to get married and then honeymooned in Antigua.

But the marriage did not survive the winter and the cooler weather. Spain emptied and the Hunts were left alone. They decided to go to Gstaad for Christmas and the rest was history.

Suzy Miller never returned to live in Spain after that Christmas, and Hunt was left alone in the house. She returned twice to agree the divorce conditions with her husband and then to pack up her belongings. The next time she came to Spain, she was Mrs Richard Burton.

The following spring of 1975, Hunt was a single man again and started to paint Marbella red. For a few months he was out of control, falling into swimming pools at parties and being banned from nightclubs.

Now he had his own villa, which meant free accommodation and food for his freeloading friends. They started arriving from England and many of them appeared never to want to leave.

Hunt realised he needed a bigger house. He also needed some help to keep himself in order; in the absence of a regular girlfriend, things were getting out of control.

He found that in Anita Todd, a very attractive multi-lingual Dutch woman, who had married IMG executive Ian Todd. Given that her husband managed Hunt's affairs at IMG, he knew her well.

She had recently separated from Todd and left the marital home. As the 24-year-old had nowhere to stay, Hunt invited her to be his Girl Friday in Marbella.

As soon as she arrived, he asked her to find him a larger house. After a month-long search, she found a luxury villa outside Marbella, overlooking the sea. It belonged to Jackie Lane, the 37-year-old half-Austrian, half-British Hollywood film actress who was married to Prince Alfonso of

Hohenlohe-Langenburg. Prior to her marriage, Lane had dated Glenn Ford and Elvis Presley, and in 1966 caused a sensation by posing nude for Hugh Hefner's new British edition of *Playboy* magazine. Now, she was pregnant with her first child and wanted to move back to England for the birth.

The villa had five bedrooms and three bathrooms together with a large swimming pool, and it fitted Hunt's requirements precisely. It also had a garage, where the Porsche could be locked away in case Lord Hesketh's representatives arrived to reclaim it.

Hunt agreed to take the villa and Lane accepted straightaway. Hunt moved in within a month.

Anita Todd moved in as housekeeper and his PA. Immediately, there were rumours of an affair but Hunt denied it and was even moved to issue a statement to that effect. He said: "We know what people will think, but there is no romance in it. She is strictly a housekeeper. It doesn't pay to fraternise with the staff. It would only lead to aggravation which would become a big pain in the arse. If you're going to sleep with your housekeeper, you may as well make her your wife. And I've already been through that. I have no steady girlfriend now, though there are several girls among my close friends." Unfortunately, no one believed him.

Whatever his arrangement with Anita Todd, it certainly was not exclusive. Whilst in Gstaad the previous winter with Suzy, he had met the 32-year-old British actress Joanna Pettet, and they enjoyed a friendship. Pettet, however, was also married to someone else at the time, which meant the friendship did not develop. She was famous for having appeared in the 1967 James Bond spoof called *Casino Royale* with David Niven, Ursula Andress and Peter Sellers. She, too, had posed nude for the British edition of *Playboy*.

Hunt said of the period: "It's nice to look at pretty girls, but you can't just look at them forever. You've got to talk to them sometime and, for me, it's important for a girl to be able to communicate. I like women with open minds and nice personalities, and I like fun people. But it takes me a long time to get to know someone, to establish trust. Only then can I relax."

Around this time, Hunt also acquired his first dog – an English Alsatian he called Oscar. Almost from the start, he and Oscar became inseparable. Oscar was a free spirit and never on a lead. Hunt trained him to stay by his side, come what may. At night, Oscar planted himself on his master's bed and did not move. By day, he went running with his master and then watched as he played tennis. When Hunt dived in the swimming pool, Oscar sometimes did too; but generally, he refrained from getting wet.

John Watson feels that Hunt's relationship with Oscar portrayed a totally different man from the one on the tracks. He says: "[Hunt] was a very loving, caring man and I first saw it in the manner in which he and his beloved Oscar related. It was one man and his dog. Very often, people are better able to express their emotions through animate objects. I understand that very well."

Hunt was pleased when Oscar was granted probationary associate membership at his golf club and allowed to follow him on his daily round. Some days, Hunt played with Sean Connery and some nights, they played backgammon until the early hours, with Oscar always looking on. Hunt soon acquired two other dogs to keep Oscar company on his long absences abroad.

The only downside Hunt found to living in Marbella was the travelling. There were few direct flights from the airport to the places he wanted to go. Nearby Gibraltar airport was just as bad.

It meant he had to fly to London, Paris or Frankfurt to connect, adding to the hassles. But Hunt had his own way of handling the thousands of miles he flew annually. He said: "I always make a point of relaxing when I travel. That's the golden rule. No matter what the difficulties and the problems are – and there are always a lot of very annoying things about tickets and standing in queues – it's always a positive disadvantage to get uptight. It gets you backwards rather than forwards, so you just take all the annoyance as they come and relax, otherwise you waste yourself while you're travelling. You have to look at the plane seat as a comfortable armchair with a good book and no telephone."

At many times in his life, Hunt was usually getting on and off aeroplanes at least four times a week. He rarely travelled anywhere but in the economy section to save money, as he said: "The tiring part about flying is going through the airports. I find that I can take catnaps easily on a plane journey and I can wake refreshed."

When he was in Marbella, he craved the company of his English friends. A frequent visitor to the new house in Marbella was Mike Hailwood. Hunt had formed a very close relationship with Hailwood in 1973 and 1974 until Hailwood left Formula One. The two were hedonists and enjoyed each other's company immensely. Ian Phillips understood the relationship precisely, as Hunt and Hailwood were the two people he admired most in life. As he says: "James and Mike were kindred spirits. Mike was just the finest gentleman that I have ever met in my entire life. He was the seven times world motorcycle champion and lived the most extraordinary lifestyle, and James wanted a part of it. Mike was also the hardest drinking man I've ever met, and I think James picked up quite a bit of that from him as well."

The two men laid siege to Marbella's night spots and became the talk of the town. Hailwood's occasional presence helped Hunt to settle after Suzy Miller's departure. And as Hunt's Formula One career developed, Marbella proved the perfect haven for a few years. But most of all, it enabled him to keep the millions of dollars he was earning away from the clutches of the British tax man.

SPAIN AND TAX EXILE

SHUNT

CHAPTER 18

Marriage to Suzy and Richard Burton to the rescue

James gets out of a hole

A few weeks after arriving in Marbella, James Hunt began rethinking his life. He was only 25 and, for some reason, he suddenly decided he should be married. No one knew what was going through his head but, whatever it was, it was not the soundest thought he had ever had.

Hunt had already given many people his views on marriage and expounded his belief that conventional thinking on the subject was wrong, especially with regard to racing drivers. He thought it was a "stupid myth" that drivers had to have a stable home life in order to cope with the stresses and strains of racing.

But his move to Spain seems to have changed his mind. Initially, he was lonely, and, within a week of arriving, he appears to have bought into the "stupid myth" and gone actively looking for a wife. Maybe his change of mind was caused by his sudden loss of form on the tracks. He told his biographer Gerald Donaldson that he wanted a woman to "help my career and ease my life in exile."

In fact, the last thing Hunt needed was a wife. His lifestyle meant he met a lot of women, and it wasn't unusual for him to have sex with more than two of them in a day – often complete strangers. His sexual appetite was voracious and, until he met his second wife, Sarah Lomax, years later, he never found a woman who could keep up with him.

His search for a permanent partner was short. Hunt began playing tennis at the Lew Hoad club in Fuengirola, where, at the bar one day, he set his eyes on Suzy Miller. Like him, Miller had just moved to Spain for a lifestyle change and was without friends. She had been modeling non-stop in London for two years and had made some money. She had also attracted the attention of some unsuitable boyfriends and had moved to Marbella for a change of pace.

Miller was a striking woman who always made a brilliant first impression, especially on men who appreciated willowy, small-breasted blondes. The two fell into easy conversation and, a few extraordinary months later, she was Mrs James Hunt.

Miller was not classically beautiful but had the effervescent appeal of an English country girl. Her looks, presence and effect on people were very much the same as the late Princess Diana's. Princess Diana, also never classically beautiful, managed to captivate everyone she met – and Miller had exactly the same effect.

Barely 24, a year younger than Hunt, she had spent much of her childhood in Southern Rhodesia with her expatriate parents as well as her twin sister, Vivienne, and a brother called John. As a child, she took piano lessons and became a concert standard pianist. She also was an excellent cook.

Her father, Frederick Miller, had been a high-ranking officer in the British army and then a lawyer and barrister employed in the British colonies. Her childhood had been spent in a number of different countries. But it was under the African sun, with her father working as a judge in Kenya, that Suzy developed into a truly attractive young woman; a real 'head turner' as Hunt would later describe her to his friends back in London.

By the time the family returned to England, she was a young woman. Frederick Miller bought a farmhouse in Basingstoke, Hampshire, but Suzy, Vivienne and John all moved to London. Without any obvious career prospects, Suzy soon signed up for some modelling work and found she was constantly in demand. As well as being good looking, she had an easy personality and was at home in any social circle. She had an instinctive warmth and gentility, although she was not an intellectual of any sort.

In Marbella, James and Suzy began seeing a lot of each other. Hunt was still living out of a suitcase in a hotel, and she had an apartment on the coast overlooking the sea. Their mutual isolation was what initially drew them together into their marriage.

Miller was very different from Hunt's previous girlfriends. Undemanding, she was quiet and had a thoughtful manner. At first, Hunt attempted to treat her like all his previous flings – in a casual manner – but she bridled against it. And the more she bridled, the more Hunt wanted her. She was not prepared to be his casual girlfriend.

Like many women approaching their mid-twenties, Suzy wanted a husband. The fact that Hunt was a famous racing driver held no appeal at all, but she saw him as perfect husband material.

Miller had no affinity for motor racing whatsoever. She had left modelling because she had recognised how shallow a world it was and, from what she could observe, racing wasn't that dissimilar. She was desperately keen to have children, and all she really wanted was a serious relationship with a suitable man. Content to devote her life to one man, Miller imagined a partner who would provide her with security and whom, in return, she could look after.

Hunt, however, just didn't get it. And Miller quickly threw him out. Back at his hotel, James suffered a serious shock to his system. For the first time, he found himself feeling hurt and lovesick. Realising that he actually might be in love with her, he said: "I talked myself back into her affections."

But Hunt had learned little and soon ended up back at the hotel once again. The relationship continued with its ups and downs, and the more she rejected him, the more he desired her. It was an old trap, and Hunt fell right into it.

After a three-week separation, which included the weekend of the British Grand Prix at Brands Hatch, he found himself intensely missing her. All he could think about that weekend was being naked in bed with her – and this time, his thoughts were not of lust but of love. Over the three days, he became more and more obsessive in his thoughts.

On the evening of Sunday 20th July 1974, he arrived back in Marbella. He had flown in from London after retiring halfway through the race. He drove straight from the airport to her apartment and proposed marriage. As he remembered: "Knowing that the prospect of marriage would swing Suzy around, I went back to her and proposed." It was a desperate measure and reflected the extent of his infatuation. He had truly lost his senses. Suzy accepted without hesitation and immediately telephoned her parents and sister with the news. She watched as a sheepish Hunt also telephoned his astonished parents. The engagement was properly announced a week later and a wedding date set for the end of the Formula One season, in October. The roller coaster had started, and there would be no getting off.

Suzy wanted to get married right away, but that was impractical, and Hunt wanted to catch his breath and put some time between the engagement and the wedding day.

Immediately after the proposal, he expressed some regret to his friends, saying he was not quite sure what he was doing. Although he wanted Miller to be his girlfriend, he found he was still sexually attracted to other women. Miller, however, was perfect at family occasions and for parading as his partner. She added a great deal of value to him, and he knew it. So he resolved to try his best to reform himself in order to make the relationship work.

But there were inherent problems. He loved having sex with her, but found that it was over quickly. Hunt was a sex addict before the term came into common usage, and he was unfaithful to her almost from the start.

But Hunt found that, once he had proposed, there was no escaping "Miss Miller's clutches", as he put it. And at that time, he did not even particularly want to escape. He enjoyed home life with her very much. He was in love with her, or so he thought, and was undeniably proud of having landed her.

Friends at the time conceded that Hunt was unsure of himself where women were concerned, and his interest in them typically extended no further than the bedroom. He had a giant appetite for sex and looked to feed wherever he could. On a physical level, he was unequalled. Emotionally, however, he was an amateur. According to his biographer and friends, he would often suggest in conversation that he was not sure what love was. Later in his life, he denied ever having been in love with Suzy or, indeed, even with his second wife. The only woman he ever professed to have loved was Helen Dyson, his girlfriend at the time of his death. But no one truthfully knows if that would have lasted, despite all Hunt's protestations to the contrary. It seems he just wasn't that sort of man. As biographer Donaldson astutely observed: "The emotional component of a relationship for James was still virgin territory."

The engagement party was held at his brother Peter's apartment in London. It was attended by the two families and most of the Hesketh team. Many of the invitees were very surprised. Hunt's former girlfriend Taormina Rieck had married in the intervening years and was also there. He was still close to Rieck and had attended her wedding the year before. Now, Hunt stood before her confessing that he didn't know what he was doing and that he didn't want to marry Suzy. He said to Rieck: "I don't know why I'm doing this." To which she retorted: "Well, why the hell are you, you silly clot?" He allegedly told her that, as he looked around at the happy family scene, he realised that it had gone too far and he couldn't get out of it. She remembers him appearing very weak and confused. It was at odds with the confident Hunt whom everyone knew. As Rieck now puts it: "I could see he was very confused."

The situation was not helped by the attitude of Lord Hesketh, which some say bordered on the irresponsible. Hesketh encouraged the union and even offered to pay for the wedding, which he duly did. He then appointed himself to organise the event, and transformed the wedding into one big party for himself and his friends. Although Hunt had known Hesketh for only a little over 18 months, he was named best man.

Suzy was Catholic, which dictated a Catholic church, and Hunt converted to Catholicism for the ceremony. The wedding was held at the Church of the Immaculate Heart of Mary, better known as the Brompton Oratory, in Kensington. The grand setting was entirely appropriate for the society wedding of the year.

Hesketh arranged a full orchestra to play the music, and the invitations stressed that nothing short of full morning suits were required. More or less every racing driver of distinction was invited, including Graham Hill, Stirling Moss, Jackie Stewart, John Watson and Ronnie Peterson.

The prospect of a wedding had been haunting Hunt since the engagement party. It had also been dominating his thoughts during the closing races of the 1974 season. Realising that the prospect of a permanent partner had not improved his performance in the cockpit, Hunt was well into having second and third thoughts about the marriage by the time the season ended. According to Donaldson, he wanted desperately to cut and run and get out of the whole dreadful situation, but was too chicken to do it. Seeing no way out, Hunt turned to drinking.

For the full four days leading up to the wedding, he was never once sober. The night before the ceremony he had hardly any sleep, as he stayed up most of the night drinking himself silly in preparation for the big event. And, on the day of the wedding itself, the situation was an utter farce. At 6 o'clock that morning, Hunt woke up and poured himself the first of many beers. Before leaving to go to the church, he knocked back a couple of bloody marys in quick succession in order to keep him going until lunch. By the time he walked up the aisle, he was hopelessly intoxicated. Some say he had done it deliberately because he would otherwise not have been able to go through with the ceremony. As Hunt himself would later say: "I just couldn't handle the whole scene, so I went out and got blind, roaring drunk. For four days, I went on the most stupendous bender of my life."

At a time when what was really required was some clear thinking and decisive action, Hesketh and Bubbles Horsley indulged Hunt through it all. Horsley reassured him that every prospective groom was nervous before getting married, and Hesketh lectured him on his obligation to perform as expected of him and to not let people down. Hesketh employed some ridiculous analogy and convinced him that he would be disappointing his many fans if he pulled out. Hunt, of course, was too inebriated to argue, and Hesketh continued to assure him that "it would all work out in the end."

Hesketh now vehemently denies having encouraged the marriage. He said to Christopher Hilton, one of Hunt's biographers: "I think the truth of the matter is that James had rather changed his mind by the time he got to the church, and he wouldn't have been the first or last person to have done that and survived." But Hesketh admits: "He said it to me on the way to the church, and I said: 'It's a bit late now.' It was a very big wedding. I said: 'You know, everyone feels like this.'" Shirking responsibility for what happened, Hesketh says: "I think it's probably always easier to shift the blame onto others, and I've got a broad pair of shoulders." He does, however, concede that: "I'm not sure James was perfectly suited for married life, really."

As for Hunt, he would say afterwards that he remembered little of the event. At the wedding reception, Hesketh and Horsley supported him when he had to stand up. According to other guests, he was virtually incoherent as he addressed the invitees and it was all rather embarrassing. Suzy just smiled her way through it all, convinced it would be different now that he was a married man. Given how much he had had to drink that day, the portents were not auspicious.

The following day, they left for their honeymoon and, once more, the occasion proved to be anything but straightforward.

Horsley had also married just a few weeks earlier and the two men planned a joint honeymoon in Antigua, in the Caribbean Sea. While both their brides had dreamed of a romantic honeymoon on the golden sands of Antigua alone with their new husbands, the two men seemed to prefer each other's company. It was an entirely selfish gesture.

What Donaldson called the "essential incompatibility" of James and Suzy was immediately apparent by this deliberate arrangement of Horsley's presence in Antigua. It was no accident of dates. Hunt simply didn't want to be alone with Suzy for a fortnight. He knew she would want conversation and he knew it would have little to do with motor racing, which was all Hunt lived for.

The honeymoon happened, and that was the best that could be said of it.

When they returned to Spain as man and wife, things did not improve. Hunt was absent most of the time. Suzy just wanted them to settle down and enjoy each other's company. She longed for a relationship, followed by three children and a settled family life. Having found a rented villa to move into, Miller desired nothing more than to be a wife and to build a home. The result, however, was catastrophic: the harder she tried to please him, the more he tried to shake her off.

The new Mrs Hunt did attend some motor races during 1975 and did her best to be a racing driver's wife. But, mostly, she led her own life and her husband led his. He became consistently unfaithful and was not particularly good at hiding his infidelities. And she learned not to ask. Hunt recalled later: "It was a matter of clashing lifestyles and personalities. I am very much into racing and doing my own thing, and I move very fast. She wanted a slow pace, a good solid base and a solid relationship. Ironically, these were the very things I married her for in the first place."

Within a few months, Suzy realised that the marriage was not going to work. Still, she was prepared to give it time in the unlikely event that she was wrong. At races in early 1975, Suzy admitted she was "bored stiff", saying to friends: "I literally felt like a spare part. I was just there for the show."

The couple began to spend more and more time apart. Sensing that the union was coming apart, Hunt's parents, Wallis and Susan, travelled to Marbella for a long stay to try to make running repairs to the marriage. Upon their arrival, their son was absent, and he appeared only sporadically thereafter. Susan Hunt was entirely on Suzy's side. She knew precisely where the fault lay, conceding: "Suzy is absolutely gorgeous, most of his girls are. But I can see that, for James, to be married is impossible. His lifestyle doesn't suit it. I'm bound to say I love him dearly, but I'd hate to have him for a husband." Susan Hunt had just about summed it up.

Hunt tried to explain what had gone wrong: "I thought that marriage was what I wanted and needed to give me a nice stable and quiet home life, but in fact it wasn't. And the mistake was mine. I really wanted to go racing on my own, and it wasn't much fun for Suzy to sit at home and wait for me all that time. It was also a terrible hassle for her to come racing because race meetings were probably the most relaxing time in my schedule. The rest of the time, you tend to be leaping on aeroplanes once a day and that made it even worse. It's bad enough organising one person to get on an aeroplane; organising two gets to be twice as much hassle. It got to the point where it was a problem for Suzy to come travelling and a hell of a deal for her to stay at home. It was making life miserable in the extreme for her and, since I felt responsible for her, it was making me miserable too."

Despite that, as far as his personality would allow, Hunt desperately wanted to please her. Whatever he said later, he was clearly in love with her. As he said: "If she stayed at home while I rushed around the world, it was boring for her. If she came with me, it was no fun for her. I was always looking over my shoulder to see if she was there, and she was always struggling to keep up with me. It was a heavy deal for both of us."

Hunt knew he had to get out of the marriage and he prayed for a miracle. The miracle he hoped for, quite simply, was that she would meet someone else. Hunt did not want to desert her and was also wary of the money situation. In the case of a divorce, Suzy would have been entitled to a large share of his wealth, which he had moved to Spain to protect. A divorce would have relieved him of half of his UK£100,000 net worth just as he had started earning good money. He literally couldn't afford a divorce.

Meanwhile, Suzy began to feel the same. Facing the possibility that James was not for her and that she had likely married for the wrong reasons, she wanted out as well. Nevertheless, Suzy remained supportive and sympathetic to Hunt's feelings. But her understanding only heightened his sense of responsibility for her, as he said: "I was very, very anxious not to hurt her. There are nice ways and nasty ways to do things, and I hope I can never be a hurtful person."

The marriage may as well have ended there and then, but it dragged on for another eight months as Suzy looked for a new partner. Finally, despairing of the likelihood of a miracle, Hunt offered to buy Suzy a smart apartment in London and to give her an allowance, with a divorce to follow when it suited them. He was prepared to pay heavily to get out of the marriage, but she didn't need the money and was reluctant to make it official. Suzy was certainly not going to get divorced and be single again – that was not on the menu at all. So they continued to live together in Marbella although, by July 1975, they had for all intents and purposes gone their separate ways. However, publicly, outside of the Formula One paddock, no one knew or suspected anything was amiss.

Only one journalist, David Benson of the *Daily Express*, guessed anything was wrong. He had heard stories of rows between the Hunts in the Marbella Club. It prompted him to send his photographer, Douglas Morrison, to Marbella for a photo shoot in the first week of November for a later article. When Morrison got there, he thought it very odd that Suzy had just flown back from the United States, where she had been for the past four weeks after the US Grand Prix, while Hunt had gone straight home. Morrison went with Hunt on the 35-minute journey to Malaga airport to pick her up. The couple were friendly but it was not the homecoming of a husband and wife who had not seen each other for three weeks. Later that evening, Morrison overheard a heated argument between them about the cost of transatlantic telephone calls on her hotel bill. The hotel bills added up to nearly US$8,000, with two thirds from telephone costs. Morrison thought it very strange that, after such a lengthy period apart, the first thing they did was argue about the telephone bill. When Morrison reported all this back to Benson, Benson sensed a story might be in the air, although he couldn't quite believe that Hunt would want to let a woman like Suzy go so easily.

In reality, they had put on a togetherness act in front of Morrison. The truth was that they were barely speaking, although there was no animosity. It was as if they had agreed to an amicable parting.

Hunt took up with Jane Birbeck while he was in London and met with a succession of other girls when he was elsewhere. But he was careful to be discreet, as he didn't want anything in the newspapers that might upset Suzy or the Miller family – or his own family for that matter.

In the end, it was Suzy who made the move, over Christmas of 1975. Hunt had secured his future with a new drive at McLaren, and Suzy had seen him through the crisis when the Hesketh team folded. Fatefully, they both went to Gstaad for Christmas with friends. Gstaad was the place to be at yuletide. At that time of year, it was an absolutely magical place. Gay and festive, it was a veritable playground for the rich and famous. Coincidentally, Richard Burton and his wife, the actress Elizabeth Taylor, were also spending the winter holiday season in Gstaad, at a villa called Chalet Arial.

Burton and Taylor were the most famous married couple in the world.

They had met in 1963 while both were on set filming *Cleopatra*, the biggest movie of the day. Taylor was playing the title role and Burton one of her suitors, the Roman general Marc Anthony. They went to bed together on their first evening on set, and the rest was show business history. They were married in 1964; she was 32 and he was 39.

Taylor was a major Hollywood actress – by far the bigger star of the two – and Burton was the quintessential British actor. The marriage helped his career enormously and he soon overtook his wife in stature as her career began to fade as she neared 40.

The marriage was a huge success for ten years and was characterised by Burton presenting Taylor with bigger and more expensive diamonds as the years went on. In those ten years, Burton spent almost US$15 million on jewellery for his wife. But Burton's large capacity for alcohol and Taylor's eccentric prima donna behavior doomed the marriage. She was a sophisticated American and he was, essentially, a simple Welsh boy.

They divorced ten years later, in 1974, but almost immediately got back together. A year after the separation, on 10th October 1975, they bizarrely remarried during a safari holiday in Botswana. She was 43 and he exactly 50 – they were married on his birthday.

When they got back to London from Botswana, Taylor threw Burton a 50th birthday party in the famous Orchid Room at the Dorchester Hotel on London's Park Lane. 250 guests attended and drank as many bottles of champagne. Burton was on the wagon and sipped mineral water all night, looking miserable at his own party. As he was prone to unpredictable personality changes when he drank, Burton daren't drink in public. All his drinking tended to be done in private.

In the winter of 1975, Burton and Taylor had resolved not to work and had planned to spend quality time together to attend to their new marriage. They cleared off nearly four months from their respective schedules but soon realised that more time together actually had the reverse of the intended effect. Although it was clear they were still in love, the remarriage had been a disastrous mistake.

In December, Burton checked into the Wellington Clinic near the famous Lord's Cricket Ground, in North London, for treatment for malaria and alcohol addiction. Afterwards, he and Taylor flew to Gstaad for Christmas. The marriage was already a disaster, and they spent less and less time together as Taylor flitted in and out of Gstaad that winter. Even when they were both together at Chalet Arial, they slept in separate bedrooms in separate wings of the house.

In Gstaad, Miller and Hunt also went their separate ways. Hunt was in serious training for the 1976 Formula One season and spent all day at the gym or running. At night, he didn't drink and, consequently, didn't socialise. Without alcohol, Hunt was a different man. But Suzy knew he was surreptitiously seeing local girls during the day. Miller ended up very depressed for the first time in her life, and spent most of the days on her own.

She first set eyes on Richard Burton as they were going opposite ways on a ski cable lift. Burton turned to his assistant, Brook Williams, and asked him who the "vision was that had just passed by." Of all the magnificent women in Gstaad that Christmas, and there were many, Burton was struck down by the sheer presence of Suzy Miller. 'Transfixed' would be a better description, as he would say later: "I turned around and there was this gorgeous creature, about nine feet tall. She could stop a stampede."

Luckily for Burton, Williams knew exactly who she was and was acquainted with her socially. Williams was the son of the playwright Emlyn Williams, and he acted unofficially as Burton's aide-de-camp. He knew everybody. As Burton recalled: "I was wondering when she would turn up again, but Brook knew her a little and my luck was in."

His luck had him running into her again a few days later on a snowy street in Gstaad. By then, Hunt was out of the way completely. He had flown to São Paulo to compete in the Brazilian Grand Prix in the opening race of the 1976 season. It was his first race for the McLaren team. Williams took the opportunity to invite Suzy to a party they were attending that night.

Williams couldn't help but notice the way Suzy lit up when she received the invitation. Burton had never heard of Hunt, but Suzy was well aware that Burton formed one half of the most famous married couple in the world. His marriage to Taylor, however, who was also at the party, was no obstacle for Burton.

At the party, Burton sat at one end of an overcrowded table and Suzy was at the other end of another table. As the party became more crowded and more people squeezed on the benches, Burton and Suzy found themselves next to each other and were introduced.

Burton was captivated by her that night, particularly as she, having lost a contact lens, ended up crawling around on the floor to look for it amongst the guests' feet. Burton thought this hilarious.

Williams invited her to come to the house the following day and, after that, Suzy started visiting Chalet Arial regularly to meet Burton. The affair between Burton and Suzy began almost immediately. He was 50 and she was 26. It was Suzy's first dalliance since her marriage to Hunt. The age gap appeared large but, as Burton said: "She was mature far beyond her years."

Although both their brief marriages were effectively over, the union was immediately problematic. As far as the outside world was concerned, both the Hunts' and Burtons' marriages were happy. But Burton needed Suzy Miller desperately – his life was a mess, he was drinking heavily again, and he needed to be taken care of.

From the day they were introduced, Burton and Suzy became virtually inseparable. Burton remembered: "She started coming to the house two, three and then four times a week."

Taylor noticed the fresh-faced and uncomplicated Englishwoman coming to the house and quickly guessed what was going on. Miller and Taylor were two very different women with very different talents and interests, but, despite the predictable rivalry, Taylor instinctively recognised that Suzy was something special and witnessed the way she fussed over her husband. One evening at the château, in a particularly memorable exchange, Taylor said to Suzy: "You'll only last six months with Richard." To which Suzy replied: "Perhaps, but those six months will be very worthwhile."

Taylor, to her surprise, found that she was rather relieved at Burton's seriousness about Suzy and at the acknowledgement that her marriage to him was finally over. She went straight out to a local discotheque and hit on a 37-year-old flaxen-haired Maltese advertising executive called Peter Darmanin, whom she brought back to the house to stay with her.

In the third week of January, Burton had to leave for New York to start rehearsals for a new play. He was due to replace Anthony Perkins for a three-month stint as the lead in Peter Shaffer's *Equus* at the Plymouth Theatre, on Broadway.

When Burton went to New York, Suzy went with Brook Williams to Lausanne; to the home of playboy Gunter Sachs, one of the richest men in Europe. Burton had arranged with Sachs for Suzy to stay with him to give him time to tell Elizabeth that their marriage was over. He didn't want his relationship with Suzy turning into a media feeding frenzy, which he knew was easily possible. Burton knew she would be safe and have a good time at Sachs' extraordinarily lavish home by the lake in Lausanne. When Burton left for New York, Taylor stayed in Gstaad in residence Chalet Arial, continuing her affair with Darmanin.

Throughout it all, Suzy had been keeping Hunt fully informed over the telephone of her developing affair, and to say that he was delighted would have been an understatement. In fact, when she had first told him that Burton had invited her to go to New York, he had simply replied: "Fine, off you go." In any case, he had been spending any free time he had in London with Jane Birbeck.

A week later, Burton, now settled into a suite at the Lombardy Hotel near the Plymouth Theatre, called Suzy and told her he believed it was safe for her to come to New York, even though he had still not told Taylor of the situation. The truth was that Burton missed her desperately. The two spent two weeks together discreetly in New York. When people asked her what she was doing as part of Burton's retinue, she told them she was a friend of Brook Williams'. If Hunt was asked why his wife was in New York hanging around Richard Burton, he admitted there were strains in the marriage, but no more than that. No one guessed that Suzy was Burton's new girlfriend.

It was a heady time. Burton excited the city with his pre-opening performances as psychiatrist Martin Dysart. *Equus* was a gruelling drama about a boy who blinds six horses because they witness his love-making and the wretched provincial psychiatrist whose patient he becomes as a result. The role of the psychiatrist had previously been played by Anthony Hopkins as well as by Anthony Perkins. But Burton eclipsed them both, and was immediately signed up for a Hollywood film version for a payday of a million dollars. His pay for three months on Broadway was US$250,000.

The sums of money Burton earned were a huge surprise to Suzy. Her new boyfriend was paid some thirty times more than her husband. After two weeks, Miller left for England to visit her parents.

In mid-February, with the media still unaware of the split, Burton called Taylor, who was still in Gstaad, and asked her to come to New York. He told her he had something very important to say. He had also organised a 44th birthday party for her on 27th February.

Burton was incredibly nervous and didn't feel able to tell Taylor about Suzy over the telephone, mistakenly believing she would be upset.

When Taylor got to New York, she also checked in at the Lombardy. Later that evening, Burton told her about his relationship with Suzy and asked Taylor for an immediate divorce so he could marry his new girlfriend. He omitted to mention the birthday party he had planned for her a few days later. Taylor was not at all upset about Suzy, as she had been enjoying the pleasures of an affair of her own. She told him she was already aware of his affair with Suzy, but was furious that Burton had made her travel all the way across the Atlantic to tell her about it. Taylor screamed at him: "You mean you brought me all this way to tell me that?" The two had a furious row which failed to subside even when Burton told her about the birthday party he had planned. Taylor thought he had made that up when he had seen how angry she was.

Storming out, Taylor returned to her room. She called her assistant in Los Angeles and asked for a flight to be arranged for the following day to the west coast. On impulse, she then called the room of *Equus* producer Alexander Cohen to see if the birthday party story was true. He confirmed that it was, and she told him to cancel it. She was unrelenting in her belief that Burton had called Cohen to tell him what to say after she had left his room.

Her fury with Burton was not abated, and the next call was to a lawyer called Aaron Frosch telling him to draw up two sets of divorce papers – one for her and one for Burton. She told him to set tough terms, believing Burton would do anything to dissolve the marriage quickly. On that score, she was entirely right. In the end, Burton surrendered almost all of his assets to her.

The next day, she flew to Los Angeles and straight into the arms of former boyfriend Henry Wynberg. She found she hardly missed Burton at all. When Taylor was asked by journalists about the swap of partners and her new relationship, she said: "What was I expected to do? Sleep alone?"

Journalists started to report on the relationship between Suzy Hunt and Brook Williams, and, in his fabled gossip column in the *Daily Mail*, Nigel Dempster revealed it to the world. Dempster reported the break-up of the Hunt marriage and wrote that Suzy had flown to New York where she was "being escorted by Emlyn Williams' son, Brook, who is one of the Burton entourage." It was news in itself that the Hunts' marriage was over, and David Benson found himself in trouble for being scooped by Dempster. So Benson, remembering what Douglas Morrison had told him, immediately rang Peter Hunt in London. James, meanwhile, was in transit to Johannesburg for the South African Grand prix.

Benson recalls: "I immediately rang Hunt's brother Peter in London. He professed to be astounded by the report, denied it absolutely and said he knew nothing of this man called Williams. He told me that there was nothing unusual in the fact that Suzy was in New York while James was in South Africa, that they were both friends of the Burtons and that Richard and Elizabeth had invited them both to visit them when they were in New York."

Peter told him that was the reason that Suzy was staying in Burton's hotel.

But Peter Hunt was lying to Benson; he knew exactly what was going on. But Benson respected Hunt and accepted his denial. He rang the *Daily Express* news desk and told them there was no truth in Dempster's story. The denial only stood for a day.

As soon as Taylor had left for Los Angeles, Burton called Suzy and told her to return to New York straightaway. As soon as Suzy got to the Lombardy, he decided not to waste the party and used it to celebrate the astounding reviews he was receiving for his performance in *Equus*. Burton was at the very peak of his acting career and the toast of Broadway. This time, he dispensed with any discretion, and Suzy was openly on his arm.

Manhattan can be a very small place, and Burton and Suzy made no attempt to hide their closeness. But, initially, American reporters were completely baffled as to who Suzy was.

Burton did not care to enlighten them and enjoyed the press' discomfort at them not being able to caption the many photos of the two appearing in the four New York daily newspapers.

Eventually, the journalists worked out that the striking blonde was the wife of racing driver James Hunt, and that she had clearly broken up Burton's marriage to Elizabeth Taylor. There was no bigger media story than that in the last week of February 1976.

In New York, after his performances, Suzy and Richard would dine with friends or on their own. Burton took her to the same bistros and restaurants to which he had taken Elizabeth Taylor ten years earlier. Burton was immensely proud of his new girlfriend's magical effect on people. When he walked into a restaurant with her on his arm, people applauded. When she excused herself, the women of New York followed her into the restroom to get a closer look at the green-eyed English beauty who had enraptured New York society overnight.

With the news suddenly out, and Suzy and Burton no longer a secret, Hunt was in for a shock when he landed at Johannesburg airport for the South African Grand Prix. When Hunt got off the plane, he drove to the

Sleepy Hollow Hotel where he was staying before he moved to the Kyalami Ranch Hotel for the race. He was followed by journalists who had flown in specially to work on the story. The hotel was staked out by a throng of jostling journalists and photographers – none of them interested in the race. Alastair Caldwell remembers: "Suddenly we had huge media interest. We had the *Sydney Morning Herald* and the *Punjabi Times*, we had every daily newspaper in the world, even Mexico. All were trying to interview us and talk to James. They were being flown in by the plane-load."

Benson was furious with Peter Hunt, who he realised had been very economical with the truth. He decided to phone Hunt direct, but Hunt also proceeded to tell him a pack of lies. He told him that he had been speaking to Suzy the night before and that there was nothing between her and Burton. Benson recalls: "Hunt had never lied to me to my knowledge before and I'd known him from his very early days in Formula 3 and done a great deal to promote his career. So I had every reason to believe James. I suppose, deep down, I liked Suzy so much and I thought that they made such a good couple that I wanted to believe James. He was rather jovial about the whole thing.

I advised him: 'Well, look James, if you are really telling me the truth about Suzy, I suggest the best thing you can do is to ring Suzy and tell her to get on the next plane and come out to South Africa and be at your side. At least it'll take the steam out of the publicity whilst you're running up to the Grand Prix. He told me not to worry. Nevertheless, I instinctively suspected that Hunt was not really telling the truth and I fed my feelings back to the *Daily Express* news desk."

The *Express* news desk contacted its own bureau chief in New York, a man called Ivor Key. Key investigated and confirmed Benson's suspicions, writing a story headlined: 'Off We Go Again – Booze, A Beautiful Girl And Another Burton Bust-up'. The article read: "Off we go once more on the Burton marriage merry-go-round. First, Richard Burton is back on the booze, with racing driver James Hunt's 26-year-old wife Suzy at his side. Second, Liz Taylor is packing her bags to go home to mother in Los Angeles. Third, Suzy Hunt has said she is considering divorce, although her husband, now in South Africa, says that's news to him."

When that story was published, Benson got back on the phone to Peter Hunt. He recalls: "'Look, Peter', I said, 'I have had a great friendship with you and James and this story about Suzy is bouncing around the world and must come out in the open sooner or later. Why not tell me straight exactly what is going on? It's perfectly obvious that this is no friendly little deal of Suzy staying with Burton in New York.' Peter replied: 'All right, David, I'll square with you. Suzy wants to marry Burton. I think she's a very silly girl, but there it is. She's told James and he has said he won't stand in her way.' I grumbled about not being told that at the start and immediately phoned James in South Africa, where he confirmed the story and gave me a quote about his co-operation if Suzy asked for a divorce."

Benson then wrote a story that appeared on the front page of the *Daily Express* on 26th February 1976, headlined: 'Suzy To Marry Burton.' Benson and the *Daily Express* were now back on top and leading the world with the story. The story read: "Suzy Hunt, wife of British racing driver James Hunt, is seeking a quickie divorce in America so that she can marry Richard Burton. This follows the actor's latest break-up with his second-time wife Liz Taylor. He and 27-year-old Suzy are staying at the same New York hotel. Burton, too, was said to be in a hurry to get a divorce." The article then contained everything the Hunt brothers had told him.

The article legitimised the story, and it seemed that suddenly everyone wanted to know how Hunt felt about his wife keeping company with Richard Burton. Hunt pretended to be desolate. At the gates of the hotel, he read out the following statement: "Naturally, I am perturbed by all the publicity about my wife in Europe and America, but I must concentrate 100 per cent on the Grand Prix. If there is a problem, it is just going to have to wait until after the race. Meanwhile, I'm far too busy sorting out the car and keeping myself fit." With that, he handed out the press releases and immediately sprinted off on a six-mile training run, followed by puffing hacks who soon gave up the chase.

It was one of the most satisfying workouts of his life. He was finally free, exactly 16 months after his wedding day in London. In fact, the Miller-Burton relationship that had developed so quickly into a proposal of marriage and a request for a quickie divorce came as a huge release.

Meanwhile, Suzy and Burton found they couldn't leave the Lombardy Hotel because over 50 reporters and photographers were at the front door.

As the news broke, Burton decided to break the ice with Hunt and called him in Kyalami, effectively to apologise. Hunt remembered Burton being rather embarrassed and tongue tied on the telephone, which he found strange. In truth, Burton couldn't quite believe that Hunt was being so casual about letting go of his beautiful wife. He expected him to be bitter towards him and devastated. But he simply said to Burton: "Relax, Richard. You've done me a wonderful turn by taking on the most alarming expense account in the country." A bemused and somewhat relieved Burton replaced the receiver in his hotel room and turned to Suzy and smiled. She said to him: "I told you James is fine about all this." Burton still could not understand.

James and Suzy had effectively split some six months before, in July 1975, so it was by no means traumatic. He said at the time: "Her running off with Burton is a great relief to me. It actually reduces the number of problems I have to face outside my racing. I am mainly concerned that everyone comes out of it happy and settled." In fact, there was no disguising Hunt's utter relief at what had transpired, as he confessed: "I prefer to be on my own at races because, really, there's enough to do looking after me. It's more than I can handle to keep myself under control at a race meeting without trying to look after someone else as well and have more responsibilities and worries. I find that, if I want an early night before a race, or if I want a couple of hours to cool off and relax before dinner, I can do no better than to read a book or listen to music and therefore it's better to be on my own." Resolving not to get tempted into marriage again, he told journalists: "Meanwhile, it is probably a good thing that I am still technically married. I have that as a safety valve. It will stop me from doing anything silly again."

The intense media interest carried on all weekend, and Hunt was as equally prominent on the front pages of the newspapers as he was on the back. Eventually, Caldwell smuggled him out of the hotel to stay with the retired South African tennis player, Abe Segal, a friend Hunt had made in London. As Caldwell recalls: "We hid him there and James went off with this tennis player to a very nice house and played tennis. Then, when he turned up at the track, we could muscle the journalists out of the pit road and keep him more or less isolated." Caldwell adds: "James loved every minute of it."

After writing his world exclusive piece, the news desk told Benson to get out to South Africa. Benson knew Abe Segal well and spoke to Hunt at length at his house. He was virtually the only journalist with access. When he had that covered, off it was back to the mundane business of reporting the race. Benson remembers that the compulsory seat belt law was about to be debated in parliament and his news desk instructed him to get a reaction to it from motor racing people in the paddock. But Benson soon found a better story to occupy him. Ironically, at the same time as Hunt was splitting from Suzy, Niki Lauda was also breaking up with his fiancé and long term love, Mariella. He discovered Lauda was with his new girlfriend, Marlene, at Kyalami. But every reporter was obsessed with the Suzy Hunt story and had overlooked it, leaving Benson with another exclusive.

Hunt flew home to London then Spain, and planned to call into New York on his way to the US Grand Prix to sort things out with Suzy and to meet Burton. Benson got wind of this and tackled Hunt about it on the day before he flew out, asking: "James, I understand you are going off to New York. Are you going to see Suzy?" Hunt told him: "I have spoken to her on the phone and I am hoping we can have lunch together tomorrow and talk over the whole problem and the question of Richard Burton. It's all very personal and there's nothing else I can say right now." When they put the phone down, Hunt took a taxi to Battersea and flew by helicopter to Heathrow to catch a Pan Am flight to New York.

In reality, it was a brief stopover on his way to Los Angeles airport. As news got round New York that "the husband" was flying in, reporters filled up the Lombardy lobby and pounced on Hunt once they recognised him. He was shocked to find himself surrounded by photographers and journalists asking him questions while his wife was upstairs in Burton's suite. Suzy eventually appeared and they went off in a taxi together to meet Burton. It was basically a meet-and-greet, with nothing of substance discussed. But, perhaps a bit ironically, Hunt had wanted to meet Burton to "approve him" as suitable for his wife. At that first meeting, Hunt was impressed by Burton's sensitivity. Burton even thanked Hunt for having given him Suzy. Thoroughly approving of Burton, Hunt said he hoped to meet him again soon.

When they returned to the Lombardy, the number of reporters and photographers had doubled, and Hunt hightailed it back to JFK airport to catch his flight to Los Angeles.

While Hunt was away, his mother, Sue, had got in on the act. She was trapped by baying reporters at a lunch she was attending to promote the sending of cards for Mother's Day, which wasn't as popular then as it is today. She told the journalists that she could not take the rift in her son's marriage lightly. She said she didn't know whether there was the possibility of a reconciliation, but did say that she was very upset about Suzy becoming involved with Burton: "I like Suzy very, very much. I am very fond of her and terribly sad for her. My upbringing has been for the stability of marriage and the family, but I realise and fully understand that marriage breakdowns can happen. And I can understand that in James' case particularly, it is [due to] his dedication to motor racing. He was dedicated to Suzy but to motor racing as well. He's always been an odd fellow, James. They were very desperately in love when they married; they really were. But, with James' character, it was a mistake for him to be married at all. I'm quite convinced that whomever he had married, the same situation would have arisen. Suzy was a delight, James is just not the marrying kind."

And there the frenzy ended, with the last word going, perhaps fittingly, to Hunt's mother.

In late March, Hunt spent some days in Marbella with Suzy and sorted out the logistics of the split. Free of the responsibilities of their relationship, Hunt also confessed to her the anguish he had gone through over the marriage, recognising that, where he liked "consuming life in a rush", she had wanted the exact opposite. Suzy assured Hunt that she did not want a divorce settlement and that Burton would take care of the financial arrangements for her. All their joint possessions stayed with Hunt, including the piano, and Suzy left with her personal possessions in a few suitcases, which she dropped off in Switzerland at Burton's house in Celigny.

And that was that. A few months later, they met for coffee at a restaurant in Malaga and bid farewell to each other as man and wife for the last time.

Suzy stopped off in London to see her parents on her way back to New York from Marbella. Up until then, she had not spoken to any reporter about the events at all, nor, indeed, has she spoken to them since. But Peter Hunt owed David Benson a favour after the terrible lies he had told him. Expecting the favour to be paid, Benson was rewarded with an exclusive chat with Suzy. So Benson travelled to Hunt's office for a sit-down with her. He was the only journalist ever to do so in the 36 years that have followed.

Benson recalls what happened: "As an old friend, she greeted me with a warm embrace. I took notes on the interview, writing down the precise words she wanted to appear: 'You are the first newspaperman I have talked to about the break-up. You understand the difficulties I have in discussing my private life in public so I want to talk to you about them and, then, if you print them, that will be it once and for all.' Suzy was particularly distressed about a report in a rival newspaper that suggested she had given Richard Burton a ring – 'I want to correct that. I didn't give Richard a ring and I wouldn't do anything like that; its too vulgar. Also, Richard did not break up my marriage to James, it was already over when I met Burton, and James had already asked me for a divorce. All I want now is to complete the separation with as much dignity and friendship as possible. James and I are still good friends, and I hope we will remain so. I did not go to Spain to try and effect a reconciliation. The home that you knew us in, David, we were only renting, and the lease ran out. James has now rented a new house and he was moving all of our things out of our old home. It was the right time for me to collect my things and sort them out."'

When Benson asked her what had gone wrong in the marriage, she told him that James was just not ready for it: "'His racing career put enormous demands on him and, at this stage, his career must come first. He tried awfully hard not to hurt me. Fortunately, everything has turned out for the best for all of us. James is happy and I am happy. It sounds corny, but put this down David, he [Richard] is a very special person and we are very, very happy together."'

Suzy confirmed to Benson that she and Burton intended to get married, but, because of the legal problems with various divorces, she didn't want to have it printed at that time. Benson agreed to this informal embargo.

The resulting story was another world exclusive for the *Daily Express* and it was covered over a double-page spread on Saturday 24th April. It was a genuine exclusive in the old tradition of Lord Beaverbrook, the late owner. Benson never saw Suzy again.

Over the spring, Burton telephoned Hunt several times in the interim to sort out the details of the divorce. Hunt was surprised how well they got along and was charmed by Burton, who he found was not at all like the man portrayed in the press. Hunt said: "He was a very nice guy, not at all the monster the press made him out to be. He called himself my father-in-law, and he's been a very nice father-in-law ever since."

With the divorce pending, Burton and Suzy made a trip to England so that each could meet their respective families. The meetings were a huge success. Burton and Suzy's father, Frederick Miller, became great friends and found that they shared similar interests. Miller, like Burton, was very well read and owned a considerable library of books, which Burton loved perusing. Sharing similar literary tastes, Burton and Frederick would go for long walks in the Hampshire countryside discussing books they had read and owned. Only Suzy's brother, John, who lived in Los Angeles, was absent but Burton did meet Suzy's twin sister, Vivienne van Dyke, and Vivienne's young daughter, Vanessa.

Equally, Suzy got on very well with Burton's Welsh family, and his sisters particularly admired the subtlety with which Suzy kept Burton from drinking. The Burtons and the Millers could not have been more compatible.

Whilst the Burton family met with her approval, many of his friends did not. In Marbella, Suzy had become accustomed to the people who surrounded James. She put up with them because they were mostly old school friends who had known him long before he was famous. But she was not prepared for the mass of hangers-on and sycophants that surrounded Burton. Where Hunt's friends had been quality people, she recognised Burton's camp followers as mostly low-quality individuals. She felt they just told him what he wanted to hear and encouraged him to drink. She got rid of them all, one by one – even upsetting Brook Williams, who had been responsible for their meeting.

Suzy found that she had also to get used to the many people who accidentally kept calling her Elizabeth. But these were mostly minor problems and, despite the age difference, Burton and Miller were a perfect foil for each other, providing exactly what the other needed.

Suzy was quite unambitious and didn't crave fame or fortune in the slightest. She wanted Burton for exactly who he was. Equally, Burton loved the quiet and unassuming, quintessentially English woman. He was delighted at the seemingly endless happiness she exhibited in sitting and listening to his stories and poetry, all of which were rather good. She was an all-attentive, all-adoring audience, and Burton loved it. He also loved listening to her play the piano, marvelling in her ability to play faultlessly any piece of music he chose.

She also kept him sober. Asserting that she planned to have children with him, she did her best to ensure that their father would be around to see them. Burton wasn't a pleasant drunk, and his personality would change for the worse after even one drink. She had been used to a drinker like Hunt, who simply became increasingly sillier as he drank. But Burton was an altogether different proposition, and she realised she had to keep him off it entirely. Burton did later readily admit that she had saved him from the brink of self-destruction.

In June 1976, the divorces of both Taylor and Burton and Hunt and Miller were formalised in Port-au-Prince, the capital of Haiti, in South America. There, foreigners could be divorced in a day, although the status was not always universally recognised.

Burton paid all the legal costs and, as predicted, Taylor took him for almost everything he had. Taylor even delayed signing the divorce papers until she got precisely what she wanted. Demanding and getting all the jewels, the paintings and almost all the property – everything she hadn't got in the first divorce two years earlier – Taylor left Burton with the half million dollars he had earned in 1976, since the split, and the three thousand books he kept in the library at his house in Switzerland. Taylor decided she didn't want the house, purchased by Burton in 1957, when he had first moved away from Britain.

After dealing with Taylor's demands, he signed a prenuptial agreement with Suzy that guaranteed her a million dollars in cash plus a suitable house if their marriage failed. After his divorce, however, he realised that he didn't actually have a million dollars in cash, so he bought her a half million dollar insurance policy on his life. She was well-provided for, and the divorce didn't cost Hunt a penny.

On Saturday 21st August, Suzy and Burton were married in Arlington, Virginia. Virginia was one of only three states in the United States that recognised a Haitian divorce. They exchanged simple gold bands, and the wedding service, conducted by Judge Frances Thomas Jr, lasted precisely four minutes. Almost immediately, they stopped using contraception and began trying for a child.

At the precise moment of their wedding, Hunt was celebrating in Scotland. He was playing golf at Gleneagles. No one who was witness to his demeanour that day would have believed he had just lost one of the world's most beautiful women to one of the earth's most seductive men. For the record, he told a local journalist: "Richard Burton came along and solved all the problems. I learned an awful lot about myself and life, and I think Suzy did too. We all ended up happy, anyway, which is more than can be said for a lot of marriages." For Hunt, it was the final release. As he said afterwards: "For the first time, I am mentally content with my private life. Suzy is largely responsible for that." Meanwhile, across the Atlantic, Burton gushed about his new wife to anyone who would listen. It was hard to believe that the new husband and the ex-husband were indeed talking about the same woman. It must have been the most pleasurable divorce and remarriage in history.

Burton simply couldn't have been happier after his marriage to Suzy. As he told journalists: "Although I like to be thought of as a tough, rugby-playing, Welsh miner's son, able to take on the world, the reality is that this image is just superficial. I am the reverse of what people think. Suzy is a crutch to me. Without Suzy, I might very easily have been dead. When I met her, I was on the edge of self-destruction and Suzy saved my life. I met her just when I was putting my hand up for help for the last time."

An amazing friendship then broke out between all the parties. Later, Elizabeth Taylor was in New York at the same time as Burton and Suzy. She had a new boyfriend, a screenwriter called Harvey Herman. The two couples went out to dinner twice and had a great time. In truth, however, Taylor never warmed to Suzy, mainly because Taylor could see how happy she made her ex-husband – a man with whom many thought she was still very much in love.

But Hunt truly liked Richard Burton, and would do anything to make him happy. When Burton and Suzy travelled to Marbella, they stayed with Lew Hoad, the former Wimbledon tennis champion, at his club – where Hunt and Suzy had first met. They socialised with Hunt whenever possible, invited him for dinner, and Hunt even brought Sean Connery along with him on one occasion to please Burton, thinking that he might enjoy having a fellow actor at the table. Bringing Connery turned out to be a mistake, as Burton and Connery soon discovered they had nothing in common. But Hunt and Burton generally got along really well together.

Burton also mixed easily with all of Suzy's friends. Although she denies it now, claiming they hardly knew each other, Bette Hill, the widow of Graham and mother of Damon, became one of Suzy's closest friends. They had met in 1974 on the Formula One circuits and were taken with each other. Suzy had rushed to Bette's side when her husband was killed in an aircraft accident in November 1975 and, equally, Bette had comforted Suzy during the split from Hunt. Suzy used to invite Bette Hill out with Burton to social occasions whenever they were in London. At the Evening Standard Drama Awards in 1977, Burton passed her a note that said: "Thank you for saving Suzy for me." The marriage was clearly a long-term commitment, and Suzy loved New York life and the arts. She loved going to dinner at the apartments of people like musician Leonard Bernstein. She got on very well with him, as she did also with composer Jay Alan Lerner, and moved easily in their company.

After the wedding, they moved into Burton's house in Celigny, and Burton bought a new holiday home in Puerto Vallarta. He had lived in Celigny, an unfashionable small quiet village near Geneva, with his first wife, Sybil, and then Elizabeth. The house was called Le Pays de Galles, which in translation means the 'Country of Wales.' It was an unpretentious house and had been extended over the years. Suzy extended it further and added her touches.

Burton had a grand piano installed for Suzy, and she played for at least two hours a day. Music filled the house whenever they were there. He spent most of the day reading and she was happy as his companion. When they had to travel to another location for filming, the only luxury Burton demanded in his trailers was a baby grand piano for Suzy to play.

The relationship thrived for the next five years, and Burton hardly ever drank. When he did fall off the wagon, Suzy quickly pulled him back up. On their fourth wedding anniversary, in August 1980, Suzy gave Burton a portable bookcase that held over 100 hardbacks and could be put on a plane just like an ordinary suitcase. It meant he could easily take part of his library with him when he travelled; he was overwhelmed with joy.

But, triggered by health problems, Burton's lifestyle soon changed. Like many people who reform and stop bad habits, he succumbed to terrible illness. In March 1981, the love story started to unravel.

They were in Los Angeles when Burton suddenly collapsed. He had chronic pains in his arms and was suffering from a viral infection. He was rushed to St John's Hospital in Santa Monica.

An expert neurosurgeon was flown across America, from Florida, to treat Burton. The diagnosis was serious: Burton was suffering from severe degenerative disorders in his cervical spine. He required immediate major surgery or the results would be fatal. However, the operation had to be delayed until Burton first recovered from the viral infection. The doctors in Santa Monica managed to keep him alive, and it was a full month later that a team of four surgeons operated on him.

What they discovered when they opened him up was grave. The whole of his spinal column was coated with crystallised alcohol. The surgeons had never seen anything like it. They had to scrape it off before they could rebuild the vertebrae in his neck. It was a dangerous and delicate operation, carrying with it the risk of paralysis.

Suzy camped at the hospital day and night, and Burton's family flew over from Wales during the recovery period. He was not expected to survive the operation but, somehow, he did. When he emerged from hospital, he was a physical wreck. Unable to take painkillers for his back due to their harmful side effects, Burton suffered huge discomfort in the aftermath of his operation.

The ramifications from the illness gradually started to destroy his marriage.

Burton became irascible and unpleasant, and Suzy struggled to cope as his nurse. He was a very difficult patient. Wracked with pain, Burton failed to appreciate Suzy's efforts to support him, and, by the time he resumed taking the painkillers, it was too late.

For the first time, Burton found his wife less than perfect, and her attentive ways were becoming a burden. She tried her best and seldom let him out of her sight, constantly running her fingers through his hair for assurance as she always had. She brought him chicken soup and tea continually, as it was all he could eat and drink. But they started to argue, and the arguments often became violent. Feeling the force of Burton's thunderous temper, Suzy became worn down by his constant abuse.

It was at this point that Suzy decided she had had enough. When he was back to full health, she left his side for the first time and rumours immediately circulated that there were marital problems. In truth, Suzy had finally reached the end of her tether and was exhausted after Burton had attacked her verbally one time too many. Finding him increasingly difficult to live with, Suzy simply began to fall out of love with him. The perpetual fight to keep him sober was a losing battle and, faced with the recognition that she had no future but as a widow if he continued to drink, she decided to bow out.

After a few weeks, she sent him a short telex saying she was not coming back and wanted a divorce. He was with the actor Franco Nero when he received the message and immediately went on a drinking session like none before. As he drank himself into oblivion, wanting to die, the torn-off telex from Suzy lay nearby.

When the news got out that Burton and Suzy were to divorce, there was immediate speculation that he and Elizabeth would get back together. Burton held a drunken press conference at the Dorchester Hotel in London, telling reporters: "Susan my wife? Taller than a ghost – and just as remote, I may say. She is so English; hopeless, hideously remote."

If there was any hope of getting back together with Suzy, these words had removed it. And the final straw was when Burton was reported to have been seen flirting with Elizabeth Taylor, who was on stage in London, and it emerged that they had spent a night together. Before that, Suzy would have returned to Burton had he asked her; but that sealed it.

At the beginning of 1983, Burton returned to Port-au-Prince in Haiti for a divorce from Suzy; much as he had seven years earlier when seeking a divorce from Taylor. Suzy was given US$1 million in cash and their holiday house in Puerto Vallarta as a settlement. He kept his home in Celigny and the rest of his money.

The reason for the quickie divorce soon became apparent; Burton, it seemed, now wanted to marry another – a pretty Englishwoman called Sally Hay, a film production assistant. 34-year-old Sally was even more attentive than Suzy but in a less intrusive and more intelligent way. He quickly married Sally when he returned from Haiti. But it was to be a brief union.

Suzy had built a new life for herself in California, but she was in England on Sunday 5th August 1984 when the news came through that Burton had died at his house in Celigny from a sudden brain haemorrhage the previous evening. Suzy was with her friend Bette Hill watching Bette's 24-year-old son Damon compete in a Formula Ford race.

Suzy was overcome with grief at the sudden news, and Bette was at a loss as to how to comfort her. Out of desperation, she phoned Alan Jay Lerner, the 66-year-old world-renowned composer who lived in Chelsea, London, with his wife, the young actress Liz Robertson. Robertson, who was only 30, was also a great friend of Suzy's. At their home, the Lerners soothed the grief-stricken Suzy as much as they could and put her to bed with a tranquiliser.

The following day, Suzy was composed enough to telephone Sally Hay. Hay told her exactly what had happened, and the two women spent a long time on the phone reminiscing about Burton's life. It seemed that, upon reflection, Suzy now deeply regretted the divorce and wished she had been there in his final moments – she had truly loved him.

But Suzy was sensible enough to agree not to attend the funeral in Celigny, and decided to mourn Burton at a memorial service at the Wilshire Theatre in Los Angeles to be held on 24th August.

Hunt was in Germany at the Nürburgring, commentating on the race for the BBC that day. It was an emotional race for him as he watched his friend Niki Lauda, now driving for his old team McLaren, desperately battling with his teammate Alain Prost for the race and the world championship; it was just as he and Niki had done eight years earlier.

When he heard the news of Burton's death, Hunt tried immediately to contact Suzy, knowing that she would be overcome with grief. Failing to get through, he didn't manage to speak to her until a few days later. As he drove away from the Nürburgring that night, he reflected on how his life had indeed turned full circle. It had been a desperately sad day.

SHUNT

CHAPTER 19

The first win 1975
An instant injection of credibility

James Hunt was gunning to win a Grand Prix in 1975. The 27-year-old was now Formula One's established golden boy, but he had never won a Grand Prix and in truth, few pundits expected he would ever do so.

He had won a Formula One race in 1974 – the Daily Express International Trophy at Silverstone – but it was non-championship and didn't count. Moreover, Hunt readily admitted that the victory at Silverstone was down to his Firestone tyres, which had been infinitely superior to the Goodyears. The truth was that the 1974 Hesketh 308 hadn't been much of a car, but on the Firestones it was as good as any other that day. For 1975, though, as Firestone withdrew from Formula One, the team was forced onto Goodyears.

But money dominated the early months of the year. The team badly needed to win a Grand Prix in order to secure its future credibility as a top team. But the obstacles were multiplying. In 1975, Lord Hesketh stopped funding the team and told Bubbles Horsley he would have to rely only on what money was in the bank, plus prize money and sponsorship, to sustain the team.

Formula One was costing Hesketh nearly US$600,000 a year; a price he was no longer prepared to pay. Development costs for the car and driver salaries were half of that. Such costs hadn't existed when the team started in 1973. Moreover, Harvey Postlethwaite planned another new car for 1975 and was spending US$160,000 designing the new Hesketh 308C. Hunt was being paid a retainer of US$150,000 a year to drive the car. Having now created a monster that was financially out of control, Hesketh felt powerless to stop it.

The economic downturn seriously affected Hesketh's businesses, and he soon ran out of cash. There were no longer millions in the bank. A private individual, however enthusiastic, could not afford that sort of outlay on his own. The amount was close to what the giant Philip Morris tobacco company was spending on its participation in Formula One. Faced with the high expenditure coupled with the weakening US dollar, the Lord declared the need for Hesketh Racing to become self-supporting.

Hesketh talked a lot about the lack of money at the beginning of 1975. In previous years, he had found it vulgar; but no more. After two years of uncapped spending, Hesketh signalled an end to the good times for the team: "Entertainment is being cut to a minimum. Yachts are out, and all the money available is being spent on the racing car. We'll still have fun, though perhaps fun is now related to success."

Acknowledging that 1974 had not been a good year for the team, he said: "We did very badly last year and I can't afford a repeat of that performance. We have got to win some races and money, or else." Hesketh sold his helicopter and, realising he had to set an example, began driving a Vauxhall car supplied by Hunt's sponsor. In lieu of cash, Horsley gave Hunt Lord Hesketh's personal Porsche 911 Carrera road car as part payment of his salary. Hunt took it to Spain, lest the Lord changed his mind and tried to claim it back.

Hesketh was serious when he told the team they must win races in 1975 to survive. The prize money from FOCA for winning a Grand Prix was worth an extra US$30,000 a time to the team. Without sponsors, the team could only survive by earning more prize money. For reasons best known to himself, Hesketh didn't want any sponsor's names on his car. But any other form of income was acceptable.

For much of the season, Hesketh became a two-car team for the first time. It was all about money and it kept the team alive by hiring out a second car to rent-a-drivers. Alan Jones, Torsten Palm, Harald Ertl and Brett Lunger all participated in the rent-a-driver scheme. Their wealthy backers ponied up as much as US$15,000 a race to rent out the team's second car. Between them, these four drivers effectively paid the bills for the 1975 season.

Bubbles Horsley took full advantage of the demand and was wheeling and dealing to keep the team alive. He managed to sell 12 races to four drivers in 1975, bringing in nearly US$150,000 – half of the team's costs. In Monaco, he even ran a third car and had two paid drivers. Horsley's efforts were aided by the exchange rate, with the rapid decline of the value of the British pound enabling foreign sponsors to get a very good deal out of Formula One. But nobody in the team cared about the second drivers. They just wanted the money to spend on Hunt's car.

The team was also helped by the times. 1975 was the last of an era of low-cost Formula One, in which teams could race for a season for as little as US$200,000. From 1976 onwards, costs exploded and almost doubled in one year. They doubled again by the end of the decade.

Hesketh also broke new ground by being the first Formula One team to get into merchandise sales as a serious money-making venture. They began selling replicas of the iconic clothing items worn by the team at races. Tens of thousands of t-shirts with the Super Bear logo were sold to fans, and profits from sales of such merchandise contributed at least US$30,000 to that year's budget. Horsley can remember taking cash from the sale of the t-shirts to pay for an urgent engine rebuild at Cosworth. Hunt had been wearing a patch on his overalls which read: 'Sex is a high-performance thing', which helped propel merchandise sales even higher.

Hunt's salary was also vulnerable to the cutbacks. He had agreed a salary of US$150,000 for 1975 but knew it was unlikely to be paid. He also knew it was too much money. So Hunt was forced to earn his own money away from the tracks. He was able to charge something like US$3,000 to US$5,000 a day for personal appearances and, since there were only 14 races in 1975, he had plenty of free days to sell. To help the team pay its bills, Hunt also let Horsley keep his share of the prize money, which came to US$70,000. It was eventually paid back to Hunt in instalments the following year. And the Porsche officially became Hunt's when Horsley sent him the logbook.

Horsley finally managed to get a budget together and the team now looked forward to going racing.

In truth, Hunt's status as a driver was outgrowing the team. He did occasionally get above himself and act like a superstar. When that happened, Hesketh and Horsley told him they were seriously considering hiring a cheaper driver who might win them some races. The barb was aimed in the right direction and was semi-serious.

Lord Hesketh was an amazing character. He may have occasionally acted like a buffoon, but in reality he was a very perceptive individual. He recognised that his driver was enjoying his fame and indulging in life's pleasures perhaps just a little too much. But, in truth, Hesketh had long ago realised that 1975 was going to be his last year in Formula One and he dearly loved his driver and wanted more than anything for him to succeed with another team after he had left. He was determined that Hunt leave the team in the very best shape for the future.

Hesketh was no prude and was prone to indulgence himself, but seeing that his driver was indulging to excess, Hesketh said: "The trappings of his style of life don't necessarily interfere with his job of being a racing driver, but possibly they do with winning races. Yes, sure, he has the raw talent, but so does everybody else in this game. Other qualities must be added beyond talent. If he doesn't work out, we can always find another driver."

The words were spoken in earnest, and there is little doubt that Hunt was chastened by him. Despite his fame, he knew that if Hesketh dumped him, there was no guarantee he could get a drive elsewhere.

The season started at the Argentinian Grand Prix on 12th January. Inflation was rampant in Argentina and there had been some doubt whether the race would take place. The race organisers were desperately short of cash and only just managed to pay the teams their starting money. Hunt was quiet all weekend and focused entirely on his racing, seemingly aware that 1975 was a make-or-break season for him. In his first race on Goodyear tyres, Hunt qualified sixth on the grid driving a modified car that was dubbed the Hesketh 308B.

The new chassis was a vast improvement on the old, and in the race he went from sixth to third and then overtook Niki Lauda's Ferrari to be second to pacesetter Emerson Fittipaldi's McLaren-Ford. Hunt mounted a furious challenge on Fittipaldi but fell back at the end, coming in six seconds shy of the Brazilian.

He could so easily have won, but second place at the opening race was a brilliant start to the season. It came with US$14,000 prize money. The money helped pay for the team's two-week stopover in South America until the Brazilian Grand Prix on 26th January.

As soon as the race was over, Hunt and Fittipaldi – along with Suzy and

Fittipaldi's wife, Maria Helena – boarded a light plane and headed for Fittipaldi's beach house on the Brazilian coast. The house became Hunt's favourite place, to which he would return many times, but now, on his first visit, he launched into all the available activities, including tennis and running on the beach. Fittipaldi, astonished at Hunt's high level of fitness, said: "James was always very fit physically, very trim and one of these drivers who surprised everybody when he got to Grand Prix racing."

The Fittipaldis and the Hunts were great friends, as Fittipaldi recalls: "I spent quite a lot of time with Suzy. She was a great lady and I enjoyed James and Suzy together."

For Hunt and Suzy, it was to be the last truly great time they spent together as a couple. When the time came, they all boarded the plane and flew to São Paulo for the serious business of the Brazilian Grand Prix on 26th January.

The 1975 event was significant because it would mark the final race of Graham Hill's long driving career; he would be forced into retirement shortly afterwards. Hill had started his own team two years earlier, sponsored by Embassy cigarettes, and was running a couple of Lola cars built for him by Eric Broadley.

Hunt and Hill were great friends and shared the same outlook on life. Hill's wife Bette had also struck up a friendship with Hunt's wife, Suzy. The relationship would endure for many years, even after the Hunts were divorced and long after Graham Hill was dead.

Hunt qualified seventh on the grid alongside Jody Scheckter's Tyrrell-Ford. It was a surprise when relative newcomer Jean-Pierre Jarier put his Shadow-Ford car on pole position. Hunt brought the Hesketh home in sixth and fought off Mario Andretti driving the American-built Parnelli-Ford.

Hunt returned from South America having earned the team nearly US$22,000 in prize money and seven world championship points. But, most importantly, he had established Hesketh racing as front runners in 1975 and placed the team high up in the Goodyear pecking order for tyres.

A five-week gap until the South African Grand Prix, on 1st March, gave the team plenty of time to prepare the car. But qualifying was disappointing, as Hunt managed only 12th after his Ford Cosworth engine blew up. In the race, fuel feed problems put him out on lap 54 and Jody Scheckter won his home Grand Prix in his Tyrrell-Ford, now back in four-wheel configuration.

Hunt returned to Marbella for another six-week gap before the Daily Express International Trophy non-championship race marked the start of the European season, on 13th April. The gaps in the calendar enabled him to earn some money by making personal appearances. He earned nearly US$25,000 in those six weeks.

At Silverstone, Hunt dominated the race from pole position. He beat back challenges from Lauda, Fittipaldi, Peterson and Reutemann. But on lap 26, after setting the fastest lap of the race, he suffered another engine blow up. Lauda eventually won from Fittipaldi after Hunt retired.

He may not have gone on to win, but the morale boost from Silverstone had a wonderful effect on Hunt and the team. His dominance had been total, and the team went to the Spanish Grand Prix believing they could win it. The money situation had also eased, as Horsley was starting to run the rent-a-drivers scheme in the spare car. He did a deal with Harry Stiller to run Alan Jones in a car. The US$15,000 came in very handy.

But the Spanish Grand Prix at the Montjuïch Park circuit in Barcelona was fraught to say the least. The first day of qualifying was abandoned after it was found that many of the steel Armco barriers round the track were loose after the bolts hadn't been tightened. It was partially fixed overnight, but not to the drivers' satisfaction.

The race organisers then threatened the teams with legal action if they did not race. Fearful of the cars being impounded by the courts, the team principals ordered their drivers onto the track. But many of the barriers were still loose and the circuit was fundamentally unsafe in almost every respect.

World champion Emerson Fittipaldi was furious. He drove the requisite minimum three laps at very low speed before pulling off into the pits. To placate his drivers, team principal Ken Tyrrell got some spanners and went out himself to help fix the barriers.

Fittipaldi announced he wouldn't race and left for the airport to fly home to Brazil. Hunt qualified third behind the two Ferraris of Lauda and Regazzoni. The Ferrari team had debuted their new car, the 312T, and it had proved stunningly quick straight away.

At the start, there was an accident involving Andretti, Regazzoni, Lauda and Patrick Depailler, which enabled Hunt to lead the race for the first six laps. Wilson Fittipaldi and Arturo Merzario withdrew their cars straight away.

Hunt's lead only lasted for six laps before his car was pitched off into the barriers along with the cars of Mark Donohue and Alan Jones; all of them had spun on oil that had been left behind when Jody Scheckter's Tyrrell-Ford blew up. It was to be a race marked by accidents – no less than eight of them.

The race was then led by German Rolf Stommelen in the Lola-Ford car of Graham Hill's team. But after two laps, the rear wing broke off and the car rammed the barrier head-on. It bounced off across the track into the barrier on the other side of the road, collecting Carlos Pace's Brabham along the way. It was then launched over the barrier into a spectator enclosure. Four people, including a fireman, a photographer and two spectators, were killed. Stommelen cracked two ribs and broke his leg and wrist.

Ironically, the accident occurred on a stretch of track where the Hill mechanics had tightened up the barrier fixing bolts.

The race continued for four more laps after the Stommelen accident, and Jochen Mass inherited the lead in his McLaren-Ford. Upon realising the seriousness of the situation, the organisers stopped the race. Mass was declared the winner and Jacky Ickx's Lotus-Ford second. As the race had lasted only half distance, Mass received half points.

It was a race best forgotten, and so the Formula One circus headed for Monaco on 11th May. The future of Formula One was at stake following the Spanish race. With the organisers and the FIA panicking, extra guard rails and catch fences were erected, some kerbing was remodelled and the chicane modified.

For safety reasons, the FIA decided that only 18 cars would be allowed to start around Monte Carlo's narrow streets.

Graham Hill realised he wasn't going to qualify and gave up trying; Niki Lauda got pole and shared the front row with Tom Pryce's Shadow-Ford. The Shadow car was suddenly competitive and Pryce's teammate, Jean-Pierre Jarier, was on the second row. Hunt qualified 11th in one of his poorest-ever performances at Monaco.

It was raining at the start and Lauda led the field on wet-weather tyres. As the track rapidly dried, Hunt quickly stopped to change onto slick tyres, anticipating a drying of the track surface. The team was very slow putting on the new wheels, dissipating his advantage. The same happened to Ronnie Peterson. Lauda led by 15 seconds from Emerson Fittipaldi and Carlos Pace, with incidents going on all around the track. One of these was Hunt's accident on lap 64, where Mass came up behind him and forced him off the track; the Hesketh touched the barrier very hard. Instead of walking back to the pits, Hunt stood by the wreck of his Hesketh shaking his fist at Jochen Mass.

In the last laps, Lauda's oil pressure faded and Fittipaldi closed in. With three laps left, the gap was 2.75 seconds. However, as the two-hour maximum race time limit had been reached, the race was stopped. Lauda's win was Ferrari's first Monaco Grand Prix win in 20 years.

The Belgian Grand Prix on 25th May marked the debut of Graham Hill's protégé Tony Brise. Brise was to prove stunningly quick right from the start of his career. Lauda got pole from Carlos Pace's Brabham-Ford and won the race from Jody Scheckter's Tyrrell-Ford. Hunt went out on lap 16 with his gearbox shattered.

In Sweden, a few weeks later, Lauda completed a hat trick of victories. Since the introduction of his new Ferrari 312T car, Lauda had been untouchable; man and machine were at one. Oddly, Vittorio Brambilla in a March-Ford took pole position and led for the first 16 laps. A variety of cars took up the chase, but Lauda overtook them all. Hunt lost all his brakes on lap 22 and retired for the second race in succession, earning very little prize money.

The two retirements had a big effect on Hesketh's finances. With its minimal income, every thousand dollars counted, and as Horsley ducked and dived to keep the team alive, he thought Hunt wasn't taking it seriously enough. Horsley and Hunt came the closest they ever would to falling out. He told him the future of the team was perilous and he needed extreme performance. His concern was not without cause, as Horsley told Hunt's biographer Gerald Donaldson: "If he wanted to be on the piss all night, that was his business, as long as it didn't affect his driving. What we tried to do was focus where discipline was needed." He added after a pause: "And we did have to discipline him in both his racing and in his private life. Anyone outside your life can see you much clearer than you can perhaps see yourself. On that basis we were able to see, on occasions, that he was leading the kind of lifestyle that would not help his driving."

After Sweden, Horsley was on a mission. Back at the Easton Neston stables, he gathered the mechanics together and told them the dire position of the team. He was already running the team as an incredibly lean operation, with only 20 employees. Hunt was also at the meeting, and Horsley told him he had to muck in and quit playing the superstar. Realising it was a battle for survival, Hunt knew that the best tonic would be to win a Grand Prix. By mid-1975, the whole of the Hesketh team was well aware that it had never won a Formula One Grand Prix, and it was starting to grate.

Hunt said at the time: "There was a feeling that perhaps my living out of the country had caused a schism in the team. So now, I'm going to be coming back between races on a regular basis to just go up and visit the shop. I'm not sure anything really valuable will come of it, but there's got to be an intangible benefit to seeing the lads, keeping closer together."

The next race was in Holland. But as the team's motorhome and truck set out from Towcester for the short trip across the channel to Zandvoort, the Dutch Grand Prix showed no prospect of being about to deliver the team anything. In fact, Zandvoort's fluid, high-speed design suited the Ferraris perfectly, and so it proved as Niki Lauda and teammate Clay Regazzoni wrapped up the front row of the grid with ease. But Hunt was third-fastest, and half a second shy of the Austrian. He was the best of the rest.

When it started raining before the start, Horsley knew the team had a chance from its high grid position. He looked up at the sky and saw a tiny patch of clear sky. Just as the mechanics had been about to change the dry weather set-up on the car to wet, Horsley ordered that they leave it, believing the weather would clear up.

So whereas Hunt started with wet tyres and a dry set up – a severe disadvantage especially whilst he remained on the deep grooved wet tyres – the rest of the grid did the opposite. Horsley told Hunt that the moment the track began to dry, he was to come into the pits to change to slick racing tyres.

The cars were obscured in spray at the start. Lauda jumped into an early lead on the very wet track, pursued from the second row by Jody Scheckter's Tyrrell-Ford. Regazzoni was third, ahead of Hunt. That order remained for the first seven laps, with Hunt keeping an eye on the sky overhead. On the seventh lap, two dry strips appeared on the track and he quickly veered into the pits for the dry-weather slick tyres. It was a bold gamble. "The track was starting to dry quite quickly," he recalled, "but there were only two dry strips to begin with, with slippery wet stuff either side, which made it tricky if you had to go off it to pass anyone. But I knew that switching tyres then was the right thing to do."

It was a trick he had pulled many times before, but never quite as successfully as this. But Hunt's bold decision didn't look immediately promising, as the Hesketh dropped down to 19th in the 22-car field. But as soon as all the others were forced to stop for dry tyres, the complexion of the race changed altogether. Hunt made up the lost ground hand-over-fist as he clung to the dry line wherever possible.

The Ferraris stopped last for tyres, with Lauda getting preference over Regazzoni.

As Lauda came out of the pits after his stop, it was not clear who would lead the race; it was to be the race's pivotal moment. Lauda got out just ahead of Hunt, but without any momentum at all. The momentum was all with Hunt.

Hunt was flying down the main straight and came into the braking area for the 180-degree Tarzan corner. While the Ferrari's tyres were not yet at working temperature, Hunt's tyres – fitted six laps earlier – were. The difference was crucial as Hunt steeled himself and got right on the Ferrari's tail. Slipstreaming, he darted out and got ahead halfway round the 14th lap. That put Hunt second behind Regazzoni, who had not stopped. When Regazzoni finally pitted for his dry tyres, Hunt took the lead. Sensing a momentous victory might be around the corner, the thousands of British onlookers who had travelled over for the race went absolutely wild.

But that was certainly not the view in the pit lane; everyone thought it a matter of a few laps before Lauda and Regazzoni reasserted themselves. And that is the way it might have been if fate had not intervened. Jean-Pierre Jarier, in his Shadow-Ford, obliged Hunt by getting in the way. Somehow, the mercurial Frenchman managed to put his Shadow-Ford ahead of Lauda. It was the start of a ferocious duel between Lauda and Jarier, enabling Hunt to pull away. Jarier managed to put a cushion of air between himself and Lauda. Instead of battling with Hunt, as he had been for 28 laps, Lauda found himself battling with a backmarker. The Shadow kept the Ferrari at bay as Hunt made the most of the opportunity.

Lauda's problem soon became clear. He was on slick tyres and the car was set up for the wet. He was running with a lot more rear wing downforce than either Hunt or Jarier, which negated his power advantage. Both the Hesketh and the Shadow, which were also, as it turned out, on dry weather settings, had less wing and therefore were faster on the straights regardless of any power disadvantage of the Ford Cosworth engine. As Hunt said: "[The Ferrari] really wasn't any quicker on the straight than me."

On the 44th lap, Lauda finally squeezed past Jarier into second place. With 31 laps left in which to catch and pass Hunt, Lauda closed in for the kill. Coming under severe pressure, the Englishman looked to be facing a wretched task, as Hunt remembered: "I just settled myself down and focused on avoiding mistakes, and I was damned if I would let Lauda by." Lap after

James Hunt relaxes with a beer on the pit counter at the 1973 Austrian Grand Prix at Österreichring. He could scarcely believe the success he was having with a customer March-Ford 731 car.

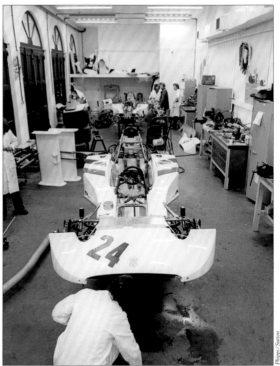

The birth of the Hesketh 308 in January 1974

Above left: The cover of the book printed by Bubbles Horsley for the launch of the team's first Hesketh chassis, the Hesketh-Ford 308.

Above: The Hesketh team work on the new Hesketh 308 chassis at Easton Neston headquarters in late April. The car was not race ready for the first two Grands Prix of the championship, so the March-Ford 731 was used instead.

Left: Dr Harvey Postlethwaite, designer of the Hesketh 308 at work at Easton Neston, in Northamptonshire.

The Brazilian Grand Prix opens the 1974 season

Right: Hunt signs autographs in the paddock next to a bikini-clad fan after the Brazilian Grand Prix on Sunday 27th January. It was a disappointing race as the March-Ford 731 handled badly on the sticky Interlagos tarmac.

The South African Grand Prix at Kyalami, 1974

Left: Playing tennis at the Kyalami Ranch Hotel with Abe Siegel on the weekend of the South African Grand Prix at the end of March 1974.

Above: Hunt with Mike Hailwood at the Kyalami Ranch Hotel. The two drivers found they were kindred spirits and enjoyed hell raising together whenever they could.

The Daily Express International Trophy at Silverstone

Left: After a stunning qualifying session, Hunt drives the Hesketh-Ford 308 to victory on race day at the Silverstone International Daily Express Trophy on 7th April 1974.

Left: Hunt receives his trophy on the podium. He had driven the entire race with the sharp stub end of the gear stick embedded in his hand.

Left: Hunt sits stranded in his Hesketh–Ford 308 after a broken rose joint forces him to retire on lap 46 during the Belgian Grand Prix at Nivelles circuit on Sunday 12th May 1974.

Right: James Hunt shows he hasn't lost his touch and duels with Niki Lauda for third place on Sunday 9th June. After 20 laps, Hunt passed Lauda and finished in third place, scoring his first podium finish of the 1974 season.

Below: Hunt takes part in a charity cricket match at Brands Hatch following the British Grand Prix on 20th July 1974. Back row from left: John Watson, Guy Edwards, Mike Hailwood, James Hunt, Graham Hill, Patrick Depailler, Peter Gethin and David Purley. Sitting from left: Jody Scheckter, Derek Bell, Niki Lauda, Jackie Stewart, Ronnie Peterson, Jochen Mass and Denny Hulme.

Phipps / Sutton

Charity Cricket Match in 1974

Peter Nygaard

Left: James Hunt stands with his fiancée Suzy Miller in his specially modified pair of racing boots at Monza on the 9th September 1974. Despite high hopes after his podium in Austria, Hunt only made it to lap two before his engine blew up.

Above: James Hunt and Mike Hailwood raced together for two years in 1973 and 1974 before Hailwood retired from Formula One. They both had the same outlook on life and got together socially as often as they could.

Below: In the paddock before the Canadian Grand Prix on 22nd September 1974, drivers and team principals, including James Hunt (far left), gathered for a briefing before the race.

The United States Grand Prix on Sunday 9th October 1974 was the championship showdown

Left: Stirling Moss with James Hunt at Watkins Glen on the day of the final race of the 1974 world championship. Three drivers – Clay Regazzoni, Emerson Fittipaldi and Jody Scheckter – all had a chance of being crowned world champion that day.

Right: Lord Hesketh, otherwise known as *Le Patron*, watches as the Hesketh mechanics prepare the Hesketh 308 at Watkins Glen. Hunt went on to finish third in the race.

Above: Chaos on the podium at Watkins Glen in 1974 as the championship is decided in Emerson Fittipaldi's favour. Race winner Carlos Reutemann celebrates while second placed Carlos Pace is interviewed by ABC commentator, Jackie Stewart. James Hunt was third and is congratulated by Marie-Helena Fittipaldi, the new champion's wife.

Phipps/Sutton

The Hesketh Racing team start the 1975 season under severe financial strain

Left: Lord Hesketh broke new ground by becoming the first Formula One team to sell merchandise. Tens of thousands of Super Bear t-shirts were sold in 1975, contributing at least US$30,000 to the year's budget.

The 1975 Argentine Grand Prix in Buenos Aires

Right: James Hunt passes a marshal's post at the Argentine Grand Prix on Sunday 12th January. It was a brilliant start to the season as he claimed second place from Niki Lauda and finished behind reigning champion Emerson Fittipaldi.

Right: Hunt enjoys a game of backgammon with Graham Hill by the swimming pool at the Kyalami Ranch hotel. The hotel, situated right by the track, was a favourite haunt of drivers.

Below: James Hunt sits in the pits as mechanics work on his car at the Belgian Grand Prix on Sunday 25th May 1975. He retired from the race on lap 15 with a shattered gearbox.

James Hunt's first Formula One win at the 1975 Dutch Grand Prix

Hesketh Racing supporters run onto the track as Hunt wins.

James Hunt leads Niki Lauda at Zandvoort on Sunday 22nd June 1975. The team foresaw the changing weather conditions.

Above: The Hesketh team mascot, Super Bear, at Zandvoort.

Below: Pure joy as he celebrates the first Grand Prix victory of his career at the Dutch Grand Prix, with second placed Niki Lauda and third placed Clay Regazonni.

Phipps/Sutton

Another podium finish at the French Grand Prix

Left: Sitting in the cockpit of the Hesketh-Ford 308 at the Paul Ricard circuit on Sunday 6th July. In order for the team to compete in the French Grand Prix, Bubbles Horsley sold Lord Hesketh's Rolls Royce to raise funds.

Below: Lord Hesketh and James Hunt unveil the new Hesketh 308C during the British Grand Prix weekend in July 1975 at Easton Neston.

Rainer Schlegelmilch

A morale boost for the team at Silverstone

Rainer Schlegelmilch

Above: Fans of James Hunt show their support at his home Grand Prix in Silverstone on Sunday 19th July 1975. He dominated the race from pole position but retired on lap 25 when his engine blew up after setting the fastest lap of the race.

Left: With team manager Bubbles Horsley at the British Grand Prix. Despite the retirement, spirits were high in the Hesketh team after his dominant performance.

The German Grand Prix at Nürburgring, 3rd August 1975

James Hunt's Hesketh 308 flies over a hump at Nürburgring. He retired on lap ten after a wheel came off the car.

Rainer Schlegelmilch

Right: American driver Mark Donohue was involved in an accident in qualifying which killed both himself and a marshall after his car plunged into catch fencing.

Mixed emotions at the Austrian Grand Prix, 1975

Far right: (From left) Second placed James Hunt. Race winner Vittorio Brambilla and third placed Tom Pryce on the podium after a rain-shortened race at Österreichring on Sunday 17th August.

Left: James Hunt talks with Tony Brise (centre) and Ronnie Peterson at the Italian Grand Prix on Sunday 7th September.

The race saw the unveiling of the Hesekth 308, which in hindsight was a luxury the team could have done without. James Hunt finished fifth and Niki Lauda third, which was enough to secure the Austrian the 1975 world championship.

Below: James Hunt with three fans at the United States Grand Prix, Watkins Glen, on Sunday 5th October where he finished fifth.

Phipps/Sutton

James Hunt is unveiled as McLaren's new driver at the end of 1975

Left: James Hunt sits in the McLaren-Ford M23 with team principal Teddy Mayer (left) and McLaren team manager Alistair Caldwell (right) after being announced as their new driver for the 1976 season.

Above: His first Grand Prix drive in the new six speed gearbox McLaren-Ford at Interlagos, Brazil.

Hunt wins first pole position at the Brazilian Grand Prix

Below: Teddy Mayer speaks to new recruit James Hunt at the Interlagos circuit on Sunday 25th January 1976. Mayer was astonished when Hunt secured his first pole position for McLaren with one flying lap. He spun out of the race on lap 33 with throttle problems.

Phipps/Sutton

Above: James Hunt with Niki Lauda at Kyalami on Sunday 6th March 1976. Hunt finished second behind Lauda in his second race for McLaren. Any doubts the McLaren team had about their new driver completely disappeared.

An unfavourable impression is left at the United States Grand Prix

Above: At the United States West Grand Prix on Sunday 28th March 1976. After being knocked out on lap four due to a collision with Patrick Depailler, Hunt stood at the side of the track shaking his fist and hurling abuse at the French driver.

Right: James Hunt, Alan Jones and Harald Ertl take an interest in an adult cinema at the Long Beach circuit, USA.

A marked change in performance and demeanor at Silverstone

After winning the Graham Hill Trophy on Sunday 11th April 1976, James Hunt appeared on the podium with Bette Hill, the widow of racing driver Graham Hill.

Stripped of a victory at the Spanish Grand Prix

Above left: Hunt crosses the chequered flag on his first victory for McLaren. Post-race scrutineering deemed the car too wide and therefore illegal according to the new race regulations, disqualifying Hunt from the race.

Above far right: James Hunt with his great friend Jody Scheckter at the Spanish Grand Prix at Jarama on Sunday 2nd May 1976.

Right: Hunt on the podium at Jarama with the King of Spain and Gunnar Nilsson before finding out the news of his disqualification from journalists. Hunt's victory was subsequently reinstated in the season after an appeal.

The McLaren-Ford M26 is unveiled in July 1976

Left: James Hunt sits in the new McLaren M26 as it is unveiled to the press. Beside him is teammate Jochen Mass (back left), McLaren team designer Gordon Coppuck (front left), McLaren Team owner Teddy Mayer (back left) and Patty McLaren, widow of the team founder Bruce McLaren. The car would not race.

1976 Monaco Grand Prix

Right: McLaren technical director Gordon Coppuck discusses set-up with Jochen Mass, James Hunt and Teddy Mayer at Monaco. The M23 was now uncompetitive after the team had concentrated so hard on ensuring the car was legal after their disqualification in Spain.

Phipps/Sutton

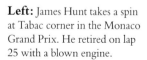

Left: James Hunt takes a spin at Tabac corner in the Monaco Grand Prix. He retired on lap 25 with a blown engine.

The British Grand Prix at Brands Hatch, Sunday 18th July 1976

Crossing the line, Hunt waves to the crowd after taking the chequered flag at Brands Hatch after the restarted race on Sunday 18th July 1976. His victory could not have been more popular with the 80,000 fans present.

The manoeuvre that caused all the trouble: A sequence of photos shot by David Phipps shows the collision between James Hunt and Clay Regazzoni which resulted in the race being stopped and restarted.

Right: Hunt chases down Lauda after the restart of the British Grand Prix. It took him 45 laps to catch his rival and overtake him.

Phipps / Sutton

Kind permission Andrew Frankl

Above: To the sheer delight of the partisan crowd, Hunt drove inside Niki Lauda on the 45th lap at Brands Hatch and passed him on the climbing approach to Druids Hill to take the lead of the 1976 British Grand Prix. He was never headed after that.

Left: Andrew Frankl, then a young journalist and photographer organised the demonstrations that led to James Hunt being reinstated in the race. As a youngster he had been involved in the Hungarian uprisings in 1956.

Above: Ferrari's Team Manager Daniele Audetto complains to the media about the controversial restart of the race and announces that he will appeal the result even though Ferrari had caused the startline accident.

Left: Hunt enjoying his British victory swigging from a bottle of Moët et Chandon champagne with another full bottle in reserve, which won't last long.

Below: Hunt celebrates his victory on the podium with Patrick Depailler (left) and John Watson (right) at the French Grand Prix at Paul Ricard, 4th July 1976.

Phipps/Sutton

lap, he kept Lauda at bay. His tactics worked and Hunt crossed the line on the 75th lap – just one second ahead. Hunt became the first Englishman to win a Grand Prix for four years since Peter Gethin in 1971.

Lauda said later he didn't try and get past Hunt in the end: "I didn't win because I wanted six points. I was driving politically for the world championship contender in those days, so six points were more important than nine." But it certainly didn't look like that as Hunt fended off Lauda during the race.

Whatever the truth of Lauda's statement, the chequered flag finally fell. Hunt had not only won his first Grand Prix and secured Hesketh's sole triumph, he had done so in style. Lauda was well beaten.

Hunt said immediately afterwards: "I could not have had greater pressure than I did in that race." And, as he remembered many years later: "I lacked experience leading races, which is why I cocked up a couple of times earlier that year. But now my education was complete. For once I didn't make any mistakes, and after that it became easier."

Lord Hesketh was in a champagne daze. Despite his brash proclamations at the start of each season, a Grand Prix victory was something he never really expected. As the winning car and driver mounted a lorry decorated with flowers, so too did the team patron. As they circled the track, on top of every sand dune, there were hundreds of union jack flags being waved by British fans delirious with joy that Hunt had won.

As the lorry rode past the pit lane, Lord Hesketh gave a minute-long two-fingered salute to the personnel of the mighty teams of Formula One, including Ferrari, McLaren and Brabham. They had lined up to watch the spectacle of what they regarded as an upper class hooray and an overbearing upper class lout, neither of whom had any business being in Formula One, actually winning a Grand Prix. It certainly didn't endear him to them, but now he could get away with it.

Hunt went straight back to the camp site, where his friends were staying amongst the sand dunes. Suzy had stayed home in Marbella and had missed her husband's triumph as well as the extraordinarily raucous party that went on late into the night.

For Lord Hesketh and James Hunt, it was the greatest day of their lives; the day their dreams came true. It had also been beneficial for Lord Hesketh's business interests: "James' win stood me in very good stead. A lot of people who thought I wasn't serious were disabused, and it made a lot of people's reputations and gave them opportunities they might not otherwise have had.

It gave me huge satisfaction."

Lord Hesketh told Gerald Donaldson that he still reaped the benefits many years later: "All these years on, it's an advantage because I now come across people whom I've never met, who were 20-ish then, who now run large institutions and who were Hesketh Racing fans. I wouldn't quite go as far as to say that it paid a dividend, but actually in the longer term of my life, it's been very useful; as well as being fun at the time." He added: "Even today, so many years later, that memory still gives me goose pimples."

For Hunt, the transition from loser to winner was even more significant. He came of age in Holland. He rose above his shortcomings and, in a rite of passage, resisted everything that Niki Lauda and Ferrari could throw at him to score a historic maiden Grand Prix victory in the red, white and blue car owned and built by Hesketh. Winning meant he had finally matured: "The race rounded off my education. I hadn't had the experience of leading races. At Zandvoort I laid that ghost to rest completely because, when the others are sitting behind, you can jolly well dictate your way of doing things. And Zandvoort was the completion of my training as a driver."

The public's perception of the team changed completely as Hesketh became a front of grid team.

But the victory in Holland masked serious financial problems. Few people knew that the team was on its very last legs when the trucks had left for Holland. Visits from bailiffs were only days away, while the British Inland Revenue department was making regular phone calls looking for its taxes.

The prize money Hunt won had been desperately needed to pay urgent bills and was gone completely by the Friday of the following week. Horsley then had to make a difficult decision: whether or not to pull the plug on the team. There wasn't enough cash even to travel to Paul Ricard for the French Grand Prix on 6th July.

As he sat at home pondering the issue, he had an idea. He went over to Easton Neston and found the log book for Lord Hesketh's Rolls-Royce. Knowing where there was a buyer, he sold the car for US$20,000. Horsley recalls simply: "We didn't have the money to go, and I saw it parked there."

In a moment of astonishing bravado, Horsley calculated that, since Hesketh rarely drove the car anymore, he would not miss it for a few weeks. Eventually, when the Lord did notice, Horsley simply told him the car was in for service: "Alexander said to me: 'Where's my Rolls-Royce?'" The subterfuge lasted until the end of the season, when Hesketh guessed what had happened.

Rather than being annoyed, he was rather impressed with Horsley's ingenuity in keeping the team afloat.

The money sustained the team for another month.

So, with a fresh US$20,000 in the coffers, Horsley was in high spirits when the team headed across France for the Paul Ricard circuit. Niki Lauda had been suffering from flu and was definitely not on top form, but it didn't stop him annexing pole position with Jody Scheckter's Tyrrell alongside him.

Scheckter had a new lightweight Tyrrell-Ford 007 with which he set a record top speed of 190 miles per hour on the straight. Hunt was third on the grid. Lauda led from Scheckter, Hunt and Mass. Hunt passed him on the eighth, and Lauda and Hunt maintained first and second to the finish. Lauda won by 1.6 seconds; second place was worth around US$22,000 to the team. For the moment, Horsley's short-term money worries were over.

For a short while, it even looked as though the situation might get better. A fortnight after Paul Ricard, on 19th July, the British Grand Prix was held at Silverstone. The race was significant because of three notable events: Graham Hill officially announced his retirement; the famous high-speed Woodcote corner was no more, with a new chicane in front of it for safety reasons; and a new lights starting system had been installed, to be used for the first time in any Grand Prix. The lights replaced the starter with the traditional national flag. Tom Pryce put his Shadow-Ford on pole. The Shadow team had been very competitive in 1975, but this was its finest moment. After the highs of Holland and France, Hunt actually had trouble qualifying and could only manage ninth on the grid.

From the start, Carlos Pace led from Pryce. Then Hunt led for eight laps, one of seven different drivers to do so, but a sudden cloudburst inundated the circuit and caused the race to be stopped. On the final lap, Jody Scheckter, Carlos Pace, James Hunt, and Mark Donohue crashed along with half the field. Fittipaldi was adjudged the winner, with Carlos Pace second and Jody Scheckter third. Hunt was fourth, although not running at the finish. Only Emerson Fittipaldi made it to the winner's podium. Ferrari protested the shortened race and the result was not confirmed until three days later.

None of the drivers were looking forward to going to the Nürburgring for the German Grand Prix on 3rd August. Since the previous race, the 14-mile track had been lined with steel Armco barriers and layers of catch fencing, but it was still dangerous. Hunt qualified ninth again and Lauda took pole with an incredibly brave lap that left everyone aghast. By lap 11, Hunt had retired after a wheel came off his car. Carlos Reutemann went on to win for Brabham.

The teams travelled to the Österreichring for the Austrian Grand Prix on 17th August. Niki Lauda delighted the home crowd by claiming his seventh pole position of the year.

Qualifying was marred by accidents and, during the final session, Mark Donohue crashed on a flat-out curve and his car plunged into the catch fencing. The car cut straight through and became hopelessly entangled. A trackside hoarding shattered into many pieces and two track marshals died instantly. Donohue was hit on the head with bits of flying catch fencing poles and the track was strewn with debris. Hunt stopped his car as another car crashed in front of him. It sent more bits of catch fencing flying everywhere – just missing Hunt's head.

Donohue, now fighting for his life, was taken to hospital with severe head injuries. He died three days later of a brain hemorrhage.

After the marshals were killed, the organisers considered cancelling the race but eventually decided against it. They went ahead with Lauda on pole, and Hunt beside him second fastest.

As the grid formed, it was raining on the far side of the track and wet tyres were mounted on all the cars. Lauda led off the start from Hunt and Patrick Depailler. Vittorio Brambilla shot through to third place.

By lap 15, Hunt held the lead for the fifth time in 1975. But when his Hesketh-Ford's engine started running on seven cylinders, Brambilla was all over him.

As the rain grew ever heavier, the Italian seized the lead and the race was brought to a halt on lap 29 as Brambilla took the flag. Having crossed the finish line, he became so exuberant he took both hands off the wheel and lost control of his car, slamming into the barriers as his March team celebrated victory.

Believing the celebrations to be premature, most of the other teams prepared for a restart. But, as the race had been stopped with a chequered flag, this was not to be and half points were awarded to all the finishers, including a jubilant Brambilla. At 37-years-old, Brambilla had won his first Grand Prix.

In the melee, Hunt was surprised to find he had placed second, earning the team another US$22,000 in much needed prize money. With the prize money, driver fees, and cash and asset sales, Horsley had scrambled together US$230,000. There would still be a deficit, but it was enough cash to get to the end of the season.

With cash in mind, the team entered the non-championship Suisse Grand Prix, held at Dijon on 24th August. There were 16 cars entered and Hunt qualified 11th and managed eighth place. Clay Regazzoni won in his Ferrari by around eight seconds from Patrick Depailler and Jochen Mass.

With the benefit of hindsight, Harvey Postlethwaite's new car, the Hesketh-Ford 308C, was a luxury the team could have done without. The car, which had cost the team US$150,000 to develop, was finally unveiled at Monza for the Italian Grand Prix on 7th September, the penultimate race of the season.

The Italian supporters were gathered in anticipation of Ferrari winning its first world championship in 11 years. Many Austrians came to Monza to support Niki Lauda and were delighted when Ferrari filled both slots on the front row of the grid, followed by Fittipaldi, Scheckter and Jochen Mass. Tony Brise delighted team owner Graham Hill by qualifying sixth in his Hill-Ford car. Hunt could only manage eighth in the new car and certainly would have done better in the old one.

On Sunday morning, it rained so hard the race was almost cancelled. At the delayed start, Clay Regazzoni led from Lauda and Jody Scheckter. There was a huge accident at the first chicane involving seven cars, of which five retired. It left the Ferraris 1-2 with Regazzoni leading from Lauda, and Fittipaldi passing Reutemann for third.

Right at the end, Fittipaldi overtook Lauda and split the Ferraris, as Lauda played it safe to make sure he secured the championship. Third was good enough, and Ferrari won the world championship for the first time since 1961 – and in front of its home crowd. Hunt finished fifth and took back a few thousand dollars in prize money to a grateful Horsley.

As the team packed up the cars and the crates to ship them to Watkins Glen for the United States Grand Prix on 5th October, there was no sense that it would be Hesketh Racing's last race. Hunt had not bothered to seek a drive elsewhere, and he confidently asserted that he would be driving for Hesketh Racing in 1976. He said: "We knew that there was no more money forthcoming from Alexander; he'd spent what he'd got for racing. But that didn't worry us too much because we felt that we were in a very good position with the success we had to get a commercial sponsor. Bubbles particularly wanted to do that because, of course, that was his future."

And Hunt believed it was his future as well. Horsley was his best friend and he loved his patron Lord Hesketh in the same way he did his parents.

Wanting to drive for the team for the rest of his career, he genuinely thought it could be a world championship contender. He also had absolute faith in the design talents of Harvey Postlethwaite.

Far from being down, the team flew across the Atlantic to New York in a good frame of mind and with high hopes for the future.

The rest of the grid might have expected Ferrari to wind back once the championship had been won, but Ferrari was in fact more determined. Having never won the United States Grand Prix, the team knew it represented a very important market for its road cars. Luca di Montezemolo, the team principal, ordered no expense to be spared to correct the historical anomaly.

Throwing caution to the wind, the team made every effort to win the race. Lauda easily got pole from Fittipaldi's McLaren-Ford. Hunt could only qualify 15th, but in the race worked his way up to fourth after a succession of retirements cleared his way.

Lauda got his victory.

THE FIRST WIN

SHUNT

CHAPTER 20

Nearly down and out of Formula One 1975

Saved by the man from Marlboro

J ames Hunt was down and out of Formula One at the end of 1975. When the season ended on 5th October of that year, he was effectively out of a drive. It was his own fault, of course, as the writing had been on the wall at Hesketh Racing since the end of 1974, when Lord Hesketh had effectively stopped funding the team. It had survived the 1975 season by using up funds left in the bank account, selling off assets, spending Hunt's prize money and renting out its spare car at races to drivers willing to pay. Hunt admitted as much to Nigel Roebuck years later: "From mid to late 1974, there was no more money really forthcoming from Alexander. He'd spent what he'd got for racing."

Although he was aware that a sponsor would be needed for 1976, Hunt knew little else of the financial difficulties at the time. However, with his retainer continually being paid late and eventually falling substantially into arrears, he didn't need Bubbles Horsley to tell him there were problems. Out of loyalty to Hesketh and Horsley, Hunt decided not to look for an alternative drive. And it was not only Hunt's but also Horsley's future which was at stake. Horsley had wagered his entire career on the survival of the team, as had the 20 or so people who worked at Easton Neston in the old stables.

Because of the success of the team, particularly after its first Grand Prix win, Hunt believed that a sponsor would be signed with relative ease: "It didn't worry us too much because we felt that we were in a very good position with the success we were getting. Bubbles particularly wanted to do that because, of course, it was his future. He knew there was going to be no long-term future with Alexander. He wouldn't just pay forever."

The truth was not only that Hesketh would not pay, but also that he could not pay. The UK£600,000 Hesketh had effectively spent on the team in his four years as a team entrant, from Formula 3 to Formula One, was his limit. In today's money, that is the equivalent of around UK£20 million and it was virtually all the liquid cash Hesketh had inherited from his father's trust fund four years earlier. Although his father had died when he was four, Hesketh had to wait until he was 21 to inherit.

When he set up the team in 1971, also at the age of 21, Hesketh was already running his own business conglomerate alongside it and imagined that the profits from the business would pay the team's bills and that the team would likewise promote the businesses. This business conglomerate model was a popular strategy in the 1970s and Hesketh initially enjoyed some success at it, but he was riding the wave of an economic boom that had begun in 1971 and was soon to come to an end. When the Arabs cut off the world's oil supply in late 1973, the global economy came to an abrupt halt and, by mid 1974, Hesketh's businesses were in serious trouble and he needed all the resources he could muster to keep afloat. Simply put, Hesketh, like many, was a brilliant businessman in boom times and a lousy businessman in a recession. And he wasn't alone. Business stars of the era, like Jim Slater and John Bentley, watched as the oil shock destroyed western economies and their companies collapsed. To Hesketh, the world had effectively stopped whilst Formula One sailed on obliviously. By early 1974, he no longer enjoyed owning his own team, and so the frivolities came to an end as well. Hunt said: "We raced off our earnings on the track and by a bit of ducking and weaving by Bubbles." As his ambitious business conglomerate slowly disintegrated, so too did the rationale of having a team to promote it.

Hesketh, in fact, was caught in a massive dilemma. He wanted to cut his losses, close down the team and clear out the stables, but he felt he owed a debt to Horsley and Hunt. If a debt was owed, it was very much the other way around, and the success of the team in 1975 made matters worse for Hesketh as it became increasingly impossible to close down a winning team.

Hunt remembered: "When it became totally obvious that there was no other way, we could have got sponsorship. Bubbles could have gone out and got sponsorship – he is very good at that. He would have got it had he been given the chance in June or July. But he was given more than assurances that a serious effort was being made in London. He was given reasonable proof and, as he was up in Towcester working 16 hours a day running the team and trying to survive on a shoestring, he didn't actually go down to London to check it all out. Alexander had been saying that he was looking for a sponsor for a year." Having come up with no prospects, Hesketh partnered with Horsley and began a more active search for sponsors. At first, Hesketh seemed genuinely keen on the scheme, saying: "They'll get a hell of an advertising campaign for a very reasonable investment."

But then began a bizarre game of cat and mouse between Horsley and an increasingly withdrawn Hesketh. Because of the team's success and the glamour of Hunt, finding sponsors willing to put up UK£250,000 proved to be little problem. It seemed that everyone wanted to be associated with the glamour boy Hunt. In fact, several deals got to the draft contract stage only for Lord Hesketh to find some reason not to conclude them.

Eventually, Hunt began to suspect that Hesketh didn't want a sponsor, either because he wanted to rid himself of the team altogether or he just couldn't stomach the idea of someone else taking it over: "Several deals came close to being signed, but he seemed to torpedo them just as they were about to happen. He'd get cold feet. He didn't really want to give it away."

Hunt thought later that Hesketh was suffering from a form of schizophrenia. He believed that one half of him wanted to continue while the other half didn't. It later became obvious that business problems were weighing on his mind and he couldn't think straight. Hunt said: "Whenever confronted with a commercial sponsor, he would shoot it out at the last minute because he couldn't quite handle it not being his team anymore. We had several sponsors ready to sign but he would not come to the meetings."

Hunt was desperately grateful to Lord Hesketh for what he had done for his career, as was Horsley, so they didn't confront him even as the situation grew increasingly more bizarre. And they continued to indulge him when, at midnight on 14th November 1975, a self-imposed deadline expired and the team was closed down.

Hunt says ruefully: "I am sure that sponsorship could have been arranged, although not at the eleventh hour. We had known for 18 months that we probably would not make it to the end of 1975. I don't think that Alexander really wanted a sponsor – for very understandable reasons. He wanted it to stay as it had been and, as he was hoping to get things together in his business, he didn't give sponsorship first priority."

The next day, Hesketh, Hunt, Horsley, Harvey Postlethwaite and the mechanics held a large press conference at Thruxton circuit in Hampshire and invited the team's fans to attend. The event was televised live on BBC's Saturday afternoon 'Grandstand' programme. To the delight of the crowd, Hunt did a few laps around Thruxton in his Dutch Grand Prix-winning Hesketh 308.

Upon being presented with a gold medal by The British Automobile Racing Club, Hesketh announced, with a somewhat bemused Hunt and Horsley looking on, that Hesketh Racing was over and the dream was dead. He said: "I'm a very lucky man in having enjoyed a friendship and a relationship with James Hunt to such an extent that he knew, several months ago, the problems that we had to face in racing next year. I am deeply grateful to James for having stayed when the going got tough. The fact that he has not secured his future drive for next year is because he believed in a dream that we all believed in. It was my honour and privilege, and still the greatest thing I ever took part in, to have been able to give James his chance." Hunt spoke afterwards: "All of us were plucked out of nowhere, particularly me. They showed great confidence in me which, considering my performance in Formula 3, was not strictly deserved. Yet they stuck by me and took me all the way. More particularly, they gave me a very happy period in my life and we've been a team of very close friends. That is something I feel will be difficult to replace." He added: "Hesketh Racing gave me and taught me everything in Formula One. And it was where my soul was."

The rest of Formula One was glad to see the back of Lord Hesketh. They had never forgotten the V-sign he had delivered them in Zandvoort.

Max Mosley wasn't among those relieved to see him go, but nor was he surprised when Lord Hesketh called a halt: "I think he had this image of being a gentleman racer, and well, of course, you just couldn't do that. Hesketh ran things in a different way. Of course, he got through a great deal of money so he was very popular with the press, but in the end the trustees put a stop to it. I just know that he ran out of money." That night, they all celebrated at Hesketh's London home in Eastbourne Terrace and forgot their troubles. Or at least they tried to.

There were only two drives available to Hunt for the 1976 season. The first was at the Lotus team, and that was far from definite. Like Hesketh, Lotus had suffered in the recession and had no money to pay its drivers. Its main asset was a contract with Ronnie Peterson, arguably the then-fastest driver in the sport. But Peterson's retainer from Lotus was US$250,000 a year and was more of a liability than an asset as a global recession raged.

At the end of 1975, team manager Peter Warr had hawked Peterson's Formula One contract around the Formula One paddock to the highest bidder in order to raise cash. Mario Andretti had been signed for the 1976 season, but Peterson's future was uncertain. There were no takers for Peterson's contract and, once he learned what Warr was doing, Peterson became disillusioned with the team. Sensing, but more likely hoping, that Peterson might leave, Warr opened negotiations with Hunt on the basis that he would agree to drive for nothing and be paid for each world championship point he scored. Andretti had already set a precedent by effectively agreeing to drive for nothing on the same basis.

The only problem was that Warr didn't much like Hunt, and the disdain was clearly mutual. But this did not stop Warr from inviting Hunt and his brother Peter out for lunch in London on a Sunday afternoon that November. The discussions went on for three hours as Warr tried to persuade Hunt to drive for nothing. Lunch was forgotten and, when Warr got to his feet to shake hands, no meal had been ordered. Warr left the restaurant without even mentioning food. According to Hunt, Warr didn't buy him lunch on purpose. As he remembered: "We went out to lunch, but didn't get any. That left me out looking for lunch in London at four o'clock on a Sunday afternoon." He said of the discussions: "They seemed to be of the opinion that their drivers shouldn't be paid. I had difficulty talking any sense to them at all."

In any case, it soon became apparent that Warr was determined not to have Hunt driving for Lotus and, after whispering in Colin Chapman's ear, he later signed the young Swedish up-and-comer Gunnar Nilsson. Hunt told people afterwards: "The meeting with Lotus comprehensively wasted three hours of my life." But Hunt wasn't a fool and knew he could use Warr's offer as leverage. He kept the illusion of a Lotus drive alive, even though that is all it was. He needed a negotiating tool to get another drive and a decent retainer with it.

Hunt's other offer was from the new, reconstituted Wolf-Williams team,

owned by Walter Wolf and Frank Williams. Williams had bought the Hes-
keth 308C that Hunt had driven in the last three races of 1975. Wolf and
Williams were now keen to see Hunt drive their blue and gold re-liveried
cars. In fact, when Bubbles Horsley had sold the two 308C cars to the Wolf-
Williams team, he had inferred that Hunt was part of the deal. But even
Hunt couldn't oblige Horsley and go along with it. Hunt believed that the
Harvey Postlethwaite-designed 308C was a terrible car. Although he had
finished in the points in all three races, he knew he had driven hard for little
reward. Believing the car was a dog, Hunt would only take the drive with
Wolf-Williams as a last resort. Still, the Wolf team was the only one offering
him a proper salary to drive.

Hunt's only other hope was Bernie Ecclestone, the Brabham team owner.
Ecclestone sensed Hunt might be out of a drive and wanted to keep him in
the sport. At the time, Ecclestone was just beginning to sell Formula One's
television broadcast rights and he sensed that Hunt would be a vital part
of that, especially in Britain. In the end, Ecclestone's instincts proved right
and Hunt emerged as the key to unlocking Formula One's true television
potential.

Ecclestone put his formidable mind towards getting Hunt a drive. He
proposed setting up a Brabham B-team whereby Hunt would drive a last
year's Brabham-Ford car with a Cosworth engine. For 1976, the works
Brabhams were contracted to run Alfa Romeo engines with the Italian car
maker paying the team's bills with sponsorship from the Martini & Rossi
drinks company. The cars would be driven by South Americans Carlos Pace
and Carlos Reutemann. But when Ecclestone asked the Italians for permission
to run Hunt in a separate team, they refused point blank. They weren't about
to have their Brabham dream team upstaged by a British playboy driving last
year's car and, in all likelihood, beating them. In the end, even Ecclestone's
genius couldn't make that deal happen. Hunt realised that Ecclestone had
placed himself in a difficult position: "I think Bernie was only doing it as a
matter of generosity to me."

And that might have been the end for Hunt in Formula One had it not
been for John Hogan. Hunt and Hogan were of a similar age and outlook
and had kept in touch since 1971 when they first met. Hogan liked Hunt's
view of motor racing as much as Hunt liked Hogan's take on sponsorship.

By 1975, Hogan had become head of sponsorship for Philip Morris
International, which had been set up to sell Marlboro cigarettes outside of

the United States. The Marlboro brand had been established outside North America by its motor racing sponsorship, which had been highly successful and very cost effective. Back then, Marlboro was playing brand catch-up in Europe and was using Formula One to get a toehold. With a budget of US$1 million a year to spend on Formula One, it was the title sponsor of the McLaren Formula One team. Hogan was in charge of making it happen and virtually had *carte blanche* from his bosses in Lausanne to get the job done.

Hogan remembers where Formula One was back then: "Emerson was king of the castle, closely followed by Niki." And the shrewd Hogan had both Emerson Fittipaldi and Niki Lauda signed up to Marlboro; Fittipaldi via the McLaren team and Lauda with a substantial personal contract said to be worth US$75,000 a year in itself. If Hogan couldn't put his Marlboro logos on the Ferrari then the next best thing was plastering them all over Lauda's race overalls and helmet, which he did.

But despite that, there was, and had been for months, doubt about how committed Emerson Fittipaldi was to the McLaren team for 1976. On paper, he was fully committed and had signed a contract for the 1976 season worth US$250,000 a year – along with Peterson's, it was the biggest salary in Formula One.

Aware of the contract, Hogan and McLaren team principal, Teddy Mayer, were certain that Fittipaldi would honour it. They were totally relaxed that Fittipaldi would drive. But Fittipaldi had three contracts with the team: one with McLaren; one with title sponsor, Marlboro; and another with the Texaco oil company, the secondary sponsor. Later it emerged that not all the contracts had been signed, making none of them enforceable. Still, there were enough signatures to stop him driving for anyone else as long as Marlboro paid him the US$250,000. But in reality, the last thing anyone wanted was an unhappy, highly-paid driver on their books.

Hogan openly admits he did not see Fittipaldi's defection coming and he is still not entirely certain whether Fittipaldi had signed the contract with Marlboro to drive for McLaren with true intent to do so. Certainly, as far as both Hogan and Teddy Mayer were concerned, signing one contract surely meant that he would honour the others as well. But Fittipaldi didn't see it that way. He believed his options were still open and was secretly negotiating with his brother Wilson and Brazilian sugar refiner Copersucar to drive for the Fittipaldi family Formula One team. The team had been founded the previous year by Wilson Fittipaldi. Hogan describes the contract confusion thus: "Emerson had signed, but not with the ferocity that modern drivers sign contracts. But Teddy was convinced, we were convinced he was going to drive." It hadn't even entered their minds that he wouldn't.

That Saturday night, the 22nd of November, Mayer was at home in Surrey when he got a call from Fittipaldi, who was in São Paulo, telling him he had just signed a contract with his brother Wilson to drive the Copersucar car in 1976. He would therefore not be driving a McLaren in 1976. He explained to Mayer that it had been his dream to drive for a Brazilian team with his name on the car.

Mayer listened, scarcely believing what he was hearing. When Fittipaldi had finished, he told him bluntly that he had a contract to drive the Marlboro McLaren and that he would sue him if he didn't. Fittipaldi politely pointed out that he had not signed his McLaren contract and was sure Marlboro would release him from its contract once they knew that. Fittipaldi had it all worked out. Mayer reflected later: "I can only say he has sold out for a bag of gold."

It later emerged that Fittipaldi had been offered US$1 million a year to drive for Copersucar. The deal was underwritten entirely by the Brazilian sugar refiner. It was a total all-in promotional contract that tied Fittipaldi to the sponsor in a way that no driver had ever before been. It would mean a huge promotional commitment. But US$1 million was four times what he would have earned at McLaren and he simply couldn't turn it down. The full details of the deal were revealed in an article in *The Sunday Times* newspaper by Keith Botsford, a legendary sports journalist of the 1970s.

The realisation that there was no valid driving contract to enforce hit Mayer like a thunderbolt, and he quickly ended the conversation with Fittipaldi. Mayer was a brusque American, totally devoid of emotion and not one to dwell on the past. But he realised that Fittipaldi's defection was a huge loss. In his two seasons with McLaren, Fittipaldi had finished first and second in the Formula One world championship. Mayer's mind was whirring as he picked up the phone to Hogan. Hogan paid the team's bills and he needed to know the news.

It was a cold night and Hogan was at home with his wife, Anne, in Reading, Berkshire. Mayer didn't waste time talking about Fittipaldi. Hogan recalls: "Teddy rang me up and just said: 'We need to find a driver.'" As far as Mayer was concerned, it was Hogan's problem. Mayer had already signed Jochen Mass. Mass, a German, had won his first Grand Prix in 1975 in Spain, and

Mayer believed he would be an adequate replacement for Fittipaldi in 1976. But Hogan, a far more astute judge of drivers than Mayer, sensed that he would not. Whilst Mayer thought the search would be for a good number two to Mass, Hogan knew he must find a star, a proper number one. In an ideal world, his first choice would have been to lure three-time world champion, the then 37-year-old Jackie Stewart out of retirement, but Hogan knew that wasn't going to happen. Stewart was one of the few drivers who fully understood why he had retired and he wasn't going to reverse his decision despite how many hundreds of thousands of dollars Marlboro threw on the table. Hogan admits, as much as he may have liked it: "I couldn't see Jackie sitting in the cockpit."

Instead, as Hogan recalls: "I knew who to get instantly – James. But I knew I had to make it look good because Marlboro and McLaren would have been just as happy with Jackie Ickx. In fact, Belgian veteran Jackie Ickx was immediately the bookies' favourite to get the drive. Well past his peak and on the slide, the 30-year-old Ickx was on the market again after leaving the Lotus team at the end of 1975. Ickx had been a star of Formula One since 1968 and made his name when he had seen off teammate Jack Brabham and given Jackie Stewart the only serious competition in the 1969 world championship. But after a few years with Ferrari, he had quickly faded and was by then a has-been.

But not to everyone. It is a little known truism that most people involved in Formula One have little clue about drivers and, even though Ickx's performance in 1975 driving for Lotus had been lamentable – finishing 16th in the world championship – he had finished second at the Spanish Grand Prix and that is what stuck in many people's minds; especially in the minds of people in Colnbrook and Lausanne, who loved the charming Belgian. But Hogan was not charmed by Ickx and, although he was realistic enough to know that it was the most likely outcome of Fittipaldi's defection, he was determined that Ickx not get the drive. He remembers: "I liked Jackie a lot. He was a great, great driver, but he was past his peak. But there was really nobody else around."

Nobody, that is, except James Hunt.

Hogan had always been very focused, and now all his focus was on Hunt. He instinctively knew there wasn't a moment to lose. In his mind, he could already envisage Ickx on a plane to Lausanne to sign a deal with Philip Morris' vice president of marketing, Pat Duffler. That terrible thought drove him on.

In the era before the cell phone made everybody instantly contactable, Hogan had no idea where Hunt was that cold Saturday night in November. First, he called his home in Marbella and found it full of hangers-on and flunkies, enjoying life at Hunt's expense. As he recalls: "I managed to get an answer from his house in Spain and speak to whoever was the phone answerer." That 'answerer' was inevitably high on a combination of cannabis and alcohol. Hogan says: "The house was always full of itinerants." One of them told Hogan: "We think he's in London." So Hogan got on the phone and tracked Hunt to Lord Hesketh's house in London. Hogan recounts how the conversation went: "So I said: 'Listen...', and [Hunt] said: 'Been expecting a call from you'. So I replied: 'I'm going to come see you now.'"

Hunt thought Hogan was joking, but Hogan jumped into his Ford Escort and drove from Reading to London at high speed. He remembers: "When I got there, he opened the front door. James was what I call 'in full Beatles mode.'"

As it happened, Hunt already knew Fittipaldi was leaving McLaren. Domingos Piedale, a very well-known figure in racing and then Fittipaldi's manager, had tipped him off on Thursday 20th November, three days earlier. Piedale told him simply that Fittipaldi would not drive for McLaren in 1976, although he was careful not to tell him who Fittipaldi would be driving for.

Hunt couldn't do anything with the information. He couldn't even speak to his friend Hogan. He knew that any enthusiasm to have the drive would compromise his negotiating position. He had already experienced Lotus trying to get him to drive for nothing, and even the great Ronnie Peterson was having trouble hanging on to his salary. The viciousness of the recession meant that drivers out of contract were in poor negotiating positions. But Hunt was very grateful to Piedale and Fittipaldi at the time: "This fine gesture by Emerson, from a business point of view, gave me warning – time to get myself ready." He added: "I knew that if Emerson didn't sign, I was going to McLaren. And I had known that since the beginning of September."

In his book, *Against All Odds*, published in 1977 to celebrate his world championship, Hunt recalls that he was confident he would be chosen to replace Fittipaldi and that he had stayed in London on Monday 15th November and cancelled his return flight to Marbella in order to await the call he knew would come.

But that simply wasn't the case. Without Hogan lobbying for him, he had little chance of getting it. Ickx had been the favoured candidate. In fact, the attitude internally at McLaren at that time was: "Anybody but Hunt." Fortunately for Hunt, Hogan's attitude was the reverse. It was "Anybody but Ickx", and Hogan was signing the cheques.

When Hogan arrived at Hesketh's house an hour and a half later, Hunt was the worse for wear and had been smoking cannabis in the company of a girl Hogan hadn't met before, called Jane Birbeck. Hunt seemed out of it and unaware of the urgency of Hogan's mission, and even less cognisant of the fact that his entire future was on the line.

At that point, as far as anyone was aware, Hunt was still happily married to Suzy Miller. In reality, the marriage was all but over and Suzy had left Spain effectively to move back in with her parents.

Hunt was behaving petulantly and refused to talk to Hogan alone, insisting he had no secrets from Birbeck even though the two hardly knew each other at that stage. On any other day, Hogan might have turned tail and left Hunt to it, but not this day. Hogan knew what had to be done – for everyone's sake.

As uncomfortable as he felt and left with no choice, Hogan laid out the deal in front of Birbeck. Hogan knew that if the details of a deal got out, Hunt's chances of the McLaren drive would be stone dead. But still, Hunt insisted that Birbeck remain present – correctly assuming that there was no risk of a kiss-and-tell in next week's *News of the World* newspaper.

Initially, Hunt feigned that he didn't want to talk about McLaren and tried to convince Hogan that he was about to sign a contract with Lotus. But Hogan knew better. He recalls: "He tried to convince me that he had a Lotus offer on the table, but I knew he couldn't stand Peter Warr, so I knew that wasn't going to happen."

Ignoring Hunt's hyperboles and antics, Hogan spelled out what was on offer: three contracts with Philip Morris, McLaren and Texaco, and a retainer of US$50,000 a year. Hunt knew vaguely what Fittipaldi was earning and told Hogan that his offer was laughable. But Hogan was deadly serious.

Even though he had been paying Fittipaldi five times that, Hogan wasn't one to throw his employers' money around unnecessarily. Hogan simply reiterated that the retainer was US$50,000 plus some success bonuses, prize money from the team and extra fees for personal appearances outside of race weekends. And that, he said, was that, take it or leave it – knowing all the while that Hunt could not afford to leave it. Hogan says now: "It was very low on the money; I pushed him down to as low as I thought he would go.

We realised he didn't have an option. We played it cool."

Hunt didn't know it at the time, but he was actually in the driver's seat with Philip Morris. Hogan admits: "I was desperate to sign him but I didn't tell him that." Hunt could have demanded three times the money and got it, but he didn't want to call Hogan's bluff.

Having made his pitch, Hogan left the offer with Hunt that night and drove back to Reading.

The next morning, when Hunt sobered up, he telephoned his brother Peter with the news. They were delighted as well as secretly relieved. Years later, it emerged that one of Hunt's biggest anxieties about driving for McLaren was whether he would be able to beat his new teammate Jochen Mass. Mass had had a formidable reputation in Formula 3 and Hunt's fear was not as irrational as it now seems.

Hunt was also overawed by his potential new team. McLaren was the most successful Formula One team of the past five years. The McLaren-Ford M23, designed by Gordon Coppuck, was a knock-off of the highly successful McLaren M16 Indianapolis car, which in turn was a knock off of the even more successful Lotus 72 Formula One car. The car had been painstakingly developed and had already raced four seasons, an unusually long time for a single Formula One car design.

McLaren itself was a very good team, well-organised and methodical. It had been founded by Bruce McLaren, a New Zealander who entered Formula One in 1966 and who had been killed while testing a McLaren M8B Can-Am sports car at Goodwood circuit in June 1970. The team survived its founder's death and carried on being run by Mayer. It operated from a factory at Colnbrook, near London's Heathrow airport, and was a top team in all three categories of racing. By the end of 1975, the team had won 15 Formula One Grand Prix, several races at the Indianapolis 500 and had dominated the Can-Am series.

On Sunday 23rd November, the whole world was informed of what was happening as Emerson Fittipaldi and his brother Wilson held a press conference in Brazil to announce that he was leaving McLaren and driving for his own Copersucar-sponsored team in 1976. At the *Daily Express*, when David Benson saw that news come over the wire, he rang Teddy Mayer, who told him: "I am very interested in James Hunt."

On Monday 24th November, Peter Hunt rang Hogan and accepted his offer. Hogan immediately called Michael Mockridge at Coward Chance,

Philip Morris' lawyers, and told him to prepare a contract.

Later that day, Hogan managed to secure permission from Philip Morris executives in Lausanne to sign Hunt. Hogan knew the British market was very important to Marlboro and, up until then, the American brand had made little impression in England. He successfully persuaded his bosses that signing Hunt could change all that. Hogan says now: "I managed to slip and slide it through, partially on the grounds that it would give us a good story – the Brit (Hunt) against the German (Lauda)."

But Hogan still had to convince the McLaren team. Apparently, team manager Alastair Caldwell did not want to accept Hunt at any price, and Hogan knew that the choice of driver was ultimately down to McLaren. Even though Mayer had ceded the decision to Hogan after the shock of Fittipaldi's defection, Mayer still had to approve his choice.

Hogan knew Mayer was a waspy character and apt to change his mind. An American lawyer, he had met Bruce McLaren in 1964, when his brother Timmy raced in the Tasman series for downgraded Formula One cars in New Zealand and Tasmania. Mayer was a graduate of Cornell University in New York. After he qualified, he declined to practice law and became his brother's manager. But Timmy died in a qualifying session in Tasmania and McLaren invited Mayer to come and work for him in England. Mayer invested money and bought shares in Bruce McLaren Motor Racing Ltd. When McLaren was killed in June 1970, Mayer bought some of his shares and split ownership of the team with McLaren's widow, Patty. In the five years which followed, Mayer had become Formula One's most successful team principal.

In truth, neither Mayer nor Caldwell, also a veteran from the Bruce McLaren days, really rated Hunt at all, although they recognised his achievements with the small Hesketh team. Caldwell described the situation as: "We had no racing driver and James had no seat. No option for him and no option for us." According to Caldwell, it was an arranged marriage in which Hogan had "forced" McLaren to accept Hunt. It was about the truth.

Persuading Caldwell, a sometimes able but erratic and stubborn manager, had been very tricky. But he and Hogan shared a bottle of Absolut vodka one afternoon that week, and Hogan quickly brought him around.

Years afterwards, Caldwell confessed to Hunt's biographer Christopher Hilton: "James was an ordinary driver to me. We were fairly hard-bitten, we were a professional racing team and the golden boy-hype business at Hesketh really meant nothing to us. They were just a bunch of wankers."

Against that background, Hogan had literally finagled Hunt into the drive using all his powers of persuasion. Hogan simply says now: "I was convinced he was the right man."

With everyone finally on board, Hogan got the deal done in record time. From hearing about Fittipaldi to signing a contract, it had taken 13 days. Hunt was represented by IMG's Ian Todd. With the deal already agreed, IMG actually played little part in the negotiations although Hunt complained that, when they did, they got in the way. At one meeting that week, after another Hunt tirade about IMG, Peter Hunt turned to his brother, exasperated, but with a rather knowing look.

Contract details took only a few days to finalise as Hogan fought to get Hunt's signature on a driving contract before someone else at McLaren signed Ickx. But it was still not done by the following weekend and Hunt stayed at Hesketh's house in London, waiting. By then, he had been in London a fortnight and his brother was worrying about his residency status as he only had 90 nights he could stay over. But Peter Hunt knew they had to get the deal done.

Hogan knew that both Mayer and Caldwell would have preferred Ickx to Hunt. Ickx also had the support of Texaco vice president John Goosens. Goosens was Belgian, and not only was he lobbying for his countryman, he was actively lobbying against Hunt.

Hunt's elation at having found a competitive drive was severely dampened by news filtering through on Sunday morning that former world champion Graham Hill and young driver Tony Brise had been killed in a light plane which had crashed on Elstree golf course the previous night. Hunt and Suzy had been great friends with Hill and his wife, Bette, and Hunt had the uncomfortable task of phoning Suzy to tell her the news. Hill had been, in many ways, very similar to Hunt. He was a handsome, womanising character with a quick wit and an entertaining sense of humour. Despite their age difference, they had been very close and had spent a memorable night together the previous year at Trader Vic's bar under the London Hilton Hotel in Park Lane. It had been Hunt's stag night, the evening before his marriage to Suzy. That night, no woman in London was safe but they had both been too drunk by the end of the evening to cause their partners any concern. Hunt was devastated by the news of Hill's death.

The agreement was finally ready to sign on Friday 5th December, and

Hogan took it round to Eastbourne Terrace to get Hunt's signature. When the deal was finally signed, Hunt, Hogan and his wife donned their finery and walked to the annual British Racing Drivers Club ball being held at the Dorchester Hotel in London's Park Lane. The Hunt-McLaren deal was still top secret as Philip Morris had yet to conclude its own promotional deal with Hunt. Hogan warned Hunt not to say anything to anyone about it. But Hunt was scheduled to make a speech and, after a few drinks, proceeded to do just that. It was not to be the only time that Hogan, over the next three years, would end his day completely exasperated with Hunt. But it turned out the speech mattered little, as Hunt had already confided in David Benson of the *Daily Express*. When Benson had it confirmed by other sources, his duty of confidentiality to Hunt ended and the story broke in the newspaper on Sunday 6th December, some three days before the official announcement.

The following Wednesday, on 3rd November, McLaren and Marlboro held a joint press conference to announce Hunt as their new driver. At the conference, Mayer took all the credit for signing Hunt and made no mention of Jackie Ickx: "When Emerson Fittipaldi rang me to say he would not be driving for us this season, I was deeply upset, more dismayed than I cared to reveal. It was a great personal relationship and it had suddenly been jarred. The mood lasted 27 seconds. I thought of James Hunt. I thought of Hunt's great talent, his courage and his technique. But most of all, I thought of his hunger. Like great boxers, a racing driver has to have that thing inside him which drives him on beyond his rivals."

It was utter nonsense but only John Hogan knew that Mayer had really wanted to sign Ickx. It had been Mayer, in fact, who coined the phrase within McLaren: "Anyone but Hunt". But John Hogan stood nearby and just smiled at Mayer's audacity and didn't care to correct him.

But Hogan's problems were just beginning. Hunt, emboldened by his new contract to drive for McLaren, tried to get as much as he could out of the promotional contract with Marlboro. But Hogan stood his ground. When Hunt threatened to walk away from the whole deal, as he frequently did, Hogan got out the driving contract and offered to rip it up there and then, inferring that maybe Jackie Ickx would be a better bet after all. Hunt just smiled at Hogan and became quiet.

When all the details were finalised and the Marlboro promotional contract was ready to be signed, Hunt, his brother and his lawyers arrived at the offices of a company called Charles Stewart Ltd, the marketing subsidiary of Philip

Morris in London. They were to meet the Marlboro lawyers to conclude the deal. The contract was about to be signed when Hunt noticed a clause that had previously escaped him – a clause regarding dress standards. The clause read that Marlboro-sponsored drivers should always be dressed in a presentable way, especially at functions away from the race track, where jacket, flannel trousers and tie were required to be worn by their drivers. It was not an unreasonable request, but Hunt shouted across the table at Hogan: "If you think I'm going to walk around in a blazer, your mistaken. I'll go and drive the Lotus." The lawyers were shocked, but Hogan was unmoved. He took Hunt outside and told him to go back in and sign the contract as it was or it was over. Hunt, by now very emotional, had to be calmed down before he could go back in. Hogan sensed this and soothed him by saying that the clause had to be in the contract but was unlikely to be enforced. And, indeed, it never was – even for Hunt's worst sartorial excesses.

Hogan, a savvy operator, worked in the real world. He could see that Hunt's natural, unkempt style fitted the mood of the 1970s. He was sure his bosses at Philip Morris would appreciate Hunt's quirky personality and not invoke any dress clauses. And he was right. The Philip Morris directors loved Hunt. When Hogan first took him to Lausanne to meet them, Hunt had no shoes on. In a much told story, Hogan took Hunt into the office of a top Philip Morris executive. After they had shaken hands, Hunt walked out of the office and, as soon as he was out of earshot, said in front of more than a half a dozen other more junior Philip Morris execs: "He's a cunt." Hogan recalls: "Everybody burst into laughter and another top Morris man said: 'You're absolutely right.'" Years later, the same scene was re-enacted in the Jim Carey film, *Liar, Liar*. It is hardly surprising, given that the story has been re-told so many times, that it has become such a classic.

It was the start of a wonderful relationship and one of the best deals Philip Morris ever did; Hunt walked the walk and smoked his Marlboros, and sales of the brand soared across Europe.

Well actually, he didn't really smoke Marlboros.

Hunt preferred to smoke Rothmans. Every night, in deference to his new sponsor, he used to transfer his Rothmans cigarettes to Marlboro's red and white cartons.

With his moderate retainer, Hunt and his brother sought ways to capitalise on his new status as a driver with a top team. IMG were good at the big picture but pretty useless at hustling for smaller deals. So Hunt and his brother took a chance and hired Barrie Gill and Andrew Marriott of the CSS agency to handle Hunt's personal sponsorships and promotional work. It was one of the best decisions they ever made and, from late 1975, Gill and Marriott gradually assumed control of that side of Hunt's life.

One potential problem was that CCS already had the John Player cigarette account in Formula One. But everyone turned a blind eye to that inherent conflict and Gill and Marriott were very good at building Chinese walls in their agency. The two men were also well known to John Hogan and had worked for Philip Morris in their very earliest days of Formula One before Hogan took over.

Hunt had been very savvy getting into CSS early and recognising the talents of Gill and Marriott. In that era, CSS were the only game in town. IMG just didn't have the specialist motor racing experience. It was CSS' success with Hunt that made everyone realise there was a market. Marriott says: "We were looking for other ways to build the business, and driver management was one of them. Peter was the accountant, he just wanted to do the money side of it, and James approached us. We immediately struck up a good relationship. In a way, we were lucky because his career was taking off and the Hesketh thing was a fairytale, and with the sponsorship just starting to boom, we were really able to capitalise on his success and his looks."

Hunt was always over at Marriott's flat at 73 Baker Street, scheming how to make some money. If not, he would be at the Shepherd's Market offices of CSS. IMG gradually had less and less to do with Hunt's affairs although its contract did not end officially until 31st December 1976.

But when the deals with McLaren, Marlboro and Texaco were all concluded and the cheque had been cashed, both Hunt and his brother Peter became worried that they could not live up to the deals they had signed. As Peter Hunt recalled: "Nobody really knew how good James was. Maybe the Hesketh was a super car and his driving was only average." Hunt himself, for all his self-confidence, was remarkably candid and realistic about his own abilities at the time: "If you want to be ridiculous about it, I wasn't to know if the Hesketh was a car that was three seconds a lap better than anything else and I was just driving it slowly, or vice versa – that it was three seconds a lap worse than anything else and I was driving it mighty quick. You can form opinions, but you don't know for sure." Despite all this, he told others that the Hesketh wasn't much of a car and that, if he got into the right car, he would start winning. But, he was careful to add, it was the sort of thing a driver does not tell the world until he is winning races.

Hunt went for a seat fitting at the McLaren factory in Colnbrook and found the cockpit of the M23 very uncomfortable. But he was assured that everything would be sorted out for the first race in Brazil, just over four weeks away. A few weeks later, in a very wet and cold testing session at Silverstone, Hunt drove his McLaren-Ford M23 for the very first time. There were two sessions at Silverstone in similar conditions and Hunt couldn't really get a feel for the car. But Alastair Caldwell was impressed and became totally sold on his new driver, saying: "It was clear after one hour of practice that we'd got ourselves a cracker."

SHUNT

CHAPTER 21

The Championship Year
January to June 1976

Just as the game appeared to be over

There was no Argentine Grand Prix to open the season in 1976. There were two reasons. The main one was that Argentina was struggling financially as price inflation spiralled out of control. By the end of 1975, inflation had reached over 300 per cent, and the organisers realised they didn't have anywhere near enough local currency to pay out the teams in US dollars. But the race was also being used as a pawn in the continuing battle between the FIA, FOCA and the circuit organisers. Bernie Ecclestone, on behalf of FOCA, was trying to squeeze more money from resistant circuit owners. An impasse was reached as the circuit owners became bolder, supported by the FIA, and Ecclestone threatened to cancel the whole series in 1976. When the owners called his bluff, Ecclestone, mindful that the race was not going to take place anyway, duly cancelled the Argentine Grand Prix. Ecclestone brilliantly manipulated the situation by cancelling a race that had effectively already been cancelled. After the shock of the cancellation, the organisers capitulated and agreed to FOCA's financial demands.

With effectively no income from TV rights, payments from circuit promoters were the teams' only form of income. It ended with the European circuits paying around US$350,000 a race and the long-haul races (outside Europe) paying around US$500,000 a race. All in all, it would mean an income to the teams for 1976 of US$5 million, less Ecclestone's agreed commission, which was then less than ten per cent. It was enough to pay a team's entire operating budget and, proportionally, drivers took a huge chunk of the available budgets in the 1970s.

The other row going on as the 1976 season got underway was that between Ronnie Peterson and Colin Chapman at the Lotus team. The two men did not speak at all in Brazil. Peterson's contract stipulated that he be paid his retainer for 1976 in full on 1st January, whether he completed the season or not. Before Brazil, Chapman, with his Lotus empire desperately short of ready cash, had paid him one-eighteenth of it, exactly US$13,800, on the basis that there were 18 races scheduled that year including non-championship events. Peterson did not care a whit about Lotus' problems and was insulted by the gesture. They spoke not a word to each other and communicated via team manager (the very same gentleman who hadn't bought Hunt his lunch), Peter Warr.

As word got around the paddock, Hunt suddenly became aware that Warr probably did not have the spare money to buy him lunch that day, which was why he had prevaricated so much when the waiters had hovered with their menus. The Lotus cash situation was indeed as desperate as it looked – Chapman was just hanging on.

So the Brazilian Grand Prix became the opening race of the season. It was held as usual at the Interlagos track, just outside São Paulo, over the weekend of the 23rd to 25th January. Brazil had been the scene of much hedonism for Hunt in 1973 and 1974, in the Hesketh days when money flowed easily. Now, in 1976, it was different – albeit not too different.

A few days before the race, Hunt took Max Mosley out on the town. He roped him into a Marlboro reception he was attending for John Hogan. Hunt knew Mosley would lighten the evening, and they set off together across São Paulo. Mosley remembers: "It was a Marlboro party and James suggested we go together. We also had with us, as one did, a driver. James said to me: 'Do you mind if I stop at one of my friends' on the way?' And I said: 'No, not at all.' So we stopped at this very posh block of flats and went up to the top floor. There was this amazing flat with an amazing view, and a very nice man. We all sat down and the nice man got out a piece of highly polished stone and laid out on it three lines of white powder. James turned to me and said: 'You don't want yours, Max, do you?' And he did both of them. We then went happily on to the party."

Recalling other typical goings-on in his time spent with Hunt, Mosley adds: "I mean, he also was just full on into women. Good for him." But his antics in 1976 were a mere shadow of what had gone on in the Hesketh days in São Paulo.

Although McLaren was not in the same position as Lotus, and even with the end of the global recession in sight, money was still very tight, as Teddy Mayer was always reminding people. The recession had seriously affected McLaren and curtailed the lavish spending of the Fittipaldi era. But Mayer had gone too far with his economising and it was affecting the team's performance.

Although the McLaren team had a reputation for engineering excellence, Hunt found it wasn't so in his experience. In fact, the lack of preparedness couldn't have been greater at the first race. There had been effectively no winter testing except for the few days spent at Silverstone in the wet. Although Ken Tyrrell and Jackie Stewart had pioneered hot weather winter testing in South Africa at the Kyalami racetrack back in 1968, Mayer was too parsimonious to sanction the money needed for a winter testing programme.

Mayer was counting the pennies and it was the least Hunt could have expected. Two weeks in Kyalami, at a cost of US$10,000, would have made all the difference to the opening races of the season. But Hunt was not even able to go to Paul Ricard in the south of France to test.

Mayer and Alastair Caldwell believed that Emerson Fittipaldi had developed the car as far as it could go and they didn't think a winter testing programme was necessary. And it was true, by 1976, the M23 was a beautifully-sorted car. Fittipaldi had been recognised as a meticulous, almost workaholic, test driver and he had left Hunt with a developed car with highly-sophisticated suspension.

But Hunt had plenty of reasons to be angry. As number one driver, it was not unreasonable for him to expect McLaren to build him a brand new chassis for the new season, to suit his physical characteristics. Instead, they gave him an old Fittipaldi chassis which had been built in 1975. Hunt was expected to drive the M23/8/2 chassis and to keep it for the rest of the season. Mayer refused to authorise the building of a new chassis on the grounds of cost. Mayer also expected to be introducing a new model.

Hunt was shocked; meticulous attention to detail had always been a McLaren hallmark. Hunt remembered: "I got to Interlagos and it was the first time I had driven the car in any sort of anger, certainly on a dry track, and Friday's qualifying practice was totally aborted."

It was clear that the car was too small for Hunt and the seat fitting at the factory had been less than perfect. Hunt was tall while Fittipaldi was tiny, and the fitting had been done in a static car. At racing speeds, it was very different. Hunt found the McLaren car "undriveable." His feet were uncomfortable on the pedals, his knees were too high in the cockpit and his elbows didn't clear the sides of the cockpit. He also complained that the steering was heavy. He said: "The cockpit was all wrong. I literally couldn't drive the car. I was in great physical discomfort."

It was obvious that a new chassis should have been built, and Hunt told anyone who would listen that the McLaren team under Mayer was a "rudderless ship", adding: "It didn't have any direction." Hunt famously told Mayer: "I'll tell you Teddy, and I've told you before, you don't know anything about motor racing whatsoever. Go and buy a new briefcase."

Hunt continued to be shocked by the unreadiness of the team and the sheer tightfistedness of Mayer; it was not at all what he had been expecting.

Hunt had expected a very competitive car from the get-go. The McLaren Ford M23 had been the outstanding car of the 1970s, competitive straight from the day it was introduced in 1973 and subsequently driven to the world championship by Emerson Fittipaldi in 1974. The car was straightforward and uncomplicated, and seemed to have unlimited development potential. Its designer Gordon Coppuck's pedigree was unmatched. He had produced the legendary M8 series of McLaren Can-Am cars, arguably the most successful car in motor racing history, dominating the American sports car series for well on five years and winning virtually every race held.

Coppuck was the first of a new breed of race car designers. He had joined McLaren from the National Gas Turbine Establishment and replaced Robin Herd as McLaren chief designer in 1968. His M23 car was successful most of all because it was kept right down to the weight limit throughout its life. It also had some clever underfloor jiggery-pokery that created extra downforce, although the team never really understood why. Coppuck had, purely by accident, designed a very clever shape underneath the car that was delivering an early version of ground effects. It was the reason the M23 was so good on slow corners at fast circuits. Alastair Caldwell would later boast that M23 was the first 'ground effects' car in Formula One. Years later John Hogan recalled: "The M23 did have a lot of plastic stuff underneath. But McLaren or Alastair didn't understand it."

One innovation for which Caldwell could claim credit was the new six-speed gearbox for 1976. Gearbox design had been a speciality of McLaren's ever since the days of Bruce McLaren. Caldwell had overseen the development of the new unit during the winter. It gave McLaren an extra gear, one more than any other team. The Ferrari flat 12 engine was generally perceived to be more powerful than the Ford Cosworth V8 and the extra gear at the top of the range was McLaren's answer to getting more speed on the straight.

Hunt also complained that the team was treating his teammate Jochen Mass as the number one driver; a role he thought he had signed up for. Hunt had history with Mass in Formula 3 from 1972 when Mass had taken over his March works drive, and Hunt now sensed that history was repeating itself.

Mass was born in Munich. He was a year older than Hunt but a far less experienced driver. He started driving competitively at the age of 21, after a career in the German merchant navy. He was a quiet, unassuming man, who spent most of his time sailing in the south of France. But after getting to know each other, the two drivers formed a close bond, as Mass said later: "As teammates, basically we got along fine. It was a very happy team."

Hunt was genuinely surprised to find that, in so many ways, McLaren was inferior to Hesketh, and that Horsley had been a much more rounded manager than Caldwell. Hunt explained: "With Hesketh, we used to spend a lot of time examining ourselves. Bubbles used to exercise tremendous discipline."

He was scathing about McLaren's approach to team discipline. He had expected a much harsher regime, as he said: "McLaren don't give me any discipline at all. They let me do exactly what I want to do; they don't take any notice of me." Hunt was particularly upset about McLaren's casual attitude to de-briefs as he said: "The debriefing sessions we have at McLaren aren't the same sort of thing at all. We discuss something if we feel like it. But (here) if nobody wants to talk, we don't… I would actually get into trouble with Bubbles if I talked to anybody else after a practice and before I had sat down he would have wrung the truth from me and we would all have had a big post-mortem."

Mayer and Caldwell were forced to defend themselves against Hunt's accusation, and Mayer said: "Possibly, Hunt's initial shortcomings were that he didn't like taking decisions. He had been in a team where all the decisions were taken for him; where Bubbles Horsley told him exactly what to do all the time. I think that it's better for a driver to learn to take his own decisions because he has more information available to him, and this is where a more mature driver will ultimately do better." Caldwell added: "As team manager, I want to be able to contribute to the choice of tyre or choice of settings on the car, but ultimately the driver has got the say, and I think initially James wanted us to do that."

In fact, Hunt came close to walking out of the team at the first race when he discovered that McLaren was not the nirvana he had expected it to be. But luckily, John Hogan was at hand to soothe his frayed nerves. Privately, Hogan was also angry with Mayer. Marlboro's budget was generous by the standards of the day – the biggest in the paddock – and Marlboro expected the money to be spent making the car as competitive as possible. Hogan wasn't at all enamoured with the penny-pinching he was witnessing.

But Mayer and Caldwell and the team were being judged too harshly. It later emerged that McLaren had spent the money developing a new car: the M26 for the 1976 season. It had never expected Hunt to race the M23. But the new M26 proved substantially slower than the M23, so its debut was aborted and the car quietly forgotten.

As the situation in Brazil developed, Hogan advised Hunt to quieten down, bide his time and to air his grievances back in Europe when the opportunity presented itself. Hunt, who had always valued Hogan's counsel ever since the Australian first began advising him in 1971, heeded his guidance. But when Teddy Mayer heard what Hunt had been saying about his team, there was a furious row. Once again, it was Hogan who intervened; this time in order to soothe Mayer. Things finally came to a head in first qualifying on Friday, when Hunt came back into the pits with a blistered thumb as a result of the heavy steering and waved it at Mayer. Caldwell, who had taken Mayer's side of the argument, realised then that Hunt had a point.

It was a pivotal moment: Hunt could either walk away from the team at the first race or McLaren could start listening to him. Caldwell decided to listen and set to work lightening the steering and modifying the cockpit surround to suit Hunt's, rather than Fittipaldi's, body shape.

The results were immediately obvious. Hunt managed to set the seventh-quickest time in the first session, with Mass fourth and Lauda fastest. The following day, as final qualifying approached, Hunt's engine blew in the morning session. The engine change didn't go as planned and the final qualifying hour began with the back of the car still in bits.

As the minutes ticked by, Hunt became increasingly angry with Mayer interfering with the set-up he wanted on the car. Screaming at Mayer to get out of his way, Hunt told him he was working on the suspension settings as best he could to suit the conditions. But Mayer told him he would have to go out with the car in the same spec in which the last session had ended. Hunt recalled: "I was going out with twenty minutes left on a five-mile track. I was guessing the settings and Mayer told me: 'You can't do that.' I told him I was driving the bloody thing. I wasn't going to be pushed around when I knew what I wanted." The quarrel took place in full view of the pit lane, in front of mechanics astonished to hear their boss being addressed in such a manner. They had never seen anything like it.

As soon as the car was ready, Hunt knew he was in trouble and likely to be sacked if he qualified behind Mass, so he couldn't have been more motivated to succeed. As he left the pit lane for his warm-up lap, there were 20 minutes left in the session. In an extraordinary few minutes, Hunt landed pole on his first flying lap with a guessed set-up and a newly-rebuilt Cosworth engine. He said: "It was my first-ever pole, which I was rather pleased about. And it impressed the boys. After that, I was very much number one."

The lap was arguably the most important of Hunt's career, and Caldwell and the mechanics were suddenly in awe of their new driver. In that five minute window, Hunt had established undoubted number one status, ensuring that Mayer would not challenge him again.

Ruminating that life could not get much better than this, Hunt felt it was one of the greatest days in his motor sport career. All of his nemeses, Mayer, Niki Lauda, Fittipaldi and Mass, had been vanquished at one stroke.

The pole position was made even sweeter by the fact that he was in Brazil, Fittipaldi's home country, driving Fittipaldi's old car. And it was even sweeter still by the fact that he had blown away Niki Lauda in his first race in a works car.

As for Mayer, he couldn't believe what he had just seen, and stood in front of the pits open-mouthed as Hunt rolled back in gesticulating wildly at him. Never before had he witnessed such amazing bravado and experienced such a conflict of emotions within a 20-minute time frame. Having been prepared to sack Hunt the minute he stepped out of the cockpit, Mayer was now ecstatic and embraced his number one driver with as much vigour and passion as he had ever shown towards another man.

But deep inside, Mayer was even more excited that Fittipaldi's nose had been rubbed in it. The resentment at Fittipaldi's abrupt departure had been gnawing away at Mayer. Hunt recalled: "In front of the Brazilian crowd, it was almost more than Mayer could take. It was not what McLaren had been used to with Emerson. But it was important psychologically because we immediately had each other's respect."

Not everyone was happy. Lauda was clearly miffed that Hunt had taken pole away from him, and the following day the two men sat on the front row of the grid glaring at each other. It was a widely held myth that the two were close friends and, although that was true later in life, they were fierce rivals in 1976 and there was much antipathy under the surface of their relationship.

Jochen Mass was also destroyed by Hunt's pole performance. He began the race believing he would easily out-qualify Hunt and be crowned the team's undoubted number one. So too had Mayer and Caldwell.

And Emerson Fittipaldi was even more crestfallen as Hunt put his car on pole in front of his Brazilian fans.

None of what had happened in those five minutes was in the script. It was the most important five minutes of Hunt's life, before, then and afterwards. Oddly enough, his greatest success was barely reported in the following day's British newspapers. Only one national newspaper had even bothered to send a representative. Of all the editors, only the *Sunday Times'* Harold Evans had recognised the importance of Hunt's McLaren debut and sent its reporter Keith Botsford out to São Paulo to report on it.

But by race day the next morning, Hunt found he was very nervous about being on the Interlagos pole. He was vomiting more than usual – caused by a combination of extreme nervousness and the amount of cocaine, alcohol and nicotine circulating in his body. Although he had completely refrained in the few days before the race, it was all still there in his bloodstream.

Hunt was particularly frightened of burning his clutch on the start line and feared he would make a poor start and let Lauda go off. It became a self-fulfilling prophecy and that is exactly what happened. Lauda went off into the lead, never to be seen again. Hunt said: "I erred on the side of safety; one thing I didn't want was to not get to the first corner at all."

Hunt was also passed by Lauda's Ferrari teammate, Clay Regazzoni. In the end, it didn't much matter as his Cosworth engine let him down once more. One of the eight fuel injector trumpets physically fell off and one of the cylinders stopped firing altogether. The engine would still have taken him through to the finish if it hadn't been for the trumpet moving around and eventually dropping into the throttle slides. Hunt had a frightening moment when the throttle jammed wide open and threw him into the catch fencing at high speed. But he managed to put the car into a spin and went into the fencing backwards.

Catch fencing, widely used in that era of Formula One, had many faults; but that day, it probably saved Hunt's life. That, coupled with his skill in spinning the car around, prevented what would have been a major accident. The manoeuvre had been so effective that Hunt was able to get his car out of the fencing with the engine still running, but the oil coolers had been ripped off and he dared drive no further.

Afterwards, Hunt was brutally honest about his race debut: "I wasn't quite quick enough; I was about five seconds behind Niki when I had trouble. A trumpet fell off and the engine started misfiring and then, not content with that, it jumped down the throttle slides which stuck it open in the middle of a great long corner. I wasn't man enough to handle that, even though it was only on seven cylinders."

Lauda easily went on to win, and his predecessor Emerson Fittipaldi brought his dire Copersucar car in 13th in front of some very disappointed fans. Jochen Mass finished sixth.

After all the drama of qualifying, Hunt was relieved when the race was over, saying: "Fortunately we got it all together, and I think everyone – particularly Teddy, John and me – breathed a big sigh of relief." Alastair Caldwell, who had favoured Jackie Ickx to replace Fittipaldi, was the most impressed and declared how glad he was to have Hunt in the team. It was high praise from the man who had once said of Hunt in 1974, during his days at Hesketh: "I was glad he didn't drive for me."

For all his faults, Caldwell was said to be one of the main reasons for McLaren's success. He was a rough-hewn, capable New Zealand-raised Brit, steeped in motor racing. He had come to Britain in 1967, after his brother Bill had been killed in a motor racing crash. Like most New Zealand motor racing exiles, he went to work for fellow kiwi Bruce McLaren. But his rise was blighted by the fact that he didn't get on with Mayer, who was McLaren's business partner at the time. In truth, Mayer didn't rate him. But when McLaren was killed in 1970, Mayer softened his attitude upon becoming the boss and, four years later, made Caldwell manager of the Formula One team.

The record says that Caldwell's appointment was a huge success and he welded together a team of mechanics with skills never before seen in

Formula One, and the likes of which have probably never been seen since. They included the legendary Dave Ryan, Steve Bunn, Lance Gibbs, Ray Grant, Howard Moore and Mark Scott. But it has to be said that Caldwell also has his critics, and they say he was made to look good by the skills of these mechanics.

When the 1976 season opened, Caldwell had considered Jochen Mass the number one driver and told the mechanics to treat him accordingly. He had never imagined that Hunt would be faster and, when it happened, he was genuinely stunned. He famously said: "This unknown bloke came in and blew Mass away." Despite Caldwell's predictions, however, the mechanics had made their own assessment, as he recalled later to Hunt biographer Gerald Donaldson: "It doesn't matter if the guy has got number one written on his forehead or tattooed over his whole body. If he's second fastest, he's number two. Period."

After Brazil, the team's and Caldwell's focus automatically shifted to Hunt. The earlier problems melted away and, once the car had been modified to suit him physically, the frustration went with it. Hunt found himself in a perfectly-developed and highly-competitive car, just as it had been left by Fittipaldi and enhanced by the new six-speed gearbox.

As the mechanics got to know him, they also began enjoying working for Hunt. Not least of all because of the amount of available women he introduced them to. Hunt drew women to the team like a magnet. Caldwell noted: "We were all as happy as pigs in shit from then on."

There was a six-week gap before the South African Grand Prix at Kyalami on 6th March, and as the team headed off to South Africa, it was with an entirely new frame of mind. As the undisputed number one, Hunt started getting the star treatment. His car had been totally rebuilt to suit him and there would be no repeat of the Interlagos fiasco; Mayer was even moved to publicly apologise to Hunt for letting him down in Brazil.

It was clear that the M23 was a competitive car that had been undermined by one-off problems in Brazil. With these problems put right, Hunt headed from Marbella to South Africa early.

By then, Suzy had left him and was spending most of her time with Richard Burton in New York. Hunt had also temporarily parted from Jane Birbeck and was playing the field, seen most often parading around Johannesburg with Paddy Norval, a famous South African film actress. All this was going on despite the fact that, as far as the rest of the world was concerned, Hunt and Suzy were still happily married.

It was while he was in Johannesburg that news of Suzy's dalliance with Burton finally leaked out. There was no bigger story for the world's press: Burton had split with his wife, Elizabeth Taylor, and was cavorting with the wife of a famous racing driver.

Caldwell remembers: "With that business of his wife running off with Burton the whole bloody press world suddenly descended on us in South Africa."

Once again, Teddy Mayer was totally bemused by Hunt's antics and his enormous capacity for the opposite sex. Mayer was a reserved character who lived quietly and soberly. When the team moved into the Kyalami Ranch Hotel, Hunt quickly dropped Norval and took up with Carmen Jardin, a beautiful Portuguese he had met at the hotel. Jardin was an exotic creature and her presence fueled the Burton–Miller saga. She accompanied him to the circuit every day, wrapping herself around him at every opportunity.

The Kyalami Ranch, adjacent to the track and basic by the standards of today, was at that time a hedonist's dream; set in rolling grass with a giant swimming pool and surrounded by low-rise motel-type buildings. It was where the Formula One circus stayed and lounged around when there was no racing. The drivers loved it, and girls were drawn in every day. Hordes of journalists were kept shepherded outside, but a few enterprising ones got in, chasing Hunt around to learn why his wife was in New York with Richard Burton and not in Kyalami with him.

The race was almost a sideshow. Qualifying was a repeat of Interlagos, except this time it was much more relaxed as Hunt, now totally comfortable with his car, effortlessly took pole – once again alongside Lauda.

Hunt was in very high spirits at Kyalami. His former team manager and close friend Bubbles Horsley had managed to resurrect the Hesketh team by running the 1975 308 cars which had been given to him by Lord Hesketh. Horsley had set up a new a business running rent-a-cars for would-be F1 drivers. The new Horsley-owned Hesketh team debuted in South Africa with German driver Harald Ertl paying US$20,000 to run. Ertl qualified his Hesketh 308 dead last and finished the race 15th; four laps behind the winner. Horsley's new team may have been hopeless, but it was very profitable, as he remembered: "We had gone from the front of the grid, from being the glamour boys, to the back of the grid and being forgotten. But on the other hand, the bank balance went from zero and filled up again." Horsley was aided by the prize money fund increase and the fact that some of the money was allocated retrospectively from the previous season's performance by Hunt in the cars. It was worth about US$70,000 to the team in all and Horsley exploited it. Hunt didn't mind and he enjoyed having his mentor and best friend around again.

Lauda dropped Hunt at the start and roared off, but Hunt gave him a much harder time than he had in Brazil. He finished second within 1.3 seconds at the finish as Lauda wrestled with a slow puncture. Mass was third, albeit 46 seconds behind, and Fittipaldi was nowhere, having retired on lap 71 from the back of the grid. It was another rout of his rivals, with the only problem being that Lauda had actually won both races and was now firm favourite to be world champion again.

The first two races, however, had lit the fuse for the 1976 world championship. It was obvious Hunt would be a contender and that Lauda may not have it all his own way.

Hunt may have dominated qualifying so far, but Niki Lauda was dominating the racing. At the height of his powers, world champion Lauda was on top of the world and enjoying both his working and personal life. Lost in all the brouhaha of Hunt's personal life, Lauda was also making waves in the European newspapers.

Lauda had left his long standing fiancé, Mariella von Reininghaus, and taken up with a new girl called Marlene Knaus. Knaus was an actress and sometime model. She belonged to one of the most respected families in Austria. Her grandfather was a renowned gynaecologist, and her father a famous Austrian painter. It was their first public appearance at the Kyalami Ranch hotel and Lauda introduced her by saying, simply: "This is my lady." Remarkably, for Lauda, the sudden dumping of his companion of eight years and the woman he intended to marry did not seem to merit any further explanation than that. It turned out that he had been seeing Marlene for at least six months during the close season and Mariella, the daughter of an Austrian brewery millionaire, had already been long gone from his life. Lauda had kept his new relationship entirely secret until Kyalami, where he introduced her to everyone for the first time. Everyone, that is, except for John Hogan, who it later turned out had known all about it.

Lauda had met Marlene the previous summer at the Salzburg home of Hollywood actor Curt Jurgens. At the time, Marlene was Jurgens' girlfriend. She and Lauda hit it off straightaway and got together after the US Grand

Prix in Watkins Glen, in October 1975.

Lauda had been away in America for three weeks and, upon his return to the apartment he shared with Mariella, his feelings suddenly struck him. As he later revealed: "I draped my jacket over the back of a chair and looked at Mariella and suddenly it hit me: this won't work." He drove away that night into Marlene's arms never to return. Lauda proposed to her that night and they went away to Ibiza on Lauda's private plane.

Back in Austria, Lauda told Mariella a pack of lies. He told her he was stressed and, because of that, demanded they end their eight-year relationship. He told her that he "no longer had time for emotional nonsense."

In truth, Mariella had become a burden and, after eight years together, he had coldly dumped her in a few minutes' conversation. Mariella was a lovely woman and had been very popular on the Formula One scene. David Benson, the *Daily Express* motoring editor, who was a close friend, later tried to explain, saying: "Lauda had simply removed the fuse on the emotional circuit in his brain."

But in Kyalami, Benson could sense that Marlene was more than a casual fling – although he had no idea how much more. It later emerged that Lauda had wanted to get married to Marlene straightaway, merely days after meeting her. But he wanted it kept a secret as he did not wish Mariella and her friends to know he already had a new girlfriend. So, the previous November, he had flown to England and met secretly with John Hogan. When he arrived at Hogan's home in Reading, he told him: "You know what I'm missing? A wife. Where can I get married in England?" It was almost comical, as Hogan remembers: "I was living out in Reading in those days, so I said: 'Let's try Reading registry office to see what happens.' So we drove up to the Reading registry office; Niki, myself and Marlene. And this very nice gentleman said: 'I'm terribly sorry. I'd love to, but I can't.'"

So Lauda's plans were thwarted and he hid away in Ibiza with Marlene over the winter. Then, three months later, they turned up in Kyalami. Lauda figured he could test the water in South Africa, away from the full glare of European journalists. But he hadn't figured on the Hunt-Burton-Taylor story making his news a complete non-event. Such was the buzz surrounding Hunt hardly anyone noticed Lauda and Marlene.

Only David Benson relayed a story back to his newspaper, which was barely interested. It was easy to see why Lauda had become so transfixed. Marlene Knaus was a very beautiful girl and wore her hair in a severe brushed back bun at the top of her head. Benson said: "I established a friendly relationship with Marlene when the other people on the racing circuit cold-shouldered her, thinking she was merely some local pick-up."

Lauda was distressed by this and decided he must make an honest woman of Marlene as quickly as he could. Meanwhile, the wives and girlfriends of the other drivers had different ideas and completely sided with Mariella as news of the new relationship leaked out in Europe's tabloid newspapers. There was still a great deal of speculation about whether Niki and Mariella would get back together again.

At a party hosted by Nina Rindt, the widow of Jochen Rindt, at her house overlooking Lake Geneva, there was an attempt to bring Lauda and Mariella together again. Helen Stewart offered to get in touch with both Mariella and Lauda and to try and heal the breach. And she was nominated by the others to directly intervene. But they were labouring under the impression that Lauda and Marlene had just met, and had no idea what had occurred the previous year in Reading.

But when news of the women's summit at Lake Geneva reached him the next day, Lauda decided to take action. He didn't want a media circus, and he knew the Austrian and German press would take Mariella's side against his. So Lauda went as quietly as he could to a registry office in Vienna-Neustadt and married Marlene. The registrar agreed to a secret marriage out of hours and, astonishingly, it remained a secret for nearly a month, by which time journalists accepted it as a fait accompli, making further speculation effectively unnecessary.

The three weeks between Kyalami and Long Beach were dominated by reports of Hunt's crumbling marriage and his sustained attempt to avoid quote-hungry journalists. After Johannesburg, Hunt flew straight back into London to stay with his parents.

He was due to drive at the non-championship Race of Champions at nearby Brands Hatch. At Brands he won his first race for McLaren, beating Niki Lauda fair and square for the first time, although Lauda had eventually retired.

But, for many, the Race of Champions was more significant for what happened off-track than on. John Surtees' new Formula One team had obtained sponsorship from the London Rubber Company, which owned Durex, the condom maker. The Durex logos on the car caused considerable embarrassment to the BBC and its then head of sport, Sam Leitch. Times were different back then and there is no doubt a large proportion of Britain would have been offended if that brand had appeared on their television screens. After qualifying, Jonathan Martin, producing the coverage, issued a statement which said: "The BBC will consider again all the implications of this new Formula One sponsorship before it confirms its decision to cover and transmit the Race of Champions." After unsuccessfully asking John Surtees to cover up the sponsors' name on his car, Martin ordered the cameras taken down, and the BBC packed up and disappeared overnight. It was too late to make other arrangements and the race would not be broadcast. The implications for the coverage of the British Grand Prix, four months later, were not lost on anybody.

At the time, the BBC was wrestling with its own crisis of conscience over the rapidly growing trend towards commercial sponsorship of sport. Formula One was the worst offender, and the BBC used the Durex situation to cancel its broadcasting contracts for 1976 whilst it considered its position towards the whole issue of sponsorship and television.

Hunt was oblivious to all of this and had other more pressing matters on his mind. He helicoptered away from Brands Hatch and went straight to London's Heathrow Airport and flew to New York to meet with Suzy and Richard Burton to discuss a divorce. After that, he flew across country to Los Angeles and Long Beach, where the first ever United States Grand Prix West was due to be staged on a converted street circuit. But by the time he arrived, Hunt felt ill and had severe stomach pains caused by nervous exhaustion.

He was suddenly a genuine world championship contender and was strangely surprised by it. Fiercely intelligent, he was often caught out by reality. Though it had always been his ambition to be world champion, when he finally had the chance to realise it, he was caught totally unaware; he didn't recognise those words associated with him in the newspapers.

The US Grand Prix West was a brand new event, a second race in America at a circuit carved out of public streets in the little-known Los Angeles suburb of Long Beach. The town was best known as the retirement home of the ex-Cunard cruise liner the Queen Mary, which had been converted into a hotel.

Long Beach was billed as an American version of the Monaco Grand Prix. In truth, the two locations shared only a proximity to water. The harbour was filthy and the surrounding buildings decrepit. Downtown Long Beach consisted of run-down motels, dirty apartment blocks and old warehouses, some of which had been converted into cinemas showing blue movies.

The circuit was worn-out tarmac bordered by concrete walls and vertical catch fencing. Long Beach turned out to be a seedy low-rent resort, and nothing at all like Monaco.

It had been the improbable dream of an improbable character called Chris Pook to hold a world championship Grand Prix round the streets of such a location. Pook was a grey-bearded expatriate Englishman. He was a chancer who was perennially short of cash but had somehow raised the funds from the Long Beach local authority to pay FOCA US$500,000 for the event. The local authority was keen to promote Long Beach's tourism, and they had watched as Pook tested the concept with lower powered Formula 5000 cars the year before.

Despite his efforts, however, there were doubts that the track could be made safe enough around its two-mile length.

Hunt didn't expect to do well in Long Beach on its tight twisty track with the guard rails inches from the action. He hated street tracks and, despite three attempts, had never managed to finish the Monaco Grand Prix. The McLaren-Ford M23 was also ill-suited to slow twisty tracks and had primarily been designed for the fast-sweeping tracks of Europe.

In qualifying, Hunt was very surprised when he qualified third behind Regazzoni's Ferrari and Patrick Depailler's Tyrrell-Ford. Lauda was having problems and could only manage fourth, once again beside Hunt on the second row of the grid. Only three tenths of a second covered the first three cars. Hunt said: "It was one of those sessions where everyone was getting quicker all the time and we were as good as anybody. The four of us had been fast, swapping times, and there was really nothing to choose between us."

Hunt made a good start in the race, passed Depailler, and set off after Regazzoni. But there was a vapour lock in his fuel system and his engine kept spluttering. It soon cleared, but his efforts came to nought on the fourth lap when, as he was attempting to overtake Patrick Depailler's Tyrrell-Ford, it moved over and pushed Hunt's McLaren off the track. Hunt was shunted head first into the wall but at slow speed so there was little damage to the car. The crowd was surprised that Hunt didn't carry on.

Instead, a furious Hunt leapt from his car, stood out in the middle of the track, only slightly off the racing line, and took to his trademark fist-shaking and shouting of abuse directed at the Frenchman. Hunt continued this tirade for three laps before he was dragged away by marshals.

Regazzoni and Lauda cruised to victory, scoring a 1-2 for Ferrari, with Depailler third.

After the race, Hunt gate-crashed the podium press conference and tackled a startled Depailler about what happened. Becoming increasingly enraged by Depailler's answers, Hunt shouted: "It was just flagrant stupidity. I came alongside you and you saw me, but you just moved over and squeezed me out. You made a complete cock-up of that corner and the first thing you should do when you make a cock-up is to look where all the others are. The first thing you must do is to bloody well learn to drive." Depailler replied: "Look, James, I am desolate at what has happened. I am so sorry." James said: "I am bloody well sorry too. Just watch it in future." Outside, Hunt told journalists that Depailler was a "crazy frog driver" who had robbed him of a certain second place.

In the end, though, most people took Depailler's side and Hunt emerged from Long Beach with very bad press. Even his friend, Jody Scheckter described Hunt's antics that day as "very foolish."

When the McLaren mechanics brought his car back to the pits, the only damage appeared to be a crumpled nose; it appeared that Hunt could have continued the race if his anger had not overpowered his reason and exaggerated the incident. Later, Hunt admitted he had made a mistake trying to pass Depailler at that corner, but he still blamed him for the accident.

So it was a still very angry James Hunt who flew back to Britain to take part in the non-championship Silverstone International Trophy Formula One race. He duly won it in style. In a display of driving perfection, he completely dominated the race in front of 75,000 almost-out-of-control, screaming fans. It was close to a repeat of 1974 and David Benson, witnessing it all, said: "James that weekend gave one of the most impressive displays of high speed Formula One driving I have ever witnessed. From the moment he went out onto the track for the first of the two practice sessions on Saturday, he was clearly the fastest man on the track. He was beautifully controlled. It was smooth, clean driving without a hint of over-exuberance."

The International Trophy had been renamed the Graham Hill Trophy, in memory of the late champion, and the trophy was presented to Hunt by Bette Hill. Hunt, as she later revealed, whispered to her on the podium: "If I can achieve only a small percentage of what Graham achieved in his life, I will be happy." Bette Hill later telephoned Suzy Miller in New York to tell her about her former husband's "magnificent day."

It was a correct description. Having spent a comfortable week at Lord Hesketh's country home Easton Neston nearby, Hunt's performance and demeanour at Silverstone was in marked contrast to that of Long Beach. Journalist Ian Phillips wrote in *Autosport* magazine: "His style was impeccable, both on and off the track, which should shut up the childish newspaper critics for good and all."

If the two non-championship races had counted for world championship points, it was not lost on Hunt that he would have been leading it. As it was, he only had six points from a second place finish to show for his troubles. Lauda already had 24 points. Hunt wasn't even second or third in the rankings; sadly not even fourth. He was by now desperate to win a Grand Prix for McLaren, as he said: "I need a victory to make Niki sweat, and I need one to know I can do it."

After Silverstone, Hunt was riding the crest of a wave. From having been a little-known playboy racing driver, he was now internationally famous – not least because of his wife's affair with Richard Burton. As a genuine world championship contender, he was now recognised wherever he went and was enjoying it immensely. When it got too much, he retreated to Marbella where he was left alone. Moreover, with his wife gone, he could smoke as much cannabis and drink as much beer as he liked; he could also sleep with as many girls as he liked – often two or three together, if it took his fancy.

Although he regarded most of the stories written about him in the media as "absolute rubbish", he told the writers he was nonetheless grateful for the coverage.

In the gap between the races, there was other good news for Hunt; somewhat less good for his rival, Lauda. Lauda had been on his tractor at the new home he was building with Marlene, near Salzburg, shifting earth and digging a hole to build a swimming pool, when the world champion lost control of the tractor and it overturned. The tractor tipped over with a load of earth piled high in the scoop. Lauda somehow fell between the seat and the transmission as the tractor rolled forward. He eventually struggled clear with earth caked over his eyes and in his mouth, but he was badly shaken and in pain. He said: "I was trying to shift a mound of earth from the meadow in front of my house when I somehow managed to tip the tractor right over on top of myself. A couple of inches either way and it would have been really serious. As it was, I was pinned to the ground and ended up with two broken ribs – all things considered, not too bad for a shunt with a 1.8 tonne tractor. But the pain was excruciating." Lauda was extremely fortunate to escape with two badly broken ribs. He was immediately bound up by a doctor and administered with routine pain-killing injections. Lauda later referred to the incident as "the ridiculous business with the tractor."

But it was a serious injury, and there was a strong chance that he would be unable to race his Ferrari in Spain at the next race. The accident caused a sensation in Italy and set in motion a series of events that totally destabilised the Ferrari team. The team had already been falling apart internally since its guiding light, Luca di Montezemolo, had left.

Montezemolo had spearheaded the revival that had culminated in Lauda's 1975 championship win and had been totally responsible for the team's renaissance after years in the Formula One wilderness.

Montezemolo had been parachuted into Ferrari by Fiat boss Gianni Agnelli at the age of 26 to effectively sideline the founder, Enzo Ferrari, and take control of the team. But Agnelli had great respect for Enzo Ferrari and wanted his *dénouement* done subtly with no embarrassment to the old man who, despite his failings, Agnelli revered. Before Montezemolo's arrival, the team had not won a world championship for 11 years. Part of the problem was the irascibility of founder Enzo Ferrari, then in his late seventies.

Enzo Ferrari was a schizophrenic. One moment he could be incredibly overbearing and pompous, a complete bully, but after he got his own way in a discussion, or thought he had, he immediately turned into a charming, warm human being whom no one could fail to like.

Montezemolo had succeeded brilliantly in sidelining him, placing the Ferrari founder in a metaphorical box where he could do no damage but still take all the credit for the team's revival.

But Montezemolo was a talented young man in a very big hurry. Running the Ferrari Formula One team, as glamorous as it was, was a small job and he was eager to move on to bigger things. As soon as he could, he quietly left the team to join Fiat. Montezemolo was effectively replaced by new team manager Daniele Audetto. Too young and inexperienced, Audetto was immediately out of his depth. He was more like a referee trying to keep order amongst Ferrari's feuding factions, all of whom came out to play once Montezemolo was gone.

Lauda described Audetto as a "fraught personality."

Montezemolo's departure left a power vacuum in the team, into which stepped a newly-energised Enzo Ferrari. The result was chaos. With Montezemolo gone, Audetto could barely control the team.

Ruefully observing what was happening, Lauda lamented Montezemolo's departure, saying: "The first hint of trouble came with the departure of my friend and ally Luca Montezemolo, who had to make a career for himself and couldn't afford to stay on the lower rungs of the ladder as team chief indefinitely. Luca was promoted closer to the seat of power in the Fiat dynasty."

The tractor incident was the spark that set off a fire. There had been much jealousy in the team over Lauda's success and, internally, his detractors wanted an Italian driver to win in the Italian car. They believed Lauda's success had been down to the car and not the driver, and they wanted him out. Lauda recalls: "The Italian press got hold of the story – you can hardly blame them – a Formula One world champion crushed by a tractor makes a pretty good copy."

Audetto made the mistake of immersing himself in these day-to-day intrigues in an effort to carve out a niche for himself, and Italian journalists started clamouring for Lauda to be sacked and replaced with an Italian. Believing the injured Lauda to be overrated, they maintained that an Italian could do better in such a good car.

Lauda said: "As soon as the news leaked out about my accident with the tractor, they sensed an opportunity to promote an Italian into the cockpit. There just happened to be a young lad around called Flammini, who had had a good result in Formula 2; he would be an automatic choice. All races I had won for Ferrari had still not silenced one particular section of the Italian press, which constantly clamoured for an Italian driver.

"Tempers ran high and, in the heat of the moment, I paid scant attention to what I said. I came out with a few choice remarks, notably to the effect that [Enzo] Ferrari could take a long walk off a short pier, and *Gazzetta dello Sport* ran that in a banner headline. All Italy was up in arms."

Lauda also offended Italy by responding to the possibility of the young Flammini replacing him by saying: "Italians are only good for driving round the church." He was so fed up with the negative publicity, he gave Enzo Ferrari an ultimatum. He would be available for the next Grand Prix in Spain, he asserted sardonically, but only "if and when Ferrari required him."

This statement successfully spooked Enzo Ferrari, who now changed tack completely and panicked at the thought of losing Lauda. Audetto and Enzo Ferrari despatched a top executive, Sante Ghedini, to drive overnight from

Maranello to Salzburg and to arrive in the early hours of the next morning at Lauda's home in order to provide regular bulletins of their driver's medical condition.

The whole event turned into an Italian farce and seriously destabilised the team. The feeling was that if Lauda wasn't fit to drive in Spain, Ferrari would replace him, probably for good. By this time, Lauda was fed up with Ferrari's politics and couldn't care less. But as he said later: "There were panic stations at Ferrari, and I was determined to do everything I could to start in the next race."

That looked nigh-on impossible until Lauda met Willy Dungl for the first time. Dungl was a world class masseur and regarded as something of a miracle-worker by Austria's winter Olympics team.

Dungl had been called in to help treat Lauda's injuries, and from that first meeting, he hardly left Lauda's side; he kept him in tip top physical condition. Lauda said in his autobiography *To Hell and Back*: "Willy Dungl has been one of the most important people in my career and my life. There is no one to touch him; he is simply a genius. His knowledge, his sensitivity, his touch, and his methods – I simply cannot imagine that there is another like him anywhere in the world." Dungl had Lauda back on the grid two weeks after the accident.

The Spanish Grand Prix that year took place on 2nd May. It was the first race of the new European season and it was being held at the Jarama circuit, just outside Madrid. By the fourth round of the 1976 world championship, James Hunt had made himself familiar to everyone; he was the centre of attention in the Formula One paddock. But despite that, his teammate Jochen Mass remained confident that he would beat Hunt at Jarama. It was the anniversary of his first Grand Prix win and he was determined to re-establish himself in the team by winning the race. It set the scene for a real needle match between the teammates, especially as Mass was fourth in the championship with seven points, whilst Hunt was fifth with six points. It had previously been established that whoever had established a lead on points early in the season would be regarded as number one driver and would then be backed up by the other driver for the world championship.

While Hunt had been getting up pole positions and making the front running in the opening races, Mass had actually scored more points: from a sixth place in Brazil; a third in South Africa; and a fifth in Long Beach. Going down to Madrid, Mass saw his chance to regain team leadership with a win.

Ferrari took the opportunity to debut its new car, designated the 312T2. It was the second in a series of what would eventually be three models of the 312T series spanning five highly-successful seasons. Lauda had it working well straightaway.

There were also hidden forces at work in Spain. Regulation changes had taken place at the beginning of the season which, up until then, had not really been enforced. At the start of 1976, both the Formula One teams and the governing body, the Fédération Internationale de l'Automobile (FIA), had become concerned that cars were getting wider and longer and going faster with more downforce, and thereby becoming more dangerous. To counter that, a revised set of measurement regulations aimed at keeping cars within specified limits and simplifying the technical regulations was agreed upon. To establish the maximum allowable width, they measured the widest car – the McLaren-Ford M23 – and declared it the limit. Likewise, the longest car was measured and its length was written in as the maximum for all cars. Alastair Caldwell remembers it all very clearly: "Our car had been measured by the authorities at the Nürburgring in 1975 as the widest. They said: 'Okay, we'll make that the maximum width for 1976.' We said: 'Come on, mate, give us a centimetre', and they replied: 'Okay, your car measured 2.9, we'll make the rule 2.10.' In 1976, the rule came in."

Coincidentally, the race was also marked by the debut of the new six-wheeled Tyrrell-Ford car, to be driven by Patrick Depailler. The six-wheeler had been designed with the new regulations in mind.

The weekend began well, with Hunt grabbing pole three-tenths of a second faster than Lauda in the Ferrari beside him. It was Hunt's third pole in four races. Mass was fourth as the two McLarens sandwiched Lauda's Ferrari and Depailler's Tyrrell. The Austrian, with Willy Dungl in attendance, seemed unaffected by his painful injury.

The start was delayed while King Juan Carlos, a keen Formula One fan, arrived in his helicopter. Once again, Hunt, fearful of his clutch, was slow to get away from the start while Lauda, high on painkillers, stormed into the lead for the first 31 laps. Hunt was again beaten off the line.

But Lauda could feel his broken jagged rib-ends grinding together under the G-forces in hard cornering and, as the painkillers wore off, he had increased difficulty controlling the car. Hunt was content to play a waiting game, knowing that Lauda's ribs simply wouldn't let him continue at that pace for the entire race. Hunt recalled later: "Niki was motoring hard at the start and I was able to tuck in behind quite comfortably. I couldn't do anything about passing him, it was just a case of waiting until his ribs started to hurt and I'd be able to nip through." And so it proved, as Hunt went past on lap 32, followed by Mass a few laps later. Mass' engine failed with a few laps to go, and Hunt crossed the line to take his first Grand Prix victory for McLaren. Lauda crawled in for second place, 31 seconds behind and in agony.

Hunt was ecstatic afterwards but totally exhausted from having wrestled the McLaren round the difficult Jarama circuit for 75 laps. On the way to the podium, he punched a spectator in frustration.

But bigger problems than a wayward spectator lay ahead in post-race scrutineering.

Peter Jowitt, a Farnborough based scientist, had been employed as a consultant by FOCA as a technical consultant. He worked for the teams and his brief was to check car dimensions, investigate causes of accidents and suggest modifications for safety. Jowitt was not a scrutineer and had no official powers at all. But he had noticed that the McLaren was 1.8 centimetres too wide across the rear wheels. Jowett innocently brought the problem to the attention of the Spanish scrutineers thinking they would merely inform McLaren of the error and ask the team to correct it. He was horrified when they disqualified the car on the basis of his discovery.

The celebrations in the Marlboro motorhome in the Spanish paddock were curtailed shortly after eight o'clock when Hunt was brought the bad news by David Benson. Hunt was stripped to the waist, wearing only a pair of jeans, talking to his teammate, some girls and his normal retinue of hangers-on. He immediately grabbed a shirt, shouted to Teddy Mayer and they ran to the steward's office in the race control tower.

Benson had extraordinary instincts for news and he had somehow sensed trouble and gone to the scrutineers garage purely on a whim. By then, it had just been announced in the press room that the stewards had ruled Hunt's car to be illegal and that he was therefore disqualified. The scrutineers had ruled that the rear tyres of Hunt's M23 extended 1.8 centimetres wider than allowed by the new regulations. After a series of measurements and re-measurements, the McLaren M23 was deemed undeniably too wide across the rear wheels. The stewards announced Lauda the new winner of the race. It was the first time the cars had been rigorously checked under the new rules, and the FIA had asked the scrutineers to carefully check the dimensions of each car.

Teddy Mayer argued with the stewards in vain. He told them that such a small discrepancy couldn't give Hunt's McLaren any advantage and that the ruling was "unbelievably harsh and unjustified."

Hunt was distraught, and tears welled in his eyes. He said: "It's stupid. It does not affect the performance of the car or make it any faster. Not even the Ferrari team protested and they were the ones who had the most to win." Lauda had already left the circuit by helicopter to the airport to fly back to Austria for further treatment on his ribs. He learned that he had been declared the winner of the race from air traffic controllers at Salzburg airport as he was landing his plane. His subsequent attitude was perfectly straightforward: "A rule is a rule. The McLaren was illegal and therefore it should have been disqualified. I am very sorry for James; he drove very well but the car was not legal. If the same had happened to my Ferrari, I would accept the ruling."

Teddy Mayer, apoplectic towards the stewards, filed an official protest and muttered something to journalists about a conspiracy by Ferrari. In fact, Hunt's car had been measured twice in pre-race scrutineering and had been found legal. But there was now no doubt that McLaren was guilty, as Caldwell freely admitted: "We [thought we] had no worries because our car was exactly the same. Like idiots, we didn't even bother to measure it – my fault – because as far as I was concerned the car had been measured and the rule based on it. However, over the winter, Goodyear developed the tyres and made them with wider sidewalls. I didn't realise that the tyres had been made this much wider. We got caught out."

Mayer, caught in a very tricky situation, put out a press release: "The entire McLaren team extends its sympathy to James Hunt." Stating he would appeal against the severity of the sentence rather than the correctness of the decision, he went on to say it was like being hanged for a parking offence. Mayer maintained that, since the minute oversight could have given Hunt no possible advantage, he should at least be able to keep his driver's points.

After his initial disappointment, Hunt became surprisingly sanguine about the entire affair, although he called his team's failure to ensure the car was the correct width "a fantastically sloppy performance." Hunt said years later: "The point was they'd taken the current widest car in the business and the current longest because they didn't want them to go much wider, like someone suddenly worked out if you had it twice as wide it would have twice as good road holding; likewise if you made it two yards longer. The point was the McLaren was the widest car in the business at the time. But McLaren didn't bother to check the width of its car because it had established the standard the previous year when it was all checked. The only problem was we were using slightly different tyres, which had a bigger bulge. And that's the widest point on the car. It was in fact 1.8 centimetres too wide, and that was purely the bulge."

On 13th May, a Spanish tribunal confirmed the disqualification but Teddy Meyer said that the proceedings were a travesty of justice as he had not been allowed to take McLaren's Spanish-speaking lawyer to the hearing. Mayer later described the tone of the tribunal hearings as follows: "The judges said: 'Do you know the rule about the width of the car?' I said: 'Yes.' They said: 'And do you realise that your car was wider?' I said: 'Yes' again. And they said: 'Right, thank you, Mr Mayer.'" Mayer was the only person called on to give evidence. Mayer launched another appeal to the FIA in Paris about the tribunal's decision.

Alastair Caldwell simply accepted the blame and admitted there was no doubt the car had been too wide. He had failed to allow for a new design of Goodyear tyres.

The usually very efficient Caldwell was mortified by his mistake, and he reacted to it by subsequently erring in the opposite direction. In fact, Caldwell's reaction to the initial oversight went on to have dire consequences for the team and for Hunt's championship bid. Back at the McLaren factory in Colnbrook, the repentant Caldwell went on a binge to make his car legal beyond doubt. Forgetting that all Formula One cars go fast by being barely legal and by pushing the envelope as far as it will go, his decisions were to cost McLaren and Hunt even more dearly than the forfeited Spanish points. Becoming obsessed with making the car legally watertight, he declared that an oil cooler modification he had made earlier in the season was also potentially illegal. The oil coolers had been moved towards the back of the car, but Caldwell ordered them to be moved forward to their original position. He also ordered the lowering of the rear wing and moved it forward as well for good measure. He then reduced the track of the car by two centimetres.

The changes rendered the car immediately uncompetitive. Hunt called his revised car: "utterly hopeless"; just how hopeless would become apparent at the upcoming Belgian Grand Prix.

The Belgian Grand Prix that year was held at Zolder on 16th May. It was a

2.6-mile tight, featureless and artificial track with few passing opportunities. It was the sort of track James Hunt despised, entirely different in character to the sweeping Spa-Francorchamps circuit where the Belgian Grand Prix had traditionally been held, but which was now excluded for safety reasons.

Amazingly, Hunt managed to top the qualifying charts on the first day of practice ahead of Clay Regazzoni's Ferrari and Jody Scheckter's Tyrrell-Ford.

Strangely enough, there had not been time at the McLaren factory for the oil coolers to be moved, so the plans were to modify them at the track. Between the morning and afternoon sessions, the mechanics shifted the oil coolers back to their old position below the rear wing. Hunt said: "We put them back virtually where they had been, under the wing, but because the wing had been moved forward, the coolers were now about an inch away from their old position."

The change was startling and the combined effect of Caldwell's modifications completely changed the car's aerodynamic set-up. So much so that, in the second session, Hunt was ninth fastest, and in the final session he was eleventh. But he managed to line up on the second row of the grid by virtue of his time in the first session – before the oil coolers were moved. The changes had turned the car into an ill-handling brute. One journalist described Hunt's revised car as a "bucking bronco." Hunt recalled: "In order to make it narrower, they unnecessarily moved radiators around and things like that. But they hadn't checked it out and completely ruined the performance of the rear wing. As a result, the aerodynamics of the car overall were hopeless."

Caldwell defended the changes: "We had several things on the car which were reasonably dodgy. You couldn't have oil fittings above a certain width from the centre of the car, let's say 80 centimetres, which meant the oil coolers in front of the rear wheels could be – could be – construed as illegal. We had a little conference and said: 'Okay, next race we must be absolutely 100 per cent safe, not get caught again. We'll narrow the car, bring the wing down just on the limit and put the oil coolers back where they were before, on the back of the car.'"

Caldwell had taken holy orders, and the car was now very legal but no longer fast enough.

From the start, Hunt somehow managed to clamber into second place behind Lauda's Ferrari. But Lauda quickly built up a huge lead and a slow Hunt was holding up the rest of the cars, which were queued up behind him.

Gradually, Regazzoni, Jacques Laffite in the Ligier, Patrick Depailler and Scheckter all passed him. He was sixth when his car's gearbox seized up and he retired from the race at exactly half distance. Lauda easily went on to win from Regazzoni for a Ferrari 1-2. Jacques Laffite came home in third place and Scheckter fourth.

After the race, there was another huge row with Hunt centre-stage but this time he was defending his own driving tactics. He had upset many of the drivers by employing some dubious driving maneuvers to stop them overtaking his slower car. Several times, Scheckter's Tyrrell-Ford was nearly shoved off the road and Laffite's Ligier was hit by Hunt's front wheel when he attempted to pass. It was also Patrick Depailler's turn to be angry with Hunt: "Hunt was driving very wild, holding everybody back. If Hunt says all these things about crazy French drivers, he should not drive in the same way himself." The drivers all had a very good point and, once again, it was not the Englishman's finest hour in Formula One.

But that was far from Hunt's biggest concern. Lauda now had 42 points in the world championship, with the next best placed driver his teammate, Regazzoni, on 15 points. Hunt was seventh in the standings with six points, with Jochen Mass ahead of him in fourth with eight points.

Meanwhile, back in England at the McLaren factory, Alastair Caldwell had no idea what had caused the car suddenly to become uncompetitive at Zolder. The team had completely lost its way and Caldwell and his men were running around like headless chickens. Having concentrated so hard on making the car legal rather than making it fast, they had briefly forgotten what Formula One was about.

The Monaco Grand Prix dawned on the weekend of the 26th to 30th May, and Hunt had other worries than the sudden poor performance of his car. Hunt was becoming increasingly disenchanted with IMG, his management agency. He telephoned his brother Peter from Monte Carlo and asked him if he would consider leaving his accounting firm to come and manage him full time. His brother was taken by surprise at the request and told him he would meet him at the Dutch Grand Prix to discuss it.

With that settled, Hunt focused on Monaco's social scene.

In his first year away from Hesketh, he was free to party anywhere he liked and he hooked up with former Formula One racer Johnny Servoz-Gavin. Servoz-Gavin had retired from Formula One in 1970 after problems with his eyesight. Now he lived on a boat in Monte Carlo harbour. Hunt and Servoz-

Gavin had been friends for years. They were joined by Philippe Gurdjian, who knew them both. Gurdjian remembers: "They were very close, and I was very close to James."

The first night in Monaco, the three young men painted the town red. The following night, they jointly hosted a huge party on the boat which ended up with many of the female guests naked.

Gurdjian remembers it fondly: "We finished the party the night before the Grand Prix at four in the morning, and they were all racing the day after without any problems. Now, it's completely different and you cannot imagine that."

That night, Hunt promised Gurdjian he would give him his helmet after the race, and he did. The Frenchman still has it today, a prized possession from that championship year. He remembers his friend fondly: "He was very friendly, he had a real face and it's a pity we don't have more guys like that."

For the serious business of racing, Hunt's car was in exactly the same specification and set-up as it had been in Zolder. When Hunt could only qualify in 13th place, they were still none the wiser about what had happened. The McLaren-Ford M23, that had been so fast earlier in the season, was now a pig to drive, and for no good reason that anyone could identify. Hunt found himself on the seventh row of the grid on a circuit where grid position was paramount. Without retirements, the cars would normally finish the Monaco Grand Prix where they had been placed on the grid since overtaking was virtually impossible.

On race morning, a desperate Caldwell ordered the removal of the airbox from the engine and found it to improve the performance of the rear wing. They had been scratching around overnight trying to find the problem, and removing the airbox was a last desperate measure. It made them look like amateurs. Up and down the pit lane, rival technical directors shook their heads. Colin Chapman of Lotus, for one, had already worked out what had gone wrong, but he wasn't about to tell Caldwell.

Hunt was dejected and knew he was finished before the race even began. The only plus point was that the brute, which is what he now called the car, handled better with a full tank of fuel, giving him hope for the early part of the race. He said: "The dreadful problem was that I was so far back on the grid I wouldn't be able to pass anybody simply because there isn't anywhere to pass at Monaco without doing anything risky or stupid. It's a pretty stupid way to have a race."

When the race started, Hunt was stuck in twelfth position, although with full tanks his car was the fastest on the track. He remembered: "I was running two seconds a lap slower than I wanted to simply because there was nowhere to pass." He quickly lost concentration and spun off but avoided hitting the wall: "I have to say that I spun the car through my lack of interest and sheer bloody frustration."

Hunt dropped to the back of the field and, clear of traffic, he found he was lapping as fast as Lauda, who was leading the race. But it didn't matter as, on the 25th lap, he was put out of his misery when his Cosworth engine blew up. For once, Hunt was delighted to be out.

From then on, it was a procession: Niki Lauda won, followed across the line by Scheckter, who was followed by Depailler's Tyrrell. Lauda now had 51 points to Hunt's six. Any notion that Hunt was a world championship contender was simply forgotten. No man had ever before won the championship from his position with six races gone.

McLaren was not the only top team experiencing severe technical problems. There were also problems at Brabham. Bernie Ecclestone seemed to have made a huge mistake in choosing Alfa-Romeo engines for the 1976 season. The cars were having to start races with ten gallons more fuel than the Ferrari- and Ford-engined cars, a weight penalty of about 45 kilos. Even with that extra fuel, they were still regularly running out of fuel if they lasted to the end the race. The team's number one driver, Carlos Reutemann, was looking to leave as a result.

Meanwhile, Alastair Caldwell was still in denial as the McLaren team travelled to Anderstorp for the Swedish Grand Prix on 13th June. Hunt was 14th in the first qualifying session, eleventh in the second session, and eighth in the final session for a grid position on the fourth row.

But between the second and final qualifying sessions, it finally dawned on Caldwell that the car's problems might have something to do with all the changes he had ordered after Spain. In the early morning, he woke his mechanics and ordered the car put back to its previous specification and set-up, except for the oil coolers which couldn't be changed at the track. Hunt recalled: "We decided in desperation to put the car back exactly to Spanish settings, but it made no difference to the car at all." Hunt had a dreadful time and spun a total of six times in practice and qualifying.

But for once, Lauda was not dominant. Jody Scheckter qualified on pole with Mario Andretti's Lotus alongside him. In the race, Andretti stormed off into the lead but was penalised a minute for a false start. So Scheckter led, and on the 46th lap Andretti's engine blew up. Scheckter and Depailler finished 1-2, Lauda was third, and Hunt fifth. He was awarded two hard-earned points as he wrestled his way around the Anderstorp track. Those two points earned in Sweden were to prove absolutely crucial six months later. Afterwards, he told journalists that he considered it his best performance of the year; a mark of how bad the car really was. Lauda came third in his worst result of the year, but was still leading Hunt by 47 points. Hunt said: "My best drive of that year; I finished miles behind in a very undriveable car and, with hindsight, it was absolutely crucial to winning the championship because it got me two points. And I won by one."

Of course, nobody saw it that way at the time. Back at the factory in England, Caldwell and the McLaren mechanics were panicking. Teddy Mayer put them under intolerable pressure, and they all feared for their jobs. Hunt had suspected what was wrong from the start but Caldwell simply wouldn't listen. Now Mayer was listening, as Hunt recalled: "It was one of the problems I had with McLaren; trying to persuade them to do anything. Straightaway, I said to them this 3/8 inch on the rear track is screwing up the car. Something fundamental has changed, so why don't we put it back to exactly how it was for Spain, except to be within the width limit?"

The mechanics had already put the car back to the Spanish Grand Prix configuration – apart from re-mounting the oil coolers. But Caldwell was sure that the mounting of the oil coolers wasn't the problem as, outwardly, there was nothing to suggest that it could be. Hunt said: "They had been moved so minutely from their old position relative to the wing, that we couldn't believe it could be that."

For once, it was Teddy Mayer who was right about a technical issue. At this stage Mayer was so frustrated that he even considered firing Caldwell, taking direct control of the team himself and promoting one of the mechanics to be the new team manager. Caldwell, under extreme and unrelenting pressure from Mayer and, against his better judgment, put the oil coolers back to where they had been. Mayer, convinced he was right, authorised an expensive test session at the Paul Ricard circuit in the south of France to test the car in the revised configuration. Caldwell remembered: "We went down there with a car and James."

When the team got the revised car to the Paul Ricard track, it was clear within a handful of laps that Mayer had been right and that they had sorted the problem simply by reverting to the pre-Spain specification. Caldwell told Hunt's biographer Christopher Hilton the fascinating manner in which the discovery was made, at least as he remembered it: "We ran with the coolers on the back, James driving, then put them on the side and James went a second and a half quicker."

Hunt, however, was not immediately convinced, believing that the changing track conditions were affecting his time. As he told Caldwell: "No, no, no. It's not the car, it's me. The track is cleaning up, the tyres are working better." Caldwell told him: "Ah well, just to check, we'll switch them to the back again." Hunt said: "No, no, no need to do that." Caldwell responded: "Well, we'll do it anyway." The mechanics moved them back and Hunt went out again. When he returned, he asked: "What happened there?" Caldwell replied: "You were two seconds slower again." Hunt still did not get it and said: "The track's worse, it's not the coolers, they have no effect at all." Caldwell said: "Okay, we'll change them back again."

Hunt was becoming increasingly angry, and said: "I won't drive the car", to which Caldwell said: "Oh yes, you will." The mechanics changed the coolers and, as Caldwell said: "James went one and a half, maybe 1.8 seconds quicker. That proved it to us."

But many of the people present at the test session that day say that Caldwell has rewritten history in his version of the events. In actual fact, they say things happened the other way around, with Caldwell not believing the changes and Hunt forcing him to make them. They say Caldwell was miffed over the cock-up he had made, and was attempting to change the narrative of what happened.

Caldwell made his comments to Hunt's biographer after Hunt was dead and therefore unable to set the record straight. But before he died, Hunt had always been very clear about his version of what happened: "It took me until the French Grand Prix and we were still struggling disastrously until finally I persuaded them [to make the changes]. They did it overnight and we stuck it straight on the pole."

Despite the successes, Caldwell always seemed to have something against Hunt and was frequently scathing of his abilities as a test driver, saying: "James was not a good test driver: lazy, never interested in testing, and the results he gave us were dubious." He added: "He tried to be professional. But he was always lazy. We should have hired a more competent test driver and got the car quicker. Then, on race day, we could have dragged James in on his leash, strapped him into the car and let him loose like a mad dog."

But Peter Collins, the former team principal of Lotus and a close personal friend of Hunt's, said: "James was an extremely intelligent individual who thought about the science of motor racing. From my memory, James was very voluble about the problems after Spain and just wanted the car returned to its previous spec."

Harvey Postlethwaite who had worked with Hunt at Hesketh between 1973 and 1975, also disagreed strongly with Caldwell's remarks: "James could talk about racing cars, about driving, understeer, and oversteer, whatever. He was a super guy to work with; very English, very pragmatic, intelligent. One realised how technically good he was. He understood racing cars and he did not believe in the bullshit, and I found that refreshing."

The McLaren mechanics discovered that changing the position of the oil coolers by less than two centimetres had been enough to upset the extremely sensitive pressure area under the rear wing and disrupt the airflow. It was a lesson in aerodynamics the team was never to forget. Soon after, the McLaren-Ford M23 was a potential race winner again, and Hunt could feel it.

In six weeks, McLaren had almost ruined its world championship chances by its own hand. So much so that Hunt no longer considered himself in contention for the world championship title, as he said: "We lost Belgium, Monte Carlo and Sweden as a result of that, which was extremely crucial to the championship. We were totally uncompetitive."

Worse still, the team had a public relations problem on its hands. Caldwell and Mayer had told the world and the FIA that the two centimetres by which the car had been too wide had actually made no difference to its performance. But, since it had reduced the width of the car, the car had actually become uncompetitive. The discrepancy did not bode well for the team's chances of winning its upcoming appeal against the disqualification. Between the Swedish and French races, there were scores of newspaper articles on the subject – most of them condemning McLaren.

The French Grand Prix was scheduled for the 4th July, a three-week break after Sweden. It would be held on the 3.6-mile Paul Ricard circuit at Le Castellet. It left plenty of time for McLaren to prepare the car in its original spec. But Ferrari hadn't been idle either. It had completed a major redesign of its flat 12 engine to get more power, despite the fact that it was already the most powerful engine on the grid.

While he waited in France, Hunt checked into the Ile Rousse Hotel, which overlooked a beach full of topless bathers. He was in his element: inspecting his potential conquests by day, without the inconvenience of them being clothed, and bedding them by night. That carried on all weekend. But he overindulged in a French delicacy, then unknown in England, called *pâté de foie gras* and made himself ill. As a result, he was left feeling slightly off-colour all weekend.

In the first qualifying session, Hunt was second fastest to Carlos Pace's Brabham-Alfa Romeo. In the second session, he was fastest ahead of Niki Lauda's Ferrari. The times were the fastest of qualifying and were carried through a slower final session to put Hunt on pole position. Ferrari was caught out as it had been increasing the rev limit of its new engine in every session. Without that, Lauda and Regazzoni would undoubtedly have been sharing the front row. They also might have had some prior notice of the problems they would encounter the following day. The sense of relief that permeated through the whole team that afternoon in France was almost palpable.

Caldwell, free from the burden of an uncompetitive car, was now back at his best. In qualifying, he had noticed that the Goodyear tyres Hunt was using were behaving strangely. He spotted that once they had been on the car for a few laps, they were a lot quicker and more consistent. He also noticed that the new cold tyres were very unstable. So Caldwell gambled on starting the race with a set of part-worn tyres, which he thought would stay consistent throughout the race. For once, Hunt agreed with Caldwell's technical analysis.

None the wiser, Lauda started as usual with a new set of tyres. He made the best of the start and disappeared into the distance. Hunt bided his time in second and closed the gap gradually. Hunt could also see Lauda's engine losing oil and water out of the back, and he knew it would be just a matter of time before it blew up. And indeed, on the eighth lap, Lauda coasted to a halt with a broken crankshaft. Then Regazzoni took over the lead, using every bit of power in the revised Ferrari engine on the long Paul Ricard straights. Eleven laps later, Regazzoni's Ferrari suffered its own crankshaft failure.

Hunt led comfortably from Depailler in the Tyrrell-Ford but, by lap 40, Hunt began to feel ill and was sick inside his helmet. He barely made it to the chequered flag, with Depailler 12 seconds behind in second place. John Watson came home third and Carlos Pace fourth, but Watson was initially disqualified after his rear wing was found to be too high. Hunt knew this was a lucky win, saying: "It was all rather depressing for the first laps of the race because of Ferrari's special engines. They just disappeared from me and there was nothing I could do. It was simply just a matter of power as they whizzed off down the straight and they really got a big lead. But you have to give credit to their quality control because it handed me the race on a plate, and I absolutely needed it."

Hunt went back to his hotel with the mechanics and celebrated with the girls from the beach; although not as late as he would have liked because he and Mayer were due to fly to Paris for the appeal hearing against McLaren's Spanish disqualification.

At dawn the next morning, Hunt, Mayer and Lotus boss Colin Chapman, flew to Paris in Chapman's plane. Chapman had generously agreed to testify on McLaren's behalf concerning the invalidity of their disqualification from the Spanish Grand Prix. Dean Delamont, secretary of the Royal Automobile Club in London, was also a witness.

Chapman and Delamont argued that the penalty had been too severe, and the five FIA-appointed judges seemed to agree. Maintaining that the punishment didn't fit the crime, Mayer asked for a fine instead of disqualification. The five judges went away to deliberate for over 24 hours. But Mayer walked out of the appeal court building greatly encouraged by the impartiality of the judges, as he said afterwards: "They obviously hadn't pre-judged the matter."

On the Tuesday morning, Jean-Jacques Freville, Secretary General of the FIA, came out of the FIA building and told waiting journalists that Hunt's McLaren was "only minimally in excess." His statement read: "The exclusion incurred by the McLaren car driven by James Hunt, who had won the event, is annulled, with all the consequences that this measure entails."

Hunt's championship points were reinstated and the team was fined US$3,000 instead. According to Caldwell, the win in France – with the car back to the original pre-Spain specification – had been the reason for their successful appeal. He said: "I'm certain the psychological advantage of us winning the day before proved decisive. If we hadn't, Ferrari would have carried the day. They would have been able to say: 'Look, these bastards are uncompetitive because they've narrowed their car, so they did have an unfair advantage when it was wider in Spain. They shouldn't get their points back.' But we proved by winning with the narrower car that it made no difference, and the hearing said 'okay.'"

Hunt, not quite able to believe the turn of events, simply said: "It has been a pleasant surprise being reinstated into Spain."

Added to the points won in France, Hunt now had 18 extra points and Lauda had lost three. In the space of two days, Hunt had effectively moved 21 points closer to Lauda. With Lauda now at 52 points, Hunt was up to 26.

At the halfway point in the season, winning the world championship no longer seemed as impossible as it had only 48 hours earlier.

SHUNT

CHAPTER 22

Fiasco at Brands Hatch 1976
A fantastic British feeling

The British Grand Prix at Brands Hatch in 1976 was always going to be a grudge match between James Hunt and Niki Lauda, and Ferrari and McLaren. Enzo Ferrari kicked off the hate when he told Italian journalists that the decision to reinstate Hunt into the Spanish Grand Prix results was "a wicked verdict" and that the perfect revenge would be for his cars to trounce McLaren at their home race.

Newspapers were full of inevitable speculation about Hunt's chances of winning the British Grand Prix. The last English, as opposed to British, driver to win it had been the late Peter Collins, driving a Ferrari in 1958, some 18 years earlier.

When James Hunt arrived at London's Heathrow airport from Marbella to compete in the British Grand Prix he was greeted by a crowd of enthusiastic fans, and it gradually began to dawn on him just how popular he had become. He had arrived for ten days of non-stop activity before the race on 18th July.

His sponsors, Texaco, Vauxhall and Marlboro made the most of Hunt's presence, arranging various promotional events throughout the week. He had also agreed to appear at some charity events. But the highlight of the week for him was a *Rolling Stones* concert at Earl's Court, where Hunt found himself in greater demand even than Mick Jagger.

He was also the star turn at a big televised event at the Albert Hall called 'Grand Prix Night With The Stars.' The event was organised by CSS and promoted by Barrie Gill and Andrew Marriott on behalf of John Webb, who decided he needed something big to promote the Grand Prix. It was dedicated to the Graham Hill Memorial Fund, as Marriott remembers: "We came up with the concept of 'The Grand Prix Night With The Stars' and we knew people in those days, and we managed to get it televised on the BBC." They even persuaded legendary BBC producer Ernest Maxim to produce it. The Albert Hall's private boxes were packed with celebrities in evening dress who had paid UK£500 for a box.

Marriott had planned for Hunt to be there to take a curtain call on stage and was surprised when he approached him back stage on the night and said: "I play the trumpet, you know. I can do something on stage." He then added: "I tell you what, I'll play them my trumpet." A sceptical Marriott humoured him, but Hunt insisted and took to the stage during a gap in proceedings. Hunt was introduced by celebrity astronomer Patrick Moore, who had just done his own impromptu performance of what he called his "soft-shoe shuffle." Moore reached for a trumpet left behind on the bandstand by Chris Barber, who had done an earlier turn. "You're supposed to be good at blowing your own trumpet," he said, "so try this one." The audience laughed, expecting a comedy routine. But Hunt took the trumpet and the band began to play. As the event was live, Marriott was worried sick and remembers: "He did this trumpet thing and I think a lot of people will remember that forever. It was absolutely fantastic, the highlight of the evening, and yet another side to him."

It fact, it was a memorable moment as Hunt, dressed in t-shirt and denim jeans, played as good as any professional. The audience roared with undisguised approval. Afterwards, Peter Hunt said: "I had hell of a job convincing the BBC, who were recording the show, that James really was a good enough trumpet player to perform on TV. He learned to play at about 12 or 13, when he was at Wellington. He was in the school orchestra and the school band, and played solo at concerts."

But Hunt was self-deprecating about his abilities afterwards, saying modestly: "You have to be very good to make a nice noise completely solo on the trumpet, and I'm just not good enough."

One person sitting at the Albert Hall that night was Stuart Turner, public affairs director of Ford of Britain, who had last witnessed Hunt's shenanigans at Vallelunga, when he had disrupted the Formula Ford race there in 1968. He said: "Now I have seen everything: James Hunt playing the trumpet at the Albert Hall." Turner went home that night utterly bemused that the thuggish young man he had met and chastised eight years earlier had just played trumpet solo at the Albert Hall in front of eight thousand people live, and millions more on television to boot.

Aside from the fun and games, there was also some more serious business, as Hunt had to drive a Vauxhall in the Texaco Tour of Britain. The Tour was a big promotion for both Texaco and Vauxhall, two of his biggest sponsors. With its mix of race and rally style driving on public roads and with special stages at race tracks, the event attracted celebrities as well as race drivers. CSS had set up the deal and Hunt was being paid US$25,000 to do it.

Hunt drove a Vauxhall Magnum, a sporty version of the Vauxhall Viva – then the most popular car in Britain. His co-driver was BBC radio presenter, Noel Edmonds. Edmonds was an amateur race driver and car buff who also flew his own helicopter. Edmonds remembers: "We got in this car and off we went. I was navigating and James did all the driving. It was my job to make sure the car was ready for the races and to get James in the right place at the right time, which was not easy."

In truth, Hunt and Edmonds, although they furiously denied it at the time, did not get on too well. The problem was that, right at the start of the event, Hunt had insulted Edmonds' then wife, Gill. Hunt didn't understand why Edmonds had brought along his wife and thought she was getting in the way. When Edmonds told him she was part of his support team, Hunt laughed in front of her. Edmonds recalls: "I remember him being extraordinarily rude to my wife. Gill really loved motor racing and of course she thought James Hunt was wonderful, but he was a sexist bastard." He adds: "He just seemed to delight in dismissing her involvement and her presence."

With two colourful personalities in the same car, the newspapers had a field day and sensationalist headlines captured every incident-packed day, or so it seemed – there were soon reports of crashes, clashes with the police and altercations with other motorists.

Hunt eventually began wondering why he had agreed to participate in the strange event in the first place. Sensing that he had been forced into it by Texaco and Vauxhall, he sought to end the charade as soon as he could. He drove wildly, reasoning that a crash would allow him to retire and retreat to his parents' house for some peace and quiet. The wrong tyres were fitted to the car early on and Hunt lost control, slamming into a tree on a timed section over a stretch of forest track.

Edmonds was astonished at what happened: "James was not good at driving on the loose stuff. The tree we hit, you would have missed and I would have missed. When we went into this tree, it was a phenomenal experience – he hit it absolutely square on. We came down this straight bit and I said: '90 right.' He was on the brakes and we just went straight into a bloody big tree. We hit it so hard and so square that if we'd had a rear seat passenger, he could have changed gears for us. The engine came into the cockpit. I think he was really embarrassed."

Hunt wanted to retire the car there and then, but Edmonds said it could be fixed. The disagreement escalated into a furious row between the two men, with Edmonds winning and the car being attended to overnight.

In fact, the car actually had to be replaced with an entirely new one, which was against the rules and a sure sign that they should have retired. But Hunt and Edmonds were the stars of the event, and Vauxhall was going to use any means possible to keep them in the race. The next day, newspaper reports said that Hunt apparently had behaved like a "spoilt child" when Edmonds tried to have the car repaired in order to continue in the rally. Although Hunt would later describe the altercation as an "amicable and reasoned discussion", it most certainly was not.

In another incident, Hunt and Edmonds were stopped by the police for speeding whilst trying to make up lost ground. Hunt became immersed in another argument, and it didn't look good in the following day's newspapers. He later admitted: "I won't say I behaved very well on the Tour, but the outcome was a combination of circumstances and sensationalist reporting. The combination of circumstances was the fact that several separate small incidents happened; taking them into a combination made them quite big, and then exaggerating each story individually made the whole thing very big. That's really what happened."

Edmonds saw it differently, thinking that the newspapers actually understated what happened: "We were chased by the police and I remember us driving down public roads in excess of 120, 130 miles an hour, and I was so cripplingly ashamed of what was happening that I tried to have my arm out of the car covering my name – because all the people we were cutting up, no, I mean scything through – there were people ending up on pavements and all sorts of things – the only name they would have seen painted on the side of the car was mine."

In the end, the two men fell so far behind with all the incidents that they had to retire from the event early. Fed up with the Tour, Hunt returned to his parents' house in Surrey for a few days to himself. He said: "I realised I had been living my life up to the red line, and I had drained myself completely. The peace and quiet was like a cocoon to me. I needed my solitude. I needed to wind down totally before cranking myself up to the intense pitch which is vital to a good result in the race."

It was a wise decision as the 1976 British Grand Prix at Brands Hatch was set to be a serious showdown between Hunt and Lauda. It was all so different from just six years prior, when he was competing in the Formula 3 race supporting the British Grand Prix and walking around the paddock with his shirt off, completely ignored by the spectators. As he walked around Brands six years later, he hankered after anonymity. With that in mind, he sought out his old friend from 1970, Tony Dron. Dron was still driving in Formula 3 and, as he sat in his car on the starting grid, Hunt walked out of the pit lane to be with him.

Brands Hatch was packed every day from Thursday to Sunday for the Grand Prix weekend. The maximum capacity was around 80,000, and it had been years since the race had attracted so many spectators. The attendance also benefited by the fact that the race was not being televised live. As expected, the BBC had withdrawn from its planned live broadcast because of the Durex logos on the Surtees cars. Embarrassingly, it was revealed that the CSS agency had brokered the deal with Surtees. But even Bernie Ecclestone supported John Surtees' decision to keep the Durex logos on the cars. He knew that if he allowed TV broadcasters to dictate sponsorship deals, it would be a catastrophe for the sport. The deal was worth US$120,000 to Surtees, and his team would close without it.

It was all very difficult for CSS and its directors, Andrew Marriott and Barrie Gill, because CSS also represented John Player, the cigarette brand. CSS had also brokered a deal for John Player to sponsor the whole Grand Prix as well as the Lotus team. Marriott recalls: "Our biggest client was John Player Special (JPS), and we were managing the Grand Prix for them. Another client was Durex."

The whole future of the CSS agency was threatened over the affair as Peter Dyke, the head of John Player's sponsorship division, screamed down the phone to Marriott: "You've screwed us, you've screwed our TV coverage."

But Gill and Marriott managed to save the situation. They approached ITV and asked if it would be interested in broadcasting the race. ITV was very interested indeed. The BBC had a lockdown on Formula One because of its alliance with European Broadcasting Union, which then held the contract with the FIA for TV rights. ITV's head of Sport, John Bromley, saw this as an opportunity to break the BBC's domination of the sport. ITV was interested but was not about to clear its prestige Sunday afternoon schedule for a motor car race. Marriott remembers what happened: "Barry and I went to see John Bromley, and we said: 'Any chance you could put the Grand Prix on ITV?', And John said: 'Not live, but if you shoot it then we'll do a deal and put it on the following week.' And so that's what we did, and we got out of jail."

CSS called in every favour and gathered together enough cameras and crew to make an excellent film of the race, which was shown the following Saturday on ITV's 'World of Sport' programme, presented by Dickie Davis. Because of all the publicity of the Hunt-Lauda fight and the start line accident, it drew a huge audience, far bigger than the BBC would have attracted live. It turned into a huge success for everybody, and Bromley had no problem with the Durex logos.

It was also not lost on Marriott that, because of the delayed start after the accident, the BBC would have not been able to carry the race live anyway as it would have run over its slot on Sunday. The huge success of the ITV broadcast also woke up the BBC to the potential of Formula One and all that it would entail a year later.

The Lauda–Hunt battle had caught the public's interest, and Hunt really was the man of the moment. The British public identified with him more than they had with any previous British driver. Hunt was loveable because he was different; different because he wore t-shirts and jeans, walked barefoot, smoked cigarettes and drank beer. His television appearance playing the trumpet had also had an enormous impact.

Both Hunt and Lauda were very anxious. Although Lauda was comfortably ensconced at the top of the world championship points table, he could sense Hunt was on a winning streak. He also knew he was hampered by his own team's politics; a disaster waiting to happen. He could lose the championship because of his own team, despite any opposition from Hunt.

Brands Hatch was not Hunt's favourite type of track, although he had enjoyed much success there. It also wasn't suited to the McLaren he was driving, as both car and driver preferred faster tracks. It was no surprise, then, when Lauda took pole and Hunt came in second, six hundredths of a second slower on the 2.6-mile track.

But Lauda's pole was not such an advantage at Brands because, as many people pointed out, it was on the wrong side of the front row. The second spot was in fact a better grid slot. Pole meant an inside run to the first corner, a drop-away right-hander. But the track at the start line was slightly banked and it was possible to slide sideways towards the verge on the slope of the road if the wheels spun at the start. Aware of this, Lauda elected, as was his right, to start from the left hand slot – the higher side – to get a long angled run into Paddock Bend.

So Hunt was effectively on pole even though he was only second-fastest. Many felt Hunt had been sandbagging in qualifying because this is what he had wanted all along; he had been playing games with Lauda, who might have been second-guessing which position Hunt would choose. Regazzoni's Ferrari had been third-fastest behind Hunt, with Mario Andretti's Lotus fourth. The 26-car grid was very competitive, achieving times that were all within three seconds of each other.

As race day dawned, the roads were jammed with a capacity crowd trying to get in. Earlier that morning, a helicopter had hit the main power cable supplying electricity to the circuit. Either by luck or good judgment, Brands Hatch's managing director, John Webb, for the first time had hired a giant standby generator for the race. When the power went out, it immediately cut in and no one noticed.

Come the start of the race, anticipation reached fever-pitch as fans eagerly awaited the battle between Hunt and Lauda. Brands Hatch has always had an atmosphere like no other circuit in the world, but that day it was unparalleled by anything seen in Britain before or since.

Hunt made his usual poor start, but Regazzoni made a storming start from the second row and ran straight into Lauda's flanks. As Hunt described it: "Clay had made a super start – a real stormer. He went up on the left of me, sliced back in front of my car and dived at the inside of Niki from way too far back. It was quite ridiculous. Niki was already turning into the corner and Clay dived in and hit him."

For a split second, Hunt was elated as it looked as though Lauda was out already at the hands of his teammate, and he calculated the damage it would do to Ferrari's morale. He remembered: "I was able to enjoy it for, I suppose, half a second because it was wonderful and extremely funny for me to see the two Ferrari drivers take each other off the road. But it quickly became obvious that I was in it too. I got on the brakes because there was no way through, and I was punted up the rear. Then all hell broke loose. I was into Regazzoni's car, which was sliding backwards, and my rear wheel climbed over his. My car was in the air, flying, and then it crashed down again on its wheels. I didn't have a chance to be frightened or to realise that I could have been on my head." That Paddock Bend accident was one of the most spectacular in Formula One history, with much of the crowd right on top of the action and the majority able to see it from the grandstands. Hunt later described Regazzoni's driving as "a serious bout of brain fade."

Hunt's McLaren had been launched into the air but it had impacted the ground squarely the right way up on its wheels. The impact with the ground, however, had damaged the car. He said: "It launched my car up in the air and, as it came down, it broke the front suspension. I had to limp in at the back of the circuit."

Amazingly, most of the other drivers had maneuvered safely around the scene of the accident, which was littered with debris. The marshals were quickly in action and, within a minute and a half, the track was totally clear.

But Hunt was heartbroken. He had driven just 140 metres of a Grand Prix he had hoped to win. However, despite the emotions, he maintained his cool and kept the engine running. He put it into gear and let out the clutch. The car moved, but the steering and the front suspension were both seriously damaged. As he limped through the part of the circuit called Druids loop, Hunt saw the red flag; the race had been stopped and a restart ordered. He remembered: "I gave a whoop of delight. I thought all my birthdays had come at once. One second I was despairing of my luck, and now it was all on again. I turned into the back road to the pits because the car wasn't steering properly. I abandoned the car and ran down the pit road to tell the lads to come and do something about it." As he was walking back, a journalist asked him a question about what had happened, and Hunt said: "Forget that. Haven't got a cigarette, have you, old boy?"

His humour hid the fact that he was in some pain as his right thumb had been hit by the spinning steering wheel whilst the car was airborne, but this was going to turn out to be the least of his problems.

Alan Henry, the well-known journalist, had a good vantage point that day and didn't believe that Hunt was still running when the red flag was shown, as he says: "I think James knew absolutely that he was out of that race, and that he'd actually stopped. He should never had been allowed to restart it, and I think the force of Teddy Mayer, particularly, bullying the stewards, got him back in."

Hunt believed differently and was genuinely unaware that it was against the regulations for him to restart. His initial thought was to switch to his spare car for the restart. But no one was quite sure whether the first race had been completely aborted. The rules were unclear about what was to happen when a lap had not been completed.

As it could have been declared an aborted start, Alastair Caldwell decided to keep his options open. As Hunt's mechanics descended on his race car to repair it, Caldwell ordered others to get the spare car ready. Hunt recalled: "They didn't know exactly which car we would be able to run at the restart." In fact, the McLaren mechanics took the spare car to the grid and put it in position while arguments went on about whether or not it was eligible.

Everyone had an opinion about what would happen next. Most of the team managers and race officials were now congregated in race control in the Brands Hatch tower, directly overlooking the start line. Caldwell and Mayer knew exactly what they had to do: to delay as long as possible. So they deliberately inflamed the argument in the control tower in order to gain their mechanics valuable time to repair Hunt's car. Every 15 minutes, Caldwell was running back and forth from the pits to the tower, reporting to Mayer on the situation with the repairs. Hunt remembered: "The stewards couldn't decide what to do because the rule book was unclear and, of course, with that, there were also a lot of Formula One team managers with a lot of words to say on the subject. The stewards were confused and the rule book was confusing, so chaos reigned."

The rule book stated: 'When a red flag is displayed, the race must stop immediately, and if there is a restart to the race, all people who are competing at the time are allowed to restart.'

The grounds for not allowing him to restart were complex, but the essence was that Hunt had not completed a lap at the time of the accident. Furthermore, he had entered the pits from the wrong direction.

Hunt's contention was that he had seen the red flag displayed and had been obeying this instruction by stopping racing immediately. The rival team managers contended that a driver is not competing if he hasn't even completed a lap. They also firmly stated that Hunt should not have entered the pits from the wrong direction, as at no time may a car be driven deliberately in the opposite direction during a race. That rule was clear.

Caldwell and Mayer argued that the obvious solution was to declare the first race null and void. For a race to be stopped after 140 metres was unheard-of in Formula One racing. But the stewards decided that the race had gone on longer, as Lauda had managed to keep moving and had threaded his car out of trouble after the initial contact from Regazzoni, and he had been the leader when the race was red-flagged.

It also became very clear that Dean Delamont, the clerk of the course, had been premature in stopping the race. Apparently, he had taken advice from his senior safety official who had been worried that cars would complete the first lap and be confronted with a blocked track full of debris. Delamont took the decision to stop the race and erred on the side of caution, but the crashed cars and debris had been cleared away by the very efficient British marshals almost immediately. With the track cleared, the race need not have been stopped at all; that it had been, was Hunt's good fortune.

As the arguments raged about what to do next, Daniele Audetto alleged that Delamont had deliberately ordered the race to be stopped in order to give Hunt a chance of restarting. On the surface, his argument was sound and made sense, but the obvious and transparent honesty of Delamont and the British officials was clear to everyone present.

All the teams were protecting their interests. Three cars – Hunt's McLaren, Regazzoni's Ferrari and Jacques Laffite's Ligier – had been damaged in the accident and, so, when the cars were called back to the grid 30 minutes later, all three drivers appeared in their spare cars. The race was ready to restart and it was officially announced over the circuit loudspeakers that the race would proceed as if the first lap had not occurred. However, this was followed by the announcement that no car would be allowed to restart that had not completed the first lap. The race, it had been decided, would include neither Hunt, Regazzoni, nor Laffite.

The Brands Hatch crowd had been watching and listening in silence. They appeared ready to accept the decision stoically. But there was a trouble-maker in their midst. Andrew Frankl, the Hungarian born publisher of *Car Magazine*, was acting as a photographer that day and was wearing a valuable circuit-issued roam-anywhere photographer's lanyard. Frankl had a history, and as a young man had been a leading participant in the 1956 Hungarian uprising against the Russians. Consequently, he knew what to do to agitate and stir up a crowd.

Frankl was on the inside of the circuit, near the pit lane. Upon hearing the announcement, he became incensed and leaned over the fence into the public area and shouted to the people to gather round. Guided by the Hungarian's natural authoritativeness, the public did as they were told. Frankl told them they needed to do something quickly in order to put pressure on the organisers to allow Hunt to start. He suggested to his crowd of attentive supporters, now at least 30-strong, that they start chanting. They decided on: "We want James."

Hearing the chant, the remaining 80,000 fans soon joined in and the words reverberated around the Brand Hatch amphitheatre. The roar of the crowd chanting in unison was extraordinary. Delamont couldn't believe it; he couldn't even hear himself talking in the control tower. After ten minutes, Frankl, who was now standing on some wooden boxes directing the proceedings like an orchestra conductor, told his people to start a slow handclap. Gradually, the crowd caught on and started clapping perfectly in time. No one had ever heard 80,000 people slow handclapping in the open air before in Britain, and it had an extraordinary effect on the mood in the control tower.

British motor racing had never seen anything like it. But it did not remain entirely good-natured. The fans soon turned nasty and began throwing bottles and cans onto the track. It was getting very ugly and the crowd in the main grandstands opposite the pit looked likely to storm the barriers in their quest to block the track and prevent a restart without Hunt. As missiles of every description rained down on the track stewards, Delamont seemed genuinely scared by what might happen next – especially if Hunt was excluded from the restart.

Hunt had been resigned to his fate, but the fans' reaction stirred the caveman instinct in him. The crowd's constant baying made Hunt determined to start the race. In the absence of Mayer and Caldwell, busy with their delaying tactics in the tower, he took charge. He ordered his mechanics to leave the spare car on the grid and to not move it off, despite the steward's orders. He told his mechanics that nothing and nobody would prevent him from starting the race – even if he was disqualified afterwards. Ferrari and Ligier mechanics, following Hunt's example, did the same.

This was the Vallelunga incident all over again, and Hunt became determined to start the British Grand Prix – come what may. He knew he had the support of 80,000 people just a few metres away.

There is no question that the stewards on the grid that day had their own agenda, and were deaf to many of Delamont's instructions coming from the control tower. They were frightened by what would happen if Hunt didn't race and appeared to be aware of the frantic efforts to get his car repaired; and they became almost co-conspirators in the delay.

Regazzoni was sitting in his car on the grid behind Hunt, and Audetto was adamant that if Hunt started in his spare car, so too would Regazzoni. Caldwell remembers that they disputed it to keep the argument going, but it was obvious they would be disqualified later. But McLaren weren't interested in running for the sake of it, as Hunt said: "We had realised that the spare car was out of the question. In the meantime, McLaren were naturally trying to keep the argument going because they were hastily getting my car repaired in the pits."

Hunt and Mayer were very conscious that if Hunt started in the spare car, he would certainly be black flagged. But a repaired race car meant all bets were off as it would almost certainly be legal.

Meanwhile, John Webb was watching with wry amusement. Hunt had been the bane of his life since he was a Formula 3 driver; always causing him trouble. Now he was the biggest star in Formula One and nothing had changed. Webb was responsible for the crowd's safety and, as the mood grew uglier and there were fears of a riot, he was the first to recognise that Hunt would have to be allowed to race – if only for purely practical reasons. He told the stewards so. He was the most capable man on the scene and his view would eventually prevail. He said: "There was indeed nearly a riot." Webb was called by the police for a meeting to warn him of impending trouble.

Webb blamed Anthony Marsh and the other circuit commentators for stoking up the crowd. He said: "He got them in a rebellious state and the police were quite anxious at that time. We couldn't do anything about it. We were the circuit owners but the meeting was being run by the RAC.

"At the time, I don't think they regarded it as terribly serious because British crowds at motor race meetings don't get out of control. It was purely the James Hunt factor. If it had been any other two drivers, nobody would have bothered too much." But the modest Webb eventually told Delamont what he would have to do to save the day.

Hunt remembered Webb's intervention well, saying: "The organisers rather than the officials decided the only way they were going to get the race started was to start me whatever happened, because [the crowd] were throwing beer cans on the track."

In the control tower, Delamont and his officials continually consulted the FIA rulebook while being watched by 30 or so people, all with a different opinion about what should happen. Delamont couldn't make any sense of what the rules actually meant. The starting grid was also thronging with people with different opinions, and, in the intense heat, arguments broke out between the teams. The arguments continued as the clock ticked on and Hunt's race car repairs neared completion. The other team managers gradually became aware of Hunt's and Caldwell's tactics of blatantly playing for time. But, by now, the team managers were on Mayer's side, as the crowd turned uglier and uglier. Hunt remembered: "The crowd went completely hooligan. I'd never known anything like it. They'd got fed up with the rules and they didn't want any more rubbish. They wanted to see a motor race."

It was close to an hour since the accident had occurred when Hunt's race car was finally pushed back on to the grid and the spare wheeled away. A new steering arm and front suspension had been fitted to his car. As Hunt admitted: "They'd put a whole new corner on it."

Caldwell returned to the control tower and now started arguing against spare cars being allowed as Audetto stared at him in disbelief, especially when a surprised Mayer chimed in as well. Audetto was screaming about Regazzoni and, although it was clearly against the rules, the stewards ruled to let both Regazzoni and Laffite restart in their spares. The stewards reasoned that the irregularities would be sorted out later.

The grid was cleared and the start of the second race was on. The cars were allowed another warm up lap and Hunt found his to be in remarkably good shape. As it came back onto the grid, the mechanics swarmed round. Hunt remembered: "The boys didn't have time to track it out but we tweaked it a bit after the warm up lap. It wasn't very good to start off with, but then the car began to settle and then started going really well."

Lauda made the best start, ahead of Hunt and Regazzoni. Carrying a full tank of fuel, Hunt's hastily rebuilt car was not nearly as fast, as he said: "You can't throw the car with full tanks because it just won't throw; it just pushes whatever you do because it's got all that weight of fuel forward."

As the fuel load started to drop, Hunt found that he could throw the car around more and go faster. At half distance, Lauda was leading but Hunt closed in on him. Hunt recalled: "I'd been catching Lauda steadily but not enough, and then I was helped by a couple of back markers trailing the field.

He got the worst of that, and about five laps after that I started stabbing at him."

As Hunt began to seek ways past the Ferrari, the fans began cheering. The noise from the crowd was so loud he could hear it above the sound of his engine.

On the 45th lap, Hunt finally drove inside Lauda and passed him on the climbing approach to Druids Hill. The crowd was wild with joy and emotions were overflowing. He said: "I knew I'd got him. I knew I was getting on top and our lap times were coming down. It was quite fantastic. We were racing at around 1 minute 19 seconds for a lap of Brands, the sort of time with which Niki and I had qualified with light fuel loads in practice."

After he was passed, Lauda didn't contest it and settled in to finish second, preserving points.

Hunt was disappointed in Lauda that afternoon for not contesting the lead: "I wanted him to race me, not just hand over." Hunt felt he had been robbed of the satisfaction of racing for it, as he said: "I will always fight and go as fast as I can to keep the other guy under pressure, and that's the fundamental difference between us – Niki will leave it and drive for his finish."

Hunt was also cross that no one had challenged Lauda for his second place. Having grabbed maximum points with a certain win, he wanted Lauda to lose points to help him in the championship race. He said: "I was a bit annoyed with everybody else at Brands, because I needed Niki to get a whole lot less than six points for second place." But Lauda remained unchallenged as the two had been going so fast that the rest of the field was well behind. Conveniently, Regazzoni and Laffite dropped out with mechanical problems, thus saving the stewards the trouble of disqualifying them.

As he crossed the line and saw the chequered flag, Hunt raised both arms aloft to acknowledge the ecstatic fans. He said many years later to his biographer Gerald Donaldson: "Brands is such an intimate circuit anyway, and you feel the crowd more than you do anywhere else. You can sense the emotion and the movement all the time, even though you are not necessarily looking at the crowd. It's there and you respond to it." He added: "It was a fantastic feeling for me, as I sat in my car, to know I had all this support – really quite incredible."

As far as Hunt was concerned, he had properly and legally won the British Grand Prix. But not everyone thought that, most notably not Daniele Audetto. In fact, initially, Ferrari, Tyrrell and Copersucar teams lodged official protests against Hunt's victory. These three teams all stood to gain points if Hunt was disqualified. Tyrrell and Copersucar eventually withdrew their protests and the stewards rejected Ferrari's claim. Ferrari said it would take the matter under appeal to the FIA court in Paris but no one took them too seriously. Since Audetto had earlier been vigorously arguing that Regazzoni should be allowed to restart in his spare car, Caldwell asked him how he could now appeal against Hunt starting again in his race car. Audetto gasped at the hypocrisy, remembering how Caldwell had reversed his own spare car argument as soon as Hunt's race car was repaired. He just stared at Caldwell and said three words: "It's my job." With that, he stalked away.

Hunt's win marked one of the greatest days in British Grand Prix history. It certainly had been the most controversial day ever seen in Brands Hatch. Afterwards, as the other drivers helicoptered away, he stayed at the track until midnight drinking with friends, who were camping nearby. They had set up a barbecue beside their tents in the car park to celebrate, and there was plenty of celebrating to do. Hunt had earned nine points, bringing his total to 35 points against Lauda's 58. He was 23 points behind as a trip to the Nürburgring loomed a fortnight hence, on the first day of August.

SHUNT

CHAPTER 23

Near Death Experience
Niki Lauda 1976

Back from the dead and as fast as ever

Niki Lauda arrived at the Nürburgring for the 1976 German Grand Prix on the Thursday morning before the race on 1st August. It was a very different track in those days. It was the old Nürburgring; 14.2 miles long and unlike any other circuit in the world. Situated in the heavily forested Eiffel mountains, west of Koblenz, it was possibly the least suitable venue for a Formula One Grand Prix. The 14.2 miles contained a staggering 177 corners. The circuit, which opened in 1920, was usually covered in mist and fog and often damp with varying weather conditions at each end.

It was without doubt the most dangerous circuit in the world. By 1976, over 140 drivers had been killed in 56 years; an average of nearly three a year. It was not until 1974, after a campaign by Jackie Stewart, that safety was addressed. Miles of catch fencing and steel guard rails were installed, finally stopping cars from flying off the circuit into the trees.

All of this was going through Lauda's mind as he sat caught up in a traffic jam outside the circuit entrance. As he sat there, stationary in his car with the window open, a fan approached him and showed him a picture of Jochen Rindt's grave. Lauda was bewildered and wondered what the point was and how he was supposed to react. Pleased with himself, the fan walked off but the incident stuck in Lauda's mind. Rindt was a fellow Austrian and had been world champion in 1970, but he was killed that same year at the Italian Grand Prix in Monza; only two years before Lauda entered Formula One. Lauda hated omens and wondered whether this was one.

It signalled the start of what would be the most difficult weekend of Lauda's life. He had been a firm opponent of the circuit on safety grounds and had wanted it closed. Thinking it far too dangerous, Lauda had voiced his concerns in public and had taken a lot of criticism in the media for his views. He was wondering what to expect at the Nürburgring and what sort of welcome he would get.

A recent television documentary had shown German fans accusing him of being "chicken-hearted" and "cowardly" because of his views of their beloved circuit. One particular fan interviewed said that if Lauda was so terrified of the ring, he should get out of Formula One. Lauda had watched the programme in Germany sitting in a hotel room on his own. Outraged by it, he said: "I was absolutely livid, knotted with rage at my inability to defend myself."

Lauda had first visited Nürburgring in 1969 as a twenty-year-old driver in Formula Vee, the German equivalent of Formula Ford in Britain. His views were very different back then, as he remembers: "We didn't think it was at all bad, only exciting." In fact, for a long time, Lauda was a big fan of the circuit and one of his ambitions was to drive the ring perfectly. He believed it offered a challenge unlike any other. In 1973, he took a BMW saloon racer round in eight minutes and 17.4 seconds, then a record time for that class of car.

Later that same year, and again in 1974, Lauda was involved in several major accidents at the circuit. It was a period when drivers were being killed on a regular basis. As lap times became faster, nothing was done about safety. Especially after Jackie Stewart had retired in 1973, the risk factor had become too high. Lauda recalls: "We were endangering not only our lives but the sport of motor racing itself by failing to do something about track safety."

Despite the installation of catch fencing and barriers, the problems at the Nürburgring were obvious. It was impossible to make safe such a long circuit, especially as much of it was tree-lined. Even with the improvements, the circuit was under constant threat of the FIA withdrawing its racing licence. Finally, in 1974, a three-year programme was launched to make safety improvements to the circuit.

1975 saw the first-ever Nürburgring lap of under seven minutes, which Lauda referred to as the "ultimate madness." Poignantly, it was Lauda himself who drove the lap, and it has not been bettered since. He said: "It was possible only because I was in a special sort of mood that day and ready to go for broke to an extent I have never permitted myself since. As I flashed past the pits, I glanced in my rear-view mirror and saw the mechanics waving their hands in the air. I knew then that I had cracked the seven-minute barrier. To be exact, my new Formula One lap record was 6 minutes 58.6 seconds. And that's how it stands to this day – no one has ever driven the ring faster."

It was a whole minute faster than when Jackie Stewart had driven his Matra-Ford in 1968, seven years earlier. He continues: "My brain kept telling me it was sheer stupidity. I knew every driver was taking his life in his hands to the most ludicrous degree."

Jackie Stewart, who won at the circuit three times, most famously in the wet in 1968, agreed with him and said: "I was always afraid. When I left home to race in the German Grand Prix I always used to pause at the end of the driveway and take a long look back. I was never sure that I would come home again."

The danger levels were so high that, at a drivers' meeting in early 1976, Lauda proposed that the German Grand Prix be moved away from the Nürburgring on safety grounds. He was hoping for a driver boycott of the circuit with immediate effect, but he was voted down as a considerable amount of money had been spent on safety precautions.

That vote was to change Lauda's life and the course of Formula One history. If it had gone the other way, James Hunt would never have been world champion and Lauda would have become the greatest driver the sport had ever seen. After the vote, Lauda was heavily criticised, which led to the television documentary.

Before Nürburgring, Lauda had been on top of the world. Comfortably leading the world championship, he looked certain to win again in 1976. It would have made him one of the few men to win back-to-back titles and to successfully defend a title. He had already amassed 61 points, while James Hunt had only 26.

He had other reasons to be pleased: the Ferrari team management was holding up surprisingly well after the departure of Luca di Montezemolo. Indeed, Lauda had just signed a brand new and highly lucrative contract with

Ferrari for the 1977 season. The contract was worth six times the money Hunt was being paid.

That new contract, signed on the eve of Nürburgring, was to save Lauda's career. But negotiating it with the 78-year-old Enzo and his son Piero had been the stuff of pantomime. Enzo was not known as '*Il commendatore*' for nothing and he loved to play the part during the negotiations.

In a major departure from Ferrari practice, Lauda had been urged by Enzo to extend his next year's contract in the middle of the season. This was not Enzo Ferrari's usual practice; he normally liked to keep his drivers on the hook until there were no other drives available, thereby limiting their bargaining ability and pushing down their retainers.

In fact, Enzo considered himself a very shrewd tactician where drivers' contracts were concerned. But this time, his street smarts deserted him. He was frantically worried about losing Lauda, who he knew was unhappy after Montezemolo's departure. He also knew he was receiving big money offers from Bernie Ecclestone's Brabham team to drive in 1977. The fact that Brabham had Italian engines made that notion unacceptable.

Enzo was also concerned that there had been friction between Lauda and new team manager Daniele Audetto, and he was desperate to get Lauda's signature on a contract for 1977. Enzo put as much pressure as he could on Lauda to sign, especially since early negotiations with Audetto had gone nowhere.

So, in late June, Lauda finally sat down for negotiations with Enzo and Piero in the back room of the Cavallino Restaurant, situated opposite the Ferrari factory in Maranello. Ferrari's son was there to interpret Enzo's Italian into English. While Lauda's Italian was pretty good, Enzo always professed to speak no English, so the role of an interpreter appeared vital to the theatre of the negotiation.

Lauda told Enzo straightaway that part of his contract must ensure that the team be limited to two drivers in a two-car team. Enzo agreed but rejected Lauda's attempt to keep Clay Regazzoni as his teammate for 1977. Enzo told him straight out that Regazzoni would be fired at the end of the season.

Enzo then asked Lauda how much money he wanted, to which Lauda replied with an amount in Austrian schillings. As Lauda recalled in his autobiography *To Hell and Back*: "[Mr Ferrari] said nothing, but he stands up, goes over to the telephone, calls his accountant, Signor Della Casa, and asks him how much so and so many million schillings are in lire? He waits for a reply, replaces the receiver, walks back across the room and sits down facing me."

Lauda recalled that Enzo was silent for a moment and then, after a pause, suddenly screamed in Italian at the very top of his voice: "You insolent pig! How dare you? Are you crazy? We have nothing more to say to each other! We are parting company as of this minute." Or words to that effect. His son rapidly translated the string of obscenities, and Lauda later recalled that having an interpreter somehow made the expletives more abstract. Admittedly, for Lauda, the spectacle of a 78-year-old man, a legend in motor racing and a hero of all Italy, shouting at him in an unpleasant manner was very disconcerting. But that was how Enzo had planned it. But Lauda had come prepared as well. Remaining completely calm, he replied in English and said to Enzo's son: "Please tell him that, as we are parting company, I'll be flying home immediately." But Piero, realising that Lauda was not joking, said of his own volition: "Sit where you are."

Lauda did sit, but the row continued until he invited Enzo to make him a counteroffer. Enzo, by now realising that his intimidatory tactics were not working, tried a new approach of conciliation and reasonableness. He replied that he could not make a counteroffer because he only wanted his drivers to be happy, and any counteroffer he made would only make Lauda unhappy. Lauda then said: "In that case, I really will fly home because there's surely no point to this if you won't accept my price and you won't make a counteroffer."

After a long pause, Enzo finally offered him a contract with a retainer at 25 per cent less than the figure Lauda had originally named; believed to be US$300,000. It was now Lauda's turn to get angry. He told Enzo that Daniele Audetto, in previous informal conversations, had already offered him much more, and added: "Are you trying to make a fool of me?" Feeling that Enzo was being disrespectful, he said: "You want to buy my services, and that is what they cost." Enzo, believing Lauda was bluffing, yelled at him again: "What is that you say about Audetto?" With that, Enzo rose and called Audetto on the telephone. He ordered him to come to the Cavallino and explain himself. He was calling Lauda's bluff. But when the hapless team manager arrived at the restaurant, he confirmed he had already offered Lauda that sum informally. Enzo scowled at Audetto, but with a twinkle in his eye. He looked at Lauda and said: "Well, if one of my employees is mad enough to offer that kind of money, I guess I'll have to go along with it. But that's my final offer."

It still wasn't high enough for Lauda, who made a counteroffer. Calling him "incorrigible", Enzo reminded him of his blood pressure. He asked if Lauda was trying to kill him with such unreasonable demands. Lauda said to his son: "Tell him you would never have been world champion without me." But Piero refused to translate it, knowing his father would explode again. Lauda later claimed that Enzo's subsequent rant, heard by the whole restaurant, lasted at least half an hour.

After he had calmed down, another half hour of relatively more reasonable negotiations followed. Finally, Enzo said: "How much do you want?" Lauda dropped his original price by four per cent and said: "My final offer."

Enzo replied: "Okay, Jew boy." And, with that, the pantomime was over.

Lauda did not take offence at Enzo's last remark and shook his hand. His new deal was worth a shade under US$345,000. As soon as the deal was agreed, Ferrari embraced Lauda warmly and openly, as if they had just enjoyed a convivial lunch together. As Lauda recalled: "The next moment he was a charming old man, the most delightful company anyone could imagine."

But Enzo Ferrari would come to regret signing that contract, which included many other Lauda demands that would later save his career after he was injured. Without it, there is little doubt he would have been fired and replaced with Carlos Reutemann, and James Hunt would have been world champion long before the final race in Japan.

As for Lauda, life couldn't have been better. He had everything he wanted. With his personal deals, he would earn over half a million dollars in 1977, guaranteed.

So it was little wonder he was starting to think more deeply about the dangers of racing at Nürburgring. For the first time, he admitted he was scared of racing at the circuit: "I'm glad to see the finish line every lap. I'm frightened, I don't mind telling you." But he added: "You either don't come or you get on with the job of racing. So I've got on with the job and I've wound up on pole position again." But not quite this time.

When qualifying ended on Saturday afternoon, James Hunt was on pole position. Lauda, with safety on his mind, admitted he was not driving as fast as he could. He was second on the grid and only a second slower than Hunt; over a seven minute lap, it was ridiculously close. Lauda summed it up: "My personal opinion is that the Nürburgring is just too dangerous to drive on nowadays."

On race morning, the weather was unpredictable and Lauda received some bad news from home. That morning the Reichsbrücke, the biggest bridge in Austria, had collapsed into the Danube in the early hours, resulting in the loss of one life. At any other time of the day, hundreds of people would have been killed. Lauda was stunned by the news and he wondered if this was another omen. He didn't like omens.

Because of the circuit's length, the race was only 14 laps and the average speed was expected to be close to 120 miles per hour. On the starting grid, it started to rain. Every driver, except Jochen Mass, chose to start on wet weather grooved tyres. Mass was totally familiar with the meteorological conditions at his home circuit and believed the track would soon be clear. When a stiff wind rose up and quickly blew the circuit dry, his instincts were proved right.

Straightaway, Mass, who started from row five, was contesting the lead as Lauda and Hunt slithered away from the start. Lauda had a terrible start and seemed to be racing in reverse, dropping as low as twentieth place on the unsuitable tyres.

By the end of the first lap, Mass was in the lead, followed by Hunt and Ronnie Peterson's March-Ford. Everyone stopped on lap two for dry tyres.

Everyone, that is, except Peterson, who was fooled by Hunt into thinking he was going to do another lap on the wet tyres and so followed suit. Hunt slowed down and let the Swede by, before suddenly diving into the pits.

After changing tyres, Hunt's McLaren-Ford rejoined the race in second place, but already 45 seconds behind Mass. Lauda also changed from wet to slick dry tyres and drove out of the pits. Speeding away on the new tyres, he tried to make up lost time on a mostly dry track that was still damp in places. But he misjudged the conditions and his Ferrari mounted a kerb with the left front wheel. The shock of the impact went right through the car and caused a tie rod to loosen. Unaware of what had happened, Lauda thought nothing of it. But Ferrari had had problems before with tie rods failing off; it was one of the car's principal weaknesses and had not been fixed.

As he approached Bergwerk, the magnesium tie rod (one of the components that secured the suspension to the engine block where it was mounted) completely broke and detached from the engine. As a result, the rear wheel mountings collapsed straight away and the car lurched to the right. Lauda was travelling at more than 130 miles per hour when it failed.

The car went sideways into the catch fencing at Bergwerk on the outside of the corner, but it lost hardly any speed at all. With the fencing unable to contain it, the car slammed into the embankment behind and went airborne. It bounced back onto the track with Lauda helpless at the wheel. The car slammed down hard on the track and the fuel tank became detached and flew through the air, spilling lighted fuel on the track. The stunned Lauda was stationary in the middle of the racing line and looked around wondering what would happen next. It was too dangerous to move. The next car through was Guy Edwards' Hesketh-Ford. He managed to avoid the Ferrari and stopped beyond it when he saw the burning fuel and realised that Lauda was still in his car. Then the Surtees-Ford car of Brett Lunger came through. Lunger was completely unsighted and smashed straight into the Ferrari with Lauda still inside. The Ferrari burst into flames and the two cars travelled at least 90 metres down the track from the force of the impact. Harald Ertl's Hesketh-Ford then piled into the wreckage of both cars.

Amazingly, Lunger and Ertl were unhurt and they leaped from their cars to help Lauda, who was now in serious trouble from three impacts. His car was a fireball, and Lauda was waving his arms in front of his helmet to ward the flames away from his face. His helmet was askew and had been half wrenched off his head in the accident.

Now all of the cars behind Lauda stopped. Because the track was so long, the medical and fire rescue were nowhere nearby and it was up to the drivers to rescue Lauda.

Arturo Merzario in a Williams-Ford was the last to stop and, by then, some marshals had arrived. But they had no fireproof clothing. Edwards, Lunger and Ertl were doing their best but couldn't get Lauda out of the flames. Merzario rushed along the road and, without thinking, dived straight into the flames with only his overalls and flameproof balaclava to protect him. In a moment of incredible foolhardiness, the Italian went in with total disregard for his own life. As quick as a flash, Merzario unbuckled Lauda's seatbelts. However, as he did so, Lauda's helmet came off and the flames licked his face.

It was inexplicable that Lauda's helmet had come off without killing him. But it later emerged that Lauda was wearing a specially modified AGV helmet with extra foam padding to make it more comfortable to wear. The extra foam had compressed when pressure was put on the helmet, and it had easily slid off his head after the accident. The modified helmet was almost certainly not legal, leaving his face exposed to the fire. Max Mosley stamped on this practice when he became president of the FIA, and remains convinced that drivers are their own worst enemies when it comes to safety, as he said: "When the crash happened, it just came off. And of course that was the attitude in those days." Bizarrely, David Benson wrote in the *Daily Express* that: "In the force of the impact, Lauda's head had momentarily shrunk and his crash helmet had briefly expanded." That was one way of putting it.

Meanwhile, Harald Ertl had found a fire extinguisher and had no choice but to squirt it at Lauda to put out the flames. It was then that Lauda breathed in some of the toxic fumes. With the fire temporarily out, Lunger leaped onto the top of the car and lifted Lauda out. Amazingly, Lauda stayed on his feet and staggered around in great pain. Meanwhile John Watson, Emerson Fittipaldi and Hans Stuck, all of whom had been behind the accident, stopped their cars and ran down the road to help. Finding Lauda wandering around the track, Watson walked him to a dry area and lay him down.

All the drivers gathered round him for support as he lay by the side of the track. Watson put Lauda's head between his own thighs and cradled it. The other drivers carefully removed his flameproof balaclava but could see he was badly burned. Although still conscious, Lauda remembered nothing of the accident itself. He continued speaking – in Italian to Merzario and in English to Watson. He asked Merzario how his face was.

An ambulance was on the scene in less than three minutes and Lauda was taken away. Luckily, there had been an ambulance stationed at Adenan bridge, near where the accident had happened.

By this time, the red flag had been shown to the rest of the field and there was a loudspeaker announcement in the pit lane that a serious accident had blocked the track at Bergwerk, the most northerly corner of the circuit. The leading cars came round and parked in front of the pits ready for the restart.

Only the seven drivers who had witnessed the accident and its aftermath knew the extent of Lauda's injuries. The accident had happened a mile or so behind the front of the pack and they were behind Lauda before the accident. Although Edwards and Merzario had witnessed the horror of the accident, they got back to the start line just in time for the restart and did not speak to any of the other drivers. Neither did Watson, Fittipaldi or Stuck. That being the case, the only news that reached the pits was that Lauda had been walking around after the crash. As he got back in his car for the restart, Hunt believed that Lauda had escaped serious injury. He said: "He was taken off to hospital and obviously wouldn't be racing again that day, but we thought he'd have his burns patched up and we'd see him at the next race in Austria. That was what we felt then; there were no alarm stories so one was able to get into the car and go racing again with no qualms."

Chris Amon, the 33-year-old veteran driver, had arrived at the accident just after it happened and, when he stopped his Ensign-Ford and saw Lauda lying by the side of the track, he was horrified. According to Amon, he didn't think the Austrian would survive. He drove back to the pit lane and retired on the spot, saying he was finished with Formula One. Amon had also been witness to how slowly emergency services had responded to Lauda's accident. He spoke to no one and left the circuit.

The biggest loser from the restart was Jochen Mass. Mass had made the right choice of tyres, established a big lead and was certain to win the race. Now it was all for nothing and, as Hunt said: "Fate intervened and ruined it for him."

Hunt cleared his mind of everything but the task at hand, and streaked into a lead that remained unthreatened. He called that first lap "probably the most aggressive piece of driving I did all year. I was absolutely determined to get as big a lead as possible, and everything turned out right."

It was dry and this time there was no uncertainty about tyres. Hunt was ten seconds clear at the end of the first restarted lap, as he remembered: "I put in a blinding first lap and the others were spinning and falling about all over the place which helped me, so I virtually had the race won by the end of the first lap. It was only a matter of controlling things from the front."

Hunt was followed home by Jody Scheckter's Tyrrell-Ford, with Mass coming in third. By the time he finished, he was half a minute ahead of Scheckter. He would later call the victory one of his most satisfying drives. But his abiding memory of the day was seeing Teddy Mayer's reaction: "McLaren had never won at the ring and it was tremendously gratifying to me to see him so happy."

With no competition from Lauda, the victory had brought him to within 14 points of his rival.

Meanwhile, Lauda was airlifted off the track in a helicopter and, upon seeing the extent of his injuries, doctors anaesthetised him. Lauda had endured his injuries incredibly bravely, being fully conscious for over three quarters of an hour. As he drifted off, the last thing he would remember was the clatter of the helicopter blades as they took off. He was taken to Mannheim Hospital.

Lauda's own personal aeroplane pilot, Hans Klemitinger, anticipating events, flew to Vienna the moment he saw his boss being put in the helicopter. Lauda's wife Marlene was herself recovering from a miscarriage and suffered from low blood pressure, but Klemitinger knew she would want to be at her husband's side. She was already at the airport when Klemitinger landed and they were at the hospital within hours of her husband's arrival. Marlene said later: "At the time, I had no idea how badly injured he would be. I was told he was alright, but that he was in hospital. It was not until I spoke to the doctors and was allowed to see him that the shock hit me."

A team of six dedicated doctors and 34 nurses tended him. His injuries were diagnosed as first to third degree burns on his head and wrists, several broken ribs, and a broken collarbone and cheekbone. Much more serious were the poisonous fumes and toxic gases he had inhaled. His windpipe and lungs were scorched, and the build-up of fluid in his lungs was life-threatening.

That night, the doctors thought he was going to die. But after only four days in intensive care, hopes started to emerge that he would pull through. While there had been no single great injury, serious damage had been done to his lungs and to his bloodstream, which was poisoned as a result of inhaling the fire extinguisher fumes, smoke and petrol vapour. The burns on his face, head and hands were severe, although not critical.

When Hunt heard on Monday morning that Lauda was fighting for his life, he was devastated. Although they were rivals and not great friends, he said: "It was suddenly very important for me that Niki should live, in a way I hadn't realised. And I felt awful because there was nothing I could do about it. There I was, sitting at home, enjoying life when I didn't even particularly want to; I wanted to go and help or do something, and I couldn't."

Marlene Lauda was entirely unprepared for the ordeal she faced. For four long days and nights, her husband's life hung by a thread. She moved into a hotel near the hospital, visiting her husband for only an hour at a time. Each visit to the hospital was accompanied by a barrage of flash bulbs and journalists looking for answers to questions and hoping to record her anguish. She told one: "I was deeply shocked by the accident but it gave me my first real understanding of motor racing. Before that, I had no idea of the dangers of the race track. I used to smoke maybe one or two cigarettes a day, but from the time of the accident, I have become a chain smoker. I know that this is not good for my health, but it helps me through the crisis."

On Wednesday, a priest was brought into Lauda's room to give him the last rites. Wavering in and out of consciousness, it was clear that Lauda did not like the intervention of the priest. He said afterwards it damaged his morale and determination to live. He survived by sheer force of will, although some people did suggest that the reading of the last rites was a ruse by Lauda to mislead Hunt about the extent of his injuries.

Immediately after the accident, newspapers, especially in Germany, began writing tasteless articles speculating on the extent of his burns, relying on very sketchy information that had been ferreted from hospital staff. Journalists at the German newspaper *Bild* were particularly shameless. In an article with the headline: 'My God, where is his face?', one journalist wrote: "Niki Lauda, the world's fastest racing driver, no longer has a face. It is no more than raw flesh with eyes oozing out of it. Niki Lauda has survived...but how can a man exist without a face?" The story went on to forecast what life would be like for Lauda, continuing: "Horrible as it may sound, even if his body recovers completely, he will not venture into public for six months at least. It will be 1979 before they can build him a new face. By then, nose, eyelids and lips will have been refashioned. But the new face will not bear the slightest resemblance to the one he had before. Lauda the racing driver will only be recognisable to his friends through his voice and his gestures."

It was all third-hand speculative nonsense, but it sold a lot of newspapers that week. It also influenced Enzo Ferrari, who entered into panic negotiations with disaffected Brabham driver Carlos Reutemann to replace Lauda immediately.

A few days later, Lauda was airlifted to Salzburg Hospital nearer to his home. There, he would begin his astoundingly quick recovery.

No official statement was ever released by Ferrari as to the cause of the accident. Only Ermanno Cuoghi, Lauda's chief mechanic, was left to provide any explanation. As for Lauda, he said: "I recollect nothing. Not a damn thing. Except a big, black hole."

After many skin grafts, Lauda's face was made reasonably presentable and his eyelids were rebuilt with plastic surgery. But angry scars remained, and no attempt was made to replace the missing half of his right ear; Niki jested that it made it easier for him to talk on the telephone.

The accident would have no lasting effects on Lauda, although he admitted he was unsure of the psychological effects. Since then, he has only had one flashback to the accident, in 1984, when he inadvertently smoked a cannabis cigarette which caused hallucinations and memories of the flames. He then had complete and accurate recall of what had happened after the accident, and replayed it in his mind. He remembers: "Suddenly, it hit me: Nürburgring and the intensive care unit."

Despite the histrionics from *Bild*, Lauda was always unconcerned with the physical changes to his face and body, as he said: "My talent for overriding my emotions by staying detached and objective served me well. There was really no point in having a complex about losing half an ear. Take a good look at yourself in the mirror – that's you, that's the way you are. And if people don't like you that way, you might as well forget them. I'm not going to have cosmetic surgery. As long as they function unimpaired, I don't feel the need."

Remarkably, Lauda also seemed to come into a similar awareness about his marriage. Nearly 15 years after the accident, he decided to get a divorce from Marlene. At the family house in Spain, he recalls: "I took her out for a walk and I said to her: 'Listen, I think we should get divorced' and she said: 'I think that's a good idea.'"

Having expected a somewhat more robust reaction, Lauda admitted he was taken aback. His attitude to her was: "Oh really?" to which she replied: "I've got my life" and he said: 'Okay, tell me what you want. You can have anything you want.'"

Her demands were modest, as she told him: "I want the house, I want the donkey, I want the cat and the dog and the three chickens." By this time Lauda was annoyed at how easy it all was. He had expected a fight and outrageous demands. He replied: "Fucking fine, help yourself woman, couldn't give a shit."

Lauda later confided in John Hogan, the man he had enlisted to help him get married all those years ago, that: "Well the dogs, the horses, and cats, and donkeys, and all the other shit: that's what drove me mad anyway. Then I realised I'm stuck with two houses in Austria, fucking aeroplanes, cars, all this fucking shit that I don't want anyway. And she's got the stuff I want."

Lauda spent the next 15 years reliving his playboy years. He finally fell for one of his airline stewardesses, Birgit Wetzinger, who donated him a kidney that he badly needed as a relic of the accident. In 2008, they had twins a boy and a girl. They married in 2009.

SHUNT

CHAPTER 24

The Championship Year
July to September 1976

Better than Clark, as good as Stewart

When James Hunt arrived in Austria for the eleventh race of the 1976 Formula One world championship, he couldn't have been on a greater high. No drink or drugs were needed to sustain him that golden weekend in the middle of August.

The setting was the 3.67-mile Österreichring circuit, and it looked magnificent within view of the glorious Alps. Located 60 miles from Graz and laid out on the foothill slopes of the Alps in beautiful countryside, it was arguably the most beautiful circuit on the Formula One calendar.

Europe was enjoying an unprecedented heat wave that summer, with over 60 days of unbroken sunshine since late May. Not a drop of rain had fallen in that time.

It was even hotter in Britain, which had not seen weather like it in recent times. The good weather was set to last for another two weeks. It seemed as if the sun was shining on James Hunt.

Hunt was now the biggest celebrity in Britain and one of the most famous sportsmen in the world. His marriage, divorce and succession of girlfriends, combined with his extraordinary success on the track, had made him a national hero. It was enhanced even more by the fact that he had taken on and beaten the 'German' enemy, Lauda – even though Lauda was Austrian. Although the war had ended 31 years earlier, it was still very fresh in the minds of the many 50-plus-year-olds who had fought in it. They were rooting for Hunt with the same enthusiasm as if the war was being fought all over again.

Without question, Hunt was at the height of his powers and more popular than any Formula One driver in history. The situation had even forced his employers to come out and issue a statement saying as much; Hunt was tickled pink by the accolades as Alastair Caldwell said: "I think Britain now has another Jimmy Clark situation with James Hunt. He is a super driver." Hunt was mightily flattered by the comparison with Clark. But that didn't stop him remonstrating with Caldwell for having referred to his hero as 'Jimmy.' 'Jim', Hunt told him, was the proper moniker. Teddy Mayer was even more effusive towards Hunt. He had never been known to praise a driver before, not even Fittipaldi, but now Mayer went so far as to say that Hunt was the best driver the team had ever employed: "Of all the drivers we've had, James has the greatest talent by far, in fact. He possibly makes more mistakes than, say, Emerson Fittipaldi, but he is certainly quicker than Emerson ever was when he drove for us. I think James is as consistently fast a driver as anyone I've ever seen."

Mayer wasn't finished and went on to compare Hunt with yet another of his heroes: "I would begin to compare his talent with Jackie Stewart's in his ability to win races driving a car that, in my opinion, is about the same as many others. Drivers like Jimmy Clark generally won races because they had superior cars. I think James' car is good, but I don't think it's any better than several other cars. Possibly it's more reliable, but it's quick because James is quick."

The praise was justified, as Hunt had won the last three Grand Prix races on the trot – four, if the reinstated Spanish win was counted. He was now a firm second in the world championship with 44 points; within 14 points of Lauda's score of 58. A championship bid that had looked impossible just four weeks ago now looked highly plausible.

What's more, he was about to race on Lauda's home territory and in his rival's absence. Lauda had been knocked out of the championship and no one, at that stage, thought he would return before the end of the season. So, at that moment, with five races to run, Hunt look certain to be world champion in 1976.

The joy was compounded because it was now clear that Lauda had survived his accident and would not die.

There had also been some doubt about the seriousness of his internal injuries when it emerged that Lauda had called in a Catholic priest to administer him the last rites. The suspicions of insiders were raised because Lauda was a confirmed atheist and, apparently, apart from when forced by his wife Marlene (for christenings, wedding and funerals), had never been known to step inside a church in his life.

It had been suggested by those who knew him that he was perhaps playing mind games with Hunt. Wanting Hunt to believe he would not be returning, he might have been trying to convince people he was more seriously injured than he really was. Certainly, while his outwards burns were horrific and disfiguring, they were not life threatening. And when, two weeks after the accident, it leaked out that Lauda was sitting up in his hospital bed, signing autographs for the nurses and watching the Austrian Grand Prix on television, it didn't square with the administration of last rites by a priest just a few days earlier.

Ferrari had withdrawn its cars from the Austrian event, ostensibly as a mark of respect for Lauda. The decision had been made by Enzo Ferrari who, at 78-years-old, had made his comeback absolute. There was now no doubt that he was back in charge and calling the shots after the departure of Luca di Montezemolo.

Enzo announced he felt cheated by what had happened at the Appeal Court in Paris and at Brands Hatch in the British Grand Prix. Enzo threatened to boycott Formula One until such a time when "the rules were enforced and justice prevailed."

Bizarrely, Enzo also blamed Lauda personally for casing the crash at the Nürburgring, thereby absolving his own engineers of any blame for the mechanical failure that was known to have caused the accident. James Hunt, speaking to reporters, called Enzo Ferrari: "an old man behaving like a child."

Daniele Audetto, on Enzo's instructions, even suggested that the Grand Prix at the Österreichring should be cancelled out of respect for Lauda. It would have suited Ferrari perfectly had that happened. But the campaign to cancel the race incensed the organisers, and the compassionate plea was greeted with cynicism by those accustomed to Enzo Ferrari's reputation for manipulating situations to his team's advantage.

Lauda, in his hospital bed, was also upset by attempts to cancel his home race. He told reporters what he wanted more than anything at that moment was "a feeling of continuity and trust." Troubled by what Audetto had said, he was also dismayed that the Ferraris had been withdrawn, as he knew this would aid Hunt significantly.

Huntmania may have been raging in Britain that summer, but it was not at all apparent in Austria as Lauda lay in hospital. In fact, what was immediately noticeable was that Lauda's absence greatly reduced the number of spectators at the race. The promoters were enraged when Enzo Ferrari withdrew the entire Ferrari team; they had been expecting a replacement driver at the very least. As it was, the loss of Clay Regazzoni decimated the Swiss contingent, who usually travelled to see him race. The organisers also lost the enthusiastic Italians, who poured over the borders between Austria and Italy to support the Ferrari team.

Despite the heat elsewhere in Europe, it rained for both qualifying days and, because the land was so dry, the water rolled off the hills and gathered in pools behind the circuit. But none of it affected James Hunt, who turned in a time that gave him his easiest pole position yet. The fast circuit suited him and his car perfectly. He would later set a new lap record at an average speed of 137.83 miles per hour.

With Lauda gone, Hunt looked around and found an unfamiliar bearded face alongside him on the front row. Ulsterman John Watson had put his Penske-Ford car on the front row of the grid. It was Watson's best moment in a stop-start career that had seen him drive for five different teams in three years with no noticeable success – apart from having an obvious talent for driving a car fast. In 30 races in the previous three years, he had scored points only twice; the highlight being a fourth place in Austria, in 1974, driving a Brabham.

But he had come good in 1976, signing on as number one driver for the Penske team. Since then, he had visited the podium twice already. Penske was a well-funded team run by American auto industry entrepreneur Roger Penske and managed by Heinz Hofer, a very precise German. It was a poignant race for the team as, a year earlier, Penske's partner and number one driver Mark Donohue had crashed on the morning of the race. The victim of a tyre failure, he was critically injured and died later that day in hospital.

Watson had taken Donohue's place in the team and it had been his big break. Although he was on the front row, however, he must have been dispirited when he came in a whole second slower than Hunt. Hunt attempted to excuse the Ulsterman for being so much slower, saying: "I knew that Watson was quite capable of going as fast, it was just that I'd got organised, had a new set of tyres fitted and gone quick before he had a chance to build up speed."

Rain threatened again on race day, slightly delaying the race start. But as the dark skies turned blue, the cars lined up on the grid. Frightened of running cars in the rain, the organisers informed the drivers that the race would be stopped if it rained suddenly. The high speed circuit, when wet, was too dangerous for cars on slick tyres, designed for dry running.

From the start line, Hunt got away first for a change and led Watson. It was the briefest of leads as Watson quickly passed him and the cars swept down the long straight from the top of the hill.

For two laps, Watson, Hunt, Ronnie Peterson (now driving a March-Ford), and Jody Scheckter's Tyrrell all diced for the lead. It was the closest racing Formula One had seen for years. Scheckter took the lead for one lap until a pattern formed with Watson, Peterson and Swedish driver Gunnar Nilsson's Lotus-Ford ahead of Scheckter and Hunt.

It soon became apparent that there was a problem with Hunt's McLaren. It was understeering on full tanks. Hunt recalled: "I was having a real struggle to stay on the road." Then Scheckter had an enormous accident at the top of the hill on the 14th lap, as the front suspension broke on his car. The Tyrrell-Ford comprehensively destroyed itself, luckily without injury to the driver. Hunt put his head down and proceeded to wring the maximum performance out of his badly-handling car. He set his fastest lap of the race, indicating just how hard he had tried.

The understeering problem turned out to be due to a damaged front wing, and Hunt could do nothing to stop John Watson winning his first Grand Prix. Hunt was fourth behind Laffite and Nilsson.

The real drama followed the podium ceremony as Watson, complying with the terms of a bet, shaved off his perennial beard in public to reveal a clean shaven look, which he was to keep from then on.

Hunt was less than delighted with his fourth place, although Niki Lauda, sitting up in his hospital bed, reportedly whooped and hollered as the chequered flag fell. The score, he quickly worked out, was: Lauda 58, Hunt 47. Later that week, Lauda spoke to winner John Watson on the telephone from his hospital bed and thanked him personally for beating Hunt. He told him: "Anything to stop Hunt getting points."

Hunt went back to Marbella in the gap between races and started his birthday celebrations before flying to Amsterdam to travel to Zandvoort. His 29th birthday fell on the 29th August, which was the Sunday of the Dutch

Grand Prix. His family, including his brother Peter, traditionally travelled out to Zandvoort, which was an easy car journey from Britain.

Soon, Hunt was locked in conversations with his brother and John Hogan over his commercial future. He desperately tried to persuade his brother to come and work on his affairs full time and to give up his accountancy career. Although his brother would not do that, he did say he would form a department at his firm to look after Hunt's financial affairs. They jointly decided to appoint Andrew Marriott and Barrie Gill of the CSS agency to handle his sponsorships. Those deals were now worth more than US$200,000 a year and his biggest source of income. CSS had been doing that unofficially anyway for the past two years, but Hunt had to pay two commissions on the deals, both to CSS and IMG. That had been bothering Hunt, especially as IMG had brought him no deals.

John Hogan recalls: "The brothers eventually decided on a compromise whereby Peter stayed with his firm in London and handled James' affairs from there." Peter Hunt immediately took over responsibility for his brother's accounts, paperwork, his diary and handling his fan mail.

When he had thrashed out his deal with his brother, Peter Hunt arranged to meet with representatives of Mark McCormack to work out an arrangement to operate jointly until its contract expired at the end of the year.

It was terminated on an amicable basis. Hogan says: "For James, it meant that he was able to be freed from the high-pressure American business approach and to operate more easily with his brother."

Gill and Marriott gradually assumed control of that side. Despite the potential conflict of CCS already having the John Player cigarette account in Formula One, Gill and Marriott had worked for Philip Morris in the very earliest days of Formula One sponsorship and could be trusted to avoid prospective biases.

Hunt was also very content to be working with Peter. He said: "I'm fortunate to be able to work with Pete, who is a chartered accountant and now runs a little department within his firm which looks after people like me and one or two other drivers and sportsmen. He does everything as far as my management is concerned. Pete deals with it entirely and only the important things are discussed with me for decisions. He administrates the whole deal and wet-nurses me as well. When I want more socks, I phone up from wherever I happen to be in the world and they send someone out to Marks and Spencer's to buy me more socks. So that side of it is great. It means I can concentrate entirely on getting on with my job, and when I'm not working, I can relax entirely. I don't have to keep rushing into an office and checking on who has paid and who hasn't, and keep track of my mail. It's all done for me."

A year earlier at Zandvoort, Hunt had won his first Grand Prix driving the Hesketh, a masterful performance during which he was chased hard by Lauda, who was then on his way to winning the world title with the Ferrari. That race marked Hunt's coming of age as a driver. Then, winning had been a fresh concept to him in Formula One, and he slowly became confident about leading and winning a Grand Prix under pressure. Now, a year later, the situation was different: Hunt was expected to win.

Niki Lauda was making a remarkable recovery and called Hunt on the telephone from his hospital bed to wish him a happy birthday. The two men chatted for a long time.

Observers were surprised about the phone call and felt Lauda was playing mind games with Hunt. Hunt claimed later that he felt a growing emotional bond with the Austrian as he fought back from his accident. It was a feeling he had not experienced before. But that didn't stop him enjoying and taking advantage of Lauda's absence.

With Lauda absent, Hunt was finding a new rival at every race. In Holland, it was a resurgent Ronnie Peterson who was finally finding his form in the works March-Ford car. Many observers still regarded Peterson as the fastest man in Grand Prix racing, and had done so since Jackie Stewart retired at the end of 1973.

Peterson had left Lotus at the beginning of the year after only one race. When team manager Peter Warr had refused to pay the money due on his contract, Peterson had simply walked out. He was as disgusted with Warr as Hunt had been with him when he invited him to lunch and then left him hungry.

After listening to Peterson describe his situation with Lotus, Hunt was thankful that his lunch date with Warr had been such a disaster. The last place he would have wanted to be in 1976 was driving for a down-on-its-luck Lotus team and, even worse, being told what to do by Warr.

So when Hunt looked around on the front row of the grid in Holland, he saw Peterson's familiar blue and yellow helmet and felt somewhat reassured; it was a feeling he never had with Lauda. But this time, it was different. Peterson was on pole and Hunt second fastest; the March-Ford was eight hundredths of a second faster than Hunt's McLaren-Ford. But what vexed Alastair Caldwell wasn't so much that Peterson was faster, but that Hunt had endured handling problems in qualifying with a severe lack of traction and understeer due to a tyre problem.

After qualifying on Saturday afternoon, there was a bizarre scene in the pit lane when Hunt's close friend Jody Scheckter rowed fiercely with his team principal, Ken Tyrrell, over US$500. John Hogan had arranged for Marlboro to sponsor a pit stop competition whereby two cars would come into a simulated pit area, change all four wheels, and then go around the circuit. The winner got US$500 provided they lapped within ten per cent of the fastest qualifying time. The Tyrrell mechanics got Scheckter away in the lead, but because of a crowded pit lane he could not complete his lap within the ten per cent time limit and forfeited the US$500 even though he had won. He said to journalists that he was not prepared to plough into people merely to win US$500.

But Ken Tyrrell flew into a rage when Scheckter balked at completing the lap in time. There was an ugly scene in the pits as the two men yelled at each other. The incident was witnessed by Hunt, who took Scheckter's side in the argument and was horrified by Tyrrell's attitude. From that moment on, Hunt took against Tyrrell in an animosity that would last the rest of his life.

On race morning, Tyrrell and Scheckter refused to talk to each other, and the South African driver told reporters that he would be leaving the team at the end of the year.

In the race, Hunt botched his start as usual, spinning his wheels and letting Peterson pull away in front. To add to the ignominy, John Watson came through from the second row and overtook Hunt at the end of the pit straight in full view of everyone.

Hunt bided his time in third as Peterson and Watson scrapped for the lead. His McLaren was understeering again as a braking air scoop worked loose. Despite that, Hunt overtook Watson on lap seven and Peterson for the lead on lap 12. Afterwards, he said he simply took advantage of mistakes by both drivers.

Hunt said: "I didn't really do any serious passing of anyone during the whole race but it put me in the lead, which was the best place to be because I had a real problem with the understeer. It meant that the onus was now on Watson to get past me if he could. I think, if he had got past me, he would have left me."

In fact, Hunt had to drive as hard as ever to block Watson from getting past. In terms of car handling, the Ulsterman was easily faster, but Hunt was simply better at blocking than Watson was at overtaking. In the end it didn't matter, as Watson coasted to a halt on lap 48 when his gearbox broke. Watson's demise was a signal for Clay Regazzoni, in the lone Ferrari entered in the race, to take up the chase. Hunt got in a panic because he feared Regazzoni might have instructions to punt him off if he couldn't get past. Hunt recalled: "Boy, was I in a panic. I was something like ten seconds ahead of Clay and I didn't want him to get within reach." By the end, Hunt won the race barely a car's length ahead of the Ferrari – too close for comfort. Hunt was absolutely elated and threw both arms aloft as he had the previous year, and nearly put his car straight into the barriers as a result.

John Watson remembers it as a classic race: "I had a car which was quicker over a whole lap, but he had a car which was fractionally quicker down the straight because we were running different levels of down force. He successfully defended his position with a fair degree of firmness. It was a classic duel of two Brits in Formula One."

Hunt's victory was a disaster for Lauda; there would be no more whooping and hollering or congratulatory phone calls. Regazzoni's failure to overtake Hunt was telling, and Enzo Ferrari was said to have decided on the basis of that performance alone to sack the Swiss driver as soon as he found a replacement. The championship score now read: Lauda 58, Hunt 56.

As Hunt began to win more and more races, he also became more and more disgusted with the amount of money McLaren was paying him. He was actually earning much less than he had at Hesketh the year before, when the team had been on the breadline. At Hesketh, he had been paid extra by sponsors for every promotional day. But at McLaren, they were all *gratis* as part of his retainer. He had picked up around US$70,000 from such promotional outings in 1975 but hardly anything in 1976. With his share of prize money, he looked set to earn US$100,000; exactly the same as he had at Hesketh.

Hunt decided to have it out with Mayer straight after the podium celebrations. They had a brief but furious row, with Mayer telling Hunt to "fuck off" and Hunt saying: "I might just do that." Of course, neither men meant it, but Mayer was sticking to his contract. As Alastair Caldwell remembers: "James and Teddy were always on about money. It got to the stage where James decided we weren't paying him enough, although he'd been only too happy to come and drive for us for nothing at the beginning of the year. By now, of course, he'd decided he was a superstar who needed paying a lot of money. That became a constant source of friction."

With his friends waiting outside to celebrate his birthday, Hunt decided he couldn't be bothered with it. John Hugenholz, the Zandvoort circuit manager, presented Hunt with a giant birthday cake in the shape of the track. It was meant as a token to mark his birthday and as a celebration of his win the year before, but it now became an ever more poignant and appropriate symbol of all he had achieved.

His mother and younger brother David had journeyed to Holland for James' birthday and had been watching the race from the grandstands. Anxiety gave way to relief and delight when they belatedly realised he had won the race.

Afterwards, Hunt and his English friends built a huge camp fire in the sand dunes of Zandvoort. They were joined by his family and they celebrated into the night and passed out on the sand, incoherent with drink. His need to celebrate his birthday along with the anniversary of his first win combined with his latest victory all inevitably took their toll.

The following morning, Hunt returned to London and caught a plane for Toronto and travelled to Quebec for a Formula Atlantic race in the quaint town of Trois-Rivières. He had been offered US$10,000 to race in the Formula Atlantic series, which was the North American equivalent of Formula Two. Three fellow Formula One drivers, Patrick Depailler, Vittorio Brambilla and Alan Jones, also made the trip.

The Formula One drivers found themselves facing a young Canadian called Gilles Villeneuve. Villeneuve had sold his house to fund his racing and had become the leading Canadian driver at the age of 26. Hunt was Villeneuve's teammate in the Ecurie Canada March team. The Canadian was desperate to make his mark in front of the Formula One stars. Despite struggling with an unfamiliar car with peculiar handling characteristics, he qualified on pole; five places ahead of Hunt.

But in the actual race, Hunt gained confidence with every lap and finished third. Alan Jones was second behind the young Villeneuve, whose pace impressed everybody from Europe.

So much so that, after the race, Hunt called Teddy Mayer and John Hogan in England and recommended they sign him before anyone else did. Mayer eventually did sign Villeneuve, but after one race lost him to Ferrari.

John Hogan remembers it well: "As soon as he came back, he said to me: 'Hogie, I promise you, that bloke is the dog's bollocks. He blew me off fair and square.' So on James' word, we did a deal with Villeneuve to hold him."

After his Formula Atlantic experience, Hunt travelled south to the Michigan International Speedway to take part in an IROC saloon car race on the oval and earn himself another US$10,000 for his trouble.

The IROC series used identical, modified Chevrolet Camaros that were regularly raced by top American drivers in something akin to a celebrity series. Hunt managed to qualify his Camaro on pole at an average speed of nearly 150 miles per hour. It was his first experience of driving on an oval, and he found he was good at it. Oval driving is all about courage and nerve, and Hunt possessed those two talents in abundance. But he found that driving on an oval on his own and racing against 20 others cars whilst doing so were entirely different propositions.

Unable to manage, and trying too hard, he crashed into a concrete wall at 150 miles per hour. He had a very narrow escape from serious injury when a piece of metal guard rail pierced the cockpit of his car. The car was badly damaged, and Hunt told the organisers exactly what he thought of IROC's safety standards.

Hunt was shaken and surprised at his inability to race other cars on an oval track. He said: "I got in the race and didn't have a clue because of all the high-speed drafting. I was right out of my depth. To tell you the truth, I was scared shitless." However, that didn't stop him from accepting another US$10,000 offer to race later in the year.

After his brief American sojourn, Hunt returned to Europe to compete in the Italian Grand Prix at Monza. Whilst Hunt had been away, stories appeared in Italian newspapers speculating that the Texaco fuel used by McLaren–Ford was illegal. Texaco took precautions and double checked that its fuel was within the regulations. The maximum octane allowance was 102. However, the rules were vague and allowed teams to use the octane rating of the best available fuel in their country of origin plus one octane. The best available in Britain was 101 octane, which meant 102 octane would be the maximum allowed. But Ferrari was subject to other measurements prevailing in Italy, as were Ligier in France. In those countries, the top grade of fuel available was only 100 octane so Ferrari was limited to 101 octane. Hunt said: "The rules are very complicated and they are difficult to understand, but they state that you can use the top grade of commercially available fuel in the team's country of origin plus a tolerance of one octane."

Those complicated rules would almost cost Hunt the world championship.

And there was other news overshadowing the arguments about the strength of the petrol – as Niki Lauda came back from the dead.

SHUNT

CHAPTER 25

Back from the dead
Niki Lauda returns at Monza

On Wednesday 8th September, Niki Lauda's close friend David Benson flew into Salzburg airport. He was there to meet Lauda and to travel with him on his private plane to Milan airport and onto Monza circuit for the Italian Grand Prix. Lauda was accompanied by his wife, Marlene, and Willy Dungl, his fitness trainer.

Benson got an exclusive interview with Lauda on the flight and scooped the rest of the world's press. How he did it no one knows to this day, but it was an amazing coup for the *Daily Express* newspaper, and the first and last time Lauda talked intimately about the accident and his recovery.

He told Benson during that flight: "A lot of people have said that they think I am crazy to go back to racing so quickly. They say that a man with a face that is not like that of a human being but like a dead man's skull should want to give up immediately. People who think like that are those who would probably be very happy to be ill and stay at home and not have to go out to work. This is not my attitude to life.

"I do not enjoy life unless I am active and have something to do and look forward to. I must work. If I have an accident in my work then my aim must be to recover as soon as possible with all the help of modern medicine. Once I had decided to go on, then I had to make a comeback as quickly as possible.

That is why I am here at Monza.

"Let's go back to the beginning – on Sunday 1st August at Nürburgring. I can't remember the race from the moment I left the pits after making a tyre change at the end of the first lap. I drove about ten kilometres before the crash, but I can't recall them.

"The first thing I remember is the sound of the helicopter engine starting up. I asked the pilot where we were and where we were going, and he told me we were leaving Adenau Hospital near the track to fly to Ludwigshafen Hospital about 45 minutes away, where they had a special burns unit. This must have been about 35 to 40 minutes after the accident.

"Daniele Audetto, the Ferrari team manager, told me that at Adenau Hospital I was not unconscious and that I told him in detail where my road car was parked in the paddock, that Marlene, my wife, was coming in my plane to Cologne and that he should telephone her and say that I was alright and ask her to find me a good hospital – the best.

"Audetto told me that together we agreed to Ludwigshafen but I don't remember anything about it. My memory only really starts with the hospital and the helicopter. Now, up to the accident I would say I was unlucky. I didn't like the Nürburgring, the conditions that day were bad and there had been all the problems about whether we should race there or not. Then, finally, came the accident.

"From that moment, all the bad luck turned to good luck. First the four drivers pulled me out of the car and then, at Adenau Hospital, they said I was too critical for them to touch. So they sent me to the best hospital in Germany. Remember, that it was a Sunday afternoon but when I got to Ludwigshafen burns unit, the boss of the whole place just happened to be there at the time.

He took one look at me and immediately decided that the burns on my face were secondary to the burns in the lungs. So he sent me to the intensive care unit in Mannheim. There, my luck was still good. The youngest professor in Germany, a man who will take over the big Munich hospital on 1st November, just happened to be working that Sunday. His name is Professor Peter and I owe him my life. He did everything absolutely right and never made a wrong move.

"You must realise that the medical knowledge about treating lung damage is not as great as in some other areas. If, for example, I had been given oxygen – which would seem logical for someone with damaged lungs – I would have been dead immediately.

"They showed me my face in a mirror. I looked at myself and I could not believe it. I looked like some grotesque animal because my whole head and neck were swollen to three times the normal size. You would not believe it could be a human being. I'm told that his is because I had been in 800 degrees of heat in the fire and the body had pumped excessive liquid to the burned areas. I was swelling up even as I looked in the mirror and then my eyes closed and I was blind for five days. Everything was a big mass of nothing.

"The lungs were in bad condition, and when they X-rayed me on the Tuesday, they were getting worse. The thing they were worried about most was the oxygen count in my blood, which was below the life maintaining level of a figure of eight. It went down to a figure of 6.8 – so in theory there was no more life.

"The doctors said and told my wife that there was no hope that I would survive. On the Sunday night, they put a tube down my throat into the lungs and connected it to a vacuum pump to drain off the liquid and the infections.

"This was critical because if the pump was used too much, it would destroy the lungs. From the Sunday night, my brain was always functioning but I felt that my body was giving up. I could just hear voices very far away and a little out of reach. I concentrated on these voices to stop myself becoming completely unconscious.

"I wanted to keep my mind awake to start the body working again. I knew that if I gave up mentally then I would be dead. My life was also saved because I was very fit before the accident. And as I have never smoked in my life, my lungs had maybe an extra per cent capacity which helped me work against the infection.

"All the time I was listening to the doctors and trying to cooperate as much as possible – no matter what personal pain it would cost. For example, they could only use the vacuum pump to my lungs for about an hour at a time. But when I felt the lungs filling up, then I called for them to switch it on, even though the pain was enormous. The doctors told me that it was the first time that anyone had asked for the pump to be switched on themselves. But I knew that I could only survive if I followed every instruction of the doctors.

"My wife Marlene was marvellous. It was very shocking for her but never once did I feel what she was going through when she was with me at the hospital. She would hold my hand and keep on telling me that I was going to get well again. She must have been terrified by my face but she only made me feel that I was a great man and gave me the will to get well. So many women would have cried or have become hysterical. I discovered that there was a much greater depth to Marlene than even I had realised.

"I do not believe in a personal God, but I believe that there is something more than this life. And I live by the rules. My strength to live after the accident came from this, from my own mind. And from my wife.

"At one point, I was asked if I wanted to see a priest. So I said: 'OK.' He came in and gave me the last rites, crossed my shoulder and said: 'Goodbye my friend.'

"I nearly had a heart attack! I wanted someone to help me to live in this world, not pass into the next. So I clung on to the voices and to my wife's strength. I would not let myself become unconscious, because I was afraid that I would die.

"Three days after the accident, the lungs began to get better. My blood count though was still bad, with the oxygen at the 6.8 level. This stayed the same for a week.

Nobody knew if my system would start working again and produce enough oxygen for the blood. If it didn't re-start, then they could have changed my blood every so often but they knew that I would then only have one or two years in which to live. So they put new blood into me and waited to see the reactions.

"After four days, it slowly improved and they changed the blood again. But now my system is working and I'm back to normal with the right amount of oxygen in my blood. They do not have to change it any more. My lungs and my physical fitness have been certified as being 100 per cent. In fact, I feel better now than I was before. My training programme is entirely up to me and to my own willpower. That was when I took the decision to go to Monza. I've been running day and night and have been taking physical exercises for 12 hours a day.

"Fortunately, I have with me 24 hours a day Willy Dungl, who is a world expert on the treatment of athletes and rebuilding of their bodies after they are broken. He has brought me on with massage and exercise every day, until we have built my body up to a point where I can complete a full 65 minutes' physical training session. He is a practical expert who works with a doctor and looks after every detail of my day including my times of rest, the kind of food that I eat and how much exercise I can stand.

"The doctors checked me yesterday and said that I was in perfect condition.

I have tried my Ferrari and my attitude to racing has not changed. I like being back in the car, I love driving it. And I feel very happy. I love my sport and I love my job. The accident was bad thing to have happened, but now I just look forward to getting back into racing again.

"Motor racing is dangerous, we all know that – and when my accident happened, I was not that surprised it should have happened to me. This may surprise people who don't understand racing, but it is true. In the kind of job I have, it is the risk I must take.

"The problem I have had to face since the accident is whether I would enjoy my motor racing again and what effect it would have on me. No one can discover this until they have been through an experience like mine. I have found that I love the positive side of motor racing. So why should I give it up?

"I have not raced for over a month and when I climb into my car there will be enormous pressure on me because it is Italy, and Ferrari is the 'king' and we have three cars entered for the race. But I will not let this pressure affect me. I may only finish in 15th place, but now I know that I am ahead of my programmes and when we go to Canada and North America, I'll be in a position to win and to keep my world championship."

The interview appeared almost verbatim in the *Daily Express* of Friday 10th September, the day Niki Lauda reappeared at the Monza track; it had been less than five weeks since he had crashed out of the German Grand Prix and been airlifted to hospital. His return to the paddock at Monza was only thirty-three days after the accident. He had missed two races and ceded 12 world championship points of his lead over Hunt.

Statistically, the two rivals were now even as both drivers had now completed exactly the same number of races during the season. Lauda and Hunt were within two points of each other in the championship table.

Willy Dungl had got Lauda's body back in shape, and Lauda wanted to return to Formula One as soon as he could properly hold a wheel. He believed that lying in bed thinking about the accident was counter-productive. He said: "I wanted to get back to work as soon as I possibly could."

Lauda admits it was a difficult decision to come back so quickly, as he said: "Many people would have thought it fitting for me to spend the first few months after Nürburgring 1976 in a darkened room surrounded by peace and quiet." He was right, and they had. Lauda's arrival was greeted with pure amazement.

His return was highly courageous, and it could not have been lost on him that donning a racing helmet so soon after the accident would make the scars on his face ultimately much worse and more visible for the rest of his life. Lauda said: "My matter-of-factness in automatically resuming my career as soon as all systems were go was disconcerting; some thought it betrayed a lack of dignity, others found it downright unappetising."

Hunt found it all rather unconvincing, saying: "I know that little fucker. Only Niki could take the last rites and come back at the Italian Grand Prix." John Hogan, a sponsor of both Hunt and Lauda, agreed, saying: "Niki, who'd never been to a church in his life, wouldn't know what the last rites were if they hit him in the head."

Hogan now believes that Lauda overstated his injuries in order to get a psychological advantage over Hunt and to lull him into false sense of security. But Lauda was obviously still very frail and weak, and it was clear he should not have been there. In today's strict medical environment, he would not have been allowed to race. Although they were hidden by bandages, his face and head were still visibly disfigured. He kept his cap firmly planted on his face, but the disguise wasn't enough to allay the serious doubts about his fitness to race – doubts being expressed even within his own team. Hogan said: "He looked horrible: blood and puss all over him."

In the pits, Lauda's wife, Marlene, kept attending to her husband's face and stroking it to give him reassurance. She had her sewing kit and was constantly modifying Lauda's new flameproof balaclava for maximum comfort. She wanted there to be no irritation to the sensitive new skin grafted around his eyes. Everyone was deeply impressed by Marlene's devotion. David Benson wrote in Saturday's *Daily Express*: "I am conquered by her courage. Here is a woman truly worthy of a very great sportsman." He added: "Marlene is a delightfully warm person. Her handshake is firm. Her eyes are steady and constant. They are the eyes of a woman who could inspire a man to great things."

And that is exactly what she did that weekend.

It seemed clear that the Ferrari team didn't want Lauda back. They thought he was finished and wanted him gone. As Lauda recalled: "They didn't know what to make of a defending champion with a disfigured face who carried on as if everything was quite normal."

His quick return also caused all sorts of confusion for Daniele Audetto and Enzo Ferrari. In Lauda's absence, Enzo had hired a replacement, Carlos

Reutemann. Reutemann had fallen out with Bernie Ecclestone and had abruptly left the Brabham team, probably sensing that a more competitive Ferrari drive might be available after Lauda's accident. It was.

But ironically, news of Reutemann's appointment inspired Lauda to return quickly. Enzo could not have chosen a bigger motivator; Lauda truly detested Reutemann. He admitted: "We never could stand each other." The notion of Reutemann inheriting his drive spurred Lauda on, as he said: "Instead of taking pressure off me, they put on even more by bringing Carlos Reutemann into the team."

Reutemann's premature signing had been fuelled by all the hysteria in the Italian press. It was a huge error and caused immense problems. With Lauda back, the team had to enter a third car for Reutemann at Monza. It breached Lauda's new contract and, as a result, Enzo Ferrari had to beg Lauda to waive the clause for Monza. Lauda agreed, but only for one race, believing he would soon see the back of Reutemann. Inwardly, Lauda was furious with Enzo and Audetto, as he said later: "To the outside world, Enzo Ferrari and his company were standing by their slightly singed world champion but, from the inside, the pitiful insecurity of each and every one of them was palpable. Tactics took precedence over trust. Ferrari kept telling the world how solidly they were behind me but, in private, they were at sixes and sevens."

The fact that Lauda had signed a new contract for 1977, before his accident, put him in a very strong position. He said: "If I hadn't had that contract, they could have ground me down mentally and turned me out to pasture. It was my one piece of good fortune that [Enzo] Ferrari had been so anxious to get me under contract for the following season."

The McLaren team was unaware of the politics raging within Ferrari, and had problems of their own to worry about. McLaren was not only fighting Ferrari for the world title, but were battling the entire Italian nation. In a fair fight, there was no doubt that Hunt could beat Lauda. But Teddy Mayer knew that the Italian Grand Prix was unlikely to be a fair fight. He knew the Italians would join forces to nobble Hunt.

There wasn't long to wait; it started as soon as the McLaren team's trucks reached the Italian border. There was nothing wrong with the paperwork or the trucks, but the Italian border guards decided to take rather a long time signing off on there being nothing wrong. A day and a half was lost at the border, eating into precious time at the track to prepare the cars.

And when the trucks finally did pull into the Monza paddock, they found a hostile reception from all the Italian speakers. At the circuit gate, as they entered the park, they saw fans holding up banners that read '*Basta con la Mafia Inglese.*' Translated, they said: 'Away with the English Mafia.' And whenever James Hunt appeared in public, he was loudly booed.

But all this was nothing compared to what would happen in scrutineering, which was outright Italian chicanery. The FIA seemed powerless to intervene as the Italian scrutineers pored over Hunt's car. It seemed they had already decided how to hinder him. But even they had no idea how effective they were to be as the rains fell from the skies rather conveniently for Ferrari.

The first qualifying session on Friday was wet, and Hunt spun off and damaged the nose of his car. When he walked back to the pits, the Italian fans erupted in the grandstands with joy. It was unseemly as they spat on him from the stands.

Meanwhile, Niki Lauda, with the Italian crowd right behind him and willing him on, got back into a car for the first time since his accident. On Friday, he had employed his normal mental preparation tactics, which included an objective review of his emotions to ensure he was mentally "well primed" before going out to qualify. But then it all changed for Lauda: "When I climbed into the cockpit at Monza," he recalled, "fear hit me so hard that all self-motivation theories flew out the window." Lauda's lap times were poor, and he admitted later that he had lied to journalists, including David Benson whose interview had been published only that morning, about his state of mind. Truthfully, he had been "rigid with fear" during qualifying and the rain had been "terrifying."

Lauda explained later: "I had to play the hero to buy myself enough time to sort things out. The fact is you have to play the hard man on occasions, whether you actually feel like one or not. It is really all a game of mental hide-and-seek; you would never be forgiven if you blurted out the truth at an inopportune moment. You would be finished."

That night, alone in the quiet cocoon of his hotel room, Lauda reviewed his performance and tried to identify what had gone wrong. He had been trying to drive as he had before the accident and it wasn't working. Feeling insecure, he said: "I had got myself into a stupid tangle."

His overnight analysis helped him, as he put it, re-programme his brain for the following day and eliminate all the pressure he felt. Managing to repress his anxiety somehow, Lauda told himself to "drive more slowly." He said later: "And that's what I did. I started slowly, then gradually built up speed until, suddenly, I was the fastest of the Ferraris – faster than Regazzoni and the newcomer Reutemann. I had managed to prove in practice what I knew in theory: I could drive as well now as before the accident."

Lauda was fifth fastest by the end of the session. For some reason, both the Ferraris and the McLarens had been slow, but Lauda was fastest of the five. He had out-qualified both his Ferrari teammates, causing Reutemann and Clay Regazzoni considerable embarrassment; not to mention James Hunt, who could only manage ninth place on the grid. There was no excuse for Hunt, as Monza was a fast circuit that suited the characteristics of his car.

Jacques Laffite put his Ligier on pole followed by Jody Scheckter's Tyrrell-Ford, Carlos Pace's Brabham-Alfa Romeo and Patrick Depailler's Tyrrell-Ford.

During the Saturday session, fuel checks were made by the scrutineers in the pits. Forewarned Texaco had made absolutely certain that the McLaren's fuel was legal, which they measured at 101.2 octane.

Lauda's miracle return became a sideshow compared to the events that followed on Sunday morning. Overnight, the Italian stewards analysed the McLaren's fuel and found it was 101.6 octane, not 101.2, but allowed for discrepancy, saying it was within the allowed limits.

Then, feigning ignorance of the rules, the Italians telexed the FIA in Paris and asked the governing body for clarification of its own ruling. The message in the telex was vague in the sending, which was deliberate, and even vaguer in the reply. The secretary of the FIA's sporting division, the CSI, replied and said the maximum allowed was 101.

So on Sunday morning, the Italian stewards announced that the Hunt's and his teammate Jochen Mass' fuel was illegal and that their Saturday times would be disallowed. Only their Friday qualifying times, run in the wet, would count. The cars were sent to the back of the grid. They also disqualified Saturday times for John Watson's Penske car. The Penske team had no argument, as their fuel was almost certainly over the allowed maximum. They had pushed the rules to the limit and imported special fuel from the United States. Team principal Roger Penske had it specially flown in from their fuel sponsor, Union 76.

The organisers' clear intention had been to put the cars out of the race completely. The disallowed times effectively meant that Hunt, Mass and Watson would not be allowed to start; their sub-two minute, rain-affected qualifying times on Friday were not fast enough to get in the race.

But even before all this happened, there was an even more bizarre incident – one in which Italian police came to the McLaren pit and took Alastair Caldwell away. They arrested him on suspicion of importing illegal fuel into Italy. It was a trumped up charge, and Caldwell's theory was that Ferrari wanted him out of the way when the stewards made their fuel announcement. As Caldwell would later recount to James Hunt's biographer Christopher Hilton, Enzo Ferrari had been able to manipulate the situation by calling a friend in the local station: "[Enzo] Ferrari had obviously said: 'We need to get rid of Caldwell completely because he'll go bananas. He's the man to worry about. What can we do? We'll pretend that the fuel has been illegally imported, we'll tell him that and have him arrested on this basis.' We had Texaco fuel, which had been brought in a truck from Belgium certainly imported correctly with the right paperwork, but that didn't matter. They had an excuse to lock me up."

Caldwell was put in a cell at Monza police station for over two hours until a Texaco technician brought the customs paperwork that proved the fuel had been correctly imported. Caldwell emerged from incarceration only to be hit with the shock that Hunt was out of the race.

Meanwhile, in the absence of Caldwell, Mayer had stormed the stewards' office with Texaco's analysis in his hand, demanding to know what was going on. The Italians showed him the telex they had received from the FIA; but, crucially, they showed him only the reply and not their original message. It was deliberate underhanded skullduggery as the scrutineers had always known exactly what the rules were. If they hadn't, they had the very articulate Teddy Mayer on hand to remind them.

Waving the telex in his hand, the Italian chief scrutineer sent Mayer away fuming. His number one driver had been properly nobbled.

Hunt was initially furious with Texaco and with John Goosens, who headed up Texaco's racing effort in Europe. Goosens was adamant that Texaco had done all it could, but Hunt was having none of it. John Hogan remembers: "James' demeanour didn't get on particularly well with John Goosens. He couldn't figure James at all." But Hunt got on very well with Texan Tom Cottrell, a top executive of Texaco in the United States, who was in overall charge of the oil company's European operation. When Hunt clashed with Goosens, he turned to Cottrell for support. Hunt liked Cottrell's straightforward approach to sorting out problems. As he recalled, Cottrell's solutions always began with his favourite saying: "I come from a place where a man puts his pants on one leg at a time." Cottrell eventually defused the Hunt-Goosens standoff by appointing veteran executive Neil McCann to liaise directly with Hunt and to avoid clashes with Goosens. McCann commanded a great deal of respect, and had been friends with Mike Hawthorn and Peter Collins.

That morning, in Caldwell's absence, Mayer was continually on the telephone to Paris asking the FIA officials exactly what was going on.

Hunt was apoplectic, not so much because of his exclusion, but by the scrutineers' assertion that he was a cheat. The implication by their actions was that the team had not competed fairly throughout 1976. Hunt recalls: "The implication that we had been cheating annoyed me enormously. Not only had we not been cheating, but running a high octane fuel would not help unless we had increased the compression ratio of the engine to match the increased octane rating. You have to modify your engine accordingly, and we certainly hadn't done that – we could have run 150 octane petrol and our engine wouldn't have given an ounce more power. Our fuel was totally legal and we had gone to a lot of trouble before the race to make sure that it was, but to have that understood by the general public was more than one could ask. So this mud had been thrown, and some of it was inevitably sticking."

Both Mayer and Hunt realised what was going on but were powerless to do anything about it. They appealed the stewards' decision straight away, which proved to be a mistake as the matter then became sub judice in the eyes of the stewards. They subsequently refused to discuss it further, as Hunt remembered: "Because we appealed, we couldn't discuss it further so I was stuffed out of the race. You can't run the Grand Prix a month later; and by putting me on the back of the grid, the argument could only be sorted out later."

The fuel situation was later clarified and corrected by a statement from the FIA, but by then it was too late; the damage had been done. Hunt laughed when he saw the statement and said: "I was frustrated even more when the CSI put out a press release saying that everything was alright and that the McLaren team hadn't been cheating."

Added to what had happened in Spain and Britain, the Italian press ran huge headlines announcing: 'McLaren cheats', and the coverage was being read around the world. Mayer said: "I think Ferrari began to believe that if James could beat them, we must be cheating; and they began to try and find excuses."

371

It was later found that the Italian fuel checks had been wrongly interpreted by the stewards.

But at that moment, the Italians believed that Hunt, Mass and Watson were out. But then something equally bizarre happened. Before the exclusions, three drivers hadn't qualified for the race: Brett Lunger's works Surtees; Arturo Merzario's Williams; and Otto Stuppacher's private Tyrrell. Gradually, all three drivers withdrew to make way for the disqualified drivers and, much to the chagrin of the Italians, Hunt, Mass and Watson were back in the race.

But Hunt would still have to start the Italian Grand Prix from the second to last row of the starting grid. Hunt was so angry, he even thought about withdrawing. But realising it would be a fruitless protest, he focused on trying to get some points – although he knew he could no longer win outright.

But his heart was not in it, and by the 12th lap he was in 12th place when he came together with Tom Pryce's Shadow and went off the road. His McLaren-Ford went into the sand and beached with its rear wheels spinning wildly. The sand traps, which were gradually replacing catch fencing, decelerated cars very effectively and slowed the McLaren so that it stopped just in front of the barrier. Hunt jumped out of his car and walked round checking for damage. Seeing it was intact, he pushed the car out of the hole dug by the spinning tyres. But he was then prevented from getting back in the car by the Italian marshals. For once, the Italians were abiding by the rules; although they didn't please Hunt. But the longer time went on, the less relevant it became. Hunt said: "They wouldn't let me get back in. They pounced on me. But it wasn't really worth making an issue of it because, firstly, the car was stuck in the sand and, secondly, I was now completely out of the race even if I could have restarted. It was then hopeless trying to gain points as far as I was concerned."

All this was going on against a backdrop of hissing and booing Italians. It was more like feeding time at a zoo than a motor race as they started throwing the contents of their picnic baskets at him.

Hunt was stupefied with frustration and wanted a fight with the whole Italian nation as he began his long walk back to the pit lane. During that walk, he made up his mind that his accident had been the fault of Tom Pryce, so he decided to have it out with the young Welshman after the race. The blame culture and revenge-seeking was a throwback to his public school background. When it surfaced, it exhibited the worst elements of his character. The truth about the accident was that Hunt had become distracted when he went into the corner and had braked far too late, with the inevitable result.

Convinced that Pryce had blocked him, however, Hunt stormed up to him after the race and shouted: "You are a brainless moron", adding in for good measure that he was "absolutely brainless." Almost immediately afterwards, as he cooled off in the motorhome, he knew he had been wrong. He went to find Pryce to apologise. He said later: "I just made a mistake." His high emotional state after the race had been made worse by his walk back to the pits, where he had been spat upon and booed by the Italians. He called them "animals" and explained: "They were spitting and hissing. I wanted to confront them but thought better of it." In the end, Hunt confessed: "I must admit I was quite pleased to get out of there unscathed. The propaganda campaign against me in the Italian press was really quite incredible; a very heavy deal. They really hated me in Italy, to an extent that was quite unbelievable. Anybody would think it was I who had caused Niki's accident."

Hunt later described the entire incident in his book *Against All Odds*, which was published a year later. It was an interesting insight into the mind of a top driver and the manner in which decisions are taken on a race track. He said: "Going out of the first chicane, I missed a gear and Pryce was going to come up alongside me. I could see that, but rather than fight him – we were all in a hurry and wanted to get on with the race – and take the inside line going into the next corner, I took the normal line. But he came hurtling up the inside, outbraking me, racing me into the next corner. That really took me by surprise because if he got past me again all he was going to do was hold both of us up. We would have both gone quicker if he had followed me. I had to fight it out with him then because I'd had a hell of a job passing him already, so I decided to go for it. When we did get to the corner, he was inside me, I couldn't get in and I went off the road of my own accord. It was my fault, but at the same time I had to fight. I took the decision when he arrived alongside me to fight him out, and it didn't come off. But I still think it was the right decision because, had I let go then, I would never have finished in the points. It was a calculated risk. In different circumstances, you adjust the size of the calculation. At Monza, it was always a risk whether I would finish the race because I had to really try hard. If by half distance you are getting into the points, the first six places, then you adjust yourself and reduce the amount of risk you take because you've got more in the bank to protect."

Meanwhile, Lauda, unaware of all the drama, had enjoyed a steady race and managed to finish fourth. It was the bravest driving performance ever seen in Formula One – before or since. When he took off his helmet after the race, his fireproof balaclava was soaked in blood; his head and face wounds had opened up. The repercussions for the scarring on his face would be enormous. But he had done what he came to do, and had increased his championship lead. Hunt not finishing had been a huge bonus. Lauda's courageous comeback had exceeded all expectations, not least those of his English rival.

Hunt was full of praise, and any ill feelings towards Lauda from the past were genuinely put aside as the two men became temporary friends again and started speaking everyday on the telephone. Hunt said: "To virtually step out of the grave and six weeks later to come fourth in a Grand Prix is a truly amazing achievement." He added: "Niki drove a typical Niki race; well-contained within himself and within his new limitations."

As they conversed, Lauda and Hunt found they had much in common: both were serial womanisers with a passion for sex and women, although Lauda did not share Hunt's fondness for drink and recreational drugs.

The race was won by Ronnie Peterson in the March-Ford; the first win by March in almost five years and the first for Peterson since he left Lotus. Regazzoni was second and Jacques Laffite third in his Ligier. The three points Lauda won for finishing fourth in Italy gave him a five-point lead over Hunt, with Lauda on 61 points and Hunt on 56.

If he couldn't win, Hunt was delighted by Peterson's return to the winner's circle. Ronnie Peterson was the driver he admired most in Formula One, as he said: "Ronnie is an absolutely straight driver. He doesn't need to do anything silly because he's that good." But he did have some advice for Peterson and told him why he thought he had never won the championship in spite of clearly being the fastest driver for the past five years: "His physical fitness is perhaps suspect, and I would think Ronnie's problem is his inability to make the right decisions when he is setting up the car." It was typical Hunt honesty about his favourite driver.

When the race was over, Ferrari team manager Daniele Audetto was very embarrassed by what had gone on that day. He confessed admiration for Hunt, saying that the crowd's hatred had been directed at the McLaren team and not at Hunt personally. Audetto then decided to make some predictions about what would happen in the last three races. He predicted Hunt would win the United States Grand Prix at Watkins Glen, finish second at the Canadian and third in Japan. Lauda, he said, would win the Canadian Grand Prix, finish second at the Japanese and not score at all at Watkins Glen. How he knew all this was beyond anyone's guess, but his predictions were widely reported around the world and taken seriously by many.

Audetto also praised Lauda's teammate, Regazzoni, predicting he would finish third, second and first respectively. But it was all typical Italian false praise as Enzo Ferrari had already decided to fire Regazzoni and replace him permanently with Reutemann after Monza.

Audetto's ultimate prophecy was that Lauda would take the championship by one point from Hunt, 76 to 75. But interestingly, Audetto's prediction took no account of the outcome of Ferrari's protest against the British Grand Prix and the mountain that Hunt still had to climb to win.

The future for Hunt might have meant that things could only get better – but first they would have to get much worse.

SHUNT

CHAPTER 26

The bittersweet October 1976
To the wire in North America

James Hunt flew back to London's Heathrow airport from Milan and then caught a flight to New York America, where he earned another US$10,000 competing in his second IROC race of the year. He then flew to Toronto and tested at Mosport for a few days prior to the Grand Prix, and then back to Spain via Heathrow. A few days later, he flew back to Toronto to get ready for the race at the Mosport track on the 3rd October.

It was an extraordinary schedule motivated by his desire to earn some extra money and spend a few days at home in peace before the end of the summer and the run-in to the championship-deciding races.

When he finally got there, Hunt was looking forward to having a marvellous time in Canada, playing squash and enjoying the country's many attractions. His libido seemed to be at its highest, as he had a different woman on his arm every evening and was even indulging during the day where he could. There was an embarrassing moment at the Mosport track during testing when he seduced the circuit manager's wife while her husband was standing nearby. Getting on very well with the woman, Hunt spotted an empty ambulance by the pits with the doors unlocked and invited her inside. Meanwhile, her husband strolled up the McLaren pit to have a word with Caldwell just as the ambulance was rocking on its shock absorbers in the background. Back at the hotel in the evenings, Hunt was also busy seducing the singer of the band that was entertaining in the hotel lounge.

But Hunt should never have been in Canada at all. In going so early and not attending the upcoming FIA Court of Appeal in Paris, he made a catastrophic error of judgment that would cost him dear.

The hearing had been called in Paris after Ferrari had appealed Hunt's win at the British Grand Prix, arguing he should have been disqualified after the race was restarted. Hunt was the principal witness and, arguably, the only witness who mattered. He was simply too lazy to go and was overconfident about the result, as he said: "I didn't see how they could possibly throw us out because it was an open and shut case as far as the legalities were concerned." But he admitted later: "I was a little nervous of the outcome."

Much of the blame for Hunt's absence at the hearing lay at the feet of Teddy Mayer. Mayer was a trained lawyer and must have known how important Hunt's testimony would be, but he still wasn't able to exert his authority over the driver and make him attend.

Hunt said later that he didn't want anything negative distracting him from the last two races in North America. He was in a very confident mood and was totally focused on the world championship. He wasn't sure he could beat Lauda for the title, but he believed he would run him close.

Hunt was up for the fight. At that point, Lauda was only five points ahead with three races to go. He said: "I was all set to give it a go. I was fired up and wanted to drive, and the only place I could be on my own to get on with the job was in the car. So I enjoyed my driving there more than ever because it was such a relief. The rest of it I hated."

But the joy he felt was about to be undone as the FIA Court of Appeal in Paris got underway to consider an appeal by the Ferrari team as to whether the Hunt's McLaren-Ford should have been disqualified from the results of the British Grand Prix. The hearing was in front of a six-member panel of judges composed of FIA delegates from France, Germany, Spain, Brazil, Switzerland and the United States of America.

Ferrari's arguments were presented by its team manager Daniele Audetto, accompanied by two lawyers. Audetto stated that, after the accident at the start of the race, Hunt's car had been abandoned by the driver and was being pushed by the McLaren mechanics while the race was still in progress, and was therefore incapable of completing the first lap.

McLaren's defence, presented by Teddy Mayer and a lawyer representing the British Royal Automobile Club, stated that Hunt stopped only when he saw the red flag being displayed and that the car was only pushed after the race had been officially halted. Hunt, they maintained, could and would have completed the lap had he felt it necessary.

Teddy Mayer brought with him to the proceedings a heavy video cassette machine and a recording of the race, supplied by Barrie Gill's CSS agency. This, he thought, substantiated McLaren's claim beyond doubt. Caldwell agreed: "We had clear video evidence of him driving the car, the video was taken to Paris and a CSS producer swore that this was untouched film."

But, without Hunt, it was still all hearsay and they effectively had no case. Moreover, his absence annoyed the six judges immensely; it smacked of arrogance.

Ferrari made no such mistake, as Niki Lauda showed up to give evidence. Although Lauda had not really been involved, he was nevertheless present to give what evidence he could. Having travelled from Vienna to Paris for the hearing, Lauda arrived at the hearing with a blood soaked bandage on his head. Since his wounds had healed by then, it was pure Italian theatrics to gain the court's sympathy. In top form, Lauda was very persuasive and appeared to sway the judges.

Additionally, Lauda was portrayed, very effectively, by the Ferrari lawyers as a victim. If Hunt had been there, he might have countered the argument. But he wasn't and he didn't.

The hearing took 11 hours, completed in one session, and the next day the secretary of the FIA delivered the verdict. It was simple: Hunt was disqualified from the results of the British Grand Prix and would lose nine points. To make matters worse, Lauda was promoted to winner and gained three points.

All in all, Hunt had effectively lost 12 points. The points score now stood at Lauda 64 and Hunt 47; a 17-point difference. And it was all the English driver's own fault.

Hunt was playing squash in Toronto on a Tuesday afternoon when he heard the news. Somehow, a call from a Canadian journalist got through to him and he was handed a piece of paper by a club staffer that read: "Call me back and be prepared for bad news." Hunt knew exactly what that meant, as he said: "News is only good or bad, and it was going to be a black or white answer anyway." With that, he effectively knew the result and didn't immediately return the call. He decided to finish his game of squash first, as he said: "I wanted to think about it a bit, so I went to the changing rooms and straight down to the court. I'm pretty tough professionally and it's difficult to move me because I've trained myself to be hard – there's no mileage in letting things upset you. But boy, I couldn't hit that squash ball and I couldn't concentrate on the game at all."

By the time Hunt finished his game, word had travelled around and he had been joined at the squash club by a horde of journalists telling him more about what had happened. He described it as "a very heavy deal."

Hunt always maintained he was never given the real reason for being thrown out of the results. He said: "They never said why. In appeals prior to this, they had always stated the findings of the court and their reasons for finding it, but in this case all they did was issue a result."

There was only one possible reason in Hunt's mind: the FIA simply had chosen to disbelieve the witnesses, including the clerk of the course and the marshals. Hunt never considered his own absence to have been the reason. He said: "The fact was that my car was running and hadn't retired, and I can't see how anyone can talk about a driver's intentions because not even I knew then whether I intended to retire or not – it was totally irrelevant." But he had not been there to tell them. Now 3,500 miles away, it struck him that perhaps he had been wrong not to go to the hearing. Years later, he tried to rewrite history by saying the hearing took place a week after it did: "I was already in Canada waiting, ready to race. I have to say it was a supreme shock to me to get the news from Paris two days before practice for the Canadian Grand Prix started." But his protestations were undone by Lauda's appearance in Paris at the hearing. Alastair Caldwell remembered: "Niki was the living saint, and the silly old sod who did the deciding decided that it was unfair on poor Niki."

Principally, Hunt blamed Ferrari for having brought such an unnecessary appeal. Hunt said: "I happened to be the guy who was beating the great Ferrari machine and they didn't like it. They've done a lot of work to make sure I didn't succeed, starting with the fuel business at Monza, and now this." He added, for good effect: "Combining this news with the Italian fiasco, I felt really cheated – yes, cheated. Here I was in a position to win the world championship after ten years of effort and here I was being politically assassinated, being cheated by events over which I had no control whatsoever. It was downright wrong and there was just nothing I could do about it."

Teddy Mayer was totally shocked by the result and said: "James won the race fair and square; there was no question about that, there was no question of his car being illegal." But Hunt did admit he and the team were somewhat at fault: "Quite honestly, neither I nor McLaren took it particularly seriously because there was nothing in the rule book, no grounds in the rules that could possibly suggest that I was going to be disqualified or that it was going to be a problem. As a result, I think McLaren and Teddy Mayer didn't set up a proper defence when they went to Paris in September."

Alastair Caldwell summed it all up: "We were never any good at politics at McLaren. We got done."

As everyone assembled in Canada, Lauda and the whole Ferrari team was cock-a-hoop about the result of the appeal and some gloating in the press was inevitable. It stirred up tremendous resentment between Hunt and Lauda, and any notions of friendship or rapprochement apparent after the Italian Grand Prix were long gone.

Lauda was quoted as being "delighted at the outcome" and, elsewhere, "madly delighted." To journalists who contacted him at his home in Austria, he said it was a "proper thing" that the FIA court had done and that "at last a positive decision had been taken." Lauda laid it on thick for the press, and Hunt got very worked up when he read it.

Hunt accepted any television interview offered to him to attack Lauda and Ferrari, and Lauda responded in kind. Hunt said: "We all live in glass houses and I don't understand the self-righteousness that was shown by Ferrari saying that they never broke rules. It's alright to say those things, but to say them and believe them is something else. To display the sort of self-righteousness that Ferrari did seems to me childish."

Lauda felt that Hunt was overreacting and being malicious: "When I was robbed of the Spanish Grand Prix, James did not say anything to me or tell me that it was a bad decision. So why should I say anything to him about the decision at Brands Hatch? Sure it was a surprise to me; I did not think that the FIA would cancel his Brands Hatch win, but they took the evidence and they decided that it should be cancelled. It is very tough luck on James; he drove a very good race that day. But the decision has been made and we must accept it. We must not go on shouting about it in public."

The stage was set for a nasty confrontation as the teams checked in at the Flying Dutchmen Motel near Bowmanville, 45 miles from Toronto. Hunt described the atmosphere as "tightrope tension" as he said: "I eventually got so depressed by the whole scene that I locked myself in my room on the Thursday night and waited for Friday's official practice and the opportunity to get back to the sanity of the cockpit of my car. Once I was in the car, all the aggravation, all the pressure disappeared and I concentrated on driving. It was beautiful."

Certainly, the surroundings were. The 2.5-mile Mosport circuit is situated in idyllically magical lake land surrounded by a wilderness of trees beautifully red-brown in the early autumn. But it suffered for being under snow for most of the winter and the circuit was not well maintained. The Grand Prix Drivers' Association safety committee, led by Lauda, remonstrated with the organisers over the condition of the track. Getting no satisfaction, a meeting was scheduled to discuss it. When asked by Lauda to attend the circuit safety meeting, Hunt argued with him and reportedly said: "To hell with safety. All I want to do is race."

Lauda thought Hunt was still angry about losing the Brands Hatch appeal, and said: "We have been friends, but James broke the rules in England. If you break the rules, you are out. No argument. Now he shouts at me. This is not right. He should respect me as a driver. We have a job to do. Bad feeling only makes it more difficult."

Hunt didn't attend the official safety committee meeting and made a flimsy excuse. It severely weakened the drivers' position. The truth was that there was a real danger of the race being cancelled, and that was not in Hunt's interests at all. With one less race, he had no chance of winning the championship. But, of course, Hunt wasn't about to admit that. Drivers always maintain that safety is paramount, but on this occasion, as far as James Hunt was concerned, it wasn't.

His behaviour completely disrupted the post-Monza harmony between the two drivers. But Hunt later admitted that, for tactical reasons, he was keen to inflame the situation rather than cool it down: "I was deliberately trying to make Niki think that I was freaked out by what was happening so he would steer clear of me on the track. It was purely a professional piece of gamesmanship. If you can psych out another driver and make him frightened of you, then he's much easier to pass. I certainly wasn't about to shove him off the track, but I wanted him to think I was in that frame of mind."

Tossing aside their ethics, journalists also began to fuel the anger between the two drivers. Hunt, realising that Lauda had tried to psyche him out earlier in the year by having the last rites administered to make him think he was out of the title race altogether, retaliated. Believing he could intimidate Lauda to the point where he would let him pass on the track rather than risk a confrontation that might put both of them out, he added: "I had cultivated the idea with Niki that I was worked up and, without every saying it, made him think that."

Hunt was walking around the motel like a bear with a sore head. One night, he got into a furious row with Daniele Audetto in the restaurant. Mayer stood by while it raged on. It had all started when Audetto, a courteous man, attempted to convey his apologies to Hunt about losing the appeal. Hunt replied with two words: "Get lost." Or at least these were the words reported in the Canadian newspapers. Audetto told him he was only doing his job. The fuse was lit, and Ferrari and McLaren personnel joined in until Hunt got bored and went to bed. He said the next day: "I thought Audetto's apology was slightly gross. He didn't have to apologise because he need not have protested my win at Brands Hatch in the first place. So I explained to him in a rather terse way that I wasn't interested in his apologies."

The following day, Ferrari had a shock when the Canadian scrutineers told Audetto that the Ferrari gearbox oil cooler was mounted in an illegal position, and it transpired that it had been in this position ever since the Spanish Grand Prix. Ferrari hadn't been trying to cheat, as there was no performance advantage, but it was a mistake and it had not been spotted until Canada. The team had simply not understood the rule book properly; nor had eight sets of previous scrutineers.

Audetto was hugely embarrassed and the team quickly re-positioned the coolers, and McLaren decided not to protest. If it had, arguably Ferrari could have been disqualified from every race since Spain.

When all the drama died down, the action on the track started. Qualifying was fought out between Hunt and Ronnie Peterson's March-Ford. Peterson was now back on form. But that didn't stop Hunt taking pole position again, four-tenths of a second clear of Peterson; a huge margin. Vittorio Brambilla, also in a March-Ford and Patrick Depailler's Tyrrell were on the second row. Lauda was only sixth fastest alongside an increasingly on-form Mario Andretti in a Lotus-Ford.

Hunt was left behind at the start, bested by Peterson. For eight laps he trailed the Swede before moving into the lead. A few laps later, Depailler in the six-wheeled Tyrrell nosed through into second place and moved closer to the McLaren. It was to remain that way to the finish. Second place had become Depailler's specialty; he was to finish second five times in 1976.

Hunt admitted: "Depailler was really giving me a hard time, keeping the

SHUNT

pressure on, and if he had got past he was probably capable of running a bit quicker than I was. But he wasn't quite quick enough to attack me. My main worries in Canada were the back markers trailing the field when we came through to lap them, because you only need to do that wrong once and the guy trailing you is through and gone. The back marker moves the wrong way at the wrong moment, you have to brake, and there is a big gap on the other side of the road. So I took great precautions not to let that situation arise. I started playing the back markers against Patrick. I'd cruise, as it were, between groups of back markers because I obviously wasn't going to get away from him, so there was no hurry. Then, when we got near the back markers, I'd put on a real spurt to get as much air between him and me and to give myself a bit of maneuvering room. Soon, I was timing my arrival with the back markers so that I was ready to pass them at the right part of the circuit. I was giving it real thought and I was managing to get through better than he was, but you need a bit of luck there as well."

In truth, Hunt scythed through the back markers majestically, as he recalled: "They all gave way to me beautifully." His tactics, intended to intimidate Lauda, had clearly worked on everyone else as well.

The Grand Prix had been enlivened by the duel between the two drivers, but in the closing laps Depailler began to drop back inexplicably and there were six seconds between them at the finish. It turned out that petrol fumes had been leaking into his Tyrrell cockpit, leaving Depailler feeling intoxicated in the last few laps. He said he felt as though he had drunk a bottle of whisky. The padded lining of his helmet was wet with fuel.

Hunt was ecstatic when he passed the finish line. He had done what he had come to Canada to do. All thoughts of the Brands Hatch disqualification disappointment were banished from his head. And there was a further bonus when he got out of the car and heard that Niki Lauda, who had fought an ill-handling car with a rear suspension problem for the whole race, could only manage eighth. Lauda had scored no points, a disaster for him.

After the race, Hunt and Lauda got together to resolve their differences. Hunt may have been consciously playing up the much publicised rift between himself and Lauda to his advantage, but there comes a point in any psychological confrontation when it is difficult to isolate the truth from the tactics. Hunt realised that this point had come and that the so-called feud needed to be laid to rest permanently.

Hunt was tired of what had happened in Italy and Canada, and wanted a fair fight to the finish in an atmosphere of good sportsmanship. He genuinely didn't want to win in a state of gladiatorial confrontation with Lauda, especially after the Nürburgring accident. Hunt was deeply sorry about Lauda's disfigurement, which had caused anguish to everybody in the Formula One paddock. They knew life would never be the same for Lauda, and they could not help but confront the thought of their own mortality when confronted with his injuries every day.

As it happened, the change in his appearance never bothered Lauda one little bit. It bothered him that others were disturbed, but the superficiality of how he looked did not trouble him personally at all.

The intimate Glen Motor Inn was an ideal venue for a rapprochement. Watkins Glen is a small tourist town situated on the Seneca Lakes in New York state. It is around 120 miles from the Canadian border. Most of the teams stay in the Glen Motor Inn and the mechanics at the Seneca Lodge. The Franzese family managed the Motor Inn at the time, and were familiar with most of the members of the Formula One circus. The dining room had giant picture windows that overlooked the lakes, and at any one time the whole Formula One community could be sitting down for a meal.

So Hunt spent a lot of time with Lauda at the Glen Motor Inn. They both realised it would be better if they discussed their differences before things got completely out of hand. Lauda insisted that he had never said the things he'd been quoted as saying after the announcement from Paris. Lauda also said his derogatory remarks about Hunt at Mosport were a case of "flagrant misreporting" by a "vicious journalist."

Hunt also denied quotes about Lauda that had been attributed to him. He was adamant his anti-Lauda comments had been instances of fabrication and misquotation. After they had talked, the two shook hands and the feud was buried forever. Hunt said afterwards: "The press was winding us both up badly, and we got a bit irritated. For a few hours we hated each other, but after we got it sorted out our good relationship continued."

At the Motor Inn, they arranged to have adjoining hotel rooms. They kept their doors open and socialised together. It was a time for practical jokes and Lauda used to wake Hunt in the morning with 'Fawlty Towers'-type John Cleese impressions. At the time, 'Fawlty Towers' was Europe's top comedy TV show.

But others do not remember the relationship being anywhere near so congenial, especially John Hogan, who said: "Throughout that year, James had had sort of a testy relationship with Niki. Niki was being a little bit the Austrian brat. For instance, I'd just got off the plane in Toronto and I walked into the huge dining room at Mosport. Niki was sitting over there with the Ferrari guys, and James was sitting over there with the McLaren guys. And I walk in and Niki says: 'Hogan, come sit here.' Then James shouts: 'Hogie, over here'. So I started with McLaren then moved over to Ferrari." There were also other undercurrents afoot, as Hogan was secretly working behind the scenes to get Lauda to leave Ferrari and join McLaren to create a dream team for 1977. Hogan had sensed his chance after Lauda's accident and Reutemann's recruitment. Hunt was all for it but Lauda had balked at the idea of being Hunt's teammate. Hogan remembers: "James had no problem at all. He said: 'You gotta look at it this way', thinking about the game again, 'you gotta put the competitors somewhere, so it might as well be in the same car.' But Niki was: 'ooooough.'"

On track, qualifying was uneventful round the 2.4-mile circuit, and for the eighth time in the season, Hunt seized pole position. This time he had Jody Scheckter alongside him in the six-wheel Tyrrell, which was proving very effective in its debut season. Scheckter was improving race by race. But he had no future with the Tyrrell team after the Zandvoort incident. It was announced he was leaving Tyrrell to drive for the Walter Wolf team. Wolf had paid him US$250,000 just as a signing on fee to persuade him to make the move.

Walter Wolf, a wealthy Canadian oil entrepreneur, had by this time sacked Frank Williams and taken sole ownership of the team. He had hired Peter Warr away from Lotus to replace Williams.

Wolf, a mystery man, also explained to journalists how he had initially made his money. He admitted he had started out from very humble beginnings and become an oil trader. He admitted his fortune was down to a piece of luck when the oil crisis happened in 1973. He had owned a tanker full of oil at sea between Nigeria and Holland when crude oil prices quadrupled overnight. Wolf said: "The only bit of genius I used was to cable the captain and tell him to take his time getting to Amsterdam because the price was going up all the time."

But Scheckter's new turn of speed was not Hunt's problem; his problem was Lauda's performance. He realised that the odds were on Lauda retaining his title and said: "I hadn't given up completely because where there's life there's hope. I could only knuckle down and go after each race as it came and try to win it. If I couldn't win, I had to finish as high as I could."

During qualifying, Hunt aggravated an inflamed nerve in his left elbow and the pain became worse overnight. A doctor was called and he was given pain-killing injections before he got in the car.

Hunt may have been on pole eight times during 1976, but he had only led one first lap. That day would prove no exception. This time, he made a good start but it was still not good enough to prevent Scheckter taking the lead. And that is how it stayed for many laps, with Hunt in station some three seconds behind Scheckter. Behind them was third place man Niki Lauda, five seconds back. But Hunt knew he had to win and started focusing hard on the physical act of driving the car, something which he confessed afterwards he did not often do. It usually all came so naturally to him, and that was often good enough. But that day it wasn't. His McLaren-Ford was oversteering alarmingly round Watkins Glen's many corners. He remembered he spent 20 laps concentrating and working out a technique to go faster. He called it a "self-administered driving lesson."

He admitted afterwards that the exercise had given him huge personal satisfaction: "I got myself together. It is very important in all walks of life to be able to catch yourself when you're doing something badly and to make sure you improve." That day he was able to do it. Hunt gritted his teeth, gripped the McLaren's steering wheel more firmly, and zeroed his mind in on Scheckter, who stood between him and the victory. Hunt was determined to get him. As he bore down on Scheckter, leaving Lauda farther and farther behind, he planned ahead, looking for likely passing places and opportunities to outmanoeuvre the leader.

On lap 36, Scheckter was delayed by another car slowing for a tight corner, and Hunt tucked his McLaren in behind the Tyrrell's rear wing. As they accelerated down the straight, Hunt darted out of Scheckter's slipstream and took the lead.

But four laps later, Scheckter got in front again as they were lapping back markers. Hunt was furious with himself, losing the lead after all that work, as he said afterwards: "Jody blasted past me on the straight. I really thought I'd blown it."

Hunt's adrenaline level was high and he pressed on, determined to win. Adrenaline levels were always a Hunt problem, as Alastair Caldwell says: "He put a tremendous amount of effort into racing and he had the biggest adrenalin pump of any racing driver I've ever known. He was so excited in the car before a race that, if you sat on the side of it, you'd think the motor was running."

Within a lap, he was again within striking range. For several laps, he waited to pounce, testing Scheckter's reaction when he moved to the left and right sides of the track behind him. Finally, with 12 laps to go, Hunt forced his way alongside the Tyrrell coming into a slow corner. The two cars went round the bend side-by-side, and on the straight Hunt got past. This time, he drove like an absolute demon to put air between him and Scheckter, who he realised was a master at negotiating slower back markers.

Hunt reeled off a succession of quick laps and eventually smashed the record with a lap that was an astonishing second faster than his pole position. That sort of performance is rarely achieved in Formula One, and spectators that day got a master class in fast driving.

Hunt went across the line eight seconds ahead of Scheckter, and Lauda came in a minute behind in third.

Hunt got out of his car, exhausted and soaked in sweat from an outstanding drive. He had closed the gap to within three points of Lauda, and there was one race remaining. On the podium, he downed a cold Miller instead of the traditional champagne.

He said on the podium: "It was as tough a race as I ever had to drive. For the first 20 laps, I drove like an old grandmother and just couldn't adapt to my car. Both Jody and I were making mistakes in those opening laps. Then I got it together and I chased Jody and passed him fairly easily. I missed my gear change and got a fistful of neutrals, and by the time I had found a gear Jody was past again. But I was quicker on the straight and hauled him in."

The victory sent the whole circuit wild as they sensed the historic moment and the showdown to come in Japan. Hunt was cheered in the press room by the normally cynical journalists. He left the press room in company with David Benson and the two men were mobbed as they walked to the Goodyear hospitality marquee for a champagne-fuelled post race party. Benson recalls: "It was an intoxicating, exciting scene. At that moment I really believed that James was at last going to win the world championship. I wanted him to win. My emotions told me that he deserved to win."

Between gulping down champagne, Hunt said; "This was the most important race of my life. I simply had to win. Thank God Jody was second. That puts Niki only three points in front of me for Japan. If I win there and he comes second, I could still win the championship. We would have equal points but

I would have more Grand Prix wins."

A disappointed Niki Lauda had expected to clinch the championship at Watkins Glen but left empty handed. After the race, he went directly by helicopter from the circuit to the airport for his home in Austria. When he got there, he faced the prospect of a further operation. The skin grafts around his brow and cheeks were so tight that he couldn't close his right eye properly and it was becoming inflamed. An immediate eye operation was deemed necessary, but it could not happen until after the Japanese Grand Prix. In his grand plan, he was not even going to go to Mount Fuji but, given his performance at Watkins Glen, now that plan was torn up.

Later that night, Hunt partied like never before. On the way back to the Glen Motor Inn, going past a construction site, he stole a road worker's yellow hard hat with a flashing orange light on it.

In the bar, he cavorted with the flashing hat perched on his head and a cigarette dangling from his mouth. He had a beer in one hand and on the other arm was one of the many adoring girls in the bar that night. Also at that party were Caldwell, Mayer and John Hogan. And it was there, in that bar, that these three men conversed, plotted and came up with a plan that would make James Hunt world champion. The plan would be decisive over the course of the next two weeks.

Before the Canadian Grand Prix, Hunt had been 17 points behind Lauda, which meant that he had to take 18 points from the final three Grand Prix races without Lauda scoring. He had now reduced that to three. There was one round left. The score was Lauda 68, Hunt 65.

The maths was relatively simple: to be champion, Hunt needed to finish outright first and he would be world champion no matter what Lauda did. If he was second, Lauda needed to be fourth or lower for him to win. If he was third, he needed Lauda to be sixth or lower. If he was fourth or under, then Lauda would be champion.

And Lauda was not the only one with medical problems. The next day, Hunt went for an examination of his left arm. He had been suffering from inflamed ligaments and had had cortisone injections earlier that week. Cure before Tokyo was vital.

A showdown loomed in Japan at the eponymous Mount Fuji track.

SHUNT

CHAPTER 27

Showdown in Japan
Sunday 24th October 1976

A no-holds-barred fight to the finish

espite having been thoroughly trounced at Watkins Glen, Ferrari's complacency after the race ended was astonishing. It made no attempts to do anything special to prepare for the last race. It just packed up its cars as usual, ready to put them on the Formula One charter Jumbo jet to Japan.

But as James Hunt cavorted in the Glen Motor Inn at Watkins Glen on the night of 10th October 1976, celebrating his victory of only a few hours earlier, Teddy Mayer, Alastair Caldwell and John Hogan sat quietly musing about what to do to get an edge. Mayer, Caldwell and Hogan were having a deadly serious conversation. They were in a place in time they had never expected to be. With one race left, James Hunt and McLaren could win the Formula One world championship. His victory that day, and Niki Lauda's fourth place, meant there were only three points between them. It was suddenly all up for grabs in Japan. Hogan recalled: "James knew it was just there, and he was kind of standing on Niki's throat."

It was the kind of situation in which Alastair Caldwell was at his best. Caldwell was a tremendously competitive man, with a brain that worked in a peculiar way. Sometimes he was stubborn and hopeless, but other times brilliant and untouchable. Hogan agrees: "James always said Alistair Caldwell won the championship, not him."

And indeed what happened next dictated the eventual outcome of the championship. Caldwell had been brooding about the task in hand all evening, trying to see where McLaren could get an edge on Ferrari.

Finally, he turned to Mayer and said: "Teddy, go ring Fuji and tell them we want to be testing there on Monday, i.e. tomorrow." He told Mayer: "We'll put the car on a plane and we'll go to Fuji tomorrow morning."

Resisting the idea mightily, Mayer stared at Caldwell as if he was crazy. But the car and equipment were already packed and ready to go the airport. Mayer was also worried about the cost. The charter was already paid for, as was the airfare for all personnel, but what Caldwell proposed would cost at least an additional US$15,000 that wasn't budgeted for. He was also uncertain about track availability and getting the car through customs. Thinking the whole scheme foolhardy, Mayer told Caldwell: "No way, we're not going testing in Japan. It isn't feasible."

An exasperated Caldwell excused himself and got straight on the phone to an air freight agency in New York, which informed him of a flight leaving for Tokyo the next day. It was the only outbound plane that week with big enough cargo doors. He said he would ring back to confirm. Then Caldwell rung the Watkins Glen circuit and told his mechanics the new plan. He told them to pack the spare car separately in a crate with enough tools and kit for a two-day test session. The car would have to be ready and at the airport on Monday morning. The mechanics got straight on it.

At the circuit, the Ferrari mechanics watched the McLaren men pack up the car and immediately guessed what was going on. Daniele Audetto put in a call to Maranello; he was going to test as well. Unlike Caldwell, though, he wasn't willing to take responsibility for the extra cost on his own head.

Meanwhile, Teddy Mayer was on his way to New York to catch his plane back to London that night. When Caldwell dropped him off at the heliport, Mayer's last words to him were: "Don't send that car to Japan; it's a waste of time and money." But as the helicopter took off for New York, Caldwell shouted out: "Well, stuff you."

Mayer's comments galvanised Caldwell even more. As soon as Caldwell returned to the hotel, he rang the shipper and told him the crate would be ready first thing in the morning. The shippers were keen to help Hunt, and only too pleased to send a truck over to Watkins Glen from New York to pick it up.

While all this was going on, Ermanno Cuoghi, Ferrari's chief mechanic, had also telephoned the same shippers to ask if Ferrari could get a car on the flight as well. The shippers answered that a truck was already on its way to pick up the McLaren and that the Ferrari crate could go on as well. The problem was that Cuoghi, like Audetto, also didn't have the nerve to authorise the cost himself. Cuoghi sought out Audetto and told him what he proposed. But Audetto told him he must first get permission from Enzo Ferrari to spend the US$15,000. Enzo Ferrari couldn't be contacted until Monday morning, with the time difference giving them just enough time to meet the truck and load the car.

Without thinking, the shipping agency then telephoned Caldwell at the Glen Motor Inn and told him the Ferrari would be on the same flight but that they were waiting for authorisation from Italy.

When Audetto finally spoke to Maranello the next morning, they promised to get authority from Enzo. He gave his blessing straightaway and his secretary called the track to let Audetto know he could send the car.

Having noticed all the to-ing and fro-ing from the pit lane telephone, and understanding just enough Italian, Caldwell had worked out what was happening, By then back at the circuit, he resolved to try and intercept the call in order to stall Ferrari. He knew if Audetto and Cuoghi didn't get permission, they wouldn't risk sending the cars.

There was only one telephone in the pit lane at the time, and it was right next to McLaren's garage. Cuoghi told the security guard who attended the phone that Ferrari was expecting a call and asked him to come find him when it arrived. Caldwell, overhearing this, went over and told the unsuspecting guard to shout for him first if there were any calls, as he too was expecting one.

Caldwell later told the whole story to Hunt biographer Christopher Hilton: "He'd get a call and shout: 'Hey Alastair, telephone.' I'd go over and say: 'Hello.' The Italian voice said: 'This is Italy, this is Ferrari, we wish to talk to our team manager.' I said: 'Hang on a minute, we'll see if we can find him.'"

Caldwell could see Audetto and Cuoghi supervising the packing, but instead of calling him over to take the call, he waited a few minutes and then picked up the phone again and said: "No, we can't find him, he's playing golf." The Italian voice said: "Can you tell us where?" to which he replied: "Watkins Glen golf course. We'll get you the number."

Having provided the number for the golf course, Caldwell put down the phone. Ten minutes later, the phone rang again. The same routine followed with the security guard handing Caldwell the telephone. The voice said: "This is Italy, this is Ferrari, we can't find our team manager at the golf course." Caldwell replied: "Perhaps he's gone to the Seneca Lodge hotel. We'll get you the number." It went on in a similar vein for the entire morning, and Caldwell managed to prevent Maranello from talking to Audetto. So, when the shipper's truck arrived, only the McLaren was loaded onto it. Caldwell, Hunt and two mechanics followed to Tokyo the following morning.

When Audetto finally spoke to Maranello, he knew immediately what Caldwell had done but by then it was too late. Ferrari's cars had been loaded onto the truck and left for the charter flight.

Initially, it did occur to Caldwell that perhaps Mayer had been right about what a waste of time it was. Caldwell spent a very frustrating week trying to get the car out of Japanese customs. The customs service in Japan was notoriously difficult, and it had a particularly difficult import policy which was carried out with the utmost vigour. Caldwell remembers the problems the delay caused: "Because you weren't allowed to test on the week of the race, we had to do it all by the Saturday."

In the end, the car was released on Friday afternoon and taken straight over to the Mount Fuji circuit. But after less than a dozen laps, the gearbox seized up. It had been assembled incorrectly in England and there was no spare gearbox in the crate. But those completed laps proved incredibly important as Hunt learned the track and acclimatised himself to Japan. After the car failed, he donned his running gear and ran the track; noting all the corners and circuit characteristics.

Since the Mount Fuji circuit would be new to all the drivers, any time spent on the track in advance was invaluable. It was the first time the Mount Fuji track had hosted the Japanese Grand Prix, and it would now work to Hunt's advantage. The track had been built under the shadow of the sacred snow-capped mountain in the foothills of the extinct volcano. It was situated in the Shizuoka Prefecture, 60 miles west of Tokyo. The car journey from the capital took an hour and a half.

Mount Fuji was Japan's tallest mountain and the volcano had last erupted in 1707. On a clear day, it was easily visible from Tokyo. The 2.7-mile track had been built in the early 1960s, originally to host Nascar racing, and it had a very long main straight measuring 1.5 kilometres.

Apart from its fabulous surroundings, the circuit itself was devoid of any character and not particularly challenging to the drivers. But Hunt liked the circuit straightaway and found it suited his style; especially after two full days of preparation, which no other driver had.

As he drove away from the Mount Fuji circuit after testing on Sunday, Hunt reflected on his year. It had been incredible; no dramatist could have created a more riveting scenario or two more heroic rivals.

Between them, he and Lauda had won 11 of the 15 Grand Prix races in the lead-up to Japan. The Austrian had overcome the horrific injuries he sustained in the Nürburgring accident and had returned to racing still leading the world championship. And Hunt had fought his way from relative obscurity and from being over 50 points behind to become the man of the moment in Formula One; the man who would take Lauda down to the wire in the battle for the title.

Because of its intensity and closeness, the battle between them had made front page news all over the world and propelled Formula One into the global spotlight. Because of them, F1 was now one of the top sports in the world and every major country was to broadcast the Japanese Grand Prix live. Formula One had never before received such exposure, and it was to mark a big sea change in attitudes towards the sport. In the process, James Hunt had also become a global celebrity and was now more famous than all the previous Formula One world champions combined.

The world's media had 14 days to prepare for the showdown and all the satellites that transmitted TV pictures were quickly booked out. Bernie Ecclestone was busy selling broadcast rights for every territory; it was the first time he had experienced any real demand. It was a watershed for his burgeoning TV sales operation, which, up until then, had not even been able to give the rights away *gratis*. There could be no real loser in Japan.

The only thing that bothered Hunt was all the attention he was getting. Suddenly it seemed everyone wanted a piece of him, and all the attention spooked him. It was made worse for Hunt because Lauda was still a virtual recluse as a result of his facial injuries. Hunt fount it all rather overwhelming, and his new fame did not rest easily on his shoulders.

Uncomfortable with the attention, Hunt wondered whether it was going to his head. As he told his biographer Gerald Donaldson, he was worried he might start believing his own press: "People spend a lot of time telling you how clever you are, and it's very easy to believe. I've seen too many people become victims of such flattery and start taking themselves too seriously. That's when they destroy themselves and their personalities."

In truth, things became so extreme in Japan that for the first time Hunt found he was not enjoying his racing, as he said at the time: "I try to be myself but I worry that I've lost the ability to enjoy life. I'm a tax exile, but England is where my heart is and where my friends are. But everywhere the demands on my time are so great that already my private life is shot to hell and I feel the loss of close friends. The main problem in this business is that you lose your individuality. Whatever you do or say is watched. You are used as evidence against yourself." There were signs of paranoia setting in, but there is no question it was a difficult time.

The McLaren team stayed at the luxurious Tokyo Hilton in downtown Tokyo. Japanese hotels were then the very best in the world. The rooms were loaded with gadgetry unknown in the west and the décor was minimalist. For Hunt, the Hilton was a playground. Once in the confines of the hotel, he was unmolested. So he set out to have a good time in the few days before the race. With his privacy guarded by the hotel staff, he tried to distract himself by stepping up his physical fitness routine to new levels.

Hunt was constantly in the Hilton's state of the art gym: running, swimming and playing squash every day. In the evening, he was flexing his mental skills by playing backgammon and won over US$1,000 that week.

But the hotel's head waiter blanched when Hunt wanted to play backgammon in the main restaurant during dinner. He had already made an exception and let the famous racing driver into the restaurant with no shoes on. When the backgammon board appeared, he told Hunt the restaurant was not a "playhouse." Hunt reportedly responded: "The whole world is a playhouse" and carried on playing. The head waiter was overruled by the hotel's manager, anxious to do anything to please the eccentric young Englishman.

An added bonus of the hotel was that British Airways, then called the British Overseas Airways Corporation (BOAC), used it for its flight crew layovers and a new batch of air hostesses was arriving fresh every day. Knowing their timetable, Hunt began greeting the arriving stewardesses in the hotel lobby every morning. He would tell them his room number and invite them to a party that night, to which they would all dutifully turn up. Hunt particularly enjoyed group sex sessions, and many of them were up for it, with Hunt bedding up to four of them every night.

Also staying in the hotel was another world-class playboy called Barry Sheene, the motorcycle world champion. During the season, Hunt and Sheene had become good friends. Sheene travelled to Japan to give Hunt moral support and he came without his girlfriend, the model Stephanie McLean, whom he would later marry. McLean was a stunning woman and Penthouse Pet of the Year in 1971. But that didn't stop Sheene partying with the same fervor as Hunt and sharing the stewardesses with him. The then 27-year-old motorcycle racer regarded the trip as his last fling before getting married to Stephanie. Sheene admitted: "[Hunt and I] were both sportsmen and we drank and smoked and chased women, went to places you shouldn't go and did things you shouldn't do." Hunt was also by then officially going out with Jane Birbeck, and in some ways also regarded it as his last fling. At night, it was just sexual mayhem, compliments of BOAC.

Sheene remembered that Hunt was never out of his t-shirt and shorts, even at formal occasions: "I loved going somewhere with James because he always made me look well-dressed." In turn, Hunt took to calling Sheene 'Mr Sheen' after the spray-on furniture polish popular in England and chortled merrily every time he did. Sheene was not particularly amused, especially when the stewardesses he was wooing also began addressing him as such.

But eventually, Hunt had to turn his attention to the race and the forbidding Mount Fuji circuit and the challenge ahead of him. He admitted he was not that keen on returning to the real world after five days in the fantasy world that had been the Tokyo Hilton.

But it hadn't all been pleasure. David Gray had arrived in Tokyo a few days before to support his friend's bid for the championship. Gray worked for Collett Dickenson Pearce (CDP) and one of CDP's clients was Olympus Cameras. Gray was due at a pre-arranged meeting in Tokyo together with Olympus' European marketing director, Barry Taylor. The Japanese managers told Gray and Taylor it was about to embark on a global advertising campaign to establish the brand in world markets. Gray remembers: "We had a meeting with Olympus where they showed us the most appalling international advertising campaign written by some clapped-out Canadian copyrighters and art directed by some more clapped-out American idiots and they said: 'What do you think of it?' Barry said it would be a complete waste of money and I told them the campaign could be for a Greek airline or a typewriter company and no one would be able to tell. I told them: 'I think you should be in an arena where, although you're not really known, you could make a big impact.'"

Then Gray made his pitch: "There's an arena that is about to happen, here on Sunday were you can conjoin with the major brands of the world and be part of it." To his eternal surprise, the Japanese bought the idea and authorised Gray to go ahead.

The deal with Hunt was quickly approved by Barry Taylor, who not only headed up marketing in Europe but had helped Gray sell it to his Japanese bosses. Gray says: "I'll never forget him, he was the most brilliant client, a brilliant marketer and he was the one that actually said: 'We will do it.'"

Gray did a quick deal with Peter Hunt to get an Olympus logo on Hunt's race overalls for the weekend. The deal was for US$10,000 for the race. It was unorthodox, and Peter sowed the patches on his brother's overalls himself before qualifying started. Gray remembers: "I persuaded Olympus to put a badge on his overalls, and I said to them: 'If he wins the championship, you will be on the front page of every newspaper all over the world.' So he did, and they were."

But it almost didn't happen, as John Hogan walked into the Marlboro hospitality area just as Peter Hunt was sowing on the patches. Hogan was not happy at all and stared around the room at the conspirators. Gray remembers: "In the middle of it, Hogan walked in and said some choice words to us." He said to Gray: "You can't just sow that patch on. We own James' overalls." Feigning outrage, Hogan then quickly agreed to it. He was aware Marlboro was underpaying Hunt substantially, especially in view of what he had achieved, and didn't want to stand in the way of him making some extra money.

The Olympus deal was vital because it became permanent and was worth US$90,000 a year to Hunt for the rest of his career. It was the first big money deal of his championship year.

By contrast with Hunt's early arrival, which had also proved very lucrative, Niki Lauda arrived in Tokyo at the last possible moment. In those days, Lauda was not interested in girls nor the casual sex that was so easily available around the circuits. In direct contrast, he was enjoying married life with his wife, Marlene, in Vienna.

When he did finally arrive, Lauda was feeling rather down and depressed. He really did not want to be in Tokyo and longed to be home in Graz. He had never planned to be there. He was sure he would win the championship in

Watkins Glen and then be able to recuperate at home from his much needed eye operation. The euphoria of his comeback had worn off, and he admitted the physical and mental trauma of Nürburgring was suddenly getting to him. He knew the Fuji weekend would be stressful and inevitably full of drama. But even Lauda had no idea just how stressful and dramatic it would turn out to be.

Alastair Caldwell had been in full battle mode from the moment he arrived in Japan. He would have worn war paint had it been appropriate. He was determined to win and thought about nothing else from dawn to dusk. As far as he was concerned, the contest with Ferrari was a battle with no rules. His attitude was completely different from that of Daniele Audetto, who treated Mount Fuji just like he would any other race. But Caldwell knew this was the battle of his life, and there was a world of difference in the two men's attitudes towards what had to be done.

Flush from his successful prevention of Ferrari testing, Caldwell started some rumours that the Fuji track's tarmac surface would begin to deteriorate and break up as early as Friday. To this end, he instructed the mechanics to make up dummy metal screens for all the intakes of the team's spare car. Caldwell then had all the brake ducts, radiators and air intakes covered by these screens, and a tarpaulin was placed over the car as it was held under close security by guards on shift both day and night. This interested Ferrari and particularly intrigued Lauda when he arrived in the McLaren pit garage to greet Hunt.

When Lauda turned up on Friday morning, Caldwell slipped off the covers. When Lauda saw what they had done, he pretended not to notice but immediately rushed back to the Ferrari pit with news of what he had seen. Daniele Audetto immediately instigated a crash programme to do the same for the three Ferraris in the garage. All Friday morning was taken up with the modifications, and every open orifice on the three Ferraris was covered up with fine mesh grilles.

Just before qualifying, Caldwell removed all the screens and Lauda realised he had been fooled. He had wasted a lot of his team's valuable preparation time on a load of concocted nonsense.

Compared to the race, the two qualifying days were entirely uneventful with neither Ferrari nor McLaren dominating – as had been expected. The John Player-sponsored Lotus team proved to be the most-improved team of the year, with Mario Andretti taking pole and Hunt managing second-fastest time alongside. Niki Lauda and John Watson's Penske-Ford were side by side on the second row. Jody Scheckter's Tyrrell-Ford was fifth and Carlos Pace was sixth; one of his best showings of the year in what had otherwise been a disastrous 1976 for the Brabham team with its thirsty Alfa-Romeo engine.

Hunt and Lauda were very close, separated by only 0.28 seconds. Clay Regazzoni was seventh in what would be his last race for Ferrari after Lauda lost the battle to keep him as his teammate. Carlos Reutemann, Lauda's teammate for 1977, did not appear at all after Lauda threatened to walk out if he replaced Regazzoni for the few remaining races of 1976 – as had been Enzo Ferrari's intention.

Despite his good performance in qualifying, Lauda was clearly tired and jet-lagged. Hunt's two weeks in Japan meant he was totally acclimatised.

But having Andretti on pole was good for Ferrari. Andretti, who was half Italian, felt the need to tell journalists that – despite his origins – he was neutral and would do nothing to influence the outcome of the race either way. But he also pointed out: "Hunt's got everything to lose. You don't have to be a mathematician to work it out. Lauda just has to beat Hunt, but Hunt's got to beat him – and all the rest of us. He's got to win." But Andretti's comments were the least of Hunt's problems. The poor weather forecast for Sunday was becoming one of the primary concerns.

Up until then, the weather had been relatively good and the only drama had been caused by the sheer number of journalists, print and broadcast, demanding interviews. Such was the interest in the Hunt-Lauda showdown that the media contingent was nearly eight times the normal number. Nearly 1,000 media personnel crowded into Mount Fuji, and everyone wanted to talk to Hunt.

But race day was to bring dramatically different weather. As the drivers looked out of their bedroom windows, it was hard to imagine a worse storm. The weather had closed in, and even the volcano was obscured by low clouds. The whole of the surrounding countryside was shrouded in thick drifting fog. It had been raining all night.

As the dawn rose, the organisers dispatched hordes of men in grey cagoules and armed with wide brooms to sweep the track of water. From time to time as the fog rolled in, it hid the army of circuit sweepers from view.

In the morning warm-up session, several cars crashed and one of them even aquaplaned off the main straight. When Niki Lauda took out his car, he knew he was in deep trouble. Lauda was very worried about his eyes in the wet and the reduced visibility. He had missed his chance to have the corrective operation and was reluctant to bring it to anyone's attention lest he should fail a medical inspection and be stopped from racing altogether. It was a legacy of the accident, when both his eyelids had been burnt away. He had sought the advice of six different specialist eye surgeons on how best to proceed. Eventually, a Swiss surgeon had taken skin from behind Lauda's ears to graft on as new eyelids. But they weren't perfect, and the right eye in particular was a problem. The doctors advised him not to race in Japan, telling him he needed an urgent operation on his right eye and that it would close properly only after further skin grafts.

Hunt was a member of the drivers' safety committee with Lauda, and the two now joined forces to tell the organisers that there couldn't be a Japanese Grand Prix as it was far too dangerous for the drivers. With the exception of Brambilla and Regazzoni, all the drivers voted against racing.

Caldwell was absolutely adamant that Hunt drive, and said to him: "James, don't be an idiot. You can't win the championship unless there is a race." James simply responded by saying that safety came first, and that he and Lauda would not race. Jochen Mass agreed with Hunt.

In fact, Hunt was so adamant he would not race in the conditions that he said: "I would rather give Niki the title than race in these conditions."

As the day wore on, however, the race was not cancelled so Hunt told Lauda they should try to have the race postponed. However, postponement didn't appear to be an option that the organisers would entertain. Slowly, the drivers' moods began to change, and Ronnie Peterson, Tom Pryce, Vittorio Brambilla, Clay Regazzoni, Alan Jones and Hans Stuck all fancied their chances on a wet track and decided they should get on with it. When Hunt heard this, he knew he was fighting a lost cause; once a few drivers lined up on the grid, others would surely follow. Especially as their team managers were threatening them with the sack if they didn't race.

Meanwhile, with the race still in doubt, Hunt was behaving very bizarrely. At one point he came out, jumped over the pit lane counter, dropped his overalls to his ankles and proceeded to take a pee in full view of the crowds in the grandstand. The spectators, many of whom had high powered binoculars trained on him, applauded him after he finished. He waved back. Half an hour later, Patrick Head, then technical director of the Walter Wolf team, accidentally walked into the wrong garage. Thinking it empty, he was surprised to find Hunt inside, with his racing overalls once more down around his ankles and a young Japanese girl kneeling in front of him with his penis in her mouth. Hunt laughed when he saw him, but Head hummed and hawed and quickly left in a daze not quite believing what he had seen. He was clearly disturbed by having witnessed such a graphic sex act from a leading participant so near to the start of an important race. But when Head recounted the story at dinner later in Tokyo, he found that no one was shocked by Hunt's pre-race preparation antics. They had become the norm.

The team managers usually took little notice of the drivers, but this time they were worried. In normal circumstances, as the weather was so bad, the race almost certainly would have been abandoned. But these were not normal circumstances. The organisers had spent over US$1 million to stage the event and would have to refund the spectators, who had paid high ticket prices. The circuit was full of television crews from all over the world who had booked expensive satellite time to broadcast the race live. From a financial point of view, there had to be a race. There were nearly 80,000 people rammed into the circuit, and the world championship had to be decided. There had never been so much pressure to hold a sporting event to schedule.

As the Formula One cars remained motionless, covered in tarpaulins in front of the pits, the team managers huddled with organisers and race officials in the first floor of the race control tower. It was plain to everyone that it was too dangerous to race. The time scheduled for the race start came and went. The pressure from the television crews was relentless.

The pressure on organisers was immense. They sought the opinions of both Hunt and Lauda, asking them if they wanted to race. Lauda didn't want to race. Hunt was ambivalent, but still agreed with Lauda. Hunt had decided to defer to Lauda, and told him that he personally felt they should wait and race the next day. But he told Lauda he would race if the race was held, saying: "Everyone was still arguing and expressing their point of view. Mine was to not race, to have it another day or something like that. But you get a few weak people to break the strike and then everybody's at it."

After further discussions, Hunt changed his mind again and told Alastair Caldwell that he and Lauda were withdrawing from the race, whatever decision the organisers made.

Bernie Ecclestone was getting frantic. He had taken some big money from the TV companies to broadcast the race. If there was no race, he faced having to give it all back.

The grandstands, which ran the whole length of the main Fuji straight, were packed with fans sitting silently beneath a sea of umbrellas. The crowd sat motionless and in absolute quiet, a perfect demonstration of Japanese reserve. There was none of the Brands Hatch mayhem; it was a different world.

Caldwell started ruminating and decided to get the crowd agitated. He got a mechanic named Lance Gibbs to stand and blow his whistle to get them roused. Caldwell knew that most Japanese carried whistles. The gesture worked, and they all brought out their whistles and started blowing to put pressure on the organisers. With Gibbs' encouragement, they also started shouting.

As the crowd became increasingly roused, the organisers became more and more nervous. Bernie Ecclestone also frightened the organisers by telling them they could have a riot on their hands if there was no race. Ecclestone, by now frantic with worry, told them: "You've got to hold the race. You'll have a riot. They'll tear down the stands."

Caldwell believes that the fans and their increasing agitation, admittedly stirred up by him, was a strong factor in eventually getting the race started.

Lauda remembers: "We all refused to drive in the prevailing conditions. We sat in the race official's trailer and told him 'no go.' At that point, the organisers had decided there would be no race. But they were being stalled from making an announcement by Bernie Ecclestone and others."

At four o'clock in Fuji, it started to get really dark. Ecclestone told them: "The race must start."

Caldwell had noticed Lauda's demeanour and guessed there might be a problem with his eyes in the wet. He knew it was now or never, and if the race was cancelled or abandoned then McLaren might lose the title race by default. So he literally grabbed Hunt by his overall lapels and told him, if the race was on, he would drive. A shocked Hunt agreed. Lauda was now in a difficult position.

The race should have started an hour and a half earlier, and in another two or three hours the Mount Fuji circuit would be in darkness. Finally, a decision was made and announced over the loudspeakers: the Japanese Grand Prix would begin in five minutes. Vittorio Brambilla led the drivers out to their cars.

Lauda, Emerson Fittipaldi and Carlos Pace were all determined not to race and would just do a few laps to please their team owners. Lauda said: "We went to the start so that our respective teams could pick up their starting money, but then we would pack it in. Because nothing changed: everything was just as dangerous as before, and the fact that it was getting dark could hardly help matters."

The drivers went out and did some exploratory laps and then came back in to vote again. Another drivers' meeting voted by a substantial majority that the circuit was too dangerous, but the organisers overruled them and decided to hold their motor race. But the new worry was the light.

They opened the pits and the cars trickled out one by one to take up their positions on the grid. Hunt again told Caldwell that he wasn't driving, and again Caldwell told him he was. Hunt said to Caldwell: "Alastair, fuck this, I'm getting out." Caldwell retorted: "Get out of that car and I'll break your fucking neck." John Hogan witnessed this and remembers: "James replied: 'Oh, alright.' And that was it." But Caldwell wasn't completely reckless and did recognise the dangers. He told Hunt that if he wasn't happy after the warm-up lap, he could come into the pits and retire without consequences but warned him that his championship bid would be over.

So the race officials took the decision away from the drivers, and the showdown in Japan finally got underway. Niki Lauda would start the race and see how conditions were. He said: "At the start, the feeling was absolutely unbearable. I was sitting there panic-stricken, rain lashing down, seeing nothing, just hunched down in the cockpit, shoulders tense, waiting for someone to run into me."

In the gloom, the cars were pushed out to the starting grid. Lance Gibbs drilled holes in the visor of Hunt's helmet to stop it fogging. He placed down a plank of wood on the tarmac so Hunt could walk to his car with dry shoes.

Once Hunt was in the cockpit, it felt damp as he wiped water off his steering wheel.

Hunt started as favourite to win the race as the in-form driver with a high grid position. From the start he went straight into the lead and, with a clear track in front of him, sped away easily. Hunt had made the best start of his life, and his McLaren's heavy spray covered everyone in his wake. The other drivers all had to contend with spray and fell further back. As only he could see where he was going and the other 24 drivers were navigating blind, Hunt sought to maximise the advantage he had earned.

Lauda was losing positions on every lap and was clearly in some sort of trouble. As Caldwell had suspected, his eyes were not up to it. There was so much standing water on the track that Lauda could hardly control his Ferrari, he simply couldn't see through his damaged eyelids. He couldn't have continued even if he wanted to. He said: "Everybody was skating and spinning; it was crazy. Looking at it this way, it seemed only sensible to drive into the pits and give up."

After two laps, he stopped. He had been unable to see and couldn't blink his eyes, which ruined his focus. It was too dangerous to continue. As he pulled to a halt, his four mechanics shielded the cockpit and he told them he had decided to retire from the race. Cuoghi said they could blame engine failure but Lauda wanted none of it, and he'd tell the truth to whoever asked – but, of course, not the whole truth. Without making excuses or offering explanations, as he didn't want the trouble with his eyes to stop him from racing in the future, Lauda admitted: "The rain has totally destroyed me."

The truth was that he should never have come back that season. His eyes were poor and he was physically unfit, but he would never admit he was unable to cope with the conditions that prevailed at the start of the race. Later, as the track dried, he rapidly began changing his mind, but by then it was too late.

Lauda sat on the pit counter, cross-legged next to Daniele Audetto, watching events unfurl. As he remembered later: "It was a miracle: after twelve hours of solid downpour, the rain stopped – about a quarter of the way into the race. If I had only held out that long, driven slowly and avoided being hit, there would have been no problem putting my foot down, which was necessary to clinch the title. As it turned out, fifth place would have been enough. Sadly, hanging on patiently was more that I could manage that day."

Three other drivers – Emerson Fittipaldi, Carlos Pace and Larry Perkins – also withdrew after a couple of laps.

As Hunt sped past the finish line for the third lap, he was shown the McLaren board, which read: 'Niki Out'. Straightaway he knew why, but Hunt felt no emotion or pleasure at his rival's demise. Lauda's behaviour that season had earned his total respect.

Hunt maintained his lead and, surprisingly, Vittorio Brambilla was now in second place in his March-Ford. On lap 22, Brambilla actually tried an overtaking maneuver on Hunt, but as he drew alongside he inevitably lost control of his car and missed Hunt's by a few millimetres. He went off the circuit in a shower of mud.

As Brambilla departed into retirement, the conditions started improving with every lap. By lap 23, the two McLaren-Fords led 1-2 with Mass tucked up in second place, guarding Hunt's flank. The cloud cover was lifting, taking with it the rain, and a strong breeze was beginning to dry out the track. Speeds picked up accordingly, and the gaps between cars shrank appreciably. But the drying track meant the wet-weather tyres were unsuitable for the new conditions and were starting to overheat. As the track dried, Caldwell kept out a permanent pit sign with 'cool tyres' written on it. He needed Hunt to drive through the puddles to get the tyres home. Jochen Mass immediately understood, and began searching for the puddles to drive through.

Hunt was so focused and preoccupied with winning the Grand Prix that he failed to give any consideration to the state of his tyres. He either ignored the sign or didn't understand it. With remarkable candour, Caldwell told Hunt's biographer Christopher Hilton: "James handled the race very badly. He disobeyed clear instructions. In previous races, we'd suffered the same problem: you went from a wet track to a dry track and the wet tyres overheat. They've so much more rubber on them and when they begin to slide around in the dry, the rubber boils and starts to rip off. The sign was to get the drivers to drive in puddles on the straight bits of the track. That kept the temperature down and, while you'd get less grip, the tyres certainly lasted longer.

"We hung this out to James and Jochen, who were travelling in line astern. Jochen saw the sign and immediately turned right, nearly hit the pit wall in a big cloud of spray. Then lap after lap they came down the straight together, James running clear and open in the dry, Jochen in the wet. In the end, we were waving this sign over the pit wall."

Mass continually sought out the wet areas of the track to keep the tyre temperatures down. As the pace of the race dropped dramatically, his tyres kept in good condition. Mario Andretti was also searching out the puddles.

Mass was getting frustrated because, having preserved his tyres, he caught up with Hunt and could have easily passed him and won the race. But he knew he couldn't with what was at stake, although Hunt could still have been champion from second place. In the end, it didn't matter as a frustrated Mass lost concentration on lap 35 and glanced a barrier, bending his front suspension and being forced to retire.

So by two thirds of the race distance, Hunt was still the comfortable leader. But his tyres were degrading fast and he was slowing. Patrick Depailler's six-wheeled Tyrrell-Ford started to catch him up. The six wheeler's tyres were coping well as Hunt's rubber deteriorated rapidly. Depailler soon passed Hunt and so did Andretti.

Andretti's tyres were in great shape as the wily American kept them cool by driving through the standing water. Like Hunt, Depailler hadn't and his tyres were worn out. Within two laps, his Tyrrell-Ford was forced into a pit stop for six new tyres, and Andretti took the lead.

There was now a tricky decision to make and the McLaren team decided to leave it to Hunt whether to pit or not for new tyres. Depailler did pit and that lifted Hunt to second and Andretti to leader, making his decision even trickier, as Caldwell recalled: "We had two signs for bringing drivers in. The first said 'In' and was compulsory. The second sign was an arrow offering the facility of coming in if the driver wanted to. Both signs were well recognised, James knew them, so there was no doubt about what we were doing."

Because of the changing conditions, the arrow was up from Lap 25 and the mechanics waited on full alert with four new tyres and the jacks primed and ready to lift the car. Mayer said: "Only James knew the true state of his tyres. We didn't because we couldn't."

Caldwell and Mayer felt Hunt should decide when to stop. Hunt thought the opposite and began gesticulating furiously each time he passed the McLaren pit.

Inevitably, Hunt's front left tyre wore through the canvas and began leaking air, slowly deflating. But still Hunt stayed out. A tyre change pit stop would cost at least 35 seconds, and Lauda would win the title by default if Hunt finished fourth or lower.

The call for a tyre change could have been made much earlier by the pit crew but it was now too late.

It was a very tricky situation for team principal Mayer and team manager Caldwell. Whatever they did, it could be the wrong decision. It seemed better not to tempt fate, so they didn't make a decision at all.

Hunt said afterwards: "The team had all the information about the rate of tyre wear. They'd seen what happened to other cars and they should have told me what to do. Instead, in response to my frantic requests for information they hung out the arrow, like a huge bloody question mark."

But fate was to prove kind to James Hunt that day, although he didn't realise it at the time. On lap 68, as he came off the last corner, his left hand front tyre blew out the rubber that had finally worn through. It was the perfect position to have a blowout and Hunt simply turned his car into the pit lane, controlling it masterfully.

The decision had been made for them. The McLaren team mechanics, who had been anxiously waiting lap after lap, were ready. When he stopped,

Caldwell and a mechanic didn't bother with a jack – they physically lifted up the car for the tyre change. Caldwell played it safe and put four new wet tyres on the car instead of slicks. The four new tyres went on in 27 seconds and Hunt spun his wheels and got back in the race. As Hunt drove down the pit lane, the Ferrari mechanics went wild believing he had lost the race. They waved their arms and cheered with undignified pleasure.

During his stop, Clay Regazzoni passed Hunt to take second, Alan Jones passed to take third and Depailler passed to be fourth. But Regazzoni and Jones were on old worn tyres, and Depailler soon went past both of them to be second.

In his head, Hunt knew his pit stop had been too long and that he had lost the championship. He would need a miracle to get the third place he needed. A red mist descended and, on fresh tyres and with nothing to lose, he drove for his life. From a man pacing himself to the finish, Hunt was now racing to win. He gave it everything he could: "I went out in mid field but of course everyone was on different laps, it was one of those confusing races. I had flown round the track at huge speeds as one would, as I was on a set of fresh wets and everybody else was on bald wets. And the track was dry so even those who had changed a few laps earlier were a lot slower because they were already overheating. The only thing I could do was shut my eyes and floor it, and pass as many cars as I could."

Under his helmet, he was silently cursing his tyres, his team, his general luck and, most of all, the weather.

The McLaren pit board told him he had rejoined in sixth place. He needed to make up three places in eight laps. He flung caution to the wind and passed Regazzoni's Ferrari and Jones' Surtees-Ford easily.

As neither had changed tyres, they were easy meat for him, just as they had been for Depailler. He swept down the short hill at the back of the pits and simply drove round the outside of both of them on the tight left-hander, the only slow corner on the track. Hunt thought he was fourth but didn't realise that McLaren lap scorers had made a mistake: Hunt had been fifth when he left the pits. He was now third but didn't know it. He then went after Depailler as fast as he could.

The tension in the pits heightened as the other teams were well aware he was third. To them, it seemed impossible that Hunt could have changed his tyres and been back in title contention again. McLaren finally worked it out and, on the penultimate lap, the mechanics hoisted the 'P3' sign over the pit counter. But Hunt either didn't see it or didn't believe it.

Mayer thought he had done it, but Caldwell still wasn't sure. The last lap was a nail biter for both men.

As the chequered flag came out, three cars flashed past – Andretti, Depailler and Hunt. Although Depailler and Hunt were both a lap down after their pit stops, it all added to the drama as, at the end, Hunt was 100 metres behind the Frenchman's Tyrrell. Andretti had made it through on one set of tyres to win; he had preserved his tyres perfectly and proven what a fine driver he was.

Hunt was livid as he drove the slowing down lap, believing he was fourth and that he had lost the championship by one point. He was furious that Mayer and Caldwell hadn't pulled him in for an earlier pit stop for new tyres. He held them entirely responsible for losing the championship.

Hunt came down the pit lane blipping the throttle, furious and ready to vent that fury. He climbed out of the car and made a grab for Mayer, planning to flatten him for his stupidity just as he had Dave Morgan all those years ago.

Caldwell could see Hunt was angry, and disappeared back to the garage. He was fed up with Hunt and thought: "I'm not putting up with this crap. Why should I get abused?" In truth, Caldwell wasn't sure whether Hunt had finished third or fourth and would wait for others to clarify it.

Hunt vented on Mayer. Although Mayer could hear Hunt, Hunt still had on his helmet and his ears were blocked so he couldn't hear Mayer. Knowing Hunt couldn't hear, Mayer made three-finger gestures at his driver and smiled. Confused by the sight of a team owner who didn't look like he'd just lost the championship, suddenly it dawned on Hunt he might be champion after all. Mayer stood there shouting: "You're world champion."

Behind him, Colin Chapman and the Lotus mechanics were climbing over the pit wall onto the track to congratulate Andretti, who had snatched the lead ten laps from the end to win the race he had started from pole position. It was the teams's first and only win that season.

A confused Hunt held back any celebrations until it dawned on him that he had indeed finished third and was world champion. As Mayer told him what had happened, Hunt said: "I want proof." Hunt would not allow himself to believe it until he had seen the lap charts and had confirmation from the officials that there were no protests on hand.

By this time, Hunt was engulfed by well-wishers and no one could see him or his car as people pressed congratulations. But all he wanted was official confirmation that he was third, and kept shouting: "I want proof, I want proof." His supporters lifted him onto their shoulders but then, in the chaos, promptly dropped him. As Hunt picked himself up from the floor, he demanded a drink and glared at Mayer whilst he drank it.

Hunt was sick with worry after all the disappointments, protests, changes and disqualifications during the season. He said afterwards: "I was absolutely determined not to think that I was world champion and then get disappointed, because there were 300 good reasons why something should have gone wrong. It was only really when I checked the laps and when the organisers said I was third – and there were no protests in the wind – that I allowed myself to start half-believing it. "

In fact, later recalling standing on the podium beside Andretti, he said: "I still didn't feel that confident when they put me up on third place on the rostrum because I wasn't sure I wasn't going to be dragged off there at the last minute, so the championship win came to me slowly."

Long afterwards, whilst reminiscing with journalist Nigel Roebuck, Hunt said: "The thing was that the pit signals I got were not consistent. Suddenly it said fourth, which wasn't right because I had passed someone for third. But with their track record for handling things in a crisis and a panic, I wasn't prepared to believe them because I had had too many disappointments already that year with things happening after the race. So I basically didn't accept that I was world champion because everything happened so quickly."

As he got off the podium, Hunt went to the press room to chat with the print journalists. Later, as it was getting dark, he said: "When I came out it was pitch black to see that everybody had gone, organisers and everything; everybody had had enough. When I realised everybody had gone, I realised nobody was going to take it away from me because there was nobody there, nobody was interested. So then I believed it. I thought I must be world champion."

For Alastair Caldwell, it was a bittersweet ending to a magnificent season. He was furious with Hunt for what had happened in the closing laps. He was adamant it would not have happened had he obeyed instructions. Caldwell never understood why an intelligent driver like Hunt disobeyed him to his obvious disadvantage. He didn't discuss it with Hunt at the time. With the championship won, it seemed churlish. Ten years afterwards, they had a short conversation in which Hunt dismissed his concerns.

Caldwell later unloaded his frustrations on Christopher Hilton, a patient journalist who liked to listen and enjoyed a good relationship with Caldwell, saying: "I was irritated, because in books and the media, James said we didn't bring him in for new tyres when we should have done – that we were idiots because we didn't run the car properly, we always gave him the wrong pit board and so on. In fact, we gave him exactly the right information all the time. We could never have stopped the car for tyres and won the world championship, so it was up to him – and we told him that all the time.

"My opinion is that we handled the race perfectly. There was nothing else we could have done.

Regazzoni and Jones did the same thing as he'd done and stayed out, and both wore their tyres to the air. They came to a walking pace because of that, and James was able to pass them."

Afterwards, Hunt disagreed entirely with Caldwell: "I knew from well before half distance that there were going to be tyre problems later on, and I started asking the McLaren pit as best as I could without a wireless. I had seen plenty of people going in and out of the pits changing tyres, so they had all the information and, in a situation like that, you watch the other cars and see how quick they are going on fresh rubber as to hot rubber or wets. They have all that information and I didn't have any. As it was, their response to my frantic request, which they did understand, was to hang me out a huge question mark and go: 'What do we do?' So the only thing I could do then was to stay out, and it very nearly cost me the championship because when I did come in I already had a blown front but I also had a slow puncture; two corners had a flat tyre and they couldn't get the jacks under it. It was a huge panic to get me a new set of tyres."

In the end, it didn't matter. Somehow, after all the drama, Hunt had won it and he wanted to get back to the Tokyo Hilton to really celebrate. But the narrow roads around the foot of Mount Fuji, some 60 miles from Tokyo, meant that the traffic was jammed solid after the race, so the 300-odd members of the Formula One circus stayed put at the track and begun the celebrations with Hunt in a room rented by Marlboro.

John Hogan was exhausted by what he had witnessed. He couldn't believe the lad he had met barely five years earlier had become world champion. Hogan's judgement about Hunt had finally been vindicated.

In the corridors of Philip Morris International in Lausanne, he was the hero. Hunt's win had meant more exposure for the Marlboro brand than they could ever have dreamed. It was Marlboro's most successful marketing campaign ever, and Hunt was responsible for it all. From Lausanne came the message to Hogan that he was not to stint on the celebrating. He would pick up all the bills for the parties that started that night in Fuji and continued on into Tokyo.

But Hogan didn't party as hard as he might have. He was just glad it was all over. He had had a very difficult first season with Hunt, as he later admitted: "It was a bit like having a dog; you think you have just trained it and it's being good, and then it goes and craps on someone else's living room carpet. And that's what he did all the time. Every race there was something."

But it had all come good in the end.

SHOWDOWN IN JAPAN

SHUNT

CHAPTER 28

Reigning world champion 1976-1977

Vast riches beckon the champion

James Hunt's championship year really started when he stepped onto the Japanese Airlines Flight 421 from Tokyo to London late on Monday evening. He caught the flight along with most of the rest of the Formula One community after 24 hours of non-stop partying following his world championship victory.

After the flag had dropped and Hunt had done his media interviews, the partying got started – all arranged and paid for by Philip Morris' John Hogan.

Hogan was a winner no matter what the outcome in Mount Fuji that day. Obviously, he preferred Hunt and his own Marlboro-sponsored McLaren team to win, but, if not, it would not have been a complete disaster. Niki Lauda was a Marlboro-sponsored driver so the cigarette company would still have had reason to celebrate – just with a different driver and a different team. Marlboro could not fail to win.

Hogan had arranged it so.

And he also had some celebrating of his own to do. After nearly five years at Philip Morris, he had turned its Formula One sponsorship into a dominant one. And in turn, sales of Marlboro brand cigarettes were taking off across Europe and the rest of the world. The sponsorship was incredibly successful, and when Hunt won the world championship by one point and then straightaway lit up a Marlboro in the pit lane, it really couldn't get much better – especially for a marketing man like Hogan.

It all looked like a carefully crafted plan coming together, but Hogan knew it could all have been so different, and kept a detached reality intact around him that day. At least until the chequered flag dropped. When Hunt took third place that afternoon in Japan, Hogan knew that reality would go out of the window for the next few days.

The parties came first. As well as a huge sponsorship budget, Hogan also commanded an equally big activation war chest. That budget covered everything outside the actual running of the team and paying the drivers. In the old days, when Marlboro had first come into the sport in 1972, the activation budget had exceeded the money spent on sponsorship by as much as 500 per cent.

Now it was more modest, but there was plenty for the parties that were to follow Hunt's victory. Hunt led the celebrations from the front. And if he flagged, another world champion, Barry Sheene, would take up the cudgels. Together, the two world champions celebrated like they never had before. Girls were falling at their feet, and it was the start of a magical 48 hours for both men.

It started as dusk fell at the Fuji Lodge, a hotel adjacent to the circuit. Hogan had booked the hotel's biggest function room to get things started that night and, although the celebration was principally for the McLaren team and Marlboro guests, everyone in the paddock was invited. There was unlimited liquor and the tables were laden with food.

The festivities went on late into the night. Everyone then went back to the Tokyo Hilton, where another huge room had been booked for another party. Hunt grabbed four hours of sleep in between, but most carried on right through. For the next eight hours, people came and went and partied throughout the next day. At around 5pm, Hunt and the Marlboro and McLaren executives trooped off to the British embassy. Hunt could hardly stand up and Hogan just prayed they would get through it. Hunt was unsuitably dressed to enter the British embassy and to be greeted by the ambassador, but the normal protocol was waived for the new champion.

Then it was back to another room at the Tokyo Hilton for a very formal Philip Morris cocktail party, where all the top executives and staff of the far east subsidiaries had gathered to congratulate their champion, who looked as though he had just come in from a long day at the beach.

Looking back, Hogan now simply says: "Dear me", as if it might all have been a dream. He recalls: "We drank for two days solid." And that is about the extent of his recollection.

He does remember the Formula One mechanics loading up bottles of spirits to drink on the plane journey home the following morning. Hogan had specified an unlimited budget at both the Tokyo Hilton and the Fuji Lodge. And the mechanics took full advantage.

The plane took off late on Monday night for an overnight flight to Heathrow. By the time they got on board, the drinking carried on, but it was a subdued flight as everyone needed to sleep. Most of the Formula One community was on that plane that evening, as it had been block booked by Bernie Ecclestone's Foca Travel company.

Hunt had been booked into economy but the airline upgraded him to first class, much to the chagrin of Teddy Mayer, who gave the impression he didn't much like travelling with the hired help. And Mayer wasn't very impressed with the commotion Hunt caused in the first class lounge either. Hunt was carrying a toy gorilla that Alastair Caldwell had given to him to celebrate the championship. The gorilla was called 'Smiler' and had cymbals attached to its paws, which Hunt kept bashing together.

In the lounge, Hunt also got into an altercation with Pierre Ugeux, the new president of FISA, who was also on the flight along with some colleagues. Ugeux was concerned that Hunt wouldn't attend the annual FIA prize giving in Paris to collect his world championship trophy. Hunt confirmed their worst fears and told Ugeux that he would not. He said: "I played them along, teasing them with my toy guerrilla, letting them think I wasn't going to be there because of all the agro they had given me this season." Ugeux knew Hunt was upset by FISA rulings at Brands Hatch and Monza, but appealed to his better nature to put the past behind him. Hunt said he would consider it, and Ugeux immediately sensed a change of mind in the offing and felt better. As the prize giving was specifically in honour of the world champion, it would have been pointless without Hunt's presence, and the new president didn't want his first year in office ruined by it. In the event, Hunt had no intention of not collecting his trophy. He was contractually bound by Philip Morris to do so, but Ugeux didn't know that. So Hunt revelled in the president's discomfort, as he later admitted: "What they didn't know was that I was not going to let them down...they looked very glum for a while."

After all that, Mayer was relieved when the flight was called and they hopped on the transit bus headed for the silver and red Boeing 747.

The JAL Jumbo's captain greeted Hunt personally at the top of the aircraft steps and motioned him into the first class cabin. But Hunt wanted to be with his friends and the mechanics, and took a seat in the economy class cabin. The captain said he would keep his first class seat free and asked him to join them for dinner. In those days, Hunt always travelled economy and it didn't occur to him to book himself into the first class cabin, although by then he could easily afford it. He tended to be anaesthetised on flights by alcohol, so he had little need for any pampering. As long as the drink flowed, which it did in those days in the economy cabin, he was happy. *Daily Express* motoring editor David Benson plopped himself into the seat next to Hunt's in first class. Benson, after covering the race, had been about to leave Tokyo and fly to Hong Kong for a holiday when his news desk ordered him onto the plane at the last minute.

As Hunt entered the cabin, a huge cheer went up.

But within a few hours, the drink ran out – such was the demand from the Formula One people on the plane. Hunt had to go into first class for top-up supplies. The Japanese captain had ordered his crew to let the champion do what he wanted, and so they obliged his every wish.

In the end, as the lights in the cabin were dimmed and everyone fell asleep, completely exhausted by the non-stop drinking which had, by then, stretched out for nearly 48 hours. Hunt then went up into the first class cabin to take a seat reserved for him for dinner.

He sat next to Benson, who was now very glad he had changed his flight to Hong Kong to accompany the new world champion home. Benson was by far the most skilled reporter of his day, and definitely Hunt's favourite journalist. He knew all the top Formula One drivers personally and had stayed at their homes, enjoying time with their families. And, in those days, the *Daily Express* was the top British newspaper, with the *Daily Mail* then a distant second. Just as he had during his flight with Niki Lauda a few months earlier, Benson got a good exclusive that night. The captain came by to chat about the race, and the crew served them a special dinner of shrimps to start, followed by chicken princess with duchess potatoes. Hunt alternatively slurped beer and red wine with his meal as the stewardesses danced up and down the aisle with constant refills of both glasses. Hunt told Benson that he was looking forward to getting home to see his dog Oscar, and that he was going to thank Lord Hesketh personally for what he had done for his career.

After they had feasted Hunt got to his feet and did some slapstick comedy routines for Benson and the other first class passengers as the Boeing started to make its descent into Anchorage airport for refuelling. The captain let Hunt make the announcement that the plane was beginning its descent and Hunt put on the best Japanese accent he could muster.

In those days, the Boeing 747 100 series had nowhere near enough fuel capacity to make it in one hop from Asia to Europe so a mid flight stop was necessary.

When they took off again, Hunt went into the back of the plane to speak with Max Mosley. He and Mosley looked for free seats so they could stretch out. Later, he went back to his seat and David Phipps took a photograph of Hunt seated next to his best friend, Chris Jones, asleep. The Phipps photograph caught everyone's imagination and Jones achieved his 60 seconds of fame when the photo was published around the world.

Barry Sheene and Pam Rowe, the photographer, had cuddled up together and gone to sleep and earlier Sheene had been trying to persuade her of the merits of joining the mile-high club.

Hogan remembers: "It wasn't an outrageous flight and everybody was just very, very happy."

As the plane descended into Heathrow, Hunt woke up with the worst hangover of his life, but he had no regrets about what had happened – although, indeed, it took him a long time to remember what had happened.

When the plane landed at around 9 o'clock in the morning, Hunt emerged from the Boeing 747 blinking and carrying his toy gorilla. A posse of photographers ambushed him at the foot of the Boeing's steps. British Airports Authority staff whisked everyone through the VIP disembarkation exit. And they had good reason, as a huge crowd of fans had gathered outside the customs hall. Hunt was greeted by more than 2,000 people waiting to welcome home their champion. The reception was on an even grander scale than when *The Beatles* had returned from America in 1963.

Amongst the 2,000 fans were his mother and father, Wallis and Sue. As they were publicly reunited, all three of them were embarrassed as the flashbulbs went off. After hugging his mother, he hugged Jane Birbeck, now seemingly his official girlfriend. It was a surreal experience, as Hunt recalled: "I hadn't expected my family to be there and it was the most unnerving thing to have to say 'hello' to them in front of all those people.

It was all quite overwhelming." Sue Hunt slightly lost the plot and was totally out of her comfort zone. The adulation for her son was something completely new to her, and not something she particularly cared for. She came from the real world, and this was far from real. Hunt remembered: "It was a bit of a heavy deal, with mother freaking out and everything – that's what really threw me."

As Sue hugged and kissed her son, it was all broadcast on television. To an ITN news crew, she said: "He's done it. He's done it. I'm elated, absolutely elated. It's magnificent." Then she added: "He may be the world champion but he hasn't changed. He's still my naughty James." Indeed, he was.

Sue Hunt couldn't help recalling all those moments in the garage with the Mini, the difficult conversations with his father and the written off minivan and Fiat 500. She was baffled that the son whom they had almost written off was suddenly the most famous sportsman in the world. She couldn't quite connect the two scenarios, and she felt as if it was all happening to somebody else.

The normally reserved and cautious Hunts had thrown caution to the wind and had decorated their house in Belmont in a gaudy display of union jacks and other patriotic embellishments. It was entirely out of character, but Wallis and Sue just couldn't help being caught up in the emotion of it all. For both of them, it brought back patriotic war memories, and it was the Brits against the Huns all over again; notwithstanding that Lauda was Austrian. Few people in Britain made the distinction. But, as in 1945, the right side had won and, for Wallis Hunt in particular, still carrying with him the legacy of his wounds from 33 years before, that made his son a real hero.

A press conference followed, and this time Hunt couldn't quite believe what was happening. His mother and father sat beside him as literally hundreds of journalists looked on and lights flashed in front of then. He thought he might have been dreaming, as he said: "In most situations I feel in control, but, when I get out of control, I'm not sure whether I'm doing or saying the right thing – not because of what people want to hear so much as the difficulty of what I want to say to them."

After the press conference, ITV's news service, ITN, got lucky and managed to get an exclusive with Hunt and the Hunt family in those few hours when everyone wanted access to them. That was because of Mary Richardson, who worked for ITN. She was the wife of John Richardson, one of Hunt's three closest friends. She had invited Wallis and Sue to watch the race live at

ITN's studios in London. They had eagerly accepted the offer as it was by no means certain that BBC would stay with the race live for its duration, and they wanted to see what transpired, good or bad. So ITN effectively owned the parents and, with the parents, came the son.

Richardson took charge of Hunt, and he travelled back into London in an ITN car. They were headed for a champagne breakfast laid on for him at Jane Birbeck's flat in London. She was sharing a plush apartment with her sister and her brother in law, and it was Richardson who suggested they go there first.

ITN was filming all the way and, thanks to Richardson, had by far the best coverage. Hunt just went along with it, much to the annoyance of rival networks, especially the BBC, which had to take ITN's dregs that day. The BBC was particularly galled because it thought it owned Formula One. It had supported F1 through all the dark days when no one was interested. Now, on the day that everyone was captivated, it had lost out to its rival.

The car trip with John and Mary Richardson became a high speed chase, as jealous journalists and photographers, many of them on motorcycles, pursued the ITN car.

When they finally arrived at Birbeck's flat, Hunt longed for some peace and quiet. Richardson recalls: "James was completely tired, but still on an adrenaline high and very happy. We barged through all the reporters and got inside the flat and opened the champagne. The enormity of what he had achieved still hadn't hit him." Richardson remembers: "He had gone out and proven he was the best in the world in his chosen sport, but yet he came back and all he wanted to do was sit down and have a drink and a bit of a smoke with his mates."

The Hunt family and the Richardsons had breakfast whilst Hunt brought them up to date with all the events of the previous weekend. Around lunch, he went off to the bedroom with Jane, and everyone else left to give him some peace and quiet. He went straight to sleep for eight hours. When he woke, the two went out for dinner.

The Hunts went home to Belmont and the Richardsons split up, with Mary going to the ITN studios to prepare the exclusive footage she had shot that day for the evening news. ITN made a fortune that day syndicating the footage all over the world.

On Wednesday morning, Hunt went to his brother's offices to discuss the multitude of offers that had landed on his desk in the few days since he had won the championship. In the afternoon, John Hogan had him at work giving interviews to favoured journalists and broadcasters.

With that over, James was free to return to Spain for a long weekend and was booked on the 9 o'clock flight that Thursday evening. Inevitably, he was running late but Iberia, the Spanish airline, decided to hold the flight for the new world champion. Hunt found everything was different being world champion. As it happened, the McDonnell–Douglas DC9 was almost completely empty: with only Hunt, two journalists and three other passengers in an aircraft that could seat 250.

The flight was due to land at 1am at Malaga airport. Despite that, it seemed that every British expatriate living in the area had decided to welcome him back at the airport. A huge crowd, led by his immediate neighbours, greeted him with champagne at the exit of the customs hall and there was an impromptu party in the airport.

The drive to his house took an hour. When he got there, more neighbours and expats he didn't know were inside, having set up another party. Hunt, by now refreshed and wide awake, loved it and didn't go to bed until well after 8 o'clock on Friday evening.

Later that morning, his friends from home arrived. John and Mary Richardson, Chris and Suzy Jones, and Malcolm and Frances Wood all flew into Marbella airport that Friday morning. It had been a long planned weekend, win or lose the championship. That weekend was the last one he would have for himself until Christmas.

James Hunt was now public property, or at least he was Marlboro's property. And he didn't seem to mind. As his daily pay rate from Marlboro was over US$3,500 a day, he was ready for as many days as Philip Morris wanted to pay him for. Hogan says now: "I must say I was in total admiration. Philip Morris had this and this organised for him, and James' feet didn't touch the ground for a whole month. He behaved impeccably throughout and was a very good boy."

Hogan stage managed the whole of the next month for the benefit of the world's media. The value to the cigarette company of those few weeks was immeasurable. It received publicity that was probably worth US$500 million, dwarfing the money it had actually spent that season.

Hogan remembers: "We went off on a whirlwind tour of Europe, and in those days there used to be a lot of car shows at the end of the season. We bounced around all the car shows."

Hunt's first official assignment was at the London Motor Show at Earls Court, where he was mobbed by his British fans. Then he flew to Cologne for another car show and then back to Britain for a rendezvous with his fans.

At Brands Hatch, Hogan and John Webb got together and organised a celebratory binge for fans at an event Webb called a 'Tribute to James' day. Over 15,000 fans turned up to celebrate with their world champion. Hogan also ordered Niki Lauda to fly in. The meeting of the two rivals on friendlier terms sparked acres of newspaper coverage around the world, not to mention hours upon hours of TV coverage, especially in mainland Europe. Hogan was doing it for the publicity, and Webb was turning a nice profit.

Rather predictably, the animosity between Webb and Hunt flared up again, and Hunt ended up in the Brands Hatch kitchens instead of being guest of honour in the hospitality suite.

Angela Webb had offered him a suite to entertain his guests for lunch alongside suites where circuit sponsors were also being entertained. Hunt was issued with a certain amount of tickets. But the trouble started when he filled his suite with twice as many guests as had tickets. It was full and guests were still arriving when Webb called a halt. The trouble began when Jane Birbeck's sister could not gain admittance after the doorman refused her entry on Angela Webb's orders. Hunt was called over and grabbed 'Vic the doorman' by his lapels and said: "Let her in, you fucking little man." The doorman told Hunt: "I'm under instructions from Mrs Webb not to let anybody else in."

Hunt then shook the doorman and lifted him off the floor by his lapels. Sensing trouble, Webb relented and the rest of Hunt's ticketless guests were admitted. But the suite was so full that Hunt asked Angela Webb whether there was anywhere he could have his lunch in peace and she led him down to the Brands Hatch kitchens. Hunt said to her on the way down: "The pigs outside were better behaved than the pigs upstairs." Webb replied: "And whose fault is that James?" She also berated him for his attack on Vic the doorman and insisted he apologise to him personally. Hunt later apologised to Vic but not to Webb nor his wife Angela, who he believed had started the trouble.

At a press conference later, John Webb told journalists he never rated Hunt, saying: "He was really abusive to Brands Hatch staff and caused an awful lot of problems. The fact that he became world champion was, I think, more luck than ability." But after his tribute day, Hunt went around to the marshall's posts that are situated all around the circuit and said 'thank you' to everyone. And Angela Webb, in turn, thanked him.

The next day, all the newspapers picked up the story and, for a brief moment in time, 'Vic the doorman' achieved national fame and his views were quoted everywhere.

Hunt didn't care what Webb or the newspapers thought, and carried on with his European tour. Next he was fêted by the city of London. His father used his connections and he was made a 'Freeman of the City of London.' The honour was conferred upon him and the chain of office put round his neck in the presence of a beaming Wallis Hunt.

Then he was off to Lausanne to the Philip Morris International offices, where PMI executives thanked him profusely for his contribution to its bottom line. And he was honoured in Switzerland by the Lausanne local authority who felt he was one of their own.

The following evening it was back to London, where Hogan threw an exclusive party for McLaren employees. Patty McLaren, Bruce's widow, was guest of honour.

After a fortnight, Hogan relaxed his grip just for a day and allowed Hunt to go to the huge General Motors factory in Luton, Bedfordshire. The sprawling plant made Vauxhall cars and Bedford trucks and employed thousands of people. Hunt went for a lap of honour around the site on a Bedford flat truck, as if he had just won a race. He then formally launched an advertising campaign that had been built for him, with the catchline: "Take my advice. Test drive a Vauxhall." As a result of that campaign, Vauxhall sold many cars in the last quarter of 1976.

Whilst Hunt was in London, Marlboro arranged to sponsor a party to celebrate the fifth anniversary of the opening of the Ladbroke Club casino in London's Mayfair. Richard Burton was a member of the club, and turned up with Suzy. By now, Hunt and Burton had become good friends. But, despite the presence of two of the most famous people in the world, it was Suzy who attracted the most media attention and was asked for the most autographs. Neither man was surprised, and gave each other knowing looks. They had long become accustomed to being overshadowed by their beguiling wife.

After that, at the request of Bernie Ecclestone, Hunt flew to Linz in Austria to open the Jochen Rindt Racing Car Show. Hogan didn't mind, as it was an excuse for a huge round of promotional events in Austria, Lauda's home country. The crowds were enormous outside every venue, and Austrian newspapers carried little else but news of Hunt's visit to their country. Lauda was sat at home recuperating after his eye operation and not particularly enjoying reading wall to wall coverage about his rival everyday in Austria's newspapers.

From Austria, he flew to Switzerland for a few days in Geneva for Philip Morris parties and receptions. Geneva was a good place for the international media to gather, and Hunt did scores of one-to-one interviews for newspapers and magazines spread over several days.

Then he returned to London via Munich and went straight into the judging for Eric Morley's Miss World contest. The Miss World contest was a very big deal in those days and scored the highest audience ratings on ITV every year. The judges were all famous people and it was considered a great honour when Morley invited Hunt to be one of them. Hunt couldn't have enjoyed himself more that evening, and the smile never left his face. Photographs of him and the new Miss World appeared in virtually every newspaper in the western world.

He went straight to Dublin, then Essen and onto Vienna. The Vienna trip was to open the Niki Lauda Racing Car Show at the behest of Lauda. Racing car shows in the seventies were very profitable events, and there were at least a dozen of them held in Europe across November and December. Hunt attended most of them that year. The public flocked to them until they lost popularity in the eighties.

Hunt left Vienna and went straight for Zurich. Much of his schedule was dictated by awards that all sorts of people wanted to bestow on him. So Hogan went with the flow and organised his schedule around the awards ceremonies.

Some of the awards and their names seem laughable now but, back then, Hunt was keen to scoop up all of them, especially if Marlboro cigarettes was paying his contracted daily rate of US$3,500. He couldn't get enough of the ceremonies, as sometimes the organisers of the events paid him another US$5,000 on top of what Marlboro gave him. On one promotional day, Hunt was paid by three different companies for effectively attending the same event.

John Hogan was well aware of what was happening but turned a blind eye to it, and paid Hunt for whatever days he was billed by his brother. Marlboro was reaping enormous rewards for winning the world championship, and Hogan didn't care about Hunt's occasional double or treble billing.

Back in London, Hunt attended the Royal Automobile Club (RAC) prize-giving lunch. Normally, that event would hardly have been noticed. But Hunt decided to cock a snoot at the RAC for past slights dating back to his Formula 3 days. He was still bitter about how he had been disqualified at Brands Hatch in October 1971, when, although clearly guilty, he felt he had been singled out by the RAC stewards for punishment as an example to others.

So he decided to inflict misery on the RAC and turned up for its awards ceremony in jeans, a t-shirt and, on this occasion, sandals.

It's impossible for anyone, even tradesmen, to get into the RAC club without a jacket and tie. Hunt wanted to be stopped by the doormen and had decided to leave immediately if he was barred entry, leaving the club's directors to explain his absence at the dinner.

But the RAC directors were cleverer than that and, suspecting there might be a confrontation, decided in advance to let him in and instructed the doormen not to react at all. There would have been difficulty turning him away since the dinner was in his honour. Hunt had calculated he had the advantage and revelled in his revenge, although he was surprised how easily they acquiesced.

The annual British Racing Drivers' Club (BRDC) dinner dance at the Dorchester Hotel was altogether different. The Dorchester had no dress code, so there was no question of him not getting in.

Hunt had no grudge against the BRDC but decided that, having got away with it at the RAC, he would dress in jeans and an open-necked shirt and test the BRDC's resolve.

Adding to the contrast was his date for the evening: French model Valentine Monnier, who was in a beautiful pink chiffon evening gown and looked tastefully stunning in a way that only French women can. She was a total contrast to Hunt, and people had difficulty knowing where to look with this unlikely pairing of people. Monnier was on her way to becoming one of the world's top models.

Gerald Lascelles, the Queen's cousin and the president of the BRDC, decided it was all too much and told Hunt exactly what he thought of him. But Hunt was already drunk and didn't even know who Lascelles was. He proceeded to get increasingly more drunk and, by the time the Duke of Kent presented him with the BRDC award, he had no idea what was going on.

It was no surprise when he later got into a scuffle with another BRDC member, who raced saloon cars. The member's face was cut in the altercation and a gin and tonic spilt down his jacket. The driver retaliated, and as another guest tried to intervene, his glasses fell off and Hunt stamped on them. The farce continued when the intervenor informed Hunt he was the solicitor of the man with whom he had fought. Hunt's reaction was to punch the solicitor as well and, by all accounts, both client and solicitor were on the floor nursing wounds inflicted by the world champion.

Seeing the carnage beneath his feet, Hunt momentarily sobered up and apologised to the two men profusely. Amazingly, they picked themselves off the floor, forgot their injuries, wiped away the blood and were instantly charmed. According to a witness, the solicitor simply said to Hunt: "Think nothing of it." Hunt jested that they should call it "a racing incident", and they all laughed. Deciding enough was enough, Monnier led her boyfriend home to bed.

To Hunt, it was just a jape. More serious were the explanations he undoubtedly must have had to give to Jane Birbeck the following day, when the next morning's newspapers printed photographs of him and Monnier whooping it up.

By the next day, Hunt had recovered sufficiently to appear on the BBC for a live interview.

He went from London to a presentation in Bologna and, after that, he opened Giacomo Agostini's motorcycle show, also in Bologna. At every event he attended in Italy, he needed at last twenty policemen on hand to control the crowds. Hunt marvelled at the contrast to when he had last been in Italy for the Italian Grand Prix, when he had been booed at every opportunity. As he said: "I was the villain at Monza, but when I went back after I had won the championship, you would have thought I was the biggest hero ever to come into Italy."

In the end, the police would only allow him five minutes at each event – such was the frenzy he created. The presence of him and Agostini together in Bologna created a mini-riot, which led the Italian news bulletins that evening and was treated as a national incident.

The show was followed by a round of press interviews in Milan, where he had flown to attend the annual Autosprint magazine awards. Hunt, however, was very cross with the hypocritical attitude of the Italian journalists, saying: "They treat racing like a religion, get very passionate, and are fed a complete load of rubbish by their press."

The Milan trip, generally, was not a great one. John Hogan's rental car was broken into while he and Hunt were attending an official Marlboro lunch in the city. Both his and Hunt's passports and visas for Poland, their next stop, were stolen. Hunt's diary was also taken. With the British consul unwilling to issue quick replacements, they sneaked over the Italian border without papers to Switzerland, where they found the British consul in Geneva much more amenable. Everything was replaced quickly and Hunt was able to continue his tour virtually uninterrupted.

The biggest loss from the robbery proved to be his diary. As a tax exile, Hunt was allowed only 90 night stopovers in Britain a year and kept detailed records to prove his whereabouts to the British Inland Revenue. He had to recreate the diary from memory. It wasn't easy.

Hunt was exhausted by the non-stop pace, and the frustrations of the stolen passport brought it home to him. As he said: "I feel like a bloody ping-pong ball being bounced all over the place. Everybody is tugging at me from all sides and I seem to be moving in a world that's gone completely mad." But he knew he was a very well-paid ping pong ball, and endured it.

The robbery was the only sour moment in the whole two months. With barely a blip in the schedule, Hunt was off to Geneva for a press conference and then more one-to-one interviews.

With the frenetic schedule, Hunt was often giving interviews with up to ten journalists a day and was being shuffled here, there and everywhere by the very serious Philip Morris PR people, who realised they were hot and that this was their one moment to reap the rewards of it. Consequently, a host of exclusive James Hunt interviews began appearing around the world and his image graced countless magazine covers.

The only respite came when he flew down to Marseille for three days testing at the Paul Ricard circuit in the south of France. Alastair Caldwell wanted to try out the McLaren M26 that he had been developing over the winter. Hunt pronounced it a dog and slower than his M23, so Caldwell decided to start 1977 with the old car.

But the big one still awaited Hunt. The one award he desperately wanted to win was the BBC Sports Personality of the Year. Jackie Stewart and Graham Hill had won it before him and he desperately wanted it too. He was dressed in a very fetching purple suede jacket and white heavy polo necked sweater, fashionable at the time. He was very much the British hero and hot favourite when he took his seat at the BBC Television Centre to hear the results. But, just like Lewis Hamilton would be 32 years later, was visibly shocked when the Olympic skater John Curry's name was called instead of his. He later said to producer Jonathan Martin: "Why didn't I win? I don't understand." Martin said to him: "Well, James, all the women voted for Curry – they like him." Hunt looked at Martin and said: "And they don't like me?" He was affronted and simply didn't understand how a Formula One driver champion could be beaten by a skater.

He had better luck with the Sports Writers' Association, which named him the Daily Express Sportsman of the Year and 300 people cheered him as he arrived to receive the award at the Savoy hotel. This time, there was no sign of Valentine Monnier. Jane Birbeck, sensing the competition, was dressed to the nines in a stunning gown which left little to the imagination. She certainly delighted the motor racing establishment with her look that night.

By then Hunt was getting very tired and even his legendary reserves of energy were being depleted, as he said: " My personal freedom is something I had worked for for so long, and now it seems completely gone. I am simply not my own man anymore."

In mid–December, he flew to Paris with John Hogan for the FIA Awards, where the championship trophies were officially bestowed on the winning drivers. By the time they got to Paris, Hogan was exhausted and close to a breakdown. He said he was too tired to accompany Hunt to the prize giving. He remembers: "I flaked out and I said to James: 'Listen, you're on your own, I'm not doing this.' I went to sleep in the hotel and James said: 'I'll go.' God knows why he was so bright eyed and bushy tailed. Anyway, he went." And so on 17th December, he finally got his hands on the world championship trophy and saw his name engraved upon it, where it would remain for all time. He was the 37th winner and couldn't have loved it more. Hogan recalls: "I heard him come back at about 3 o'clock in the morning."

The two men had to catch a 6am flight for the final engagement of the tour in Brussels. They were picked up by Belgian Claude Begoine in his Rolls Royce at Brussels airport. When the Brussels promotion was over, Hunt and Hogan got on the plane for London, where Hunt turned round to Hogan and said: "Hogey that's it, I'm outta here." With that, it was over and Hogan didn't see him again for four months. As they shook hands at Heathrow, it was a signal that the mission the two had hatched exactly a year ago had been accomplished. It was an emotional moment, and both men had come a long way together in those 12 months.

Hunt went from Heathrow to his parents house to spend a few days with them before Christmas.

When Hunt got back to Marbella a few days later, he went to bed and stayed there for two days recovering and getting ready for Christmas and the New Year, Hunt said: "I have never been so relieved to get to my home and my dog, and I had a very quiet Christmas." He vowed never to put himself through that again, and he stopped taking John Hogan's phone calls for a few weeks.

Back home in Spain he contemplated the events of the past two months and he realised there was a serious downside to the career path he had chosen. Up to winning the world championship, it had been all positive and he had never believed there would be such a drawback. But the number of promotional events that he had been forced to attend was almost inhuman; sometimes he was doing three or four events a day.

Although many of the events were choreographed and private – designed to impress and entertain a few important people – there were also some highly public events which he found draining and depressing. As he explained: "I am still very new to this, and the massive invasion of privacy is worse than being at school." He was getting rather fed up with having to sign as many as 500 autographs in a session, something that could take two hours even at full speed. At one point, he asked John Hogan not to organise any more such events and told him forthwith he would be charging Philip Morris per autograph instead of per day. On the plus side, he admitted it was "a wonderful ego trip" but warned people close to him that his "ego was getting seriously over-fed."

Even close friends changed because he was now a famous celebrity. When he wanted a quiet supper in front of the television, or to be on his own, he would find himself the centre of attention at a dinner party for ten or 12.

He also could not believe the number of gifts that were showered on him. But, with every gift, came a problem – especially with the expensive, useless ones. He instantly became responsible for them, which was often a nuisance hundreds of miles from home. He said: "What do I do with them? I don't want a lot of useless bowls cluttering up my life."

He was also fed up and got annoyed with the constant sycophancy: "I get incredibly embarrassed when very successful men come up to me and start gushing. Okay, I have done a good job in a racing car, but some people get it all out of proportion. I don't want to abuse people. I don't want to start believing all the flattery. It can lead to bad behaviour, and I could end up a very objectionable person.

"Still, there's a temptation, when the seventy-fourth person grabs you and gives you an earful of bullshit, to tell him: 'Fuck off and leave me alone.' But that person's probably travelled three hundred miles and especially wanted to talk to you. You need their support and it's nice to have, and it's not their fault they've caught you at a bad moment. They didn't mean any harm, you have to remember that. But sometimes it's very wearing, very tiring.

"Short of locking myself up in a room, I can't get away from it. And the problem is that the nice people don't often come up and talk. It's the pushy ones who barge through and make you perform. You feel like some sort of mechanical toy. When they confront you, it's like throwing the switch and you're supposed to do or say something clever."

And he had another problem on his hands. People, all sorts of people, were throwing money at him.

Straight after his world championship victory, Paul Hamlyn, the well known publisher, who owned his own eponymous imprint, offered him a deal he couldn't refuse to write an autobiography of his winning season. Hamlyn put US$75,000 on the table; payable when a final manuscript was delivered. It was an extraordinary offer, and more than what Philip Morris had paid him to race that year.

Hamlyn explained that Hunt would not have to write the book himself. Instead, they would hire a ghost writer to do the job. He would simply have to spend a few hours answering questions into a tape recorder, and the writer would do the rest – but it would be his book.

The idea had merit, and his brother liked the number that Hamlyn had quoted as the advance. It was at that moment that Peter Hunt truly realised his brother's earning potential over the following years as the reigning world champion. Up until then, Hunt had believed he would be able to earn around US$500,000. But now he revised that to US$800,000. The cachet of being world champion was making a huge difference to his earnings already.

Peter Hunt estimated that James had earned US$150,000 in the ten months up to the Japanese Grand Prix as an ordinary driver – but he had managed to trouser the same amount again in the last two months of the year as world champion. And the offers kept piling in. It was no longer necessary to go out and promote his brother. A single decal on the front of his overalls now went for US$60,000, up from US$5,000 just a few months before. It was an extraordinary change in earning power, and it took everyone by complete surprise.

Much of it was down to CSS. Barry Gill and Andrew Marriott had immediately seen Hunt's potential when he entered Formula One in 1973, and they signed Hunt to personal deals with car manufacturer General Motors and Aurora, which made slot car racing kits. Vauxhall was one of CSS' proudest deals, as Marriott recalls: "He was driving a car with a Ford engine and we did a great deal promoting Vauxhall cars." Marriott can still not believe they pulled that off – Vauxhall paid Hunt US$120,000 a year and Aurora paid around US$50,000.

Gill and Marriott were both journalists and they set up Hunt with a string of regular motor racing columns in newspapers all over the world. Marriott saw it as extra exposure for sponsors, and there was rarely a column where all of Hunt's sponsors were not mentioned at least once.

Hunt had been extremely savvy signing up the CSS agency so early. The agency had been founded by Marriott, Gill and publisher Michael Tee. From late 1974 onwards, they effectively built the agency around Hunt, and the relationship came into its own in 1976 and 1977 and endured until he retired in 1979.

But, crucially, the agency was kept out of the book deal with Hamlyn, as Peter Hunt did not want to pay it commission on the deal. CSS received up to 20 per cent of every deal in which it was involved and, despite the strong editorial background of Marriott and Gill, plus Michael Tee's publishing connections, Peter decided to do it himself and save the cash.

But Peter Hunt, so efficient in financial matters, was immediately out of his depth, and, with no external support from CSS, he floundered. The book was important to James, not only for the money, but because it could be important to his image and reputation, and would define his world championship year. But it was now early November and the book needed to be ready in four weeks to be out for the crucial two-week buying season before Christmas. Hamlyn owned a printing plant and it would take a few days to print and bind once it was written and typeset.

Hamlyn contacted Eoin Young, then arguably Formula One's top journalist, to be Hunt's ghostwriter. Young was a New Zealander who had come to Britain with Bruce McLaren and worked for him in his start-up motor racing team. When McLaren was killed in 1970, Young had written the seminal book on him, and it had been acclaimed everywhere. Every self-respecting motor racing fan had it in their bookcase. Hunt was attracted to Young because he had been one of the original founders of the McLaren team. But that fact also made Hunt unattractive to Young, as he told Hunt's biographer Christopher Hilton: "I had been with Bruce when we started the McLaren team, and I didn't think James and his public school behaviour would have found favour with Bruce. I regarded his off-track indolence as a disservice to sport – no class."

Years later, Young confessed he had never wanted to do the book at all for the simple reason that he "didn't like James Hunt." Young said: "I thought he was obnoxious – a pop star in a professional sport that perhaps still regarded itself as amateur." He added: "I was somewhat surprised when I was invited to write the book."

But the more Young resisted Hunt's blandishments, the more Hunt wanted him. Young was finally signed to do it for a fee of around UK£5,000. He was assisted by Maurice Hamilton, an Irish journalist, who later became a very gifted radio commentator. For his own reasons, Hamilton disliked Hunt even more than Young.

Hamlyn left it to Young to deal with Peter Hunt, who controlled access to his brother. But Peter didn't understand the processes of publishing at all, and inevitable chaos ensued.

Young flew to Spain immediately and booked himself into the Marbella club, not far from Hunt's home. Over a period of a few days, before Hunt set off on his promotional tour of Europe, Young taped interviews during the day and transcribed them at night, aided by a secretary.

It took Young a further ten days to complete writing the book, and he sent it to Peter Hunt by the end of the third week in November. The process was not to prove a happy one, as the plans kept changing every few days. Young became frustrated. The impossibly tight deadline was not conducive to frequent changes of direction. Peter Hunt didn't like the way some of it was written and he wanted changes. Young made the changes and duly sent the pages back to Hunt and didn't hear anything else. He got paid and he didn't really care.

Anyone who knows Peter Hunt is aware his general manner can be an acquired taste. But he is a very proud man with a sense of tradition. Some believe that it was his brother's attitude that contributed to many of James Hunt's problems with journalists in 1977 and 1978. One well-known journalist says of the problem: "Peter simply didn't get it and tried to impose his views on people."

People had mixed views, but one fan was John Webb, the managing director of Brands Hatch. Webb had a lot of time for Peter Hunt, saying: "Peter was a very able accountant and he did absolute wonders for James. I had a very high regard for Peter and he was most certainly the architect of most of James' career." David Gray echoes Webb: "We became really good mates and I still see him now. He is lovely and a marvellous man, and he looked after James incredibly well too."

Early on, it became apparent to Young that there was no chance of the book coming out before Christmas, but Peter Hunt refused to accept this until the last minute, when the project was quietly shelved. Young says that the publisher also panicked when a book called *Hunt vs Lauda* appeared, written by David Benson. That was unlikely to be true; the reality was that they simply ran out of time. There was too much going on in James' life at time. And the Benson book was well written but poorly produced as a thin, unprepossessing paperback and not a threat at all.

Fully refreshed straight after the New Year, Hunt flew to Argentina for the Grand Prix on 9th January. But he had not enjoyed the Christmas and New Year celebrations with the same carefree manner he was used to. He found even his closest friends treated him differently now that he was world champion. He said: "Physically I reckon I'm alright for the first race, but mentally I'm not ready yet. I need more time to get my mind sorted out and concentrate absolutely on my driving." He stayed in South America until after the Brazilian Grand Prix. When he arrived back in Europe at the end of January, he was straight back into the promotional activity, but this time for Texaco. The oil company suddenly woke up to the hot property that was James Hunt. He wearily threw himself into it again, and said: "I can tell you, the business of being champion is nearly as tough as trying to stay champion on the track. It's almost a relief to get back to the simple life on the circuit, but I realise that isn't the way I should be looking at it."

The most important social event was a gala dinner at the Europa Hotel in London, where the prestigious Tarmac Trophy was to be presented. This award came with cash; some US$6,000. It guaranteed James' attendance.

At the time, the event was the equivalent of the modern day Autosport magazine dinner, and over 300 members of motor racing's great and good came together to honour him, including Teddy Mayer, Alastair Caldwell and his team of eight mechanics. But many people felt that Hunt dishonoured the very formal occasion by turning up in his trademark jeans, t-shirt and an anorak.

It was now very noticeable that at some events he dressed up and others he dressed down. The hosts came to see it is disrespect when he chose the latter for them.

The Tarmac event in particular is remembered by virtually everyone who was there, and the Duke of Kent was noticeably uncomfortable handing Hunt the trophy and the cheque. But everyone also recalls his amusing acceptance speech.

Whereas Hunt usually got away with his informal attire at the Europa Hotel, he was criticised to his face by his contemporaries, who felt he had let down motor sport. Hunt may have been immune to embarrassment but he didn't like personal criticism any more than the next man, and it bothered him for weeks afterwards. He said: "I refused to be shoved around and if that meant calling a spade a spade and not toadying to middle-class ego-massaging and being dressed in jeans and t-shirt, so what? I wasn't prepared to truss myself up in a monkey suit and I always thought I turned out cleanly and comfortably dressed. The whole point was that I was basically getting on with my life in my own way and I didn't really care about what anyone thought. Even though it made a lot of people dislike me intensely, I said to myself, 'stuff it. I'll do it my way.'"

Andrew Marriott believes Hunt's behaviour at the motor racing establishment was deliberate. He says: "I always saw him as the Mick Jagger of motor racing, and he was probably a lot cleverer than most people thought." He was certainly getting noticed.

On his way back to Europe from Brazil, he called in on Scandinavia – at Sweden, Denmark and Finland – and did events for Vauxhall and Texaco.

Although Texaco had woken up very late to the huge potential of Hunt's win, the oil company sought to catch up fast and to associate itself with his victory. It commissioned the London advertising agency, Collett Dickenson Pearce (CDP), to film some commercials of Hunt with the comedy duo Morecambe and Wise. The two commercials, written by CDP's star copywriter, Ron Collins, were very witty and are now regarded as masterpieces by advertising aficionados.

The first advert was full of non-stop quips, including Eric Morecambe addressing Hunt as 'Jane' and, when corrected, telling him: "It's the way you walk." The punch line to all the ads was: "You can trust Texaco. The world champion does." Andrew Marriott remembers: "They were done at Silverstone and they were very funny."

Hunt also appeared on the 'Morecambe & Wise' show in a short two minute sketch. The sketch featured Hunt, as a chauffeur, driving Eric and Ernie in the back of a Mini. Hunt picks them up, pushes the seat forward and they climb in the back. He then proceeds to drive them at full speed, knocking over road signs and barriers. When they get to their destination, he lets them out and, just as they are leaving, he grabs Eric Morecambe and says: "Hey, what about a tip?" Morecambe replies: "Certainly. Leave the women alone."

Despite the success of the Morecambe and Wise commercials, many believe a commercial he did with 76-year-old actor and comedian Fred Emney was his best work. David Gray agrees: "Fred, a huge fat comedian, played the head of Texaco and James said to him: 'Good afternoon, sir, my name is Hunt', and Fred said: 'I can see that from here.'" It was a play on words that would not be tolerated now but was acceptable then, as Gray says: "People were falling about. It was just brilliant."

CSS also roped in Sue Hunt for a series of newspaper adverts. She was surprisingly game and was especially pleased when she received a US$2,000 fee. The adverts featured the unforgettable catchline: "As used by Mrs Hunt and her son." It was a brilliant advert by Ron Collins, and no agency had ever brought a sportsman's mother into it before.

Hunt's relationship with his sponsors proved to be excellent right up to the day he retired. Much of that was down to Peter Hunt, who was much more comfortable with corporates than with the media. Hunt paid tribute to his brother's handling of them: "My main sponsorship contracts are Marlboro, Texaco, Vauxhall and Goodyear. I enjoy a very good relationship with them, and Pete is one of the most important reasons for that because the big company people respect how efficiently my affairs are run. It makes it easy for them to deal with me, and I believe that has helped me enormously. I honestly believe that if one of the traditional sports management organisations had been handling my affairs and been rushing in with the hard sell, I wouldn't have the two years contract with Texaco that I have now. I'm sure it's because they respect the way our business is carried out."

Hunt achieved a good reputation for honouring his responsibilities to sponsors as he said: "I hate being involved with promotions if the guy who hired you hasn't done a good job of setting it up because it reflects badly on you. It doesn't satisfy me just to get my cheque at the end of the day. That's the nice thing about my sponsors – they give me sensible work to do. I can see the value in it for them, and it means one goes away at the end of the day satisfied that one has been of worthwhile value for money. It's most important."

Hunt was so popular and so effective that Philip Morris was forced to raise his basic retainer by 500 per cent, to US$250,000, for 1977. By initially signing a one-year contract, he had put himself in a very good position to negotiate for the following season. He also expected to earn at least another US$250,000 from prize money and personal appearances for Marlboro. There were also huge amounts of cash from Texaco and Vauxhall. Olympus, the Japanese camera company, paid him US$100,000 in a personal sponsorship deal.

Bernie Ecclestone, observing all this and realising that Hunt would become the best paid Formula One driver in history in 1977, decided to play a joke on Jackie Stewart. Stewart had now been retired from Formula One for four years and was earning some US$500,000 a year as a commentator and sponsorship ambassador in the United States. Stewart considered himself motor racing's top earner, and often boasted he was earning more in retirement than the drivers currently racing. To annoy Stewart, Ecclestone offered Hunt US$1 million in exchange for the rights to all his income for 1977. The offer, Ecclestone made public, was never serious but he liked the publicity and he loved piquing Stewart.

After the Brazilian Grand Prix, the Hamlyn book project was revived again after the publisher demanded its advance back. Hamlyn had paid US$25,000 up front as well as paying Young US$10,000 and, in the absence of a manuscript, wanted the US$35,000 repaying.

Peter Hunt panicked at the thought of having to tell his brother that not only had he wasted all those hours with Eoin Young, but it would also cost him US$35,000 – not to mention forfeiting the rest of the US$50,000 Hamlyn had promised.

Peter Hunt rang Eoin Young in a panic, saying they had to update the book for a June publication date. He told him he wanted two more chapters on the first two races of the season to freshen up the manuscript and to make it different from the Benson book. Young, feeling cocky and wanting to teach Peter Hunt a lesson, asked for US$3,000 a chapter to finish the job. Hunt told him that under the contract he had to do it as part of the original fee. Young said to him: "What contract?"

In all the haste and confusion of the previous year, Peter Hunt had forgotten to get Young to sign the contract before he had been paid the money. It was an extraordinary lapse for an accountant of Peter Hunt's reputation. Knowing there was no contract, Young said to him: "I suggested if you could find a copy of the contract with my signature on it, I would do the chapters for nothing." Hunt appealed to his better nature, saying it would be only a matter of spending two hours with his brother. Young responded with something to the effect of: "Peter, has it ever occurred to you that I don't want to spend an hour after each race with your brother?"

Hunt was appalled by Young's attitude, and found another journalist called David Hodges to finish off the book with new chapters. Hodges actually re-wrote the entire manuscript at the same time. In the end, it was a very good book, one that his brother could be proud of.

When the season started properly in South Africa on 5th March 1977, James Hunt breathed a sigh of relief as the promotional trips ended and he could get on with the serious business of racing again. As he said: "The last three months have been absolute bloody. You don't have any idea what it means being world champion. Since Japan there was hardly a single day when I did not attend at least three public functions. I just worked 14 to 20 hours a day."

But Hunt wasn't complaining. He had, by the beginning of 1977, over US$1 million in his bank account in cash, plus another US$500,000 in investments bought for him by his brother. But he was keen to tell people he was not just racing for the money, saying: "I do my deals with the team and my sponsors, and to an extent that's the end of the story. I get my percentages as I race, and, the better I do in races, the better I do financially.

"The races are still a sporting effort for my own personal achievement, and I really don't think about the money too much. Obviously one attempts to capitalise, but also to find a happy medium. One wants to win races, one wants to live a nice life, one wants to make as much money as one reasonably can without becoming a sort of machine."

But it's fair to say that, by the beginning of March 1977, that is exactly how he felt.

REIGNING WORLD CHAMPION 1976-1977

SHUNT

CHAPTER 29

Girls, girls, girls, then Jane
But faithful to none of them

James Hunt was a man totally incapable of being monogamous or faithful to one woman. In modern parlance, he would be described as a sex addict and there is no question he had a big appetite for sex.

But during all this time, he was very rarely without a regular partner. Over his life, he probably knew seven women who could be classed as partners, two of whom he married. These were Taormina Rich, Chantal Lacluse, Suzy Miller, Valentine Monnier, Jane Birbeck, Sarah Lomax and Helen Dyson. Of those, he had been in love with only Rich, Miller, Birbeck, Lomax and Dyson, the only relationships that were to last any length of time.

But apart from love, the relationships all had one thing in common – he was faithful to none of them. The five principal partners also had one thing in common – they were all blonde. He generally only dated blue-eyed blondes, and he liked small to medium-breasted girls with longish legs and flat tummies. He was rarely seen with a dark-haired girl. In fact, Chantal Lacluse, a vivacious dark-haired Polish girl with whom he lived for a year and a half, was the only exception.

Surprisingly, none of the many other women with whom he became intimately acquainted ever 'kissed and told' publicly. Consequently, very little is known about his sex life. Aside from an article in a Dutch magazine, there was no account of any woman speaking publicly about intimate details of their relationship.

But one who did speak anonymously to Hunt's biographer Gerald Donaldson long after James Hunt was dead, said he was a "sensitive and highly-skilled lover." She told Donaldson: "He was always attentive to his partner's needs. Indeed much of his satisfaction came from giving pleasure. The only problem was that his desire to please often out-stripped my needs."

Many of the girls with whom Hunt was known to have had relationships with during the seventies now flatly deny it. The laws of libel, of course, prevent authors disputing that, however obvious it may have been to the contrary.

But it must be noted that many of the denials this author encountered were accompanied by a twinkle in the eyes of the deniers, which made the denials very difficult to take seriously.

One such repudiator, who is now a well-known journalist, flatly denies there was ever a sexual relationship, but admits that she took Hunt to meet her mother.

The fact that he never suffered from 'kiss and tell' newspaper exposure is unusual considering the number of women he bedded, including married ones while he too was married. There are also no illegitimate children, which, considering how many times he had sex and with how many women, must be considered a minor miracle.

One close friend, who insisted on anonymity said: "Calculating how many women he slept with during his 30-year career as an accomplished and prolific swordsman is impossible, but I'd say it was at least 5,000." So he was not in Warren Beatty's class, but not far off. But, as Tony Dron, his close friend from his Formula 3 days, says: "If you were as good looking as him, and women threw themselves at you on a regular basis, what would you have done?"

Although promiscuous from the age of 16, he never really got going until after his marriage to Suzy Miller ended. With her gone, Hunt threw caution to the wind and placed no constraints on his sexual proclivities. His only restriction was his on-off relationship with Jane Birbeck, but she lived far away in New York and, at that time, no one really knew anything about her. Birbeck was beautiful and exactly his sort of woman. He knew he was falling in love with her, but that didn't stop him sleeping with as many women as he could from early 1976 onwards.

Hunt's only problem, if it was a problem, was that he was usually only attracted to wholesome, nice girls. He usually had no time at all for the flashy, busty and tarty airhead types. And the type of girls he liked did not always want to fall into bed with him. At races, he was very successful with women and, for those that resisted his charms, he had a fallback line that always won a girl over. He would tell them: "But I might be killed in the race."

When Hunt was driving for the Hesketh team, Bubbles Horsley overheard Hunt using the line. It was just before a final qualifying session and there was danger of his driver not even qualifying for the race, so he leaned over to Hunt, who was sitting strapped into his Hesketh car with his helmet on, waiting to go out, and said: "Going to die in the race, are we? Well we'll have to go a lot quicker in qualifying then, won't we?" Horsley remembers that Hunt was very embarrassed and went out and drove faster than he had ever done, and easily qualified.

Apart from on the race track, Hunt's main means of meeting women was by socialising in London's west end. When in England, he was a regular in the pubs, bars and nightclubs in the Kings Road. He particularly loved chatting up cute, young, English waitresses in restaurants, and there were many of them working in London at a time before large-scale immigration started. After a few drinks, he thought life was a huge joke and found everything very funny. It was immensely attractive to women, and girls loved being around him. He radiated what was described by one friend as an "attractive *bonhomie*."

In Christopher Hilton's book about Hunt, called *Memories*, many people reflected on Hunt's sexual prowess. Before he died, Nick Brittan said: "He was larger than life, boisterous and excessive in nearly everything he did, and he had a rather delightful arrogance." But Brittan was not always an admirer, and added: "There's a fine line between supreme confidence and arrogance, and James teetered on the brink."

Ian Phillips was a regular in the Kings Road in the early seventies, and remembers: "James was the darling of Chelsea and the west end." But Phillips declined to socialise with him when he became world champion, saying: "We lost touch because he moved in circles I didn't want to move in. All manner of people want to know you when you're the champion." But Phillips understood the temptations put in Hunt's way, and he understood Hunt. As he says: "I'll pose the question: if you were 29, good looking in a macho sort of way, had the public school certainties, the bravery to drive a Formula One car and win in it, had the money and the adulation, what constrictions would you have accepted? If he pursued and caught beautiful women, wouldn't you? It wasn't even adultery. He was divorced, not married."

Chris Witty, the well-known motor sport PR man, told the following story, and it rings true: "He'd go into a bar and, if there was a pretty girl and an ugly girl, he'd always have a bet with the mechanics that he would pull the ugly one – because she didn't expect to be bonked that night and he couldn't be bothered to spend all the time chatting up the pretty one."

Jochen Mass, his teammate, also recounted an anecdote that reflected Hunt's view of women at the time: "There was a girl called Mercedes, and she worked for Spanish television. She said: 'Can I do an interview?' He said: 'Not a problem', and they stood him beside the camera. And as she was asking him a question, he asked her (on camera): 'Do you fuck?' She said: 'Thank you, James', and walked off. Sometimes, he just went over the edge with statements and things like that."

James Hunt was never afraid of frankly discussing sex and his requirements, even with journalists. He said sex for him was a therapeutic form of relaxation. He called it a "form of communication." He said: "I don't usually have sex before a race because I am very definitely concentrating. I find that it is the communication between two people that makes it worthwhile, and, before a race, I am pretty uncommunicative. However, if, say, I have an hour or so to spare before dinner on the night before a race, then I can enjoy the physical release. But I will only do it with someone who is fully understanding." But, of course, he broke all his own rules as frequently as he made them. He liked nothing better than to have sex immediately before the start of a Grand Prix. As the famous story goes, he had sex just before the most important race of his life – at the Japanese Grand Prix of 1976 – only minutes before getting into his car.

But he never behaved so crudely with Jane Birbeck. They had met a year before, when Birbeck was having an affair with Mark McCormack, the chairman of International Management Group (IMG), the world's biggest sports sponsorship and management agency. Physically, Birbeck ticked all Hunt's boxes and he couldn't take his eyes off her the first time they met, which was at a backgammon tournament in Marbella.

But there was a problem as McCormack was not a man Hunt could afford to upset. Hunt was also a client of McCormack's company, as was Jackie

Stewart.

McCormack and Birbeck had met at IMG's office in London, and the 45-year-old American was a legend in the sports industry and the most powerful man in sport. He was manager to all of the world's top golf and tennis stars and an author of the best-selling book, *What They Don't Teach You At Harvard Business School*. The book sold millions based on the precept of how to negotiate a deal. But he was also married to Nancy Breckenridge and had three small children, who lived in Cleveland. Breckenridge was a stay-at-home housewife, bringing up the children and never accompanying her husband on his travels. Her husband was very discreet, and she never asked and was never told about what he got up to.

McCormack was very rich, worth at least US$20 million personally through his ownership of 100 per cent of the shares of IMG. He spent his life travelling on IMG business, making deals and looking after his clients.

But Hunt, after chatting to Birbeck for some length while McCormack was occupied in a business meeting, could sense that she was uncomfortable about seeing a married man with three children. But then Hunt, too, was a married man, and so he decided to bide his time before taking the relationship any further. But, by all accounts, she had captivated him that day.

After their first meeting, when it was time to leave the Marbella Club, Jane told Hunt she was returning to London with McCormack the following day but invited him to look her up.

When he was in London again, he did look her up; and so began a relationship that would last for more than half a decade. But it all started off very slowly and very properly, which was unusual for Hunt. It was a full six months after they met that he and Birbeck went to bed together. Hunt had wanted to make sure that McCormack was off the scene completely as he was genuinely frightened about the damage he could do to his career. Only when that was certain did he proceed.

Birbeck had no idea about this and she didn't realise that McCormack's fearsome reputation preceded him. In the sports business, he was nicknamed 'Mark the Shark', and with good reason. Many a promising young tennis player had had their careers terminated by 'The Shark'. Hunt, aware of his reputation and having been warned by Jackie Stewart, did not want that to happen to him.

Recalling how long it took Hunt to make his move, Birbeck told Gerald Donaldson: "I was sure he was gay because he never made a move on me for so long. It was a rather bizarre courtship. We had plenty to talk about, but that's all we ever did. He liked conversation and would talk endlessly to me on the telephone. When we got together, we'd have supper and talk into the small hours. There was no deep urge, particularly on his part, to make a permanent relationship."

Birbeck was 24 years old at the time and a stunning woman. Her beauty was always understated because she always dressed like a tomboy, but when she got dressed up, she was a very impressive woman indeed. Hunt's friend John Richardson described her as "a very cool, a very English, ice maiden." Hunt quickly nicknamed her 'Hot loins', which got shortened to 'Hottie'. The nickname was picked up by the British media and she never shook it off. Richardson remembered: "The name stuck, and the press picked it up and ran with it." Gerald Donaldson described her as "adventurous and fun-loving…with very obvious feminine charms."

Like his wife Suzy, Jane was the daughter of a military man, also a brigadier, called Nigel Birbeck. The family was well-off and she was educated at a boarding school in Kent. Nigel Birbeck was renowned as a former deputy fortress commander of Gibraltar, where the family had lived for a long period. Jane Birbeck spent her teenage years on the Costa del Sol. When the family moved back to Britain, they took up residence in Buckinghamshire and she started to spend a lot of time in London. She worked as an au pair for a while before taking a secretarial course.

From the end of 1975, Hunt and Birbeck were seeing each other regularly when Hunt was in London. She avoided Spain, as Hunt was publicly still married to Suzy Miller and was living with her at the Spanish house. The last thing she wanted was to be known as was the girl who broke up his marriage.

But when Miller got together publicly with Richard Burton in early 1976, there was no further need for secrecy and the two of them became an item and began being photographed together. At first, no one knew who Birbeck was; and Hunt wasn't in a rush to enlighten the paparazzi.

But the relationship was serious and passionate from the start. She also had a very fierce independent streak, which Hunt adored as an antidote to Suzy Miller's neediness. He felt the failure of his marriage was primarily because he could not cater to Miller's need for constant attention. Birbeck required none of that, and was a total opposite to Miller. Although she lacked Miller's poise and ethereal presence, Hunt liked Birbeck's bohemian style and her undeniable sex appeal. He said about her: "She has a strong personality, the strongest one I've ever met and the only one who could stand up to my strength, which is why we have such a good balance. I've never wanted to use or abuse women, but if you have a stronger personality you can't help but be the dominant one, and the moment that happens you have no relationship. I don't want someone to live for me."

Birbeck also understood that marriage wasn't on Hunt's agenda after the fiasco with Suzy Miller.

The marriage to Miller had made him realise he needed an independent woman on his arm. There was initially no question of Birbeck moving in with him. He didn't want it and neither did she. But Hunt often felt lonely on his own in Marbella and so he did what many single men do when faced with that situation – he got a dog. Well three dogs to be precise.

They were called Oscar, Gypsy and Barbarella. But only one of them really mattered, and Hunt formed a connection with Oscar that was to endure for 14 years. Hunt's relationship with Oscar transcended any human relationship he ever had. With Oscar, he found a true connection, and a serious bond developed between them.

Oscar was supplied by a British vet, who was introduced to Hunt by Mary Richardson. He was immediately taken to Spain. It was the start of an enduring and rewarding relationship, as Hunt and Oscar became inseparable on the beaches, the mountain roads, tennis courts and golf courses of Marbella. Oscar was never on a lead and followed Hunt everywhere, jumping into the passenger seat of his Porsche 911 Carrera and leaping out when they reached their destination, just as a human companion would. Hunt would frequent cafes and restaurants that welcomed Oscar and, where possible, Oscar liked to sit at the table as well. Hunt said: "Oscar is very special."

One golf club, the Aloha, sent out a memo to members banning dogs from the course. But the memo actually stated that the ban did not include Oscar because he was better behaved than some of its members. Richardson remembers: "James' relationship with Oscar seemed far closer than any human relationship he ever had. He was completely devoted to that dog."

The relationship with Birbeck, however, was initially not so smooth.

When Hunt declared his love for her and she for him, she was very wary of his reputation and didn't feel ready to move in with him to share his life. She declined to come live with him in Spain and carried on with her job in London, later moving to New York at the end of 1976. Birbeck was remarkably candid to Donaldson about their relationship. She told him that he was a "spoiled brat", something she didn't realise at first. She was also well aware that he was incapable of being faithful to her. She would open the European newspapers and magazines sold in New York and see a photo of her boyfriend with a glamorous woman on his arm. She told herself it was because she was not there.

Hunt slept with so many women that year it is impossible to recall them all. In truth, he didn't know all their names either. He had a fling with 19-year-old Charlene Shorto, the Brazilian socialite, and they were an item for a while. Shorto was the sister of Baroness Denise Thyssen, who was married to Baron Henri Thyssen, the iron and steel heir who also owned the world's most valuable art collection. Hunt met her in Marbella, where the Thyssens lived and where she was staying with her sister. Shorto was later the muse of fashion designer Valentino and became a leading figure in Europe's fashion industry.

It was at this time that Hunt also took up with Valentine Monnier, a supermodel and budding actress. She was a blue-eyed blonde who appeared on the cover of the American *Cosmopolitan* magazine in the summer of 1977. Monnier wore a gold evening gown for the shoot and was briefly America's best paid model. Later, she became a minor actress. Monnier was a serious rival to Birbeck at the time, and Hunt considered leaving her for Monnier many times.

But ultimately, Shorto and Monnier were just two of many during 1976 and 1977. At the French Grand Prix, Hunt hooked up with then 16-year-old Ruth Caldwell, a very bright girl and the daughter of McLaren team manager, Alastair Caldwell. Because of his respect for her father nothing happened between them, but they certainly had a good time together.

But, despite all the dalliances, he always came back to Birbeck. And there was no doubt, despite what he said later, that she was the love of his life.

But Birbeck took a long time to adjust to her boyfriend's chronic unfaithfulness. Hunt tried to hide it from her, but there were too many affairs. He was a very good juggler, but he just had too many balls in the air. When she was at his villa in Marbella, Birbeck would continually pick up the phone and, on the other end, presumably upon hearing a woman's voice when she said 'hello', the caller would just click off.

They had terrible rows in Spain, and Hunt admitted that Birbeck would "throw terrible tantrums and lapse into silent sulks and not speak to him for several days." She was initially angry at what she called his "lack of consideration."

Birbeck never spoke publicly about it but it was often impossible to hide her disappointment, and she had to endure some pretty humiliating and sometimes public put-downs due to his chronic unfaithfulness. But she was not alone.

The Hunts and the Sheenes were very good friends during this period. Both men were world champions in cars and motorcycles in 1976. Barry Sheene's girlfriend and later wife, Stephanie McLean, had to put up with the same kinds of problems as Birbeck. They had both met their partners in 1975 and both quickly realised they were serial womanisers, incapable of being faithful. Both McLean and Birbeck were of similar age and looks. McLean was regarded as one of the most beautiful women in the world. The two women often got together and discussed their joint problems with their boyfriends, but Stephanie MacLean did not have to endure the humiliations of Jane Birbeck.

There was no more public and no more humiliating put-down than when Hunt's one night stand with a Dutch journalist was written up and published all over the world in the Dutch weekly entertainment magazine *Nieuwe Revu*, in July 1977.

It all started in March 1977, when Hunt scheduled an appointment at his villa in Marbella with Alissa Morrien, a blonde journalist from Holland. It was for a lifestyle article with photographs. But what Hunt didn't know was that Morrien was on permanent assignment from her magazine to sleep with famous men, write up the experience and rate their performance in bed for the magazine's readers. The magazine had a circulation of 200,000 and was only published in Dutch.

Morrien flew into Marbella and checked herself and the photographer into the Marbella Club, which was situated not far from Hunt's house.

Hunt spent the day with her by his swimming pool. During the interview, Morrien stripped down to her bikini and lay sunbathing on a sun lounger as they talked about his life. Hunt thought the behaviour odd for a journalist, as he said later: "I thought it was slightly strange when she started to divest herself of her clothing." She questioned Hunt about his sex life, and he admitted to having many girlfriends despite his permanent relationship with Birbeck. At noon, they got into his Porsche and sped off to a harbourside café at San Pedro for lunch.

When they returned, he went out for his afternoon run and Morrien attempted to joined him but fell back with a severe cramp after a few hundred metres and returned to the house.

When Hunt returned after 15 minutes, he took a bath, and the interview continued with him naked and Morien sitting on the loo seat, tape recorder in hand. It is clear that Morrien could not stop staring at Hunt's penis, even when he asked her to look away. When he told her: "I will get shy if you don't avert your gaze", she admitted she carried on looking through a mirror. In truth, Hunt found it amusing and had no idea it would all be reported later.

After his bath, he invited her out for dinner with two of his neighbours.

Morrien described part of the dinner: "James put his hand on my knee and began stroking my leg. He told me: 'I'd love to stroke you all over your body', and I replied: 'I'd love that.'" Morrien sent her photographer back to the Marbella Club and remained with Hunt that night. Hunt said later: "I had dinner with her and the rest is up to your imagination."

Well not quite, as little imagination was subsequently required. Afterwards, by the time she had left and when he was informed what Morrien did for a living, he said: "It never occurred to me that I was being a gullible idiot. But I am pleased to have been able to help Miss Morrien with her journalistic inquiries. I was on good form and look forward to reading my official rating."

But when the article was published, it was relatively harmless and stopped short of describing what happened that night when they went to bed. Surprisingly, it has never before been translated into English, and this is how it reads in full:

The doorman of the Marbella Club Hotel, where, in the high season, I heard only the beautiful, the rich and the famous of the world are allowed, knows immediately what I'm talking about when I ask where the villa of James Hunt is located. 'La Casa de James Hunt', the doorman says to the driver of the taxi that he has ordered for me. The taxi drives away carefully on the bumpy road to the secluded villa where the Formula One world champion lives. Due to the heavy tax on his income, Hunt had to leave the United Kingdom.

It is ten o'clock in the morning. The bright, but not yet burning sunlight creates an atmosphere that is totally different from the drizzly-driven wet weather I have left behind in the Netherlands. The birds chirping are a delight as I have not heard them in years.

At the beginning of the driveway stand three tremendous-looking, barking dogs. A German Shepherd, a Great Dane and a Dachshund. When I get out, they do not bite – fortunately.

Long, slim, blonde and barefoot, I see James Hunt with his dogs: Oscar, Gypsy and Barbarella. Acknowledging me, Hunt runs back into the house with the dogs behind him. I walk into the house after him, directly to the large sunny terrace.

'A bit of drama going on here,' he says in his very English voice. 'My housekeeper is meeting someone at the airport and I'm not that domestically inclined.' I notice his voice is beautifully modulated.

Hunt is not often at home. Apart from racing and testing, he is always away on promotional tours and making promotional films for his sponsors.

He has not swam in his pool on the terrace this year, and it has flies and wasps floating in the water. The mattresses on the chairs and sun loungers are soaked from the early morning rainfall. In the house, he has a Neil Diamond album playing. 'That thing is running?' he says, laughing, when his eye falls on my tape recorder. 'It is recording', I tell him.

I have no idea what kind of impression I am making on him.

'Have you ever been shy?' I ask.

'I am,' he says, 'especially in big groups of people. I do not like big spaces. The last year has been worse because now everyone looks at me, which is very heavy and it makes me nervous.'

'You freak out sometimes?' I ask.

'Until now, no,' Hunt says, grinning. 'But lately, I sometimes feel that it could happen. The fear of rooms with many people is not so bad because, if it becomes too much, I simply leave...but in the last eight months, so much has changed. I do not know which way I will go. So much happens at once that I hardly have time to take it all in. If everything goes too fast to notice, I have to teach myself how to adapt, and that is not easy.'

James Hunt is often described as a playboy or, as I read in a magazine, a Don Juan. In the time that the young eccentric Lord Hesketh sponsored him, he travelled with the Hesketh Racing team in a private jet, a helicopter and a green Rolls Royce. And, at the Monaco Grand Prix, there were two luxury yachts and Dom Pérignon champagne flowed copiously like water and tea was served in Limoges porcelain. And, of course, there were beautiful women.

'Do you treat women differently than men?' I ask.

'I think everyone does to some extent,' said James thoughtfully. 'I do not mind, certainly not with women whom I like...'

'And women whom you do not find nice?'

'I treat them not at all.'

'Why not?' I ask.

But James did not answer because he is distracted by Oscar, his German Shepherd. 'Oscar, what have you got there?' he cries and goes to the dog to get something out of his mouth. 'He is my youngest,' he says. 'He is just one year old.' Meanwhile, Valerie, the housekeeper, came back from the airport. When she sees James with his dog, she winks at me and says: 'The most important person in his life.'

But I do not want to talk about dogs.

'Why not?' I ask James again. He sits back down and thinks. Its obvious that he tries to use his dogs to evade my questions.

'As you can imagine,' he says unashamed, 'there are many women interested in me for what I am. I treat women differently than men because I'm in the right way to defend against the charms with which they come down on me.'

James Hunt was married to Suzy Miller for sixteen months, the woman who now is married to Richard Burton and is expecting a child. By marrying and divorcing, James says he came to realise that he loves friendship and is not a fan of the traditional roles of men and women. His current girlfriend, the beautiful New York resident Jane Birbeck, is with him because of that.

'I treat her like a man,' says James. 'And she would not want otherwise. Therefore, we also agree with each other. She is independent and she does her work and I do mine. I don't want a slave because I have a housekeeper, and I also do not want someone who follows me all the time, because I already have a dog.'

'Are you saying that sometimes you love her?' I ask.

'Yes,' says Hunt, a little surprised. 'Not as often and not in a ponderous way, but we say it now and again. It has taken a year before we said it to each other, however after eight months we already knew. You should always be very sure before you say it.'

I tell him: 'I've never known what it means.'

'That's right,' says Hunt. 'It could mean anything. The only thing we currently do is enjoy the friendship we have and hope that, in a couple of years, when I withdraw from racing, we still feel the same for each other. But we are both aware that, by then, our time may have passed. She may have met another, or me.'

'Are you jealous?' I ask.

James does not answer the first time, as he is distracted: Gypsy is showing romantic interest in Oscar.

'Gypsy, don't,' James calls, laughing. 'You're a girl…Oscar, bite her', he laughs.

'Are you jealous?' I ask again.

'Now, that's an interesting point', says James Hunt. 'The last eight or nine years, I never have been. I have no reason to be jealous because I have everything I want.

But, my friend, I am sometimes a little jealous when I think what she is doing in New York...but I know what she does, so really it's no problem. I think you're always a bit jealous when you love someone, and that is very important to me.'

'Have you ever thought you could not really love someone?'

'Yes, I was worried about it. For a few years it is not bad, but then, you still wonder whether you'll ever love someone and therefore I find it nice that I'm a little jealous.'

'Do you tell her everything?' I ask him.

'All that she wants to know,' James says diplomatically.

I ask again: 'You conceal things that you think are painful for her?'

'I think so, but it's never been presented as she would not ask me such things. She is too intelligent. She would not like to be in the position where I tell her something that would upset her...But I always try to avoid lying.'

The housekeeper has returned, and brings us two giant cups of coffee.

I am trying to feel completely at ease with James and, while we are posing for the first photographs on the edge of the pool, we get close to each other. Despite his blonde hair, he has very dark eyelashes. There is a mutual understanding developing between us, and we both know that in the course of the day we both expect more than a light touch.

'It is dangerous to be interviewed by you,' says James. 'You make talking to someone too easy.'

That does not stop him from inviting me to lunch at the port of San Pedro.

We drive to the port in his Porsche. Hunt does not like to be noticed in his car. My legs are raised high as the seat does not go back. He has bare feet and his safety belt on as he safely speeds the car over the bumps in the road. He says he does not plan to be killed in a road car.

'Were you shocked by Lauda's accident?' I ask.

'Not really,' says Hunt. 'You know it can happen, we are mentally prepared and we know the risks. It's just sad that your friend is injured, but professionally it does not matter. But if, for example, three major accidents in quick succession were to happen, we should start worrying because then something has changed. The only way to protect yourself against the dangers of a race at Grand Prix level, is simply not drive. Whether you ride hard or soft does not matter. I drive better when I drive very hard, because then I concentrate better. But most accidents happen because of something with the car. Drivers do not make mistakes, they make errors, but mistakes do not cause serious accidents statistically. When you make a mistake, at least you have the car under control. But if one wheel of your car flies off, you have no control anymore.'

James is quite serious about his job and now he talks at a stretch, and he forgets that he has ordered a sandwich and I forget my omelette.

'Your omelette is cold,' says Hunt. 'But maybe you'll find that good.'

I put a bite in my mouth and say that I have read that he wants to be world champion again. Many people think that Lauda would have been if he had not had his accident.

'That's right', says Hunt. 'Autocourse, for example, a directory of races, set an annual ranking of their own and have Niki placed first and me second. They love to be controversial, but I am very satisfied.'

I ask him: 'Would it not have been an elegant gesture to surrender your title to Lauda in view of what happened?'

James gets indignant: 'That's a ridiculous question. If we're not racing then we could just as well all go home at the start of the season.'

Calmer, he says: 'Niki and I both have a very good year behind us. He had the sympathy of the audience and he knows he could have been world champion. Moreover, he has learned a lot since the accident. He is less closed and he now enjoys more of his life. Like me, has become aware that in life there is no time to lose. As for me, I find that I am world champion right now. If you have the string of statistics, you will see that no one has lost the world championship. After all, he has won four Grand Prix races and I've won seven of last year. It would have been ridiculous if I had won half of that number. And I have a chance this year, but it may be that this year it is Niki.'

It is time for James' daily training. With stopwatch in hand, he runs the distance back and forward from his house to the main road. 'I'm fitter than I actually need to be,' he says, 'but I force myself to do it every day. It's more a mental workout.'

Oscar declines to join his master this time. 'He's too lazy,' he says. 'Once he sees me press the stopwatch, he falls on the ground.'

I try to run it with him; I want to see how far I get. Except that I'm hobbled, as I am not wearing training shoes. I get a cramp after a few hundred metres and go back. James disappears behind a hill in the road. The sun is already setting, and slowly I walk back to the house and sit on the grass in front of the door.

Drowning in sweat, James returns fifteen minutes later. At the gate, he presses his stopwatch and stands on the grass next to me. His face lights up with pure joy as he tells me he has broken his own record. Panting and breathless, he reaches out to my hand to help me to get up.

'Your skirt looks great on your legs,' he says. 'Very sexy.'

'Shall I show you the rest of the house?' James asks, still out of breath from the run. I nod and ask myself if he will push me onto the bed when showing me the bedroom, but he doesn't do that. His house is beautiful, though not cosy. It is rented and it

contains furniture belonging to other people; a deep sofa made of light material with orange and green flowers on it.

There are some pictures of James in his racing car which remind me of a boy's room.

'Do you think of yourself as a man or a boy?' I ask.

'A boy', he says promptly. 'That is logical because all my life I have done nothing other than have fun. I have never outgrown it.'

'You have worked very hard as well, haven't you?' I say.

'Yes, very hard', says James. 'I have been working for eleven years as a professional driver and only in the last three years have I started to earn money.'

'The last two years I have started to see myself as a woman,' I say.

'How old are you?' asks James.

'Thirty-one', I reply.

'I am twenty-nine,' he says. 'Maybe in about two years I will feel like a man.'

He has undressed and climbed into the bath that he had been filling. I have flipped the lid of the toilet down so I can sit on it.

'Do you mind looking the other way?' asks James, when he stands up in the bath to wash himself. 'Otherwise, I will become very shy.'

'Yes,' I say, smiling, because the wall opposite the bath consists entirely of mirrors. James is laughing too.

'Now I am ready for anything,' says James after he has put on clean clothes, combed his hair and put a necklace with a coin around his neck.

We will be going out to dinner with two friends of his. James and I are sitting on the back seat of their car.

During the drive, he puts his hand on my knee. Softly, he begins to tickle my thighs as he sums up the courage to do so. 'All day, I have been looking at your legs,' he says.

I have to laugh about his. 'You are stroking nicely,' I say.

'I would like to stroke you all over your body,' he says.

I say: 'That sounds wonderful.'

While we are sitting at the bar in the restaurant, my legs are being tickled again.

He tells me: 'I am doing it in a way that nobody will notice.'

'I actually find it nice when people can see,' I say. That comment makes James laugh. 'But doing this in secret is nice too. Is it possible to stroke my legs when we are sitting at our table?'

Enjoyment, Enjoyment!

That is exactly what he does even while we are having a serious conversation, poker faced.

Later on, when we are lying on the bed, I hold James to his promise.

The article, although never translated, received wide coverage when it appeared. But its content was exaggerated and readers were lead to believe that Morrien had described Hunt's sexual performance, taking readers through all the nuances of his lovemaking. She hadn't, and she didn't rate his performance either. But the article left no one in any doubt that they had made love. Morrien later told friends that Hunt was an expert lover and very satisfying.

What Jane Birbeck thought to all this has been never been recorded, but it certainly seemed to play a part in her decision to come to live with him permanently in Spain.

In fact, there were two triggers. Birbeck found she was pregnant in mid 1977, while she was still living in New York. When she told him on the telephone, she expected trouble. But the opposite happened, as she told Gerald Donaldson: "When I found out I was pregnant, I became terribly excited and rang him up to discuss it. When I told him, he just assumed I would come back and there was no more discussion. He appeared in New York to pick me up and we set up home in Spain."

Birbeck's pregnancy was the trigger for them to live together, and she gave up working in anticipation of the baby. By then, Hunt had put down more permanent roots and given up his rental villa and bought an old villa in San Pedro that needed renovating. Birbeck took charge of the renovations, as she said: "We got the builders in and made the house all nice."

But the domestic bliss was disturbed when Birbeck suffered a miscarriage. The miscarriage changed all their plans, but the pain of it brought them closer together. And so began one of the most tender periods in Hunt's life, when he stopped being unfaithful and became more devoted to her. She found his new sensitivity irresistible, as she said: "His sensitivity to my feelings became one of James' most endearing qualities." She says she learned so much about herself from him and that he helped her "grow up."

David Gray remembers Hunt's time with Birbeck as his happiest: "They were both very funny together very. It was all extraordinarily funny, and he was very loyal to her."

The relationship with Birbeck was to last for five years and would be the most enduring of his life; it spanned his remaining time in tax exile in Spain and his return to Britain.

GIRLS, GIRLS, GIRLS, THEN JANE

SHUNT

CHAPTER 30

A desperately disappointing
title defence 1977
Over the top behaviour costs him dearly

A s soon as the 1977 season opened, it was clear that Jody Scheckter, apart from Niki Lauda, would be Hunt's new main rival. But there would be many rivals that season in an extraordinary year of close racing, when any one of seven drivers could easily have been world champion. Scheckter's decision to join Walter Wolf's new team from his established perch at Tyrrell looked a good one. Patrick Head, the young Wolf designer who had designed the new Wolf-Ford WR7, was a coming man. Head, virtually unknown in 1977, was to become the dominant Formula One car designer of the eighties and nineties.

However, by the time Scheckter arrived at his new team, Head had resigned. But fortunately for Scheckter, he had left behind his new car, the Wolf-Ford WR7, a legacy that Scheckter was to exploit most effectively during the season.

The 1977 season opened in a hurry with the Argentine Grand Prix on 9th January. The race had only been confirmed on the calendar a few days before Christmas, after the financial problems that had caused its cancellation in 1976 had been resolved.

It was a very different James Hunt who arrived in South America in 1977. A year earlier, he was a new boy in the McLaren team but now he returned as world champion. He was now being paid US$250,000 a year by Marlboro to drive. Only Emerson Fittipaldi and Niki Lauda were earning more. It was the first time in his life that he believed he was being paid what he was worth. The bonus structure was also impressive. With that carrot in front of him, he had attended every promotional event and party that Marlboro's John Hogan requested. In truth, it was not too much of a burden for, despite his complaints, James Hunt loved being world champion.

Hunt just couldn't say 'no' to a press conference or a personal appearance, and the day before the Argentine Grand Prix weekend, Hunt spoke to the local Buenos Aries media to help sell tickets. The organisers got a bit of a shock when he turned up at the press conference in bare feet, dirty jeans and a t-shirt. He was also unshaven, many years before it was fashionable.

Buenos Aries was a city that prided itself on formality. The following day's newspapers carried little information about the race, but focused heavily on the disrespect shown by Hunt for the city and its citizens. The articles mentioned his unkempt hair, the bags under his eyes and his constant yawning.

The coverage didn't bother him at all. He was more bothered about the high temperatures, which hovered around 38 degrees. The circuit was set in open parkland on the outskirts of Buenos Aires and track temperatures were to reach nearly 50 degrees during race weekend.

Out at the circuit, there were soldiers and police everywhere. They were toting automatic rifles and sub machine guns backed up by shotguns, tear gas and even some light artillery. The circuit looked more like it was preparing for a war rather than a Formula One Grand Prix.

The Argentine government feared that an extremist group might use the Grand Prix as a platform for a national incident. The extremists were, at the time, very active, protesting about the economy and an inflation rate that exceeded 300 per cent annually.

The worries were heightened because Argentina was scheduled to host the World Cup soccer tournament in 1978. Should the Grand Prix have been disrupted, it was likely the soccer governing body FIFA would have cancelled or reallocated the World Cup tournament. The government was taking no chances.

For the McLaren team, it was business as usual. Time had seemingly stood still as the team wheeled out the McLaren-Ford M23 model for its fifth season of racing. The new M26 had again proven to be slower than the older car in testing.

The two-model dilemma had cost McLaren dearly, both in competitiveness and cash, and there was no solution in sight. Hunt explained the essence of the dilemma: "Most teams introduce a new car because they bloody well need it and therefore are prepared to speculate, to chuck away the old car and get on with the new car on the theory that the old car wasn't good enough, even if it means struggling with the new car for a couple of races. McLaren's problem was that the old car was brilliant and carried on being brilliant, and a new car was not necessary."

It made the development programme slower than it should have been, as Hunt explained: "When you've got a car that can win races, why change for the sake of change?" It was good advice that the team ultimately didn't take.

As reigning world champion, the number 1 graced Hunt's car as he pulled out of the pit lane to join the first practice session of 1977. Although only three months had passed, much had changed. As well as Scheckter's move to Wolf, Ronnie Peterson had left March and joined Tyrrell, and there were a pair of new six-wheeled Tyrrell-Fords for him and Patrick Depailler.

Team Lotus had two new Lotus 78s, the first ground effect cars, for Mario Andretti and Gunnar Nilsson. John Watson was now ensconced at Brabham after the Penske team shut down. Clay Regazzoni had joined the small uncompetitive and underfunded Ensign team. When Hunt learned of this, he thought to himself: "There, but for the grace of God, go I." Had Fittipaldi not left McLaren, it might easily have been Hunt's predicament.

Niki Lauda appeared dejected at the first race. He had lost the battle to keep Regazzoni as his teammate and now had a co-driver he didn't like – Carlos Reutemann. Lauda and Regazzoni had been far closer than people knew, often flying together to races and spending social time together. Lauda now viewed Reutemann as a rival he had to beat, not a teammate.

What had not changed was the fractious relationship between Lauda and Enzo Ferrari.

Lauda now regarded him as a buffoon, and the two were at loggerheads all winter. When he had withdrawn from the Japanese Grand Prix and lost the championship, Lauda believed that Enzo had behaved disgracefully, as he recalled: "There was none of the legendary Ferrari greatness about him. It was less than dignified and he reacted like any other team boss who sees his chance slipping away." In Tokyo's airport lounge, Lauda and Enzo had had a ludicrous telephone conversation, which Lauda described as "heartless." According to Lauda, Enzo Ferrari made all his decisions based on what he read in the Italian newspapers. The newspapers had called Lauda a "coward", and Enzo had believed it. This naturally infuriated Lauda, who said: "At 78, and with a lifetime of intrigue and distorted information behind him, he was far too removed from the essential issue. He could only sit and read his newspapers."

It was revealed that when Lauda had returned to Italy after Japan, Enzo had offered him the job of team manager. His object was to sack Lauda as a driver and to stop him driving elsewhere. In another pantomime session with Enzo, Lauda threw his contract at him and said he was off to drive for McLaren. Frightened, Enzo called in his advisers and they, who only half an hour earlier had advised him to sack Lauda, now advised him on how to persuade him to stay.

When he returned to the meeting, Enzo informed Lauda that while he could stay on as a driver, Reutemann would be the team's number one. Lauda, tired of arguing, simply shrugged his shoulders and left. It was at that moment that he decided not to sign a new contract with Ferrari for 1978. He would take Ferrari's money in 1977 and see what developed.

As the 1977 season opened, James Hunt seemed to carry on where he had left off three months earlier: he was second fastest to Depailler's Tyrrell-Ford in the opening session of practice; fastest in the afternoon session; and faster still the following day, taking pole position – the ninth of his career. John Watson put himself alongside Hunt on the front row of the grid in his first race with his new Brabham-Alfa Romeo. Surprisingly, Scheckter was a disappointing eleventh and Lauda fourth. But no one remembers any of that. The qualifying sessions were dominated by an explosion in the pit lane on the first day. The bang rocked the pits and caused panic amongst soldiers and police who were convinced that an extremist bomb had been deployed. The noise caused Teddy Mayer instantly to drop to the floor, expecting a hail of bullets to follow as soldiers tried to shoot the bomber. Mayer said: "I knew that if it was a bomb, there would be bullets spraying everywhere."

But it was no bomb; it was a fire extinguisher bottle and a Lotus driver. Mario Andretti had had a lucky escape from death, probably the luckiest in Formula One history. Andretti found himself with no brakes and was blinded by oil flying through the air. With the driver now a passenger, the car hurtled down the track out of control. While Andretti was lucky in not having been killed by the explosion, he was doubly fortunate in also surviving the resulting accident. When the car came to a rest, his only grievances were sore eyes and tingling feet from the force of the explosion against the pedals.

In most Formula One cars, the fire extinguisher bottle was situated under the drivers' seat. The Lotus extinguisher was in the nose, and no one had ever considered the safety implications of it exploding. After the blast, pieces of Andretti's black car rained down on the pit lane and bounced across the track. But there was no sign of the car. The force of the blast had blown the nose off the car and ripped open the aluminum chassis, tearing off the brake cylinders and the oil radiator.

The entire paddock was shocked by what had happened and amazed that Andretti was still walking around. Opinion was divided in the paddock as to what would have happened had the extinguisher been located under his seat. Andretti seemed totally unmoved and was cracking jokes all day about the incident. James Hunt was deeply concerned; the horrors of what could have happened to vital bits of his anatomy if the extinguisher had exploded in his car were not lost on him.

On race day, Argentine weather forecasters proved very unreliable. While the forecast had called for heavy rain, it turned out to be a scorching hot day. On such days, Hunt took salt tablets but he had forgotten to bring them from Europe, and none could be obtained locally in Buenos Aires. He said: "The most important thing before a race like this is to make sure your sugar, salt and liquid content is topped up, and I had forgotten my salt tablets. The only thing I could get hold of was medical saline solution, the stuff they feed into your arm through a drip. It was disgusting. I drank one bottle on the Saturday night and one on the Sunday morning, and I didn't stop feeling sick until Monday night. I felt as though I was going to be ill all the time. It really screwed up my stomach."

Other drivers fitted thermos flasks in their cars filled with cool water. Hunt had orange juice with glucose in his, or at least that is what he told people. No one was quite sure.

When the race started, John Watson went into a commanding lead as Hunt made another of his poor starts, even falling behind Lauda's Ferrari. But he soon took the place back from Lauda and followed Watson closely around. The Irishman's tyres started to go off quite early on, and Hunt took the lead relatively effortlessly.

Hunt pulled away and already looked victorious. But on lap 32, he lost his steering, went straight on round a corner and ploughed into the catch fencing. A bolt had broken in the rear suspension. When Hunt arrived back at the pits on the pillion of a motorcycle, he was unsure what had pitched him off. He just said: "I was onto the quick bit of the circuit when the rear suspension broke."

He watched the rest of the race from the pits as Watson again led briefly and allowed Carlos Pace in the other Brabham-Alfa Romeo to go ahead. The two Brabhams were first and second and in command of the race. Scheckter in the Wolf-Ford was third after a mighty drive through the field.

Hunt was astonished at how much the Brabhams had improved and how powerful the engine was: "The Alfa in that Brabham was considerably more powerful than the Ferrari; it really was. It wasn't a heavy car but it used masses of fuel, so it used to start a race very heavy but in the latter part of a race with no fuel load I had no chance against them on the straights."

But they were not always reliable, and Watson's Brabham retired while Scheckter passed Pace's Brabham, which was having handling problems, to win with Reutemann's Ferrari third and Emerson Fittipaldi fourth. It was a personal triumph for Fittipaldi, and one of his best ever results ever in the Copersucar car. There were three South Americans in the first four, which pleased the crowed immensely.

Hunt was delighted for Scheckter, who was his closest friend in the paddock. The friendship had started in Spain, where he lived when he first started racing. Scheckter was another talent Teddy Mayer had let slip away after he debuted for McLaren in 1972. He ran only one race before being snapped up by Tyrrell, effectively to replace the retiring Jackie Stewart. When Scheckter moved to Monte Carlo, the two men kept in touch. Both were highly intelligent and enjoyed each other's views on life, as Hunt admitted: "I like people with good minds, I find it stimulating, and Jody has an exceptionally sharp brain. He's very funny but it takes him a long time to get it out because he's not an educated guy." Many read that as an insult, but Hunt continued: "Because of his intelligence, he was aware that he lacked education. He felt he was at a disadvantage and therefore he was very defensive, but he's got over that now. He's got his confidence."

Hunt advised Scheckter on his career and told him he thought his friend Harvey Postlethwaite was a good car designer. Hunt hadn't known about Patrick Head, apart from when Head had caught him in the Mount Fuji garage with a girl.

Hunt was aware that Scheckter had suffered at Tyrrell because the Frenchman Patrick Depailler was number one, and everything was done Depailler's way as a result. After the Zandvoort incident Hunt never thought much of team boss Ken Tyrrell, as he said: "I think Jody was being inhibited because Ken wanted to do what Patrick said all the time, and it wasn't necessarily what Jody wanted." But despite Postlethwaite, Hunt doubted the wisdom of signing for Wolf: "I wondered if he had gone for the money instead of the best drive. Mind you, I don't know whether there were any obvious championship-winning drives available to him."

The whole of the Grand Prix circus stayed on in South America for the fortnight before the Brazilian Grand Prix on 23rd January in São Paulo. Hunt had many friends in the city, which was awash with cocaine. A few years earlier, Hunt had formed what he called the São Paulo Diving Society. Having nothing to do with water, it actually referred to a popular sexual pastime called 'muff diving', which apparently Hunt found was to his taste.

Max Mosley remembers it well: "It was actually going a bit far. You've heard the New Zealand expression, 'Oh, he's a muff diver.' James was the honorary president of club."

Hunt resolved to have a very good time at the São Paulo Hilton, just as he had at the Tokyo Hilton. But his main entertainment theme for 1977 was surprisingly staid; he was obsessed with playing backgammon, often against Bernie Ecclestone.

A marathon game was held in the São Paulo Hilton before the 1977 Brazilian Grand Prix. It started on the Thursday afternoon and continued until the next morning, a few hours before the opening qualifying session at the Interlagos circuit. The players quickly grabbed breakfast and Ecclestone finagled the Argentine police to give the world champion a police escort, of which the rest of the players in his retinue also took advantage.

It was a ludicrous way to prepare for the race, and on the first day of qualifying Hunt was really unwell and in no fit state to drive the car. By the final qualifying the following day, he had recovered and managed to secure pole position for the first race of the year. The McLaren-Ford, suited to long straights and fast bends, easily looked the best car on the São Paulo track.

But the newspapers the next morning were dominated by Hunt's off-track antics. During qualifying, a Brazilian journalist from the *São Paulo Times* had been wandering up and down the pit lane. He rested his foot on the sidepod of the McLaren M23 as Hunt sat in the pit waiting to go out to qualify. Hunt didn't care much for this and, when the journalist asked him for a quote, he said jokingly: "All Brazilians are cunts." Not realising just how to the point the Brazilian media operated, Hunt was confronted the next day with a headline which read: 'James Hunt says all Brazilians are cunts.'

The quote quickly spread around the world, and John Hogan soon had executives from Philip Morris in New York on his back for an explanation. While Hogan may not recall precisely what he told them, he certainly remembers the experience, saying: "The phone lines were hot between São Paulo and New York over that one."

The race organisers were also behaving strangely and, overnight, the unexpected happened. The organisers, apparently ignorant of Formula One's subtleties, ordered the track to be washed down with pressure washers. They were seemingly unaware that, during a Grand Prix weekend, vast amounts of rubber are deposited on the track and that all race tyres are designed with this in mind. With all the rubber wiped off, the increased friction with what was now fresh tarmac meant that Goodyear's tyres would not last the race distance. This unsettled Hunt, who made another poor start from pole position and was passed by Carlos Pace's Brabham-Alfa Romeo, which stormed through from the third row of the grid. Reutemann's Ferrari also got past. Hunt took second back from Reutemann on the third lap. Three laps later, Pace made a mistake and Hunt dived past his Brabham to take the lead.

The 80,000 South American crowd, made up of Brazilians and Argentines, was in a frenzy of disgust as the British driver, who had two days earlier called them all cunts, passed their two local heroes with apparent ease; Argentines also had never cared for the British due to the constant arguing over the sovereignty of the nearby Falkland Islands.

During the overtaking maneuvers, Hunt had damaged the nosecone which dramatically altered the handling of his McLaren-Ford, but he still led Reutemann by four seconds, with Jochen Mass third and Mario Andretti's Lotus-Ford fourth. Mass crashed and took four other cars with him into the catch fencing, and Andretti started to close up on Hunt and Reutemann.

By half distance, the inevitable happened as Hunt's tyres became worn out by the bare tarmac. As his lead shrunk, with the memory of Mount Fuji still fresh, he decided to stop for new tyres. He remembered: "I reckoned I could go three seconds a lap faster on new front tyres, and there were twenty laps left. It would be worth the pit stop."

The pit stop took fourteen seconds and Hunt came back into the race on Niki Lauda's tail in fifth place. A lap later, he had passed the Ferrari and

Watson's Brabham-Alfa Romeo to take third, a long way behind Reutemann and Tom Pryce's Shadow-Ford, which had benefited from all the accidents and retirements.

Six laps later, tyre wear started to wreak havoc with the field as Pryce's car stopped and Watson's was also out. But Hunt couldn't catch Reutemann, who was 11 seconds ahead at the finish. Somehow, Reutemann's tyres had lasted even though, as he admitted later, they only had two laps left in them. The victory was a massive relief for Reutemann, as it had been a long time since he had crossed the line first. Niki Lauda was not so pleased; he had barely been noticed in the first two races of the season.

Hunt was happy to come away with six points but knew in his heart he could easily have won had it not been for niggling problems out of his control.

The South African Grand Prix followed a fortnight later, on 5th March. After São Paulo, Hunt was on a high and enjoyed himself a little too much on the South African Airways flight from London. He was travelling to South Africa early to do some testing at Kyalami the week before. Hunt usually flew economy class to save money, but it was full so he was upgraded to first class. The clientele in that section were not used to his antics. Whereas in economy, he found he could get away with any sort of behaviour and no one batted an eyelid, it was not so in the front of the plane, where a member of the De Beers family was sitting. The popular British singer of the time, Leapy Lee, was also aboard.

Immediately, Hunt indulged himself from the first class drinks trolley. He was soon paralytically drunk and encouraged Leapy Lee, then a well-known personality, to serenade the other first class passengers with his hit single 'Little Arrows.' Lee declined, but Hunt sang it anyway. The other passengers, particularly one female member of the De Beers family, was so thoroughly fed up with Hunt she asked the captain to radio ahead to the airport and report Hunt's behaviour.

As Hunt had not been rude to anyone or even unpleasant – just raucous and noisy – there was little the police could do. But they were well aware who he was and decided to make his entry into South Africa as difficult as possible, perhaps hoping to provoke a reaction for which they might arrest him.

On his arrival, Hunt and his luggage were thoroughly searched and he was questioned closely by customs officials. They appeared to be looking for recreational drugs, but found none. He was carrying a copy of *Penthouse* magazine, which contained within it an article about him and Niki Lauda. *Penthouse* was illegal in South Africa, and the police considered arresting him for that. But thinking better of it, the magazine was simply confiscated.

News circulated that Hunt had been detained, and journalists gathered at the airport exit to see if he came out. Still drunk, he told them that South Africa was a "police state" and "very rude to foreigners." But he added that it didn't matter because, "the South African girls are terrific and I'm available." His words were picked up by a wire agency and printed on the front page of every single newspaper in South Africa the following day.

He also told the journalists that his detention made him late for his first promotional engagement at a women's circle dinner, where he said he was to be guest of honour. Whether that was true or not, no one knew.

Recovering quickly, Hunt was at Kyalami early next morning to test the new McLaren-Ford M26 car. But the test was curtailed quickly when a brake caliper failed and destroyed a tyre at high speed. The M26 went off the track at around 140 miles per hour, broke through rows of catch fencing and stopped just in front of an earth bank. Hunt told local journalists covering the test sessions: "I investigated the catch fencing rather more thoroughly than was comfortable, and fortunately it worked very well."

Hunt didn't know why McLaren were persisting with the M26. He thought they should focus on the M23 for a sixth season of development. But Caldwell was adamant that it wouldn't be good enough, sensing it was at the end of its development potential.

But Hunt knew the M26 was a dog as soon as he drove it, as he said later: "I can tell you in ten laps if a car is worth pursuing. I could do the ten laps, come in and say: 'Throw it away, start again', but no-one's ever got the balls to do it."

Hunt's view of the M26 was: "Let's not mess about with it; it's not going to work, forget it. Make another one and we'll see if that works." But Caldwell didn't rate Hunt's opinion.

A week later, after much hedonism at the Kyalami Ranch Hotel and, as if to emphasise his point, Hunt scored yet another pole position; it was his third in a row in the old McLaren-Ford M23. Carlos Pace was second and Lauda third fastest, with Patrick Depailler making up the second row of the grid in fourth slot.

Hunt led from the start until Lauda blasted past on the long straight on lap seven. A few laps later, very keen to impress his home crowd, Jody Scheckter came up behind him.

As Scheckter's Wolf pulled alongside on the inside of the entry to the corner, Hunt refused to give ground and they negotiated the corner side by side, wheels banging together as Hunt gave way to his friend.

Afterwards, Hunt was surprisingly sanguine about Scheckter's maneuver considering the way he had pursued Patrick Depailler at Long Beach the year before. He dismissed it as nothing: "Oh, it's all right if it's wheel-to-wheel. It's when you get a wheel between the others that it gets a bit dodgy."

Hunt hadn't forgotten Depailler, however, and when he fell back into the clutches of the Frenchman, he shut the door on the Tyrrell-Ford in the middle of a corner and Depailler almost went into the barrier. But Hunt, somewhat shocked at the near miss, quickly gave way to him and then ran to the finish in fourth place as Niki Lauda's Ferrari won the race. It was his first victory since his accident and a seminal moment for the Austrian.

Lauda's victory seemed to cheer up Hunt, as he said: 'I was very pleased that Niki won the race. In my opinion, he has been driving as well as ever since Canada last year and I have been expecting him to win ever since. The pleasing thing is that this will silence once and for all the critics and non-believers who were stupid enough to think he had lost his nerve."

After the race however, there was little celebrating when the drivers learned that Welshman Tom Pryce had been killed on lap 23 in a freak accident. Pryce was in the wrong place at the wrong time when two marshals had irresponsibly run across the track to put out a fire in Pryce's teammate's car. It was not a life-threatening fire for Renzo Zorzi, whose car had pulled off at the start of Kyalami's long straight.

One marshal made it across but the other carrying a heavy fire extinguisher didn't. The marshal, a South African called Jansen van Vuuren, was hit by Pryce's Shadow-Ford and killed instantly. Pryce was knocked out by the impact with the extinguisher but his car carried on at around 160 miles an hour down the straight. It eventually hit a barrier and glanced off straight into the path of Jacques Laffite's Ligier. Both cars were buried in the catch fencing. A shaken Laffite stepped out of his car, but it turned out that Pryce was already dead from the impact with the marshal's fire extinguisher.

Lauda's mechanics found a piece of Pryce's suspension lodged underneath his Ferrari, but Hunt had not seen the accident and did not know about it until afterwards. When he heard of it, he was stunned that such a thing could happen on a Formula One standard track. He said: "Until there are professional marshals trained to a high standard and with suitable experience, there will be unnecessary deaths or injuries in motor racing. The sport should provide the facilities and money for professionally-trained and experienced marshals, and if it has taken Tom's death to impress this upon the authorities then he will not have died in vain."

Apart from not getting any results, Hunt had had a magnificent start to the season. His McLaren-Ford M23, breathed on over the winter by Alastair Caldwell and his men, was unexpectedly competitive and he felt that the championship was his for the taking.

To make that point, Hunt returned to Britain the following week to compete in the non-championship Race of Champions Formula One event at Brands Hatch. Around half the regular drivers competed and the only notable team not to enter was Ferrari. John Watson did the duties for Brabham-Alfa Romeo while Carlos Pace stayed in Brazil.

But the result didn't matter as, on Friday evening before the race, Carlos Pace was killed in a light airplane crash in Brazil. On Saturday morning, the news came through to the Brands Hatch paddock and the Brabham team owner, Bernie Ecclestone. Ecclestone was absolutely devastated by the news. Not only had Pace been his driver, he had also been a very close friend. It was the closest relationship Ecclestone had had with a driver since Jochen Rindt had died.

Although Pace had only won one race and had not been in Formula One for very long, his stature was far greater than his achievements. He was universally popular and beloved in a way that drivers like Carlos Reutemann were not. After he died, the principal Formula One circuit in São Paulo was renamed in his honour.

Ecclestone did his best to mask his emotions, and when Watson asked him if the Brabham team would withdraw from the race, he told him: "The guy was doing what he wanted to do and he would have wanted us to race." Ecclestone was a hard man, but Pace was the fourth driver he had lost in seven years. That evening, away from the track, he broke down with pure grief.

Watson went out on the track that afternoon to qualify. He drove a devastating lap and got pole. Hunt had not really known Carlos Pace well at all, but he felt the sense of unease that hung over the paddock that day. The next day, Hunt saw off the challenge from Watson and won the race with ease. His confidence could not have been higher as he flew off to New York to meet up with his girlfriend, Jane Birbeck, who was working at a picture agency representing photographers. After a few days with Birbeck, he then took the red eye flight to Los Angeles. From there, a car picked him up and took him to Long Beach, where he was to be paid US$10,000 by the promoter Chris Pook for a few days' work making personal appearances to promote the United States Grand Prix West.

Hunt was dubious about the job as he had heard less than complimentary things about Pook, who some people regarded as a chancer. Consequently, Hunt wanted his money in advance. But Pook fobbed him off and Hunt told him he would not do the work until he was paid. Hunt was only reassured after speaking to Bernie Ecclestone, and he agreed to wait until qualifying for his money. Pook was planning to pay him from ticket receipts.

Worried by Pook's refusal to pay him, Hunt also called John Hogan, who was in London at the time. As Hogan remembered: "He phoned up from Long Beach and whimpered about the situation, and I could sense then he was just about to go off the rails." But interestingly, Hunt didn't tell Hogan the real nature of his dispute with Pook.

Hogan's legendary sixth sense sniffed a problem, and he called up Patrick McNally, who then worked in promotions for Philip Morris. Hogan recalls: "I said to Paddy, who was on holiday: 'Paddy, go out there and hold his hand', so that's what Paddy did."

McNally was so good at hand-holding that Hogan appointed him Hunt's permanent minder; a job he did for two years. McNally was a former top journalist whom Hogan had lured to Philip Morris. He would later go on to head Allsport, the circuit trackside adverting agency. He also invented the Paddock Club hospitality concept and would make a great deal of money.

Hogan was surprised to hear about the dispute with Pook: "James shouldn't have been paid for it anyway. There was no need to be paid; it was our promotion."

When race weekend got underway, on Friday 1st April, interest was high thanks to Hunt's efforts in the previous two weeks. But Formula One was short two of its best drivers, and the mood was sombre as people realised that Tom Pryce and Carlos Pace, both undoubtedly future world champions, would never again grace a Formula One paddock. Alan Jones, the young Australian, replaced Pryce, and Hans Stuck Jr was in Pace's car.

Unfortunately, the race also marked the end of James Hunt's period of dominance in Formula One, and he was never again to be the main man. Lauda had regained that crown and underlined it with a brilliant pole position. Hunt wasn't even in the battle for pole, finishing up eighth on the grid. Even Emerson Fittipaldi's Copersucar bested him.

Lauda was now fully back to his best after his brilliant victory in South Africa. He had seen off the challenge from Carlos Reutemann for team leadership.

Hunt's lack of form was not completely explained by his distaste for street circuits and tight tracks. Whether Hunt was affected by his now public falling-out with Pook is unclear. It had been resolved when Pook handed him some cash, but the unseemly wrangling had left him in a dark mood. Hunt was angry with Pook because he had put his heart and soul into the promotions and spent a hectic week in California. Some days there was nothing Hunt hated more than being under-appreciated, and this was one of them. But with McNally and Hogan on hand, he got through the weekend intact emotionally, although it was a low point.

Unaccustomed to his low grid position, Hunt's McLaren hit the rear wheel of John Watson's Brabham-Alfa Romeo and he was launched into the air. Watson remembers getting a full view of the underside of Hunt's car for a brief scary moment as it soared over his head. The car landed square on all four wheels and, amazingly, Hunt carried on and managed to finish seventh. Scheckter, Andretti and Lauda battled for the lead, which Andretti eventually won. Andretti's victory marked the beginning of the ground-effect era in Formula One, although no one knew it at the time.

McLaren was all at sea again after its American debacle. Caldwell and Mayer decided it was entirely the fault of the long-in-the-tooth McLaren M23 – forgetting the dominance of the car in the opening races of the season. So the McLaren-Ford M26 was finally wheeled out for a race debut, 18 months after it had first appeared. But the car was effectively already out of date, made obsolete by ground effects. It was no M23, but just about held its own in 1977.

The Spanish Grand Prix was held over the weekend of 7th-8th May, and in qualifying Hunt managed to launch his new car into the air again, this time off the front wheel of Watson's teammate Hans Stuck Jr. Stuck was not as sanguine as Watson had been. When Stuck tackled Hunt outside the Marlboro motorhome, Hunt looked round, sneered at him and walked into the motorhome without a word, slamming the door right in Stuck's face.

Andretti won his second victory of the year from pole position as Hunt, starting in seventh place on the grid, retired on lap 11 with a broken engine after making no impact in the race. Hunt was further annoyed when his teammate Jochen Mass got fourth place in his old M23. Battling hard to beat Mass in qualifying, he became convinced that bringing the new car to Spain had been a huge mistake.

For the Monaco Grand Prix on 22nd May, Hunt reverted to his old McLaren-Ford M23 car, but development had stopped on the car. Not that it mattered. Hunt hated Monaco and had never done well there. His driving style and McLaren cars were simply not suited to tight street circuits.

Hunt had another problem at Monte Carlo. It was the perfect hedonist's playground, and he was the ultimate hedonist. He was welcome on every yacht in the harbor, and it seemed that he managed to visit most of them over the weekend. Unable to remain sober, his performance was affected the day after. No driver could get away with such behaviour at the Monaco circuit, which requires the sharpest concentration and maximum rest at night in order to succeed.

John Watson got pole with his Brabham-Alfa Romeo and Jody Scheckter won the race. Hunt's engine blew up halfway through on lap 26. The race also marked the debut of young Italian Ricardo Patrese, who had replaced Renzo Zorzi in the Shadow team. Patrese would become hugely significant in Hunt's life in later years.

With Monaco and Long Beach out of the way, Hunt started looking forward to the rest of the season. The Belgian Grand Prix on 5th June was almost a bun fight as 32 cars competed for the 26 starting positions. Competing in Formula One had never been so popular or so cheap. It seemed that anyone and anybody could buy a second-hand car and an old Cosworth DFV engine and enter a Grand Prix.

Mario Andretti was starting to become dominant in his Lotus-Ford 78, with its sliding skirts controlling airflow under the car. It was called 'ground effects' and Colin Chapman and his aerodynamicist Peter Wright had discovered ground effects completely by accident the previous year and grafted it onto the Lotus 78 design. Although the car was a compromise on tight circuits, it had vastly superior grip. As the car was developed, Andretti and his young Swedish teammate, Gunnar Nilsson became more competitive. At Zolder, Andretti got pole and Nilsson was third. Only John Watson could get close to the Lotuses and he split them on the grid. Hunt was back in his

McLaren-Ford and could only manage ninth on the grid.

Race morning dawned and it was raining. Hunt was desperate for an edge, as he knew his car was uncompetitive. He gambled on starting on dry slick tyres, but the gamble failed and the rain persisted. Andretti took out Watson on the start line, leaving Nilsson to win the race. It was as simple as that. Hunt came in seventh.

Getting on for halfway through the season, Hunt believed he was driving better than he had done in 1976, yet his season was becoming a shambles. The team, buoyed by what had occurred in 1976, were lulled into a false sense of security by the underlying notion that they had time to turn it around. In truth, Hunt had been very lucky in 1976 and lady luck wasn't going to favour him two years running.

Hunt was perhaps the first to realise that 1977 was not going to be a repeat of 1976. Sensing that the demise of the M23 meant he would never again be competitive, he wanted the team to develop a whole new car for 1978 with ground effects built in. On the track, Hunt could see what Andretti and Nilsson were doing with the extra grip of the Lotus 78. But McLaren no longer had the technical expertise to design a good new car. Gordon Coppuck, now in his forties, was a much less potent force than he had been. He simply didn't grasp the ground effects concept at all. Equally, while Alastair Caldwell was a mighty fine engineer, it stopped there.

Teddy Mayer's era at McLaren was also running out. Mayer was past his best and McLaren would never again be successful with him in charge. Hunt was stuck at his peak, and found himself in his prime on the tail-end of Mayer's glory days. It was not a pleasant place to be. In fact, Hunt likened Mayer in 1977 to General Robert E. Lee at the battle of Gettysburg in 1863. It was an unusual comparison, but in hindsight very prescient.

Mayer was all washed up, although he would not finally exit Formula One until a decade and many millions of wasted dollars later, as he tried desperately to recapture the glorious mid-seventies.

Lauda and Scheckter were fighting for the world championship, and Hunt was down in ninth place with barely a handful of points. But publicly, in an uncharacteristic display of loyalty, Hunt now defended his team and Mayer to the hilt, saying: "I know the only thing that will convince them that this is bullshit is for us to get a few results. All I can say until those results come is that I intend to retain my championship." That may have been a forlorn dream, but he added: "What people don't realise is that winning is easy.

Losing is the thing that's bloody hard work." It certainly was at McLaren.

At the Swedish Grand Prix at Anderstorp, the M26 at last began to show some promise. Hunt qualified third behind Watson and Andretti but the race was utterly dominated by Frenchman Jacques Laffite in his V12 Matra-engined Ligier car, which suddenly came good. With Laffite's victory, 1977 was shaping up to be a year when no particular car or driver dominated. Six teams and seven drivers – Andretti at Lotus; Laffite at Ligier; Hunt at McLaren; Lauda and Reutemann at Ferrari; Peterson at Tyrrell; and Watson at Brabham – were all capable of winning races.

The diversity at the front was playing into the hands of Niki Lauda, who was ever-present at the front but by no means the fastest. But he failed to finish in Sweden, and Hunt only managed twelfth. To Hunt's chagrin, Mass was second in the old M23 car.

At the French Grand Prix, held at Paul Ricard, Hunt sensed a real return to form. He liked the track and was entirely familiar with its special quirks. Mario Andretti was unstoppable in his Lotus and took pole, but Hunt was right next to him in the best showing for the M26 yet.

In the race, Hunt got away cleanly and led for the first four laps. It was the first time he had actually led a race in four months. But, failing to heed the wisdom of experience, he had been overindulging on *pâté de foie gras* again and was ill throughout the race and fell back to third. Poor old John Watson led most of the race but ran out of fuel on the last lap, and victory was inherited by Andretti, who was beginning to look as though he might be world champion as Lauda struggled in fifth. Watson was disconsolate afterwards, and Hunt hugged him and told him he felt his pain. As for Hunt, he had learnt none of the lessons of the past. Every time he was in France he overindulged on *pâté de foie gras* and paid the price.

At the midpoint of the season, Hunt had not won one race. He tried to put his troubled season behind him and resolved to enjoy himself. The 1977 British Grand Prix was at Silverstone and, despite Lord Hesketh's money worries, it was the perfect excuse for a week of festivities, bingeing and consuming large quantities of Moët et Chandon champagne. A huge number of Hesketh and Hunt cronies descended on Easton Neston, the beautiful Georgian house three miles from the Silverstone circuit.

The race was notable for the debut of a new type of car in Formula One. The Renault RS01 took advantage of rules that allowed teams to run a 1.5-litre turbocharged engine instead of a three-litre atmospheric engine. It was debuted by Jean-Pierre Jabouille. It was the start of an engine revolution that would eventually break the Ford Cosworth DFV monopoly. But that was still years away, and for the time being Jabouille had to cope with the huge time delay between pressing the throttle pedal and the car actually moving.

Hunt thought it a novel idea but had many other things on his mind. He was enjoying himself with his friends, and his morale was boosted by the in-house fan club who was cheering him on. But others were not so happy with the British world champion. Some unknown figure had stickers made up which read: 'James Hunt is a Steaming Turd.' They were being sold outside the pit lane and appearing everywhere. There was one on the side of Jody Scheckter's Wolf -Ford car and even one on the nose of Hunt's own McLaren M26, which seemed not to bother him a bit.

The prevalence of the stickers reflected Hunt's unpopularity with journalists, who felt he had changed since becoming world champion. One journalist who felt strongly about him at the time was *Autosport's* Nigel Roebuck. Roebuck said: "In his racing days, I never much cared for him. He had about him a posse of hangers-on to set your teeth on edge. They were not in any important sense offensive people, but they maddened you with their vacuous self-importance. The Marlboro motorhome was like a school common room of the worst kind."

In fact, Roebuck dreaded having to enter the Marlboro motorhome, where, as he said: "The loud and patronising retinue of Hunt worshippers would applaud and laugh uproariously at whatever James said or did. So whenever you went in there to ask him a question you'd get a facetious answer, given for the benefit of his audience. I found it all very uncomfortable and eventually I thought: 'Well, that's it, I'm not going to bother anymore.'"

But Roebuck always suspected that this was not Hunt's real personality, as he said: "Glamorous, successful, footloose and free, he was an obvious target for celebrity leeches. But there always lingered a suspicion that James himself did not really belong."

Many other prominent journalists detested him, including Peter Windsor and Maurice Hamilton.

In1977, Hamilton was just beginning his career and one of his jobs was to provide editorial material for a bi-monthly publication called *James Hunt Magazine*. It was the official publication of the James Hunt Fan Club. At races, Hamilton would spend hours sitting outside the Marlboro motorhome waiting for Hunt, as he recalls: "He knew why I was there and that it was in

Above: Hunt enjoying a cigarette on the pit wall during qualifying for the Japanese Grand Prix at Mount Fuji, on 24th October 1976. Hunt smoked 40 cigarettes a day until the latter days of his life. At the time, many athletes smoked and it wasn't regarded as a problem.

The German Grand Prix at Nürburgring, Sunday 1st August 1976.

Above: Niki Lauda looks pensive before the German Grand Prix, the race which would place his career and life in jeopardy. On the right, he appears on the pit wall with Jody Scheckter and James Hunt.

Victory at the Dutch Grand Prix closes the gap between Hunt and Lauda

Right: James Hunt celebrating on the podium after a first place finish at Zandvoort. The result brought him within two points of Niki Lauda in the world championship standings.

Below: Celebrating another victory at the Canadian Grand Prix at Mosport on Sunday 3rd October 1976.

The United States Grand Prix, 10th October 1976

Left: Hunt on the podium at the United States Grand Prix at Watkins Glen for the seventh time that season. It put the world championship in his grasp.

Left: The McLaren team celebrates another win for James Hunt at Watkins Glen, which brought him within three points of championship leader Niki Lauda.

Below: With Niki Lauda and the world motorcycle champion of that year, Barry Sheene, on the pitwall of the Mount Fuji circuit.

Bottom right: A comical message from Alastair Caldwell for his driver about the need to wear in new brake pads.

Showdown at the Japanese Grand Prix, 24th October 1976

James Hunt poses for David Phipps during qualifying at Mount Fuji with the mountain itself in the background.

Hunt ahead of teammate Jochen Mass at the start of a very wet and dangerous race at Mount Fuji.

Peter Nygaard

Right: Teddy Mayer holds three fingers up to James Hunt, signalling that he finished in third place. At this point, Hunt believed he had finished fourth due to an incorrect pit board and was angry about what had happened with his pit stop for fresh tyres.

Phipps/Sutton

Phipps/Sutton

Peter Nygaard

Top right: The McLaren team prepare a pit board to askHunt whether it is time to switch to dry tyres due to the changing weather conditions at Mount Fuji.

Left: Teddy Mayer and Alastair Caldwell hold out a pit board telling their driver to call into the pits for a fresh set of tyres.

Left: On the second leg of Japanese Airlines Flight 421 from Tokyo to London via Anchorage, Hunt finally fell asleep exhausted from celebrating. (Clockwise from left): Chris Jones, John Hogan, Alastair Caldwell and James Hunt.

David Phipps / Sutton

Getty Images

Solo Syndication

Above left: Sue Hunt is reunited with her son at London's Heathrow Airport on 26th October 1976 upon his return from Tokyo after winning the 1976 Formula One world championship.

Above right: Hundreds of fans made their way to Brands Hatch for the tribute meeting celebrating the new world champion. Hunt's popularity in Great Britain was at its height.

James Hunt, with Barry Sheene, is mobbed by fans and the media whilst being paraded at Brands Hatch after becoming the new world champion.

Below: The new world champion is interviewed by journalists at London's Heathrow Airport on 26th October 1976.

Getty Images

The 1977 Argentine Grand Prix at Buenos Aires

Above: With Teddy Mayer and Ray Grant prior to the start at Buenos Aires. He retired from the race on lap 32 and ploughed into catch fencing after his rear suspension broke.

Above: In the McLaren pit at Interlagos posing with a female fan, Sunday 9th January 1977.

Peter Nygaard

The 1977 United States West Grand Prix at Long Beach, California

Above: Hunt's McLaren M23 is launched into the air after hitting the rear wheel of John Watson's Brabham-Alfa Romero. The race marked the end of his period of dominance in Formula One.

David Phipps/Sutton

Above: James Hunt with George Harrison at Long Beach on Sunday 3rd April

Above: James Hunt was a backgammon fanatic and carried a board with him for impromptu games with people like Bernie Ecclestone (left) and Teddy Mayer (right).

Left: Jane Birbeck consoles her boyfriend at the end of the United States West Grand Prix.

The McLaren-Ford M26 debuts at the 1977 Spanish Grand Prix at Jarama

Left: McLaren mechanic Gary Anderson pushes Hunt's McLaren M26 back into the pits after his retirement at the Spanish Grand Prix, Sunday 8th May.

Below: Racing in the McLaren M26 for the first time at Jarama. Hunt made no impact in the race and retired on lap ten with a broken engine. He was further frustrated by the fact that teammate Jochen Mass finished fourth in the M23.

The 1977 Monaco Grand Prix

Left: Hunt on board a private yacht with world motorcycle champion, Barry Sheene, at John F. Kennedy Plaza at the Monte Carlo harbour on Sunday 22nd May.

Below: Hunt sticks up two fingers to the photographer David Phipps at the Monaco Grand Prix. He loathed the street circuit and was led astray by the hedonistic pleasures of the principality the night before the race.

Left: Hunt with Niki Lauda at the Belgian Grand Prix. Hunt only managed seventh in the McLaren M26 and Lauda was favourite for the title again.

Above: James Hunt loved the Paul Ricard track and brought his Mclaren-Ford M26 home in third place, his best showing of the season so far.

The French Grand Prix at Dijon-Prenois, Sunday 3rd July 1977

The British Grand Prix at Silverstone, 1977

Above: 100,000 ecstatic British Fans cheer for Hunt as he crosses the line in first place in his McLaren-Ford M26 at the British Grand Prix on Sunday 16th July 1977.

Above: Journalists felt that the world championship had gone to Hunt's head. An unnamed journalist had stickers made which read: 'James Hunt is a steaming turd' that appeared everywhere in the paddock, Hunt himself seemed not to care.

Above: Hunts' biography of the 1976 season was finally published In mid 1977. It sold 177,000 copies.

Left: Hunt with Stirling Moss after a disappointing Dutch Grand Prix at Zandvoort on Sunday 28th August. Hunt crashed out of the race after a challenge for the lead from Mario Andretti.

The United States Grand Prix at Watkins Glen, Sunday 2nd October 1977

Hunt drives home his second victory of the season at the United States Grand Prix.

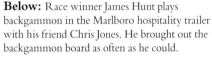

Below: Celebrating his Watkins Glen victory in this famous photo by David Phipps after the race finished. He appears alongside a *Penthouse* magazine promotions girl with cigarette and a beer in hand.

Below: Race winner James Hunt plays backgammon in the Marlboro hospitality trailer with his friend Chris Jones. He brought out the backgammon board as often as he could.

David Phipps/Sutton

Left: James Hunt finished 1977 with a flourish as he drove to victory in the last race of the season in Japan, with the iconic Mount Fuji in the background. The weather was rather better than the year before.

The last season with McLaren in 1978

Above: James Hunt finished fourth in the Argentinian Grand Prix on the 15th January, only three seconds behind second placed Niki Lauda's Brabham-Alfa Romeo. It was a more competitive start to the season than Hunt expected.

Above: Proof that Hunt could wear a suit and tie came at this early-season Marlboro sponsored event.

Above: Competing in a cycling race with Niki Lauda round the Jacarepagua circuit at the Brazilian Grand Prix on 27th January 1978.

Left: At the start of the South African Grand Prix, 4th March, he retired from the race after he "simply lost interest and spun off."

With Ronnie Peterson, Mario Andretti and Patrick Depallier on the pit wall at the Argentine Grand Prix on 15th January 1978.

Right: James Hunt stands by his retired car at the United States West Grand Prix at Long Beach, Sunday 2nd April, after he struck the wall before the pit straight on the sixth lap and knocked his right front wheel askew. Distraught, he blamed himself for making a "stupid mistake".

Above: Playing backgammon with Patrick McNally, who looked after him at races for Marlboro in 1977 and 1978.

Above: Teddy Mayer with James Hunt and his team-mate Patrick Tambay at the Monaco Grand Prix on Sunday 7th May, 1977.

Above: In an effort to find downforce, McLaren experimented with an unusual front wing configuration on the McLaren M26 during practice for the Spanish Grand Prix. Hunt went on to finish sixth in the race. It made Marlboro's John Hogan happy, but the car was no faster.

Above: With Brabham team owner Bernie Ecclestone on the weekend of the Swedish Grand Prix, which saw the debut of the Brabham-Alfa Romeo fan car. Hunt and Ecclestone always had a special relationship.

David Phipps/Sutton

Above: Although he would have preferred to have Giles Villeneuve as his teammate, James Hunt eventually warmed to his new teammate for 1978, a Frenchman called Patrick Tambay. They are photographed at Paul Ricard together.

The French Grand Prix at Paul Ricard, Sunday 2nd July

Racing in the French Grand Prix in what would be his best performance of the year, Hunt managed to finish third but was sick in his helmet for the third time in a race after over indulging with *pâté de foie gras* in local restaurants.

Above: Hunt at the British Grand Prix before spinning off on lap eight. The race was a disaster as Hunt's car spun right around at high speed without warning, causing him to crash into the Armco barrier. Hunt blamed both himself and the tyres.

Peter Nygaard

Above: Stripped down to his underpants at the 1978 German Grand Prix at Hockenheim on 30th July 1978.

Left: Hunt with Teddy Mayer and Alistair Caldwell, posing for David Phipps' camera at the British Grand Prix.

Tragedy at the Italian Grand Prix, Sunday 10th September 1978

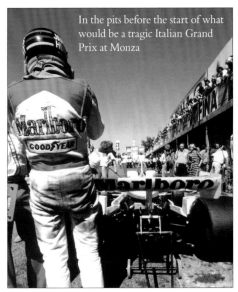

In the pits before the start of what would be a tragic Italian Grand Prix at Monza

David Phipps/Sutton

Above right The immediate aftermath of the seven-car accident which would eventually lead to the death of Ronnie Peterson. Hunt immediately climbed on top of the wrecked Lotus and tried to pull Peterson out.

Right: James Hunt, Professor Sid Watkins, Bernie Ecclestone and Colin Chapman run back to the scene of the start line accident which would claim the life of Ronnie Peterson.

Above: Ronnie Peterson lies in the centre of the track after being pulled from his burning Lotus 78. The amount of time taken for doctors to attend to Peterson was inexplicable. Italian Police were being overzealous, stopping anybody from the reaching the driver.

Right: The funeral of Ronnie Peterson on Friday 15th September 1978. (Back row): Tommy Peterson, Barbro Peterson and Erik Edvardson. (Clockwise from bottom left): Ake Strandberg, Emerson Fittipaldi, James Hunt, Gunnar Nilsson, John Watson, Niki Lauda and Jody Scheckter.

Solo Syndication

Left: The McLaren team poses for pictures at the United States Grand Prix. For the final two races of the season, the team were sponsored by Lowenbrau beer, another subsidiary of Philip Morris.

The Canadian Grand Prix at Circuit Île Notre-Dame, Sunday 8th October

Right: Hunt with Patrick Tambay (left) and Formula One doctor, Professor Sid Watkins (right), at the United States Grand Prix. Hunt finished seventh.

In the Canadian Grand Prix, Hunt drove his worst-ever qualifying performance to be 19th on the grid and then retired from the race on lap 51. He finished 13th in the World Championship standings with only eight points. Hunt called it "a disastrous season."

Above: At the Canadian Grand Prix, James Hunt is strapped into the McLaren M26 by mechanic Ray Grant for his final race with McLaren. He had repaired his relationships with Teddy Mayer and the mechanics, who pinned a note on his steering wheel that read: "This is the last one, good buddy – it's been a great three years." The McLarens ran in Lowenbrau livery for the final two races.

1979: A short spell with Walter Wolf Racing followed by sudden retirement

Left: James Hunt in his Wolf Racing overalls at the United States Grand Prix at Long Beach, on Sunday 8th April.

Below: Hunt drove for Walter Wolf Racing in the Argentine Grand Prix at Buenos Aires, on Sunday 21st January, before retiring on lap 41. The race was a serious wake up call as Hunt discovered he had lost some of his zest for Formula One.

David Phipps / Sutton

Left: In the Wolf-Ford WR7, which Hunt privately referred to as an "ill-handling pig", at the South African Grand Prix in Kyalami, on Sunday 3rd March. It was to be the only race of the season that Hunt finished, driving home in eighth place.

Right: At the United States West Grand Prix on Sunday 8th April 1979 at Long Beach. Hunt did not even complete the first lap after his gear box broke on the start line.

Below: James Hunt racing in his last ever Formula One race at the Monaco Grand Prix, on Sunday 27th May 1979. He announced his retirement two weeks later.

Bottom: Hunt contemplates stepping into a Formula One car for the very last time in the Monaco pits on the race morning of 27th May 1979. Few people knew of his plans.

his best interests to talk to me. I didn't then know him well enough or have enough clout to tell him to stop pissing about."

When Hamilton finally got the see Hunt, he and his friends made fun of the young Irishman.

Hamilton says: "I thought he was a right sod."

One journalist thought to be Peter Windsor called Hunt's behaviour: "Flagrantly petulant, insolent, rude and immature."

Ian Phillips was editor of *Autosport* in the years Hunt was successful in Formula One agrees with his colleagues that he was not a particularly pleasant man in those years. Phillips and many others believe that that success affected him for the worst as he says: "He lost the plot basically. We used to see him now and then, and we'd be civilised. But..."

Phillips blames the hangers on that used to surround him in those days. He says: "He had an entourage of people around him and he enjoyed his fame and his money. I suppose these days you'd call them hangers on. He liked to be around mates, he was not good on his own, but you know what happens, you get to a stage when you've achieved things and suddenly a load of sycophantic toss pots turn up tell you you're wonderful. It's the intoxication of fame."

Alan Henry, thought that Hunt went from being "immensely genial company in the early seventies to becoming a bit tiresome, partly because he surrounded himself with some tiresome people."

Even Jackie Stewart was critical of his behaviour, saying in 1977: "James Hunt would be all right when he grows up."

Hunt heard all the criticism and was surprised how vehement it was but he didn't have time to worry about it, as he said: "I certainly don't expect to be loved wherever I go, but I do sometimes feel that the press make their own decisions about people and it is very difficult to change their minds."

Alastair Caldwell, said: "James was always sure of himself, but he became even cockier and a lot of people didn't like it. He was a bit of a smart-ass. No doubt about it. But he was getting frustrated by so many journalists asking him so many stupid questions. Some of the good ones knew how to ask sensible questions, but they were in the minority."

Caldwell took some of the blame and said: "James' problem with the press was partly the team's fault, because the atmosphere at McLaren at the time, mostly engendered by me, was like a fortress mentality. We were not sympathetic to journalists, mostly because most of them were just so asinine and you had to be asinine to talk to them. You needed a company asshole, a PR person to talk to them, and we didn't have one."

Hunt tried to excuse himself by saying: "Don't forget, I came from nowhere. I'd just won my first Grand Prix in the year before I became world champion. So I was pitched pretty heavily in at the deep end. When I was driving everything was fine, but all the rest of it, what people expected of a world champion, really got to me. It was a huge change and all I could do was operate in the only way I knew – which was not to compromise myself. I just had to get on with it, in my own odd style."

Bubbles Horsley took a different view and said Hunt had always been exactly the same but that no one had been listening or bothered before – as he explained: "I don't think he changed at all. He always said and did what he felt like. I just think he had a bigger audience. More people were listening and he was taken more seriously – which was probably a great mistake."

Roger Benoit, the veteran Swiss journalist, then also starting out, said later: "He would not ask himself if he should say something, he would just say it. He never worried about saying the wrong thing, like some other drivers who only want you to write nice things about them. James was not a member of that club. He was no ass-licker." Benoit, unlike many of his colleagues appreciated that.

But ordinary fans attending the British Grand Prix knew little of such matters, and cared even less. He had 30,000 cheering fans on the Saturday of qualifying, and he put the M26 on pole position for the first time. Inevitably, John Watson was alongside him in the Brabham-Alfa Romeo, and Niki Lauda lurked just behind them, with Scheckter fourth. Andretti was nowhere on a track where grip was not particularly at a premium. Jabouille qualified the turbo Renault 16th and impressed no one.

Hunt had trouble with his clutch on the start line, and Watson got ahead and stayed in the lead for 49 of the 68 laps. Then his car started to suffer from fuel starvation and he retired. Hunt inherited an easy lead and crossed the chequered flag in first place, cheered on by ecstatic British fans. It was his first victory of 1977. Afterwards, Hunt admitted that for the second race in succession, Watson was the fastest man in Formula One. He said: "It was cruel luck and I really felt sorry for him." But, he added with a twinkle: "I was still very happy to see him go."

The race was also marked by the Formula One debut of Canadian, Gilles Villeneuve. Hunt had been directly responsible for putting Villeneuve into

Formula One and the McLaren team. Villeneuve, driving Hunt's old M23, looked as though he would finish fourth in his first race. But a faulty engine temperature gauge meant an unnecessary pit stop after which he was 11th, where he stayed to the finish.

Hunt was once again on top of the world and thought a good end-of-season run could still deliver him the world championship.

The day after his triumph, he played in a charity cricket match at the home of Earl Spencer, father of the future Princess of Wales. He drove straight to Althorp Park from Easton Neston. He was playing for the Duke of Gloucester's XI, against the Lord's Taverners' XI. Some three thousand spectators crowded into Althorp that day to watch him play.

Straight after that, he flew to Monte Carlo to play in a lucrative backgammon tournament. As he walked round Monaco, unmolested and virtually unrecognised, for a moment he considered leaving Spain and moving closer to his friend Jody Scheckter. But he decided he would become bored too quickly and shelved the idea.

After Monaco, Hunt went home to Marbella for a few days and Niki and Marlene Lauda came to visit. He then flew to England for the launch of his book *Against All Odds*. With the publication of his long-delayed 1976 season memoirs, he could finally collect the rest of his advance from publisher Paul Hamlyn. Hunt was five hours late for the start of the party due to an airline strike, but the book was nevertheless a huge success and easily earned Hunt's advance for the publisher. It sold 175,000 copies before the end of the year and ended up in the Christmas stockings of many of Britain's delighted schoolboys.

The book may have been a success, but Hunt's career was going in the opposite direction.

The next four races in Germany, Austria, Holland and Italy saw him retire four times in a row. It was a devastating sequence. In Germany, he was third when his fuel pump cracked. In Austria, where he was on pole position, his engine failed. At Monza, after a supreme effort, he put his car on pole in the final minute of qualifying. Looking set to win on a very fast track ideally suited to him and his car, he spun it, damaged the steering arm and was out.

The Austrian Grand Prix was marked by the maiden Grand Prix win for both a driver and team. It was a very rare event when Alan Jones won the Shadow team's only Formula One victory. It marked some welcome relief for the team after Tom Pryce's death only a few months before. It also highlighted what might have been for Pryce and Shadow. Hunt was very pleased for Alan Jones, whom he liked.

Of those four races, Hunt had shown the most promise in Holland, two weeks before his Italian Grand Prix flame out. The Dutch Grand Prix at Zandvoort now had a special place in his heart. It had been the scene of two back-to-back victories in 1975 and 1976. But 1977 was not to be remembered for what he did on the track.

It was the weekend of his birthday, and he managed to qualify third after Andretti on pole and Laffite beside him. Lauda was fourth. Hunt had a terrific start and actually led the first four laps. But on lap four came one of the worst moments of his career. He had a coming together with Mario Andretti's Lotus at the exit of Tarzan bend. Tarzan is the only high-banked turn on all the Formula One circuits and is especially tricky, even for brave drivers.

Andretti was chasing down Hunt after a poor start; he easily had the faster car and Hunt was defending his position. Andretti had a big grip advantage from his ground effects.

Hunt was leading and Andretti challenged him on the outside of the Tarzan corner. Andretti was going to use his superior grip to drive right round him. The two men disputed the corner and neither would yield.

Andretti, lacking Hunt's straight line speed, remembered: "I couldn't get him clean going into the corner. I had a few tries on the inside and I baited him to chop me off on the outside and I just took a nice arc on the outside. I was totally alongside of him at the exit and he just ran right over my right front wheel." Hunt crashed out, but Andretti drove on. A few laps later, Andretti retired as his Ford engine blew up.

In the pits, Hunt blew his top. Before Andretti's own retirement, Hunt approached Lotus team owner Colin Chapman and delivered a tirade. He shouted at Chapman: "Your driver will never win the world championship until he learns not to hit people on the track." It was an astonishing display of impoliteness and disrespect to Chapman, the most revered figure in Formula One. Andretti was furious when he heard of Hunt's exchange with Chapman, retorting: "He's a silly jerk. James Hunt is champion of the world right? The problem is he thinks he's king of the goddamned world as well." Hunt insisted that Andretti's choice of a passing place, so early in the race, was absurd: "It was his race, he had the best car and, sooner or later, he was going to get by me easily."

As Andretti told a journalist after the incident: "Hunt said to me: 'Well, the thing is in Formula One you're not expected to pass on the outside.' I said: 'Well, where I come from you pass wherever you can.' I thought he was making a stupid statement, actually. I told him: 'I deserve that piece of real estate as much as you do, and so you have to drive accordingly.' He ignored me, drove right into me and is trying to blame me because I wasn't supposed to be there. I had him and he didn't accept it."

Back in the press room, Hunt was ridiculed for coming out with the statement 'We don't pass on the outside in Formula One.' There was laughter.

Nigel Roebuck had strong views about what happened in Holland: "Mario had been all over him, lap after lap. They came out of the corner more or less side by side with James still slightly ahead, but with Mario's front wheels alongside James' cockpit. James really did what Michael Schumacher does a dozen times a year these days – it was just as if Mario wasn't there, he just took his car right out to the edge of the track leaving Mario nowhere to go but off. They touched and, as it turned out, that was the end of the race for both of them."

Roebuck attempted to get Hunt's view of the incident afterwards and found him almost deranged: "I remember him screaming and ranting and raving, so then I went to see Mario. Mario was every bit as angry, but quiet. It was a very vivid thing."

Afterwards, when Hunt could see he was not winning the argument, he changed tack and said his mirrors were dirty and he couldn't see Andretti coming up behind him. It was yet another paddock incident in which he did not come out smelling of roses.

The noise Hunt was making in Zandvoort provided cover for the eventual race winner Niki Lauda to conclude a deal with Bernie Ecclestone to switch to the Brabham-Alfa Romeo team for the 1978 season. It was Lauda's revenge for the way Enzo Ferrari had treated him. The Alfa Romeo-engine Brabham had been highly competitive during 1977 and looked a good bet for 1978. But Lauda knew the news that he was leaving for another Italian-connected team would infuriate Ferrari, so he kept it secret until the world championship was decided. As it was, Lauda had spent most of year avoiding Enzo, who had been chasing him to sign a new contract once he started besting Reutemann.

Lauda's move to Brabham also signalled another milestone in Formula One history. He negotiated himself the first million dollar a year salary. Ecclestone seemed to be itching to read that headline and, as a consummate dealmaker, he was almost desperate to be the first team owner to pay it. Lauda sensed this and used it to his advantage. Ecclestone had more than doubled Lauda's salary in order to secure him.

Lauda would later take enormous pleasure in hurting the 78-year-old Enzo Ferrari. He was quoted as saying: "I was happy that my departure would be a slap in the face for Enzo Ferrari."

Undoubtedly angry with Enzo for the way he had treated him after his accident, Lauda was even more upset with the "self-serving advisers" who surrounded him and exploited his age. After he had signed, and purely for his own amusement, Lauda finally opened negotiations with Enzo and, as he admitted in his autobiography *To Hell and Back*: "I really enjoyed turning down the most generous offer [Enzo] surely ever made." But when he told Enzo he didn't want to stay at the team, Enzo assumed it was a bluff. Later, it emerged that Enzo and his advisers had been totally unaware of his negotiations with Ecclestone.

By the United States Grand Prix at Watkins Glen on 2nd October, any chance James Hunt may have harboured of retaining his world championship was gone. As expected, Niki Lauda's fourth place was enough to see him crowned world champion for the second time. Lauda had only won three races all year but picked up six second place finishes along the way. In the absence of a dominant driver, Lauda's consistency won him the championship. In truth, Andretti, Reutemann, Watson, Scheckter or Hunt could just as easily been champion had things gone their way.

But Hunt tried his very best right to the end. He wrung the neck of his McLaren M26 at Watkins Glen and put it on pole, beating out the ultra-quick pair of Brabham-Alfa Romeos of John Watson and the resurgent Hans Stuck who, aware his drive was up for grabs in 1978, was trying to impress the boss.

Race day at Watkins Glen proved to be cold and wet, but that didn't stop 100,000 American fans pouring into the circuit to see if Mario Andretti could win the race and if Lauda could clinch the championship. Lauda, driving for points, didn't really feature, and the race proved a battle between Hunt and Mario Andretti. The two had long forgotten their differences at Zandvoort.

Andretti was well behind as the race drew to a close, but he drove the last laps like a demon. At the start of the penultimate lap, Andretti and Hunt were 6.5 seconds apart. At the start of the last lap, it was 1.5 seconds. Andretti had driven a lap five seconds faster than Hunt. That woke up Hunt, and in the end he cruised in over the line some two and a half seconds clear.

The hugely entertaining American race reflected the whole season. It was rare to have so many contenders for the title, and it made for a vintage year of Formula One. Whereas 1976 was the most dramatic season on record, 1977 was the most enjoyable for fans.

By finishing fourth at Watkins Glen, Lauda put the 1977 title beyond doubt. So just before the penultimate race of the season, the Canadian Grand Prix, the Brabham team announced that Niki Lauda would be its number one driver in 1978.

The announcement drove Enzo Ferrari into a state of apoplexy, far worse than anything Lauda had imagined. They had a furious exchange of words over the telephone. After he put down the phone, Lauda, who was used to Enzo's tirades, was shocked at the venom. He was so shaken that he even considered withdrawing from Mosport but, fearful of the legal ramifications, decided to honour his contract.

When he arrived in Toronto, he began to wish he hadn't. He was astonished to find that Ferrari had entered a third car for the young Canadian Gilles Villeneuve, who was to replace him in the team in 1978. Ferrari had spirited Villeneuve away from the hapless Teddy Mayer, who had failed to take up the option he had on the young Canadian driving prodigy. It was an extraordinary lapse by Mayer and inexplicable to James Hunt, who had brokered the original deal between Villeneuve and his team.

Lauda had had a contract with Ferrari in which it was stated that the team would always comprise only two cars, forbidding a third from being entered. Lauda had insisted on the stipulation because he considered the team incapable of running more than two cars competently. Enzo hated the clause, but Lauda had insisted.

Entering Villeneuve in the Canadian Grand Prix was a clear breach of the contract signed in June 1976, but Enzo had been in a difficult situation as Villeneuve insisted on driving in his home race and McLaren had already promised him a car for that race.

Lauda was astounded and told people that, had he been asked, he probably would have agreed to it. But he was incensed when he was not told and had to discover it for himself when he arrived and saw Villeneuve's name on the side of the third car.

Lauda attacked Daniele Audetto in the pits. Audetto called up Enzo and handed Lauda the telephone receiver. The two men had another furious row over the crackling transatlantic line. Lauda slammed down the phone and went to cool off.

As he had already been paid his full retainer, he decided to leave the team there and then. Lauda walked out confident in the knowledge that Ferrari had been the first to breach the contract. He immediately flew back to Europe and missed the final two races of 1977. Hunt was fully behind Lauda's decision to quit early, saying: "You can only put up with so much agro." A rancorous Enzo Ferrari also sacked Lauda's head mechanic, Ermano Cuoghi, after guessing that he would follow Lauda to Brabham.

The hatred was palpable, although Lauda eventually changed his view of Enzo Ferrari. As the years passed, he put his irascibility down to old age and poor advisers. Six years later, they were reconciled when they met at the Imola circuit by accident. By then, Enzo was 84 and Lauda 35. The two men hugged for at least five minutes, all differences forgotten. They reminisced, and Enzo told Lauda he had scored 15 wins in a Ferrari, 12 second places and 23 pole positions. He told him he had driven 3,292 miles leading races and scored 248 world championship points. Enzo loved his racing and, in the end, Lauda loved Enzo.

Lauda even came to love the Ferrari GTO he had been given as his company car when he joined the team. Only 213 were ever made, and today Lauda's car is worth more money than he ever earned at Ferrari in his entire four seasons with the team combined.

As it happened, Hunt wasn't too displeased to see the back of Lauda for the final two races. It made his job much easier as he sought to salvage something from a very disappointing season which had seen him score six pole positions and gain only two victories.

In Canada qualifying, Hunt was second on the grid next to Mario Andretti on pole. Peterson was third and Nilsson fourth on the grid. The race started as the grid order, with Hunt running second to Andretti and the others nowhere. But when Hunt came up to lap his teammate, he managed to collide with him despite Mass waving him through. Mass continued on, but the collision pushed Hunt into the most serious accident of his entire career.

Mass was on the right hand side of the track as Hunt got in his slipstream, desperately chasing after Andretti with no time to lose. An impatient Hunt veered left but Mass went left as well to get out of his way. Mass braked to let Hunt through; but Hunt, not realising what was happening, ran straight into the back of him. Hunt lost control and went through the catch fencing, which couldn't hold the car, and hit the concrete wall head on in excess of 100 miles per hour. Observers at the scene who witnessed the force of the accident thought Hunt was dead.

The car was completely written off and Alastair Caldwell, attempting to find some humour in the situation, described the condition of the car as "turning left at the dashboard."

Hunt said: "This was by far the worst accident of my Formula One career. I was very lucky not to have a broken leg or worse. My legs were trapped but by removing the steering wheel and wriggling out of my shoes I managed to extract myself from the remains."

He had had the luckiest of escapes.

But far from rejoicing, Hunt got out of his car extremely angry at his teammate, whose car did not appear to be damaged. Hunt did his usual trick of standing at the side of the track and moving into Mass' line when he appeared, which caused the driver to maneuver to avoid him at high speed. It was incredibly foolhardy. For three laps, Hunt stood at the side of the track shaking his fist at Mass. When a marshal ordered him away from the track, Hunt turned round and punched him in the face. The marshal fell down and Hunt suddenly realised what he had done. He picked up the poor American marshal and took him back to the pits, apologising profusely along the way. Professor Sid Watkins, the Formula One doctor, witnessed that incident and was impressed by Hunt's quick apology: "Most people do not realise the enormous mental and emotional effort these young men put into their performances."

But despite his efforts to make good his actions, Hunt had gone too far for the stewards and they were determined to punish him. He was fined CDN$2,000 for assaulting a track official and CDN$750 for being on the track.

The marshal, who had accepted Hunt's apologies initially, was approached by a lawyer who had witnessed the incident and was convinced to sue. Hunt settled out of court quietly with a confidentiality clause in the agreement. But friends later said it had cost him US$5,000.

Mass was very upset about Hunt's behavior, especially when he learned that he had bad-mouthed him around the paddock. Mass said: "He thought I blocked him deliberately, which is stupid. He opens his mouth very quickly, which is unfortunate."

Journalists watched aghast at Hunt's behavior and they all sided with Mass. With the fines and the marshal's intention to sue, this was an incident that could not be brushed away. In the newspapers the following day, two of the more memorable headlines read: 'Hunt the Punch' and 'Prima donna's punch-up.' The incident made headlines worldwide. Jody Scheckter eventually won the race, but no one seemed to remember. The South African was amazed at the lack of coverage for his win. Mass limped in in third, having driven an excellent race in the circumstances. Patrick Depailler was second.

Hunt couldn't get across the border to the United States quick enough, as he headed for Europe before flying to Japan for the final race of the season on 23rd October.

Mario Andretti, by now the dominant drive in Formula One, was easily on pole position and Hunt was once again second on the grid. The race would be between these two. But Andretti did not even last the first lap and Hunt drove an uneventful race to victory, leading from start to finish. Carlos Reutemann was second over a minute behind, and Patrick Depailler third.

But the race was almost stopped when Gilles Villeneuve's Ferrari ran into Ronnie Peterson's Tyrrell-Ford and took off into a spectator's enclosure, killing two of them. It was a huge incident and there was little celebrating on the podium thereafter. The accident also caused the cancellation of the following year's race.

Not that Hunt was on the podium. Along with Carlos Reutemann, he rushed straight to Tokyo airport to catch an early flight home. The promoters had promised him a police escort to the airport after the podium celebrations. But when the police escort didn't appear as arranged, Hunt just left. Patrick Depailler was left on his own to spray the champagne in front of a bemused 80,000 fans.

It had been a hugely frustrating year for Hunt and a disappointing title defence in a season that had held so much promise. Perhaps if things had been just a little bit different, Hunt could have been champion again. As he said, he almost won three more races in Argentina, Austria and Canada. Hunt himself was astonished he had done so well, saying: "The M26 really was an awful car and still, to my amazement, I won three Grands Prix in the M26."

He reflected: "The galling thing really about 1977 was that I should have finished on a hat trick. But still, to win two out of the last three was still what

I call only just compensation for my efforts for the year." He had finished the season strongly and what happened in the first half upset him even more, as he said ruefully: "I had a disastrous first half of the season and it got a bit better by the second half, but by then it was too late." He added: "We won three but we didn't do much finishing between them."

John Hogan remembers Hunt being mightily fed up when they went to lunch shortly after the season ended: "He was a little bit pissed that he could have won the championship a second time. He was going quite well, but then they brought out the M26 and it was just going nowhere. Had they stayed with the M23, he probably would have had a big chance. He was a bit pissed when they didn't focus on that. So I think he felt that he kind of gave it away in 1977. Although he always said: 'I won the championship once, what's the point in winning it a second time?'"

But his second-half performance showed he had every reason, as he flew back to Britain, to believe that he could win the title again in 1978 with a fully sorted-out McLaren M26.

But Hunt was about to embark upon the most disappointing and frustrating year of his life.

SHUNT

CHAPTER 31

A fear of death takes hold 1978

Danger sparks morbid thoughts

James Hunt had always taken the possibility of dying in a racing car quite lightly. He told people he would keep going full speed until the day he retired, regardless of the risk. Immediately after becoming world champion, he said: "Life's too short – it certainly can be in a racing driver's career – to relax. And you don't stand any less chance of getting killed if you relax." Sometimes it seemed as though the accidents never really happened to him.

While he was flippant about the possibility of dying in a racing car, he had clearly thought about it deeply; although perhaps not too deeply. According to Hunt, he had weighed the odds of dying alongside the risks involved in racing a car and found them to be in his favour. As he said before he was world champion: "The danger aspect is the biggest cloud on my horizon, and a constant heavy thought at home. But it's not something you dwell on in the emotionally charged atmosphere of a circuit. One has to weigh the odds, the risks involved as well as one can, and look at life and see if it's worth taking the risks for the time being. Once you have decided it's worth those risks, it would be counter-productive to worry about it. In fact, worrying about it would be very bad for your driving. You might as well give it your best while you are racing, and then stop at the right time." But how he could have made such a determination is unclear: seven times in his career, Hunt

489

had accidents that should have killed him. In fact, all seven were more likely to have killed him than not. The fact that he survived them was, each time, a miracle in itself. Seven serious accidents in a 13-year racing career is not a great survival statistic but somehow he wasn't concerned. In fact, some of those accidents were simply the result of careless actions, reflecting just how reckless he was in the early days.

From his first serious accident on 26th October 1968, when he ended up in a lake at Oulton Park, to the last really serious one on Friday 2nd June 1978, when he went into a barrier at Jarama and was nearly crushed by his own left front tyre, he was incredibly lucky. On the first occasion, he suffered no more than a cut on his head and, on the last, merely a bruised hand. Strangely enough, the most grievous injury Hunt had ever received in a car was in a road accident, in which he had a head-on collision in his Mini road car whilst returning from a race at Brands Hatch. It was the only time he ever ended up in hospital from something he had done in a car. Even his skiing accidents were far more serious than any motor racing accident had ever been.

But he thought it counterproductive to even think about it until an accident happened, or so he claimed: "Once an accident has started happening, you've just about got time to say: 'Shit, I'm having a shunt.' You can't usually do anything about the fact that you are having an accident, but you might have time to get the car to go in backwards rather than forwards, which hopefully would be better. Basically, you have just got time to get your head down and brace yourself." That was all the thought he believed it required until 1978.

In the early days in Formula 3, his rivals considered him a brave competitor, as one said: "He frightened himself and he was at the same time a brave bastard." Hunt didn't disagree, saying: "I intend to keep going full chat until the day I retire because it makes sense; an accident which starts at 165 miles an hour is as bad as one that starts at 170." There is no question that in the earlier part of his career, he took a cavalier attitude to death and injury.

He brushed aside all such worries until Sunday 10th September 1978, when he was intimately involved in an accident that befell Ronnie Peterson. Peterson was a close friend, and his death affected Hunt profoundly. They had known each other since they raced together in Formula 3. Hunt pulled Peterson out of his car on the Monza grid and laid him on the tarmac while they waited for the medics. Despite the terrible injuries to both his legs, some 27 breaks in all, Peterson was fully conscious and there was eye contact between the two drivers as Hunt lay next to Peterson and comforted him on the hot tarmac of the starting grid.

From that moment until the end of his own life 15 years later, Hunt was haunted by the fear he saw that day in Peterson's face. He said: "Ronnie knew he was in trouble, and I could see he was terribly frightened." In that moment, the realities of dying or being maimed in a racing car hit him full on. An hour after the accident, Hunt was within seconds of announcing his retirement. Hunt told Postlethwaite that he really didn't want to continue, and wanted to pack it in there and then, but Postlethwaite managed to talk him out of it, persuaded him to get back into his McLaren for the restart of the race and subsequently saved his career.

That evening, for the first time, he talked with his girlfriend Jane Birbeck about dying. And in the next few days, he thought deeply about what a serious accident would mean to his way of life. Birbeck remembers him saying that he wanted everybody to have a big party if anything happened to him.

A driver can accommodate many conflicting emotions, and the art of driving a race car fast is in many ways mastering the emotions. But once genuine takes hold, everything alters. Hunt had suddenly lost the protection of the 'It won't happen to me' syndrome. When that protection was replaced by the belief that it might, he decided to quit.

But he had to balance the risk against his other ambition, which was to win another championship; something that was well possible in 1977 and 1978. But in the same way that serendipity had enabled him to win in 1976, it now worked against him in these two years. In 1976, he had said: "I don't see myself racing on into the 1980s. It is too dangerous. I am not going to carry on risking my life indefinitely. I will only continue as long as I think I can win. There are too many other things I want to do." He elaborated: "More than anything else, I want to retire alive. So the sooner I achieve my goals, the quicker I can retire."

Hunt was very intelligent and he, more than any other driver, realised full well what the risks were. He demonstrated a level of thinking about what he was doing and how he was going about it. As Peter Warr says: "It gave rise to some of the casual remarks he made like: 'I'm only going to do this until I'm World Champion, cash in and then quit' thing. You don't hear those sort of remarks from people who don't think about it."

When Hunt finally did retire, his youngest brother David asked him for financial help in becoming a racing driver himself. Although James could well afford it, he refused point blank to give him any money.

When he left school, David worked in various odd jobs to make money to go racing – just as his elder brother had done. He got as far as Formula 3000, driving for Eddie Jordan, before giving up because of lack of money. David Hunt thought the danger factor was the reason that James wouldn't help him; he believed James would feel responsible if anything happened to him. Indeed, aside from withholding cash, Hunt tried his very best to end his brother's career. Hunt directly appealed to Eddie Jordan to drop him from his team on more than one occasion. Jordan recalls: "James used to ring me up and say: 'Why are you running that wanker?'" It was not in his nature to be deliberately destructive and, in any case, Jordan believed David had a talent worth pursuing, as he says: "He wasn't his brother but he was a good driver." Jordan believes now that Hunt was desperately frightened for his brother. The fear was borne from a realisation, belatedly, of just how lucky he had been. Ian Phillips, who by then had left *Autosport* and was working for Eddie Jordan agrees with that assessment: "James was a hugely intelligent man for all the play acting and this, that and the other, and he worked out how to go racing with the least amount of risk."

Long after his death, James Hunt's eldest son Freddie took up racing but it is unlikely he would have been able to if his father had still been alive. James certainly wouldn't have given him any money, just as James' own father hadn't before him. In fact, before Hunt died, he made his attitude clear: "I would discourage [Freddie] because if he was going to be any good he would do it in spite of anything I said, and if I managed to put him off he wouldn't have been any good anyway. The first thing you need is massive motivation from within. You'll never be any good at anything unless you have that." But it was mainly fear of anything happening to his brother or his son that prevented him from supporting either of them in their racing endeavours.

From September 1978 onwards, risk was constantly on his mind. Hunt wrote as much in his book *Against All Odds*: "The way I looked at it, I made my decision at the beginning of each season that I was there. You work out the risk and then you make your decision: 'Do you want to take risk or don't you?'"

What he wrote next, at the peak of his powers and three years before he retired, is telling: "It is a very specific risk, and the risk isn't the way you drive the car; it's whether you get in it or not. Because the difference between driving a racing car fast and slow is, in racing terms, probably two seconds a lap. Two seconds a lap slower is terribly slower than you'd normally do. At an average circuit that might be a difference in average speed of, say, four miles an hour. So what it means is the accident at when you're going flat out two seconds a lap quicker – shall we say you have an accident at 170, the other one's at 166 – well, the car's not really going to do a lot different between those two, so the accident's the same. And if a car fails, you don't really put a lot more strain on it; they are designed to do it. If they are going to break, they break anyway, and from a driver's point of view, I was more inclined to take the risk."

Ian Phillips best summed up Hunt's attitude, saying: "I think James mentally planned out what he wanted to do and how he was going to achieve it, and the moment he achieved it, that was the end of it." Or as Max Mosley said: "There's a fine line between being brave and being stupid, and James wasn't stupid."

The time to quit was nearing.

SHUNT

CHAPTER 32

The end of the road with McLaren
1978

A devastatingly poor year

If 1976 and 1977 had been vintage years in Formula One for different reasons, 1978 was to work out very differently. It was a year when one team would dominate and effectively be unbeatable.

James Hunt started out in 1978 less than optimistic. He was angry with McLaren team principal Teddy Mayer. What troubled Hunt was the continuing battle of wills between Mayer and the team manager, Alastair Caldwell, and some of the buffoonery Hunt believed the two men displayed whilst running the team. Although both were highly capable in their own ways, they were continually clashing. Mayer owned the team but they effectively ran it as equals, which led to a weakened chain of command.

This weakness manifested itself when they failed to sign the young Canadian Gilles Villeneuve as Hunt's teammate for 1978. Villeneuve was Hunt's protégé. On his advice, Mayer had taken an option on Villeneuve for 1978; but he let it lapse. So the rising star left McLaren behind and signed for Ferrari.

Villeneuve had been primed to replace Jochen Mass, who was moving to his friend Gunter Schmidt's German ATS team. Instead, Mayer signed Frenchman Patrick Tambay to replace Mass in the team.

However, Mayer was not entirely to blame for losing Villeneuve. Philip Morris had been dead set against Villeneuve as the sponsor, seeing no marketing

495

value in having a Canadian driver promoting its Marlboro cigarettes. Its opinion mattered because Philip Morris effectively would have paid Villeneuve's not inconsiderable salary. But Hunt felt Mayer should have put the team first and signed Villeneuve anyway.

Hunt discovered afterwards that Mayer, aware that Marlboro would not pay, wanted Villeneuve to drive for nothing and would not pay the young Canadian a salary. A disgusted Villeneuve, who was very highly paid to race in his native Canada, simply turned his attention to the many offers he was receiving from elsewhere.

In any case, Mayer and Caldwell were just as keen on the clean-cut Frenchman Patrick Tambay to replace Mass. Convinced that Mayer and Caldwell knew nothing about drivers, Hunt now understood why they had wanted to sign Jackie Ickx instead of him in 1976. Tambay was a quick driver but not in Villeneuve's class. John Hogan remembers the saga well: "It's where sponsorship does get in the way sometimes because, in Phillip Morris' world, a Canadian was no good for them at all. And that really was the issue because we had Patrick Tambay hovering in the wings and he was French – a big attraction to us. James said early on: 'I promise you, he's not going to get the job done. Villeneuve's the way to go.'" Hogan added: "One of the consequences was that Ferrari got on the phone to us at Phillip Morris and said: 'If you can't find a hole for him, we'd really like him.' So we said: 'Well, maybe.' So that's how that transfer happened. There wasn't anything mysterious about it as it happened. It was a surprise only because we kept it quiet. That's why it was a surprise."

Hogan believes now they might have done it differently: "He was certainly a spectacular driver, absolutely spectacular. Whether he would have done better and therefore lasted longer in a cool, calmer McLaren environment, I don't know. Commercially, for McLaren-Marlboro it didn't make any sense, and you're sometimes forced into things because of commercial considerations."

Hogan did however sign Villeneuve to a personal Marlboro contract, indicating that there were other politics afoot in Villeneuve going to Ferrari of which Hunt was not aware.

Hogan's explanation didn't stop Hunt telling anyone who would listen that the team bosses had no clue about the relative merits of different drivers. When the criticisms got back to Mayer, it caused tensions between them. But by then it was too late – Villeneuve was already ensconced in the Ferrari team. Hunt was right about Tambay he was completely inexperienced and not anywhere near as fast as Villeneuve. Hunt simply could not understand the attitude of Philip Morris, and told John Hogan what he thought. As Hogan admits: "Oh, James thought we were nuts. Yeah, and he told us all the same. He told Teddy, told me, told everybody: 'You're nuts, this guy is the future.'" The loss was a watershed for the McLaren team and marked their passage from being a top team to an also-ran.

But by then the team had other problems to worry about; namely, ground effects.

Right from the beginning, it was clear that 1978 would be Colin Chapman's and Lotus' year. Mario Andretti should have won the championship in 1977, and only bad luck had prevented it.

To underline Lotus superiority, Colin Chapman hired Ronnie Peterson away from Tyrrell to return to the team he had left two years prior. Peterson had left because of money troubles but he was tempted back by Chapman whose problems had eased as the global recession ended. The seat was available because the young Swede Gunnar Nilsson had been forced to retire early when he developed cancer.

In all truthfulness, though, it almost did not matter who the drivers were that year. James Hunt joked that even Jackie Ickx could have won the world championship in the Lotus.

Lotus would have a new car for 1977, called the Lotus 79. Until it was ready, it would rely on the older Lotus 78 model. The 79 employed full ground effects, and the 78 only partial ground effects. For six races, the other teams could take their chances.

The Lotus 79 worked by creating a partial vacuum of air beneath the car, which sucked it into the ground and enabled much higher cornering speeds. For ground effects to work, it needed a system to keep the air from escaping from underneath the car's flanks. Chapman and Peter Wright, a then unknown aerodynamicist, solved this problem by bolting on strips of brush heads to the bottom of the car's side panniers. The strips actually brushed along the ground and kept air underneath the car, thereby ensuring the integrity of the partial vacuum.

None of the other teams really understood what Lotus was doing, and as the season progressed they just bolted the same type of skirts to the sides of their cars without really knowing why. In fact, apart from Chapman and Wright, only one other man in the paddock understood the concept. This was former Wolf designer Patrick Head, now working with Frank Williams.

Head would eventually design a better car than the Lotus and would come
to understand Chapman and Wright's concept better than they did. But that
was at least a year away, and for now Formula One was a Lotus playground.

But Lotus' rivals were not entirely without hope. Ferrari also had a secret
weapon. It had signed a deal to race on Michelin tyres for 1978, ditching
Goodyear tyres for the untried French rubber. Michelin, the French tyre
company was new to Formula One and no one expected much from it. In
fact, pundits thought Enzo Ferrari had made a big mistake. Michelin introduced
a new tyre construction to Formula One called the radial; Formula One tyres
traditionally had been made of cross-ply construction.

Another change in 1978 was the amount of money suddenly sloshing
around. The recession was well and truly over, and the world economies
were booming once again. Driver salaries were going up every year, and
team budgets were beginning to head skywards. The number of teams wanting
to enter Formula One was also multiplying.

Formula One was also beginning to receive the benefits of increased
television exposure. There was at last some income from the sale of TV
rights. The effects of Hunt's championship victory in Mount Fuji in 1976
were being felt. Demand for live Formula One coverage in Europe, especially
Germany, meant that for the first time Bernie Ecclestone could get cash for
the rights.

The Brabham team owner was appointed chief executive of the Formula
One Constructors' Association (FOCA) and handed the job of officially
negotiating television contracts. He had been doing the job unofficially
for years. The teams had been doing this outside of the FIA's control and it
would eventually lead to conflict with later FIA president Jean-Marie Balestre.
It also marked the beginning of the Max Mosley-Bernie Ecclestone alliance
which would so benefit Formula One commercially in the years ahead.

Money was flooding into top teams like Lotus, and there was enough to
pay Andretti and Peterson the US$500,000 a year retainers they now
demanded. Just two years earlier, they had not earned even half of that.

So it was no surprise when Mario Andretti dominated the Argentine
Grand Prix from pole position to the finish flag. Although still in his old
Lotus 78, the ground effects were so effective that no one could keep up
with Andretti's pace.

Only his teammate and Carlos Reutemann could get close, and they lined
up alongside him on the grid. Hunt could only manage sixth on the grid,

with Lauda fifth.

Andretti drove off at the start and stayed ahead for all 52 laps. Lauda did well in his debut race for Brabham-Alfa Romeo to finish second only 13.2 seconds behind at the finish. Hunt was more competitive than he expected in fourth, only three seconds behind Lauda and third-placed Patrick Depailler.

When it was announced over the circuit's loudspeakers that Gilles Villeneuve had driven the fastest lap of the race, Hunt sneered at Mayer and gave him an 'I-told-you-so' look.

The race marked the debut of the new Williams team with a car driven by Alan Jones; a team and driver destined to have a big impact on Formula One over the years.

Two weeks later in Brazil, on Sunday 29th January, it was Peterson's turn to take pole position. The race was marked by the debut of the new Arrows team that had been started by ex-March man Alan Rees and former driver Jackie Oliver, with Tony Southgate designing the cars. They had all come over from the Shadow team the previous year after falling out with its irascible American owner, Don Nichols. Nichols had then sued them for plagiarism and they had had to totally redesign their new car, thereby missing the first race. The team, with its new driver Ricardo Patrese, also brought over from Shadow, was not immediately impressive.

The race was dominated by tyres, namely the new Michelin radials, which caught Goodyear flat-footed. Reutemann's Michelin tyres were to prove supreme in the race and he came up from fourth on the grid to immediately claim the lead, which he held to the flag. Hunt, who had managed to get himself placed second on the grid, had a troubled weekend. He had been fined for driving on the circuit without a crash helmet on Saturday and it had put him in a black mood.

But the race was marked for the best ever performance by Emerson Fittipaldi in his Copersucar-Fittipaldi car after placing second at his home Grand Prix.

Hunt spun off and, after a pit stop to change tyres, he got stuck in the sand pit in the run-off area and couldn't get going again. He was forced to retire.

Hunt blamed his altercation on a lapse of concentration and on being held up by slower cars. He said bluntly: "I simply lost interest and spun off."

In early March, after a five-week break, Hunt returned to his favourite playground of South Africa and the Kyalami Ranch Hotel. There, he was reunited with his hedonistic friend, the former South African tennis star Abe Segal. Together, he enjoyed all the pleasures on offer, from alcohol to recreational drugs, smoking and women. To say he indulged in all four joyfully and copiously would not be an overstatement.

The two enjoyed themselves so much that South African gossip journalists began following them around, printing stories about just how good a time they were having. South African journalists had few inhibitions and recorded events far more liberally than their counterparts in Europe and America. It was seventies excess redefined.

Hunt, reading all this, momentarily had pause to wonder what his girlfriend, Jane Birbeck, back in Britain would think if she had access to South African newspapers. Luckily, she didn't.

The race was held at Kyalami on Sunday 4th March, and Ferrari and Brabham had their new cars. For Ferrari, it was the third version of the highly successful 312T series, designated the 312T3, and Brabham had its new Alfa Romeo-engined BT46. The race also saw the return of a much modified Renault turbo charged car driven by Jean-Pierre Jabouille.

Lauda put his new car straight on pole position with Andretti second and Hunt a strong third. But the race was marked by the extraordinary performance of the young 24-year-old Italian Ricardo Patrese, who led the race until lap 63 in what was only the second race for the new Arrows team. He was halted only when his Arrows blew its Ford engine.

With Patrese gone, Ronnie Peterson in his Lotus 78 battled Patrick Depailler's Tyrrell to the last lap for victory. John Watson finished third for Brabham. Lauda retired with his engine blown, as did the Ferraris and both McLarens.

Ironically, in view of what would happen later, Hunt described Patrese's race-leading performance as "extremely impressive."

Hunt returned to England to compete with the Silverstone International Trophy non-championship race on the 19th March. It was an impressive field, including Andretti and Peterson in their Lotus 78s, Emerson Fittipaldi, Niki Lauda and Patrick Depailler. Hunt usually specialised in winning these British non-championship events, but not this time. Heavy rain decimated the field and Hunt spun off. The race was eventually won by Keke Rosberg in only his second outing in a Formula One car.

On Easter weekend, on 26th March, Hunt competed in a celebrity saloon car race at Brands Hatch with, amongst others, Jane Birbeck. It was Birbeck's first time on a race track and, although she managed to spin the car right round three times during the race, she was not lapped and the car was undamaged at the finish.

A week later, it was back to serious business for the third running of the United States Grand Prix West at Long Beach, on 2nd April. This time, Hunt flew in on the Wednesday and spent all weekend scowling at Chris Pook. After last year's shenanigans, the two men were not the best of friends.

With hardly any promotion, attendance suffered. But even if fans were short on the ground, the number of competitors was not. Formula One was so cheap to compete in and so popular that there were a staggering 30 entries for the 22 available starting slots.

With the Lotus drivers still waiting for their new 79 models, it was Ferrari who proved to have the best driver-chassis-engine-tyres combination. In fact, the Ferrari team was absolutely dominant on its Michelin radial tyres. The new Michelins worked so well it left Goodyear scrambling to catch up.

Niki Lauda set the early pace in his new Brabham-Alfa Romeo. It was now clear that the Alfa Romeo V12 was the most powerful engine on the grid, although it had obvious reliability problems. But Reutemann's Ferrari set pole time and no one was able to better it on Saturday. The first three rows of the final grid were occupied by three teams, Ferrari, Brabham-Alfa Romeo and Lotus-Ford, absolutely reflecting current form. There was no place for McLaren.

After only five races, Gilles Villeneuve had already and almost effortlessly established himself as one of Formula One's top stars. Hunt had an accident in qualifying which curtailed his running time.

Hunt was frustrated for the whole weekend. On Saturday, he had a furious one-to-one heated argument with Teddy Mayer in which he called him a "non-believer", implying he didn't believe in talent. Hunt was still furious that Villeneuve had been lost to Ferrari. For Hunt, Villeneuve should have been made his teammate, and not the nice but slow Frenchman with whom he had been saddled. He also maintained that Mayer had tossed Ferrari a huge stick with which to beat McLaren. Hunt was in no doubt that Villeneuve would soon be out-qualifying his teammate Reutemann.

Hunt simply couldn't comprehend Mayer's decision and was incandescent as he walked round the dusty paddock muttering to himself about the team's huge own goal. It was at Long Beach that he resolved to leave McLaren at the end of the season. Hunt told friends he couldn't continue to work for someone whom he didn't respect. He told Villeneuve the same, and that kicked off a chain of events that would see Hunt meeting Ferrari secretly later in the season.

A beautiful California day dawned for race day and around 75,000 fans showed up to the race. The start had been moved from Ocean Boulevard to Shoreline Drive in an effort to avoid any first corner accidents. It worked, and everyone got away more or less cleanly, although John Watson nearly took off Reutemann. This enabled Villeneuve to lead the field.

The order from the start was Villeneuve, Watson, Lauda, Reutemann, Andretti, Alan Jones, Hunt and Peterson. Villeneuve was driving superbly. But not so Hunt. On the sixth lap, he struck the wall before the pit straight and knocked off his right front wheel and was out. Hunt was distraught and blamed himself for making a "stupid error."

It was the race that marked the ascendance of the new Williams team and showed off exactly what a talented car designer Patrick Head was. His new Williams-Ford FW06 was the class chassis, and Alan Jones could easily have won the race.

On lap 39 Villeneuve, the race leader, had a coming together with Clay Regazzoni's Ensign-Ford car and was lucky to escape injury. Then Jones fell back after a front wing component failure and the leading contenders retired for one reason or another, leaving Reutemann to inherit victory from Andretti, who picked up some easy points in second. Jones still managed to set the fastest lap of the race on lap 27, underlining the car's potential.

It was a whole five weeks before the Monaco Grand Prix on 7th May, and Hunt went home with Jane Birbeck to Marbella to get fit before the grind of the European season started. It was the calm before the storm.

The Formula One circus assembled in Monte Carlo unseasonably early on the first weekend of May, and 30 cars turned up to compete for the 20 grid slots available for the race.

With so many cars wanting to get in the race, qualification became a problem even for some of the better known drivers. On this occasion, notables like Clay Regazzoni and Jochen Mass failed to qualify.

On his Michelin radials, Carlos Reutemann was dominant in qualifying but was hounded by the two Brabhams. Hunt qualified well in sixth.

Hunt's usual hedonistic activities were curtailed by his girlfriend's presence, and John Hogan corralled him to do some promotional activities for Marlboro. Hogan needed Hunt to attend a reception at Prince Rainier's palace on the hill, but Hunt wouldn't be coaxed out of his t-shirt and shorts. Although Hogan finally got him to wear a blue blazer over the t-shirt, Hunt didn't tell his girlfriend where they were going, and she too was dressed for the beach. Prince Rainier didn't seem to mind, though, and Hunt remained typically oblivious to what other people thought – although Birbeck was mortified.

The Grand Prix was a tedious affair, as it often was over the narrow streets. Hunt made a good start but a suddenly slowing car forced his McLaren-Ford off the racing line and he brushed an Armco barrier lining the streets. He was forced into the pits and the M26 was patched up. But the suspension had been irretrievably damaged and it totally collapsed a few laps later, and he was out. The race was won by Patrick Depailler's Tyrrell-Ford, with Lauda 22 seconds behind in a typical Monte Carlo procession to the chequered flag.

There was more lively action on the streets of Monaco later that evening. Hunt and Birbeck attended the famous Tip-Top bar along with John Watson. There were also some Formula One team mechanics there intent on some high jinks. The gathering spilled out onto the streets as the bar filled up.

The immaculately-tailored and uniformed Monegasque Police usually left the Formula One fraternity to get on with it on Grand Prix weekend, but on this occasion felt the need to intervene. They formed into a tight group and charged down the road with their truncheons extended to break up what they viewed as an unruly mob.

Hunt called it the 'Battle of the Tip-Top' and recounted to his biographer Gerald Donaldson what happened next: "Without any warning, [the police] charged down on the assembled throng, hitting out with rubber truncheons in the most disgraceful display of public brutality I have ever witnessed. If they had wished to disperse us, they had only needed to ask. But to hit girls standing with their backs to them over the head and in the face is the sort of behaviour that incites riots." People were trampled underfoot and a girl was thrown bodily over the guard rail by a policeman. Hunt was inside at the bar when it happened and Birbeck caught the brunt of it, receiving a black eye. Rushing out, Hunt lunged at the policeman who had hit her but was held back by his mechanics, who made a tactical withdrawal with their irate driver and Jane, with an ice pack on her eye.

It was a bad weekend for Birbeck, who also suffered terrible blisters from walking round Monaco in new shoes. She returned to Marbella in some pain.

Between Monaco and Belgium there was a test day at Brands Hatch when the new Formula One medical delegate Professor Sid Watkins was introduced to the drivers. It was the first formal meeting between Watkins and Hunt and they immediately began a great friendship, as Watkins remembers: "I met all the drivers then and James, of course. He was a remarkable chap, a gentleman, an absolute gentleman, a perfectly mannered guy." Watkins can't really explain what drew him to the Englishman but he admits that in all his time in Formula One, he only got really close to three drivers: Hunt, Ayrton Senna and Jody Scheckter. Watkins says: "I don't know really, it's one of things I suppose. I had it with Jody and of course I had it with Senna and James."

At the Belgian Grand Prix two weeks later, on 21st May, 30 cars tried to qualify for this race. Mario Andretti finally got his hands on the new Lotus 79, a totally integrated ground effects car, and the game was up for the rest of the field. Andretti took pole and obliterated any challenge from Reutemann and Lauda. Once the Lotus 79 took the field, the championship really was over. Peterson followed Andretti home second in the old Lotus 78, and Reutemann and Villeneuve trailed in after them. Hunt had by now realised that he was going to be out of it in 1978. He qualified sixth and retired on the first lap after his first brush with Ricardo Patrese, whose Arrows car hit him in the rear at the start. Hunt's McLaren was launched into the air and crashed back down all askew. Fittipaldi and Lauda also went out in the incident.

After Belgium, Peter Hunt did his first big deal away from his brother. Olympus Cameras, which was represented by Collett Dickenson Pearce's David Gray, was desperate to become more involved with Formula One and sponsor a team. Then it was spending US$90,000 a year as one of Hunt's personal sponsors. A team deal with McLaren was impossible because of a clash of colours with Marlboro; Olympus colours were black or very dark blue, and John Hogan would not allow that on his red and white car.

Ironically, John Player Special, which was part of Imperial Tobacco, had told Lotus' Colin Chapman that it wanted to withdraw halfway through 1978. It was a strange decision as the cigarette company had already paid half its sponsorship fee and was having a very successful season. Gray remembers: "John Player wanted to pull out because I think it had budget problems. Colin Chapman said it couldn't pull out if he could find no one to replace it."

Chapman asked Peter Hunt to help, and he called David Gray. Gray and Hunt quickly did a deal with Barry Taylor and Olympus' European managing director, Werner Teuwfel, and signed it at a Hertfordshire hotel on the last day of May. Olympus Cameras paid US$400,000 for a half season and shared billing with John Player Special. Gray got in his car and raced back to London. Olympus was due to debut on the car at the next race, the

Spanish Grand Prix at Jarama a few days later, and he had plenty of work to do. So did Peter Hunt, who collected a commission on the deal. Hunt was very happy for his brother.

With the Spanish Grand Prix coming up, Hunt was scheduled to meet formally with King Juan Carlos. With that in mind, he asked Jane Birbeck to make sure she could come. Birbeck didn't need much encouragement. She had finally read some of the press coverage of her boyfriend's antics in South Africa and had resolved to accompany him to more races that year.

Jackie Stewart arranged a dinner for Formula One notables at the home of King Juan Carlos prior to the Spanish Grand Prix. As a mark of respect to the King, Hunt swapped his shorts for denim jeans but Birbeck, mindful of what had happened in Monte Carlo, dressed appropriately for a formal dinner. But when Hunt arrived in jeans, Stewart was mortified and went into a huddle with the King's aides. Together, they decided to scrap the plan for a formal dinner and turned the occasion into a buffet supper by the swimming pool, for which Stewart deemed Hunt was more properly dressed. The King remained unaware of the original plans.

King Juan Carlos owned a pet cheetah, and the event was marked when the animal pulled off Birbeck's dress with its teeth. Birbeck was wearing one of the fashionable Diane Von Furstenberg wrap dresses and the King was left staring at her in her bra and knickers. The dress was quickly recovered, with the King admonishing the cheetah. Hunt made some joke to the King about how Jane usually didn't wear underwear, which luckily the King didn't comprehend – much to Stewart's relief.

At the track, both Andretti and Ronnie Peterson were equipped with new Olympus liveried Lotus 79s. As qualifying started on Thursday 1st June, the paint was still wet after 'John Player' had been sprayed over and the new Olympus stickers applied. David Gray remembers: "We had to pick the gravel off the side pods because the paint was still wet."

Olympus got terrific value as Peterson and Andretti proceeded to smash the field in qualifying and in the race. It was no contest, with Jacques Laffite the best of the rest in his Ligier-Matra V12. Hunt qualified fourth and managed to finish sixth in the race after a pit stop to change blistering tyres.

Hunt had a lucky escape from a heavy qualifying accident after an impact with a steel Armco barrier pushed the left front wheel of his car right into the cockpit area. The tyre left black smears on his windscreen and left Hunt with a heavily bruised hand. It was a very narrow escape from serious injury.

With seven races already gone in 1978, Hunt had not managed to finish one race on the podium steps. The year was shaping up to be a disaster.

And Hunt knew what the problem was: 1978 marked a period of great change financially, logistically and technologically; a change that happens in Formula One every so often. Such change also happens invisibly and is often hardly noticeable. But when it does happen, it quickly becomes very apparent which teams have moved with it and which teams have not. Teddy Mayer had no clue the change was going on, and it was to mark the end of him as a serious force in the sport. Over the years, the phenomenon has destroyed many notable and top line English teams including Cooper, BRM, Brabham, Lotus, Tyrrell and, currently, Williams. Ironically, only McLaren eventually managed to regroup and survive this culling; the others eventually disappeared.

Hunt laid the blame squarely at the feet of Teddy Mayer, and was beginning to believe he was a buffoon. He could not put the Villeneuve affair out of his mind. He had also lost some of the confidence he had in Alastair Caldwell.

In his head, Hunt had already resolved to leave McLaren at the end of the season. After he told Gilles Villeneuve, Villeneuve told Daniel Audetto, who then informed Enzo Ferrari. This culminated in Hunt and his brother Peter having a meeting with Audetto, who by that time was head of all Fiat's motorsport activities, to discuss a Ferrari contract for 1979.

Audetto confided to them that Carlos Reutemann had been a disappointment and would be leaving the team at the end of the year. There and then, he offered Hunt a drive alongside Villeneuve for 1979. When Peter Hunt demurred, James leapt in and said he could consider it but he would want to earn the same number that Niki Lauda was getting at Brabham. Audetto was shocked, as it was twice the sum Ferrari had ever paid any driver. At least 30 seconds passed before Audetto slowly nodded his head.

Now, apparently, it seems that Peter Hunt wanted to accept right away, but it was his brother who paused. It seemed too easy. Hunt had heard horror stories from Lauda about what a monster Enzo Ferrari could be and how political the Ferrari team was. He had also heard about the venom of Italian journalists and knew he would be a target if he joined Ferrari. Hunt was not sure this was the environment for him.

Peter Hunt told Audetto they would get back to him. They never did, and Enzo turned his attention to Jody Scheckter, who he found wanted only US$500,000 a year to drive the car. Hunt had never been motivated by money alone and didn't need Ferrari's million dollars that badly.

Meanwhile, back at the track, it was getting interesting. The Swedish Grand Prix on 17th June will be remembered for just two things: the debut of the Brabham-Alfa Romeo fan car and Professor Watkins taking over as Formula One's official doctor. Watkins was permanently stationed right at the entrance to the pit lane at every race and Hunt started a tradition of saluting him every time he came into the pits, as Watkins recalls: "Every time he came in, he saluted and I got very, very fond of James." Watkins started to hang out at the Marlboro motorhome with Hunt.

Neither Hunt, nor Watkins knew what to make of the new fan car. The Brabham BT46B was designer Gordon Murray's quick answer to the dominance of the Lotus 79. Knowing it would take him a year to design and develop a proper ground effects car to challenge the Lotus, and also knowing that putting sliding brush skirts onto the existing cars was nonsense, Murray took a short cut and created the same effect artificially. He effectively created turbo charged ground effects.

Murray's solution was to box in the engine with new bodywork. Then he fitted a large industrial fan mounted horizontally over the engine. The fan sucked air from under the car, creating a vacuum and extra downforce. Murray insisted the movement of the fan was a cooling device; otherwise it would have infringed an important rule that banned moving aerodynamic devices on Formula One cars.

The car was even cleverer than it looked as the fan was attached to the gearbox; and the higher the speed of car, the harder it sucked. As it went faster, the car gained road holding rather than losing it.

The legality of the car was immediately questioned, but when Lauda only qualified third and was slower than teammate John Watson in qualifying, no one was particularly bothered. Lauda would probably have done better without the fan and the other team principals reckoned the Heath-Robinson contraption on the back of the Brabham wasn't working.

But Murray and Lauda knew just how quick the car was and were actually sand-bagging in qualifying to prevent the car from being disqualified before the race.

Hunt was totally bemused by Brabham's innovation, and the sheer lack of it in his own team. By this time, his own team manager, Alastair Caldwell, was also fed up and was entertaining offers from the Brabham team to move there. Hunt qualified his car an abysmal 14th.

At the start, Lauda got ahead of Watson to chase leader Andretti. Lauda soon got by and Andretti quickly retired. Lauda's fan car was then in a race of its own, glued to a track which was very slippery. When any oil got on the track, the Brabham remained unaffected by it. The fan sucked the car to the track so powerfully that it was virtually impossible to spin off. Lauda was entering and exiting corners at terrifying speeds. Lauda reined it back in the end and won by 34 seconds, followed by Patrese and Peterson. Hunt finished eighth.

After the race, the stewards had no choice but to rule the car was legal since the fan did contribute to cooling and could not be outlawed as the rules stood. But Colin Chapman was determined to get the car banned. He could see all his team's good work with the Lotus 79 coming to nothing if the Brabham was allowed to race. Every team could quickly copy it and get around naturally aspirated ground effects in favour of turbo charged ground effects, which is effectively what the fan car was.

The FIA investigated the car and confirmed that the fan's primary effect was to cool the car, meeting the letter, if not the spirit, of the rules. But the fan car never raced again and was voluntarily withdrawn by Brabham. It later emerged that Chapman had threatened Ecclestone that Lotus would leave membership of FOCA unless he withdrew the fan car voluntarily. Ecclestone had too much to lose and had realised that the idea was, in any case, easily copied and that the advantage would be fleeting, if at all, by the following race.

With that resolved, Formula One moved on to the French Grand Prix. Buoyed by the success in Sweden, the Brabham team's confidence was sky-high as John Watson put his car on pole position. Lauda was third, and Andretti split them. Hunt qualified fourth, a performance that surprised him immensely, especially as he out-qualified Peterson's Lotus 79 in the process.

His qualifying performance translated into third in the race and he only just managed to hold on. Once again, he couldn't resist the *pâté de foie gras* and was ill for the third year in a row. He was sick in his helmet and only just made it to the finish line.

It turned out to be his best performance of the year, and his only first podium finish for 1978.

But it was much more significant than that. It would be his last trip to the podium ever and, even more sadly, those four points would turn out to be the very last points he ever scored in his career – which still had a year to run.

The race also marked a rapprochement with his new teammate Patrick Tambay, whom he was growing to like. The disappointment of Villeneuve's exit was fading and the two enjoyed a convivial dinner after the French race. Hunt told Tambay he was designating him "Formula One's 'fastest frog'" and emptied a bottle of wine over his head to anoint him. Tambay didn't get the joke, grabbed the ice bucket and emptied the half-melted contents over Hunt.

Hogan recalls Hunt and Tambay eventually becoming great friends. Tambay was a handsome Frenchman and effortlessly attracted women to his side, as Hogan recalls: "Tambay had a certain handsomeness which attracted pit followers, team followers, and that was fine by James. So for that reason alone he got on with Tambay very well and there was absolutely no problem."

With two very handsome drivers, the supply of girls to everyone in the team increased dramatically. But on the track, any success was very hard to come by.

Back at the McLaren factory in Colnbrook, England, with Caldwell and Mayer fighting, the McLaren team was floundering around wondering what to do about ground effects. Mayer ordered sliding brush skirts to be stuck on the side of the M26 so at least the cars looked like a Lotus 79. It was the limit of the American's technical knowledge. He also ordered Hunt to stay at Paul Ricard to test the modified car, instead of going home to Marbella.

Ironically, Caldwell would later claim to have invented ground effects in Formula One with the undeniably clever underside of the original M23 car. John Hogan thought the M23 clever but dismissed Caldwell's claims, saying: "I would define the inventor as being the first guy who knows how it works; so that's why the Wright brothers invented the aeroplane, not the Montgolfier brothers."

Initially, Mayer was in total denial about McLaren's problems. He had taken to publicly blaming the driver for the faults of the car. He said pointedly to a journalist: "I can get James to talk about women, backgammon, tennis, golf, business, taxes, Spain, food, childhood, but I can't get him to talk to me about racing cars."

Caldwell also had his views on the situation, as he told Gerald Donaldson: "He needed to be competitive, and if he wasn't quick he was disappointed. I think his interest in motor racing was never that great anyway. He didn't want to work at it. He wanted it to be easy. So when it became hard work, he lost interest. He wanted to just turn up and be the star, and when that didn't happen he was not happy."

Hunt didn't like what was being said, but he would admit his motivation was waning. In truth, he was looking for a way out of his McLaren contract but couldn't see how, saying: "I find it a great struggle to slog around endlessly in a car that is so fundamentally bad that whatever you do to it doesn't change anything. I've got no peace of mind at the moment. I only get that from winning. I must win if I am going to stay in motor racing."

But he said he was still racing with the same determination and enthusiasm: "I'm still racing to win, but at the moment I'm not doing it very well. But winning can come back to you at any time and, when it comes, you've got to be ready to capitalise on it. The important thing is to not get depressed about it. I've been through far too many bad patches in my career to let something like this get on top of me." But, of course, it did.

It was not only Hunt who was fed up with McLaren. Hogan admits that Marlboro was also getting very itchy feet: "The condition of the team was basically terminal due to an outside influence which McLaren and, in fairness, everybody else called ground effects. And it just wiped everybody out. Nobody had a clue as to what was happening in terms of ground effects. You just saw how much quicker ground effects cars could be than regular cars, and it was monstrous. It was seconds a lap."

Hogan admits that Philip Morris seriously considered dropping McLaren at this point but couldn't find another team at the time: "We wanted to stay in Formula One, first decision. Second decision was which team we should be with. There was actually only Lotus, but there was no chance because they were already sponsored by a tobacco company. So we had to, in a way, grin and bear it. There were good people at McLaren. Teddy was first class: honesty, integrity and everything. He was very open and said to us: 'Listen, until we get somebody who knows about ground effects, we're fucked.'"

The British Grand Prix was on the horizon and would normally be a much-anticipated occasion for Hunt. But in 1978, he was dreading the return to Brands Hatch. He knew that the Lotus 79s would dominate and that his car would not be competitive. He couldn't stand the thought of being an also-ran in front of his home crowd.

And so it turned out.

In qualifying in the skirted M26, he was half a second slower than he had been in the un-skirted M23 in 1976. He mused that his McLaren team had actually gone backwards, and the M26 programme had been an unmitigated disaster. He wondered what would have happened if all the team's efforts had been put into the M23 and the M26 programme scrapped when it had become clear the car was a dog.

As it was, putting skirts on the M26 was very risky if the engineers didn't understand what they were doing. It made the car unpredictable.

By then, the team had completely lost direction. The team's leadership was non-existent and Teddy Mayer was having trouble with his marriage, which made his decision-making and leadership even worse. The team was in a mess, and it was getting to Hunt.

But things were only to get worse. Hunt qualified 14th at Brands Hatch. The Lotus duo of Andretti and Peterson annexed the front row of the grid. Hunt couldn't even see the Lotus 79s from the seventh row. In the race, he was running alone in ninth place when the car suddenly and without any warning spun right around at high speed, as if someone had put on the handbrake. The car flew off the tracks and ran into the Armco barrier. Hunt said: "Nothing broke. The car was handling badly and I just made a mistake." Since the start of the race, he had been experiencing understeer in right-hand corners and oversteer in left-hand corners. He blamed the tyres.

But dark rumours abounded, and people said they had seen Hunt snorting cocaine over the race weekend. The inference was that he was still under the influence in the cockpit. There was no drug testing of any sort in those days and drivers could get into cars drunk if they so desired.

In truth, Hunt was already on the slippery slope, and the decline that would continue for the next 12 years had already begun.

The German Grand Prix at Hockenheim on 30th July was another Lotus benefit. Mario Andretti was looking certain to be crowned world champion. Goodyear had got its act together and seen off Michelin's challenge, and Reutemann was being demoralised by the sheer speed of his teammate Gilles Villeneuve. Brabham had also been knocked back by the effort it had put into the fan car, which had displaced its development programme.

Hunt was just trying to finish the season so he could go home to Marbella and lick his wounds. He was desperately seeking a way out of McLaren and was even talking to his nemesis Peter Warr about driving for Wolf the following year. By then, Jody Scheckter had told Warr he was leaving for Ferrari in 1979, and Warr was desperate to sign a star replacement. And there was no bigger star in the Formula One paddock than James Hunt.

But Hunt disgraced himself again at Hockenheim. In the final qualifying session, he was running eighth when his fastest lap to date was ruined by Vittorio Brambilla's Surtees-Ford, which got in his way. Brambilla had run out of fuel and was coasting to the pits with his hand raised to warn oncoming drivers. Hunt had to slow down and was incensed. A reactionary Hunt drove his car in front of the Surtees, slowed down quickly and then braked sharply. But it went wrong, and Brambilla was unable to brake quickly enough to avoid running into the back of Hunt's McLaren. The antic had been performed right in front of the pit wall.

Jumping out of his car, Brambilla ran down the pit road ready to hit Hunt, who wisely kept his helmet on and stayed in the car when he saw the veteran Italian approaching at high speed in his mirrors. He shouted at Hunt in his broken English: "You've got to be a crazy man to do that." Brambilla slammed his fists down on the top of Hunt's helmet. The McLaren mechanics grabbed the crazed Italian and carted him off back to the Surtees pit.

But the paddock's sympathies were entirely with Brambilla. Mayer shook his head. Just as Hunt didn't want to re-sign with McLaren, Mayer didn't want him to sign either. The relationship was over.

Andretti and Peterson dominated the race until Peterson retired on lap 36 with a broken gearbox. Hunt was disqualified on lap 37 after he got a puncture and took a short cut to the pits.

By the Austrian Grand Prix on 13th August, Hunt was shot through mentally. The Lotus 79s were on the front row at the Österreichring track, and Hunt qualified eighth. But he spun off on the seventh lap and that was it, as Peterson's Lotus won.

Hunt was no longer enjoying his racing, nor did drink and drugs offer the solace they usually did. The following morning, after Österreichring, he felt increasingly disillusioned and bitter. He was starting to look much older as well; overnight, he seemed to have lost his youthful features.

For the first time, he contemplated retirement and was even considering turning down the highly lucrative offer he had received from Peter Warr at the Wolf team. Wolf authorised Warr to offer him the magic figure of US$1 million to drive in 1979. It was double what Hunt had earned in 1978.

There was also another incentive for Hunt. His friend David Gray of Collett Dickenson Pearce was keen on the deal to take Hunt to Wolf. Olympus, despite its success, was looking for a way out of Lotus and offered US$1 million to be sole sponsors of the Wolf team for 1979 on the condition that Hunt was driving. It was strange for Olympus to leave its Lotus partnership so early but Gray was fed up dealing with Fred Bushell, Lotus's finance director and was delighted when Hunt left McLaren to go to Wolf and when the sponsorship went with him. In fact, the Olympus deal was worth exactly the same as Hunt's retainer, and even Hunt could overcome his general dislike of Warr for that kind of money.

Hogan says: "He despised him. There's a French word I'm trying to think of. That famous incident when he didn't buy him any lunch; that was Peter to a tee." But Hogan adds: "But Peter was very efficient at running a team. James had a high regard for his technical ability. He was not a great admirer of Warr as a person but admired him in technical sense. He used to call him 'the pubic warr' [after the rivalry between the pornographic magazines *Playboy* and *Penthouse* in the 1960s and 1970s]."

In truth, Hunt was not overly enamoured with the prospect of working with Warr, but he liked the chance of rejoining Postlethwaite again. Although Postlethwaite was vastly overrated and never actually designed a successful Grand Prix car, Hunt rated him and, more importantly, liked him.

By then, Hunt could have afforded to retire. He had made about US$2 million in his three years at McLaren and thought that would be enough to sustain him for the rest of his life. But joining Wolf seemed to be like getting a new lease on life, even if it was to turn out to be illusory.

Hunt tried a Lotus before he signed for Wolf, but he just didn't think the car was safe. This would come back to haunt him when he heard what Colin Chapman said upon learning of Ronnie Peterson's death: "Oh no, not another one."

So before the Dutch Grand Prix at Zandvoort, on the eve of Hunt's 31st birthday, it was announced he was moving to Walter Wolf Racing in 1979.

The early announcement, he said, would give McLaren plenty of time to find his replacement, sparing them of the agonies they had suffered with Emerson Fittipaldi three years earlier. Hunt said at the press conference: "I decided that, on the professional level, I had grown stale with the McLaren team. Our relationship had gone as far as it possibly could, but this new team is a tremendous stimulus. I think they're going to provide me with a challenge that I so desperately want.

"I've still got it in me to be a winner. I know it's still there even after a year like this. I am convinced that once I get back into the right car the good results will come. My aim is to be world champion in 1979 so that I can go out of this business on a high. That's the way I want to retire."

John Hogan believes that Hunt had realised he hadn't earned as much as he probably should have done, and that the million dollars was the main attraction.

Now that he had announced he was leaving, Hunt's relationship with the team suffered and he was constantly rowing with Mayer and the mechanics. Immediately, Mayer signed Ronnie Peterson to replace Hunt, as Peterson was disillusioned about his status at Lotus playing second fiddle to Andretti and wanted out again.

Ironically, with the announcement made, Hunt's relationship with Teddy Mayer improved dramatically. The pressure was suddenly off and Mayer knew he had Ronnie Peterson's contract in his back pocket. John Hogan recalls the thaw with great affection: "James had this sort of British sense of humour which Teddy appreciated. After that, they were always ribbing each other all the time." Hunt started to socialise with Mayer and his wife in Surrey, and attended many barbeques, lunches and dinners in those last few months of 1978.

Hunt managed to qualify tenth at the Zandvoort track, which was by now considered an excellent outcome.

He finished seventh at Zandvoort, but that in itself was a minor miracle considering his state of mind and the disarray of the team. Mario Andretti won the race from pole position, and Ronnie Peterson was second, with Lauda third.

The Italian Grand Prix was to prove the most traumatic of Hunt's career. Mario Andretti was on pole but Ronnie Peterson had a difficult qualifying and had to start the race in his spare car, an old Lotus 78. Gilles Villeneuve qualified second.

At the start, the race began before all the cars had joined the grid. The middle of the field was travelling faster than those stationary at the front. There was a huge pile up and Peterson and Vittorio Brambilla were badly injured. Brambilla had head injuries and Peterson's legs were broken in 27 places.

Three hours later, the race restarted and was won by Andretti from Villeneuve. But both were penalised and dropped to sixth and seventh, respectively. Lauda was declared the winner. But sixth place was enough for Andretti to be crowned world champion; an achievement that paled when Ronnie Peterson died on early Monday morning.

At the United States Grand Prix at Watkins Glen, on Sunday 1st October,

Mario Andretti returned home as the newly-crowned world champion and put his Lotus 79 on the pole in front of over 150,000 fans who had come to celebrate his championship. Andretti headed the Ferraris of Reutemann and Gilles Villeneuve and the two Brabhams of Niki Lauda and John Watson. Bobby Rahal made his Formula One debut as Wolf ran two cars for the first time. Hunt qualified sixth in a car that was running the livery of Lowenbrau beer, another subsidiary of Philip Morris.

At the start, Andretti jumped into the lead, but on lap three Reutemann went past, along with Villeneuve a lap later. They pulled away. On lap 23, Villeneuve's engine blew and Alan Jones earned a deserved second place finish. Reutemann was never headed and came home almost twenty seconds ahead of Jones. Jean-Pierre Jabouille was forth for the rapidly improving Renault turbo charged car. He scored the first points for Renault and the first for a turbo charged engine. Hunt finished down in seventh place, one lap behind the leaders.

The Canadian Grand Prix, at the new circuit around the parks of Montreal, was a sombre affair. According to the organisers, exactly 72,632 spectators paid to get in on race day, attracted by their local hero Gilles Villeneuve who, on cue, scored his first Grand Prix victory. It was a sort of triumph for James Hunt who had been responsible for bringing Villeneuve across the Atlantic into Formula One.

It was James Hunt's final race for the McLaren team and, by then, as the season began to run out, he had repaired his relationship with the mechanics and also with Teddy Mayer. Before the start, the mechanics pinned a note on his steering wheel that read: "This is the last one, good buddy – it's been a great three years."

He drove his worst-ever qualifying performance to be 19th on the grid and then retired from the race on lap 52 when one of the wheels came loose and he went off on the grass. There was time for one last altercation with a marshal as he crossed the track, but this time no punches were thrown.

By season end, Hunt was 13th in the world championship with only eight points – exactly the same as his teammate Patrick Tambay. It was six fewer points than in his next-worst year, with Hesketh in 1973. His car had retired in ten of the 16 races. Six of the retirements were due to accidents. Hunt called it "a disastrous season."

As soon as the season was over, he headed off to Australia and the Tasman series to drive a Formula 5000 single-seater at Winton for a fee of US$25,000. He was booked on Malaysian Airlines and took with him an entourage that included McLaren mechanic Ray Grant, his friend John Richardson and his brother Peter.

The flight to Australia via Kuala Lumpur was just a 24-hour drinking session. Hunt, who could barely stand by the time he arrived at Melbourne airport, was greeted by a party of dignitaries, journalists and a brass band playing uplifting music very loudly. He quickly learned his arrival was being televised live. Although Hunt was paralytically drunk, as he would say later, he "rose to the occasion." To disguise his condition, he said he adopted a "composed and thoughtful look" as if considering the full gravitas and import of the questions being posed to him. In reality, he was trying to steady himself to keep from falling off the chair. Afterwards, the Australian public was said to have been "impressed with his articulate and knowledgeable answers."

At the Winton circuit, north of Melbourne, 15,000 Australians attended the 30-lap race to see him win it easily. It was his first victory in 12 months, and the very last of his career.

THE END OF THE ROAD WITH McLAREN

SHUNT

CHAPTER 33

The death of Ronnie Peterson
A devastating weekend

On Sunday 10th September 1978, James Hunt effectively made the decision he would retire from Formula One racing. Although he would carry on for another eight months after reaching his decision, his heart was no longer in it after that fateful day. Only a few days earlier, retirement had been very far from his thoughts as he signed a new US$1 million a year contract with the Wolf team for the 1979 season.

The sequence of events that changed his mind started on Thursday 7th September 1978, when his friend, Ronnie Peterson, stepped off the plane at Milan's Linate airport just after lunch. Peterson had flown in from Nice after spending the previous week at his apartment in Monte Carlo, which had, for tax reasons, served as his and his wife Barbro's home for the last five years – since he stated earning big money. He was in Italy for the Grand Prix at Monza, due to take place that Sunday.

James Hunt and his girlfriend Jane Birbeck weren't far behind them, coming in from Marbella.

Meanwhile, the McLaren transporters bringing Hunt's car had left the Colnbrook factory on Monday evening and would arrive at Monza on Wednesday evening. The Lotus transporters carrying Peterson's car had also left the team's headquarters at Ketteringham Hall, near Norwich, on Monday

SHUNT

evening and would arrive at the circuit late on Thursday morning, after taking a more leisurely drive.

It was a poignant weekend for both men. Hunt had just learned that Peterson would be replacing him as number one driver at McLaren for the 1979 season, and they were due to discuss it at Monza. There was no acrimony, as Hunt had already announced he was leaving McLaren for Wolf.

The weather was warm and sunny and both drivers were relaxed when they arrived at the Villa D'Este, the fabulous hotel on the banks of Lake Como where they were staying.

Villa d'Este was once a favourite retreat of the European aristocracy and was the perfect antidote to the hectic atmosphere of Monza. It was surrounded by ten acres of private parkland and garden and had perfect views all around of Lake Como from its sloping lawns.

Unusually, Barbro was not with Peterson that weekend. She hadn't been well and had decided to stay home with their young daughter, Nina. In contrast, Jane Birbeck had given up her job and had been travelling with her boyfriend all summer.

Barbro's more frequent absences from the tracks had sparked rumours of difficulties in their marriage, and the Formula One rumour mill said the couple was not getting on so well. It was true that Peterson was going to his other home in England after the race and not back to his wife. The marriage problems may or may not have been true, but there were other good reasons for Barbro not to be at the track.

Whereas James Hunt's future may have been settled, Peterson's situation made it a tense and difficult race. Although he was regarded by many as the fastest driver in the world, he had never won the world championship. This year he had been capable of winning it, but a variety of political factors meant that only in special circumstances would he have been able to do so. It was because of such factors that he had announced he was off to McLaren. The announcement had increased the tension within the team.

In the past two races, in Austria and the Netherlands, Peterson had scored 15 points to the nine of his team leader Mario Andretti. Suddenly, Peterson had catapulted himself into contention for the world championship after Andretti had dominated earlier in the season. Andretti went to Italy on 63 points; Peterson had 51. Peterson could still win the championship mathematically, but that was the last thing team owner Colin Chapman wanted.

Despite the fact that Peterson had been the dutiful teammate and perfect number two, deep inside the situation rankled. Peterson believed that, in a fair fight, he could beat Andretti to the title. Peterson was 12 points adrift from Andretti, with a possible 27 to play for. Nowadays, the two drivers simply would have raced it out to the championship. But back then, it was different: drivers were gentlemen and team orders were obeyed. Andretti had bluntly informed the press that team orders were in place, ignoring Colin Chapman's advice not to overdo it.

Chapman had been doing all he could to help Andretti, even sandbagging Peterson's car in qualifying by putting in too much fuel.

Peterson could win if Andretti dropped out of the race, but if Andretti was behind him and running, he would be ordered to move over. There were no other contenders. The next nearest driver was Niki Lauda, but he was 30 points behind and well out of it with only three races to go.

The situation was made even more complicated by the fact that Andretti and Peterson were very good friends and had holidayed together with their wives many times. It made the inevitable tension between them impossible to bear.

It was also a lot worse than anyone realised at the time. As Andretti admitted years later, the two friends weren't talking at all in Italy. Although Peterson would not disobey team orders, their natural racing hunger had turned them into unspoken enemies since the previous race, when the Monza showdown had loomed. A bizarre, unnatural ambience reigned.

Andretti says now: "Peterson was one of my best teammates. When you can live in that same environment, operate, drive and still respect each other, that's a great thing. I admit things weren't the same as usual at Monza because of the tension. We were both a little uptight and hardly said a word. And that bothered me."

And that was the real reason Barbro stayed away. She knew Dee-Ann, Andretti's wife, would be there. For the wives, the situation would be very awkward. Barbro liked the Andrettis and didn't want their relationship to be destroyed over one race. But Peterson and Andretti bore no real grudges. In their air-conditioned John Player motorhome that weekend, he and Andretti were in boisterous mood.

More than anything, Peterson was upset with Colin Chapman. Although intent on honouring the agreement he had made pre-season with Chapman, to support Andretti's title campaign, he was angered by Chapman's efforts to ensure he played second fiddle, especially by manipulating his fuel load in qualifying.

He had caught Chapman out at the French Grand Prix. During practice at Paul Ricard, Peterson had been very quick and clearly embarrassed a much slower Andretti. Chapman ordered the Swede into the pits and told the mechanics to fill his tank half full, just as the fastest times of the day were being set. Normally, Peterson wouldn't have noticed some extra fuel, but he was so much quicker that day that it was clear Chapman had taken it upon himself to weigh him down with more fuel. Peterson's manager at the time, Staffan Svenby, remembers the tactic well: "Ronnie was not too happy about this at all." With Peterson weighed down, a slow Andretti was still beaten to pole by John Watson in his Brabham-Alfa Romeo; Peterson trailed in fifth. It was astonishing that he should be beaten by the clearly inferior Brabham, which had no ground effect."

Peterson, though happy to play second fiddle, was distraught about being slowed down artificially. He could do little about it, though: he had signed for the team because it had the fastest car. The ground-effect era was starting and the Lotus 79 was one of the most dominant cars ever seen in Formula One. So upset was Peterson, he resolved there and then to leave Lotus, and he joined McLaren after just a year.

By Monza, Peterson's patience was wearing thin and he was itching to flaunt his speed. Clive Hicks, Lotus' tyres and fuel manager during the 1978 season, recalls that Chapman was continually reassuring Andretti during Monza weekend that Peterson would not threaten his championship: "I overheard Colin saying to Mario: 'Don't worry, he's only a racer.'"

In Hicks' view, Peterson was definitely the faster driver. It became apparent once Peterson drove the new Lotus 79 for the Spanish Grand Prix at Jarama, in June. Andretti had received the first new car; a huge improvement on the old Lotus 78, which had only had partial ground-effect. The 79 was fast straight out of the box.

By accident or design, only one car had been available early in the season. Andretti was being protected by Chapman because of their longstanding relationship and the work they had put in to make the ground-effect cars such a success. Hicks says: "Once Ronnie got his car, he was so much quicker than Mario. At Brands Hatch, I was told by Chapman to put 'A' compound tyres on Ronnie's car. They were rock hard and should have slowed him down, but he was still quicker."

When Peterson announced at the Dutch Grand Prix, two weeks before

Monza, that he was off to McLaren, Chapman was even more determined to make sure Andretti won the world championship. The last thing Chapman wanted was the champion's number one gracing the McLaren the following year.

Chapman was enormously proud when his cars wore the number one sticker, as they had done when Lotus won the 1963, 1965, 1968, 1970 and 1972 drivers' titles.

Rex Hart, Peterson's chief mechanic that season, remembers: "Ronnie was looking forward to the race. He had won in Austria a month earlier and was in good form. We'd also had a one-two, Andretti and Peterson, two weeks before at Zandvoort. The cars were going well and we had high hopes."

But there were effectively two camps in team Lotus that weekend – Peterson's and Andretti's – with Chapman the biased referee. But no one could have imagined the result. Bob Dance, the Lotus chief mechanic said: "Chapman was anxious that Mario should win the race and was very concerned that, if he didn't win, his chances of the championship would take a severe knock. If Ronnie won, it would be a difficult scenario to contemplate."

And then there were the race cars. Andretti's contract stated that he had exclusive use of the two cars. For 1978, it meant that Lotus had to take four cars to each race. For some reason, Chapman had only built four new 79s, reasoning he could use the old 78s in a crisis. That decision not to build a fifth chassis was to lead to Peterson's death by a series of tragic coincidences.

It had started a month earlier, when Andretti had damaged one of the four 79s after a crash on the opening lap of the Austrian Grand Prix. For some reason, the car had not been repaired, so Peterson went to Monza with the old car as spare. If something went wrong, he knew he could not use Andretti's 79.

The 78 was outdated by then, but if Peterson had an accident and damaged his car he would probably have no choice but to race it, as the team was desperately short of 79 spares. The 79 had removable side-pods, which gave the team huge control over levels of down force and download distribution. But it was very difficult to repair.

Had Chapman organised the spare car situation that way, or were his excuses genuine? An unhappy Peterson suspected they weren't.

On Friday morning, Peterson woke at the magnificent 16th-century Villa d'Este and everything felt right with the world. He got into his silver Rolls-Royce Corniche, which had been provided for the weekend by the Milan

Rolls-Royce dealer. He began the 30-minute drive south to Monza Park with his manager Staffan Svenby in the passenger seat.

Andretti and Chapman, who were also staying at the hotel, went separately to the circuit in Andretti's identical Corniche, also provided for him.

James Hunt, also staying in the Villa d'Este, didn't have quite the same luxury mode of transport. The McLaren team were taken to the circuit in McLaren's American built GMC minibuses, which had been driven over from England.

Peterson jumped straight into his Lotus 79 for the practice session, but after a few laps slowly rolled down the pit lane and back into the garage. The Cosworth engine had blown up. The Swede climbed into the old 78 and went back out, only to return shortly afterwards. "No use driving this old machine," he said. "It's too slow and it's a waste of time to set it up, as I'm driving my race car tomorrow."

With that, Peterson joined Andretti in the black John Player motorhome where the American was giving an interview. All Andretti recalls now is Peterson fretting about losing his sunglasses. He says: "Nobody had seen them, so he forgot about them, sat down and off-handily began to talk about practice. For him, it had gone from good to bad to worse: second-fastest in the first session before an engine blew up; back in the old 78 for the second; failing back brakes and clutch slip on Saturday morning and most of the afternoon."

Peterson recounted a funny story about the 78: "As well as everything else, there was this lizard in the car. I kept trying to reach it to put it out of the car, but it kept getting away from me. It was still there at the end of practice."

When Hunt and Peterson finally got chatting that day, the Englishman filled him in on what he might expect at McLaren, but Peterson was clearly looking forward to the prospect of his number one status at McLaren in 1979. Hunt couldn't bear to tell him the truth: that the politics at McLaren would be little better than those at Lotus.

Andretti and Peterson left the circuit at the same time that Friday evening and, as racers will be racers, staged an unofficial Rolls-Royce race back to the Villa d'Este. As they left Monza Park, the two drivers looked at each other through their windscreens and, signalling to each other, raced back to Villa d'Este neck and neck. Staffan Svenby was in the front seat of Peterson's car, with Colin Chapman in the back. Svenby remembers Chapman being 'dead scared' and screaming at Peterson to slow down.

According to Chapman, the Swede won the Corniche race; but as Svenby remembers it, Andretti won.

When Svenby went back to his room, he could see the cars in the courtyard below parked side by side: "I could smell burning rubber, so looked out of the window and there were these two Rolls-Royces, one white, one silver, and the tyres and the brakes were still smoking."

Later that evening, Svenby and Peterson joined the Andrettis and Chapman for an awkward dinner in the hotel restaurant, discussing the day's events. Andretti and Peterson retired early to their rooms.

Peterson was up with the lark, and drove Svenby to the circuit. The dinner had somewhat lightened the team mood.

But his run of bad luck at the circuit was not over. In qualifying, he suffered with brake problems before a gearbox oil seal failed and lubricant leaked out onto the clutch. His mechanic worked hard and Peterson went back out, eventually lapping the 3.6-mile circuit in 1 minute 38.256 seconds. Peterson's time put him fifth, alongside Williams' driver Alan Jones. Andretti took pole alongside Gilles Villeneuve, with Jean-Pierre Jabouille's Renault in third place, Lauda in fourth and Peterson in fifth. Hunt could only manage tenth. The Swede, however, refused to be downbeat: "Everything went wrong," he admitted, "but I never give up. The race is not over until the man jumps up and down with the chequered flag, and I will drive flat out till I see him."

Early on Sunday morning, Peterson, once again up early, drove to Monza with Svenby. He had wanted to reach the circuit by 8:30am to beat the traffic.

During morning warm up, the rear brakes on his Lotus 79 suddenly failed at the second chicane and he crashed. He said soon afterwards: "When I came to the second chicane, the brakes didn't work and I went straight on. I don't know how many layers of catch fencing I went through until the car stopped. The catch is badly smashed and I guess I'll have to drive the old one in the race." As Peterson suspected, the car could not be repaired in time for the race. There was a faint hope that Andretti might release his spare car, which was standing unused in the pit.

During the session, Andretti, Chapman and Peterson discussed whether Andretti's spare 79 would be available. But it soon became clear that the idea was a non-starter, and Peterson resigned himself to using the 78. It was his death warrant, as the 78 was a much flimsier car with little protection at the front.

"Of course we wanted the car at the warm up," Svenby went on, "and it was Colin who made the decision, but the number one had the first call. There is no question in my mind that Colin wanted Mario to win the championship. He was American, and Ronnie was going to leave the team." It was a vital moment. Days later, the ramifications were lost on no one.

Other members of the Lotus team were equally aware of Chapman's intentions. Rex Hart said: "He wanted to sell Lotus cars in America, and Andretti was an American."

Peterson shut himself in the team's motor home to examine his legs, which had been bruised by the impact. He was unhappy about using the 78, but went along with the decision. While the championship was still open, he wanted to have the best possible chance of winning. A short time later, he returned to the pit garage and got into the 78 to get the pedals adjusted.

At 3 o'clock, 24 Grand Prix cars trickled out onto the Monza circuit for the scheduled start 30 minutes later. The formation lap was led away by Andretti and Gilles Villeneuve's Ferrari. As they arrived back at the start line, the starter raised the Italian flag.

He flicked on the red light as the first few rows of cars settled on the grid, and flicked to the green light before all the cars had finished settling. It created a wild staggered rush, compounded because some cars were already on the move before the green. But before the back of the grid had negotiated the Parabolica, let alone come to a standstill, the flag fell and the race was on. Villeneuve and Lauda got away quickly but Andretti and Peterson hesitated, believing a false start would immediately be called. Brambilla's Surtees was travelling at around 80 miles per hour when the green light flicked on, and it almost immediately brought him up to Hunt on the fifth row. The back markers were already doing around 50 miles per hour and several of them cars passed the midfield cars. All the moving cars were still in second or third gear when the race began.

The wide starting grid at Monza funnelled abruptly into the short straight leading to the first chicane, and compressed the field. Peterson was caught and swallowed by at least half the field. Jody Scheckter's Wolf-Ford was moving much faster and moved from left to right across the track to avoid hitting the Lotus and Hunt's McLaren, which was on Peterson's right. Peterson moved slightly to the right and Ricardo Patrese's Arrows was on the right side of the track, intent on going past. Patrese cut in behind Scheckter and left Hunt's McLaren with nowhere to go.

What happened next is disputed to this day. Hunt claimed Patrese hit him

– forcing him into Peterson – but Patrese rejected that version: "I was not involved because I was in front of the accident. Ronnie had a very slow start in the t-car and everybody came from behind very quickly. There was a touch between Peterson and Hunt, and the accident happened."

Video tapes show that Hunt was forced into Peterson's Lotus and then launched airborne, pushing the Lotus 78 at high speed into the barriers. Hunt's McLaren was then hit by other spinning cars.

The 78 was the wrong car for a frontal impact accident. In fact, the chassis was very vulnerable to a frontal impact. It was made of aluminium honey-comb with fuel tanks in the side extensions, unlike in the 79 where they were mounted behind the driver. Worse still, the 78 suffered from fuel pick-up problems and had been modified with the installation of a fuel catch tank in the cockpit footwell. The catch tank exploded in the impact and created a fireball as it impacted with Peterson's feet, pushing the chassis metal and pedals into his legs.

The Lotus had too much momentum as Brambilla's Surtees ran straight into it, pushing it back the other way and catching seven other cars in the chaos. It had all happened in an instant, and the Lotus ricocheted back onto the circuit before coming to a halt in the middle of the track. When the cars eventually stopped, Peterson was trapped in the burning Lotus and Italian driver Brambilla was unconscious.

Hunt was straight out of his car and on top of the Lotus, struggling to get Peterson out of the car. A policeman grabbed a fire extinguisher and put out the flames quickly before marshals took over.

Twisted metal and pedals were trapping Peterson in the car, and Patrick Depailler kicked the steering wheel out of the way as Hunt tried to lift the driver. Hunt said: "I tried to pull Ronnie clear but found one of his legs trapped between the steering wheel and what remained of the chassis. Flames and smoke enveloped the whole car again but the marshal flattened them and, with additional assistance from Clay [Regazzoni], we managed to wrench the steering wheel clear. I picked up Ronnie by the epaulettes of his uniform and dragged him clear of the car."

Hunt put the Swede down on the tarmac and sat with him, looking round for any signs of a doctor. Brambilla was laid down beside him unconscious. The Italian's injuries looked far more serious than those of Peterson.

Hunt stayed with Peterson and talked to him, avoiding looking at his injuries. Peterson propped himself up on his elbows but his legs were covered.

Hunt said: "I was reassuring Ronnie, but I knew that his injuries must be pretty severe as there was nothing left to the front end of the car."

The amount of time it took for doctors to attend to Peterson was inexplicable. The Italian police were being overzealous and stopping everyone, including the doctors, from reaching the injured drivers. This included Professor Sid Watkins, the recently appointed Formula One doctor, who was stationed at the race control building, a five-minute walk from the medical centre. When the accident happened, Watkins had immediately set off on foot to help, but was stopped by the police. They had formed a barrier across the track and were letting no one through. Watkins didn't have the authority to pass through, and was helpless in the hands of the Italians.

Assuming Italian doctors were on hand, and having no idea as to the severity of the injuries, Watkins assumed he was not needed and began the walk back to the medical centre, where the injured drivers were to be taken.

The Monza medical centre was located at the back of the paddock. The medical facilities were quite good by the standards of the day. The centre was run by six doctors trained in anaesthesia and trauma care. There were five ambulances and two mobile intensive care units around the circuit, staffed by more doctors and nurses.

There was also a helicopter ready to take any injured drivers to the Ospedale Maggiore Hospital at Niguardia, which was ten minutes away by air. Watkins reached the medical centre at the same time as the ambulance containing Peterson. But the injured drivers had been let down by the circuit; 18 minutes had passed between Hunt's removal of Peterson from his Lotus and the arrival of the ambulance at the crash scene.

A disconsolate Hunt walked back to the pits and whacked a policeman who wanted his autograph. With so many of the teams' cars involved, all the mechanics were waiting anxiously for news of their drivers. Rex Hart remembers: "I was in the pits, where we'd gone after leaving the starting grid. They'd done the warming up lap and come onto the grid. The cars went, but then we heard the noise and knew something was going on. A great cloud of smoke went up and, a minute or so later, someone came along and said Ronnie was involved in it. The news then filtered through slowly."

Journalists questioned Hunt about what happened and straightaway he blamed Ricardo Patrese, insisting that his Arrows had hit his car, saying: "Patrese, with nowhere to go, without warning, barged over on me, pushing me into Ronnie. In the ensuing sandwich, my car flew up in the air and slid sideways down the middle of the track. Behind me, all hell broke loose." Shock was beginning to set in from what he had seen, and Hunt didn't want to go to the Marlboro motorhome. Seeking some peace and quiet, he went to the Wolf team motorhome.

The paddock and media centre were in a chaotic state. The journalists present were already hailing Hunt as a hero who had saved Peterson's life. That annoyed Hunt intensely, as he told them in the Monza paddock: "Don't make a big hero thing out of this. I happened to be one of the first on the scene. I was dressed in a fireproof driving suit, so I didn't have to do anything brave." But they persisted and he became incensed, saying later: "They had spent the whole season knocking me, and then all of a sudden they were quite unjustifiably acclaiming me as a hero, which I found very embarrassing. When you're down, they kick you and then they kick you again. When you're up, they go right over the top."

Back at the medical centre, it was mayhem. Watkins remembers: "There was a huge crowd of *tifosi* outside the security rails of the centre and spilling over the access roads. Ronnie was quite conscious and rational but both his legs were badly smashed, and he had some superficial burns on the shoulder and chest. We got several intravenous infusions up into the arm veins and his blood pressure was surprisingly normal. The medical team were busy splinting the leg fractures, many of which appeared to be technically compound. Ronnie was talking sensibly. He was very anxious that I should come to the hospital as soon as I could, and that I promised. In fact, he said: 'Please don't leave me, Prof.'"

But Watkins was committed to helping all the injured drivers. Brambilla, who had been hit by a wheel, had a severe head injury. At the time, it looked far more serious than it was. He was suffering from left-side paralysis of his limbs, but was stable. Brambilla would go on to make a full recovery. Hans-Joachim Stuck, who had briefly been knocked out after being hit by another tyre, also had a severe headache and was told he should not join the restart.

Peterson was eventually taken to a waiting helicopter on a stretcher, where crowds of *tifosi* pushed and shoved to touch the injured driver. As Peterson was stretchered to the helicopter, he was fully conscious and resting upright on his elbows, talking to people. Ake Strandberg, who saw him into the helicopter, said: "He was still in his race overalls and you could tell one leg was crushed. Ronnie told me: 'It really hurts', and that was the last thing he said to me." Reine Wisell, a fellow Swede, also spoke to

Peterson. He was calm and sanguine, recalls Wisell, saying: "It's shit about
the legs but they fixed up Graham Hill, so they must be able to fix me. I'll
be ready for next year."

Rex Hart recovered Peterson's helmet and gloves from the medical centre,
and said: "We had his gloves and helmet back immediately after they'd taken
him away. There were virtually no burn marks on them." Staffan Svenby
took Peterson's Rolls-Royce Corniche and drove to the hospital, arriving
shortly after the helicopter.

James Hunt was talking to Harvey Postlethwaite in the Wolf motorhome.
Postlethwaite made him a cup of tea and tried to calm down the agitated
driver. Hunt had seen the extent of Peterson's injuries and had been with
him for nearly half an hour after the accident. As Postlethwaite remembers,
Hunt's hands were shaking and his voice was trembling with emotion. He
was in no condition to drive his car again that afternoon. Nonetheless, when
the restart was called, he duly got back in his car.

While Peterson was on his way to the hospital, Colin Chapman immediately
began a clean-up of his own, aware of what could happen if a driver died in
Italy. Whilst he had no reason to believe it would happen, he wasn't taking
any chances. Since the Italian authorities had no reason to suspect that
Peterson's injuries were life-threatening, they had no interest in impounding
the Lotus – although, 24 hours later, they would.

Chapman quickly arranged for two mechanics to drive the Lotus truck
back to England immediately, with the damaged car on board. Rex Hart
remembers: "Because of the problems Lotus had had at Monza when
Italian officials confiscated the cars after Rindt, Clark and Von Trips had
come together, the two mechanics were told not to stop until they reached
France. They just about had time to wash their hands before they left."

Chapman ordered the mechanics to dismantle the car and get rid of it
when they got back to the factory. Rex Hart remembers the car was in "a
hell of a mess" but still in one piece.

Chapman's biographer, French journalist Jabby Crombac, said the Lotus
boss grew extremely bitter about the fact that Peterson had been in the 78.
Crombac said: "The foot box on the new 79 was much stronger than on the
78, and if Ronnie had been driving a spare 79 instead, it is quite likely that
his injuries would have been less severe. What made Colin particularly angry
was that Peterson's spare 79 was not ready to take to Monza."

This anger was directed at the team's personnel, whom Chapman believed had not worked hard enough to get the fourth 79 ready for the Monza race. Crombac was very close to Chapman, and it seemed to confirm that there was no conspiracy to deprive Peterson of a spare 79.

While plans were being made for the second start, Peterson was being X-rayed over at Niguardia. Svenby phoned Barbro Peterson at home in Monte Carlo as soon as her husband arrived at the hospital. He gave her the news but said the injuries weren't life-threatening, and they decided Barbro would remain in Monaco with Nina before travelling straight to Milan early the next morning. Brabham team owner Bernie Ecclestone arranged for a private plane to pick her up at Nice airport.

After the initial X-rays were completed, the Niguardia doctors advised Peterson that his injuries were creating a problem with the blood supply to his legs. The doctors apparently advised Svenby that they should consider amputating the badly damaged leg to avoid complications, but Peterson said to Svenby: "I want to be able to drive at Watkins Glen. Please make sure I can."

Svenby consulted with Swedish doctors on the telephone for a second opinion. Peterson agreed to go ahead with the tricky operation to fix his badly damaged legs. Svenby said: "He was okay about it. After all, there weren't so many options for him."

The operation could not take place immediately because the specialist surgeon was not on duty and couldn't be contacted. He finally arrived at 7 o'clock.

Meanwhile, the re-started race was delayed again when, on the warm-up lap, Scheckter's Wolf flattened the Armco at the second Lesmo corner and the barrier had to be replaced. The crowd became aggressive and began throwing bottles. With the light fading, the race was shortened to 40 laps.

Hunt eventually got back into the spare McLaren but was in no mood to drive and, without thinking, burned his clutch out at the restart. Shoving the gears in manually, crash style, he circulated for a few laps then retired with an electrical problem. Mario Andretti's Lotus was in front at the finish and, though he was given a one-minute penalty for jumping the start and demoted to sixth place, the single point was enough for the American to clinch the 1978 World Driving Championship. Niki Lauda and John Watson scored a Brabham-Alfa Romeo 1-2 with Carlos Reutemann's Ferrari third.

Andretti was crowned world champion but, with Peterson in hospital, it didn't seem the right time to celebrate. Andretti sat in the John Player motorhome, still in his overalls. The champagne was being drunk, but the talk was all about Peterson. Andretti and Chapman discussed his recovery prospects with Sid Watkins. There was absolutely no thought or discussions about him not surviving – simply about when he would be able to race again.

Later that evening, Watkins returned to the motorhome and told Andretti and Chapman about Peterson's operation, which was still in progress. The three decided to journey over to the hospital, so Watkins and Chapman set off in the Rolls-Royce Corniche with Andretti driving. He found it difficult to get past the *tifosi* lining the roads leading out of the circuit. There was no security in evidence once the race had ended. Andretti knew a short cut across the park fields to the motorway.

When they finally reached Niguardia, they found a large crowd of people outside the hospital. Peterson was still in surgery, but all appeared to be going well. Watkins was invited into the operating theatre, and he reported that surgeons were working on the last fracture to Peterson's legs. "I talked to the anaesthetist and Ronnie's vital signs were all fine," he says.

Watkins continues: "The blood transfusion with the correct blood group was in progress. Looking at the X-rays, I counted about 27 fractures in both legs and feet. The surgeon in charge indicated that he thought all was going to plan and that they would be finished shortly. Thereafter, Ronnie was to be transferred to the intensive care unit where Brambilla had already taken up residence."

Watkins then updated Andretti and Chapman on Peterson's condition, while Svenby contacted Barbro to update her on the situation and confirm the arrangements for a helicopter to bring her from Linate airport to the hospital in the morning. At around midnight, Andretti and Chapman returned to the Villa d'Este, while Svenby and Watkins decided to stay close and checked into a nearby hotel. Svenby said: "At that time, it didn't occur to me that anything would go wrong."

Mike Doodson, the well known journalist, remembered Colin Chapman returning to the hotel: "Chapman came back from the hospital with a look of relief on his face. We thought that it was going to be a long recovery as he'd been very badly hurt; but at some point he'd be back in a Formula One car."

Back at their hotels rooms in Monza, the Lotus team members, after watching television footage of the Swede lifting himself up on his elbows in the ambulance and talking to people, were also convinced that Peterson was going to be okay. The Lotus mechanics were not worried and they had no thought of Peterson not surviving his injuries. Rex Hart said: "We had a few beers and that sort of thing. No one thought Ronnie would die."

But strange things happened during the night, and it soon became clear that something was wrong. Hospital insiders were relaying disturbing reports to the media about Peterson's treatment. Word got out that a mistake had been made in setting the bones and that a cover-up was in progress.

Svenby telephoned Barbro with a progress report, but she told him that she had been receiving calls from journalists – many of them Swedish – giving her various different reports about her husband's condition. Svenby, who had just come from the hospital, told Barbro to ignore them. The pair decided that Barbro should disconnect the telephone in order to prevent the calls. But she didn't.

At 4am, Svenby was woken by the telephone in his room. It was Watkins; he had just received a call from the hospital advising him that Peterson's condition had worsened. The pair left for the hospital immediately.

Watkins' and Svenby's accounts differ slightly about the moment they received the bad news. According to Watkins, it was Svenby who rang him: "Staffan woke me by telephone to say that the hospital had called to tell us things had taken a bad turn for Ronnie."

At the same time, somebody, saying he was a doctor, telephoned Barbro to tell her that he thought the Italian doctors were killing her husband. Watkins says he was never able to find out the caller's identity, but it was suspected that he had impersonated medical staff in order to get into the hospital. But the caller was right – Peterson was in trouble.

Watkins and Svenby rushed to the intensive care unit and were met by a neurosurgeon, who informed them that Peterson had developed breathing difficulties and was now being ventilated on a machine to try to keep up his blood oxygen levels. "A chest X-ray showed that he had developed multiple emboli [small obstructions blocking the blood vessels] in his lungs," Watkins said. "His kidney function had also declined and urinary output had deteriorated. He was unconscious, and neurological examination showed that he had signs of severe brain damage."

Watkins then examined Peterson himself and found fat globules obstructing the small arteries in the retinas of both eyes. Watkins said: "The outlook was pretty hopeless."

Svenby went off to telephone Chapman to inform them of the growing crisis, and Chapman called Bernie Ecclestone. By the time Chapman and Ecclestone reached the hospital, Watkins had devastating news: neurologists who had come in to do brain electrical recordings had reported no activity and had indicated brain death. It was 6:30am. It was clear that the end was near and, by dawn, Peterson was dead.

By now, Barbro had started her journey from Nice to the hospital, so Svenby was unable to inform her of the situation. At Milan's Linate airport, the Lotus team members were also waiting to make the journey home when news of their driver's death came through. The newspaper vendors started shouting: "*Peterson e morti*".

Watkins said: "Having seen him on television at our hotel the night before, we couldn't believe it. It shocked everybody. I remember Mrs Peterson arriving at Milan airport in the early hours, and the plane just turning around and taking her home. She didn't even get off the plane because there was nothing she could do." Hunt was deeply shocked and leaned on Jane Birbeck for support at the airport. He said he thought of Peterson as "indestructible."

Peterson's friend Ake Strandberg had been at the hospital all night. When he walked out into the dawn of Milan, he recalled later: "I wondered why the trams were still running. I couldn't understand why they hadn't stopped. For me the world had suddenly come to a standstill."

Mario Andretti was devastated. His reasons for not giving Peterson the spare car had been racing ones. If he had known what was going to happen, he would have handed it over, no question.

The next day, he recalled how he heard the news: "I was in the car on my way to the hospital with my wife and we were quite relaxed. Obviously we felt very sorry for Ronnie – I mean he'd had a bad break – but in a couple of months he'd be okay. I'm on the autostrada and I get to the booth and the gentleman there says: 'Hey, did you hear Ronnie Peterson just died?' I said: 'No'. 'It was just on the radio,' he said. And I went to the hospital and I couldn't believe it. It was the furthest thing from my mind that he would die from those injuries. I mean, they were severe, no question, but they just didn't seem to be life-threatening. So that was a huge shock, to say the least."

Some time afterwards, Watkins received word from Italian doctors that Peterson's autopsy had confirmed fat embolism as the cause of the Swede's death. Fat globules were identified in his lungs, kidneys and brain.

By this time, many people in Formula One were questioning the competency of the staff who had treated Peterson. Even today, Andretti feels that poor treatment was the cause of his friend's death: "I felt that fate was so unfair to Ronnie Peterson; to lose his life in a way that he shouldn't have because, you know, I don't think those were life-threatening injuries. I don't think he received the proper care in Italy."

Fredrick Petersens, a friend of the Swede who had visited the hospital on the Sunday evening, claimed afterwards that conditions in Niguardia hospital were questionable. "It was dirty and all over the floor were cigarettes," he reported. "Something had gone wrong, there was little doubt about that. Peterson should not have died from those injuries. The surgeons appeared to have bungled the repair of his legs, a very complex operation."

Some people thought the surgeons should have waited to operate until he was more stable. Other people think he should have been flown to Austria or Switzerland to a hospital experienced in mountaineering fractures. A leading Swedish surgeon said later: "You don't operate on a guy in that condition. That's rule number one, by the book. You stabilise him first, make sure he has all the life support systems. You don't just go in there and operate. That's how these embolisms start. Any doctor in the Austrian or Italian Alps would have understood that because that's what they're dealing with every day. They let the patient rest, sort out what needs to be done, and they wait."

But Svenby insists the medical treatment Peterson received at Niguardia did not contribute to his death. "It was so ridiculous," he said, "there were a lot of rumours about the hospital, but it had a record of treating road traffic accidents (where broken limbs are common) and was probably one of the best places for him to go. I have no complaints. The guy who operated on Ronnie was a top Italian surgeon. It was just so unfortunate."

Svenby continues: "With hindsight, it's easy to say that his leg should we been amputated, but Ronnie wouldn't have wanted that." Peterson's friend Lars Berntson later told Johnny Tipler, who wrote a very fine book about him years later: "If they'd amputated, Ronnie's life wouldn't have been worth living. Racing was his reason for living. It was all or nothing. So you could say what happened was a blessing in disguise, because I could never imagine Ronnie hopping about with crutches or prosthetic limbs."

Watkins agrees with Svenby and insists that Peterson got the best treatment, saying: "Niguardia hospital was a major trauma centre level 1." Max Mosley adds: "It was important to all of us that Sid was there, because we would all have said that the Italians screwed up like they did with Jochen Rindt. But Sid was there and was able to say it was an act of God; Ronnie was just unlucky."

Colin Chapman ordered an aircraft to fly from Britain to collect Peterson's coffin. It was flown back to Sweden with Staffan Svenby and Ake Strandberg on board.

Four days later, hundreds of people lined up outside the church in Peterson's home town of Orebro, Sweden, as Formula One paid its final respects to the Swede. Emerson Fittapaldi, James Hunt, Niki Lauda, Jody Scheckter, Ake Strandberg and John Watson carried his coffin, while Peterson's close friend, countryman and fellow racing driver Gunnar Nilsson, who by that time was in the advanced stages of cancer and too weak to help bear his friends remains, followed on behind. Upon his return to London, Nilsson went straight into hospital. He was never to leave and died a few weeks later, on 20th October, at the age of 30.

Andretti did not attend Peterson's funeral. After Monza, he and Dee-Ann spent a couple of days in Florence before flying back out to New York. There was a USAC race in Michigan the following weekend, in which Andretti had committed to run. Qualifying took place on the day of Peterson's funeral.

Chapman sent two aeroplanes full of Lotus staff over to Sweden. Poignantly, at exactly the same time, cars and equipment were being shipped to the airport for the journey to the United States for the next Grand Prix at Watkins Glen. Whatever trauma hit Formula One, and Peterson's death was one of the biggest, the show always went on.

In Italy, as Chapman had feared, a legal investigation into the accident got under way. But, as Chapman had disposed of all the evidence, it did not get very far and he never faced any investigation or charges over the car. Using video tapes, Italian police charged the race starter and Ricardo Patrese with manslaughter.

The drivers, angry at Peterson's death and looking for someone to blame, set up their very own kangaroo court with Hunt taking on the role of 'Hanging Judge Jeffries'.

There was high emotion, and the Grand Prix Drivers' Association safety committee was formed with Hunt, Niki Lauda, Emerson Fittipaldi, Jody Scheckter and Mario Andretti sitting on it. It quickly decided on Hunt's say-so that Ricardo Patrese was guilty of dangerous driving and should be banned from competing in the next race at Watkins Glen. And that is precisely what happened.

Patrese had a reputation for being arrogant and had been criticised previously by drivers for overly-aggressive driving. But he stated firmly that he was innocent, and urged the committee to watch the film of the incident. But Hunt was adamant: "For me, the responsibility for the accident is completely Patrese's." Patrese knew he had not hit Hunt.

Patrese was proved right, and three years later he was cleared of any blame by the Italian courts. Italian judges studied the video tapes carefully, which seemed to show that Patrese's Arrows did not hit Hunt's McLaren. But it had forced the McLaren into the Lotus when Hunt swerved to avoid contact with Patrese's aggressive driving.

Patrese may have been overly aggressive but it was proved to be a racing incident – a conclusion on which everyone, including Hunt, eventually came to agree. If Patrese hadn't driven as aggressively as he had, Peterson would still be alive; but that was Formula One, and all the drivers – including Peterson – knew and understood those risks.

Ricardo Patrese's career continued and eventually he competed in more Formula One Grand Prix races than any other driver. But Patrese's reputation suffered badly from the incident and its aftermath, and he never forgave Hunt for the disrepute. He said: "Inside myself, I knew I had no reason to be unhappy because I knew I did not cause the accident. But I think what the drivers did to me on that occasion is very difficult to forgive."

Years later, a repentant Hunt tried to speak to him to clear the air, but Patrese considered the damage done and therefore irreparable. Patrese refused to speak to him and stepped to the other side of the Formula One paddock whenever he saw Hunt. Patrese's attitude was troublesome to Hunt, and remained so until his death. When Hunt died, he and Patrese were still bitter enemies but, as Ecclestone summed it up years later: "At the time, James believed what he'd done was right. He thought he had to jump up and blame somebody, which wasn't really necessary because it was an accident. And it wasn't really the cause of Ronnie's death anyway. Nobody dies from a broken leg."

James Hunt was awarded the Golden Shield by the Royal Swedish Automobile Club for his part in rescuing Ronnie Peterson.

SHUNT

CHAPTER 34

Sudden retirement and gone 1979

The flag comes down on a career of contrasts

James Hunt went into 1979 with no illusions – it would be his last year of racing. He had been traumatised by the death of Ronnie Peterson and he no longer wanted to take the risk of being killed or maimed in a race car. He would drive one more season, primarily for the money and secondly in the hope that a competitive car could enable him to leave the sport in a blaze of glory.

Despite all his reservations about safety after Peterson's death, he was still looking forward to the season ahead with his new team. Whatever he had thought of Peter Warr in the past, he eventually came to the realisation that he was a good organiser and administrator. And Warr had agreed to pay Hunt a great deal of money for his services, which more than made up for not buying him lunch four years earlier.

Hunt's US$1 million salary would be paid in two equal instalments, due by 1st May and 1st November. John Hogan also agreed that Marlboro would organise a personal sponsorship deal worth US$125,000 a year. Along with other personal deals, Hunt hoped to earn about US$1.5 million in his last year of racing. In 1977 and 1978, he had cleared over US$1 million a year all in and paid very little tax living in Marbella as an ex-pat.

The money may have been good, but what Hunt didn't know was that

Walter Wolf was entering his own period of decline. He had business problems similar to those of Lord Hesketh in 1974. Oil prices had collapsed and so had exploration. His company's services, so in demand ten years earlier, were no longer wanted. Wolf was also guilty of hubris; he had believed his own press cuttings. His personal spending was over US$2 million a year plus what he spent on the Formula One team, and it was unsustainable.

To take some of the financial strain, Wolf had signed his first commercial sponsor, Olympus Cameras, to help pay the bills. Peter Warr had lured Olympus over from Lotus. The camera company had almost exclusive branding on the car and the deal was worth US$1 million a year, which effectively paid Hunt's salary. There was not much left to spend on the team.

But whatever his enthusiasm for his new team and season, Hunt's motivation was suspect. In truth, Hunt no longer believed in Formula One as once he had. Now, three years after his world championship victory, he was disillusioned and worn down by the politics at McLaren. The 1978 season had been terrible, and he had become very aware of Teddy Mayer and Alastair Caldwell's limitations. He loved them as people, but they too had come to believe their own press cuttings.

Hunt would have retired at the end of 1978 had he not been offered so much money by Warr. But he was still ambitious. He wanted to win the world title again and he firmly believed he could do it with the Wolf team, whose car was designed by ex-Hesketh technical director Harvey Postlethwaite. Hunt had maximum faith in Postlethwaite's skills.

But the Argentine Grand Prix in Buenos Aires, on 21st January 1979, was a serious wake up call. He found he had lost some of his zest for Formula One. The failure of the 1978 season had hit him hard, and Wolf was no Hesketh. Every time he looked at Peter Warr, he found he still remembered the lunch he never got in 1975. Hunt himself was also no longer quite the golden boy and, as much as he told people he detested the epithet, he now rather missed it. Gilles Villeneuve was the new star of Formula One. Hunt's friend Bubbles Horsley had also closed down his rent-a-driver team and was no longer around for moral support. The rising costs of Formula One had scared away most of the privateers, and the prize money allocation system had been changed. Now only the top teams received cash, driving out all the smaller participants. The Hesketh era that had started in 1973 and lasted five years was well and truly over, and the new system meant it would no longer be possible to do a Hesketh.

In truth, the James Hunt era was also coming to an end, but he was still lingering on. Hunt felt it keenly. To use a modern slogan that was unknown back then, it would be fair to say that Hunt was essentially "past his sell-by date".

The new season was all about the new people, the young people. Hunt had turned 30 and he was no longer in that category. He felt that keenly, as well.

Formula One was coming to be dominated by the French. The oil company Elf had done a brilliant job nurturing young French drivers, and seven of them now dominated the grid. Patrick Depailler moved from Tyrrell to Ligier to be partnered with Jacques Laffite in the French team. Ken Tyrrell's team had started its long decline and the cars were in the hands of two more Frenchmen, Didier Pironi and Jean-Pierre Jarier, chosen by oil sponsor Elf. Jean-Pierre Jabouille was joined by Rene Arnoux at Renault, now a two-car team for the first time. The seventh Frenchman was Patrick Tambay, who was now getting into the groove at McLaren, where John Watson had replaced Hunt after Peterson's death. Niki Lauda had been joined at Brabham by another rising star, Nelson Piquet. Elsewhere, Carlos Reutemann had switched to Lotus from Ferrari and Clay Regazzoni had joined Alan Jones at Williams, which was also a two-car team for the first time in the team's short history.

Jones and Regazzoni were set to be the sensations of the season in sensational cars.

There was a serious changing of the guard going on in Formula One, but it was all happening too quickly. Ground effects technology had totally changed the game and few of the current designers understood it fully. Simultaneously, two other major technical changes besides ground effects were occurring that were just as significant to lap times. First, the Renault turbo engine was now working extremely well with the single turbocharger being replaced by twin KKK turbocharger, virtually eliminating the throttle lag that had plagued the cars. The other change was the arrival of Michelin radial tyres. These were exclusive to Renault and Ferrari, as the rest of the field was on Goodyear cross plies.

The changes were too sudden, and the established order was being swept away too quickly and to the detriment of the show. There was a dearth of established stars performing at the front. Lauda, Hunt, Andretti and Fittipaldi were still there, but they were all suddenly in uncompetitive cars and effectively back markers. It was not to be a vintage year for anyone, and eventually the world championship was won by the driver who got the most points – not from winning – but from finishing second, third, and fourth weekend in, weekend out.

Somehow, the advent of ground effects technology had sucked the life out of Formula One, and even Jody Scheckter would have admitted he was not the best driver that year.

If James Hunt thought the McLaren M26 was a dog, the Wolf WR7 was a whole lot worse. Privately, Hunt called it "an ill-handling pig", saying that was a complimentary view of the car. But he was careful to keep his real thoughts private. Publicly, he said: "The car is suffering from a drastic oversteer problem which we cannot do anything about."

There were also doubts about the standard of preparation of the car. In qualifying, the nose cone flew off and came back into the cockpit. He had to duck as it flew over his head at high speed, narrowly missing his helmet. Hunt was surprised at the quality of the technical set-up at Wolf, bearing in mind that Warr and Postlethwaite were in charge. He began to have second thoughts about Postlethwaite's capabilities. There had always been doubts about the Hesketh team's success and whether it was due to the brilliant car or the brilliant driver. No one, least of all Hunt, really knew the answer to that. Only now was he beginning to work it out.

Hunt eventually qualified 18th and drove round at the back of the field for 41 laps before the electrics failed, causing the engine to cut out. He found retirement a merciful relief and headed to the airport to spend a week at Emerson Fittipaldi's beach house. From that moment on, he knew there was going to be no fairytale ending to his career, and all of his thoughts were on getting himself out.

As expected, the French were totally supreme at the opening race. Laffite and Depailler were first and second on the grid, and first and fourth in the race. Laffite was also blowing away the more experienced Depailler.

The French Ligier-Ford cars were designed by newcomer Gerard Ducarouge. He had refined the ground effects theories pioneered by Lotus simply by designing a car with massive side panniers and maximising the area under the car. It was very crude but highly effective. Combined with the Ford Cosworth engine, the speed of the cars was only limited by the ability of the drivers.

Fittipaldi's beach house on the Brazilian coast was a dream, and Hunt forgot the troubles that were constantly revolving around in his head. But even the week at the beach house felt different from the carefree days of the past; he was no longer carefree. It slowly began to dawn on him that he had seen his best years, and they were behind him. It was time for the second act of his life; and it did not include being a Formula One driver.

On 4th February, at Interlagos for the Brazilian Grand Prix, he manhandled the Wolf-Ford up the grid to tenth place. It was a magnificent performance, and he was alongside Fittipaldi on the fifth row. Fittipaldi had also used his supreme talent to get his Fittipaldi-Ford car in that position. On the grid, the two glanced at each other with knowing smiles.

The second race of the season was totally dominated by the Ligier Fords of Jacques Laffite and Patrick Depailler, this time scoring 100 per cent; 1-2 in the race and in qualifying. For Wolf, it went from bad to worse. After a few laps, Hunt attempted to change gear but found himself waving around the little gearstick as it came off in his hand. It hadn't been tightened up properly. As he struggled, unable to change gears, the steering rack also came apart – apparently for the same reason. He quickly retired the car, having lost all confidence in his mechanics.

Hunt scurried off straight to the airport to return home to Spain via Heathrow. He was missing Oscar, his German Shepherd, at home in Marbella. The direct connection he had with that particular dog never ceased to amaze him. The dog went everywhere with him when he was at home.

It was a whole month before the next race in South Africa on 3rd March, and in the break Hunt resolved to do the best he could for Wolf and to make his last season as memorable as possible despite the limitations of his team and car. But in his heart of hearts he realised there was nothing he could do to make the Wolf go faster. His only real hope was a new car Harvey Postlethwaite had designed. But the team's growing cash shortage had made the new car late.

He resolved to cut down on his drinking that month and he stopped the drugs altogether; he was training harder than ever before. In truth, he had suddenly lost the taste for both alcohol and drugs. His sudden abstinence from drink and recreational drugs caused him some health problems and he had strong withdrawal symptoms that became apparent at the next race in South Africa, on 3rd March.

At that race, his views on the capabilities of his mechanics were shown to be correct and this time the consequences would be catastrophic.

During the first qualifying session, his Wolf-Ford's brakes failed as he pressed hard on the pedal for a corner. The brake failure was total, and he was left helpless as the car headed straight for the steel barrier.

In that brief moment, Hunt thought he was going to die and visions of François Cevert's accident at Watkins Glen suddenly flashed through his mind.

But somehow the car spun to a halt without hitting anything. Miraculously, the Wolf-Ford was completely undamaged. Hunt was in shock and had never before experienced total brake failure at high speed. He was also in double shock at the enormity of the accident he didn't have.

He staggered out of the car and barely knew where he was. Realising he had had a very lucky escape, he then couldn't stop thinking about the look of fear on Ronnie Peterson's face as he had lain on the tarmac at Monza. The Cevert and Peterson flashbacks in quick succession spooked him and made the shock more severe. By chance, Jackie Stewart, commentating for the SABC, the South African Broadcasting Corporation, was nearby and went out to see if he was alright.

Stewart quickly realised that Hunt was anything but alright. He saw he was in a state of extreme shock and walked with him back to the pits. As Hunt pulled out a cigarette, his hands were shaking so much that Stewart had to light it for him.

Stewart described Hunt as "a truly frightened man" after the accident. He said: "James was physically shaking, which is something I had not previously ever seen in a racing driver. I walked with him down the pit lane right after the incident; he was clearly considerably affected by it and was physically incapable of holding the cigarette in his hand steady. It was a major shake."

Rob Walker, the legendary former team owner, was working with the Wolf team as a consultant. Hunt adored Walker and had huge respect for his achievements in Formula One in the sixties. He sat down next to him, wanting some immediate advice. Hunt's overwhelming feeling was that he should retire on the spot, return to Spain and forget the money.

Walker remembered him being all set to retire, as he told Hunt biographer Gerald Donaldson many years later: "That day in South Africa, we had a great deal of trouble getting him back in the car. In fact, I did it myself, by talking to him about religion. I said that God would protect him whatever happened and, as long as he knew that, it would be all right."

From previous chats, Walker knew that Hunt was getting to dislike motor racing but he told him there was "just one mind in charge of him, and that mind was not his but from above. And as long as he put himself in the hands of that one mind, it would be absolutely safe."

Hunt was genuinely moved by what Walker said and, 15 minutes later, he got back into the car to carry on with qualifying. Walker confessed: "He was rather unwilling."

The incident made up Hunt's mind and he decided he would retire as soon as he had received his retainer from Wolf for the first half of the season. The first person he told was David Gray, who was attending the race with Olympus Cameras. Hunt wanted to see what Gray's reaction would be. As Gray recalls: "He just said to me: 'I'm stopping.' And I said: 'Why's that?' And he said: 'Because I don't want to go on. I just don't want to go on. I think it's better if I don't.'"

Gray was unperturbed and said he was sure Olympus would understand: "I told him I thought I thought it was an incredibly brave decision. It wasn't a problem for me and it was a brilliant decision for him." Hunt told no one else about his decision that day.

But he did recount the dreadful experience of the crash and the flashbacks. The Wolf mechanics couldn't understand what all the drama was about when the car was returned to the pit lane unmarked. And that was part of the problem.

There is little doubt that, without the presence of Jackie Stewart and Rob Walker, Hunt would have walked away from Formula One that day. Instead, Hunt somehow managed to qualify the Wolf-Ford 13th fastest. The race marked his only finish for the year, as he brought the car home eighth.

Whereas in previous years he had loved Kyalami and staying at the ranch playing tennis with his friend Abe Segal, now he couldn't wait to get out and fly home to Marbella.

The race itself was interesting because Jean-Pierre Jabouille put the turbo charged Renault on pole position for the first time, aided by the high altitude and his Michelin radials. The Michelins were supreme at Kyalami. But it was Gilles Villeneuve and Jody Scheckter who dominated the race, with Villeneuve first. There was a five-week gap before the next race for the United States Grand Prix West, at Long Beach, on 8th April.

By the time of the Grand Prix West, tensions were becoming apparent between Hunt and Olympus' head of marketing in Europe, a man called Werner Teuffel. The relationship with the camera company overall was proving to be a success, but it was being undermined by personal tensions. As David

Gray recalls: "I went whizzing around the world to virtually every single race and Olympus got a lot out of its association with James."

But Hunt took a strong dislike to Teuffel, as Gray adds: "Werner believed he was pretty good and James didn't. He used to arrive with his entourage and they clashed. James just hated him and it was awful. Werner ran Europe and he was quite able. But he found Formula One smelly and eventually he got bored with it, so he didn't come anymore."

There were also tensions in the team and especially between Harvey Postlethwaite and Hunt.

Harvey Postlethwaite now had the new Wolf-Ford WR8 ready. Unfortunately however, it was slower than the WR7 and the brakes were a disaster. But Hunt was determined to develop it and chose to use it in the race.

Driveshafts were a real problem at Long Beach and almost took the life of Jean-Pierre Jabouille. In early Saturday qualifying, Jabouille broke a driveshaft on his Renault on the curved straight and hit a concrete wall at 180 miles per hour. With a badly sprained arm, he was out of the race. Qualifying was a battle between Ferrari, Ligier and, surprisingly, Lotus. As was usually the case at Long Beach, the circuit was littered with broken cars by the end of each session. Carlos Reutemann, in the second Lotus, held the pole until the very end of the final session, when Gilles Villeneuve bumped him. The weather was surprisingly overcast and cold.

After a slow start, the Long Beach race was proving a success and had attracted 100,000 fans, aided by having an American world champion. Not many Formula One races attracted 100,000 people on race day, but Long beach became one of them and Chris Pook's reputation was redeemed. Suddenly, he became a respected member of the Formula One community.

Sunday was sunny and warm, just in time for the race. After an aborted start, right from the restart Villeneuve led teammate Jody Scheckter home. It was the Canadian's second consecutive win and the third Long Beach win in a row for Ferrari. Villeneuve was leading the world championship after four races. Hunt did not even complete the first lap after his gearbox mashed up on the start line.

This led to a furious row with Warr and Postlethwaite over the state of the car's preparation. The two men were defenceless, as Hunt had only finished one race in four and all his retirements had been down to the mechanics making mistakes. Postlethwaite later admitted to Hunt biographer Christopher Hilton: "It would be very easy for me as a designer to say that our car was perfect and that the driver was an idiot, but we didn't give James a competitive car."

For the first time, Warr told Hunt that the team was having a funding problem as Walter Wolf's business deteriorated. But he assured him his own salary was ring-fenced and coming from Olympus. Postlethwaite said: "The car was barely competitive for a number of reasons, probably because at that stage the team was underfunded." He added: "We were struggling to cope in the era of ground effects." Hunt seemed unconcerned about the financial problems; he had seen what Postlethwaite had done under similar conditions at Hesketh.

The European season began with the Spanish Grand Prix on 29th April at Jarama circuit. Hunt was back in the Wolf-Ford WR7, as the WR8 had proved to be such a dog in testing. Hunt managed to qualify 15th but stopped his car on lap 27 of the race after the brakes began to fade and he became frightened of what might happen. Hunt said the Wolf's brakes were so poor, he "decided to call it a day." Ligier was back on top of Formula One and Patrick Depailler won the race from the Lotuses of Reutemann and Mario Andretti.

During the weekend, there was yet another row. Finding it unconstructive, Postlethwaite admitted later: "When you have a driver who is close to hysterical, it has a terribly unbalancing effect on the rest of the team, and it wasn't a very pleasant situation for us or for him. He was, by that time, a fairly disruptive influence. The problem wasn't only the team; part of the problem was undoubtedly James." Postlethwaite admitted his relationship with Hunt had, by that time, deteriorated significantly: "He had it in for me because I think he saw me as the guy who couldn't give him the car with which he could exit brilliantly from his career." Peter Warr was disgusted by Hunt's attitude in failing to help make the Wolf competitive. As Warr told Christopher Hilton, he "concluded that Hunt was driving for the money."

Hunt denied that accusation and said: When you're driving an uncompetitive car and you're a top line driver, and you are used to a good car and then you go into a bad one, it is difficult to maintain the interest and to maintain the competitive edge. But I am an instinctive, natural competitor which meant every time I got in a racing car, I can say with my hand on my heart that I tried my best." He insisted to journalist that he was still motivated and told Nigel Roebuck: "I'd been very well trained at Hesketh racing by Bubbles, who taught me to recognise when things were going badly, the car wasn't working well. We were in double figures on the grid and I taught myself how to recognise that problem and to prepare myself so that I always delivered in the car."

But try as he might, he realised the Wolf car was really a dog. When he saw Walter Wolf he suggested he rename the team, as the current moniker was no longer appropriate. Wolf did not see the funny side of Hunt's remark. The situation was not helped by the lack of rapport between Wolf and Hunt. Wolf was a narcissist and Hunt didn't have a narcissistic bone in his body. They were just not compatible people. It was only the soothing presence of Rob Walker that kept the Hunt–Wolf show on the road.

As Hunt stopped his car in the Jarama pit lane, he irrevocably decided he had had enough of racing it. His relationship with Peter Warr was strained after all the car failures, and he finally realised that his friend Postlethwaite was not the car design genius he had initially believed him to be. He wondered why he had taken six years to work that one out.

That evening, Hunt told Jane Birbeck he was definitely retiring and they discussed the change this would mean to their lives. After Birbeck, the first person Hunt called to tell the news was John Hogan. Hogan advised him not to be hasty and to think it through. If he was still determined, then he should seek specialist media help for the announcement. Hogan was careful to advise his friend that the manner of his exit would be important for his reputation and image, as well as his money-earning ability after he quit. He also reminded him that his Marlboro personal sponsorship deal would be cancelled when he stopped racing.

Hunt told Hogan that the exact timing of the announcement would depend on when he received the first half of his retainer from Walter Wolf, some US$500,000. His contract required him to complete at least eight races to qualify for the money, which meant it wouldn't be until the end of May. Hunt told Hogan that the news mustn't break before his announcement. Hogan was used to keeping secrets, and Hunt knew he was the one man in the gossipy world of Formula One who could be trusted. At that stage, only Hogan and David Gray knew of his intentions, although Rob Walker and Sid Watkins had guessed that the end was near.

Hunt was very pensive when he entered the paddock gates of the Zolder circuit for the Belgian Grand Prix on 13th May. He was well aware that this was his penultimate race in Formula One and he wanted to enjoy it.

Qualifying was dominated once again by the Ligier-Fords of Jacques Laffite and Patrick Depailler, who annexed first and second on the starting grid. The surprise of qualifying was young Nelson Piquet, showing his potential by qualifying third in the Brabham-Alfa Romeo. Piquet was starting to get the better of his team leader Niki Lauda, who seemed almost as dispirited as James Hunt in a car that was now uncompetitive. Harvey Postlethwaite appeared to have the Wolf-Ford WR8 performing properly and the WR7 was finally retired for good. Hunt qualified ninth on the grid alongside Carlos Reutemann, but his mind was on his retirement announcement.

In those days, public relations people were thin on the ground and all Formula One PR was handled by journalists in their spare time. It created an incestuous relationship between media, teams and sponsors; all of which were all represented by the same people. It effectively corrupted the coverage of Formula One, as the normal separation of what is called 'church and state' did not exist as it did in every other sport. It is a legacy that still continues today.

So Hunt was forced to choose a journalist to handle the announcement. He realised that this was fraught with danger. The only journalist he knew well enough was Eoin Young, who had worked with him on the book *Against All Odds*. During the writing of that book, Young had been very discreet and nothing had leaked out prematurely. Young was one of the few writers in the press room not prone to gossip.

Deciding to trust Young, Hunt sent Jane Birbeck off to the press room to find him. He handed her his pass so she could get in and she found him sitting at his temporary desk, looking out over his half moon reading glasses at his manual typewriter, trying to change a ribbon. As he struggled with the task at hand, she invited him into the Wolf motorhome for a meeting with her boyfriend. Young was delighted to leave his desk and the ribbon problem behind.

When they arrived at the Wolf motorhome, Hunt was alone in the back room smoking one of his usual Rothmans. In his biography of Hunt, Gerald Donaldson records Young's vivid account of what happened next: "The atmosphere was ominously quiet. He checked that the door was closed so no one could hear, then told me he was planning to announce his retirement at Monaco and asked if I would help him put together his tell-the-world announcement."

Young was shocked to say the least and immediately thought the job too big for him. So he recommended one of the big London PR firms. But

Hunt told Young that he hadn't received the first half of his retainer and felt he couldn't trust a London PR agency not to leak the news early, which meant that Walter Wolf would likely not pay him. Young told him his unexpected retirement was bound to turn into a media circus. Young was also cautious about accepting the task as he was sure the news would leak out early and Hunt would blame him for the leak.

But Hunt was persuasive, telling Young that, after having worked with him on the book, he felt he could trust him. Young eventually agreed to give him advice, beginning with the suggestion that the Monaco Grand Prix should be the last place to make such an announcement.

Together they decided he would make his announcement on 6th June at a central London hotel that Young would book. Hunt had to go out and qualify, and they agreed to meet later to finalise the arrangements. It was perfect timing, as there was no Swedish Grand Prix that year. After the deaths of Ronnie Peterson and Gunnar Nilsson, interest in Formula One in Sweden had faded and the race had been cancelled. It meant the whole month of June was empty and it would give Peter Warr the maximum time to find a replacement driver.

Later that night, Eoin Young made his way over to the hotel where Hunt and Birbeck were staying. Hunt had been smoking cannabis and was confused. Birbeck tried to give some order to the proceedings. Instead of discussing the details, Hunt rambled on about motor racing being dangerous. He told Young: "I am having to try harder to do worse, and I can't see an end to it." He admitted that, although he had decided to retire, in his heart of hearts he really didn't want to but "felt he had no choice."

Hunt told Young he had done some calculations. He reckoned that his normal life expectancy might be 75 years. And, at 31 years old, he had 44 more years left. He said: "If I continue racing for another five years, it would take up just over ten per cent of the rest of my life." But he thought the odds were only about even that he would still be alive at the end of the five years. He concluded: "I reckoned I'd had a fair crack at the whip. I'd done six seasons in Formula 1, and I thought that was enough for anybody. I didn't want to end up in a box or permanently injured. The main thing was self-preservation."

Young told him he would make his retirement announcement as painless as possible and they agreed a fee of US$1,000 for the work necessary, which was essentially comprised of writing a press release, hiring a venue and sending out an invitation. Hunt agreed to pay for the hotel and any additional expenses Young incurred. With that, Hunt declared the meeting over by climbing into bed, and a bemused Young took his leave while Birbeck muttered apologies for her boyfriend's somewhat eccentric behaviour.

Drivers generally hated racing at Zolder, but Hunt suddenly felt much more relaxed after making his decision and finalising the arrangements with Young. But he was full of angst that the news would break early and Wolf wouldn't pay him his retainer.

The team had high hopes for a podium at Zolder but it didn't materialise, with Hunt chasing around in the middle of the field whilst Jody Scheckter was grinding out a victory in his Ferrari. Hunt drove a fine race for 40 laps, enjoying himself for the first time in a race that season, but suddenly it all came to an abrupt stop as the Wolf lurched sideways and went off the track, hitting a steel barrier very hard. The car bounced back into the middle of the track and Hunt survived yet another accident in one piece. While a good result at Zolder might have meant he wavered from his decision, the accident reinforced his resolve to retire. Hunt told a journalist afterwards: "I don't know what caused it, but I think it might have been a tyre. For some time the steering had been getting heavier and heavier." He no longer actually cared;

Hunt received his first payment from Wolf a week later, and the Monaco Grand Prix would be his last race.

Walter Wolf was a strange animal and his actions could never be predicted. Hunt told people he was about as far from Alexander Hesketh as one could imagine, although he admitted the two did share some characteristics. Whilst he loved Alexander Hesketh, he felt nothing for Walter Wolf and he didn't feel he owed Wolf anything.

The Monaco Grand Prix on 27th May marked Hunt's seventh race on the streets of Monte Carlo in a Formula One car. It seemed an age since he had been scared to death at the wheel of his March–Ford 731 in 1973. A lot had happened in the interim, and he had achieved all he set out to in Formula One.

At night, as he hopped from one yacht to another moored alongside John F. Kennedy Plaza, the memories of the Hesketh days came flooding back to him. Those days were long gone but the memories were fresh. With a deep longing for the past, he confronted the reality that not only were those days gone forever, but that soon he too would be gone from Formula One.

He qualified tenth and shared the fifth row of the grid with Alan Jones' nimble Williams-Ford FW06. His performance convinced him he was still competitive. There was no doubt he could be on pole position, he thought, if all the drivers were equipped with the dreadful Wolf WR8.

Jody Scheckter was rampant in his home town and scored a rare pole position and then won the race in his Ferrari. Clay Regazzoni showed how far Williams had come by finishing second. For Hunt, his second to last Formula One race ended after four laps when he broke down outside the Tip-Top bar, where he would be celebrating with Jane later. Another drive shaft broke and put him out, making it an astonishing seven retirements in eight races for Wolf. It was a damning indictment of the team, and Hunt felt nothing about leaving it midway through the season. As he walked through Monaco to get back to the pits, he wondered which poor sod would replace him in the team, a misery he would not wish on any other driver. As he said: "It was over and I knew this was my last race, and I hated that car, anyway. I felt no sadness at all, just immense relief." He retired a few months short of his 32nd birthday.

But Hunt had one more commitment to fulfil: driving in a non-championship event, effectively a time trial, at Donington Park on 3rd June on behalf of circuit owner Tom Wheatcroft. It would be his last competitive drive in a Formula One car and, with that completed, he could retire.

The race was originally intended to be a full non-championship race, but the FIA would not grant the new circuit the appropriate licence and all but five teams withdrew from the event, with only Hunt, Mario Andretti, Nelson Piquet, Alan Jones and Rupert Keegan competing. The event was designed to showcase Donington's capacity to run Formula One cars on the track, which had been re-opened by Wheatcroft. Without an FIA licence, it became a time trial. Wheatcroft was staging the event to benefit the Gunnar Nilsson Memorial Fund, for which Hunt had been a prime mover. Hunt set the second fastest time in the trial after Alan Jones, with Mario Andretti third.

With that over, Hunt walked away from Formula One and from the 20,000 British fans in attendance who had no idea that they would be the last to see Hunt in action in a Formula One car.

That same evening, Hunt rang Peter Warr to tell him he was finished and that he would need to find a new driver. Warr didn't try to dissuade him. Upon putting down the phone, Hunt then rang Postlethwaite. Postlethwaite told him he wasn't surprised, and actually apologised for the terrible performance of the team and the cars.

Five days later, on Friday 8th June, Hunt finally announced his retirement in London to a very crowded press conference. His eight-year Formula One career, relatively short in modern terms, had brought him ten wins in 92 Grand Prix races, and was now over.

There was silence as the journalists took in the news. He had been one of the luckiest drivers, having turned his performances, which were by no means outstanding, into a Formula One world championship. All his victories were won in a three-year period, and he might easily have been world champion again in 1977 had he enjoyed the same kind of luck he had in 1976. But many drivers with better performance records had failed to become champion, including Stirling Moss with 16 wins and Carlos Reutemann with 12. He was the first world champion to retire in mid-season.

At the press conference, Hunt said was full of regrets: "I wanted to have a really good final year. It wasn't a matter of thinking about the Championship or anything. I wanted a good, competitive car with which to win some races. I was never the type to get pleasure from simply being a racing driver."

Then, in a comment which would make Peter Warr and Harvey Postlethwaite wince when they read it, he said: "It's become clear to me that our car will never get there. " Perhaps realising he was on dangerous ground, he added: "It's nobody's fault in particular, just one of those things. And if you haven't got an absolutely competitive car these days, you can forget it. Quite frankly, it's not worth the risk to life and limb to continue under those circumstances."

However he dressed it up, it was a damning indictment of the Wolf team. The comments made Frank Williams and Patrick Head smile. They were about to unleash the Williams FW07 on Formula One, which was what the Wolf car might have been if Walter Wolf hadn't been so stupid and sacked them. Both Williams and Head were quite candid later in their concession that they never would have left Wolf if they had not been fired.

In the next morning's newspapers, there was some debate about how much money Hunt had made in his career, and whether it would be enough to see him through to the end of his life. By walking away, he was turning his back on US$80,000 from Marlboro and US$500,000 from Walter Wolf. He had perhaps earned around US$3 million in his entire career and had managed to keep hold of most of it after moving to tax exile. He was certain it was enough: "I have made plenty of money out of racing. But it's not material achievement that's so important. What matters is achieving the way of life that suits you so you're happy. I think happiness is the really important thing." The sentiment was genuine, as money had never been really important to him. If it had been, he would have slogged his way around the rest of the season in the Wolf: "My ultimate goal, since I was 18, was to make a happy, well-balanced life for myself. Racing has always been a means to an end for me – the chance for me to find material freedom in life. And that is what I look forward to now."

When asked what he would do immediately, he was very honest and said: "It comes as a great relief to stop racing, and I look forward to just relaxing for a while. Then again, as with anything in life, the pleasures and relaxations are short-lived because they're soon replaced by a rush of other worries and problems. There are highs and lows and dreads and fears however you live your life, whether you're a racing driver or a clerk in an office. But I look forward to life after racing. I'm now taking the big step into a world that is unknown to me."

For the past 13 years, his life had been nothing but motor racing and he was a fully paid-up petrol head, but he said: "I feel no sadness at all, just immense relief. That's over now and I'm not sentimental. I don't dwell on the past. My goal is to make a mellow, well-balanced life. I need and am stimulated by ambition, but at the moment I'm happy marking time – just keeping busy chasing my tail."

John Hogan believed it was a mistake for Hunt to retire and told him so. He thought his lack of success on the race tracks had overpowered his sense of reason and he was making a hasty decision. There was little question that the sheer boredom of the 1979 season had played its part. It cannot be over-emphasised how much the advent of ground effects sucked the spirit out of Formula One.

But it was Bubbles Horsley who probably came up with the best analysis, saying of Hunt that the "damaging effects of self-indulgence were being compounded by fear." Horsley confirms that Hunt had become frightened by Formula One, and he didn't want to kill himself whilst unsuccessful. According to Horsley, Hunt knew his career was in decline, that he wasn't in the right team, that he wasn't succeeding and that his talent hadn't yet declined. Horsley told Hunt's biographer Gerald Donaldson: "It's rather like a film star who's suddenly getting bum scripts, but he needs to do it because that's what he does. He needs the money, and therefore he does it. But in the end, the scripts got so bad..."

Harvey Postlethwaite wasn't surprised by his friend's retirement, as he said at the time: "If anything, I think the decision came too late. If it had happened earlier we'd all have been able to get out of it better."

The season rolled on after Hunt retired, and the young Finn Keke Rosberg replaced him in the Wolf team. Rosberg was the best available driver without a drive after he had walked out on the uncompetitive ATS team at the end of 1978.

The team was relieved to have a more cooperative driver. They had become fed up with Hunt and were glad to see him go. When he left, there were a few tears shed as well as some rubbishing of the former world champion behind his back, as the team began a PR offensive to repair its damaged image. Back home in Spain, Hunt couldn't care a damn what Warr and Postlethwaite were saying. He knew the record spoke for itself. Postlethwaite said: "Formula One doesn't pardon anyone. Everybody exits Formula One out of the back door; you never exit out of the front. It doesn't happen. Everyone exits from the back door because it's that sort of business." He added: "My own reaction is that it's best forgotten. I prefer to remember him in the Hesketh days rather than subsequently."

In his first race at the French Grand Prix, Rosberg qualified 16th and brought the car home ninth. It was no better or worse than Hunt would have achieved in the car.

The race itself marked the first win for a turbo charged car in the modern era as Jean-Pierre Jabouille won his home Grand Prix from pole position. And Hunt missed a true racing spectacle. The race marked the fiercest ever battle fought for second place between Gilles Villeneuve's Ferrari and René Arnoux in a Renault Turbo, both shod with Michelin radials. During the final laps, they touched wheels and frequently swapped positions. Villeneuve eventually took the chequered flag less than a quarter of a second ahead of Arnoux. Villeneuve said it was his "best memory of Grand Prix racing."

The British Grand Prix at Silverstone went ahead for the first time in seven years without James Hunt and, inevitably, the crowd was smaller and Easton Neston quieter. For the second race in succession, there was a new winning team on the top step of the podium. A new era was beginning, as Alan Jones took pole position in the new Williams-Ford FW07. That domination continued in the race until Jones retired. His teammate Clay Regazzoni went on to score Williams' first ever win.

Peter Warr and Walter Wolf were stunned by the Williams' success. It was only two years earlier that they had shown Frank Williams and Patrick Head the door.

Meanwhile, Keke Rosberg had realised the Wolf WR8 was a dog, and he struggled all weekend to do anything decent with the car.

After the fiasco of Niki Lauda's accident at the Nürburgring in 1976, the German Grand Prix was now firmly established at Hockenheim. The new era was confirmed as Jones and Regazzoni scored a Williams 1-2. But Jody Scheckter was piling on points, getting fourth place, and was seemingly the world championship favourite as the success of Williams made it unlikely that anyone else could get enough points to beat him. Alan Jones had left his challenge too late and was not a threat.

It was proving a terrible year for the established teams. Hunt's old team, McLaren, with John Watson and Patrick Tambay driving were struggling almost as badly as Wolf. Brabham and Lotus were also experiencing the doldrums, with Williams, Ligier, Arrows and Renault in the ascendance.

On 12th August, Alan Jones won the Austrian Grand Prix at Österreichring, marking a third consecutive victory for the Williams team. The ground effect Williams FW07 was an outstanding car, every bit as good and destined to be every bit as pivotal as the Lotus 72, McLaren M23 and the Ferrari 312T had been earlier in the decade.

Rosberg in the Wolf WR8 just kept sinking, and the Finn wished he was elsewhere. Like Hunt before him, now Rosberg was thinking of quitting and was worried about his career prospects from continuing to drive the Wolf.

On 26th August, at the Dutch Grand Prix at Zandvoort, Alan Jones won his third consecutive race and the Williams team's fourth race in a row. Jody Scheckter battled his Ferrari up to second as he edged closer to being crowned world champion. In any other year, Jones would easily have been world champion, but his poor performance in the first half of the season had made that impossible. Even though he had only won twice after Holland, Scheckter merely needed four more points to ensure the driver's title.

Italy closed ranks for the Italian Grand Prix at Monza on 9th September, and Scheckter and Villeneuve scored a Ferrari 1-2 to give Scheckter the world championship title. It was the end of the European season, and the Italian fans went wild with the perfect result.

The Canadian Grand Prix on 30th September was held for the first time at a street and park circuit in Montreal. Mosport had lost the rights to stage the race after Bernie Ecclestone had rowed with its owners. Significantly, Niki Lauda walked away from Grand Prix racing halfway through the weekend. Lauda had become disillusioned with Formula One circulating in an uncompetitive Brabham-Alfa Romeo. Feeling very much like Hunt, he said: "My heart was not in it anymore."

The Lauda-Hunt rivalry since 1976 had transformed Formula One from a secondary sport into a primary one, and the two drivers were to be bitterly missed. Both would receive huge financial offers to return to the sport in the years ahead. By 1979, however, Lauda had started an airline business called Lauda Air and had bought himself a US$18 million Boeing 737 airliner. It seemed his heart was now in flying rather than racing.

Ironically, his decision to leave coincided with the debut of a brand new Brabham-Ford. Brabham ditched the Alfa Romeo and appeared with new Cosworth-engined cars. It appeared that Lauda had made his decision too soon as the car was instantly competitive, with Nelson Piquet qualifying it fourth on its debut.

With its two biggest stars gone within a few months, Formula One was in a spiral. There were only two world champions left in Formula One, Mario Andretti and Emerson Fittipaldi. Fittipaldi was now a footnote in the sport after three seasons at the back of the grid, and Andretti was fading fast in an uncompetitive Lotus.

Alan Jones easily won the race on the new circuit from pole position. In a seriously low point for the Wolf team, Keke Rosberg could not even qualify his car. When James Hunt learned of it, he was glad he had retired; it could easily have been him humiliated in the penultimate race of the season.

He said: "The common theory that I'd lost interest driving the Wolf in 1979 was immediately completely destroyed by the fact that Keke Rosberg, a young man with a lot to prove and everywhere to go, was put in the car and was very substantially slower than I had been in it, in the same car." Hunt felt vindicated after Wolf's fiasco in Montreal and said: "I always delivered in the car and...I tried my best."

By this time, Rosberg was seriously looking for an exit from the Wolf team, as it had become dreadful.

The Formula One circus packed up its crates and headed to New York for the final race of the season at Watkins Glen on 7th October. From pole position, Alan Jones in the Williams was totally dominant and would have won but for a rain-affected race that saw his team botch a pit stop to change tyres and force him out of the race with a damaged wheel. Gilles Villeneuve gave a virtuoso performance in the wet to win the race.

But there was a triumph of sorts for Keke Rosberg in the Wolf. He qualified 12th and managed to manhandle the Wolf-Ford up to a podium-challenging place. But it all ended with an accident on lap 20 when he tried to challenge Didier Pironi's Tyrrell for the pace and cocked it up, sliding wide and almost taking Pironi out as well. The world championship was won by Jody Scheckter, with Villeneuve second. It was Ferrari's swansong as it began its own long period of decline; one that would end 21 years later.

At the end of 1979, Teddy Mayer realised that McLaren was in serious trouble. John Hogan would have yanked Marlboro's money away from the team if he could have found anywhere better to put it. Mayer made a desperate bid to recapture past successes and tried to lure James Hunt back into the team. Mayer, with Hogan's approval, offered Hunt US$1.5 million to return. It would have made him the highest-paid driver by far. But Hunt was enjoying his retirement and declined. Although he did say that if the sport was made safer, he would reconsider; and that "no" was not definitely "no." And that was that.

Jackie Stewart was commentating for ABC Television in the United States during 1979, and Hunt's retirement was big news across the Atlantic. Stewart found the words to make the most intelligent and incisive analysis of why Hunt had retired: "You would have likened James' rise to that of someone in the pop music industry rather than in sport. It was a very sudden rise to adulation and big money and the good life. It's hopelessly intoxicating and very confusing. Your entire world is fantasy and candy floss. There's no substance to it, and unless you're very careful you get carried along on this magic carpet ride. But there's a side to this business which I think has gotten to James – driving a racing car endlessly, testing chassis, developing tyres, sitting in searing heat for an unacceptable number of hours, presentations, cocktail parties and dinners with people you don't want to be with – I think all this has troubled James, along with the pressures on his private life. He wants to do things his way, but unfortunately you can't. If you're going to stay in the sport, you have to compromise. Or you can do what James [did], which is to retire…I don't believe he thinks it's worth all the compromise, and I think he's making the right decision."

During his career, Hunt had also talked about retirement far more frequently than any other driver. Getting out had always been in his head, from as early as 1973. He said in 1976: "It is my ambition to retire, but I want to do it from the top, not from the dreaded slide down. When I retire, my ambition is to go back to being a normal person – one who likes other people, whom other people like."

That he had done. David Gray still regrets Hunt's early exit and feels he would have turned into a David Beckham or a Tiger Woods if he had stayed active longer: "He was a world figure. If he had carried on with it, he would have been a Beckham I think."

SHUNT

CHAPTER 35

The psychology of a champion
A low tolerance for indolence

No racing driver is easy to analyse. But assessing the psychology of a racing driver like James Hunt is near impossible. The closest he ever came to getting a professional assessment was when his second wife, Sarah, took him to see specialist marriage counsellors in 1985. The counsellors, attempting to analyse his psyche, told him he was a "cold fish who had difficulty showing love and affection." He also saw a psychiatrist in this period. In truth, an accurate assessment was to prove difficult even for the most skilled psychiatrist.

Hunt was a very intelligent man and probably understood his own problems far better than any professional analyst. But he never discussed his deep down psyche with anyone. It was simply not his style. That remained buried deep within him, and there it stayed.

Hunt appeared to race on his nerves. His propensity to vomit before a race seems to have indicated as much. He made no attempt to hide it and would often do so in front of people quite openly. Although he suffered from nerves, in actuality he suffered no more from nerves than any other driver. Other drivers simply handled their nerves differently from Hunt.

In the early days, when his consumption of alcohol and cigarettes was lower, it was less pronounced. But the truth was that the vomiting was a false clue to his personality. After 1969, it was never just about his nerves. It was about his high intake of alcohol and cigarettes, which facilitated an over-production of adrenalin, which then led to the vomiting. The mixture of all this in his body simply triggered a chemical reaction in his stomach to such an extent that he could only release it by vomiting before taking to the track. His total lack of embarrassment meant he didn't mind who witnessed it either.

No top sportsman has ever consumed as much alcohol or smoked as many cigarettes as Hunt, neither before nor since. He did both to excess. After his Formula Ford days he began smoking between 40 and 60 cigarettes a day for most of his life and, although he said he did not drink in the few days before a race, this was often not true.

The only other top athlete known to smoke as much as Hunt and still perform at the top level was Dutch soccer player Johan Cruyff, who smoked 30 cigarettes a day.

Tony Dron disagrees with this analysis and remembers that all the drivers used to smoke in those days: "Personally, I don't think it had any affect whatsoever on our performance. We weren't really aware of the outside world and what was going on. Everyone smoked then." 'Everyone' included Stirling Moss, who actually had a contract to promote the cigarette brand called Craven 'A'.

But Dron's analysis may be faulty in light of sophisticated medical research that was not available then. It is now well-known, well-documented and widely accepted that smoking is not conducive to professional athletes. Smoking regularly causes an athlete's airwaves to become blocked and it becomes tougher for oxygen to circulate around the body to reach vital muscles, which leads to respiratory problems. While smoking was much more common in the past and, in the short term may not have appeared to present such a problem, it would inevitably prove highly disruptive over the longer term.

Alcohol consumption has its own problems. As alcohol stays in the system for about three days after a drink, this means the human body will suffer dehydration for the duration of those days. This leads to headaches, nausea and a lack of concentration, and cramps are even more common. If the muscles don't receive enough fluids, they become tired and injuries are much more likely to happen – so the effects are two-fold.

These days, an athlete's hydration level is tested by something called an osmolarity test, which measures urine samples for water. But the test was not available when Hunt was driving. If it had been, he most certainly would have failed every time. This condition explains his desperate desire for a drink every time he stepped out of the cockpit. That desire was sometimes overwhelming and it often led to some embarrassing incidents. The worst case was after he won the 1976 Spanish Grand Prix at Jarama. It had been a tiring race and he was handed a bottle of Orangina (bottled orange juice) in the crush of getting out of his car. He was on his way to the royal box for the presentation when, as he explained: "I'd just won the race, I was tired and thirsty and this drink was the only thing I had in the world. This guy knocked it out of my hand and I punched him. It was a terrible thing to do because the poor guy hadn't meant to, but I didn't have time to think about it. I felt awful about it afterwards and tried to find him to apologise, but I couldn't find him. I'm not a punchy person normally, but I'm always punchy when I get out of the car."

But Hunt had misread himself; he wasn't punchy simply upon getting out of the car, but had a deep need for liquids caused by his extreme dehydration due to his various lifestyle choices.

His only thought when he won the world championship was getting a drink, and he was captured on film desperately asking for liquids when he got out of his car in Mount Fuji in 1976.

The nutritionists that abound in modern day Grand Prix racing would have recognised and sorted out this problem, and Hunt's life would have been very different. But there was none of that in the mid-seventies and the condition was never treated.

Bubbles Horsley was generally thought to be a good team manager who got the best out of Hunt when he was at Hesketh. But, in many ways, Horsley let his friend down by not insisting that he give up cigarettes and alcohol altogether. Horsley was another victim of the prevalent ignorance about the affects of both substances on sportsmen. He explains: "We never stopped him carousing. If he wanted to be on the piss all night, that was his business as long as it didn't affect his driving. What we tried to do was focus where discipline was needed, and we did have to discipline him in both his racing and in his private life. Maybe discipline isn't really the right word. Anyone outside your life can see you much clearer than you can perhaps see yourself. On that basis we were able to see, on occasion, that he was leading the kind of lifestyle that would not help his driving, so we tried to keep him on the straight and narrow."

But it wasn't enough, and there is little doubt that Horsley would have acted differently if he had understood that it was the combination of adrenaline, alcohol and cigarettes that was most likely causing the vomiting. He might also have better understood the need to keep his driver constantly hydrated while he was in the cockpit.

Jean-Pierre Jarier, who raced with Hunt in the seventies, believes that more discipline was needed in the Hesketh days: "James had no limits and he drank with Bubbles Horsley and the gang. Unfortunately, he paid a big price for that."

The condition sometimes manifested itself when Hunt retired from a race early. There was a world of difference between an abrupt stop after an accident and a controlled stop where he had a lap to think about it. The oversupply of adrenaline was then at its peak. Hunt seemed to recognise the situation in himself, saying that his adrenaline overload often took the form of excess ire: "When the race suddenly stops, whatever happens – an accident or a mechanical problem – I'm always in a highly emotional, discharging state. To open that emotional door at the end of four or five days is obviously a great relief. I think it's a normal and human way to behave, and if it upsets anyone that's unfortunate. But it can put me a bit out of control."

To explain it to himself, he felt it was necessary – or at least that is what he told journalists – to build himself up to an emotional peak of tension in order to achieve his best performance. That process, he said, began on a Wednesday before a race so that, by Sunday, he had worked himself up into the desired state of readiness, at which point he vomited. He never once mentioned the effects of smoking or alcohol in that process, which indicates either that he was ignorant of it or that he deliberately didn't want to address it. He said: "I'm very nervous and you have to be nervous to the right amount. I've got to the point now where I can control it. I can make myself more nervous by thinking about the race, and if I'm too nervous I deliberately stop thinking about it. Now all that requires a lot of mental effort, a lot of concentration, a lot of introversion. When you're driving, you have to be in total control of your emotions. It must be purely practical work. Otherwise you're playing with a dangerous thing."

In fact, many of Hunt's dramas were chemically- rather than emotionally-induced, as was generally believed. They seemed to arise when the chemicals inside his body became mixed up, but he always dismissed them as momentary lapses of emotional distress, common in a racing driver's psyche.

And 'momentary' was the key word. Because it was momentary, he got away with it. As he confessed: "Anger dissipates very easily in me, it's not something I notice. My mother pointed it out a few years ago. I've never been a ventral person, which is odd, out of character for somebody who's very naturally competitive. I get angry when people treat me unfairly, or what I perceive to be unfairly, but after getting angry I then get on with my life. I'm too much of a forward-looker to dwell on past aggravations, and I think that was the case there."

Alastair Caldwell, his team manager at McLaren, admitted he had never seen a driver as nervous as Hunt. "Before a race, a lot of my drivers pretended to be sleeping. Either they would be overcome by adrenaline or, in an attempt to control it, they would go into a passive mode and try to lower their metabolism by dozing. But James couldn't keep still. He would pace around the garage, chain-smoking cigarettes, putting his helmet on, then taking it off again and he nearly always threw up in the pits. It would get worse when we brought the car out onto the grid. Just before the start, he would get so uptight that the car was actually shaking on the grid. If you sat on the sidepod with him in the cockpit, his legs would be going up and down like jackhammers and you would think the engine was running. He was banging against the inside of the car, physically shaking and banging."

Teddy Mayer, the McLaren team owner, often witnessed what he called "James' emotional kettle boiling over." As he recalls: "I suppose it's not a bad way for a driver to be. They've got to have some fire and determination and at least if he blows off steam, it's gone. If he carried it around bottled up, it could do all sorts of harm. So I don't see that as a particularly bad characteristic. It might be unpleasant for a few moments, but you can learn to live with that."

But Mayer didn't make any attempt to prevent Hunt drinking alcohol or smoking. Ironically, it was BBC producer Mark Wilkin who first made an effort to change Hunt's ways, and Hunt responded very positively. At Wilkin's first ever race at Monaco in 1988, Hunt turned up merry, swigging from a bottle of rosé. Wilkin calmly took the bottle and replaced it with a bottle of water. Later, he told Hunt he was a much better commentator when sober and Hunt took it to heart. The difference in the standard of his work when he stopped drinking is clearly evident upon reviewing old TV tapes. Wilkin had a much better and more decisive relationship with Hunt than did any of his team bosses when he was racing.

It wasn't just Mayer who got the abuse; his other team principals, Bubbles Horsley and Peter Warr, also suffered from it and really had only themselves to blame. Horsley said: "We were all on a learning curve [in 1973], and when I made mistakes on the management side, he was very hard on me, accusing me of costing him races and so on. It would get quite heated, but, after I learned my trade, I would give him a hard time. I'd say: 'Look, you're not going to make it if you carry on like this. You're wasting our time. A lot of money is going into this and you're letting the side down.'" When it got down to the real, base emotional level, Hunt always responded and Horsley was gradually able to mould him into something more acceptable. One of the more persistent problems was Hunt's "me-against-the-world attitude", which was something he could not shake. He definitely felt let down when driving for the Wolf team in 1979, as Peter Warr explains: "When his car broke down, he'd jump out shouting: 'This car's a fucking heap of shit.' You'd just reel under the shock of his onslaught."

Harvey Postlethwaite was exposed to it for most of the four out of seven years he spent in Formula One, and says: "He was never cool, calm and collected, and he'd always be losing his temper and complaining and whinging and moaning before a race."

Hunt must certainly have been aware of it himself, but he made no attempt to alter his response to pressure. Jochen Mass, his teammate at McLaren in 1976 and 1977, was in a very good position to witness all this but doesn't think fully Hunt understood his own psyche at all: "You have a lot of footballers who go wrong because they can't take the pressure, but James was good with that. He could live up to that. He just searched for something within himself, he was constantly running after something. I don't know whether he knew what it was."

Maybe it was because it all came too easily to him. Hunt's approach to motor racing was very different from that of the mainstream. He was an effortlessly gifted sportsman, who, if he hadn't made it in Formula One, would have succeeded at the highest level in up to a half a dozen other sports. As top journalist Peter Windsor put it in 1976, Hunt had an "above-average belief in himself", which was putting it very mildly. Windsor wrote: "All racing drivers appear to be egoists, but with Hunt it is more so. He depends on his almost disassociated self-confidence, which sits easily on his casually clad shoulders." Or as Caldwell said: "James had a fantastic ego, but then of course all racing drivers do. He believed he was king of all he surveyed." But Hunt was by no means a narcissist. Despite the self-belief, he had virtually nil self-regard, and it was this inherent contradiction that made him the complex and complicated man he was.

Hunt always dismissed any criticism of his over-developed ego. He believed it was confidence and lack of pressure that had helped him most in his endeavours. He blamed most of his problems on pressure, and never gave a thought to lifestyle as a contributing factor.

The situation was confused because he often spoke gobbledygook to journalists, who typically printed exactly what he said without fully understanding it. Like all clever and intelligent people, sometimes Hunt liked the sound of his own voice rather too much, even when it was making little sense. This is demonstrated all too clearly in his book *Against All Odds*, written in his own words in 1976. Whilst much of it appears to offer concise and considered wisdom, some of it is utter nonsense, with the author seemingly unable to differentiate between the two – which is perhaps the way Hunt liked it. For example, he writes: "I think most people who win the world championship do [feel confident], because you've reached the ultimate pinnacle and it gives you a new dimension of confidence; you feel very on top of the world. And I was pretty confident through that half of 1976 too, when I was knocking off win after win. But to sort it all out gives you a new relaxed confidence and this all helps you in sport, so long as you maintain your mental preparation and your competitive edge, and building yourself up right with that sort of tension, to be relaxed is vital. It does give you a little bit more relaxation. And I think that probably, yes, for sure, I was driving better. I had everything and I was really enjoying it."

No one denies that Hunt was full of self-belief and utter confidence, but what made him such a confusing character was the sliver of disbelief that ran through his character and which sometimes became apparent upon those rare occasions when he talked about it. It was the belief that he couldn't do something until he did it. It seems to explain his relative underperformance right through his days of Formula Ford, Formula 3 and Formula 2.

All his team managers have something to say about getting the best out of him, and much of it relates to qualifying. Although he scored a race win and came very close to winning three or four other races in his first three years of Formula, Hunt never really got a sniff of pole position. And it appeared to be the result of a complete lack of confidence that he could actually be the fastest driver of all. It also seemed to relate to the fact that he had nothing to prove at Hesketh in Formula One. He continually performed better than the team expected, and there was little motivation to be a better qualifier. He appeared to be frightened of the front row of the grid.

Bubbles Horsley eventually worked this out and often told the story of the techniques he used to motivate Hunt during qualifying. When the car was stationary in the pit lane with the driver aboard, Horsley would tell the mechanics to work slowly, knowing it would infuriate Hunt, who would then get worked up and perform better. Horsley admitted: "He'd be straining away at his seatbelts, saying: 'What's going on?' He'd be waving and gesticulating and you'd see the anger in his eyes. You'd nod to the mechanic, drop the car and say: 'It's okay now.' He'd go out and do a blistering lap, and come back and give us a bollocking – 'incompetent amateurs.' We didn't do it every time because it wouldn't work."

Another trick was to use false pit boards. If Horsley thought Hunt could go faster out on the track, he would change lap times on the pit board. He sometimes showed his driver a slower time than he had lapped in. Horsley said it always managed to speed up Hunt.

Alastair Caldwell also worked out how Hunt's mind functioned, and practiced his own form of psychology. He said: "James needed distraction to keep him from getting too excited. Sometimes, I used to get Teddy to have an argument on the grid about money because that was James' favourite subject. They would have this huge row about hotel accommodation or first-class airline tickets and that took his mind off worrying."

But Hunt proved all his qualifying detractors wrong when he went to McLaren in 1976. He had never before scored a pole position, and had only been on the first row twice and the second row five times. Considering how fast he was, particularly when he had the Firestone tyre advantage in 1973 and 1974, it was a poor performance. But all that changed at McLaren, when he planted it on pole first time out in the dying minutes of qualifying at the Brazilian Grand Prix. He scored a further eight poles that year out of 16 races and went on to take six poles in 1977 in a much less competitive car, and 14 in his career. As soon as he had managed to get one pole position, he found it became very easy.

Hunt had another, even bigger problem with winning races; a problem he was very happy to talk about. His first win should have been in 1973, at the very last race of the year in the United States at Watkins Glen. He had a superior car and a tyre advantage but he wasn't psychologically equipped to do it. And it took him another year and a half to win a race.

In truth, his first win, in his third year of racing, in 1975, when he had lost his tyre advantage, was fortuitous; weather conditions had favoured him. But it gave him a taste, and when he got to McLaren, he was able to win frequently – ten times in all. But all his wins came in two of his seven years of racing. And they only happened after he had convinced himself he could do it.

Hunt was only too well aware of this side of his psyche, as he said: "You've got to remember, I had a pretty funny career up to Formula One and I didn't have any real practice at leading races – and you need practice. At first, I was cracking under the pressure. I was so worried about leading and was so busy telling myself to be careful, that when I got to the next corner I was still talking to myself and not concentrating, and I would do something silly and throw it all away.

"I finally worked out that you had to just sit and relax and get on with it, just drive in the normal way you do when you're not leading."

That reality manifested itself in the first half of the 1976 season. Hunt fully realised he was battling against himself just as much as he was fighting Lauda. He knew he was the faster driver but that, psychologically, he couldn't win. As he said at the time: "I was behind Niki and we were very closely matched. He just had the edge, but it was only a tiny edge. And I always said half of that edge was the fact that he was on a winning streak and I was not. It only needed a tip of the scales, and the scales tipped in my direction."

And that tipping of the scales happened at the Spanish Grand Prix in 1976, and the difference in his outlook was the difference between night and day: "I felt relaxed leading and under pressure if I was not. That's a good way to feel because you're in command, in charge."

The benefit of having eased the pressure manifested itself at the last three races of the 1977 season, after Niki Lauda had become world champion and the pressure was off Hunt. He admits that he drove far better in that situation than ever before. He won two races out of three and believed he would have won all three but for a mechanical failure: "The championship was all over so I was without pressure, I was completely at the top of my form. I was very confident with myself, I was driving very, very well and you know it was much more the lack of pressure than the aggravation. I was very stimulated anyway and I was enjoying myself, and when you're a sportsman enjoying your sport, it's got to make you play better."

It demonstrated a lack of consistency in his character and the total reverse motivation of most sportsmen; when he knew he could no longer be champion, he upped his performance level.

It suggested a totally unstructured thought process, which of course manifested itself more than a few times when he was commentating for the BBC in the years 1980 to 1993. It also goes some way to explaining his irrational verbal attacks on people like Ricardo Patrese, where, although Hunt would later regret his words, in many cases the damage was done and could not be undone.

It was the same with Ken Tyrrell, whom he perpetually criticised because of an incident involving his friend Jody Scheckter. John Hogan witnessed many such incidents, but remained, albeit with a few reservations, a huge admirer of Hunt's ability to "read the game." He says: "James was always absolutely black and white about somebody's ability. Totally black and white: 'that guy is a wanker; that guy is good; that guy is acceptable.' I mean if he went through them all, you'd be surprised."

Very surprised. He was a huge, huge supporter of Jackie Stewart. But he had this thing about Frank Williams and used to say: "Frank is a fucking idiot, he doesn't know the first fucking thing about motor racing, not a clue. If I ever get a lot of money, I'm gonna buy Williams so I can fire Frank."

And he meant it. But that was James Hunt.

THE PSYCHOLOGY OF A CHAMPION

SHUNT

CHAPTER 36

The return to Britain 1979
Time on his hands and nothing to do

etirement brought its own problems, and not the sort of problems that James Hunt expected at all. If he had looked forward to blissful days in Spain with nothing to do but swim and walk his dogs, he was soon disabused of that notion.

As soon as he had time on his hands and nothing to do, the attractions of Marbella faded away and he began to wonder whether they had in fact ever existed at all, except in his mind.

After he retired, he became much closer to his girlfriend, Jane Birbeck. He had far less choice in girlfriends as, when he had lost his racing career, he had also lost his arena for making sexual conquests. Suddenly there were far fewer opportunities for conquest, and that was something else he had not thought of. So there he was, ensconced in Spain with Birbeck, with absolutely nothing in his diary for virtually the first time in his life. Hunt had enormous amounts of energy and found this a wholly unsatisfactory situation. Neither of them had jobs, and Marbella became the perfect breeding ground for misery.

Aside from lack of availability, he had also lost some of his appeal as a swordsman. Although he still had his looks, the fact that he was no longer a racing driver meant the girls did not fawn over him as once they had.

It only took a few months for the rot to set in. Within weeks, Hunt became aware of the fact that he had never truly liked living in Spain, as John Hogan recalls: "I remember he came into my office one day and we went to lunch. It was pissing down with rain, and he said to me: 'It's a horrible day, but this is the best country in the world, even when it's like this.' I realised then that he was on his way home."

Hogan adds: "Sunshine is wonderful but, if you have no particular purpose sitting in it, it can be pretty damn awful. I believe that he really hated it. I don't think he ever enjoyed what I call the semi-colonial, incestuous cocktail party circuit. In fact, he often told me he despised it."

The truth was that Hunt was English to the core, and loved his country. It was the part of him that had so attracted him to Lord Hesketh in 1972, when they first met. Hunt's sole motivation for leaving Britain had been tax. He had been unprepared to pay tax on his income at over 90 per cent, and that had driven him to Spain. Now that his earnings had been reduced dramatically overnight – to effectively zero – the tax no longer applied and he could move back to Britain without penalty.

But his brother, Peter, was more cautious. He informed James that there were still opportunities in retirement for him to earn around US$500,000 year if he worked reasonably hard. Peter asked him bluntly whether he was really prepared to pay some US$400,000 of that to the British Inland Revenue. There was also the little matter of his annual unearned income from the US$5 million fortune he had built up when he was racing and on which he had paid no tax.

Peter Hunt warned him that the British Inland Revenue would scrutinise his affairs on his return to Britain and squeeze him "until the pips squeaked." Peter Hunt was quoting the words of Denis Healey, the former chancellor of the exchequer, whose ludicrous "squeeze the rich" tax policies had forced Hunt abroad in the first place.

But, once again, luck played its part in James Hunt's fortunes. Coinciding with his decision to retire and, just as he was making the decision to come home, there was a change of government. Margaret Thatcher ended the reign of Harold Wilson and his cohort Jim Callaghan, and ousted Labour in 1979. The general election result was resounding, with the Conservatives getting a 43-seat majority and 54 Labor MPs losing their seats. The overall swing of 5.2 per cent was the largest since 1945, and gave the Conservatives a workable majority But 11.5 million people still voted Labour despite the damage Healey had wrought.

When it came to power, the Labour government that had forced Hunt to Spain in 1974 was a total disaster for Britain. Healey's tax policies had forced over 250,000 high earning Britons, like Hunt, to move abroad. All the talent had been pushed out, with the resulting economic loss. If more moderate tax polices had been instigated of, say, a top rate of 50 per cent, Hunt would have stayed and the British exchequer would have been US$1.5 million richer, not to mention the economic benefit of having Hunt spending his money in Britain instead of Spain. Multiply the Hunt experience by 250,000, and it is easy to work out what Britain lost.

Sir Geoffrey Howe became Chancellor of the Exchequer under Margaret Thatcher and soon reduced the top rate of tax to 60 per cent, effective April 1980, with the promise to reduce it further as economic conditions improved. It was perfect timing for Hunt as he laid plans to return home.

In fact, Howe created the perfect economic environment for Hunt's return. There was a notable shift to indirect taxation and an abolition of exchange controls. Two years later, Howe's 1981 budget defied conventional economic wisdom by deflating the economy. Howe wanted to finally defeat inflation, which was a problem for Hunt and his depreciating capital. Inflation went from 11.9 per cent in spring 1981 to 3.8 per cent in February 1983, which suited the former world champion just fine.

With the ideal conditions in place for Hunt to return home, he finally persuaded his cautious brother it was the right thing for him to do and that his fortune would not be too depleted by the decision.

Explaining his decision to return, Hunt said: "I am English. I always intended to come back to Britain to live. It is my home, where my family and friends are, and I prefer the English culture and way of life. There are quite a few things wrong with the country but, on the credit side, in terms of freedom and law and order and general pleasantness, it's the best place in the world to live."

Concurrent with planning his return, he also started to plan his life after racing. When he retired, he had around US$3.5 million in the bank and another US$500,000 worth of assets. To secure himself an income for the future, he decided to invest half of his liquid cash in three business ventures. His most lucrative investment was a property development company he started with Bubbles Horsley. The company invested in commercial property – mainly offices, shops and factories, with a few residential developments whenever the opportunity arose.

Horsley proved to be very good at property, and the venture made some serious money. It was also a boom time and there was easy money around. Some of Horsley's deals made big profits very quickly, and, for seven years, the business boomed.

He also invested in a 14-court squash club in Munich, Germany, with external partners. While his involvement there was purely a financial one, he had more hands-on participation when he planned a new nightclub in Marbella named after his dog, Oscar. After he left, his partners ran the business.

He also planned to marry Jane Birbeck when they were settled again in England although, to all intents and purposes, he was already married to her. They were living together full time and were trying for children. He said: "I realised that I needed responsibility. That's why Jane and I are trying to have our baby. Then I would have a real meaning to my life. Someone to take care of. We both love children and, when we have a family, if the situation is right, we will probably get married."

The marriage plans were based on a desire to please both sets of their parents, and they announced their engagement as soon as they got to England, in November of 1979. Jane was happy because she was sure it was all the commuting between Marbella and London that had caused her to miscarry so many times. Motherhood appealed to her, and she was desperate to have a baby. But she did not feel the same way about marriage, which had been entirely Hunt's idea and not hers. In fact, she was not the marrying kind at all, as she told Gerald Donaldson: "It all seemed a bit grown up and we weren't sure we were ready for it. I thought I had commitment from him and was very happy just as we were. There were moments when I thought I'd quite like to get married, but it was never a pressing issue."

In England, Hunt planned to live the life of a typical, wealthy English gentleman with a wife and family. As part of that fantasy, he wanted a place in the country as well as a London residence.

To achieve this ambition, he splashed out half of his cash on property. He paid US$150,000 for a mews house in London's Baron Court, near good sports facilities. He then spent another US$50,000 getting the builders in for a complete renovation. Gerald Donaldson says: "He wanted to participate fully in what his native land had to offer; he thought he might like to lead the life of both a country squire and a man-about-town."

But strangely, his quest for a country home led him northwards. Instead of returning to his old haunts of Surrey, near his family, he opted for Buckinghamshire, near the homes of Lord Hesketh and Bubbles Horsley. And also near the family home of the Birbecks. He wanted at least 500 acres, and he deemed Surrey "hideously expensive."

Jane's father, Nigel Birbeck, told him about a farm that was for sale, a 600-acre estate in Buckinghamshire, near the old village of Olney. Called Park Farm, it was principally an agricultural estate. It had a six-bedroom farmhouse and a huge spread of outbuildings. Hunt was also attracted by the location on the banks of the River Ouse. In fact, it had rights to a staggering two miles of coarse fishing on the great river.

The house also came with the old courtesy title of 'Lord of the Manor of Tyringham, Filgrave, Sherington and Emberton', which were small nearby villages. Hunt seemed unconcerned about his would-be in-laws being so close.

The estate also had good connections to London and was situated just off junction 14 off the M1 motorway. The junction was ten minutes away and, once on it, he could reach his London mews house within 50 minutes, outside of rush hour. He was only half-an-hour from Easton Neston and 20 minutes from Horsley's house, near Silverstone.

Hunt had all sorts of idealistic visions about living in the country, but he had not really thought it through. He decided he would run Park Farm as a working farm and, bizarrely, decided he would be the farmer. He decided that his louche days as a Marbella-based playboy were now to be exchanged for the life of a Buckinghamshire farmer. It was a truly bizarre thought process. His thinking was aided by his friend Bubbles Horsley, who encouraged him in his rural fantasies. Lord Hesketh also approved of the plan.

But like the Horsley/Hesketh plan to marry Hunt off to Suzy Miller five years before, the scheme was to prove calamitous. Both Hesketh and Horsley had achieved much together, but they had also had moments of failure in their partnership. The two together were capable of incredibly poor judgment, and often made terrible decisions about small and big matters that blighted their lives.

Their advice and encouragement to Hunt to buy Park Farm proved to be one of these. It was so terribly obvious to everyone else that Hunt was not cut out to be a farmer. But Horsley could be terribly dismissive, it was one of his less endearing faults, and told his friend not to listen to the naysayers. Unfortunately the naysayers, as they had been in the case of the Suzy Miller marriage, were right.

Horsley advised Hunt to enrol on an agricultural course at Cirencester Agricultural College. Horsley himself had studied estate management at Cirencester before deciding to become a Formula One team manager. Horsley was adamant that Hunt should learn modern farming management techniques and the modern methods of breeding cattle.

As Hunt loved animals, it seemed the right way to go. But Horsley couldn't have given poorer advice to his friend if he tried. Hunt truly loved animals, and the idea of breeding them and then killing them was totally abhorrent to him. If Horsley believed that his friend could breed cattle and subsequently send them to the slaughter house, then he was on cloud cuckoo-land. Hunt was a man who went to great lengths to rescue spiders from the plughole. It was never going to happen, and his career as a farmer was over before it even started.

Hunt couldn't even bear to kill rats and vermin, the sort of things farmers have to do to keep an estate in order. Hunt felt very strongly that all the animals residing on his estate should be left alone.

He also told the local fox hunters that they could no longer hunt on his land. Naturally, this caused considerable strife locally, not least with his would-be in-laws, as the land was on the route of a well-known and traditional fox hunt called 'The Bicester and Warden Hill Hunt.'

But Hunt was adamant that it was no longer going to happen.

Such changes lead to big problems in local communities, and James was not ready for the resentment it caused. These sorts of incidents and disagreements sour the joy of caring and living in a rural environment, and Hunt's neighbours were soon sour on him. For Hunt, there was no way back from the fox-hunting ban, and he told reporters he found the idea of it "horrible." One local, quoted anonymously in the local newspaper, said: "Wait until one of them gets in amongst his chickens and he sees the slaughter and havoc one small fox can create. Then he may think differently." But Hunt, who had never witnessed the aftermath of a fox attack on a chicken coop, remained unmoved.

But the biggest problem in what became a local saga was that one of Hunt's principal opponents was his would-be father-in-law, the brigadier Nigel Birbeck. Birbeck was a formidable man and just happened to be secretary of the Bicester and Warden Hill Hunt. The complications this altercation caused for his daughter were immense as the two men stopped talking for a while. It also added to the tensions in his and Jane's relationship.

Park Farm also had a big tradition of keeping horses. But if there was one sport that Hunt didn't participate in, it was horse riding. As a car man who actually enjoyed the smell of petrol, he just couldn't see the point; and the smell of manure never excited him at all.

In truth, he was as unsuited to the life of a country squire as one could possibly be. He found the surrounding villages to be seriously boring, and the village of Olney was perhaps the one place in Britain where no one recognised him at all.

He decided to keep the villa in San Pedro as a holiday home and planned to split his time between all three. He decided that Oscar's future would be at Park Farm and that his other two dogs would remain in Spain. Oscar began his six months in quarantine, which proved a very difficult time and added to the stresses of the period.

And so began his new life in retirement, and it was not a happy time. Hunt made the classic mistake made by many wealthy people of overcomplicating his life and trying to live up to the amount of money he had in his bank account.

Advised by Bubbles Horsley, he got it completely wrong. Horsley was a brilliant team manager, but not so great as a life adviser. It was to set the scene for years of unhappiness.

Six months after the move back to England, the subject of marriage was off their agenda and Jane decided to pursue a career full time. She started a photo agency business called 'Domino'. But soon after starting the agency, she closed it down and went to work for Mark McCormack at the London office of IMG. She said: "Mark created an opening for me at IMG at about the same time as James had planned the wedding. And I said to James I'd rather have the wedding later because I'd just been given this job. And that was it really. It was finished. We never talked about marriage again. It was just sort of quietly ignored. We missed our moment."

And after that, his relationship with Jane Birbeck slowly began to deteriorate, as she later freely admitted to Gerald Donaldson. She began drinking too much and worrying about what was happening to her, as she said: "I felt he was just pulling me down."

Retirement wasn't proving to be all James Hunt had thought it would be, and he didn't have enough to do. In truth, as soon as he realised that, he should have made the move back to motor racing – as Niki Lauda would do a year later. And it wasn't as if there wasn't opportunity. Hunt's chance came when Teddy Mayer approached him at the end of 1979 and offered him US$1.5 million to make a comeback with McLaren for the 1980 season. He turned it down, believing he had not given retirement long enough. In truth, he had been spooked by the chances of getting killed. He had had plenty of time to reflect in the six months he had been away on just how lucky he had been. He counted seven times he should have been killed in his race car from Formula Ford to Formula One, and he wasn't so sure he would be eighth-time lucky. Although retirement had been miserable, it was better than being dead.

It wasn't only McLaren that needed him; Formula One did as well. From the halcyon years of 1975 to 1978, the sport had collapsed into a period of unremarkableness. Thanks largely to Lauda and Hunt, those three years of rivalry had transformed Formula One into a top global sport. Gone were the days when the BBC weren't interested in it. It was now being sold as pure entertainment. But all the entertainers had gone, and the most charismatic man on the circuits was Jody Scheckter.

Hunt told journalists who got wind of Mayer's offer that he would consider coming out of retirement if the sport was not so dangerous. The rejection was a huge mistake, and again the hand of Bubbles Horsley could be seen in it.

But in refusing McLaren's offer, Hunt was playing a dangerous game. He was 34 and the clock was ticking. With the shortage of genuine stars in Formula One, he was at his peak attractiveness, and the folly of turning down such a lucrative return was proved when Lauda came back a year later to take the McLaren seat and win another world championship. Whatever advice he was getting and whomever from, it was wrong; just plain wrong.

THE RETURN TO BRITAIN

SHUNT

CHAPTER 37

Disaster on the ski slopes 1980

Return to racing is thwarted by events

O n 28th February 1980, during qualifying for the South African
Grand Prix, Alain Prost crashed his McLaren-Ford M29B heavily
into the barriers at Kyalami and got out of the car clutching his
wrist in obvious pain. He had broken his wrist and could not start the race.
It would be six weeks before it healed sufficiently to drive again.

The United States West Grand Prix at Long Beach, California, was a
month away on 30th March, and that left the McLaren team with a big
problem. The American races were important for Marlboro, and there was
no obvious calibre of driver around as a replacement for Prost. Not unnaturally,
Teddy Mayer immediately thought of James Hunt.

Knowing Hunt's retirement was not working out, Mayer asked John Hogan
to tempt him back into Formula One. He had seriously missed Hunt when
he had left McLaren at the end of 1978. His replacement, John Watson, was
a very able driver and as quick as Hunt on his day. But Watson was not in the
same superstar class, and Hogan was not generating anywhere near the same
amount of media coverage for Marlboro.

Hogan lost no time contacting Hunt and asking him to take Prost's place
in the race. He knew the publicity surrounding Hunt's return, albeit for one
race, would be huge.

583

Hunt was tempted by the offer but not keen to come out of retirement so soon, if at all. So he asked Hogan for US$1 million for the single race. Hogan had a very big budget, but US$1 million was out of the question. But Hogan, who had anticipated paying Hunt US$100,000 for his return, thought it through and decided that the publicity generated for Marlboro would be so huge that he counter-offered US$500,000 for the one event.

Hunt quickly decided it was too much money to turn down for what would be one week's work. He figured that the Long Beach circuit would be safe enough for a single outing, even though the British tax man would take US$200,000 of the money now that he was back in Britain and paying UK taxes. So Hunt told Hogan he would do it and started training hard.

Then, at the end of the first week in March, he did something really stupid. He was on a skiing holiday in Verbier, Switzerland, with a large party of friends along with Patrick McNally, who worked for Marlboro. The party included a Marlboro-sponsored team of acrobatic skiers, called the 'Marlboro Hot Dog Ski Team'. Hunt was drinking heavily that day. In the afternoon, he was taking incredible chances on the snow whilst under the influence. His luck finally ran out when he tried to do a back flip on a snowboard while completely out of his mind on alcohol he had consumed at lunch.

He fell down awkwardly in the snow, and the resulting impact detached the ligaments in his left knee. When it happened, he was so groggy from the effect of the drink that he couldn't actually feel the pain and so he tried to get up. Getting up did even more damage to his ligaments. Gerald Donaldson described it as follows: "He was still under the influence of his lunchtime anaesthetic."

But Hunt, completely oblivious to the extent of the knee damage, attempted to carry on in the snow, making the injury significantly worse. John Hogan reflects: "If you ski when you're drunk, it's worse than driving when you're drunk. You will definitely hit something."

Eventually, he realised he was badly injured and lay down. He was taken to a nearby hospital on a stretcher. The hospital in Verbier was accustomed to all sorts of ski injuries but rarely had doctors seen such wholesale damage to knee ligaments. Unaccustomed to receiving inebriated patients, they were equally horrified when they realised that Hunt was drunk and slurring his words. As the 'lunchtime self-administered anaesthetic' wore off, the pain became increasingly worse. It was clear that it was a very nasty injury and there would be no more skiing for quite a while.

McNally phoned Hogan to tell him that any comeback at Long Beach was also out of the question.

The Swiss doctors decided to operate and knit the knee ligaments back together. When he came round after the operation, Hunt found the pain unbearable, and a morphine pump was set up by his bed. The doctors confirmed that he had endured the worst sort of ligament injury possible, and it would mean months in a full-length leg plaster cast and, when that came off, many more months in rehabilitation therapy. The doctors told Hunt to cancel his plans for the rest of 1980. But that, of course, fell on deaf ears.

He was forced to stay in the hospital in traction for 12 days. As he lay immobilised in hospital, he was attended to by Jane Birbeck, who did what she could to relieve the boredom.

At the time of the accident, Jane Birbeck was trying to get herself straight and give up alcohol and cigarettes. By now, she was deeply in love with Hunt to the point of unhealthiness, and was distressed by the pain he was suffering.

But, as she witnessed the extent of his pain and felt unable to help, she withdrew into herself. She also started losing her own battle to give up drinking. As she told Gerald Donaldson: "I didn't go to see him in the hospital as often as I should have. I was terribly selfish. When he needed me, I really wasn't there for him because I was trying so hard to straighten myself out."

Things improved when he came got out of hospital and got back to Britain. When he got home, the time he spent in bed wasn't entirely wasted as he and Jane took the time to talk and to get to know each other better. But whilst she was able to confide in him and discuss her problems, he found it very difficult to open up. Convinced that his innermost feelings should remain private, Hunt didn't feel comfortable discussing them, especially with women. It was not in his nature to ask for help to overcome a personal problem. His sense of self-reliance had become so highly developed that he had never learned how to need anyone.

Determined to cheer himself up, he decided to attend the United States Grand Prix West at Long Beach, where he should have been driving but for the accident. Getting there with a cast that was almost the full length of his leg was difficult and painful, but he managed it with the aid of crutches. It was a stupid decision to go to the race and, even though his knee was immobilised by the plaster, the stresses of a long flight did not help the healing process.

He was to be deeply affected by what had happened during the Grand Prix.

After he had been rendered unable to drive, McLaren gave the seat to a young, up-and-coming driver called Stephen South. But he wasn't good enough to be able to qualify. John Watson, then McLaren number one, could only qualify 21st, although he did drag it up to fourth in the race. The McLaren-Ford car, then in M29B designation, had not improved since Hunt's exit.

But all that was secondary compared to what happened to Clay Regazzoni in the race. The Swiss was driving an Ensign-Ford. Ensign was a small team run by a character called Mo Nunn, who had originally been inspired by Lord Hesketh to enter Formula One, albeit with far less success. Regazzoni was down on his luck and at the end of his career. He was racing simply because he enjoyed it. He couldn't give up the drug it had become to him. For Nunn, Regazzoni was a star, albeit a fading one, who drove for nothing and gave the team some resonance.

But it all went wrong for both of them on lap 50 of the race, when the car's brakes completely failed at the end of the long, high-speed straight where Regazzoni was doing in excess of 165 miles per hour. Although there was an escape road at the end of the straight, precisely to cope with this sort of failure, it was unfortunately already occupied by a retired car that the marshals had failed to move. The Brabham-Ford of Ricardo Zuniño had stopped after a first lap accident. Regazzoni hit Zuniño's car and bounced off it into the steel Armco barrier. He was immediately unconscious, as the huge impact had knocked him out. He regained consciousness as the marshals lifted him from the car, but was in terrible pain. He was rushed to hospital and operated on, but it was hopeless. He would never walk again. Regazzoni had been paralysed from the waist down.

Seeing the accident scared Hunt out of his wits, and he resolved there and then to make his retirement permanent. He was well aware it could easily have been him instead of Regazzoni, without brakes and helpless to control the crash. He just couldn't imagine a life of paralysis and not being able to have sex. At that moment, he finally defined a question that had been vexing him for the whole of his adult life: whether he preferred sex or motor racing.

Meanwhile, back in England, Birbeck was suffering from miscarriage after miscarriage as they tried to conceive a baby. A baby would have altered the course of their personal history, and Hunt put his formidable intellect to the problem. They discussed for many hours how a baby was made and what Jane's problem might be.

But the accident and his hospitalisation had done permanent damage to the relationship. She revealed: "We were still very close – there were moments when we were incredibly close – but I just thought that something went out of our relationship after that."

In the background was the absence of Hunt's dog Oscar, in quarantine. Hunt adored the dog and every hour thought about Oscar's forced imprisonment, and it troubled him. Both master and dog missed each other desperately.

He found he could speak more freely to outsiders than he could to Birbeck. One of his confidants at the time was April Tod, the young tennis journalist who had presented him with a garland at Rouen all those years before. They met again at a party with both their legs in plaster. She, too, was nursing a nasty leg injury from a skiing accident, and they compared notes. Hunt couldn't immediately remember her until she reminded him of their first meeting and that memorable kiss. Tod – then 28 – was, and still is, an extremely attractive woman with a warm, endearing personality. She remembers: "I had just come back from skiing and had a skiing injury, and there was he on crutches and I was on crutches, so we sat and chatted about our various injuries and he was really sympathetic. From that moment onwards, we bonded and we were always great friends."

John Hogan doesn't recall him being particularly depressed over the skiing accident, as he says: "I think he quite enjoyed that. He was hobbling around on his one leg – although it was very painful." Hogan and Birbeck's entirely varying accounts of those times indicates the ease Hunt felt with his male friends, and the unease he felt communicating with Birbeck, the closest companion he ever had.

One brief respite from the agonies was Hunt's debut for the BBC Grand Prix programme on 18th May. With his leg still in plaster, he managed to get to Monaco and enjoy his customary good time, free from the driving duties although hobbled by his crutches. He was sozzled the entire weekend, including during the live television broadcast, where he deeply upset Murray Walker by resting his cast on Walker's lap for the entire two-hour duration of the broadcast.

In the end, he spent nearly 12 weeks with his left leg encased in plaster. When the plaster finally came off, his leg was set in a straight position and he was faced with months of physiotherapy to get it back into proper working

SHUNT

order. After that, he went to San Pedro to recover but was in pain he could hardly bare. The Spanish heat meant he could not sleep at nights, making him very depressed.

The treatment in itself was also very painful, and Hunt rushed the process as he couldn't believe it was taking so long. The rush made the injury worse and he injured his ligaments again, which necessitated another operation.

The change in his circumstances was profound. Only a year earlier, he had been a top racing driver at the peak of fitness, and now he was virtually a cripple. It was not what he had expected in retirement. He later described the whole thing as a "shattering experience." He was also taking a cocktail of prescription drugs to relieve the pain.

Jane Birbeck was shouldering the burden of all this, and, as his fitness deteriorated, so did his mood. He descended into the condition known as 'black dog'. He admitted later: "Poor Jane. My brain became so addled with pain I couldn't talk to her. But as much as she wanted to help, there wasn't much she could do."

Upon recollection, Hunt was sanguine about what had happened to him, saying: "An ordeal of pain is something very personal. It has to be seen through alone."

The injury and its painful aftermath changed their relationship completely. They saw new sides of each other. It was a turning point in his life, which coincided with his change of status from golden boy racing driver to fallible ordinary citizen.

He didn't know it then, but it was the moment that his life would begin its long descent into a downward spiral he would not pull out of for nearly ten years – by which time Jane would be long gone.

Birbeck was by then approaching her thirties and beginning to wonder what the future held. Despite all the advantages and being blessed with extremely good looks, she had done nothing with her life. And she was full of regret that, after so long resisting her boyfriend's bad habits, she had sunk to his lows, drinking and smoking to excess. She worried she had developed an addictive personality as well.

And now, at this crucial moment in her own life, her boyfriend had been crippled in both mind and body at a time when they had three houses to look after and no income.

She told people that Hunt's enforced immobility meant he couldn't work off his frustrations physically. He also began to suffer from chronic insomnia

588

exaggerated by the heat of Spain. The insomnia, a new experience for him, would afflict him for the rest of his life.

To relieve the boredom, he drank through the day and night and was continually high on marijuana. As he withdrew into himself, Jane Birbeck's life began to fall apart. They both believed a baby would rescue them, but that baby was destined never to come.

But there had been some bright spots: Hunt had very successfully started a broadcasting career with the BBC, launching a second career after racing. But, when the season ended, melancholy set in once again, as did the bleak British winter.

By the end of the year, they were spending most of their time at the London house and were thoroughly miserable. Donaldson described their domestic situation as "far from blissful." Just before Christmas, Birbeck had yet another miscarriage. As she said later: "At Christmastime, we couldn't have been more depressed. The whole of 1980 was a wretched year."

It would get worse before it got better.

SHUNT

CHAPTER 38

Fleetwood Mac, the BBC
and all that 1980

A television great emerges

J ames Hunt predicted exactly when he would retire and also predicted
that there would be a second act to his career, saying: "As [motor racing]
winds down, I'll wind myself into something else." And that is exactly
what happened.

From that point of view, the timing of his retirement proved to be perfect.
Television sport was in its infancy in the mid–1970s and Formula One was
almost an afterthought in British schedules. But that was about to change,
and the catalyst for the change had been Hunt himself. His world
championship victory at the Japanese Grand Prix in Mount Fuji in 1976
had awakened interest in the sport around the world. Like every other
broadcaster, the BBC had carried it live and had cleared the schedule to do
so. It had been rewarded with huge ratings. The ratings woke up BBC bosses
to the potential of the sport and, for the first time, they took it seriously. So
1976 was a big watershed globally, when Formula One and television finally
found each other. Before that, the BBC only covered a few races a season,
cherry-picking the British, Monaco, Italian and, sometimes, Belgian Grand
Prix races.

Raymond Baxter was the BBC's motor racing commentator at the time.
But Baxter was more famous for presenting a science programme called

591

'Tomorrow's World' and he didn't really know much about Formula One. In truth, Baxter's racing programmes weren't very good, as he sometimes only had silent pictures to commentate on and no source of oral information.

Murray Walker says now: "It wasn't Raymond's fault because he sat in the presenter's seat doing the best job he could in circumstances beyond his and everybody else's control." Nevertheless, as Walker points out, the black and white images and Baxter's distinguished tones made the programmes absolutely memorable in their own way.

In 1976, a producer called Jonathan Martin oversaw the BBC's motor racing coverage. Martin, who at the time edited 'Sportsnight' and 'Match of the Day' would later be responsible for producing the highly successful 'Ski Sunday' programme.

After the Mount Fuji ratings success, Martin got the green light for a regular Sunday evening programme he called 'Grand Prix'. 'Grand Prix' was a 30-minute highlights programme which was broadcast on BBC 2 at 9:30pm after every Formula One race from 1977 onwards. The initial budget was minuscule and Martin managed to secure exclusive F1 rights for the BBC from Eurovision. At the same time, Martin launched 'Ski Sunday'. Just as Hunt had made Formula One popular, Franz Klammer had done the same for skiing. Martin called skiing and Formula One "sit in your armchair admire-and-marvel television."

Bernie Ecclestone, who ran FOCA, the team's commercial operation, was delighted to see Formula One get a regular slot on the BBC, although in those days he did not control the European TV rights, which remained firmly held by Eurovision.

The two new programmes were also the result of a dramatic increase in the quality of sports event broadcasting around that time. Martin says the quality before that was terrible, and only the Americans and Italians could do it properly: "In those days, I only dared broadcast Monaco and Monza live."

Martin co-opted Murray Walker to be anchor commentator right from the start. Raymond Baxter was thought to be too busy to take on the commitment, but it was more likely that Martin didn't want him, which was a surprise given that Baxter was then in his heyday and a big television personality.

Walker was born into motor sport commentary and his father, Graham Walker, was a successful motorcycle racing commentator for BBC radio in the thirties. Both father and son were also successful motor cycle racers. Murray Walker started commentating in 1949. But it was always a part-time occupation until 1977. A former military man, Walker graduated from Sandhurst and served in the Royal Scots Greys during D-Day. He ended the war with the rank of Captain, commanding tanks. After he was de-mobbed, he entered the nascent adverting industry and became a highly successful copywriter and was credited with penning the famous line: 'A Mars a day helps you work, rest and play', although he always denied it. He became a principal in the Masius agency for which he worked, and was part of the team that built it into 54 offices around the world. Walker, along with his partners, made a great deal of money when they sold the agency in 1982.

In between, Walker became the voice of motorcycle racing and expanded into car racing as second string to the famous Raymond Baxter, and used to commentate on the BBC's Saturday afternoon motor cycle scrambling broadcasts, which had a sizeable cult audience

Walker was an unknown when Martin plucked him from obscurity, but he was to prove an inspired choice. As was the choice of music for the introduction to the new programme. Martin's assistant producer, Bob Abrahams, chose the first 40 seconds from a *Fleetwood Mac* instrumental called 'The Chain'. It became the show's theme tune, which endures to this day. Martin remembers: "Bob had a good ear for music, and I wanted something that reflected motor racing. The first time I heard it, I just jumped at it – it was absolutely right. The first few seconds are threatening in anticipation of the start (as they are sitting on the grid) and then it bursts into life as the cars go off – it just explodes." Martin adds: "It has stood the test of time."

The opening title sequence was also stunning for its time, and featured the helmeted headshots of Niki Lauda, Jody Scheckter and Mario Andretti followed by the team principals Ken Tyrrell, Bernie Ecclestone and Colin Chapman, and action sequences. When the 40-second sequence stopped, Murray Walker burst into action. As he says: "Every time I hear that music, I get butterflies because I know that, when it stops, I start."

For Formula One fans, Martin's Grand Prix programme on a Sunday night was a little piece of heaven on earth. It just didn't get any better than that for the 800,000 or so people who used to tune in.

Initially, Murray Walker did not travel to the races, as everything was done in the BBC studio at Television Centre at Shepherd's Bush. But he soon received permission and the expenses allocation to be able to attend all 16

Grand Prix races. He was in the Formula One paddock from Thursday to Saturday, and back in the studio by Sunday morning to watch the live broadcast carried by the Eurovision satellite. Eurovision was the amalgamation of most of Europe's public broadcasters, and had an overall deal to broadcast Formula One in Europe at the time. It had signed a deal with the FIA years before.

Walker remembers: "The race was edited to 30 minutes and shown in the evening, with me doing a live commentary to the edited version." A journalist called Mike Doodson was always at the track to tell him what was going on over the telephone. By modern standards, it was ramshackle; but it worked extremely well, as anyone who can remember those programmes will testify.

Many Formula One fans at the time tried to avoid hearing the results of the race until they watched the highlights programme. It was brilliantly edited by Jonathan Martin, and fans got an absolute treat sitting in their armchairs. When James Hunt retired midway through 1979, Martin immediately wanted to hire him. But Martin, aware of his reputation as a hedonistic rabble-rouser, wondered if it would work. As a precursor to that, he invited him to be a guest pundit during the live broadcast of the 1979 British Grand Prix. Hunt didn't feature much, but, when he did, Martin found his contribution enthralling. Whatever the potential problems, Martin resolved to pair Hunt with Walker for the following season.

Martin was attracted by Hunt's manner of speaking and his clear and precise diction, which was tailor-made for television. The authoritative public school accent he had acquired in his five years at prep school commanded instant respect. He says: "It was easy to listen to his voice. He had clear diction and a good vocabulary."

But hiring Hunt was easier said than done. Both he and his manager, his brother Peter, valued his services very highly. When the three men met to discuss a deal, Martin reputedly offered Hunt US$30,000 a year to do the 16 races. He only wanted Hunt for the race, so it was effectively 16 days' work. At US$2,000 a day, Martin thought his offer reasonable. But the Hunt brothers just laughed. Peter Hunt told Martin it would have to be a six-figure number. Martin remembers: "James came in with all this film star stuff." Hunt had told Martin that he could easily earn between US$5,000 and US$10,000 a day opening supermarkets, and wanted a comparable figure from the BBC. He vaguely hinted US$100,000 a year might do it. But the hint was big enough for Martin to know that a deal was his if he wanted it. This was an unprecedented salary demand for BBC Sport, and Martin had to use all his persuasive powers to get approval from Alan Hart, then BBC head of sport. Hart had to go the controller of BBC1, Bill Cotton. Luckily, Cotton was a motor racing fan and soon agreed to pay. The eventual fee agreed to was nearly US$70,000 a year. Martin had put his career on the line for Hunt, and he had to make it work.

Martin was attracted to Hunt because he knew it was his win in Japan that had started all the excitement. He describes him as "abrupt, focused and friendly all at the same time", and recalls his impressions at the time: "I didn't feel it represented a risk in the sense that we could already see from his interviews that he was a natural communicator."

But Martin was naturally worried about Hunt's reliability. He had heard all the stories, and knew Hunt was a playboy who liked a drink. He was also worried about his long-term commitment. But the money on offer made it attractive enough for Hunt to take it seriously and be reliable.

And these were misnomers Hunt had inherited; contrary to his reputation, he was in fact reliable. When he contracted to do something, he was meticulous about turning up on time and giving it 100 per cent. But that wasn't his reputation, and once the deal was announced, it seemed that everyone Martin bumped into had a Hunt horror story to tell him. But somehow Martin's instincts told him it would be alright on the night.

After Martin had Hunt's signature on a contract, he told the news to Murray Walker. He thought it would be welcome news. But Walker had established his own comfortable and solitary niche on the show and clearly liked it that way.

Walker says it came as a "bombshell" when Martin told him what he proposed. He recalls: "Jonathan told me that there would now be two commentators and that the other would be James Hunt."

Walker was shocked and had to sit down. When he left Martin's office, he says his reaction was a mixture of "fear and resentment" – fear because he thought he would be fired and replaced by Hunt; and resentment because he didn't much care for his new partner.

Walker really believed that Hunt's appointment was a precursor to him being fired, and he suspected that Martin was simply letting him down lightly. He remembers thinking to himself: "The next thing that'll happen is that they'll be saying: 'Thanks for all you've done, Murray, but we want a younger man who has actually done it.'"

But nothing could have been further from Martin's mind, and he didn't realise he had upset Walker until he read about it in Walker's autobiography years later.

The fact was that a new era of twin commentators was beginning in televised sport, and Martin was using Formula One as an experiment to see how it worked. But Walker couldn't see that, as he says looking back: "I feared I would lose a job I loved."

Walker hardly knew Hunt at all. He was not his sort of person, and they had had only what Walker calls "casual conversations" in the past.

Hunt said Walker's fears, which he learned about later, were baseless as he never had any designs on his job and Martin had no intention of firing him: "The last thing I wanted to do was handle a whole race because that would not give me time to look around, to assess, come out of the commentary box door and have a listen with my own ears to hear what the engine's doing." In fact, Hunt revealed later that he would not have taken the job if Walker had not been the main commentator.

Initially, Walker didn't have much time for Hunt and was very frank about what he thought of him in his autobiography, published in 2003: "As a person, he was arrogant, rude, overbearing, drank too much and was certainly not my idea of someone with whom I wanted to share the microphone. I was totally incompatible with him."

As Walker recalled in his book, *Unless I'm Very Much Mistaken*, which sold 1.1 million copies: "Two people could hardly have been more different in terms of age, temperament, background and attitude. James was a free spirit, with a highly volatile and forcefully opinionated personality and a fearsome temper, who did not think or act like other people. And how about me? At 57, I was more than old enough to be his father, and unhappy about being paired off with someone I thought was lazy and unprofessional and whose private life I did not admire. We were a seemingly ill-matched couple with a potentially disastrous future." He added: "I was pretty averagely cross with James for a lot of the time. I didn't admire his lifestyle and his arrogance, and it wasn't just me."

The first programme they did together was effectively a dress rehearsal at the Daily Express International Trophy race at Silverstone. By then, the event was a shadow of its previous self and was no longer a Formula One race. It was exclusively for Formula 5000 cars and was won by Eliseo Salazar, the Chilean driver. Walker remembers it well: "I summed it up as brightly as I could and turned to James and said: 'And what did you think of it, James?' 'What a load of rubbish,' he replied." Walker was audibly shocked by his bluntness, but had to agree with the initial assessment.

It was the sixth race of the season by the time Martin had finalised his new deal with Hunt, and the partnership proper, which would endure for nigh on 13 years, began at the 1980 Monaco Grand Prix. The BBC's Monaco commentary box was effectively on the pavement opposite the pit lane. Hunt and Walker sat on deck chairs just behind the temporary steel Armco barrier, which was sheltered by a canvas top in case it rained. The canvas was more to protect the equipment than the commentators. Jonathan Martin sat behind them with a cardboard screen to shade the sun from the screens. A few feet away, the cars blasted past on the warm up lap and the noise was deafening. Walker was wearing an earpiece for the first time so Martin could tell him how to interact with Hunt if he needed to. It's probably fair to say that Martin was quite nervous about the pair's first outing together.

Five minutes before the race was due to start, there was no sign of Hunt, and Martin was getting anxious. As for Walker, he was praying Hunt wouldn't turn up at all. But with two minutes to go, Hunt arrived. He was a mess and it didn't appear that he had been to bed. Unshaven, barefoot and drunk, he was wearing a dirty t-shirt and a frayed pair of cut-down jeans. But worst of all, he arrived swigging directly from a bottle of French rosé wine.

For good measure, he was on crutches and his leg was in a plaster from a skiing accident the month before. Mouthing apologies for being late, he immediately sat down and rested his long plaster cast on a horrified Murray Walker's lap.

Walker was totally stunned and cast Martin some very dirty looks. With no confidence in the situation, Walker couldn't believe Martin had been stupid enough to hire Hunt and feared what would happen in the next hour and forty minutes.

As Hunt polished off his wine, a friend handed him another full bottle and Walker looked on in disbelief. In truth, Walker thought Martin had lost the plot that day, and he couldn't have been more disgusted with his producer and new co-commentator.

But Walker needn't have had any fear as, to his absolute astonishment, Hunt was brilliant from the very first moment Walker handed him the microphone. In those days, there was one microphone which was shared so that the two men could not talk over each other. Martin insisted from the start that there be one microphone. Walker, who commentated standing up, would cue in Hunt and hand him the microphone when the action demanded an expert comment. Whatever his personal feelings, Walker was generous with the microphone that day and Hunt could have had no complaints on that score. Walker remembers: "I stood up during the race, going berserk with excitement; James sat down and was calmly authoritative in that wonderful public school voice of his."

As soon as the race was over, Hunt astonished Walker again. When the chequered flag dropped, Hunt was gone. Monaco had established a pattern that would endure for 13 years: Hunt would arrive at the very last possible moment and would then desert the commentary box the moment the race ended.

Jonathan Martin was absolutely delighted when the race ended, and remembers: "James' essential broadcasting characteristics were there from the start. He was on air because he had been there and done that and was speaking with authority, and therefore the public listened. It's no good having expertise if you can't communicate it, and James could. His use of language just flowed, and of course he had a broadcasting voice."

Walker may have been seething underneath, but even he had to acknowledge Hunt had made a devastating debut at Monaco. When he looked at tapes of his broadcasts both before and after partnering with Hunt, he conceded how much better they had become. He says: "You had my practical race-reading ability alongside his personal acumen, political clout, inquisitive mind and provocative attitude, and suddenly you got a partnership which people tell me worked brilliantly well."

Martin agrees: "What he brought to the microphone was a complete honesty. The best thing about him as a commentator was that his opinions were based on good judgment. Occasionally, he and I had discussions about what he'd said because I wanted him to justify it, and he always could very easily. He wasn't controversial just to be controversial." Martin adds: "He enjoyed it. It gave him enormous satisfaction, I think."

Martin has a good way of describing the Walker-Hunt broadcasting relationship: "Murray's job was to read the race and describe the action, and James' job was to navigate the race."

After a while, when Walker realised that Jonathan Martin's intentions were honourable and that he was not going to be sacked, he started to warm to

Hunt and to see his good side.

It was also essential that they worked together as a team as it was not easy being Formula One commentators in those days. Both men were peering into tiny monitors, with Mike Doodson sitting behind them supporting them with information. Doodson, who was in the commentary box for all 13 years of the Hunt–Walker partnership became an integral part of it.

The thawing in the relationship between Walker and Hunt proved a slow process as, just as it began to warm up, Hunt would do something that upset Walker and a period of coolness would follow.

Hunt never ceased to amaze Walker, and he remembers in particular the day he found him in the studio intently reading some books: "He had these sex manuals that he used to carry around with him and he would sit diligently reading them. It was instructive stuff, and it was very difficult not to read them over his shoulder, I can tell you." Hunt, as Walker recalls, was not in the least bit embarrassed and asked him if he would like to borrow one. Walker shuddered and walked away shaking his head.

Walker prided himself in being a team player, and he travelled to the races with the BBC crew and stayed at the same hotels. But Hunt's whereabouts were always a mystery, and there were often races when he was not in contact all weekend and no one even knew if he was in the country. As Walker remembers: "In fact, it became something of a joke: 'Has anybody seen James?'"

It was funny but it irked Walker, who was meticulous about his homework before races. When Hunt eventually did turn up, he always famously greeted Walker with the same line: "Right then, Murray, who's on pole?" In the early days, Hunt usually didn't know who was on pole and had done no research before a race. So he tried to crib from Walker's own meticulously researched notes. But Walker invariably snatched them away, much to Hunt's chagrin. As Walker told Gerald Donaldson: "My attitude was that I had sweated blood to produce these itemised details which I can refer to at a moment's notice and I'm damned if I'm going to let this lazy interloper benefit from all my hard work." Walker added: "I deeply resented the fact that this chap was not putting his all into it." But Jonathan Martin disagrees, saying: "James did a bit more research than he ever let on, and liked Murray to think that."

But Walker, who received a lot of criticism from the Hunt family for his candid views after his autobiography was published, adds: "I don't want to give the impression that we couldn't stand the sight of each other. James always had enormous charm. There was no animosity. We always got on. But what I didn't do in the beginning was respect him."

Martin thinks Hunt did it deliberately. "He was a guy that lived on adrenaline and I think he loved the tightrope nature of live broadcasting, slipping into the commentary box just before the start of a race, when the mouth goes dry and the palms start to get wet and it's pressure time."

For all that, in 13 years, only once did Hunt not turn up for a race. It was at the Belgian Grand Prix in 1989 at Spa-Francorchamps, and Walker was forced to do the race on his own.

Roger Moody, Martin's successor as producer, was frantically phoning round to find him. Hunt later apologised and phoned Moody 20 minutes before the end of the race, saying he was ill in bed with food poisoning from eating Belgian *pâté*, a delicacy of which he was particularly fond.

But Moody later found out that wasn't true; at least the bit about being ill. Hunt had enjoyed a particularly wild night out with two girls, believed to be Belgian nurses, and had carried on drinking into Sunday afternoon. Jonathan Martin, who by then had been promoted to head of sport at the BBC was apoplectic when he found out. But he let it go after he found that Hunt himself was mortified at what had happened and decided the remorse he felt was in fact punishment enough.

It was a wise decision and Hunt never let him down again.

In fact, from that moment on, the situation improved immeasurably and Walker really warmed to Hunt. As Walker got older, he had increasing difficulty coping with the demanding conditions commentators had to put up with on the circuits, and mistakes began to creep into his commentary.

Hunt often stood up for Walker and defended him when he was criticised for making mistakes. Later, the mistakes became part of the Murray Walker legend. Hunt understood how difficult it was. The truth was that the viewer at home often had a better view of the race than the commentators, who were working in cramped conditions alongside other broadcasters from around the world, staring into small monitors.

When he heard the criticisms, Hunt said: "Look, it's bloody difficult to get it right. I certainly get confused from time to time. It's not easy. Why people insist on criticising him I don't know. The trouble is all Murray ever hears in this country is criticism. He's a tremendous enthusiast and he does a hell of a lot for the image of the sport."

Walker was delighted when Hunt stood up for him.

But one problem endured, and that was Hunt's relentless and unending criticism of Formula One drivers. Hunt was uncompromising in his opinions throughout the 13 years he was broadcasting, and successive BBC producers – Jonathan Martin, Roger Moody, Charles Balchin and Mark Wilkin – were loathe to rein him in for fear of ruining the magic and chemistry of the Hunt-Walker partnership. They all recognised that the conflict between the two men was part of the charm.

Hunt genuinely thought it was his role to be the outspoken expert, and he had a list of drivers he didn't rate and whom he subjected to endless criticism. At the top of the list was undoubtedly Italian driver Ricardo Patrese. Patrese was Hunt's nemesis from 1978 to almost the end of his life. Hunt had an on-air vendetta against Patrese, and it all stemmed from the death of Ronnie Peterson in September 1978.

Hunt held Patrese fully responsible for Peterson's accident and subsequent death. It later turned out that Hunt was wrong in his assessment and that he was just as much to blame for Peterson's death as the Italian – not that blame needed to be attributed because it was clearly shown to be a 'racing incident' that unfortunately resulted in the death of a driver.

It was one of the biggest errors of Hunt's life, but it was real and it continually annoyed Murray Walker, who was a personal friend of Patrese's. Walker remembers: "I only had to say something complimentary about Ricardo Patrese for James to fiercely gesture for the microphone. I would give the mike to James who would then spew vitriol and bile over Patrese."

Walker admits that, after a while, he deliberately began to annoy Hunt on air: "I would say: 'Well meanwhile, on lap 54, Ricardo Patrese, who has won six Grands Prix, scored eight pole positions and finished second and third in the world championship, has moved up to fourth place.'"

With only one microphone between them, an infuriated Hunt was unable to retaliate.

The criticism of Patrese ceased in 1992 but had endured for 12 years before that, causing the likeable and popular Italian immense distress. And it was another of those incidents where no measure of accountability could be forced from Hunt. Mark Wilkin, his last producer, says merely: "James was emphatically right or he was emphatically wrong, there was nothing in between."

Hunt would go to elaborate lengths to prove he was right about Patrese and he spent hours poring over race reports and lap times, performing mathematical calculations which showed that Patrese was 0.94 seconds slower than his teammate in one season, then 1.14 seconds slower the next year.

John Hogan admits that Hunt passed "total misjudgement against Patrese" as he says: "It was weird. And it went back to the Peterson thing, and that was a bit stupid and very extraordinary because his judgement of drivers was usually so sound."

John Richardson believes Hunt's outspoken commentating stemmed from his childhood and his strong sense of self-sufficiency. Acknowledging that no one was ever able to penetrate it, Richardson says: "He was always very intransigent and he had his own ideas, and he wouldn't be afraid to tell somebody that they were a complete idiot if he felt that they were."

John Watson, who otherwise holds Hunt's memory in great affection, says: "I had my reasons to think it's James putting the boot in – whether it was directly because of 1978 or just James being James. I think he went on to the point where he had to make a public apology. It was perceived as personal and, certainly, at one Grand Prix, he did have to make a grovelling apology. He wasn't criticising from a balanced point of view. I think the BBC received many complaints about James' unyielding negativity towards Ricardo Patrese who, from the public's point of view, was not perceived in the way that James was portraying him."

To Hunt's credit, as he gave up alcohol and mellowed in his last few years, he recognised this, and the criticism of Patrese ended. But it still frustrated Murray Walker: "My attitude was that I'm not here to argue with James Hunt on the merits or demerits of Ricardo Patrese, I'm here to tell people what's actually happening in this race."

There was one comical moment amongst it all, as Mark Wilkin recalls. At the German Grand Prix in 1992, Hunt discovered that the media centre at races had staff that produced detailed statistical information. Hunt had never visited a modern day media centre and barely knew it existed. He had been used to the table-clothed, trestle tabled rooms of the past, where journalists tapped on their portable typewriters. The advent of the computer and ISDN lines had turned them into high-tech communications rooms. Wilkin remembers: "He came up to me in Germany and said: 'I've found this marvellous place called the media centre, they've got all sorts of things in there you know.' 'Yeah, I know.' 'They've got charts of everybody's lap times for every session.' I said: 'Yeah, I know.' 'It's marvellous,' he said. 'Do you know, this is absolutely fantastic because I can now prove that Patrese is a cunt rather than just telling everybody.'"

But although Patrese consumed most of Hunt's attention, Murray Walker had only to mention a name on Hunt's so-called 'hate list' and he would immediately launch into a searing attack.

Of the Brazilian driver Nelson Piquet, he said: "The problem with Piquet is that he's never grown up. He's only racing for the money to keep his 45-metre yacht afloat. What I can't understand is why he doesn't drive faster just out of self-respect." Of Alessandro Nannini, he said he "lacked brainpower behind the wheel"; Mauricio Gugelmin was "slow in all the lesser formulae, even slower in Formula One and had no reason to be there"; and Rene Arnoux was a "menace to other drivers." Moreover, Andrea de Cesaris was an "embarrassment to himself, his team and the sport" and a driver who "never looked in his mirrors"; Alain Prost's motivation was "suspect"; and Jean Pierre Jarier was a "French wally – always has been and always will be." He also called Jarier "pig ignorant" live on air.

Nigel Mansell took exception to Hunt's coverage of his world championship in 1992 and subsequent move to the United States. Hunt regarded Mansell as a "whinger" and someone who was "undeserving of respect." Mansell even threatened the BBC with legal action if Hunt didn't moderate his views.

It was not only drivers who came under Hunt's attack. He also had a go at the team principals, some of whom he considered to be "clowns" and wasn't afraid to say so. Ken Tyrrell was furious with Hunt when he proffered advice on how to run his team more effectively. Hunt had taken against Tyrrell after a long-forgotten incident with his friend Jody Scheckter in Holland in 1976. Hunt made Tyrrell pay for this many times over with his barbed comments on air. But Walker was furious and said: "I cannot imagine anyone less likely to have done such a thing than the experienced and honourable Ken Tyrrell."

Hunt was also scathing about Frank Williams and, although respectful on air, privately told friends that Williams was a "wanker."

Walker didn't agree with any of the aspersions made by Hunt. To him, Grand Prix drivers were heroes and were to be revered. But to Hunt, they were something different altogether – because he was one of them. Walker visibly winced when Hunt delivered his harshest criticisms, but was scared of interjecting on air as he knew Hunt could respond vigorously, potentially initiating an on-air argument.

Hunt was unrepentant: "I simply describe things as I see them. If someone makes a cock-up, then I say it's a cock-up, rather than watering it down. It's as if I'm sitting at home with my mates, watching the Grand Prix on the telly. All I'm doing is colouring it in for them because I can see things they might not pick up."

But Walker just did not feel it was right: "I did not regard it as my right to criticise the drivers; James was fiercely condemnatory whenever he got the chance. With his knowledge and experience of what it was actually like to race a Formula One car, he had every right to do so, although he was often vindictively unfair in my opinion."

Walker simply glossed over his more controversial statements.

Wilkin recalls an almost comical moment in the partnership when both Hunt and Walker each decided that the other was getting too much 'microphone time.' It was at the Belgian Grand Prix in 1991, and a brief power struggle took place, as Wilkin recalls: They had both obviously been thinking about it for a while and had decided to confront the producer and have it out. James said to me: 'It's not fair, Murray is doing too much, we need to redress this balance and it's your job to sort that out.' So I said: 'Yes, it is absolutely. I will sort that out.' At the same race, Murray came to me and said: 'I've been thinking, it's not fair. James is doing too much and you really need to sort that out,' and I said: 'I've noticed that, Murray. I'm going to have a word with him.' "Afterwards, of course, I said nothing to either of them. But after the race they both came up to me and said: 'I don't know what it is you said but it worked a treat, absolutely perfect this time round' – both of them convinced."

Wilkin could barely contain himself but had to take the complaints seriously, as he didn't want to upset the on-air talent. Wilkin says: "I said I understood and agreed with them both, and I did absolutely."

Wilkin hopes he dealt with the disagreements diplomatically, but says: "James used to sometimes bang his fists on the table like a child and say: 'Tell Murray I do the replays', and occasionally Murray would venture into giving opinions and I'd say: 'Not yours; you don't get opinions. You tell us what's happening.'"

There was also a huge conflict of interest for the BBC to deal with. Throughout his commentating career, Hunt was retained as a consultant by John Hogan of Philip Morris on US$50,000 a year. He was therefore very attached to McLaren and spent all his time in the Marlboro motor home.

Marriage to Suzy Miller and Richard Burton to the rescue

Below: James Hunt and best man Lord Hesketh on the day of the wedding. Hunt had been having serious doubts about the marriage ever since the engagement party, and decided the solution was to get himself inebriated.

Above: The official engagement photograph: The couple met whilst they were both living in Marbella. Unlike Hunt's previous girlfriends, Suzy Miller was undemanding, quiet and had a thoughtful manner.

Above: Hunt with Graham Hill at his stag night, which was held at Trader Vic's under the London Hilton in Park Lane, London, on 17th October 1974. It was the night before his marriage to Suzy Miller.

Left: James Hunt and Suzy Miller on their wedding day on 19th October 1974 outside the Brompton Oratory Catholic church in Kensington, London.

Bottom right: The bridal Rolls-Royce, complete with a helmeted Hesketh bear.

Below: Graham Hill and Stirling Moss at the wedding of James Hunt and Suzy Miller. More or less every racing driver of distinction was invited, including Jackie Stewart, John Watson and Ronnie Peterson.

Press Association

Above: Hunt with Richard Burton and Suzy Miller. As far as the outside world was concerned, both the Hunts' and Burtons' marriages were fine but Suzy had kept Hunt fully informed of the developing affair on the telephone. To say that he was delighted would have been an understatement.

David Phipps/Sutton

Below: James Hunt and the new Mrs Richard Burton photographed in Marbella, Spain, on 1st October 1976, when Richard Burton came to visit his new wife's ex-husband.

Above: The couple relax at the Monaco Grand Prix on 26th May 1974.

Press Association

Right: Hunt surrounded by young fans at Great Ormond Street Hospital, London, in 1977. He visited the hospital to help with a fund-raising appeal. He pioneered Formula One's long standing association with the hospital.

Solo Syndication

Hunt strikes a pose and rides Lord Hesketh's Suzuki superbike around Monte Carlo at the Monaco Grand Prix in 1973.

Solo Syndication

Mirrorpix

Above: Five well-dressed grid girls hold up a delighted James Hunt at the British Grand Prix on 18th July 1976. **Left:** Hunt with Noel Edmonds prior to the start of the Avon Tour of Britain, 1974.

Above left: Jane Birbeck and James Hunt were first introduced by Mark McCormack, the chairman of IMG, the world's biggest sports sponsorship and management agency. Birbeck was going out with McCormack at the time. They had a great time together at Monte Carlo in 1977.
Above right: Hunt and Jane Birbeck in the pits at the Monaco Grand Prix on 22nd May 1977.

Left: With Barry Sheene and his future wife, Stephanie McLean, after the 1976 British Grand Prix on 18th July. McLean and Birbeck found common ground in their womanising and became firm friends.

Left: Hunt at London's Heathrow Airport with Jane Birbeck after flying in from Montreal after the 1977 Canadian Grand Prix.

Above: James Hunt and Jane Birbeck pose for a *Daily Mirror* photographer in Marbella shortly after Hunt retired in May 1979.

Above: Hunt and Jane Birbeck share a moment of domestic bliss at home at their London mews house.

Solo Syndication

Right: At home in Marbella.

Mirrorpix

Above: Hunt and Jane Birbeck pose at a press conference to promote the opening of Birbeck's new gym on King's Road, London in 1982. Hunt was very generous to his ex-partner after the split, and agreed to become an investor in the gym.

James Hunt with girlfriend Jane Birbeck pose for the cameras for a PR shot at the Monaco Grand Prix in 1977. Their relationship lasted for five years.

David Phipps / Sutton

Below: James Hunt and Sarah Lomax at the Portuguese Grand Prix at Estoril on Sunday 21st October. The pair met whilst Lomax was holidaying with girlfriends in Marbella.

Right: James Hunt and Sarah Lomax on their wedding day in Marlborough, Wiltshire, on Saturday 17th December 1983. Some of his friends declined to attend as they were loyal to Jane Birbeck and felt the marriage was not appropriate.

Below: James and Sarah Hunt at the launch of an anti-drug campaign supported by celebrities on 3rd September 1986. Ironically, they both enjoyed to drink, smoke and indulge in recreational drugs in a way that perfectly matched eighties hedonism. However, they were both firmly against hard drugs.

Left: James Hunt was a favourite with *Daily Mirror* readers. In 1974, he posed for a series of glamour shots with model Susan Shaw.

Below: Hunt was romantically involved with budding actress and supermodel Valentine Monnier for several years during the 70s. She appeared on the cover of the 1977 September issue of *Cosmopolitan* at the height of their romance.

Hunt with Pam Rowe at the Monaco Grand Prix.

COSMOPOLITAN

September 1977 $1.50

Margaret Mead Talks About Men, Women, Marriage, Work, Sex, and Drugs in a Myth-Shattering Interview

How Much Sleep Do You Really Need?

The Second or Third Time Around— With Men You Never Previously Considered

Plain Jane into Gorgeous Model

Women in the All-New FBI

How to Be a Lover Who Lasts by the Author of The Sensuous Woman

Vivien Leigh: The Troubled Actress Who Played Scarlett O'Hara— From Anne Edwards's Candid Biography

The Subsidized Girl (What It's Like to Have a Man Pay Your Bills)

Ann-Margret: Her Glitter Is Now Pure Gold

How You Can Turn a Man Off While Trying to Turn Him On (You Silly Girl)

Two High-Protein Short Stories! Delicious. And a Frothy Short Novel for Dessert

Above: Hunt and Helen Dyson with his trusty Austin A35 van, which he bought for £900 and used to transport his budgerigars to shows around the country.

Above: With his last girlfriend, artist Helen Dyson. The pair met while she was working as a waitress in a hamburger restaurant.

Above: James Hunt hosted a table for his friends at the annual BRDC dinner in December 1977. (Clockwise from bottom left): John Richardson, David Zelkowitz, Margaret Birrell, Patrick McNally, Jane Birbeck, James Hunt, Anne Hogan, John Hogan, Mr and Mrs Peter Hunt and Mary Richardson.

Left: Enjoying a round of golf in Marbella. Hunt was a born competitor and excelled in a wide range of sports from an early age.

Above: Hunt on the tennis court in South Africa. He was a very keen tennis player and had played racquet sports constantly from the age of six.

Right: On crutches and his leg in cast following a ski accident at the annual Marlboro ski weekend. He appeared at the United States West Grand Prix West at Long Beach, California, on 30th March 1980. It was less than three weeks after the accident which had detached his knee ligaments and he travelled the Atlantic in a full-length cast.

Solo Syndication

Above, left and below: James with his beloved German Shepherd Oscar at home in Marbella, Spain. Oscar was a remarkable dog and was Hunt's constant companion for over 14 years. Oscar was the only dog allowed into BBC Television Centre.

Mirrorpix

Rex Features

Above: James Hunt with some of his prize-winning budgerigars. Eventually, he had 140 budgerigars in his garden. They were said to be worth nearly UK£60,000 and included rare species such as Normals, Cinnamons, Opalines and Spangles.

Above: Hunt talks with Sarah Ferguson at the 1985 Monaco Grand Prix.

Above right: James Hunt, in typical dress mode, wanders around the paddock at the Austrian Grand Prix on 17th August 1986.

Right: In the nineties, James Hunt travelled everywhere in London by bicycle. He would keep a change of clothes in his haversack and would change into them when he arrived at his destination.

Right: James Hunt and Niki Lauda in 1992. The two stayed good friends long after they retired from racing.

Below: James Hunt with Murray Walker and Mike Doodson in the commentary box at the Swiss Grand Prix at Dijon-Prenois on 29th August 1982.

Left: One year into his commentating career for the BBC. Exhausted after the Spanish Grand Prix on Sunday 21st June 1981, he is pictured sleeping in the McLaren motorhome.

Right: BBC producer, Mark Wilkin (left) produced the Grand Prix programme for the last five years of Hunt's life. Wilkin is photographed here with VT operator Simon Barton. Wilkin and Hunt were both Wellington College boys.

With his sons Tom (left) and Freddie (right) at the British Grand Prix at Silverstone on Sunday 16th July 1989.

Press Association

Above: Holding his youngest son, Freddie, in front of the paddock area.

Left: Freddie Hunt, the youngest son of James Hunt, at the British Formula Ford Championship at Snetterton on 2nd June 2007. Freddie was the image of his father both physically and mentally. He raced in Formula Ford and Formula 3 categories for three years.

Keith Sutton

Right: James Hunt and his fellow world champions gather for a photograph at the Australian Grand Prix at Adelaide on 4th November 1990. (From left to right in back row): James Hunt, Sir Jackie Stewart, Denny Hulme. (From left to right in front row): Nelson Piquet, Juan Manuel Fangio, Ayrton Senna and Sir Jack Brabham. Alain Prost declined the invitation to be photographed for reasons best known to himself.

Left: With Marlboro McLaren team principal Ron Dennis at the Belgian Grand Prix at Spa-Francorchamps on 25th August 1991. The two men were on the same wavelength and great friends.

Rainer Schlegelmilch

Left: Hunt with Ayrton Senna outside the famous San Lorenzo restaurant in Knightsbridge, London, on 1st April 1991. Afterwards, Hunt gave Senna a lift in his Austin van, but not before Senna tried to break the lap record round Cadogan Square in the vehicle.

Below: With Alessandro Zanardi, Hakkinen's teammate at the European Grand Prix at Donington Park on 11th April 1993. Hunt was helping out his old friend Peter Collins at this race.

Above: Mika Hakkinen, driving for Peter Collins' Lotus team in his second year of his Formula One career gets advice prior to the start of the Australian Grand Prix at Adelaide on 8th November 1992. Hunt was hired by John Hogan to mentor his young drivers.

Above: John Hogan sensed something special in Hunt from the first day they met, and secured him his very first sponsorship deal. Patrick McNally was James Hunt's Marlboro-appointed minder from 1977 to the end of his career.

Above: Nigel Mansell, unveiling his own waxwork at Madame Tussauds, is visibly moved during a minute's silence for James Hunt on the morning after his death on Wednesday 16th July 1993.

Above: Suzy Miller, by then divorced from Richard Burton, and Graham Hill's widow, Bette Hill, outside St James's Church in Piccadilly, London, following James Hunt's memorial service on Friday 29th September 1993.

Above: Sarah Lomax and her two sons, Tom and Freddie Hunt, and her mother, Rosemary Lomax, at her ex-husband's memorial service.

Above: Jane Birbeck and Daley Thompson leave the memorial service at St James's church. The former girlfriend of Hunt was dating the athlete at the time.

Helen Dyson, James Hunt's last girlfriend, leaves his memorial service at St James's church on Friday 29th September 1993.

Above: At a Mother's Day lunch at the Tower Hotel, London, hosted by the Greeting Card and Calendar Association on 17th March 1976, Mrs Sue Hunt joined other mothers of famous people. (Back row from left): Mrs J A Wilkie, mother of Olympic swimmer, David Wilkie; Mrs H Zavaroni, mother of singer Lena Zavaroni; Mrs B Stracey, mother of boxer John H Stracey; Mrs Janicwiez, mother of boxer Richard Dunn; and Mrs O'Sullivan, mother of actor Richard O'Sullivan. (Front row): Sue Hunt and Mrs K Rantzen, mother of Esther Rantzen.

Left: Renowned author Christopher Hilton penned two books about Hunt after the driver's death.

Above: Tim Hunt, the youngest of the Hunt brothers, now lives in New York, where he is director of the Warhol Foundation. He is pictured with wife Tama Janowitz, an American novelist.

Right: David Hunt in 1988. He was the youngest of the Hunt brothers and raced cars in his youth.

Above: (From left): Four journalists who were very important to James Hunt during his career: Ian Phillips, Eoin Young, Gerald Donaldson and David Phipps.

And there was therefore a natural bias towards McLaren in his commentary. It was not deliberate, but just the way it was.

As Christopher Hilton noted in his biography of Hunt, which includes an excellent chapter about his time at the BBC: "James was wedded to McLaren and wedded to Marlboro in every way possible. That was his virtual sole source of information."

But John Hogan never saw it as a conflict: "He kept in touch with us, he became part of the family because of his BBC commitments and so he was always in and out of the hospitality suite because he knew the girls and that was part of the attraction. And we always used to talk about young drivers, always, always, always: who was a wanker, who wasn't; who was good, who wasn't. And the existing drivers: who was good, who was bad."

Hogan says the retainer was paid for his work with young drivers, not for him to say good things about Marlboro or McLaren on air. "It was the way Marlboro used to work, we were always bringing in new drivers and I just felt that we needed a bit of serious expertise in that area. So we'd say to him: 'We've got a young Dutch driver that our Dutch office is really keen on, can you go and look?' 'Oh yes, I'll go to Holland. Don't worry.' And that's how we used him."

Life quietened down a little when Mark Wilkin took over as Grand Prix's producer in mid-1989. Wilkin and Hunt were much more compatible, as both were old boys of Wellington College and therefore had some shared values. Wilkin managed to do as Bubbles Horsley had 16 years earlier: to maintain a friendship with Hunt but still keep his distance as his boss and maintain discipline.

Wilkin joined the BBC in 1978 as an engineer, but admits he wasn't very good at engineering. He says: "I discovered that making programmes was far more interesting than engineering."

He joined BBC Sport in 1985 and it was his dream come true. He loved sport and lived for it. Four years later he was producing 'Ski Sunday' and 'Grand Prix' about two of his favourite sports. He says: "I have travelled all over the world and I've been lucky enough to enjoy my job, every day of my job, every day since then."

Wilkin got the 'Grand Prix' assignment as a direct result of the exodus from the BBC to SkyTV in the late eighties. As all his more senior colleagues left to take Sky's shilling, he was left in prime position for promotion, and the BBC had perceived that skiing and motor racing were similar sports –

presumably both being fast and participated in by people wearing helmets. He remembers: "I took over Ski Sunday and Formula One all in the same year because other people left, and you know that's the nature of all these things, isn't it?"

Wilkin was a friend of Tim Hunt, James' brother, and often visited the family home in Belmont, although he never got to meet James, who was always away racing. Wilkin first met Hunt at the Wimbledon tennis championships where he was working and Hunt, an avid tennis fan, was a guest of the BBC. Jonathan Martin wanted to test Hunt as a tennis commentator.

Wilkin's first race was at Monaco in 1989 and he remembers: "I'd gone out with Murray and an engineer and I didn't see James at all. We were sitting in the commentary box on Sunday and then we went on the air and I still hadn't seen James."

Wilkin had been briefed by his predecessor, Charles Balchin, on what to expect and he wasn't too concerned. But he admits, as it was his first race, he was anxiously scanning the track looking for his arrival. He recalls: "Eventually, I see a lone figure in a pair of shorts, no shoes and no shirt and a shock of blonde hair, holding a bottle of rosé wine and staggering across the grid looking for the gap to jump over the fence in order to get up to the commentary box on the outside of the circuit."

Wilkin was ready and had rehearsed in his mind how to handle Hunt: "As he came in, I said: 'Hello, James. I'm Mark, let me take that from you,' which was the bottle of wine. I replaced it with a bottle of water and he went on to give us one of the sublime performances that he used to do every week. He disappeared at the end of the race, just after the cars crossed the line, and I didn't see him again that weekend. But as time went on, we became firm friends and I saw a lot of him, both at the track and away from the circuit."

Wilkin resolved to sort out Hunt's on-air drinking and he gradually phased it out. Wilkin trod cautiously and says: "I never really had a row with him. We used to have some fierce arguments, but they didn't develop into screaming matches. They were genuine debates. The worst really was that first time when I didn't know him and I thought: 'What on earth am I going to do?' I was thinking: 'I should've done something to avoid this situation' and yet, twenty minutes in, he's making lucid and pertinent comments. I did say to him: 'It's best to be sober' and 'You're actually much more interesting when you're sober', and I think he got that fairly early on and he took that on board."

But one incident made him realise that Hunt's capacity for alcohol was so enormous that the odd bottle of rosé wine really made little difference to him. It happened at the 1991 Australian Grand Prix, which coincided with the final of the Rugby World Cup between England and Australia. Wilkin says: "James and I were in Adelaide, and he said to me: 'What are you doing for the match? Why don't we watch it together?' So I went to his hotel. We had dinner and we spun it out with a few bottles of wine. Anyway, by the time we'd finished the match, we had 11 empty bottles of wine kicking around, and that was just the two of us. We had started at ten and we finished at five. I didn't drink my share, it's safe to say. I had to get back to my hotel after that and I was supposed to give a report to Murray about what happened in the match. I couldn't remember the second half at all. I knew we'd lost."

But while life in the commentary box may have been getting smoother, life outside it was not. Hunt was paid generous expenses and made his own flight and travel arrangements, sending the bills to the BBC to pay. He did not fly with the BBC nor sleep at the BBC-booked hotel, preferring to make all his own arrangements.

Hunt's expenses were always a running sore with all of the BBC producers for whom he worked. They were difficult because they were so large, and Wilkin says they were always inflated. Diplomatically, he explains: "Let's just say he used to claim for things that I knew he hadn't spent."

The relationship between Walker and Hunt may eventually have developed into mutual respect and liking, but, as Wilkin says: "It went through some trying times along the way."

Now Walker firmly believes that Jonathan Martin was totally right to put them together, as he says: "We may not have had the greatest respect for each other at the start, but our skills complemented each other perfectly, the viewers liked our partnership and, as time went by, we rubbed the corners off each other, grew together and worked even better."

And Walker admits he was not exactly perfect himself: "I must also have irritated James immensely by my attitude in the box. I was immensely fired up, totally focused, literally on the balls of my feet, oozing adrenalin, and all the time I wanted to be the one pouring out words about what was happening. I thought James slowed things down and he thought I talked too much. He may well have been right."

There were one or two occasions when the two almost came to blows in the commentary box; incidents that both Murray Walker and Mark Wilkin readily recall: "I was, as ever, standing up and in full flow, giving it plenty when James, sitting beside me, decided it was his turn. Instead of languidly waving his hand for the microphone, he grabbed its wire and gave a sharp tug. It flew out of my hand into his, and while he calmly got on with whatever it was he wanted to say, I was seething with rage at being cut off in my prime. I regard myself as someone who is hard to anger, but I actually held my fist back when I saw Mark Wilkin wagging a reproving finger at me and silently mouthing the words: 'No, Murray.' I backed off, and it is just as well I did, for that would have been the end of a great partnership."

Wilkin admits that there was never a dull moment when Hunt was commentating and never a period when he could say the show was "settled." Jonathan Martin says there was much more animosity between the two than anyone realised: "There were many times at the end of a race when I thought they were going to go outside and thump each other."

Eventually, as the ratings went up, the BBC Grand Prix programme went live on Sunday afternoons and live commentaries were done from European events, although Walker and Hunt were still mostly studio bound for races outside Europe. The duo however always gave the deliberate impression that they were actually trackside in the country hosting the race, although they always stopped short of saying so in order not to mislead. But they definitely never said they weren't.

One Sunday, Hunt made a monumental cock-up as he and Walker were sitting in front of the screen commentating live at Shepherd's Bush on the 1991 South African Grand Prix that was taking place in Kyalami, 4,500 miles away. Suddenly and for no reason, Hunt launched into a withering attack on the evils of the white South African government. Walker remembers: "He was fired up about apartheid and we were about halfway through and James suddenly starts banging on about the evils of apartheid, which wasn't at all relevant to the South African Grand Prix and wasn't conducive to good relations between South Africa and Britain, exemplified by the BBC."

It was politically provocative material, and Wilkin ordered Hunt to get back to the subject of the race, and Hunt did, ending his diatribe by saying: "Anyway, thank God we're not there."

Wilkin and Walker just hung their heads in despair as Hunt looked quizzically at them, not realising that he had blown their cover.

Another tricky moment was at the Australian Grand Prix in 1985, which was recounted by Murray Walker in his autobiography. The host broadcaster, Channel 9, were making maximum efforts and Walker and Hunt were also doing the race commentary for Channel 9 as well as the BBC. Its show was produced by David Hill, one of Australia's top TV executives. The qualifying was being broadcast for Channel 9's benefit, and was not on the BBC.

Hunt took an instant dislike to Hill and was sulking when Walker handed him the microphone during qualifying. Hunt put the microphone down and simply said: "I've got nothing to say."

The producer quickly switched to a commercial break and Hill, the consummate professional, just leaned across to where Hunt was sitting, looked him in the eye and said: "Pick the fucking thing up and say something." Hunt, not used to such direct talk, looked at Hill and did as he was told. After he had got over his surprise, Hunt started seething in his seat. When the session was over, Hunt approached Hill and said: "I'd like a word with you. I've never been spoken to like that by anyone in the whole of my life and I don't like it." Hill replied: "I don't give a fuck what you like, as far as I'm concerned you're a hired hand, and if you don't like it you can fuck off."

The tense situation between Hunt and Hill continued over the years and only ended when Hill was posted to the UK to become head of Sky Sports. Walker witnessed all this and was mildly amused by it, particularly by Hunt's discomfort at being forced to work with Hill: "We were never the greatest mates out of the box because we were so different, but as the years rolled by he changed, very much for the better as far as I was concerned, and I must have too. We both mellowed."

John Hogan is adamant that the difficulties were just part of the creative process and that Hunt was one of the finest sports commentators ever: "James was the only driver I've ever seen who had the vaguest idea about what it actually takes to be a racing driver. Others, like Niki, could say so, and so might be good. But they couldn't tell you why. James' big strength was that he could articulate the game. More than anyone, James had that ability to articulate and communicate. That's why he was such an outstanding TV commentator."

Ian Phillips agrees with Hogan: "He became incredibly good in the commentary box, he was intelligent, he understood what was going on and he made the effort. He wandered round the paddock, saw and spoke to the people."

Martin says: "For all his laid-back irreverence, James could be intensely serious when the moment demanded. That was what made him such a good commentator. His act was simple enough really: A great performance received tribute, a poor one rebuke." Martin was often amazed at the expertise Hunt brought to the job: "He would poke his head out of the commentary box, cock an ear and listen to the engine note of a passing car."

There was no better example of that expertise as when he was describing the duals between Ayrton Senna and Alain Prost in the late eighties. At the German Grand Prix, at the height of the Prost and Senna battles, he said: "To run at the front in Grand Prix racing, and to stay there, is mentally exhausting. The brain gets tired before the body does. I mean, you've only got to look at some of the geriatrics tooling around nowadays to see who's got tired brains." The then producer Roger Moody braced himself as he expected Hunt to name the drivers he considered to have 'tired brains'. But he didn't, and Moody breathed a sigh of relief.

But Hunt didn't always get it right. One of his last commentaries was for the European Grand Prix at Donington Park on 11th April 1993. It was pouring with rain and, during the build up to the race, Hunt forecast that there would not be a lot of overtaking in such appalling, difficult wet weather conditions. He couldn't have been more wrong, and the first lap proved to be the finest exhibition of overtaking mastery in Formula One history, with Ayrton Senna starting the race in fifth and overtaking Michael Schumacher, Karl Wendlinger, Damon Hill and Alain Prost on a single lap to lead into lap two, and then to go on to win the race.

Regardless of that, when he died, Hunt was regarded as being unmatched in his analysis of Formula One racing by Nigel Roebuck, who knows a thing or two about Formula One himself.

According to Roebuck, Hunt could never be accused of artificially romanticising Formula One, of which today's commentators are often guilty. Hunt told Roebuck in an interview: "I won't compromise myself by saying things I don't mean." After thinking about that statement, he added: "What tends to happen, in fact, is that I compromise myself by saying exactly what I think."

Jonathan Martin, who rose to be head of sport at the BBC in 1981 and is now enjoying his retirement, recalls: "James was able to communicate his experience, and he could communicate. I'd say he was one of the top broadcasters of his generation, and I'm not saying that because he's dead. I used to say that while he was alive."

Peter Scudamore, a former jockey who commentated on horse racing for the BBC when it had the rights, was quoted as saying: "I hope over the years I'll get to be as good as Richie Benaud or James Hunt or Geoff Boycott." It was praise indeed.

Televised sport probably never had as great a combination as Walker and Hunt – neither then nor since. Even Mark Wilkin would probably admit that the combination of Hunt and Walker was unmatched, and puts the pair's successors in the shade.

At the time that James Hunt made his television debut, only cricket's Richie Benaud had successfully made the transition, and most people had forgotten he used to be a player.

Hunt became the first top British sportsman to go into television, and he paved the way for a whole swathe of retired sportsmen and women to become highly paid presenters and commentators. His BBC contract was then said to be worth US$70,000 a year, and was certainly the third most expensive single personnel item on BBC Sport's profit and loss account after David Coleman and Harry Carpenter. He was up there with Morecambe and Wise and other top people on television in the seventies.

Only John McEnroe, Gary Lineker, Geoff Boycott and David Gower spring to mind as truly comparable, great sports commentators. Would Hunt eventually have done a Gary Lineker and become a household staple earning millions? Mark Wilkin believes so, and he also believes that Hunt would have been able to restore his fortunes as one of the BBC's top salaried presenters, earning as much as he had when he was a driver.

Wilkin says: "We paid him a fortune but he was a world champion, you know, and we hadn't hired people like that before."

That fortune was paid back many times during those glory years of 1980 and 1993.

SHUNT

CHAPTER 39

Goodbye Baby Jane
The end of the affair

O nce he was back in England, and as 1981 wore on, the novelty of being a retired racing driver soon faded. Hunt began to experience withdrawal symptoms and he became increasingly restless. And when he became restless, his consumption of alcohol went up accordingly. Jane Birbeck also found herself drinking too much. The depression caused by his skiing injuries, and the subsequent complications, had fatally wounded their relationship, and a parting of the ways was now only a matter of time.

Even the solution always came back to the same problem: apart from his job at the BBC, which effectively occupied him for only 50 days of the year, he had nothing to do. As he freely admitted: "Having nothing to do made me feel very frustrated. It's not easy for a man of my energetic disposition to sit around twiddling my thumbs."

He also realised, rather belatedly, that he was not cut out to be a businessman: his nightclub and squash club were absorbing his cash and showing no signs of making a profit. He and his brother Peter decided to exit the businesses, and, selling his shares back to his partners in both ventures, he made a loss on both. However, his successful property venture with Horsley continued.

Predictably, the farming experiment at Park Farm was also quickly over. But the booming property market meant that, after just a year and a half of ownership, the farm was worth much more than he had paid for it. He had paid UK£1 million and sold it off in two lots for close to UK£1.25 million. When that was done, he moved back to London full time with Jane. He went to Formula One races in Europe every other weekend, and his only other activity was promotional work for Olympus Cameras and Marlboro. For reasons best known to himself, Peter Hunt had dispensed with the services of the CSS agency and, with it, the chance of other promotional contracts.

The BBC commentating role was vital in maintaining Hunt's sanity, as it gave him a sense of purpose. But against that, he had fallen out of love with the sport. Now that he was no longer a driver, he disliked being in the Formula One paddock. The care-free atmosphere that had always prevailed in the paddock was now replaced with a cold-edged business one. He was annoyed that the female groupies no longer had access to the venue. The groupies had been his main source of sex, and now that they were gone, so too was much of the appeal of being there. As he said: "With the modern pass system, there aren't any women around and you have to go outside." He had become so used to having casual sex with women at the back of empty pit garages, that he resented the new rules intensely. Having to search for girls outside the protected paddock fences, he found that, even though he had retired, people still treated him as a driver. He explained: "What really made it particularly unpleasant was that people, especially the general public, were still treating me like a driver. This was specifically one of the things I was trying to get away from. So there I was, walking back into the fire, having just got out of the frying pan."

Outside the paddock, he found larger quantities of girls who wanted to sleep with him, but the quality was considerably poorer. Nevertheless, during the summer of 1981, he was chronically unfaithful to Jane Birbeck. They had been together for close to six years and Jane had miscarried nine times during that period. They had, by then, given up hope of a baby. In the end, she was glad. As the incompatibility became readily apparent, she became anxious to leave the relationship. But that was easier said than done as their lives were so completely intertwined.

She also realised she was on the way to having an alcohol dependency, and she would not be able to stop drinking whilst she was going out with him. And as much as she loved him, she yearned to get back to a normal life.

She had always overlooked his infidelities, as there were just too many of them, and she accepted him for what he was. As long as she didn't specifically know about them, she was okay about it. But she stopped going to races because she could no longer look people in the eye.

The end finally came in a way she never could have imagined. Hunt returned from a Grand Prix that summer after allegedly having slept with seven different women during one weekend – and some of them were not particularly pleasant girls either. He just couldn't help himself, and was full of remorse and disgust at his own behaviour.

When he arrived home that Sunday evening, he burst into tears and confessed to Jane what had happened, telling her he could not live with himself any more. He said he was tormented by his sex addiction and that it would be best if they parted.

Although Jane knew it was happening, the confession unnerved her. As she told Donaldson: "It was a pretty horrible time and I think I fell apart for a few days. But there was no acrimony and we were both very loving towards each other. We planned how to help each other through the transition. It was very bittersweet."

Once that was sorted out, Hunt started acting very bizarrely and planned visits to both their parents' homes to inform them of the break up. He then told Jane he would like Bubbles Horsley to negotiate with her over the financial and logistical side of the split. That was a surprise to her because she had not expected there to be any financial or logistical side to it, save for her eventually moving out of the mews house.

But Hunt insisted and, according to her, as recounted in Donaldson's biography, she and Hunt and Horsley sat around the kitchen table at the London mews house drinking wine. Jane was amazed when Hunt offered her the house they were sitting in as a gift, and said he would give her UK£2,000 a month for six months as a transitional allowance. The house was by then worth as much as UK£200,000 and it was an extremely generous settlement he had no obligation to make. When he asked her what she would do, she told him it was her ambition to start a gym in the Kings Road. He then agreed to invest in that as a partner.

Hunt quickly moved out into temporary accommodation and started looking for a new house of his own. Despite all this, the break up was not absolute; there was a brief reconciliation that lasted just over a month and, after that, Hunt left for good.

He was now homeless and only owned his property in Spain. Jane agreed to house him while he searched for a home in the Wimbledon, Barnes,

Twickenham and Richmond areas. He saw those areas as the ideal compromise between town and country.

He eventually found what he wanted in a private road in Wimbledon. It was almost next door to the All England Club. It was a beautiful, but slightly tatty, house in Wimbledon, and the asking price was around UK£200,000. Built in the 1930s, the private lane sat on the edge of Wimbledon Common. It had a very large garden but needed urgent refurbishment. He decided to buy it when he saw the obvious joy Oscar was having in the garden as he viewed it for the second time.

As soon as he closed on the deal, he set to work recreating all the rooms and facilities that a 30-something bachelor required, including a snooker room and a giant whirlpool bath in the garden.

The purchase of the house, and the obvious pleasure it gave him, was the first sign of light at the end of his personal tunnel since retirement.

By year-end, he had rid himself of the rich man's appendages that he found he didn't need. He was a confirmed bachelor again, with no ties to anyone and with a resolute determination to play the field; but this time with no feelings of guilt. But he grew increasingly disgusted with himself by the quality of women he was picking up for casual sex. While he knew the solution to that was another permanent relationship, he was far from ready for it.

It was also a time of change in Formula One. The sport had been through a very bad patch with the advent of ground effect cars, which had sucked the life out of it. Formula One was missing its two stars and, that autumn, there were very serious moves afoot to bring back both Niki Lauda and James Hunt to the sport. Hunt was still only 34 and in his prime.

Bernie Ecclestone tried to lure Hunt to drive for his Brabham team with a reported offer of US$5 million for one year's work. Driver salary inflation had run riot in Formula One with the shortage of top drivers, and Ecclestone's offer was 100 times what Hunt had been paid in 1976, only six years earlier. The size of the offer made him think very clearly about his future and everything he had been through. But he had been spooked by what had happened to Clay Regazzoni at Long Beach the year before. He had also not completely recovered from his skiing injury, to the extent that he had difficulties with the clutch in his Porsche. After much soul searching, he declined Ecclestone's offer, but with a heavy heart. He had no idea if he was right to do so, especially when Ricardo Patrese, his nemesis, got the drive instead.

He said at the time: "I gave it serious thought, but I have decided to carry on living the easy life. There is no point in risking your neck for money you don't need. You can't spend a fortune if you're dead." And at that time, he really did not need the money. The British economy was booming and, despite the losses in Munich and Marbella and Jane Birbeck's settlement, he was still well ahead for the year. The last thing he needed then was money – he had plenty of it.

Not so for Niki Lauda, who was desperately short of cash. He had spent the US$10 million fortune with which he had left the sport on his airline business, called Lauda Air, and the money had run out.

Lauda was planning a comeback with Hunt's old team, McLaren, and had received a similar offer. McLaren was now under new ownership, and a young entrepreneur called Ron Dennis had taken over the team. The takeover had been orchestrated by John Hogan, frustrated by the years of underperformance since Hunt had left. Teddy Mayer was effectively out and Alastair Caldwell had left to join Brabham. Gordon Coppuck had also left, and a new design team was installed with the brilliant John Barnard as technical director. Barnard also had a 15 per cent stake in the team, with Dennis owning the majority and Mayer retaining the rest.

Bringing Lauda back was Dennis' idea, not Hogan's. Hogan was unsure about the wisdom of the decision, and consulted Hunt. Hunt's Marlboro contract as a global ambassador was worth US$60,000 a year, and it now extended to giving others advice as a consultant.

Part of the new brief was to advise Hogan on drivers, and he consulted him on Lauda. At that time, no retired driver had ever made a successful return to Formula One, and Hogan wasn't sure it was even possible, as he says: "I asked James, and he was adamant that Lauda could do it. The only question in his mind was his motivation." But Hunt told Hogan firmly that, if Lauda was motivated, he could be world champion again. Hogan went away and questioned Lauda carefully about his motivations, relaying his answers back to Hunt. When he heard the answers, Hunt was unequivocal, and advised Hogan to sign Lauda. Hogan admits it was Hunt's advice that won Lauda the drive. Hogan was an enormous admirer of Hunt's ability to, in his words, "read the game." In fact, he thought there was no one better at it.

After that, Hunt warmed to his role as a driver coach for Marlboro and started working closely with Peter Collins, who by then had bought the Lotus team from the late Colin Chapman's family. Collins leaned heavily on Hunt's advice about drivers. Another Marlboro-contracted driver, Mika Hakkinen, also owes his career to Hunt's championing of him. Hunt was always in the Lotus pit talking to Collins' young drivers, including Alex Zanardi, who was then making his Formula One debut.

Hunt's championing of those two drivers eventually resulted in a third world championship for Lauda in 1984 and two world championships for Hakkinen in 1998 and 1999. Just before he died, Hunt brokered a deal to take Hakkinen to McLaren as its test driver in 1993. He got particularly close to Hakkinen, mainly because both of them liked a drink, and they often socialised away from the track. Hakkinen recalls: "I liked him a lot and he was a very great help to me."

One driver he did not support or offer any advice to was his younger brother, David, who was 21 was trying to make it as a racing driver by following in his brother's footsteps and racing in Formula Ford. But Hunt would give him no encouragement and certainly no money, for which he frequently asked. He simply didn't want a brother in motor racing. He was the only Hunt in the sport and was determined to have it stay that way. Ostensibly, he told him it was too dangerous and that if he supported him financially and anything happened, he would be wracked with guilt. So young David had to find his own way in the world.

Hunt's thinking was actually very sound, as the Warwick and Surtees families would eventually discover much later when they encouraged their younger members to take up motor racing.

Despite the problems of the past few years, Hunt was a much more settled man at the end of 1981. He was installed in his Wimbledon home and living life to his own agenda. He had Jane Birbeck as a solid friend and confidante. He loved having his friends come over to Wimbledon to hang out. There were many riotous parties in the whirlpool bath over the next few years, and the neighbours were certainly entertained by the naked women cavorting in the garden, often in the freezing weather. Hunt was enjoying a year of freedom and guilt-free sex until the next time lightning struck – as surely it soon would.

GOODBYE BABY JANE

SHUNT

CHAPTER 40

Meeting Sarah and Wedding number two

Not a match made in heaven

Sarah Lomax was just 24 when she met James Hunt in the first week of September 1982. One half of her character was her image as a glamorous, blond-haired, blue-eyed vivacious girl with a huge personality. She was very rarely seen without an open, friendly smile on her face. The other half was a chronic shyness when she was out of her natural environment.

When she felt comfortable, she was hugely gregarious but sometimes not in a way that particularly attracted people, although it certainly didn't put them off. She was no Suzy Miller or Jane Birbeck, but she made a huge impression on Hunt that afternoon in Spain.

She was just an ordinary, albeit upper-class English girl on holiday with three girlfriends on the Costa del Sol. Hunt was also in Spain on one of his periodic visits to his house and, after the official split from Jane Birbeck, completely unattached.

It was a fateful moment when he introduced himself to the four bubbly girls, three of whom had recognised him. They were all at a party on the beach. But Hunt had eyes for only one of them, initially probably because she didn't know who he was. Lomax had no interested in motor racing.

The holiday on the Costa del Sol was an end of summer fling with some girlfriends, and she was totally unprepared for her confrontation with James Hunt. As she remembered: "My friends said: 'There's James Hunt', and I said: 'Give me another clue.'"

As she later recounted to Hunt biographer Christopher Hilton: "I had no idea who he was, no idea at all. I was at school when he was racing and he had retired when I met him."

Hunt thought it was funny that she didn't know him and was amused by the contrast in her attitude to that of her friends, who were so obviously excited. He reassured her: "Why on earth should you have heard of me?" It added to the attraction between them, much to the chagrin of the other three girls, who were intensely jealous.

When she discovered who he was, she was very flattered by the attention from the 35-year-old former world champion. So much so that she proceeded to tell him her life story: how she had lived a sheltered life and been brought up in a beautiful family home, an idyllic old rectory built in the very centre of the village of Chidham. It was an old and historic house built at the start of the eighteenth century near Baydon, where her parents had a training yard for horses. She told Hunt her parents had divorced in 1972 and that, at 14, she was very badly affected by it and had resented the end of her perfect childhood in a perfect environment. She admitted she was not academically gifted and left school early to take a secretarial course. She told him she was a good horsewoman like her mother. As a traditional debutante, she travelled abroad, working her way around the sun spots of Europe. But she had rejected the good life in Europe and returned home, saying: "All the time I was terribly homesick for the countryside and country life."

Whilst she was talking, she realised that she actually had heard of him before. She had been to a motor race when she was 16, as she remembered later: "I went because I fancied one of the boys taking us." It had been eight years earlier, in 1974, at Brands Hatch for the British Grand Prix. Hunt was racing his Hesketh, as she later recalled: "I remember looking at the posters and thinking: 'I want him to win, he's good looking.'" But she didn't register his name and said later: "They were handing out stickers of James, I took one and stuck it to the back of my cheque book." Christopher Hilton said in his book: "When she got back to school, she wrote her name next to his and played one of those word games – loves, likes, hates, adores – using the letters of their names. It culminated in 'I love James Hunt.' It was no more than the sort of thing schoolgirls do, and that's proved by the fact that she forgot him so completely."

That afternoon, Hunt found he was transfixed by this girl from Wiltshire. He was overcome as he listened to her story, intently fascinated by her and not quite understanding why. After that, all of them got very drunk and, at the end of the party, somehow managed to get themselves back to the hotel.

After the holiday, and as the autumn set in, Lomax got a call from Hunt asking her out on a date. And so it began.

They found they had a lot in common. There was an instant mutual attraction, and a particularly strong sexual attraction. For her, she had found a boyfriend who enjoyed sex as much as she did. Previously, she had been unable to find anyone who could keep up with her. Sarah told Gerald Donaldson years later that Hunt thought she was a sex maniac.

Both had a huge sexual appetite, and both had found an outlet with which to satisfy it. She also liked to drink and smoke. And, in that respect, they were the perfect couple. Lomax told Gerald Donaldson: "I was smitten, totally smitten, by James. I couldn't believe he was interested in me. I remember somebody said: 'He's a celebrity and he'll soon drop you.' But he appeared to be incredibly keen." So keen in fact that when she moved to the United States he followed her, the attraction was so strong.

Lomax was working as an interior designer, and she was due to go the United States to gain experience later that year. After meeting Hunt, she was torn and didn't want to go, believing it would mean the end of their relationship. But her mother insisted and advised her daughter that her suitor's ardour would be all the more for the distance between them. Lomax had forgotten the old adage 'absence makes the heart grow fonder', and indeed so it turned out.

After she left, Hunt missed her terribly and began visiting her at weekends in Washington DC, where she was based. It was very cold in Washington that winter, but they were heady times in the American capital. Ronald Reagan was in the second year of his first term as President, and Washington was alive again after the dour years of Jimmy Carter's presidency.

Lomax was in heaven, as she recalled: "When he came to see me in Washington, people would recognise him on the street. I remember how embarrassed he was. He'd be stopped and asked for autographs. He hated it, and when people asked: 'Are you James Hunt?' He'd say: 'Guilty.'"

Hunt was as besotted with Lomax as she was with him, and they began writing love letters to each other. She remembers: "He wrote me wonderful letters and I wrote him back." Hunt bought her a bicycle so she could get around Washington more easily.

On one of his Washington weekend stopovers, Hunt proposed to her and asked her when she would return to England. After the engagement, she decided to return home in the spring of 1983. He picked her up from the airport and took her straight back to his house at Wimbledon, and she never left. As soon as they officially got together, it was time for the madness to start. It was almost as if someone had said: 'Let the party commence.' And it wasn't to stop for nigh on five years.

On the surface, the two were very compatible. Hunt wanted to settle down and get married, and so did she. The age difference was only 11 years and they were from similar backgrounds. She told Donaldson: "All I wanted to do when I was a kid was to get married and look after my man. And this is what James thought he wanted, the normality of a family home."

Like her mother, she had gone to secretarial college and was well organised, practical and kept a very good home, as she said; "James thought I could give him security and stability. He loved the home I kept. He loved my cooking. I think he couldn't believe his luck when he met me: a country girl who could keep a great home."

That combination was unusual at the time, and, if that was the script to which they had adhered, they would have lived happily ever after. But instead, they went on some wild, hedonistic non-stop parties in the quiet environs of Wimbledon. As she explained very vividly to Donaldson: "He wanted to party. I could party with him. I could be outrageous. We were both certainly outrageous. We were total soulmates. I was in love with him. We laughed and we had a really wonderful time."

They were enjoying themselves so much that they didn't get around to getting married until just before Christmas that year, on Saturday 17th December 1983, in a registry office at Marlborough, in Wiltshire, near where her mother Rosemary lived.

Not everyone was happy that he was marrying Sarah, and his parents were not overly keen. They thought their son should settle down with a more sober character. They were worried about their son's increased consumption of alcohol and his drug taking. They had liked Jane Birbeck and would have much preferred it had he taken that direction.

Many of his old friends declined his invitation to the wedding as a sort of invisible protest. They felt it was too soon after Jane and they were loyal to her. Some were also disgusted with how he had gone off the rails and acquired new friends they didn't particularly care for.

Hunt was desperate to have his old friends around him for the wedding. He was very annoyed when Ian Phillips told him he couldn't make it. Phillips recalls: "I know he got peeved off because I didn't go to his wedding. One of my friends was getting married the same weekend and I felt more loyalty to go to that." But the truth was that Phillips didn't want to go and didn't like what his old friend was becoming.

In the wedding pictures, Hunt looks somewhat dishevelled in a borrowed tie and Sarah is wearing a curious green wedding dress that makes her vaguely resemble a morris man. She had cut her long blond hair into a short bob, fashionable at the time, and dyed it a darker shade. They looked a very odd couple indeed as they stood on the steps of Marlborough registry office. The wedding day had none of the glamour of his 1974 marriage to Suzy Miller, and certainly Sarah Lomax would not be running off into the arms of Richard Burton.

Stirling Moss, who met all Hunt's wives and girlfriends over the years, agrees: "Suzy was absolutely drop dead gorgeous and she was exactly what I thought James would have married. Sarah was not the one that all the guys were trying to grab, I mean, 'cor! where did you get that one?'" Susie Moss disagrees with her husband: "Maybe he wanted a more real person. Maybe he wanted a family now, maybe he wanted to settle down, maybe he wanted a house and kids. You know, there must have been reasons."

But that day, it was obvious the golden boy had fallen far from his former gilded perch. Luckily, the wedding photos received hardly any attention in the next day's newspapers as editors had weightier issues with which to contend. The wedding day was somewhat overshadowed when news filtered through to the reception that there had been a car bomb attack by the IRA outside Harrods department store in London's Knightsbridge. Three police officers and three other people had been killed and 75 were left injured, some of them seriously.

With the marriage to Sarah Lomax came a new and formidable set of in-laws. Hunt had developed a predilection for collecting formidable in-laws. Both Suzy Miller's and Jane Birbeck's parents had been highly accomplished people and fully signed up members of the British establishment. The Lomax family was no exception. Ian and Rosemary Lomax were both accomplished horse and sports people. Her father was a master of foxhounds and a notable cricketer at county level. Her mother trained race horses and was a top point-to-point competitor in English competition and had won 41 races in the fifties. They had married in 1953 and had established a small training yard at Baydon, near Lambourn in Berkshire, which Rosemary ran whilst her husband played cricket. They lived nearby, across the border in Wiltshire. Three children followed: David, Michael and Sarah.

Both parents became famous when her father played cricket for England and her mother became the first woman officially to train a winner at Royal Ascot. Her success came with a horse called Precipice Wood, which won the King George V Stakes in 1969 and the 1970 Gold Cup. The Gold Cup success was much earned, as the horse had been stung by a bee shortly before the race. It had bolted only to be recovered, drenched in sweat and exhausted, but he still won. Rosemary was also a successful trainer of jump horses, and her horses competed in the Grand National. In those days, the training licence was in the name of her husband since it was not until 1967 that the Jockey Club granted permits to women, at which time she took out a licence in her own name. The perfect family came unravelled when her parents divorced in 1974.

After the wedding and honeymoon, Hunt and Lomax just carried on partying where they had left off. She told Donaldson: "James said he married a wild, drug-taking sex maniac." They drank, they smoked and they indulged in recreational drugs in a way that perfectly matched eighties hedonism at its best. Perhaps unsurprisingly, they gave each other the same nickname: 'The Beast.' It was totally appropriate for the way both of them behaved. They were both beasts, with the money and the ambition to indulge their fantasies. They chain-smoked joints and woke to glasses of vodka by the side of the bed to help them face the day.

They were two people totally out of control and with too many hanger-on friends who indulged them. Their parties at the 1930s house, right by the home of the tennis championships and on the edge of Wimbledon Common, went on until dawn every Friday and Saturday night. A big whirlpool bath was installed in the garden, and the high jinks in that bath can only be imagined. Certainly the neighbours recall naked whirlpool bath parties in the garden, which were rather shocking for suburban Wimbledon.

In truth, all sorts of things went on at that Wimbledon house during that period. She once told another famous racing driver who raced with Hunt in the seventies: "I can walk into a room and immediately identify the girls who like to do tricks." What she meant no one really knows. Sarah said: "I was in a continual state of excitement, never pausing for thought."

There is no question that the two of them were extraordinarily close for a period. Although he later gave interviews saying that his last girlfriend, Helen Dyson, was the only girl he ever loved, it simply wasn't true. For a period of two years, when they first met and married, he was totally in love with Sarah and obsessed and besotted with her wild ways. In 1984, he took her to the Monaco Grand Prix, where the two of them had the most marvellous time. She remembers: "He took me into the tunnel and said: 'You ought to experience this.' This is the closest ever you'll get to what it feels like to be in a racing car going at that speed. And as a driver, you have to be completely focused.' He wanted me to experience it."

She also found she liked motor racing: "The only time I've known adrenaline is out hunting, and you don't think about anything else at all. You can't. Imagine that in motor racing: it's got to be the fastest, most dangerous sport. When you're standing in the tunnel at Monte Carlo and if you're having the worst crisis of your life, you're going to forget that crisis."

Sarah loved being Mrs James Hunt but found she became totally dependent on her husband. Whilst she thrived at home and was in her element in an environment in which she felt safe, she didn't like being the centre of attention at the formal functions she was obliged to attend as his wife. As she explained: "I hated parties, too shy, couldn't cope at all. To walk into a room full of people still fills me with absolute fear." But she coped, as she said: "It was different when I was on James' arm, someone charming and ravishingly good-looking, because everybody wanted to help."

But many of Hunt's friends simply didn't like her and didn't think she was good enough for him. When they invited him to an event or a party, they would write on the invitation: 'James Hunt plus one', hoping he would bring someone else. But he didn't, and at the beginning of their marriage he had resolved to be a good husband and faithful to her. She remembered: "At one party, I was introduced to the hostess to whom I said: 'Hello, I'm "plus one"'. She didn't know what I meant so I said: 'Well, you addressed the card to James Hunt "plus one", and I've been Mrs Hunt for three years.' I was livid."

But the first year was a good one as the partying continued. She admitted: "I depended on him 100 per cent. James and I, two very shy, very excitable souls. He was always a very young man in terms of outlook; young in spirit."

And therein lay the problem. But even before the problem became apparent, there were to be children – as Tom and Freddie came on the scene.

MEETING SARAH AND WEDDING NUMBER TWO

CHAPTER 41

Family life, Freddie, Tom...
and the budgerigars
A false dawn as fatherhood beckons

James Hunt was always very good with children, just as he was with
animals. He had an innate understanding of them and, from the age of
28, he had wanted his own. He first started trying with Jane Birbeck. If
Jane had been able to get pregnant, it is likely that the course of his life would
have been radically different.

His understanding of children came from his skills understanding people
and situations. And much of that came from his experience with his own
family in his youth. The Hunts were unusual in that they were essentially
two families in one. His mother, Sue, had arranged her child rearing in two
halves. She had Sally, James and Peter first and, ten years later, gave birth to
Georgina, David and Timothy. It created an unusual situation. When James
was 20, he effectively had three youngsters to look after. Caring for and
providing guidance to Georgina, David and Timothy gave him enormous
experience and confidence with young children; something few other
20-year-olds would have cultivated.

When he gave up working to become a full-time race driver, he had plenty
of time to spend with his younger siblings, especially in their school holidays.
And he was effectively an uncle to them rather than a brother. When his
brothers and sisters were unhappy, he could always talk it through with them

at their level. His mother recalls: "He just knew how to do it." His skills as a communicator probably worked best on children and, according to his mother, just a few words from him could transform a child's mood. He was incredibly good at it, and that experience would pay enormous dividends when his own children arrived.

Taormina Rich, his first girlfriend, who witnessed his relationship with his younger siblings, says: "He really enjoyed looking after them, and just seeing the way he behaved with his little brothers and sisters, you knew it was instinctive in him. He was always going to be a good father."

The Hunts began trying for a baby soon after Christmas 1984, and, late in January 1985, Sarah announced she was pregnant. It suddenly seemed the most natural thing in the world and everyone was delighted that, at the age of 37, James Hunt was to be a father for the first time after so many years of trying. When it finally happened, he was surprised. After Jane Birbeck's many miscarriages, he had secretly wondered whether he was destined to be a father.

Initially, the decision to have children came about as part of a plan to rescue the marriage which, at the time, was going the way of all his other relationships. After just a year of marriage and non-stop hedonistic activity, Hunt had begun to wander and his vows of faithfulness and monogamy had worn off. He had also fallen out of love with his wife and began to see sides of her he had never before noticed. But it was not mutual. She was more in love with him than ever, and just as desperately in need of him as ever. But the marriage had begun to disintegrate before their very eyes.

Sensing this and worried about both their parents' reactions to a failed marriage, the couple decided to consult marriage counsellors. Couples' counselling was increasingly common in those days, as the divorce rate in England was alarmingly on the rise.

One of the possible options suggested to them by the counsellors was to start a family. It was not an easy decision, and they both realised that their lifestyles were not conducive to family life at all.

But they took the advice and Sarah stopped her contraception and soon fell pregnant.

To ease the housekeeping duties and prepare for the baby, Hunt didn't do the conventional thing by hiring a nanny or a housekeeper. He hired a mixture of a valet cum houseman, gardener and butler called Winston, who hailed from Jamaica and was almost as eccentric as his new employer. Hunt had met him when he was a taxi driver – he had lost his licence for speeding whilst taking Hunt to an appointment for which he was late.

Winston was in his early forties and came to the house every day. He began addressing Hunt as "boss" and was an immediate hit. Visitors to the house remember Winston as being a very charming and warm man.

There was nothing Winston could not do, and one of his tasks was dropping off and picking up Hunt from nearby Heathrow airport on his many foreign trips. Winston was quickly absorbed into the family and gradually assumed the household tasks as Sarah progressed further in her pregnancy.

The pregnancy was difficult in its later stages and Sarah went into St Teresa's Hospital in Wimbledon early to prepare for the birth. Situated on Wimbledon Downs, St Teresa's was a specialist maternity hospital and a great place to have a baby.

But once there, despite her mother's support, Sarah was frightened and felt alone. She was full of apprehension about childbirth and her ability to love her baby. Hunt recognised this and did everything he could to support her. Bizarrely, he brought a powerful stereo system and some of her favourite music into the hospital, which wasn't popular with either the nurses or the other patients.

Hunt also did his best to reassure his wife, spending many hours at her bedside talking about the coming baby. Although they had opted not to know beforehand and wouldn't have minded a boy or girl, they had a feeling it might be a boy and, if it was, they were to call him Tom. Sarah told Gerald Donaldson: "I asked James about whether I could love my baby and he said: 'Don't worry, Beast. God is a great designer and you will love that little thing when it is born.' And he was so right."

So the household was fully prepared when Tom Hunt arrived a few weeks early, on Thursday 12th September 1985. As it was the day James was due to go to the Belgian Grand Prix, it threw into disarray his plans to travel to Spa for the race.

Hunt was reported as saying after the birth: "I didn't mind a boy or a girl, but Sarah is very pleased at having a boy. But it's a daunting prospect as I have lived 37 years without responsibility." Tom weighed five and a half pounds and was a very healthy baby. That was a relief, as Sarah was a heavy drinker and smoker before her pregnancy but had totally reformed for the eight months while she was carrying.

At Tom's christening in Wimbledon, Bubbles Horsley did the honours as godfather. It was quite a tense ceremony, as Horsley was still angry with Tom's father about an incident on an aeroplane a few weeks before.

Hunt was not much enamoured of his son as a baby. Although he could relate to children once they could communicate, he wasn't so good with babies and spent much of the time away from home commentating on races, exhibiting his budgerigars and doing promotional work. He also found that being away was the best medicine for his very shaky marriage, which had not improved at all since the birth of Tom; the marriage counsellors had been wrong about that. If anything, it had become worse, with the normal post-natal problems and disruptions to the household.

Sarah recalls: "By the time the nine months had gone by and I'd gone through the process of giving birth, I was halfway changed to this new person. But James wasn't changed, and that's when things started to go wrong."

So in October 1986, barely a year after Tom's birth, Sarah announced that she was pregnant again. The second pregnancy was another attempt to improve their marriage and, in the process, round off the family. Hunt had always wanted many children and had no intention of Tom being an only child.

For some reason, they didn't seem particularly welcome back at St Teresa's – perhaps it was the loud music – so Freddie Hunt duly arrived at Mount Alvernia hospital in nearby Guildford on Wednesday 1st July 1987. Tom was just 22 months old, his father was 39 and his mother 28. Once again, the timing of the birth was very inconvenient. Hunt was about to leave for the French Grand Prix at Paul Ricard, which was followed by the British Grand Prix just a week later. Somehow, they all got through it and, when the season was over, Lord Hesketh did the honours as godfather.

James Hunt also had other things on his mind when his second son was born; he was approaching his 40th year. He was determined to mark his 40th birthday in style. The birthday party was always going to be a big affair and it didn't disappoint, becoming the talk of Wimbledon for several months afterwards.

He celebrated with a lavish event at his home in Wimbledon. The garden was virtually covered in marquees, and everywhere there were tin baths of ice to keep the champagne cold. Unlike his wedding, this celebration was attended by most of his friends. Some 300 guests turned up on the night and packed the house and garden.

The party was designated fancy dress and the theme was, bizarrely, 'bird or beast.' Hunt was drunk before the party began and put on a kilt, under which he hung an actual salami-type 18-inch sausage, which poked out underneath the kilt. When the kilt was lifted, as it was many times during the evening, it was apparent that Hunt was wearing no underpants – and two sausages were revealed. It has to be said that many of the ladies who did the peeking seemed to have viewed the contents previously. Sarah was not best pleased, but then she hadn't quite anticipated being surrounded by so many of her husband's ex-girlfriends fluttering around in revealing outfits. She was wearing a budgerigar outfit with a feather wig and false beak.

The relevance of Sarah's outfit was obvious, although her husband's was less so. Hunt told his guests that his outfit was meant to signify the famous racehorse Northern Dancer, who was now at stud. Canadian bred, Northern Dancer was the most successful sire in thoroughbred horse racing, and his offspring earned more money and won more major stakes races than those of any other.

The owners of Northern Dancer charged US$1 million each time he covered a mare. And Hunt told his guests that it was his hope, when he died and came back, to be a stud horse like Northern Dancer.

Legend has it that during the party, he may have got in some early practice. Certainly, no one would have been surprised if he did.

At the end of the party, he slumped on the bed still wearing the kilt and the salami sausage, and he awoke to find that Oscar had eaten most of it. Although Hunt said he had removed it before going to sleep, he later confessed that he hadn't and was glad Oscar knew the difference between the sausage and 'the real thing.'

Once the party was out of the way and the Formula One season over, Hunt concentrated on his parenting duties. The 40th birthday party really had been the height of irresponsibility for parents with two young children and all the responsibilities that entailed. But it precisely defined the dilemma of this 40-year-old man and this 29-year-old woman and the excesses that drove them both. They were both Jekyll and Hyde characters, albeit in totally different ways. Both were truly excellent parents but highly irresponsible adults. The incident on the aeroplane that had so upset Bubbles Horsley truly reflected just how irresponsible Hunt could be. He was now drinking more and more as the marriage deteriorated.

As Sarah ruefully told Donaldson: "He would be partying and I would be panicking, worrying about getting up to breastfeed at four in the morning.

SHUNT

I would say we can't party but he would say: 'Don't be silly, Beast, of course we can. But I couldn't do it. I just wanted to look after my babies."

But it wasn't all bad by any means. The responsible, warm and loving side of his character, masked by the excesses, began to emerge as Hunt's family matured. In so many ways, it was the perfect set up of the eccentric father, eccentric mother, eccentric manservant, eccentric dog, one small child just beginning to walk and talk, and his very young baby brother.

As Tom began to communicate, so too did his father. "As Tom grew up", said Sarah, "you could see the love in him for his children and it was lovely to see. Suddenly, here's a guy who in the 1970s was the playboy of the western world and the real man was coming through. His stage had changed and he was reverting to childhood."

Hunt became completely focused on Tom and developed his early education by reading and speaking to him. As Sarah recalled: "He was completely focused on whatever he did. I mean, if he was reading a story to the children, there was no question of anything else coming into it. No phone calls, no yapping dog or even a best friend arriving. I remember it very, very strongly."

That is, except for the family parrot, called 'Humbert the parrot', who often sat on Hunt's shoulder. The relationship with the parrot was close, as it was with Oscar. The greeting Hunt received from Humbert after he had been away had to be seen to be believed.

Sarah has so many happy memories of Hunt as a father, which she has recalled to many different interviewers over the years: "We had a baby coach that we'd bought from our neighbour, I think for a hundred quid. It was a London baby carriage, a massive big pram. It was his pride and joy. He'd push it and Oscar would be there, and every single day they'd go and feed the Canada ducks on Wimbledon Common."

At one point, it seemed as though the marriage was saved, as the presence of the children seemed to divest Hunt of his demons and to foster in him a true family man. Sarah says none of the temper that Hunt had demonstrated at the race track ever existed at home: "I've read that he was quite lively on the racetrack and once got out and decked someone, but home life was very, very calm, very relaxed and nothing like the character he needed to adopt as a racing man." Of all the troubles, he always maintained a semblance of control and a calmness that was endearing: "James did not have a short fuse at all. He used to amaze me because he could let things go. Someone would make a wind-up remark and I'd be going mad while he'd already have forgotten about it. I'd be carrying it for a week, and he'd ask: 'Why?'" She is adamant that, at home, Hunt was nothing like his public image: "You always admire people who have demanding jobs and the minute they get home they are a family man and nothing like the character they were in the meeting or whatever three hours before. It's only men who take control of their lives who can do that."

Years after his death, she gave an interview to the *Daily Mail* in which she said: "His laugh was him, and that's the side I saw most of the time as a family person. His sense of humour was wicked – *wicked*. And I loved it. We were very similar in that way."

Home life between the two of them was relatively serene.

But Sarah also recalled what she called the "naughty" times with her husband. Every time they could get away and enjoy their old hedonistic activities, they did; leaving one of their mothers and Winston in charge of the children. The mothers were only too happy to take over the duty of looking after the two "delightful" boys.

The British Grand Prix at Silverstone was always a highlight of those "naughty times" spent together. Hunt and Sarah were very good friends with a leading team principal and his wife.

The team principal was a fastidious man who liked everything just so. Sarah recalled an incident in his car at Silverstone to a *Daily Mail* reporter that reflected Hunt's naughty side. In fact, she says it was the naughtiest she can remember: "James was trying to light up a fag in his car – just James, me and his wife in it – and she was saying: 'No way, James. People do not smoke in his car. He is obsessive about things like that.' So with a glint in his eye, James ate a McDonald's and chips and then had a fag in the car. It was so childish and naughty and twinkling – I thought it was terrific. If he ever found out, he'd probably have changed the car."

Sarah recounted another trip to Gleneagles, which also proved that her husband had lost none of his daredevil spirit by becoming a father, as she told the *Daily Mail*: "We were going to a pro-am (gold tournament) at Gleneagles in the old brown 6.9-litre Mercedes. It didn't always go but it went that night, went like a rocket. We left at about 11 o'clock at night from Wimbledon, and near the Scottish borders there was a police car, a Panda car, behind us. So he thought: 'No, I'm not going to stop for that one' and he put his foot down. It was a bit hairy. We got well in front and he pulled off onto a track.

We hid behind bushes and watched the Panda go by. You could almost feel the Panda's driver saying: 'Where's he going, where's he going, where's he gone?' We then came out and James really put his foot down and overtook the Panda. James said he knew there was the changeover at the border and that the Panda car couldn't follow. It would take him a little while to phone through and get another guy on the other side to pick us up. Well, we were gone – and in thick fog. They were chasing us and we were doing 120 miles an hour in this fog, at 3 o'clock in the morning. He said: 'The best place for you is down there on the floor – lie down, think of England and don't forget I'm the highest paid chauffeur in the world.' We got away. His concentration was total and I'll never forget seeing the veins and the muscles on his forearms. I felt actually okay. He said: 'Don't look at the needle.' Afterwards, I was fine but Oscar was ill for days."

The arrival of the two boys saw Oscar really come into his own and become the star of the show, demonstrating what a truly magnificent dog he was. Oscar was one of those very special dogs that forms an innate bond with its master which defies analysis. Jonathan Martin, Hunt's boss at the BBC remembers: "Oscar was a remarkable animal. He used to go everywhere with James. I remember at Wimbledon one year, he was with him in one of the BBC caravans and James told him to 'stay'. Oscar did not move from that spot for an hour until James returned."

Oscar also sometimes went to restaurants with his master and was well known at Langan's Brasserie in Mayfair, owned by Peter Langan and actor Michael Caine. Langan, a true eccentric himself, loved Oscar and allowed him to sit at the table with Hunt. If any of his other diners didn't like it, Langan would rather ask them to leave than Oscar. Peter Langan's eccentricity made Hunt's own antics look small, but they got on famously.

There was one rather unsavoury incident, where Oscar disgraced himself by eating one of Bubbles Horsley's children's guinea pigs on a visit to his house near Silverstone. Horsley told Gerald Donaldson: "My daughter was far less upset about it than I was. I got quite emotional about the tragedy and sent James to bed with Oscar."

Despite the incident, Horsley recognised the bond between the Hunt and his canine companion: "He was a remarkable dog, no question. James thought a lot about animals and their requirements, and was very concerned about their needs. He gave Oscar the very best treatment and was also keenly interested in the welfare of other dogs. He would look at a dog and wonder if its owner was treating it well and bringing it up properly, and if the dog was getting everything out of life that it could." Nigel Roebuck, the *Autosport* journalists also witnessed this kindness to animals when Hunt rescued a dog wandering around the paddock, gave it food and ensured its well-being, going through a lot of trouble along the way.

John Watson agreed: "In his relationship with Oscar, James showed he was a very caring and loving man. When you saw James and Oscar together, you knew he was capable of great tenderness. I suspect that, for James, Oscar wasn't a dog. He was a companion. And he loved him. There was a very deep bond between James and Oscar that I only saw again in the great love and affection he had for his two sons."

As an antidote to family life, Hunt renewed his love affair with golf, which had rather faded away since he had left Spain. He became, in the words of his friends, a "golf bore". He installed a practice net in his garden to make his swing perfect and then toured the south of England's golf courses where he knew he could always engage in an interesting round against some interesting opponents. After his knee injury healed, he played almost every day.

Far less easy to explain was Hunt's ten year affair with budgerigars, which arose directly from a childhood fascination. It was an obsession buried somewhere deep in his psyche. His interest in feathered birds began when he was 12, when his grandmother had introduced a yellow caged budgerigar to the Hunt household. The bird was apparently called Rita, after his grandmother. He used Rita as his base for breeding, installing breeding cages in the attic of their new house in Sutton and making an aviary in the garden. Before he discovered racing, he planned a career breeding budgies and reckoned he could earn a very good living at it. He told Taormina Rich he would be a budgie-breeding millionaire by the time he was 30. As the eggs hatched, the whole family became involved, and the population peaked at 32 birds. But when the family moved from Sutton to the house at Belmont, his father told him the birds had to go, and so they did. If Wallis Hunt hadn't been so insistent, there is every chance that his son would have become a professional budgerigar breeder and never given any more thought to a career in motor racing.

20 year later, the budgerigars made a comeback at his house in Wimbledon. A former world champion racing driver taking up budgie breeding in retirement was faintly ridiculous. And to those who suggested as much, and there were more than a few, James simply said: "Well, why is that ridiculous?"

There was, of course, no answer to that and the questioners then felt ridiculous for having suggested it. In truth, it was just like any other hobby, and he didn't think it out of character. But even James couldn't explain to people why he enjoyed it so much; he could only assure them that he did.

He built a large 4-metre by 9-metre aviary in his garden, which was insulated and equipped with 30 breeding cages, and he bought 30 budgerigars initially. His ambition was to breed exhibition standard budgies and to show them.

He bought a 30-year-old Austin A35 van in which to transport the budgerigars around the country. The choice of vehicle, which cost UK£900, was truly absurd and reflected his total eccentricity. But he was proud of it and of his budgies. He said by way of explanation: "It really is a jolly good car and I'm very attached to it, and I chuck it about and drive it right on the limit without breaking the law."

Eventually, James had some 140 budgerigars in his garden, said to be worth nearly UK£60,000. He owned rare species with names such as Normals, Cinnamons, Opalines and Spangles. Trying to explain his enthusiasm, he said simply: "I like them because they are decorative and make a cheerful sound."

The children certainly loved them as well, and Hunt's son Freddie can recall being showered with droppings from the birds as he, his father and his brother kicked footballs around the garden. They were very happy times, indeed.

Sadly, they were not to last.

SHUNT

CHAPTER 42

Black dog and the lost decade
Off the rails in his darkest period

Few people knew about, and even fewer understood, the depression or the 'black dog' from which James Hunt suffered between 1980 and 1990, after he had retired from motor racing.

That is because he revealed it to so few people. Even very close friends, such as John Hogan and Peter Collins, were totally unaware of it. In many ways, James Hunt lived his life in compartments; he was a different person to different people. Or perhaps those people just brought out different aspects in him.

His problem was very common in successful sports people of the time; people like soccer player George Best and snooker player Alex Higgins were also victims of it. Inevitably, people who drank heavily and who had addictive personalities were more vulnerable.

By the age of 33, James Hunt had been there and done it, and yet his natural adult life span was barely a quarter complete. From then on, as he realised only too well, it would be downhill all the way. And so it was.

Ian Phillips strongly believes it started when Hunt went completely off the rails for a period after his retirement. He tries to define what went wrong: "It's something I don't understand and am never going to, but it fascinates me how sportsmen in general conduct themselves once it's all over. Some

643

do brilliantly and some go off the rails, and I think it's not unfair to say that actually James went off the rails for a little bit."

Murray Walker believed that the problems were caused by withdrawal syndrome and nothing to do with the move from Spain or his subsequent lifestyle choices, He says: "For years, he had been lionised and harried ceaselessly by countless fans and given no peace by the media. He hated being so public and when he retired he was worn out by the pressure and what had been a very turbulent lifestyle. So he drank to excess, smoked to excess, womanised to super-excess and was now literally yesterday's man."

Peter Warr thought that the problems were caused by the manner in which Hunt exited Formula One. He believes that Hunt developed a serious chip on his shoulder after he retired from racing. Warr is well aware that Hunt took against him and bad-mouthed him, as he did many people against whom he formed, sometimes irascibly, a strong dislike. Warr said: "He had it in for a lot of people, and for a time I was included in that because I think he saw me as the guy who couldn't give him the car with which he could exit brilliantly from his career; but Formula One doesn't pardon anyone. Everybody exits Formula One out of the back door, you never exit out of the front. It doesn't happen, even to Nigel Mansell or whomever. Everyone exits from the back door because it's that sort of business. One of the nice things is that James probably came the nearest of anybody to exiting through the front because everyone now has a good word for him.

"But the James of those post-championship years, when the booze and the women got to him and he had it in for everybody, that wasn't the real James Hunt, for sure. It certainly wasn't the James of his latter years, or the James I'd known in the debriefs and the on-track situations."

There is no question that retiring relatively early left a huge gap in his life, emotionally as well as physically. Suddenly his whole reason for existing had been removed and he was, in truth, no longer James Hunt. Without racing, he was someone else. And it took him ten years to adapt to the new character he was forced to become. They were to be ten long, painful years.

The problems arose because he hadn't properly thought through the ramifications of retirement. Thinking that retirement entailed simply no longer driving a race car, he was taken aback by how much more there was to it than that.

In truth, Hunt actually had no idea what he was doing, proven by the fact that he chose to retire in mid-season; an exit route few drivers have chosen and, when they have, have almost always regretted. For all Hunt's intelligence, he totally messed up his exit and had no one around him strong enough to tell him so. He was actually risking his mental health with such a sudden and jarring change in his life.

Niki Lauda, who had retired even more abruptly than Hunt, fared much better. With his flourishing airline business, Lauda had another life to turn to after retirement. Hunt, however, had absolutely nothing after his racing ended. Lauda agrees: "James had a bad time, no question. When he retired, he had nothing to do so he enjoyed himself too much."

What it was all boiled down to was that Hunt had retired from racing because he feared for his life, and that fear had destroyed the innate love he had for motor racing. In fact, he was actually more frightened of being severely disabled than he was of dying.

After he retired, the accident that befell Clay Regazzoni at Long Beach in 1980 affected him more than anything he had witnessed when he was racing. He knew that could easily have been him, and it depressed him greatly. He already suffered from flashbacks from the deaths of François Cevert and Ronnie Peterson, and they were just two of the many deaths that occurred whilst he was racing.

Aside from his racing experiences, other writers have recorded that he blamed his parents for the troubled man he had become by the time he reached his 40th birthday. They say he looked back on his childhood and the manner in which he had been brought up, and placed part of the blame on his parents for not loving him enough. But there is nothing on the record to say that this was his sincere view and no evidence to suggest it. In fact, there is plenty of evidence indicating precisely the opposite.

His mother did admit to interviewers that the family was guilty of what she called "unshared feelings" and that the deepest emotions sometimes went unexpressed in what was the busy Hunt household in Belmont in the late 1960s. Like many families in the sixties, the Hunts were not particularly demonstrative with their love and affection for each other, even though there was no doubt it existed. It was not a hypocritical environment in any sense. But Wallis and Sue Hunt were unselfish and gave up everything for their six children. Everything was funnelled into their development and they were perfect parents, as early chapters demonstrate.

Gerald Donaldson had some intimate conversations with Sue Hunt when he was writing his 1993 biography, and she revealed that she had discussed with James his problems with depression around the time of his 40th birthday.

It appears that Hunt himself had initiated a conversation with her and had sought her help with the problem he thought he had of "withdrawing into himself as a boy and his inability to form close personal relationships as an adult." Donaldson recounted: "In response to his questioning about the way he was brought up, Sue wrote James a letter. In it, she admitted that she might have treated him differently, perhaps catered more to his special needs, but she didn't recognise them at the time. She acknowledged that she was young and inexperienced as a parent, especially in dealing with boys, because she had no brothers and there were few males among her close relations. But she assumed what she was doing, the same as her parents had done for her, was best for him."

Donaldson reprinted some of that letter, in which she said, tellingly: "If we hadn't treated you the way we did, if you hadn't had the sort of upbringing you had, which you chose to fight, you might not have been world champion."

Bubbles Horsley believes the problems in his relationship with Sarah caused the deepest pits of the black dog from which Hunt suffered. As Horsley was undoubtedly Hunt's closest friend in life, his words have more resonance than most: "It was huge stress, emotional stress. He was desperate about the future. It was almost as if he had gone back to a fight for survival, like the fight he had in his early Formula 3 days."

To her credit, his wife Sarah fought very hard to help him combat the black dog. But she could make little impact, and seeing her husband in such torment and being unable to help made her depressed as well. Eventually, she began to be affected herself and suffered severe weight loss. The couple saw a psychiatrist together but, as they had found with the marriage counselling, it was ineffective.

Somewhat surprisingly, it is perhaps Hunt's youngest son, Freddie, now 23-years-old, who has the best handle on his father's ten years of depression. When Freddie himself started racing in 2007, he gave several newspaper interviews, many of which inevitably strayed into the subject of his father. He talked about his own ambitions in racing and contrasted them with his father's experiences.

Freddie, who, like his father, was not academically gifted, showed he had nevertheless inherited much of his father's intelligence and thoughtfulness with his answers. He said of his father: "He basically got to the top of his ladder and then I don't think he had given any previous thought to what would happen after that if he did get there. As a result, his depression and everything else he's done, his spiral, which everyone knows about, I think was as a result of that. I don't want to end up like he did. He got to the top, but he soon went downhill after he retired. And it took him a good few years to get his head back and to be happy again.

"Because you know what? You retire as a Formula One driver when you're what – 30, 35, 38? There's still a lot of life after that, and that's what daddy really didn't take into consideration. I don't know exactly what was going through his head, but when you're at the top, sometimes the only way you can go after that is down. Daddy drank a lot and took one or two substances he shouldn't have, both of which possibly caused the bouts of depression from which he suffered from time to time. Because depression is often hereditary, it represents my greatest fear."

These were thoughts and fears that his father had never examined in his own life. That his son had, and had already worked out the dangers, says everything about the strength of their relationship before he died. Freddie Hunt is, without a doubt, his father's son.

SHUNT

CHAPTER 43

Separation from Sarah and financial disaster

He loses his fortune and his family

According to the Lloyd's 'Blue Book', James Hunt was heavily involved as a member of the Lloyd's of London insurance market for most of the 1980s. In that period, he may well have been a member of up to 40 syndicates. For the most of the years of his involvement, he made good money – except for the last year.

Lloyd's of London was actually a market where individuals, traditionally known as 'names' came together. They were organised by brokers into syndicates to cover the risks of others for a premium fee. In the main, Lloyd's members effectively reinsured insurance companies to spread their risk. Because the reinsurance was rarely called upon, the premiums paid were virtually all profit for its members. And this practice had gone on, with very little trouble, for hundreds of years.

The members had to put up very little cash and were able to share in very big rewards. The downside was that they were liable for all the losses personally. Other retired sports personalities, such as jockey Lester Piggott and boxer Henry Cooper, were also names at Lloyd's.

There were also big tax advantages to being a Lloyd's member and the profits were liable for much lower rates of tax.

However, after the experiences of his father as the victim of an unforeseen circumstance as an unlimited partner in 1981, Hunt might have been expected to be more cautious about effectively putting himself in the same position.

But Hunt enjoyed the profits as they flowed. After his retirement, he invested more and more heavily, and there was no real reason for him to be cautious. Lloyd's of London was a centuries old institution and members had always made money.

Hunt's two main investments were in Syndicate no. 745, run by a broker called David King, and Syndicate no. 895, run by Bryan Spencer. Spencer was a colourful character, as were many of the Lloyd's brokers in those days. His nickname on the insurance market was 'Nodding Donkey'.

Hunt had been put into the syndicates by his brother Peter, who set himself up as a Lloyd's sub-agent and could therefore reap a commission on his clients' transactions. It was sound advice at the time, when being a Lloyd's 'name' was literally a licence to print money.

However, in the late 1980s the gravy train finally hit the buffers and Lloyd's went through the most traumatic period in its history. Unexpectedly, large awards in American law courts for punitive damages led to large insurance claims. The main problem was the discovery of the long-term health hazards of using asbestos in buildings. There were claims dating as far back as the 1940s and the policies were designed to cover all liabilities.

Moreover, many brokers did not behave honourably. They recruited more names, Hunt amongst them, after they knew about the emerging problems. They withheld their knowledge of the potentially ruinous claims until they could recruit more investors to take on the liabilities that were still unknown outside a small circle of people. Hunt was caught in the trap.

From reaping big dividends, Hunt suddenly found himself getting cash calls for hundreds of thousands of pounds. He was not alone and many names who couldn't pay stopped paying, and the names that could pay, such as Hunt, picked up their share of the losses. Hunt had no choice but to pay, and soon all his liquid cash was gone.

Just at the same moment, the UK property market crashed and prices were dropping like a stone. As Hunt liquidated his property investments, prices dropped and his net worth fell alarmingly. All the businesses he had set up in the aftermath of his retirement had also closed or collapsed. The nightclub in Marbella named after his dog Oscar had shut and cost him over US$100,000.

He was threatened with bankruptcy by Lloyd's if he didn't pay – so had no choice. And the liability was unlimited. It was a truly frightening time. Hunt went from being a very rich man with unlimited spending power to being a pauper in six short months.

The luxurious holidays on yachts stopped. The Mercedes 6.9-litre car was put up on blocks as Hunt could no longer afford the insurance, the tax, the maintenance or the petrol. Winston took a pay cut.

He was in such financial trouble that he tried to make a racing comeback at the age of 41. He had seen Niki Lauda come back in 1982 to earn US$12 million before he retired again. The top racing drivers were then making as much as US$8 million a year and he thought he could come back and do the same in order to solve his own pressing financial problems. But he had left it too long to make a comeback.

He arranged to test a Williams car at Paul Ricard circuit. But he was two seconds off the pace and Williams weren't interested in him. But Hunt felt he could still do it and approached John Hogan for help. He confessed to him he was broke and needed the money and begged him to help him find a drive. But Hogan thought he was crazy to consider it and wrote him a letter telling him so.

He even asked his friend Tony Dron, who remembers: "He said he thought he might try and make a return to Formula One and I just remember saying to him: 'Is that what you really want?' There was a long silence and that was the end of that."

Very soon, Hunt realised that the avenue was closed to him, and as the Lloyd's cash calls subsided, he learned that he still had a net worth of some US$3 million – enough to live on comfortably for the rest of his life if he was careful. He also had an annual income of over US$150,000 a year from his BBC and Marlboro contracts.

But he hadn't factored in his next calamity. His relationship with Sarah couldn't survive under these circumstances and, in October 1988, the façade of the happy marriage and family life finally cracked wide open. In a press release, James and Sarah Hunt officially announced they were separating, although there was no mention of divorce.

For the sake of their young children, Hunt and Sarah decided to live separate lives but to stay under the same roof. Predictably, that arrangement wasn't successful. As Hunt took up his role as a bachelor, Sarah found it unacceptable to be in the same house.

So he spent UK£350,000 of money he didn't have and bought her a house nearby, within walking distance so he could see Tom and Freddie. By then, the children were both talking and walking, and he was starting to really enjoy their company. He nicknamed them his 'little men', and indeed they were. He loved them deeply and was a very proud father and a perfect parent.

But Sarah was devastated by the official split. According to Gerald Donaldson, she told him that "she had only ever wanted a husband, children and a home of her own, and the prospect of a failed marriage was devastating."

Hunt was relieved when the split was made official but also upset as, despite his own marital failings, he had hoped that marriage and parenthood would bring him peace and contentment. But it hadn't and he had simply chosen the wrong woman with whom to spend the rest of his life. While many of his friends already knew the two of them were totally incompatible, it had taken the couple five eventful years to find out. They eventually found they had nothing in common other than their children.

When they had married, Sarah described herself as "24 going on four" but the responsibilities of motherhood had now made her more responsible. But her husband hadn't change at all. Stirling Moss, for one, wasn't at all surprised when the marriage went wrong: "I wouldn't liked to have lived with James."

In November 1989, 13 months after they separated, Sarah was granted a divorce in the matrimonial division of the High Court on the grounds of adultery by her husband. Sarah didn't want the divorce and would have been quite happy for them to have stayed as man and wife – albeit living separately.

Up to the moment when Hunt pushed her for a formal divorce, it had been a relatively amicable separation. But his insistence on a divorce meant things turned nasty, particularly when she hired herself a solicitor to handle it – and a very good solicitor to boot. Conversely, Hunt hired one that he came to believe was less good.

The solicitor turned Sarah's head, and persuaded her to go for the jugular by insisting on receiving half of Hunt's net worth as a lump sum for herself and a big monthly allowance to bring up the children. And that is precisely what she ended up getting.

The eventual terms of the divorce were ruinous, and Sarah took whatever was left from Lloyd's until Hunt was left in considerable debt. Her settlement was in excess of UK£1.25 million in cash and assets, and at least half of his annual income also went to her and the children.

Her solicitor wiped the floor with Hunt's solicitor, and even threatened to apply for a court order that would have allowed Hunt to be in the presence of his children only with another neutral adult present.

The solicitor claimed he was unfit to be alone with his children. It was a wholly ridiculous allegation and personally humiliating, but the lawyer played on Hunt's well-known drinking and drug taking habits, of which Sarah had plenty of evidence.

It was a smoking gun, and Hunt had absolutely no defence. Sarah's solicitor wrote to him asking for details of exactly what had happened on the flight to Adelaide, to the Australian Grand Prix in 1985, the month after his eldest son was born.

Hunt, remembering the highly publicised incident on the aeroplane, realised that in the face of such evidence a judge might easily grant such an order. And so he capitulated to virtually all of Sarah's financial demands, as unreasonable as he considered them to be. At worst, there was a possibility that the judge might not give him any custody rights. Hunt felt absolutely defenceless, and every time he raised any sort of objection, Sarah's solicitor brought up the issue of the custody of the children. They used the children as a weapon to nail him, and it was very successful.

Mark Wilkin, his producer at the BBC, was very close to Hunt as the divorce reached his climax. They saw each other every fortnight at races and Wilkin provided a willing proverbial shoulder for Hunt to cry on. He remembers: "James was very direct, he never really beat about the bush with anything. He'd often greet me at a race with: 'Do you know what they've done now?' He was talking about his wife's solicitors and there'd be absolute anger. The divorce was clearly ghastly for him and he would often spend the first hour of a meeting just unloading the last two weeks and you had to sit and listen and 'err and umm.' He just needed to unload it on someone."

Ian Phillips, who had never been in favour of the marriage, remembers the ordeal: "He was very bitter about the whole thing. One night in a restaurant, we were having dinner with John Hogan and Graham Bogle and he was absolutely raging about the legal system and lawyers. He was quite obviously distressed."

Bubbles Horsley remembered: "He appeared to hit bottom when threatened with losing his share of custody of his two sons."

In many ways, Hunt had only himself to blame. The aeroplane incident had severely damaged his image and reputation just at a time when he needed a good image with which to earn some money.

And at one point, he almost cracked. With people he didn't know, he completely lost his confidence and was walking around in a haze. When they came up to congratulate him on his success, he felt a complete fraud with his life in such a mess. He suddenly shied away from physical contact. He avoided eye contact and was just so embarrassed at the state in which he found himself.

But Hunt was grateful for the support and encouragement of friends like Wilkin and Phillips, and he didn't take it all lying down. He threw all his energy into defending himself. He got together comprehensive files chronicling the marriage woes and the deficiencies of his wife. He was forced to attack her personally in order to defend himself. She was by no means perfect, and the files were huge, including all the letters they had written each other and receipts and invoices detailing the money he had spent on her during the marriage. But it was all fruitless because of the aeroplane incident, and he was wasting his time.

The main battle went on for three months, and, to rub salt into his wounds at the very last minute, Hunt was presented with Sarah's solicitor's bill and had to find another £30,000 to pay for the time of the man who had tormented him. By this time, he had mortgaged the house and was in serious financial trouble. But he had no choice but to keep paying until all his money was gone. In the end, he almost gave up and stopped fighting. Every time he fought, it cost more money in legal fees, his and hers, and he was getting nowhere. His own legal bill was £40,000. In the end, he paid more than UK£15,000 in VAT on the legal bills alone.

But his main problem was discrepancy between what he considered to be the poor quality of his own case and the extraordinary quality of Sarah's. Hunt eventually sued his own solicitor in the High Court. He was so impoverished by this stage that he was actually granted legal aid to do it. The granting of legal aid showed just how far he had fallen.

As mortgage rates rose at the start of the 1990s, he found his debts had peaked at UK£800,000, which at its height was costing him more than £2,000 a week in interest to service. Even when interest rates dropped, it was costing £1,000 a week.

When the dust settled, Hunt owned his house in Wimbledon but was UK£500,000 in debt via his new mortgage. His net worth dropped to less than £400,000 and he had no cash other than what he was earning. From having had unlimited money he was now living on £500 a week and paying all his bills out of it, including Winston's salary. But it was the price of his freedom and, in the end, that freedom was very important to him.

The end of his marriage was very painful, and afterwards he considered writing a book on divorce as a guide for suffering ex-husbands. But when he looked at the confidentiality clauses Sarah's solicitor had built into the various agreements he had signed, he realised it was not possible.

He also knew he couldn't afford the time. He had been screwed financially and, as Sarah put it later and very succinctly to her husband's biographer: "James was a victim of the three 'L's: love, lawyers and Lloyd's."

But although Sarah may have come out of the marriage with no financial worries and seemingly set up for life, she was also scared of facing up to life on her own, as she said: "I was totally dependent on him, emotionally, financially, in every possible way."

With custody sorted out, his two sons came to stay with him at his Wimbledon home on a regular basis. Although very young, they knew what was going on and had the normal split loyalties of children of a broken home. As Sarah confessed: "They found it awfully hard to be equally loyal to both of us after we separated. It used to tear them apart. But Sarah proved to be an excellent mother and, despite her own feelings at the time, didn't carry it over to her children as many parents do. She encouraged them to talk about their father all the time and she responded very positively. It helped the process of adjusting to the separation.

But privately, she remained frustrated, as she said: "When I met people after we divorced, all they wanted to know was about James. It really got me down. I used to say: 'Here's his phone number, ring him up and ask how he is yourself – I don't live with him so how should I know how he is?'" It would take her at least two years to get past it.

Meanwhile, Hunt did everything he could to earn money, including as many promotional days as he could, albeit now at a somewhat reduced rate. He was always asking Mark Wilkin for improvements to his BBC contract, saying he needed the money. Wilkin helped if he could – often inadvertently. He signed off expenses he knew Hunt hadn't incurred to try and help him out of a chronic mess. Hunt knew nothing of this, of course, and he thought his expense fiddling was going by unnoticed, but Wilkin was aware of it. Wilkin says: "He was always complaining he hadn't got any money, but all through it I had huge respect for him and it grew into a huge fondness."

To raise money, Hunt licensed his name to a venture called the 'James Hunt Racing Centre', which had cost US$3 million to set up. The centre was effectively a leisure race track with small identical single seater race cars designed for the corporate market for staff and client away-days. It was all based around a private track in Milton Keynes. He was paid UK£50,000 for the use of his name, plus royalties. But these didn't amount to much as the venture quickly went bust. The idea was ahead of its time, and ex racing driver Jonathan Palmer later took up the concept and set up Bedford Autodrome based on the same idea and made millions. Hunt continued to raise money any way he could and eventually his beloved budgerigars had to be sold. He got UK£45,000 for them.

He also took any journalistic work he could find. He wrote an internationally syndicated newspaper column and worked with a new friend called Gerald Donaldson, who later became his biographer. It paid him over US$1,000 a week. Stirling Moss remembers it well: "When he lost all his money all of a sudden, he needed to work."

His meeting with Donaldson was accidental and fortuitous. He bumped into him in the Silverstone car park. The encounter was marked when Hunt told Donaldson he had read his earlier biography of Gilles Villeneuve and said he had found it an emotionally challenging read. He congratulated Donaldson on it.

Donaldson immediately suggested that he might want to consider his own biography, but Hunt nixed the idea straightaway: "No, no time for that, but why don't we work together?" And so they did. Donaldson became his collaborator for his syndicated newspaper columns, which appeared all over the world and were highly lucrative for both men.

And so began a highly enjoyable three years of co-writing, as Donaldson says: "We did them on the Monday and they were due on the Tuesday. His columns were, dare I say, extraordinarily well written, because he worked really hard on them and, if he wanted, he could be as articulate in print as he was when he spoke. It was a pretty influential column in those times."

Hunt also got lucky with a lucrative promotional contract from Shell Oil. Shell sensed that his Texaco days were now a distant memory for most people and that it could use him very effectively to sell more petrol and oil, just as Texaco had many years earlier. Unfortunately, Eric Morecambe was now dead, so that golden partnership could not be recreated.

His old friend David Gray believes that Hunt handled his financial reversals with considerable maturity: "James was careful with his money and he always had a fantastically broad bat, so he never had any sort of self-pity. His attitude was 'shit happens' and that was pretty much what he thought. He could always earn money; he was a good-looking bloke."

Publicly, Hunt was confident he could rebuild his fortune, as he told a group of journalists: "In the long run money buys freedom – the right to do exactly what you like – and that's what I shall buy myself when I retire." But as he said the words, he leant down to touch some wood.

In truth, he was by no means sure he would be able to recover from the financial calamity that had befallen him.

But out of the travails eventually some good did emerge. With far less money in his pocket, Hunt's drinking subsided considerably. He simply couldn't afford it. He also admitted for the first time that he was probably an alcoholic.

He also slowly began to realise he had to give up smoking and reduce his marijuana consumption. To help him do it, he began to read voraciously on how to cure addictions and the consequences of an addictive personality. The more he read, the more he recognised himself. He also finally realised he was a sex addict, long before the condition was ever recognised publicly. It was also the age when people were dying of AIDS, and he realised that casual sex was now dangerous and that he needed to take more precautions.

He also started some brutal fitness programmes. After a heavy workout, he would take a hot shower and then jump into a tub of ice-cold water. The brutal process was intended to strengthen the immune system and libido. He also stopped using soap and deodorant, allowing his body to clean itself naturally. He became a 'Chinese herbalist' and drank what he called 'funny tea,' a mixture of crushed ginger, lemon juice, honey and hot water.

Hogan says: "He straightened himself out by absolute willpower. The strength of character of the man enabled him to get out of it. He cut out the cigarettes, the dope and drugs, the booze and the womanising, and his sense of priorities became more well-balanced."

Niki Lauda said: "He got himself out of the shit completely. Didn't smoke. Didn't drink. I think one day he just woke and said: 'Shit. I can't go on like this.' He realised this is not the way he wanted to go on, so he was completely clean and clear. This strength was unbelievable for me."

And with the new, more sober regime, a new mood overtook him. A substantially better mood prevailed. Hunt also got back into fitness by buying an old bicycle, and he started cycling into central London from Wimbledon, stripped to the waist and carrying clothes in a haversack for when he arrived. He cycled everywhere.

The only aspect of Hunt's life that he didn't reform was his mode of dress. That was apparent on his first visit to Shell's headquarters for a meeting with Shell's top managers; he turned up on his bicycle, in shorts and trainers. When the doorman asked him if he had found a place to park his car, he asked if he could put his bicycle behind the security desk.

It was the new James Hunt. As Stirling Moss assessed: "With James, he needed to run out of money before he pulled himself together."

SHUNT

CHAPTER 44

Helen's arrival sparks a financial personal revival 1990-1993

Light in the dark tunnel again

As 1989 came to a close, James Hunt found himself in radically changed circumstances. He literally had no money; none at all. His only solution to the problem had been a motor racing comeback, and that had failed. Added to that, Britain was in the grip of a recession and property prices had collapsed. As the potential to make money disappeared, his property development company with Bubbles Horsley also wound down. Margaret Thatcher was about to fall, and interest rates were on their way up to 14 per cent. His biggest problem was servicing the loans he had been forced to take out to fund his Lloyds' losses and the divorce. The interest payments and maintenance he paid to Sarah were taking all his money, and he had less than UK£500 a week to live on.

It was by no means enough, and he was forced to borrow money from friends, including Bernie Ecclestone. One day, desperate, he rung Ecclestone and asked him for a loan. Ecclestone asked: "When do you need it?" To which Hunt replied: "Right now." And he meant right now. Ecclestone rang up to his personal accountant at his offices at Princes Gate in Knightsbridge, and asked him to arrange for UK£5,000 in cash to be left in an envelope at reception for Hunt to collect an hour later. Hunt cycled into London, collected it, took it to his bank and deposited it so his bills would be met.

SHUNT

Money was desperately short, and this was reflected by the difficulties he
had getting his Austin A35 van through its MOT test. The van needed some
welding done on the chassis, which was going to cost UK£200, and Hunt
simply didn't have the money to get it done. As the van was a necessity, he
panicked and rang his old friend Tony Dron for help. Dron arranged for one
of his race mechanics to do it for him on credit. Dron remembers: "He said
to me: 'I have been broke many times in my life – I just get on with it.'"

There were many other incidents like that, and Hunt just about managed
to cover his bills and avoid a financial meltdown. He was being overtaken by
the high interest rates, and the situation looked hopeless. But this cloud had
a silver lining, even if it wasn't apparent to him at the time.

Hunt's drop in income proved to be his salvation. It made him wake up and
take a good look at himself and the world around him. He realised that, since
1973, for nigh on 17 years, he had been living in a complete fantasy world
where money didn't matter because he had so much of it. The unlimited
supply of money had enabled him to indulge any fantasy he liked, whether
it was good for him or not – and usually, it was not.

Now that he had no money, he would no longer drink himself to oblivion
every night. He certainly couldn't afford cocaine, and even marijuana was
off the menu. He cut down the number of cigarettes he smoked to less than
20 a day.

He was literally forced to go straight, and as soon as he cut down on the
drink, drugs and cigarettes, he started to feel much healthier. He had never
felt as good as he did after just one month without alcohol. It was at that
moment that he resolved to give them up altogether. The more progress he
made, the more voraciously he read his self-help books and became focused
on overcoming his addictions.

His financial problems had ultimately ended up saving him, and he began
the last three years of his life in better shape than at any point since he was 17.

He told Nigel Roebuck, explaining the change in his outlook and his new
lifestyle: "Quite simple, really, the tail was starting to wag the dog."

He didn't try to hide his straitened financial circumstances from anybody
and, when asked, he admitted he was broke. John Hogan remembers some
very pleasant times after what he calls 'The Reformation': "We had many
pleasant lunches and dinners at a restaurant called Drones, and he used to
come out skiing at Verbier with his kids. He found he was suddenly much
happier and much fitter. He discovered that life was no different driving

662

around in an old van than it was in a large Mercedes, or indeed even pedalling everywhere on a bicycle." Stirling Moss recalls: "When his car was up on bricks, he said to me: 'That's how it is darling, you know. It's nobody's fault, nobody owes me anything, that's fine.'"

Ian Phillips was delighted to see the change in his friend: "He was only 40 and I think he suddenly asked himself: 'What am I doing with my life?' and he cleaned up his act. The drugs had gone, the drink, and he didn't even smoke."

Professor Sid Watkins, Formula One's doctor, says it is a misconception that Hunt actually gave up drinking. He didn't, but what he did do was learn to control it. Says Watkins: "At no time was he not drinking at all, but he was able control it and we enjoyed a few drinks together." Likewise, Nigel Roebuck, who enjoyed drinks with Hunt on his last flight back from Australia in 1993, recounted to Gerald Donaldson: "I asked him if he was off the wagon. James said: 'No, I've allowed myself to have a bit of fun.' And when I asked him if he really could stop it, he said: 'Yes, I really can.'"

When he dined with Murray Walker in Portugal in 1991, Walker offered him wine but Hunt declined, saying: "I've stopped, I'm off it, Walker." Walker asked why and he replied simply: "I think I've had my share."

To say Walker was surprised would be an understatement, as he later told Christopher Hilton: "I'm no psychologist, but my analysis is this: One, James suddenly had a driving need to earn money; two, the need existed because he had two things that mattered enormously to him – his sons; three, he had reformed because I suspect he knew or had been told his health was at risk if he didn't knock off the drink and other things; And four, possibly more important than anything else, he had a good woman behind him."

Walker says he noticed the physical change in Hunt straightaway: "James changed physically and he changed mentally. Before he had been dour, sleepy-eyed and flaccid, but he now became lean, ruddy-faced and, most significantly, bright-eyed. Before, you felt he wasn't with you or was seeing you through a veil. All of a sudden, he was very much there."

Walker was very enthusiastic about the change, as he told Gerald Donaldson: "He became, to me, an altogether different, enormously likeable chap whom I greatly respected. A much more charming and jolly chap who actually began to communicate with me, whereas before we had been talking to each other through millions of people by means of television, but not really communicating. James was now positively demanding the microphone, and making significant and interesting contributions to the whole presentation, and we were now producing, in my opinion, an incomparably better product."

Walker also remembers some carefree days in Portugal at Grand Prix time at the Estalagem Muchaxo in Guincho, up the coast from Cascais: It became an annual event with his two sons in the last few years of his life: "It was a very unusual place at the end of a superb bay at the extreme western edge of Europe, and I was immensely impressed with a side of James, as a warm-hearted dad, that I had never seen before. He was marvellous, marvellous.'

And then there was Helen.

Helen Dyson was 25 and working as a waitress in a restaurant called 'Hamburger Heaven', a posher version of McDonald's, with waitress service. Hunt loved eating hamburgers, and often visited the establishment after his separation from Sarah. He gradually became more and more enamoured of the young blonde who served him, with her bright personality and a dazzling but warm smile. It gradually emerged she was an artist, serving hamburgers by day and painting murals by night. She was also studying for a fine arts degree in fabric design at Middlesex Polytechnic. It turned out that she was also his neighbour. Her parents, Mike and Molly Dyson, lived on Wimbledon Common. He learned that she came from was a good Catholic family and that her father was an accountant.

In normal circumstances, he simply would have asked her out and bedded her. But he really liked her and, by then, he was 43-years-old and overly conscious of the age gap. He was also waiting for his divorce to be finalised. He delayed making any move until that was all done.

As soon as it was, almost to the day, he asked her out. They went to dinner the following Saturday. She didn't know anything about motor racing, but had guessed from people's reactions in the restaurant – he had been asked to sign autographs – that he was reasonably well known.

But in the days before the internet and Google, she couldn't really know who James Hunt was. She was still at school when he was winning his world championship. She says: "Had I known who he was, I might not have had the courage to say 'yes'. I thought he was some charming village man and that it was sweet of him to ask me out."

She claims now that she never asked him about his past and only learned of it in the obituaries and many articles published after his death. She says: "I'd have run a mile had I known that when we started seeing each other. But I think, to be honest, James was ashamed of it; he'd moved on. I didn't know the extent of it, I didn't really want to know – it wasn't relevant to our life."

Helen was entirely different from his previous girlfriends. For a start, she wasn't a big socialiser. She explains: "I didn't like all that partying and excess, so he didn't inflict it on me. I'm very much a suburbs girl. I couldn't have managed all that. And maybe James liked the fact that I was so normal."

Helen had an entirely different experience from Hunt's other significant partners, Taormina, Suzy, Jane and Sarah, as she says: "I couldn't have gone out with a man who was a womaniser. But the man I knew wasn't like that. He wanted to settle down. He couldn't have been more devoted and loving." She didn't recognise the man described in the obituaries, the manic-depressive, drug-taking drunk was not the boyfriend she had.

Shortly after his death, Helen spoke candidly to Gerald Donaldson and described her first date with Hunt: "I was in a very jolly mood. It was bit awkward at first and the conversation was stilted, but I really began to fancy him and became completely infatuated."

She discovered he was also a Catholic, a convert, but a lapsed one. He had converted to Catholicism when he married Suzy Miller – but not with any enthusiasm.

On that first date, he confessed his past to her; although obviously not all the details. She admitted she was horrified by what he did reveal. When he told her he had been married twice, she immediately began to wonder what her parents might think, even though they were only on their first date and might not even have a second. The little he told her about what Gerald Donaldson described as "his decadent past" worried her. Helen didn't want to be anyone's bimbo or mistress, which was why she was single when she met him. She had high standards and, as the evening progressed, became hesitant about seeing him a second time. But she did, and by the third date, she was utterly charmed by him and was hooked. It was now too late for second thoughts.

At the time, Mike Dennett, an old friend of Hunt's, was living with him in Wimbledon. For a long time, he was the only one of his friends to have met Helen. Dennett told Donaldson: "Helen came around to the house more and more often, and he just seemed to light up in her company. But he also seemed less sure of himself." They quickly fell in love and began what was a very happy three-year relationship, in which they often discussed marriage and children. They would undoubtedly have married, but Hunt simply couldn't afford it.

Helen remained anxious about him meeting her parents, and it was some months before the 25- year-old took her 43-year-old boyfriend round to her family home. But any fears about the age gap were completely unfounded. Her parents didn't even register it. Neither Mike nor Molly Dyson batted an eyelid when she brought him home to meet them. They knew nothing about him, and took him at face value. Helen says: They didn't know about motor racing, and they weren't the sort to read gossip."

Once that ordeal was over, Hunt visited her house regularly and they settled into a relationship. She was the first straight girlfriend he had ever had; she didn't drink or smoke to excess and she absolutely hated making drunken small talk. She didn't like him when he was drunk and told him so. And she certainly wasn't interested in taking drugs.

However, for all that, there is little doubt that Helen has slightly exaggerated the story of their three years together. Or maybe she prefers to remember it that way after all the trauma she endured when he died. According to her version of events, from the moment he met her, Hunt became a monogamous saint, which almost certainly wasn't true. However, it is clear that Helen believes he did. What is clear however is that he tried, like he had never tried before, to be faithful to her and clean up his act. And by and large, he succeeded.

Hunt told her he hadn't experienced love before, and that he thought he just wasn't capable of it. He also told her he had never been in love before, and that simply wasn't true. There was no question that he had been in love with Suzy, Jane and Sarah and probably Taormina as well.

But Helen insisted: "James told me he had never been in love and he thought that, as a person, he was incapable of it. What happened between us was absolutely magical, something I had never dreamed of either." Certainly what he experienced with Helen was similar to what he had with Jane, except now it was in much calmer and sober circumstances – which meant he was able to enjoy it this time around.

But they did not move in together for another two and a half years, until the end of 1992. Until then, Helen remained at home with her parents during the week and stayed with him at weekends.

She claims he was persistent and wanted to make the relationship more permanent, but that she resisted. But when he built her an artist's studio in the attic space above his snooker room, it sealed the deal for her and, at last, she agreed to move in with him. She told Gerald Donaldson: "When I eventually moved in with him, things went from great to simply wonderful and just got better and better. He made me the happiest person in the world." Her moving in coincided with a modest revival in his financial fortunes. Interest rates gradually started to subside and every half point of the rate put an extra UK£200 a week in his pocket.

As interest rates began falling as fast as they had risen, Hunt had some disposable income again. That trend saved him and, from 1991 onwards, interest rates were cut eight times in a very short space of time, falling from 14 per cent to ten per cent. That cut saved Hunt nearly UK£700 a week in interest payments and restored his cash flow. Suddenly his earnings comfortably exceeded his outgoings again. That is, apart from the brief blip on Wednesday 16th September 1992, when interest rates rose from ten per cent to 15 per cent and then back to ten percent all in the span of 24 hours. That was a very worrying day indeed, and Hunt didn't move from his television set as the day's events unfolded and he calculated the effect on his finances with every percentage change. He was mightily relieved by mid morning of the following day when everything returned back to normal. And from that day on, his financial position improved as interest rates began another inexorable move downwards.

Suddenly, everything was getting better in his life after 12 years of things getting worse. As one close friend put it, his life cycle first went out of reverse where it had been stuck since 1980, into neutral and then through the forward gears.

He even found his sex addiction was coming under control, the last and most difficult addiction he had to give up. Now, for the first time, he was able to say no to women who came onto him at races. He was not the saint that Helen believed him to be, but he more or less became the faithful boyfriend. The worst problem he found were old girlfriends who wanted to revisit old times.

As an antidote to his past, when he was away at races commentating, Hunt started writing love letters to Helen and faxed them over to her from the press room. For a man who had difficulty opening up and showing his true feelings, they were revelatory. After his death, Helen showed the letters to journalists and gave them permission to publish the contents. She first showed them to Gerald Donaldson, who was allowed to read them and publish their contents in his 1993 biography. Then, in 1996, she did an in-depth interview with Mary Greene of the *Daily Mail*, who was also allowed to read the letters and to publish extracts.

In an earlier letter, James committed a line to paper that he had used verbally to his other partners. It was remarkable committing it to paper, and was not complimentary to his parents: "I realise now that the feeling of not being loved as a child made me close up to any incoming love projected onto me. I do see that I cannot live without love." Of course, Hunt didn't really mean it and he could never have predicted that the contents of the letters would be made public. The letters were clearly written during a bout of guilt while away from Helen, and contained the same basic line he had given other girlfriends when he was caught being unfaithful. Tony Dron, who has firsthand knowledge of the period, is adamant that his friend was brought up in a loving atmosphere. He says it was always obvious how much his parents, especially his mother, loved him. "I don't know what they are talking about. They were just busy people."

Dyson also takes credit for Hunt's conversion to healthy living, although in truth he had started the process well before he met her: "Once he decided I was the girl for him and that he wouldn't be looking for anyone else, he began to really focus on his problems and to deal with them. All his morals and values completely changed."

In the last letter to Helen, written in May 1992, he ended with the words: "I have to make it work. I want to make it work. Also, I believe I can make it work."

But examining the contents of those faxed letters, they do appear to have been inspired by feelings of guilt. Friends at the time say he still chased women at races, and the letters may have been written as a result of that. Certainly, the line about his parents had been used before in similar circumstances. It appeared that Hunt was fighting a battle with his own conscience and trying to win. For all the fibs he may have told Helen, he certainly didn't want it that way. It was just that he had not yet quite conquered all of his own demons. But Helen is insistent: "There certainly wasn't any womanising. I suppose he just matured."

As she told Donaldson, Hunt had confessed to her that "he was unable to be faithful to anyone in the past because sex was for him just another addiction, and he needed women to get his highs." It sounded much like valediction. She then told Donaldson that Hunt had told her that he disliked social gatherings, and "only had parties or went to them to pick up women."

She told him she was willing to forgive and forget what had gone on before, but that she wouldn't tolerate it in their relationship. And so he agreed to be faithful to her.

This did not sound like the James Hunt of old, who was an inveterate party giver and would start one anywhere and everywhere. The declaration that he did not actually like parties is simply too much to swallow. But she insisted he was a completely changed man: "His letters really exuded love, he was so besotted with me. He'd found happiness – and he had really found peace."

After they moved in together, Helen describes how they hardly ever left the house. They were both at home every day and had their own working areas. She paints an idyllic picture of their life in those days. The bulk of his day was spent writing for a living. His syndicated columns paid very well, and he needed the money that they brought in.

She painted in her studio in the gallery above his snooker room. To the sound of music, she completed big murals. He helped her to sell her paintings and supported her financially as much as he could, as she says: "He used to say that he'd had his career, now it was my turn. And when I sold my first picture, he was even more excited than I was."

Helen was also thrust into the role of unofficial stepmother at a very tender age. She has never spoken about this, but it appears she enjoyed the role; although most of her focus was on her having her own family with Hunt.

But the joy of meeting Helen was tinged with the sadness of losing Oscar, Hunt's faithful companion of nearly 16 years. Oscar simply faded away from old age and was buried in the garden at Wimbledon. Hunt was devastated by Oscar's death. The German Shepherd that people often mistook for an Alsatian had been with him for most of his Formula One career, his marriage and the birth of his two sons. Oscar had lived with Hunt in Marbella, Buckinghamshire and Wimbledon. It took him two months to stop crying, and a year before he was fully over it. Oscar was eventually replaced by one of his grandsons, called Muffy. There was already a terrier in the house called Jackson, who had been owned by Sarah and left with Hunt when she moved out. But Hunt never had the same connection with Muffy as he had with Oscar. With Oscar, it was just one of those things.

In the three years they were together, Helen rarely travelled with Hunt, and she usually excused herself when he went off on trips with Tom and Freddie. During this period, Hunt took his sons on frequent visits to see Sid and Susan Watkins at their home on Tayside. Watkins was only really close to three drivers: Ayrton Senna, Jody Scheckter and Hunt, and all three used to visit Scotland regularly.

Sid Watkins is great company and one of the world's top half dozen surgeons. His wife Susan is a well-known author in the field of history and has written a biography of Bernie Ecclestone. Susan is a soft-spoken lady of immense natural charm, and Hunt adored being in their company. But the real attraction was the salmon fishing on the River Tweed.

His visits would last for three or four nights over the weekend, and he always made the journey to Scotland on the train with Tom and Freddie. Watkins remembers: "He used to come up with the boys on the train and I used to pick them up from Berwick Station. We had a large house in those days, and they had a big suite that was self-contained in which he and his little boys stayed. He really fathered and mothered them extremely well. They were sometimes real handfuls, but he was awfully good with them." Watkins was impressed with how Hunt settled down with the boys in the evenings and read them stories: "When he put them to bed, there was five minutes of prayers before lights out. Then I used to go down to the gillies' pub and drink beer with him."

Hunt used to rise early, and when Sid and Susan got up, they would find him in the kitchen: "He'd go downstairs into the kitchen and boil eggs for them, and when Susan and I came down for breakfast he'd be feeding them boiled eggs with soldiers."

Then, Watkins, Hunt, Tom and Freddie would go salmon fishing. As Watkins remembers: "The two little lads were lovely. We used to go down to the river and he'd get into the boat with the gillie, and I used to take the two youngsters off with little rods to fish for little trout. It was absolutely tremendous fun."

Hunt, as in most other things, was a highly skilled fisherman. But he always threw the fish back. He was not up for killing any animals. He also liked to indulge, as Watkins remembers: "I was fishing with him one day and we were out in the middle of the Tweed when he said: 'Do you think I could have a weed out here?' So I said: 'There'll be no inspectors around the Tweed looking for marijuana.' So he had his weed, and he used to roll it himself, very quaint."

Watkins, who only really got to know Hunt well in the latter stages of his life, has a very high opinion of him indeed, as he says: "He was a very clever, sensitive and perceptive person. James didn't grow up in a way. He was still a boy at heart, and I found that charming."

Helen enjoyed welcoming them home when they returned from these trips away. She revealed to Donaldson that they also thought about moving house, to make a fresh start in another home, but in the end decided not to. But Hunt would never have wanted to leave that home for many reasons: one being that Oscar was buried in the garden. The truth was that, at one point, Hunt thought he might have to sell the house because he could not afford to keep it, and he had pre-warned her. Ironically, he was saved by the 1992 slump in house values. Values fell to an all-time low and it became worth half what it had been just three years earlier. Hunt simply could not afford to sell it at the price it was worth, and so he held on to it.

But for all that, Helen was genuinely unfazed by his lack of money: "Neither of us cared much about money. You don't need much when you're madly in love. James wasn't materialistic. He cared about real things, important things – being a good father, being good to me."

After he realised they could stay, Hunt planned to make one of the rooms in the house into a nursery. But despite the intimate discussions about having children, he had not proposed. He was holding back until it was right and he had fully conquered all his demons. He was determined to be faithful to Helen if he married her, and that moment had not yet arrived – but he was getting there.

He was very much in love with Helen, and of that there is no doubt. Gerald Donaldson thought she was perfect: "She was wonderful, extremely good looking and well grounded, they were a perfect match."

Sid Watkins also found Helen a charming girl and enjoyed some nights out in London with them after they started living together. Watkins recalls: "I remember he came to collect us one night in a little van. He had Helen with him, so Susan and I sat in the back of the van and off we went, rattling through the streets of London to go to a fish restaurant, where he was instantly recognised and besieged by a hoard of admirers."

The family's first experience of the new James Hunt, sober, drug-free and non-smoking, came at his parents' golden wedding anniversary party at their home on 5th April 1993, two months before his death. It was very much a family occasion, and Hunt attended with Tom and Freddie.

It was the first time that his parents truly realised that they had got their son back at last. He was a normal person again, and it was obvious that Helen had worked her magic on him. The change was immediately apparent; no longer the 'life and soul of the party', Hunt was quiet and reserved. His parents had organised an informal thanksgiving service in their drawing room to give thanks for their 50 years of happy marriage. It was conducted by a local vicar, who was a friend of the family. The vicar said some prayers and Hunt's sister, Sally, read a passage from the bible. Wallis played some hymns on the piano. It was a beautiful family occasion, and Hunt was almost moved to tears. He had missed all these occasions over the years, having spent them viewing his family through an alcoholic haze. He was sad for himself and at that point saw clearly for the first time what a fool he had been. At previous family events, he had been too drunk to really know, much less appreciate, what was going on. For the first time, he recognised what a marvellous family he had and how much he had missed it.

Sue Hunt told Donaldson she thought the change in her son "extraordinary", and indeed it was. Afterwards, he wrote his mother a letter saying how lovely it had been to see the family so happy together, how pleased he was for them and how he had found it an uplifting experience.

Sarah didn't witness this, but it was all recounted to her by Tom and Freddie when they got home. She was genuinely surprised by the change in her ex-husband. Recognising that it was Helen's work, she was delighted. She even discussed it with him when they met to hand over the children on another occasion: "He told me how happy he was with Helen, and I was delighted for him. There was no more acrimony between us. He had come to peace with himself at last."

In this period of the last three years of his life, he won over many of his detractors, including Eoin Young's old assistant Maurice Hamilton. Hamilton, an immensely likeable Irishman, had moved on and become one of Formula One's leading journalists after Hunt stopped driving in Formula One. They found they had much in common and Hamilton was also a naturally talented communicator and had established himself as Formula One's top radio commentator.

Hamilton went from "detesting" Hunt to describing him as "a lovely bloke." Indeed, it went even further than that as they became very good friends and Hamilton became one of his 'confidants', sharing many long telephone conversations with him as he sought to keep on top of what Formula One had become. It was the same with Nigel Roebuck, who was Hunt and Hamilton's equivalent in print journalism.

In fact, Hunt really started enjoying his job as a television commentator in the last year of his life, and admitted his eyes had been opened when he stopped drinking. The new seriousness with which he took the job was very apparent. His new commitment inspired Murray Walker to better performances, as he readily admits. To watch the two of them in action in the first half of the 1993 season was a revelation in commitment and professionalism. Even David Hill, had he still been around, would have been impressed.

Hunt also developed a very close relationship with Ayrton Senna in the last three years of his life. Senna had no time for Hunt when he was drunk, but warmed to him when he cleaned up. At one point, when Senna was considering retirement from Formula One and thinking of taking his career to America, Hunt persuaded him not to. Senna had become frustrated after failing to make the move from McLaren to Williams in late 1992. Hunt counselled him and persuaded him his chance would come again. As it did after Hunt died.

Senna found Hunt a kindred spirit and came to rely on him for advice and support. They often dined together at San Lorenzo in London when Senna was in town. Once, after one such dinner, Senna famously took Hunt's Austin A35 van at high speed round London's Cadogan Square after midnight, saying he was trying to break the square's lap record. Hunt was frantic, believing his van would not be able to stand up to Senna's four wheel slides.

Senna said: "He was good to talk to and wouldn't give you any rubbish. He would always tell you the truth – his truth. I respected his opinions and sometimes he would convince me I was wrong. I would accept it, but I could also convince him that perhaps he didn't do justice to me, and he would accept that too. That was his great strength. James was a very special man, by his own character and personality. He was always capable of embarrassing somebody. But I liked him the way he was."

One of the last occasions in which Hunt was seen in public was the memorial service for 1967 world champion Denny Hume, held in Chelsea, London, in 1993. A former world champion, Hulme had died at the wheel of a race car the previous October after having suffered a heart attack whilst racing a saloon car for fun. Hunt had raced against the New Zealander in 1973 and 1974 in Formula One, and they had become good friends. Both he and Hulme enjoyed chasing women around the Formula One paddock.

Everyone was crowded outside before the memorial service began, and they remember Hunt arriving on his bicycle, stripped to the waist, in nothing but shorts and sandals. Nigel Roebuck remembers: "We were standing around outside the church when the former world champion rode into sight: 'Morning, chaps! Back in a minute...' And, with that, he briefly disappeared but soon he was back, immaculate, having popped round the corner to change into a suit, shirt and tie he had been carrying in a haversack on his back."

Another occasion which marks one of Hunt's last appearances in public was one of journalist Eoin Young's famous media lunches, held at the Barley Mow pub, in Surrey. Hunt thoroughly enjoyed himself and did not drink at all. Another Hunt nemesis, Ken Tyrrell, whose factory was situated nearby, regularly attended the lunches and sat opposite Hunt at his last one. The two men argued throughout the lunch and finally agreed to disagree about Formula One. Tyrrell memorably said to Hunt: "James, sometimes you should keep your mouth shut." Hunt told him: "Unfortunately, Ken, the BBC pays me to keep it open."

In mid-May 1993, a few weeks after his parents' golden wedding celebration, he invited his parents to Wimbledon for Sunday lunch with their grandchildren and to meet Helen. In the afternoon, Sue, Wallis, Helen, Freddie and Tom walked to the pond at Wimbledon Common to feed left-over bread to the Canadian geese that gathered their every spring. Sue Hunt told Gerald Donaldson she had never seen her son so happy as that day feeding the ducks with his sons and Helen. It was the last time they would see their son alive.

Sue and Wallis returned Tom and Freddie to their mother that evening in Sussex. They hadn't seen their former daughter-in-law for nearly four years, and they all greeted each other warmly.

By then, Hunt had forgiven his ex-wife for all the acrimony of the divorce and had decided to bury the past for the sake of the children. His parents did as well.

When they left the house, Wallis noticed that the whirlpool bath in the garden was covered in long grass and obviously hadn't been used in a long time. He thought it a poignant symbol of how much his son's life had changed. Seeing the long grass obstructing a part of Hunt's hedonistic past, Wallis was made glad by the thought that the bad times were over, and that it represented a new hope for the future.

But there was to be no future.

SHUNT

CHAPTER 45

Premature goodbye to a great champion
£5,000 pays for his farewell party

On Monday 21st June, James Hunt's immediate family gathered for his funeral. There were less than 30 people present and the family was joined only by very close friends. The rest would have to wait for a memorial service a few months hence.

Hunt had vaguely indicated that if the worst was ever to happen, he would like his funeral to be in Wimbledon; and the natural venue was St Mary's, an Anglican church which sits on the edge of Wimbledon Common. It has an imposing exterior and an intimate interior and it was where Tom and Freddie Hunt were christened. The service was conducted by the local vicar, Andrew Studdert-Kennedy.

Oddly, even though he was due to be cremated, intimate personal objects were placed in the coffin, including Tom and Freddie's christening blankets and Oscar's lead and collar. Helen Dyson had earlier kissed her boyfriend farewell privately before the coffin was sealed.

A trumpeter played, and Wallis and Sue Hunt, with the help of Nigel Davison, had chosen a selection of appropriate hymns. Wallis read the lesson and tried and failed to lighten the mood by saying that his son would have wanted everybody to cheer up. But it had been too soon and it had been too sudden, and the mood was very heavy indeed. Hundreds of letters of condolence had been received by various members of the family, and another few hundred more were on their way. Wallis read some out.

The coffin was carried out by the remaining male Hunts: Wallis, Peter, Tim and David, along with Mike Dennett and Bubbles Horsley. Two miles away at Putney Vale Crematorium, the coffin was incinerated and the urn handed to Helen.

A reception was held at Peter Hunt's home afterwards and it was felt to be an appropriate occasion to open a 1922 claret that James had given to his father 11 years earlier for his 60th birthday. In truth, they had all thought they would be opening it some years hence, for Wallis' funeral, not his son's. It was a desperately sad occasion.

And with that, they all drifted away to begin the rest of their lives. It had been a traumatic seven days, not least for Peter Hunt who went home to rest and reflect on what had happened. To him had fallen the biggest burden, and he had endured some pretty awful tasks and taken some difficult decisions since that fateful phone call from Mike Dennett, which had woken him up in the early hours of the previous Tuesday morning.

No words can describe the scene when Peter Hunt arrived at the house in the early hours of that morning. But Peter, as ever, took command of the situation, reserving his own private grief for later.

Peter Hunt had always carried the burden of his brother's life on his shoulders and, now, the ending of it was no different. And he had carried it stoically and served his brother well to the end of his days. Few knew or appreciated what Peter had done for James. Everything he had done had been very much for the best.

Ian Phillips did not attend the funeral but was surprised how quickly and swiftly his friend's burial was scheduled, as he said: "The whole thing was very strange, he was dead and buried within about three days. It was very fast. I don't know why and I never asked, but a few people thought it was strange." In truth, Phillips, like many of his friends would have liked to have been there for the end.

Fast forward three months to Wednesday 29th September 1993 and to the appropriately named St James's Church in Piccadilly. That day, there was a gusting wind blowing the autumn leaves off the tress and a threat of rain. A Union Jack fluttered in the wind at the chosen venue for a memorial service entitled: 'A Celebration of the Life of James Hunt.'

The church that sits in its own garden oasis in that busiest part of London had been all but destroyed by Herman Goering's Luftwaffe in the autumn of 1940. Long since rebuilt, it provided an appropriate venue for the last hurrah of James Hunt, 1947 – 1993.

In fact, St James's is one of London's premier Anglican churches situated in the heart of the West End, just west of Piccadilly Circus. It has a small market in front of it and sits tucked back behind railings, with a garden and meeting rooms. It holds regular classical concerts.

St Mary's vicar, Andrew Studdert-Kennedy, was once again called on to preside.

A large turnout was expected, but not the 600 people who turned up to pay their respects. The absolute great and good of motor racing were gathered outside that morning to celebrate the life of their friend. It was a truly extraordinary turnout, unmatched previously and one that may not be matched again. Tony Dron remembers: "The church in Piccadilly was absolutely packed out, and there were a lot of very elegant people there."

There were also plenty of photographers. Their targets were Hunt's girlfriends and partners, who were all getting together for the first time. Suzy Miller, widowed by an ex husband for the second time, was there with Bette Hill; Jane Birbeck was there with Daley Thompson, the Olympian who had replaced Hunt in her affections; and Sarah Hunt was there with Tom and Freddie and flanked by her mother, Rosemary Lomax. Only Taormina Rich, now Rieck, with her husband Peter, went unnoticed. No one but a few friends from the really old days knew who she was.

Outside the railings, a crowd had gathered to witness the arrival of so many famous faces.

Nigel Davison, the former director of music at Wellington College, organised the music as he had done on so many occasions in James Hunt's life. Davison co-opted a trumpeter, two organists, two soloists and the Wellington College Choir to create a magnificent ensemble of musicians. He created the perfect atmosphere to celebrate his former pupil's life. 600 people sang lustily along with the choir.

Peter Hunt spoke first. He extended a welcome and greeted everybody: "On behalf of James' family, it is my great pleasure to welcome you to this celebration of James' life. We would, of course, all much rather not have to be here. But it is wonderful to see a full church and so many old friends. Several things I know for sure: Firstly, that James would have loved to have been here with all his friends. He'll be absolutely livid he's missing all the fun. Secondly, that we're having lots of his favourite music – lots of trumpet, lots of noise and lots of singing. We know he liked the hymns because he had two of them at his first marriage service and three of them at his second. Thirdly, that he would have wanted everybody to enjoy the music and sing as loudly as possible. Now, a lot of you are aware that he left me instructions in his will to organise a party for his friends after he died. That party is being held this evening, and I hope James would approve. One of my hardest jobs has been trying to decide who to invite. James had so many friends, it has simply not been possible to invite all of you. Please accept my apologies if you think you should have been on the guest list. Anyway, the point is that the message to me and to all of James' family is that we should enjoy ourselves today. We all have very happy memories of him, and our aim today is to share those memories with his friends and to see lots of laughter and smiling faces. I should like to thank all of you very much for coming to this service and for all your wonderful letters, tributes and messages of support over the last few months. You have all been fantastic. I should particularly like to express my sincere thanks to Mike Dennett for all his invaluable help both to Helen and me immediately after James died, to Ron Dennis for his thoughtfulness and generosity, and to Roger Carey and his assistant Patricia for all their help, support and enthusiasm in organising today's service. My thanks also to everybody taking part in the service and for those who have helped make it possible. I am now going to hand over to my parents, Sue and Wallis. The last time the family got together before James died was to celebrate their 50th wedding anniversary, in April this year. It was a wonderfully happy day for all of us and their many friends. Since then, we have been dealt a terrible blow, but with your help we are getting through it. Let's try and make today as happy and memorable as we possibly can for James' family and friends."

His mother, Sue, in her wonderful warm English voice, made the most poignant impact by reading an incantation from Ecclesiastes, chapter three, which began: "To every thing there is a season, and a time to every purpose under the heaven" and ended: "A time to love, and a time to hate; a time of war, and a time of peace."

Innes Ireland, speaking in his role as the president of the British Racing Drivers' Club, in one of his last public appearances, read Rudyard Kipling's highly appropriate poem 'If…' which reads: "If you can meet with Triumph and Disaster/ And treat those two impostors just the same…Or walk with Kings – nor lose the common touch…"

Sally Jones, Hunt's sister, read Hilaire Belloc's family poem 'Jim', and a radiant Helen Dyson, looking every inch the widow she was not, also read a psalm.

Lord Hesketh, the man who had saved Hunt when he was at his lowest point, introduced the preface and said: "When Peter honoured me by asking me to introduce this preface, I was told that I could only speak for 90 seconds. I reminded Peter of the last time that he gave me an instruction, which was asking for James' retainer, and I recited to him at that time the two Belloc poems – or telegraphic poems – which came from a boy at prep school, which said: 'No Mon', No Fun, Yo' Son. Too Bad, So Sad, Yo' Dad.'

"I first met James 21 years ago in the paddock, if you can call it that – it was a sort of a mucky meadow in Belgium – at Chimay. I'd arrived there from Monaco, and Bubbles had resigned as chief driver for Hesketh Racing and become team manager by his own appointment. We had no driver and James had no car. Twelve months later, we lifted him exhausted from a car which had finished and broken down on the last lap at Monaco and we were classified ninth. Twelve months later, he won his first Formula One race at Silverstone and the Daily Express International Trophy. Twelve months later, he won his first Grand Prix. And twelve months later, he was world champion. It was an honour for me, in my life, to be able to call him a friend. But he was much more than that. He represented something very, very English. He was the combination of the Corinthian casual and the anarchist. Hesketh Racing gave him very little. He gave a great deal to us. What we gave him was because we were also anarchists. We didn't get embarrassed when he kept flying off while in the lead while educating himself in the craft of driving. What he gave to Hesketh Racing was the difference between being in the record book at the back of the *Autosport Annual Review* under Did Not Qualify: DNQ, DNQ and DNQ. I know that in many ways his career was dogged by criticism, which had nothing to do with his ability. And the judgment on James' career will improve as the years go by, and the turnout today, I believe, reveals his real quality. I know that the people who care about racing, the fans who are, after all, the life-blood of the sport, are the people who held him in the highest regard. And it is in his passing, in the obituaries that were written, that something of his real, international, all-time ability can be seen. I know this: that when his two boys, Freddie and Tom, by whom he put so much, grow to be men, there will be by then middle-aged and older men and women – hopefully wiser, certainly greyer – and they will come up to those two boys who will then be men, and they will see them and they will talk to them and they will touch them. And of the memory that I will always hold – of that spring day in 1974 when James overtook Ronnie Peterson with two wheels on the grass at Woodcote, a corner that no longer exists and, now sadly, the driver who no longer exists – they will speak to those boys who will then be men, and they will say, possibly with misty eyes: 'We were there.'"

Lord Hesketh's speech was extraordinary in its quality and delivery, and reminiscent of Winston Churchill in content.

Nigel Davison prefaced the second reading and said: "James was one of the most remarkable teenagers I have met in a long career of teaching. He was very single-minded and always seemed to know exactly what he wanted to achieve. He also had a very clear view of how to achieve it, which sometimes conflicted strongly with conventional wisdom. He must have been quite a trial to some of the more narrow-minded school masters. I don't think he was too interested in team games, preferring what he saw as more individual sports: squash, tennis, racquets and cross-country running. He represented Wellington College at all of them. I couldn't repress a smile when I re-read the other day what I'd written for the 1965 Wellington Yearbook about the year's cross-country running. 'With one notable, if successful, exception, the team threw themselves wholeheartedly into the rigorous training programme.' The notable exception was, of course, James. He had quickly decided that team training was not for him. It probably wasn't rigorous enough. He thought he knew best how to train himself, and events proved him right. For he either won or came first equal in every race of that year that I can recall, including a particularly gruesome and arduous inter-house match, whose finish involved wading through a large lake. James was also a talented and enthusiastic trumpeter. If he had decided to make himself an instrumental virtuoso, he might well have become the James Galway of the trumpet. As it was, trumpet playing was for him a rare form of relaxation and we spent many enjoyable half hours working away at the Trumpet Voluntary, which you didn't hear this afternoon, incidentally, or the Haydn Trumpet Concerto or, in his final term, the finale of a Mozart Concerto which he thought would be fun to play an octave higher than Mozart had ever intended. James was full of original ideas. I well recall playing the organ for his wedding to Sarah. He had planned the music in great detail. I had to bring with me a trumpeter and a soprano so there could be lots of trumpet tunes, lots of descants to the hymns and, using all three of us, Handel's 'Let the Bright Seraphim' during the signing of the register. Who but James could have chosen for a November wedding the hymn 'O Come All Ye Faithful'? I have only happy memories and am grateful for the way he once brightened my life."

Stirling Moss prefaced the next reading and talked with unconcealed affection as he said: "Well, as we have heard, James was truly unique. He was a man of immense personality and charm. A total non-conformist who was a curious mix of wit, intelligence and unparalleled stubbornness. Someone who stood firmly behind his actions and beliefs. Right or wrong, he certainly provided food for thought and fuel for debate. Whatever else he may have been, James was not boring. Never. He was definitely no saint, either. Particularly for one of my generation, his behaviour could be quite appalling. I've been with him on occasions when it was difficult to admit I even knew him – let alone that he was a friend of mine. But somehow, because it was James, one could overlook it. The contribution he made to our sport, through his television and his writing, was enormous. He brought to televised motor racing a dimension that had not previously existed. His explanations and pithy comments, often controversial, brought to the general public an interest and understanding that raised the level of Formula One far above that of being merely a spectacle. He turned moderately interested viewers into well-informed enthusiasts. He brought in thousands of extra followers and fans to our sport. Now, I never raced against James. In fact, I had to wait until later in his life before getting to know him as a friend. Over the years, he was a man that I grew to know, to like, to trust and respect. A man whose opinions and friendship I valued greatly. Like all of you here today, I miss him."

Murray Walker regarded delivering the address at James Hunt's memorial service as the "hardest thing I've ever had to do in my life." But his was the performance of the day. His voice charged with sincerity as he spoke of the man who was once his enemy but had become his friend. Walker had rehearsed the speech the day before with his BBC producer Mark Wilkin until it was word perfect. He said: "We're here today to remember and to honour James as a very special person, who in different ways has been part of the life of each and every one of us. To his family, he was a loving son, brother, father. To the motor racing world of which he was such an outstanding part, he was a great competitor, a forceful teammate, a determined and gifted rival. And to millions of Formula One fans all over the world, from Adelaide to Andover, who listened to the calm, authoritative and witty television commentaries he gave, his was the voice that made sense out of an involved and complicated sport. And to me, he was a respected and admired colleague, whose wit and wisdom added immeasurably to our joint efforts to communicate the sport that meant so much to both of us. But to everyone, James was a charismatic personality whose untimely departure has made our world a duller place. In today's world, most of us stand out like grey against black; conforming to the general standard, unable or unwilling to do their own thing, make their own mark, be their own man. This is something that you most certainly could not say about James. Quite apart from his talents, his success, his commanding presence and his natural dignity, he was an immensely likeable, warm, different kind of human being. One who made wherever he was a livelier and more stimulating and enjoyable place to be. Because James didn't think like other people. He didn't act like other people. He refused to conform to the rules that govern most of us. And he had the presence and the charm to get away with it. I bet almost everybody here could tell a personal story about something that James did or said. And they'd tell it with affection and warmth to emphasise that he was no ordinary person. The first commentary I ever did with him was on a Formula 5000 race at Silverstone. James, with his leg in plaster, lay on the floor, looking up at the monitor, at an extremely boring and uneventful race. When I handed him the microphone to sum it up, he simply said: 'What a load of rubbish!' and handed it back to me. But later, at Monaco, for his very first Grand Prix commentary, wearing no shoes, a t-shirt, shorts that had certainly seen better days, and clutching a bottle of rosé, he planted his plaster cast in my lap and sailed into the comments that were to endear him to his vast following for 13 years. Now our gathering here is to celebrate James' life rather than mourn his death – much as we all do so. And I'm jolly sure that that's what he'd like. You don't need me to tell you about his twin careers: about his 'Boy's Own Paper' leap from virtual obscurity to world champion in an incredibly short time; about how he became the nation's sporting hero and the focal point of their obsessive interest –which was something he hated, incidentally; about how he retired from Grand Prix racing far too soon, dispirited by his lack of success in an uncompetitive car, when there isn't a shadow of doubt that his talent could have made him world champion again, and again; or about how he effortlessly changed gear into a new role, as the BBC's voice of authority in Formula One. James raced in an era where it was possible both to succeed and enjoy yourself. And he did both to the full. And then he matured, to pass on his experience and his knowledge to his successors, and an enormous audience, by means of that commanding voice, presence and his natural authority. His sudden death, totally unexpected, and tragic for one so young and seemingly so fit, touched the nation like few other things in my experience. It's a theory of mine that television communicates people to the viewer like they really are. And it certainly did in James' case. I have had dozens and dozens of truly moving letters telling me that the writers felt they'd lost a real and valued personal friend, whose warmth and humour had enriched their lives, and whose experience, knowledge and outspokenness had kindled and developed their interest in Grand Prix racing. Now if my theory is correct, it's not difficult to see why. They saw James as a character, which he certainly was. They saw him as his own man, which he most certainly was. They saw him as a having a bright, breezy, lively personality, which he did. And they loved his irreverence and his provocative comments because James, anywhere and everywhere, was never reluctant to speak his mind. An incredibly clear-thinking and analytical mind, which may sometimes have produced words his targets didn't like – I didn't like some of them – but which he was always ready to defend to their faces with logic and eloquence that usually won them over. 'I'm just off to have it out with so-and-so about last week,' he'd say. And then you'd see him calmly justify his case in the paddock, when most people would have laid low and hoped that it would go away. But then he would always apologise if he felt he'd been wrong. Apropos of which, I have never known a public figure of his magnitude, of his very considerable magnitude, who was as unaffected by his success and as self-effacing as James was. Letter after letter told me how the writer had met him somewhere and been overwhelmed by the fact that he found the time to stop and just chat like any other enthusiast. You know, the paying public on the other side of the track get next to no direct contact with their heroes these days. But they got the consideration they deserved from James. 'One of the reasons I retired, Murray,' he told me, 'was that I just couldn't stand being a human honey pot wherever I went; restaurants, pubs, out on the street. Everyone wanting a part of me. No privacy. No way could I lead a normal life.' Hardly surprising when practically everything he did created national headlines at the height of his racing fame. But James was essentially a private man, and he didn't really like the ceaseless adulation. When his racing career was over, he was glad to get away from it, go about his new life

– forever accompanied by his beloved Oscar – become a truly loving father, and do something which must have seemed totally out of character to most people: successfully breed and show budgerigars. So, a paragon of humanity? Nothing to criticise? No weak points? Well, of course there were, and thank heavens too. None of us is perfect. There are people here who could write a book about James Hunt's escapades. And an immensely readable bestseller it would be, too. And when the adrenaline was running high, he could be a fearsome chap. I've seen him fell a rival competitor who angered him. I've seen him do the same to a marshal who incurred his wrath. I bet Teddy Mayer hasn't forgotten the roasting he got at the end of his Japanese Grand Prix whilst he was vainly trying to tell a furious James, who thought he'd failed, that he had in fact clinched the world championship. And I certainly won't forget the tongue lashing that an unfortunate technician got in Australia when a communication failure made James look silly. But, that same adrenaline surge gave him the selfless courage to rescue Ronnie Peterson from his blazing Lotus at Monza. Bravery can take many forms, but surely none greater than voluntarily plunging into fire to save your fellow man. James could charm the birds out of the trees, but sadly he wasn't spared hard times in recent years. Personal and financial problems had made things very tough indeed for him. But you'd never have known it. He was unfailingly cheerful and remained the kind, courteous and helpful English gentleman he had always been. And he industriously knuckled down to getting out of the trouble he was in. In his job as racing consultant, he passed on his hard-won knowledge and expertise to a new generation of drivers. Ask his friend and mentor, John Hogan. Ask Johnny Herbert. Ask Mika Hakkinen. In his job as a TV commentator, he was a friend and talented contributor to his colleagues. Ask Jonathan Martin, the BBC's head of sport. Ask Mark Wilkin, the producer of Grand Prix. Ask me. And in his new job as a journalist, he was a very welcome and lively addition to the press room; one who had shown the same dedicated determination to succeed as he had at the last three Grands Prix of 1976, where quite outstanding drives against the odds won him his world championship. On Sunday 13th June, James cycled from his home in Wimbledon to the television centre at Shepherd's Bush, gave his customary, authoritative commentary on the Canadian Grand Prix, did his column and cycled home again, seemingly his usual self. Little more than 24 hours later, to stunned disbelief, he was no longer with us. Even now, it seems hardly conceivable that we're no longer going to enjoy his ebullient presence and it hasn't, somehow, all been a ghastly dream. They say the gods take those they love early. In which case, we can only console ourselves with the knowledge that 45 years of James' life contained at least as much as 90 of anybody else's. His loved ones, motor racing, his countless friends and all those who admired him from afar are infinitely the poorer for his passing. May he rest in peace."

It was the performance of Murray Walker's life, and every word was heartfelt.

The service climaxed with 'Glory! Glory! Hallelujah!' It all fitted together perfectly, as befitted a Nigel Davison production.

Of those who attended the service, no one can forget the image of Hunt's two small boys, Tom and Freddie, at the end of the service, walking out down the aisle and smiling to each other as they went. Freddie Hunt, then approaching his sixth birthday, was shocked by the number of people at his father's memorial service. He said years later: "I knew we weren't a normal family and that daddy was special in some way, and I'd been to a funeral before so the funeral itself was no big deal. Don't forget, I wasn't quite six, so I was too young to take it all in. But when we had the memorial service and I saw how many people were there, that's when I knew he was very special to everyone, not just Tom and me."

Outside in the courtyard, friends and family mingled together as the wives and girlfriends posed happily for photographs and smiled knowingly at each other. It was a time for coming together, and Suzy, Jane, Sarah and Helen all knew things no one else knew about the man they had just honoured. They shared a common bond which would unite them forever.

David Gray, amongst a host of advertising agency people present, said: "The memorial service was amazing. It was perfect – the Wellington side of it and the English side of it."

Stirling Moss reflected the views of many when he said: "What a terrible waste because finally James seemed to have become his own person." He added: "I remember laughing because I'd been to a couple of memorial services and sat next to him, and he'd complained about the music, saying: 'Well I wouldn't have this at mine.'"

Gerald Donaldson, whose life had been devastated by the loss was very moved and said: "It was brilliantly done, there wasn't much sadness, it was a celebration of his life."

Helen Dyson said: "It will be a great comfort to all his friends to know that James was happier than he had ever been just before he died. He was famous for living life to the full, but I knew a much quieter man. He was a wonderful father to his sons and he was my best friend. He is and always will be the love of my life."

The shock was over and the sadness had subsided for most of those present. That is, except for one man who could not be joyful that day. Tony Dron, Hunt's friend and racing partner from that first year in Formula Ford in 1969, was absolutely desolate. For him, it was even worse than Tuesday 15th June, when he had first heard the news. The memorial service had brought back so many memories and now he couldn't stop crying for his friend, as he said later: "I can remember being extremely disturbed in my head, and I couldn't account for it at the time. I think that's when it sunk in that he had really gone. I was really quite distressed by the whole day. I wouldn't describe it as a happy occasion for me." That afternoon, he paced the streets of Piccadilly for hours looking at the sky and talking to his great racing buddy.

Later, many of the people present drifted over to 136 Grosvenor Road, where Peter Hunt had hired the Westminster Boating Base for his brother's farewell party. Hunt had left £5,000 in his will to pay for it. That money wouldn't be realised until his house was sold, but still the party went ahead – paid for by someone.

The party was a huge success and Peter Hunt, ever the accountant, made sure his brother's UK£5,000 was well spent and went a long way. But no man was more desolate that day than Tony Dron, as he said at the end: "And then I went home, went to sleep, got up and carried on with my life."

SHUNT

CHAPTER 46

Life after James 1993
The aftermath of a premature death

There were a lot of people interested in James Hunt's last will and
testament, not least editors of Britain's national tabloid newspapers.
It was well known that Hunt had lost all of his money in 1989 but
still managed to live in a grand house in Wimbledon; albeit with his brown
Mercedes SL500 up on jacks to avoid paying any road taxes and insurance.
The jacking up of his Mercedes had been a symbolic gesture by Hunt to tell
the world he was poor. He planned to put the wheels back on as a signal
that his financial troubles were over. He never lived long enough to do that.

The newspapers loved it, especially the *Daily Express*, which headlined its
front page: 'The hero who died penniless.'

When details of the will were published, the horrible truth was revealed.
The value of his assets, made up exclusively of his house, was UK£1.233
million but he owed the banks UK£856,000. Once all that was settled, there
then remained some UK£377,000 which was shared between his two sons
and put in trust for them. The welfare of his sons was already catered for by
an earlier trust fund that made maintenance payments to his ex-wife, Sarah.

Although his ex-wife threatened to sue the estate over disbursement of the
will and her own maintenance payments, it was all settled out of court. Peter
Hunt gathered all of Hunt's trophies and memorabilia in order to disburse

them to his sons. They were then of little value, but would be rather more valuable 17 years later.

The Hunt family had to go on without its most famous member. But one member, who was not really a member at all, faced the greatest difficulty – both emotionally and financially.

The widow who wasn't, Helen Dyson was left in a very difficult position when Hunt died. She had given up her life for him and was left with literally nothing. Her circumstances were an accident of fate. He had not expected to die and had not made a new will to reflect their circumstances. But she had no regrets and did not blame her boyfriend for her plight at all. They were not even formally engaged. She said: "He was in the process of changing his will in accordance with our marriage plans. We hadn't set a date but it was going to be soon. We would probably have married that autumn."

It now fell to Peter Hunt to deal with Helen, who was living in Hunt's house. The house had to be sold and Helen had to move out – these were the cold facts of the situation. He eased her transition by telling her she could live in the house until after Christmas and that he would somehow find her some cash from Hunt's estate so that she could put down a deposit on a flat. She was grateful to Peter Hunt for allowing her to stay until January 1994. Those months in the house helped exorcise her grief.

Despite that, there is no question that Helen had the hardest time after the funeral. She got through it by blanking out the trauma surrounding his death. She resolved to remember only the three and a half years they had been together, the last year of which had been effectively as man and wife in everything but name.

During those seven months following Hunt's death, she kept a detailed diary of her feelings day by day; it was one way of dealing with her grief. She also carried on painting in her studio and pretended her boyfriend was still in his office. Some days that summer, it really seemed as if he was, as the sun streamed in through the windows and she got lost in her own world, completely alone and unmolested. At night, she recreated the past and cried herself to sleep in their bed. She said: "I was like Miss Havisham. I was in cuckoo land."

Eventually, Helen decided to celebrate Hunt's life rather than mourn him and she entered what she calls a "euphoric stage" She said she was "so happy to be alive, celebrating life and feeling very strongly that James was with me in spirit." It helped her recover, and by the time of the memorial service, she was well on her way.

After an emotional Christmas and New Year, effectively on her own, Helen left the house one day in late January, and all her memories went with her as a removal company with a big furniture van quickly removed everything she had cherished into storage. She was allowed to keep none of it. Everything had been listed and itemised on the orders of Sarah. Helen was not granted any of Hunt's personal effects, and that hurt her.

Hunt's second wife ensured that everything was taken into storage, saying to Helen: "It's all for the boys." Helen also missed seeing his sons, Tom and Freddie, whom she adored. All she was able to take with her were her personal belongings and a gift that Hunt had given her on her last birthday. It was an art book and she had wrapped it in brown paper. Inside the cover, Hunt had written in gold ink: "To my darling Helen. May your colours soon surpass even the power and vibrancy of those in this book. With all my love, James. P. S. In the unlikely event that they don't, I will still, and always, love you anyway."

She moved back in with her parents, Mike and Molly. But at nearly 30 years of age, that was not a permanent option. Eventually, Peter Hunt came through with the money he had promised and she was able to get a mortgage on a one bedroom flat at the top of a big, old converted house in Wimbledon, less than a mile from the house she had once shared with Hunt.

She said: "When I was at our old house, I kept thinking, any minute James is going to come through that door. When I was with my parents, I couldn't help thinking that one day I'd be going home to James." When she finally moved into her own flat, his death suddenly became final. She was in her own home; a home with absolutely no connection to him, a place he had never been.

And yet, she continued to feel his presence strongly for many years. She said: "He's like a guardian angel. He has given me a lot of strength to get through. When you lose somebody, you realise we are just mortal beings. I love life. I want to make sure that when I go, there's something of me left behind. I can't waste my gifts when James was so proud of me." Ironically, she took up smoking after his death despite the fact that she had helped him give it up when he had been alive.

She said by way of a postscript on their lives: "We had mapped out the rest of our lives together. To know you're going to be with one person forever and then suddenly to have everything taken away, my whole world was whipped from under my feet."

The rest of the Hunt family carried on with their lives. Few of them had had day-to-day contact with James. He had rarely visited his parents prior to his death, and so their everyday existence was not much altered, although they all mourned in private.

The Hunt sisters, Sally and Georgina, had followed the example of their mother and had chosen to devote their lives to public service. Sally was a lay pastoral assistant in her church and Georgina was a social worker with a charity.

David Hunt ultimately failed in his quest to become a professional racing driver, and, after a test with the Benetton Formula One team, gave up. He entered business and made a great deal of money in direct sales. He bought Team Lotus from the liquidator after it collapsed in 1994. But he couldn't do anything with it and is believed to have sold his interest in it for a nominal sum when the team was resurrected in 2010. Now, he wheels and deals in various business ventures.

Peter Hunt continued with his accountancy business and won a battle with cancer. Today, he still looks after the many clients he met during his racing days with his brother.

Tim Hunt, the youngest of the brothers, looked like he was destined to be the family's highest achiever. He was head boy at Wellington and a winner of the Queen's Medal for the student who most measured up to the standards of the school's founder, the Duke of Wellington. He sailed into Oxford and shared his famous brother's good looks and was even a male model for a period. He then went to work at Christie's in London and eventually moved to New York to become a significant figure in the art world. He is now director of the Warhol Foundation. He married the American novelist, Tama Janowitz.

And so for the Hunts, life went on. That is, until 2001.

In March 2001, eight years after his son's death, Wallis Hunt died after a long battle with illness. His death was a few weeks short of his and Sue's 58th wedding anniversary. A memorial service was held at Wellington College in the chapel. He had attended the College in 1936 and was followed by his sons and his grandchildren. Afterwards, there was lunch in the college and then a rugby match. Strangely, in his address, Peter Hunt failed to mention the name of James Hunt at all.

Today, his 86-year-old widow, Sue, is matriarch of the Hunt family and living out her life in splendid isolation in Wiltshire, wishing her sons and grandchildren would visit more often, but happy nonetheless.

Jane Birbeck lives quietly and doesn't seek any attention. After she split with Hunt, she took up with Olympics star Daley Thompson and they were together for over 12 years before he married someone else. David Gray says: "She has never married. She is just as nice as she was." Apart from Gerald Donaldson, Birbeck has never spoken to a journalist about her relationship with Hunt and no quotes from her exist on the record anywhere. She prefers it that way.

Taormina Rich married Peter Rieck soon after she split with James Hunt in the mid 1980s. She met her future husband at the Monaco Grand Prix in 1970 whilst still going out with Hunt. Peter Rieck became great friends with Hunt and they socialised frequently after he married Taormina. Now, the couple live quietly in Cambridgeshire.

Sarah Hunt had a turbulent time after the death of her ex-husband. His death opened up all sorts of wounds as she battled with the family over his estate. Traumatised by the experience, she felt she had to fight her corner for her sons. She had suffered badly since the divorce and had panic attacks when in public places. Hunt's death only aggravated the situation, as she said: "It's taken me all these years to forgive myself for the fact that [the marriage] wasn't working, which was terribly important because, until I'd forgiven myself, I couldn't really go on."

She regained her sanity only when she got a job working at a local pub/ hotel as a barmaid, waitress and cook. It gave her a new focus and she gradually began to recover. She occasionally spoke to journalists and said of her marriage: "I wouldn't say I made a mistake the first time around; it was just one of those awful, sad things – our marriage simply didn't work. We really had to stop fighting. Sadly, for people like us, when you get over excitable, you go down with an almighty bump."

Her children's maintenance was guaranteed by a trust fund set up by Hunt after the divorce. But her own payments were not. She also had trouble settling down with another partner after her divorce from Hunt. She said: "I didn't believe I would ever get married again. I was 100 per cent certain that the right man, or true love, whatever that may be, could not be found again." Adding to her troubles, her father died two years after Hunt.

But the aging process was very kind to Sarah, and as she got older, the more attractive she became and eventually she started dating again. She had an 18-month affair with a wealthy Italian Count called Alex Mapelli-Mozzi and then, in 1997, she met a handsome, 49-year-old divorcee, Lieutenant Colonel Christopher Jeffery of the Royal Gurkha Regiment. They met at a local Beagle Ball in January 1997. When she met him, she said: "I knew absolutely that he was going to be my future husband and I proposed to him two or three weeks later." He was naturally very surprised, and she gave him a week to think about it. When the time had elapsed, she said to him: "How's the thinking?" He said: "Well, I think it all sounds rather nice." That was the answer she was looking for and they were married a short time later. She was far better matched to her new husband than she had been to her first. He had no children of his own and was an accomplished horseman, being field master of the hunt in the Hampshire area. Sarah said at the time: "I never dreamt that I'd have those feelings for somebody else ever again."

He lived most of the year in Nepal, where his regiment was based, and she moved there with him after the wedding. Both Tom and Freddie went to a preparatory boarding school before Tom went to Wellington College like his father and Freddie to a succession of schools before ending up at the local grammar school.

But her new husband was quickly was assigned to Nato's Allied Rapid Reaction Corp at Rheindahlen in Germany, and Sarah followed him there. Jeffery and Sarah had a son together just over a year later. They named him Charlie, a half brother for Tom and Freddie. But Charlie was only seven months old when there was another terrible tragedy.

At only 52 years of age, Christopher Jeffery was relaxing watching the 1999 Japanese Grand Prix on television when he started to feel ill and had a stroke. Having been rushed to hospital, he died two days later. He had been in England on leave for the christening of his and Sarah's son.

Sarah was effectively widowed for a second time in nine years and left with three young children without a father. The army recommended she receive her husband's full pension entitlement for life. She bought a rambling ranch-style property, which stands in two acres of Hampshire countryside with a tributary of the River Rother on one boundary. She installed a new heated swimming pool for the children and carried on as best she could. She was in the news again in 2010 when her elderly mother, Rosemary Lomax, finally passed away.

Tom Hunt went to Wellington College as planned and then onto university, unlike his brother Freddie, who was the image of his father in every physical and mental respect.

Freddie was not academic and attended seven schools in all. Like his father, he hated it. As he admitted: "There are always mischievous kids at school, and I was one of them. I wasn't always the most mischievous, but the one who got caught." Freddie found school a trial and couldn't wait until he was 18 to leave. He is now a grown up young man with a mane of unkempt hair and slightly hunched shoulders, just like his father. Fiercely intelligent, he has an open, engaging and erudite personality, with a free spirit and fiery temper. As his mother says, it could almost be his father all over again.

His first interest was his mother's sport, horses, and he took up playing polo and became an accomplished player, owning six horses. Then, he caught the motor racing bug after a visit to the Goodwood Festival of Speed. He sold his polo ponies to fund his new career. He tried Formula Ford and Formula 3. But he found he was not good enough and did the sensible thing and retired after a couple of years. But not before he had his father's signature tattooed on his back and inscribed on his crash helmet as a permanent memory.

Today, Freddie is a wandering troubadour, seeking his future and his way in life. He is so like his father it is uncanny. Nobody doubts he will make a success of his life, but they have no idea how.

Apart from Helen Dyson, BBC producer Mark Wilkin was the outsider most affected by his friend's death and it took him a long time to recover. He continued producing the Grand Prix programme without Hunt, and it was traumatic. The first race, the 1993 French Grand Prix was a serious problem for him, coming less than a fortnight after Hunt's death, as he said: "It was tough at the first race back, the French Grand Prix. It was awful to go do that without James, it really was."

Now, life has come full circle for Wilkin. In the late nineties, the BBC lost the Formula One contract to ITV. Two years ago, it came back to the BBC and Wilkin was back where he had been ten years earlier. He still remembers Hunt fondly, saying: "It's one of the things, isn't it? People who die young are forever remembered in life."

John Watson is long retired from driving and is now a TV pundit, much as Hunt was. For years, he fulfilled the same role on Eurosport until it lost the Formula One contract. He says of his old friend simply: "There was a truly decent, good man there."

Bubbles Horsley is now effectively retired. He inherited family money and made enough from business never to have to work again. He lives quietly in France with his family, but still retains an English house in Oxfordshire. Hunt's death knocked the stuffing out of his life. As it did the lives of Hunt's close friends John Richardson, Chris Jones and Mike Dennett. They all keep in touch with Peter Hunt and frequently reminisce about the good old days. But with Hunt dead, the zest has gone out of their lives.

Lord Hesketh has had an eventful life since his brush with motor racing 35 years ago. After that, he dabbled in motorcycles and then started an airline. The motorcycle firm was ultimately unsuccessful but the airline was sold for a profit. In 2005, he decided he needed a break from the past and took the drastic step of selling his family home at Easton Neston, along with all the memories of Hesketh Racing. It was sold in 2006 to a Russian oligarch for UK£16 million. Hesketh is now busy selling the rest of the land and the buildings surrounding it.

In 1989, he used his seat in the House of Lords to become a significant and active politician in Margaret Thatcher's conservative government. He held the office of Parliamentary Under-Secretary of State at the Department for Environment between 1989 and 1990 and was Minister of State in the Department of Trade and Industry between 1990 and 1991. After that, he was appointed Government Chief Whip in the House of Lords, a position he kept until September 1993.

Eventually, he all but retired from public life and now lives quietly in the west country with his wife. Now 60 years old, his three children, Flora, Sophia and Frederick, are grown up.

John Hogan rose to great heights at Philip Morris International, and, under his guidance, Formula One was used to make Marlboro the biggest cigarette brand in the world. He went on to win many more world championships with Alain Prost and Ayrton Senna at McLaren before moving Marlboro's sponsorship to Ferrari, where he won many more again with Michael Schumacher.

He retired from Philip Morris in 2002 at the age of 60 and became a consultant, working closely with Vodafone. In 2003, he accepted an offer from Jaguar Cars to head up marketing for its Formula One team but, unhappy with its direction, left a year later. He was snapped up and became a key executive at Zak Brown's fast-growing American sponsorship agency, Just Marketing, where he remains today, still making big deals and pulling levers behind the scenes.

Soon after Hunt left McLaren, Teddy Mayer sold McLaren to Ron Dennis and then made a brief comeback in Formula One and Indy car racing. He finally retired to Florida and married former photographer, Pamela Rowe. He died last year.

Alastair Caldwell moved to the Brabham team after Hunt left McLaren but it was not a particularly happy time, and he left motor racing to work with his daughter, Ruth, and started a storage firm, which is very successful today.

Peter Warr left the Wolf team and it closed down. He moved back to Lotus when Colin Chapman died, and ran the team for a few years. The team fell on hard times and was eventually sold to Peter Collins, upon which Warr effectively retired.

Harvey Postlethwaite moved to the Tyrrell team after Wolf closed down and enjoyed some success. He eventually left and set up an experimental Formula One team for Honda but died suddenly before it could enter the championship.

David Gray became a very significant force in advertising with Collett Dickenson Pearce, one of the world's great agencies. He semi retired and is now active again working on digital ventures. He is still a client of Peter Hunt's accountancy firm.

Peter Collins eventually lost control of Team Lotus, and it closed down in 1994. He had a torrid time with its new owner, David Hunt, and decided to leave Britain for Switzerland. Today, he is a sponsorship consultant and a successful driver manager. He first discovered Kimi Raikkonen and now manages Tonio Liuzzi, who drives for the Force India team.

Ian Phillips had a very successful career in Formula One with the Jordan team when it was owned by Eddie Jordan. After new owners took over, he carried on. He finally left the team this year after nearly 20 years, and is now semi retired.

Today, Tony Dron lives in an idyllic home in Cambridgeshire and works at his twin passions of writing and racing very successfully. His eyes still moisten when he discusses his old friend, as he says: "James always told me he would go until he had won or died. And that's how his life went."

Gerald Donaldson used all the access he had to James Hunt when he was alive to write an eponymous biography of the driver, which was very successful. It came out in 1994, a year after Hunt's death and was the family-approved biography. It made Donaldson a great deal of money. Now, he is a successful broadcaster, spending his time equally in Toronto and the English Cotswolds, and has since written a biography of Juan Manuel Fangio.

After his early biography of Hunt, called *Portrait of a Champion*, Christopher Hilton wrote a book called *Memories of James Hunt*, which was effectively a pastiche of stories from hundreds of motor racing personalities who had known him. Hilton has become motor racing's most prolific author and there is no racing fan who does not have at least one of his books on their shelf.

But of all the active journalists, Nigel Roebuck missed James Hunt the most. He joined Gilles Villeneuve on Roebuck's 'idol list' as he said: "I still miss the visits to that lovely house in Wimbledon, with the old Mercedes and A35 van outside, the soppy Alsatian, foul-mouthed parrot and bare-footed owner within. In an age made colourless by political correctness, he was genuinely a free spirit; it was a terrible sadness that, personally happier than at any time in his life, he left the party so early. 'It's always the bores that stay to the end, isn't it?', he would say."

Murray Walker carried on being Murray Walker after Hunt died but it was never quite the same again for him. He joined ITV Sport when it won the contract and retired from commentating some eight years later at the height of his powers. Simultaneously, he published his autobiography, which sold a staggering 1.1 million copies.

And so the James Hunt story came to an end.

Apart from one nasty postscript. In 2001, Peter Hunt was approached by Ralph Lee, a producer for the independent production company Diverse Productions. Diverse wanted to do a documentary on Hunt for Britain's Channel 4 programme. Peter Hunt didn't appear himself, nor did members of the family, but he encouraged others to do so, including Bubbles Horsley, Chris Jones and Lord Hesketh. The interviews with Jones and Horsley were not particularly flattering to them to say the least, although Lord Hesketh came out reasonably well.

But the worst damage was done by footage of the incident at the Doncaster nightclub in 1978, when Hunt was arrested for assault. The footage had previously been unseen and had been retained by the nightclub, which then released it to Diverse to broadcast it. It was very unedifying and caused considerable problems within the family. Peter Hunt even indirectly referred to it in his speech at his father's memorial service. The programme also showed a highly distasteful interview with the Dutch reporter Alissa Morrien, who had seduced Hunt in 1977 and then written about it. It was all highly distressing, and upset Hunt's mother and family greatly.

The distress had a lasting effect and, after that, the family closed ranks and effectively abandoned the Hunt legacy. They wanted the story of James Hunt to come to an end.

But that could never happen. James Hunt belonged to the fans, not his family. He genuinely was the people's champion. For all his faults and flaws, and there were many, James Hunt was a very great man. His memory can never be extinguished.

APPENDIX I

Formula One Grand Prix Career Statistics

Races Entered
93
Races Started
92
Race Finishes
44
Race Retirements
46
Races Disqualified
2
Race Wins
10
Pole Positions
14
Podiums Finishes
23
Front Rows
24
Fastest Laps
8
Points Scored
179
Laps Completed
3,930
Distance Completed
11,771 miles
Races Led
24
Race Laps led
666
Race Distances Led
2,090 miles

APPENDIX II
Other Races

1967 Special Saloon Cars

At Snetterton in 1967, James Hunt had hoped to race the Mini which he had built in his garage, but it failed scrutineering. Sources suggest that it lacked windows and that a deckchair was used to form the passenger seat. He did get to race at Brands Hatch and, according to him, probably at two further races, although there is no record if it.

Date: 8th October 1967
Circuit: Brands Hatch
Car: Mini special
Race result: retired
Participated in further races of which there are no records of.

1978 Formula 5000

In 1978, James Hunt won his only Formula 5000 race, which was at Winton in Australia. He had travelled to Australia at the end of 1978 for social reasons connected to his friend Mike Hailwood. He competed in the race for a large fee and his expenses.

Date: 28th October 1978
Circuit: Winton, Australia
Race: Rose City "10,000"
Car-engine: Elf-Chevrolet MR8
Qualifying: 1st, 54.9s
Race result: 1st, 29m 06.2s
Fastest lap: 2nd fastest, 57.0s

1973 to 1974 Sports Cars

James Hunt raced in two sports car events in 1973 and 1974.
Both were for John Wyer's Gulf-Mirage team.

Date: 3rd November 1973
Circuit: Kyalami, South Africa
Race: Daily Mail Nine Hour
Car-engine: Gulf Mirage-Ford
Cosworth M6 (no.5)
Co-driver: Derek Bell
Qualifying: 2nd, 1m 19.530s
Race result: 2nd, 349 laps
Fastest lap: fastest, 1m 20.2s

Date: 19th May 1974
Circuit: Nürburgring, Germany
Race: 1000km Nürburgring (World
Championship for Makes)
Car-engine: Gulf Mirage-Ford
Cosworth GR7 (no.7)
Co-driver: Vern Schuppan
Qualifying: 6th, time: 7m 25.6s
Race result: 4th, 32 laps

APPENDIX III
1968 to 1969 Formula Ford 1600

In 1968, James Hunt advanced to Formula Ford 1600, taking part in several closing races in the Guards Championship in a Russell-Alexis and a Merlyn Mk11A. He won on his third outing, at Lydden Hill, in Kent. James raced a Merlyn Mk11A in Formula Ford 1600 during 1969, driving in the Les Leston Championship until May. He achieved one victory at Lydden Hill and, in late summer, progressed to Formula 3.

1968
Date: 26th August 1968
Circuit: Snetterton
Car–engine: Russell-Alexis-Steele
Race result: 5th

Date: 2nd September 1968
Circuit: Mallory Park
Car–engine: Russell-Alexis-Steele
Race result: 2nd

Date: 9th September 1968
Circuit: Lydden Hill
Car–engine: Russell-Alexis-Steele
Race result: 1st, 10m 06.2s

Date: 30th September 1968
Circuit: Brands Hatch
Car–engine: Russell-Alexis-Steele
Race result: 6th

Date: 7th October 1968
Circuit: Snetterton
Car–engine: Russell-Alexis-Steele
Race result: 7th

Date: 14th October 1968
Circuit: Mallory Park
Car–engine: Russell-Alexis Steele
Race result: retired (accident)

Date: 26th October 1968
Circuit: Oulton Park
Car–engine: Merlyn-Steele Mk 11
Race result: retired (accident)

Date: 18th November 1968
Circuit: Brands Hatch
Car–engine: Merlyn-Steele Mk 11
Race result: 4th

Date: 25th November 1968
Circuit: Brands Hatch
Car–engine: Merlyn-Steele Mk 11
Race result: 3rd

Date: 27th December 1968
Circuit: Brands Hatch
Car–engine: Merlyn-Steele Mk 11
Race result: 6th

Date: 29th December 1968
Circuit: Mallory Park
Car–engine: Merlyn-Steele Mk 11
Race result: 5th

1969
Date: 24th February 1969
Circuit: Brands Hatch
Car–engine: Merlyn-Steele Mk 11A
Race result: 3rd

Date: 10th March 1969
Circuit: Mallory Park
Car–engine: Merlyn-Steele Mk 11A
Race result: 5th

Date: 16th March 1969
Circuit: Brands Hatch
Car–engine: Merlyn-Steele Mk 11A
Race result: 5th

Date: 24th March 1969
Circuit: Snetterton
Car–engine: Merlyn-Steele Mk 11A
Race result: retired (accident)

Date: 8th April 1969
Circuit: Zandvoort, Netherlands
Car–engine: Merlyn-Steele Mk 11A
Race result: 3rd

Date: 14th April 1969
Circuit: Aspern, Austria
Car–engine: Merlyn-Steele Mk 11A
Race result: 2nd (+ 1.24s), Fastest lap: 1m 08.79s

Date: 21st April 1969
Circuit: Brands Hatch
Car–engine: Merlyn-Steele Mk 11A
Race result: 7th

Date: 5th May 1969
Circuit: Lydden Hill
Car–engine: Merlyn-Steele Mk 11A
Race result: 1st, 1m 9m 54.2s

Date: 12th May 1969
Circuit: Mondello Park, Ireland
Car–engine: Merlyn-Steele Mk 11A
Race result: 4th

Date: 26th May 1969
Circuit: Snetterton
Car–engine: Merlyn-Steele Mk 11A
Race result: retired (accident)

APPENDIX IV

1969 to 1972 Formula 3

In 1969, James Hunt entered a Brabham BT21, which he had purchased, in Formula 3 meetings, and towards the end of the season drove a March 693 and Lotus 59 for an outing in each. He won at two Formula Libre meetings. Driving a Lotus 59/59A for 1970, he participated in the BARC Forward Trust, MCD Lombank and BRSCC MotorSport Shell Championships and ventured abroad to race the first time, taking in some French, Swedish and Belgian championship events. Wins this year came at Rouen and Zolder. In 1971, racing a March, he took part in events for the three British championships and again raced in France. He won four races. In 1972, before moving up to Formula Two, he entered March and Dastle cars in Formula 3 without recording a victory.

1969

Date: 11th August 1969
Circuit: Mallory Park (Lombank F3)
Car-engine: Brabham-Ford Cosworth BT21 (no.126)
Race result: 8th, 20 laps

Date: 17th August 1969
Circuit: Brands Hatch (Lombank F3)
Car-engine: Brabham-Ford Cosworth BT21B (no.157)
Race result: 3rd, 10 laps

Date: 24th August 1969
Circuit: Brands Hatch (Libre)
Car-engine: Brabham-Ford Cosworth BT21 (no.104)
Race result: 4th

Date: 1st September 1969
Circuit: Brands Hatch
Race: Guards International Trophy
Car-engine: Brabham-Ford Cosworth BT21 (no.20)
Qualifying-heat: 39.6s
Race result-heat: 4th

(Final grid = 12th)
Race result-final: retired (oil pipe)

Date: 7th September 1969
Circuit: Brands Hatch (Libre)
Car-engine: Brabham-Ford Cosworth BT21B
Qualifying: (front row for race)
Race result: 1st

Date: 13th September 1969
Circuit: Crystal Palace
Race: Reg Parnell Trophy
Car-engine: Brabham-Ford Cosworth BT21B (no.94)
Qualifying-heat: 5th, 56.2s
Race result-heat: 7th (Final grid = 14th)
Race result-final: 8th, 14m 17.8s (+22.6s)

Date: 14th September 1969
Circuit: Brands Hatch (Lombank F3)
Race: Dartford Trophy
Car-engine: Brabham-Ford Cosworth BT21B (no.46)
Race result: 6th, 15 laps

Date: 14th September 1969
Circuit: Brands Hatch (Libre)
Car-engine: Brabham-Ford Cosworth
BT21B
Race result: 1st, 17m 45.6s

Date: 21st September 1969
Circuit: Brands Hatch (Libre)
Car-engine: Brabham-Ford
Cosworth BT21B
Race result: 2nd, (+2.5s)

Date: 29th September 1969
Circuit: Cadwell Park
Race: Lincolnshire International
Trophy
Car-engine: Brabham-Ford Cosworth
BT21B (no.37)
Qualifying-heat: 4th, 1m 33.8s
Race result-heat: 3rd, 15m 55.0s
(+2.4s)
Race result-final: 4th, 39m 38.0s
(+16.4s)
Fastest lap: joint fastest, 1m 33.2s

Date: 4th October 1969
Circuit: Oulton Park
Race: BARC
Car-engine: Brabham-Ford
Cosworth BT21B (no.86)
Qualifying: did not participate
(broken camshaft)
Race result: did not qualify

Date: 12th October 1969
Circuit: Mallory Park (Lombank F3)
Car-engine: Brabham-Ford
Cosworth BT21B
Race result: 4th, 10 laps

Date: 19th October 1969
Circuit: Brands Hatch (Lombank F3)
Race: E.R. Hall Trophy
Car-engine: March-Ford   Cosworth

693 (no.95)
Race result-heat: 4th, 16m 18.2s
(+1.0s) (Final grid = 8th)
Race result-final: 10th, 32m 40.0s
(+20.4s)

Date: 26th October 1969
Circuit: Brands Hatch (Libre)
Car-engine: Brabham-Ford
Cosworth BT21B
Race result: 3rd

Date: 15th November 1969
Circuit: Thruxton
Race: W.D. & H.O. Wills Trophy
Car-engine: Lotus-Ford Cosworth 59
Race result: Disqualified (tyres)

1970

Date: 5th April 1970
Circuit: Pau, France (France F3/ Craven 'A')
Race: Coupe de Vitesse de Pau
Car-engine: Lotus-Ford Cosworth 59
(no.19)
Qualifying: 11th, 1m 26.7s
Race result: did not start (accident in
qualifying)

Date: 26th April 1970
Circuit: Silverstone (Shell F3)
Race: GKN/ Binfield Transmission F3
Trophy
Car-engine: Lotus-Ford Cosworth 59
(no.41)
Qualifying: 49.4s
Race result: 4th, 33m 21.3s (+17.1s)

Date: 2nd May 1970
Circuit: Magny-Cours, France
(France F3)
Race: Critérium de Nivernais
Car-engine: Lotus-Ford Cosworth 59
Qualifying: 9th, 50.0s
Race result-heat: 4th, 21m 28.7s

APPENDIX IV

(+9.5s) (Final grid = 7th)
Race result-final: 4th, 29m 52.3s (+9.8s)
Date: 9th May 1970
Circuit: Monte-Carlo, Monaco (Shell F3)
Race: Grand Prix de Monaco – Formule 3
Car-engine: Brabham-Ford Cosworth
BT28 (no.52)
Qualifying: 11th, 1m 36.6s
(Heat grid = 6th)
Race result-heat: retired
(rear suspension), 9 laps
Race result-final: did not start

Date: 17th May 1970
Circuit: Österreichring, Austria
Race: Preis von Steiermark
Car-engine: Lotus-Ford Cosworth 59
(no.43)
Qualifying: 5th, 2m 13.9s
Race result-heats: 3rd, 30m 55.48s
(+0.83s) & 1st, 30m 47.09s
Race result-aggregate: 2nd, 1h 01m
42.57s (+0.57s)

Date: 25th May 1970
Circuit: Oulton Park (Shell F3)
Race: British Empire Trophy
Car-engine: Lotus-Ford Cosworth 59
Qualifying: heat: 1st, 1m 40.8s
Race result-heat: 2nd (Final grid = 3rd)
Race result-final: 2nd, 51m 27.8s
(+0.2s)

Date: 31st May 1970
Circuit: Chimay, Belgium (Belgium F3)
Race: Grand Prix des Frontières
Car-engine: Lotus-Ford Cosworth 59
(no.20)
Qualifying: 1st, 3m 24.5s
Race result: 2nd, 51m 24.9s (+1.0s)
Fastest lap: fastest, 3m 19.8s

Date: 6th June 1970
Circuit: Silverstone (Shell F3)

Race: AMOC Martini
International Trophy
Car-engine: Lotus-Ford Cosworth 59
Qualifying: 2nd, 1m 36.4s
Race result: 6th, 40m 55.8s (+1.4s)

Date: 14th June 1970
Circuit: Hämeenlinna, Finland
(Finland Speed)
Car-engine: Lotus-Ford Cosworth 59
Race result: 3rd

Date: 28th June 1970
Circuit: Rouen-les-Essarts, France
(France F3/ Craven 'A')
Race: Coupe de Vitesse de l'A.C.
Normand
Car-engine: Lotus-Ford Cosworth 59
Qualifying: 17th, 2m 20.8s
Race result: 1st, 47m 20.7s

Date: 11th July 1970
Circuit: Croft (Shell F3/ BARC F3)
Race: Guards International Trophy
Car-engine: Lotus-Ford
Cosworth 59 (no.5)
Qualifying-heat: 5th, 1m 11.8s
Race result-heat: 5th, 12m 11.8s
(+2.2s) (Final grid = 11th)
Race result-final: 9th, 36m 26s (+24s)
Fastest lap-heat: joint fastest, 1m 11.4s

Date: 17th July 1970
Circuit: Brands Hatch (Shell F3)
Race: Formula 3 International Trophy
Car-engine: Lotus-Ford Cosworth 59A
(no.44)
Qualifying-heat: 1st, 1m 37.1s
Race result-heat: 1st, 16m 20.6s
(Final grid = pole)
Race result-final: 3rd, 32m 34.4s (+0.1s)

Date: 19th July 1970
Circuit: Cadwell Park (BARC F3)

709

Car-engine: Lotus-Ford Cosworth 59A
Race result-heat: 1st, 12m 45.0s (Final grid = pole)
Race result-final: 3rd

Date: 9th August 1970
Circuit: Karlskoga, Sweden
(Sweden F3)
Race: Kanonloppet
Car-engine: Lotus-Ford Cosworth 59 (no.1)
Qualifying-heat: 5th, 1m 22.8s
Race result-heat: 4th, 22m 13.8s (+3.2s) (Final grid = 4th)
Race result-final: disqualified (dangerous driving)

Date: 16th August 1970
Circuit: Knutstorp, Sweden
(Sweden F3)
Race: Knutstorp Cup
Car-engine: Lotus-Ford Cosworth 59 (no.8)
Race result: 2nd, 26m 50.0s (+0.8s)

Date: 22nd August 1970
Circuit: Oulton Park
Race: International Gold Cup
Car-engine: Lotus-Ford Cosworth 59A
Qualifying: 25th
Race result: retired (valve spring)

Date: 31st August 1970
Circuit: Brands Hatch (Shell F3)
Race: Guards International F3 Trophy
Car-engine: Lotus-Ford Cosworth 59A
Qualifying-heat: 4th, 1m 37.8s
Race result-heat: 2nd, 24m 33.4s (+2.0s) (Final grid = 2nd)
Race result-final: retired (puncture)

Date: 6th September 1970
Circuit: Zolder, Belgium (Belgium F3)
Race: Coupe de l'Avenir

Car-engine: Lotus-Ford Cosworth 59A (no.3)
Qualifying: 2nd, 1m 37.2s
Race result-heats: 2nd, 24m 45.0s (+0.2s) & 1st, 24m 26.3s
Race result-aggregate: 1st, 49m 11.2s

Date: 13th September 1970
Circuit: Cadwell Park (Shell F3)
Race: Lincolnshire International Trophy
Car-engine: Lotus-Ford Cosworth 59A
Qualifying-heat: 1st, 1m 33.6s
Race result-heat: 1st, 15m 58.4s (Final grid = pole)
Race result-final: 3rd, 44m 40.6s (+8.2s)

Date: 20th September 1970
Circuit: Thruxton (BARC F3)
Race: Europa Cup Race 1
Car-engine: Lotus-Ford Cosworth 59A (no.34)
Qualifying: 4th, 1m 21.6s
Race result: retired (water pump belt), 9 laps

Date: 20th September 1970
Circuit: Thruxton (BARC F3)
Race: Europa Cup race 2
Car-engine: Lotus-Ford Cosworth 59A (no.34)
Race result: did not start (engine).

Date: 3rd October 1970
Circuit: Crystal Palace (Shell F3)
Race: Daily Express Trophy
Car-engine: Lotus-Ford Cosworth 59A (no.21)
Qualifying-heat: 2nd, 55.3s
Race result-heat: 2nd, 9m 33.5s (+0.2s) (Final grid = 4th)
Race result-final: retired (accident), 19 laps

Date: 18th October 1970
Circuit: E.R. Hall Trophy (Shell F3)
Race: Brands Hatch
Car-engine: Lotus-Ford Cosworth 59A
Qualifying-heat: 2nd, 1m 36.8s
Race result-heat: 2nd, 16m 17.4s
(+1.0s) (Final grid = 3rd)
Race result-final: 2nd, 32m 33.8s
(+2.4s)

1971
Date: 14th March 1971
Circuit: Mallory Park (Lombank F3)
Car-engine: March-Ford Cosworth
713S (no.86)
Qualifying: 1st, 49.2s
Race result: disqualified (airbox) (finished 1st in 12m 36.0s)
Fastest lap: fastest, 49m 4s

Date: 21st March 1971
Circuit: Brands Hatch (Shell F3/
Lombank F3)
Car-engine: March-Ford Cosworth
713S (no.25)
Qualifying: 5th, 1m 56.6s
Race result: retired (fuel pipe)

Date: 28th March 1971
Circuit: Linas-Montlhéry, France
(France F3)
Race: Challenge Raymond Sommer
Car-engine: March-Ford Cosworth
713M (no.24)
Race result: 1st, 31m 57.3s

Date: 3rd April 1971
Circuit: Brands Hatch (Shell F3)
Car-engine: March-Ford Cosworth
713S (no.30)
Qualifying: 12th, 1m 43.8s
Race result: retired (throttle/ spin),
26 laps

Date: 11th April 1971
Circuit: Nürburgring, Germany
Race: Internationales ADAC 300km
Rennen
Car-engine: March-Ford Cosworth
713S (no.3)
Qualifying: 1st, 3m 05.6s
Race result: 1st, 40m 24.3s

Date: 17th April 1971
Circuit: Montjuïc, Spain
Race: Gran Premio Ciudad de
Barcelona de F3
Car-engine: March-Ford Cosworth
713M (no.10)
Qualifying: 3rd, 1m 40.4s
Race result: retired (accident), 25 laps
Fastest lap: 2nd fastest, 1m 42.2s

Date: 24th April 1971
Circuit: Pau, France (France F3/
Craven 'A')
Race: Coupe de Vitesse
Car-engine: March-Ford Cosworth
713S
Qualifying: 4th, 1m 42.6s
Race result: retired (accident), 0 laps

Date: 2nd May 1971
Circuit: Brands Hatch (Shell F3)
Car-engine: March-Ford Cosworth
713S (no.27)
Qualifying-heat: 4th, 52.4s
Race result-heats: retired (oil pipe) &
10th, 9m 58.4s★ (+1m 07.9s) (Final
grid = 20th)
Race result-final: 3rd, 34m 42.5s
(+9.5s)
★ includes 1-min penalty for push start

Date: 8th May 1971
Circuit: Silverstone (Shell F3)
Race: GKN Forgings Trophy
Car-engine: March-Ford Cosworth

713S (no.7)
Qualifying: 6th, 1m 38.8s
Race result: retired (accident), 19 laps

Date: 16th May 1971
Circuit: Zandvoort, Netherlands
(Shell F3)
Car-engine: March-Ford Cosworth
713S (no.10)
Qualifying-heat: 22nd, 1m 40.4s
Race result-heats: 12th, 32m 55.3s &
retired (accident), 14 laps
Race result-aggregate: not classified,
34 laps

Date: 18th June 1971
Circuit: Crystal Palace
Race: Chris Moore Memorial Trophy
Car-engine: March-Ford
Cosworth 713M
Qualifying: 1st
Race result: 1st, 13m 18.0s

Date: 20th June 1971
Circuit: Brands Hatch (Lombank F3)
Car-engine: March-Ford Cosworth
713M
Race result: quit after being given
1-min penalty for jumping the start

Date: 3rd July 1971
Circuit: Paul Ricard, France (Shell F3/
France F3/ Craven 'A')
Race: Trophée Paul Ricard
Car-engine: March-Ford
Cosworth 713M (no.7)
Qualifying: 5th, 1m 25.1s
Race result: 3rd, 35m 47.0s (+10.1s)

Date: 10th July 1971
Circuit: Croft (BARC F3)
Race: Rothmans International Trophy
Car-engine: March-Ford Cosworth
713M (no.21)

Qualifying-heat: 3rd, 1m 11.4s
Race result-heat: 4th (Final grid = 4th)
Race result-final: 2nd, 36m 12.4s
(+14.2s)

Date: 17th July 1971
Circuit: Silverstone (Shell F3)
Race: International Formula III Race
Car-engine: March-Ford Cosworth
713M (no.52)
Qualifying-heat: 5th, 1m 37.2s
Race result-heat: 6th, 24m 46.7s
(+15.4s) (Final grid = 6th)
Race result-final: retired (fuel metering
unit), 8 laps

Date: 18th July 1971
Circuit: Cadwell Park (BARC F3)
Car-engine: March-Ford Cosworth
713M (no.49)
Qualifying: 8th
Race result: retired (quit)

Date: 24th July 1971
Circuit: Kirkistown
Race: GKN Ulster F3 Trophy
Car-engine: March-Ford Cosworth
713M (no.12)
Qualifying: 6th, 1m 02.4s
Race result-heats: 2nd, 34m 40.2s
(22.2s) & retired (wishbone)
Race result-aggregate: not classified

Date: 1st August 1971
Circuit: Thruxton (BARC F3)
Race: Kodak 135 Trophy
Car-engine: March-Ford Cosworth
713M (no.61)
Qualifying: 2nd, 1m 20.5s
Race result: 2nd, 20m 26.4s (+0.0s)

Date: 7th August 1971
Circuit: Crystal Palace
Race: Daily Express Trophy – Petonyer

Trophy
Car-engine: March-Ford Cosworth
713M (no.17)
Qualifying-heat: 3rd, 54.8s
Race result-heat: 1st, 10m 13.2s (Final
grid = 2nd)
Race result-final: retired (accident),
1 lap

Date: 15th August 1971
Circuit: Brands Hatch (Lombank F3)
Car-engine: March-Ford Cosworth
713M (no.80)
Qualifying: 2nd
Race result: 1st, 16m 33.2s
Fastest lap: fastest, 48.4s

Date: 21st August 1971
Circuit: Oulton Park (Shell F3)
Race: International Gold Cup
Car-engine: March-Ford Cosworth
713M (no.129)
Qualifying: 1st, 1m 37.4s
Race result: 3rd, 49m 20.4s (+11.8s)

Date: 22nd August 1971
Circuit: Thruxton
Race: Echo Trophy
Car-engine: March-Ford
Cosworth 713M
Qualifying: 1st, 1m 20.2s
Race result: 8th
Fastest lap: joint fastest, 1m 20.2s

Date: 29nd August 1971
Circuit: Thruxton (BARC F3)
Car-engine: March-Ford
Cosworth 713M
Race result: 7th, 7 laps

Date: 11th September 1971
Circuit: Crystal Palace (BARC F3)
Race: Iberia Airlines Trophy
Car-engine: March-Ford Cosworth

713M (no.26)
Qualifying-heat: 1st, 53.0s
Race result-heat: 1st, 13m 42.0s (Final
grid = 4th)
Race result-final: 6th

Date: 12th September 1971
Circuit: Brands Hatch (Lombank F3)
Car-engine: March-Ford Cosworth
713M (no.177)
Qualifying: 1st, 48.6s
Race result: retired

Date: 19th September 1971
Circuit: Thruxton
Race: European Cup
Car-engine: March-Ford
Cosworth 713M (no.6)
Qualifying: 4th, 1m 19.8s
Race result: did not start (engine)

Date: 19th September 1971
Circuit: Thruxton (Shell F3)
Race: Iberia Trophy
Car-engine: March-Ford Cosworth
713M (no.6)
Qualifying-heat: 2nd, 1m 20.2s
Race result-heat: retired (piston), 3 laps
(Final grid = 24th)
Race result-final: did not start

Date: 26th September 1971
Circuit: Mallory Park (Shell F3/ Lom-
bank F3)
Car-engine: March-Ford Cosworth
713M (no.27)
Qualifying-heat: 5th, 51.8s
Race result-heat: did not start (repaired
from qualifying accident too late)
Race result-final: did not qualify

Date: 3rd October 1971
Circuit: Snetterton (Shell F3)
Car-engine: March-Ford Cosworth

713M (no.26)
Qualifying-heat: did not participate (injured in practice)
Race result-heat: did not qualify

Date: 17th October 1971
Circuit: Thruxton (BARC F3)
Race: BARC Finals
Car-engine: March-Ford Cosworth 713M (no.51)
Qualifying: 1st, 1m 22.4s
Race result: 2nd, 20m 31.0s (+0.0s)

Date: 24th October 1971
Circuit: Brands Hatch (Shell F3/ Lombank F3)
Race: E.R. Hall Trophy
Car-engine: March-Ford Cosworth 713M (no.33)
Qualifying-heat: 2nd, 1m 34.6s
Race result-heat: 2nd, 15m 54.4s (+0.2s) (Final grid = 2nd)
Race result-final: disqualified (airbox) (finished 2nd in 39m 51.0s)
Fastest lap-heat: fastest, 1m 33.6s; final: fastest, 1m 34.0s

Date: 31st October 1971
Circuit: Brands Hatch (Lombank F3)
Car-engine: March-Ford Cosworth 713M (no.27)
Qualifying: 2nd, 48.4s
Race result: 4th, 16m 42.0s (+6.8s)
Fastest lap: fastest, 48.6s

1972
Date: 5th March 1972
Circuit: Brands Hatch (Lombard F3)
Car-engine: March-Ford Cosworth 723 (no.109)
Qualifying: 4th, 1m 03.6s
Race result: 4th, 16m 10.4s (+19.4s)
Date: 12th March 1972
Circuit: Mallory Park (BARC F3)

Car-engine: March-Ford Cosworth 723 (no.1)
Qualifying: 4th, 48.4s
Race result: disqualified (air box) (finished 2nd in 16m 06.2s)
Fastest lap: joint fastest, 47.4s

Date: 19th March 1972
Circuit: Brands Hatch (Shell F3)
Car-engine: March-Ford Cosworth 723 (no.6)
Qualifying: 3rd, 1m 34.8s
Race result: 5th, 32m 07.6s (+18.6s)

Date: 26th March 1972
Circuit: Snetterton (Lombard F3)
Car-engine: March-Ford Cosworth 723 (no.212)
Qualifying: 1m 40.2s
Race result: 10th

Date: 31st March 1972
Circuit: Oulton Park (Shell F3)
Car-engine: March-Ford Cosworth 723 (no.50)
Qualifying: 1m 53.2s, row 2
Race result: retired (accident), 0 laps

Date: 3rd April 1972
Circuit: Mallory Park (Shell F3)
Car-engine: March-Ford Cosworth 723 (no.28)
Qualifying: 4th, 47.4s
Race result-heat: 5th
Race result-final: 3rd, 32m 09.6s (+22.2s)

Date: 16th April 1972
Circuit: Silverstone (BARC F3)
Car-engine: March-Ford Cosworth 723M (no.1)
Race result: 7th

Date: 23rd April 1972
Circuit: Silverstone (Shell F3)

Race: GKN Forgings Trophy
Car-engine: March-Ford Cosworth 723
(no.62)
Qualifying: 5th, 1m 34.2s
Race result-heat: 13th, 16m 05.7s
(+16.0s) (Final grid = 28th)
Race result-final: retired (accident),
14 laps

Date: 13th May 1972
Circuit: Monte-Carlo, Monaco (Shell
F3/ France F3)
Race: Grand Prix de Monte-Carlo –
Formule 3
Car-engine: March-Ford Cosworth
713M (no.40)
Race result-heat: retired (accident), 1
lap
Race result-final: did not qualify

Date: 21st May 1972
Circuit: Chimay, Belgium (France F3)
Race: Grand Prix des Frontières
Car-engine: March-Ford Cosworth
713M (no.1)
Qualifying: 2nd, 3m 15.8s
Race result: 5th, 39m 46.8s (+1.3s)

Date: 29th May 1972
Circuit: Mallory Park (Shell F3/France F3)
Car-engine: March-Ford Cosworth
713M (no.6)
Race result-heat: 8th
Race result-final: 10th

Date: 11th June 1972
Circuit: Silverstone (BARC F3)
Car-engine: Dastle-Ford Cosworth
Mk9 (no.60)
Race result: retired (accident), 0 laps

Date: 18th June 1972
Circuit: Thruxton (BARC F3)
Car-engine: Dastle-Ford Cosworth

Mk9 (no.18)
Race result: 10th

Date: 25th June 1972
Circuit: Rouen-les-Essarts, France
(France F3)
Race: Coupe de Vitesse de l'A.C.
Normand
Car-engine: Dastle-Ford Cosworth
Mk9 (no.68)
Qualifying: 9th, 2m 03.2s
Race result: 7th, 51m 32.7s (+1m
03.1s)

Date: 2nd July 1972
Circuit: Clermont-Ferrand, France
(France F3)
Race: Trophée d'Auvergne
Car-engine: Dastle-Ford Cosworth
Mk9
Qualifying: 21st, 3m 24.9s
Race result: did not start (wheel bear-
ing/ suspension)

Date: 15th July 1972
Circuit: Brands Hatch (Shell F3)
Car-engine: Dastle-Ford Cosworth
Mk9 (no.9)
Qualifying: 1m 34.8s
Race result: did not start (accident in
qualifying)

Glossary:

BARC F3 = BARC Forward Trust British
F3 Championship
Belgium F3 = Championnat de Belgique
Craven 'A' = Challenge Trophée Craven 'A
France F3 = Championnat de France
Finland Speed = Finland Speed Week
Lombard F3 = MCD Lombard North Central
British F3 Championship
Shell F3 = BRS
CC/ MCD Shell Super Oil British F3
Championship
Sweden F3 = Svenska mästerskapet

APPENDIX V
1971 to 1973 Formula 2

James Hunt first tried Formula Two in 1971 for a single race, with a car which he had borrowed from March. He participated full time in Formula Two from late 1972 until May 1973 in a number of British and European championship events as well as a couple in Brazil at the end of 1972. His best result was third at Oulton Park in September 1972.

1971
Date: 30th August 1971
Circuit: Brands Hatch
Race: Shell Rothmans International Trophy
Car-engine: March-Ford Cosworth 712M (no.17)
Qualifying: 19th, 1m 28.4s
Race result: 12th, 39 laps

Glossary
Euro F2 = European Formula 2 Championship
British F2 = John Player British Formula 2 Championship
Brazil F2 = Il Torneio Internacional de Formula 2 do Brasil
Libre = Formula Libre

1972
Date: 28th August 1972
Circuit: Brands Hatch (Libre)
Race: Rothmans 50,000
Car-engine: March-Ford Cosworth 712M (no.44)
Qualifying: 11th, 1m 26.0s
Race result: 5th, 115 laps

Date: 3rd September 1972
Circuit: Salzburgring, Austria (Euro F2)
Race: Festspielpreis der Stadt Salzburg
Car-engine: March-Ford Cosworth 712M (no.36)

Qualifying: 3rd, 1m 12.19s
Race result-heats: retired (engine), 25 laps & did not start
Race result-aggregate: not classified, 25 laps

Date: 16th September 1972
Circuit: Oulton Park (British F2)
Car-engine: March-Ford Cosworth 712M (no.15)
Qualifying: 2nd, 1m 27.8s
Race result: 3rd, 59m 27.6s (+18.4s)
Fastest lap: joint fastest, 1m 27.4s

Date: 24th September 1972
Circuit: Albi, France (Euro F2)
Race: Grand Prix d'Albi
Car-engine: March-Ford Cosworth 712M (no.29)
Qualifying: 6th, 1m 10.8s
Race result-heat: 4th, 33m 32.8s (+10.3s) (Final grid = 8th)
Race result-final: 5th, 38m 18.6 (+25.1s)

Date: 1st October 1972
Circuit: Hockenheim, Germany (Euro F2)
Race: Preis von Hessen und Württemberg
Car-engine: March-Ford Cosworth 712M (no.25)

Qualifying: 12th, 2m 05.7s
Race result: 8th, 1h 08m 18.1s (+55.4s)

Date: 29th October 1972
Circuit: Interlagos, Brazil (Brazil F2)
Car-engine: March-Ford Cosworth
712M (no.11)
Qualifying: 13th, 2m 47.0s
Race result-heats: 7th, 39m 07.59s
(+10.13s) & 5th, 38m 53.10s (+1m
13.43s)
Race result-aggregate: 5th, 1h 18m
00.69s (+17.15s)

Date: 12th November 1972
Circuit: Interlagos, Brazil (Brazil F2)
Car-engine: March-Ford Cosworth
712M (no.11 or 19)
Qualifying: 2m 43.3s
Race result-heats: 6th, 27m 19.89s
(+35.32s) & 6th, 27m 24.20s (+35.03s)
Race result-aggregate: 4th, 54m 44.09s
(+1m 06.71s)

1973

Date: 11th March 1973
Circuit: Mallory Park (Euro F2)
Race: Radio Luxembourg Formula 2
Trophy
Car-engine: Surtees-Ford Cosworth
TS15 (no.19)
Qualifying: 2nd, 42.7s
Race result-heats: retired (suspension
mounting), 21 laps & did not start
Race result-aggregate: not classified, 21
laps

Date: 8th April 1973
Circuit: Hockenheim, Germany
(Euro F2)
Race: Deutschland Trophäe
Car-engine: Surtees-Ford Cosworth
TS15 (no.38)
Qualifying:12th, 2m 04.7s (Heat grid

= 30th)
Race result-heats: did not start (fuel
pump in qualifying)
Race result-aggregate: did not start

Date: 23rd April 1973
Circuit: Thruxton (Euro F2)
Race: BARC "200"/ Jochen Rindt
Memorial Trophy - Esso Uniflow
Trophy
Car-engine: Surtees-Ford Cosworth
TS15 (no.33)
Qualifying: 6th, 1m 12.2s
Race result-heat: 6th, 34m 52.4s
(+58.4s) (Final grid =8th)
Race result-final: 10th, 48 laps

Date: 29th April 1973
Circuit: Nürburgring, Germany
(Euro F2)
Race: Internationales
ADAC-Eifelrennen
Car-engine: Surtees-Ford Cosworth
TS15 (no.28)
Qualifying: 7m 52.7s
Race result: retired (tyres), 6 laps

Date: 6th May1973
Circuit: Pau, France (Euro F2)
Race: Grand Prix Automobile de Pau
Car-engine: Surtees-Ford Cosworth
TS15
Qualifying: did not participate (accident
in practice)
Race result: did not qualify

Glossary
Euro F2 = European Formula 2 Championship
British F2 = John Player British Formula 2 Championship
Brazil F2 = Il Torneio Internacional
de Formula 2 do Brasil
Libre = Formula Libre

APPENDIX VI
1973 to 1979 Formula One

James Hunt competed in Formula One during seven seasons, driving for Hesketh Racing from 1973 to 1975. It was at the Dutch Grand Prix in 1975 that he won his first Grand Prix. He drove for Marlboro Team McLaren in 1976 and 1977, and Walter Wolf Racing in 1978 and 1979. With Hesketh, he drove a March 731 until Brazil in 1974, then a Hesketh 308 and 308B. He drove a McLaren M23 throughout 1976, which won him the World Championship. In 1977, he continued with the M23 and then the M26 to the end of 1978. In 1979, he drove a Wolf WR7 and WR8.

1973

Date: 3rd June 1973
Circuit: Monte-Carlo
Race: Monaco Grand Prix
Car-engine: March-Ford Cosworth 731 (no.27)
Qualifying: 18th, 1m 29.9s
Race result: 9th, retired (engine), 73 laps
Fastest lap: 18th fastest, 1m 31.7s

Date: 1st July 1973
Circuit: Paul Ricard
Race: French Grand Prix
Car-engine: March-Ford Cosworth 731 (no.27)
Qualifying: 14th, 1m 51.63s
Race result: 6th, 1h 42m 59.06s (+1m 22.54s)
Fastest lap: 13th fastest, 1m 53.42s

Date: 14th July 1973
Circuit: Silverstone
Race: British Grand Prix
Car-engine: March-Ford Cosworth 731 (no.27)
Qualifying: 11th, 1m 17.6s
Race result: 4th, 1h 29m 21.9s (+3.4s)
Fastest lap: fastest, 1m 18.6s

Date: 29th July 1973
Circuit: Zandvoort
Race: Dutch Grand Prix
Car-engine: March-Ford Cosworth 731 (no.27)
Qualifying: 7th, 1m 20.70s
Race result: 3rd, 1h 40m 15.46s (+1m 03.01s)
Fastest lap: not recorded

Date: 19th August 1973
Circuit: Österreichring
Race: Austrian Grand Prix
Car-engine: March-Ford Cosworth 731 (no.27)
Qualifying: 9th, 1m 36.63s
Race result: retired (fuel metering unit), 3 laps
Fastest lap: not recorded

Date: 9th September 1973
Circuit: Monza
Race: Italian Grand Prix
Car-engine: March-Ford Cosworth 731 (no.27)
Qualifying: did not participate (accident in practice)
Race result: did not qualify
Date: 23rd September 1973

Circuit: Mosport Park
Race: Canadian Grand Prix
Car-engine: March-Ford Cosworth 731
(no.27)
Qualifying: 15th, 1m 16.584s
Race result: 7th, 78 laps
Fastest lap: not recorded

Date: 7th October 1973
Circuit: Watkins Glen
Race: USA Grand Prix
Car-engine: March-Ford Cosworth 731
(no.27)
Qualifying: 4th, 1m 40.520s
Race result: 2nd, 1h 41m 16.467s
(+0.668s)
Fastest lap: fastest, 1m 41.652s

1974

Date: 13th January 1974
Circuit: Buenos Aires No.15
Race: Argentinian Grand Prix
Car-engine: March-Ford Cosworth 731
(no.24)
Qualifying: 5th, 1m 51.52s
Race result: retired (engine overheating), 11 laps
Fastest lap: 13th fastest, 1m 54.30s

Date: 27th January 1974
Circuit: Interlagos
Race: Brazilian Grand Prix
Car-engine: March-Ford Cosworth 731
(no.24)
Qualifying: 18th, 2m 37.24s
Race result: 9th, 31 laps
Fastest lap: not recorded

Date: 30th March 1974
Circuit: Kyalami
Race: South African Grand Prix
Car-engine: Hesketh-Ford Cosworth
308 (no.24)
Qualifying: 14th, 1m 17.41s

Race result: retired (cv joint), 13 laps
Fastest lap: 14th fastest, 1m 19.12s

Date: 28th April 1974
Circuit: Jarama
Race: Spanish Grand Prix
Car-engine: Hesketh-Ford Cosworth
308 (no.24)
Qualifying: 10th, 1m 19.87s
Race result: 10th, 81 laps
Fastest lap: 9th fastest, 1m 22.79s

Date: 12th May 1974
Circuit: Nivelles-Baulers
Race: Belgian Grand Prix
Car-engine: Hesketh-Ford Cosworth
308 (no.24)
Qualifying: 9th, 1m 11.53s
Race result: retired (rear suspension),
45 laps
Fastest lap: not recorded

Date: 26th May 1974
Circuit: Monte-Carlo
Race: Monaco Grand Prix
Car-engine: Hesketh-Ford Cosworth
308 (no.24)
Qualifying: 7th, 1m 27.8s
Race result: retired (driveshaft), 28 laps
Fastest lap: 9th fastest, 1m 30.5s

Date: 9th June 1974
Circuit: Anderstorp
Race: Swedish Grand Prix
Car-engine: Hesketh-Ford Cosworth
308 (no.24)
Qualifying: 6th, 1m 25.556s
Race result: 3rd, 1h 58m 34.716s
(+3.325s)
Fastest lap: 3rd fastest, 1m 27.522s

Date: 23rd June 1974
Circuit: Zandvoort
Race: Dutch Grand Prix

Car-engine: Hesketh-Ford Cosworth
308 (no.24)
Qualifying: 6th, 1m 19.95s
Race result: retired (accident/ rear
suspension), 2 laps
Fastest lap: 23rd fastest, 1m 30.37s

Date: 7th July 1974
Circuit: Dijon-Prenois
Race: French Grand Prix
Car-engine: Hesketh-Ford Cosworth
308 (no.24)
Qualifying: 10th, 1m 59.51s
Race result: retired (accident), 0 laps
Fastest lap: -

Date: 20th July 1974
Circuit: Brands Hatch
Race: British Grand Prix
Car-engine: Hesketh-Ford Cosworth
308 (no.24)
Qualifying: 6th, 1m 20.3s
Race result: retired (rear suspension/
spin), 2 laps
Fastest lap: joint 23rd fastest, 1m 25.5s

Date: 4th August 1974
Circuit: Nürburgring
Race: German Grand Prix
Car-engine: Hesketh-Ford Cosworth
308 (no.24)
Qualifying: 13th, 7m 10.4s
Race result: retired (gearbox), 11 laps
Fastest lap: 10th fastest, 7m 16.9s

Date: 18th August 1974
Circuit: Österreichring
Race: Austrian Grand Prix
Car-engine: Hesketh-Ford Cosworth
308 (no.24)
Qualifying: 7th, 1m 36.11s
Race result: 3rd, 1h 29m 46.26s (+1m
01.54s)
Fastest lap: joint 9th fastest, 1m 38.08s

Date: 8th September 1974
Circuit: Monza
Race: Italian Grand Prix
Car-engine: Hesketh-Ford Cosworth
308 (no.24)
Qualifying: 8th, 1m 34.34s
Race result: retired (engine), 2 laps
Fastest lap: 22nd fastest, 1m 37.9s

Date: 22nd September 1974
Circuit: Mosport Park
Race: Canadian Grand Prix
Car-engine: Hesketh-Ford Cosworth
308 (no.24)
Qualifying: 8th, 1m 13.736s
Race result: 4th, 1h 40m 41.805s
(+15.669s)
Fastest lap: 3rd fastest, 1m 13.984s

Date: 6th October 1974
Circuit: Watkins Glen
Race: USA Grand Prix
Car-engine: Hesketh-Ford Cosworth
308 (no.24)
Qualifying: 2nd, 1m 38.995s
Race result: 3rd, 1h 41m 31.823s (+1m
10.384s)
Fastest lap: 3rd fastest, 1m 41.104s

1975

Date: 12th January 1975
Circuit: Buenos Aires No.15
Race: Argentinian Grand Prix
Car-engine: Hesketh-Ford Cosworth
308B (no.24)
Qualifying: 6th, 1m 50.26s
Race result: 2nd, 1h 39m 32.20s
(+5.91s)
Fastest lap: fastest, 1m 50.91s

Date: 26th January 1975
Circuit: Interlagos
Race: Brazilian Grand Prix
Car-engine: Hesketh-Ford Cosworth

308B (no.24)
Qualifying: 7th, 2m 31.70s
Race result: 6th, 1h 45m 46.29s
(+1m 05.12s)
Fastest lap: 8th fastest, 2m 35.77s

Date: 1st March 1975
Circuit: Kyalami
Race: South African Grand Prix
Car-engine: Hesketh-Ford Cosworth
308B (no.24)
Qualifying: 12th, 1m 17.30s
Race result: retired (fuel metering unit),
53 laps
Fastest lap: 16th fastest, 1m 19.08s

Date: 27th April 1975
Circuit: Montjuïch Park
Race: Spanish Grand Prix
Car-engine: Hesketh-Ford Cosworth
308B (no.24)
Qualifying: 3rd, 1m 23.8s
Race result: retired (accident), 6 laps
Fastest lap: 4th fastest, 1m 25.7s

Date: 11th May 1975
Circuit: Monte-Carlo
Race: Monaco Grand Prix
Car-engine: Hesketh-Ford Cosworth
308B (no.24)
Qualifying: 11th, 1m 27.94s
Race result: retired (accident), 63 laps
Fastest lap: 8th fastest, 1m 29.58s

Date: 25th May 1975
Circuit: Zolder
Race: Belgian Grand Prix
Car-engine: Hesketh-Ford Cosworth
308B (no.24)
Qualifying: 11th, 1m 26.51s
Race result: retired (gear linkage), 15
laps
Fastest lap: 16th fastest, 1m 29.82s
Date: 8th June 1975

Circuit: Anderstorp
Race: Swedish Grand Prix
Car-engine: Hesketh-Ford Cosworth
308B (no.24)
Qualifying: 13th, 1m 26.500s
Race result: retired (brake fluid leak),
21 laps
Fastest lap: 13th fastest, 1m 29.353s

Date: 22nd June 1975
Circuit: Zandvoort
Race: Dutch Grand Prix
Car-engine: Hesketh-Ford Cosworth
308B (no.24)
Qualifying: 3rd, 1m 20.70s
Race result: 1st, 1h 46m 57.40s
Fastest lap: 4th fastest, 1m 22.00s

Date: 6th July 1975
Circuit: Paul Ricard
Race: French Grand Prix
Car-engine: Hesketh-Ford Cosworth
308B (no.24)
Qualifying: 3rd, 1m 48.25s
Race result: 2nd, 1h 40m 20.43s
(+1.59s)
Fastest lap: 4th fastest, 1m 50.69s

Date: 19th July 1975
Circuit: Silverstone
Race: British Grand Prix
Car-engine: Hesketh-Ford Cosworth
308B (no.24)
Qualifying: 9th, 1m 20.14s
Race result: 4th, retired (accident),
55 laps
Fastest lap: 12th fastest, 1m 21.9s

Date: 3rd August 1975
Circuit: Nürburgring
Race: German Grand Prix
Car-engine: Hesketh-Ford Cosworth
308B (no.24)
Qualifying: 9th, 7m 02.7s

Race result: retired (rear hub), 10 laps
Fastest lap: joint 6th fastest, 7m 10.8s

Date: 17th August 1975
Circuit: Österreichring
Race: Austrian Grand Prix
Car-engine: Hesketh-Ford Cosworth
308B (no.24)
Qualifying: 2nd, 1m 34.97s
Race result: 2nd, 58m 23.72s (+27.03s)
Fastest lap: not recorded

Date: 7th September 1975
Circuit: Monza
Race: Italian Grand Prix
Car-engine: Hesketh-Ford Cosworth
308C (no.24)
Qualifying: 8th, 1m 33.73s
Race result: 5th, 1h 23m 39.7s (+57.1s)
Fastest lap: 6th fastest, 1m 34.7s

Date: 5th October 1975
Circuit: Watkins Glen
Race: USA Grand Prix
Car-engine: Hesketh-Ford Cosworth
308C (308 for practice)(no.24)
Qualifying: 15th, 1m 43.820s
Race result: 4th, 1h 43m 47.650s
(+49.475s)
Fastest lap: 10th fastest, 1m 44.835s

1976
Date: 25th January 1976
Circuit: Interlagos
Race: Brazilian Grand Prix
Car-engine: McLaren-Ford Cosworth
M23 (no.11)
Qualifying: 1st, 2m 32.50s
Race result: retired (stuck throttle/
accident), 32 laps
Fastest lap: 3rd fastest, 2m 36.29s

Date: 6th March 1976
Circuit: Kyalami

Race: South African Grand Prix
Car-engine: McLaren-Ford Cosworth
M23 (no.11)
Qualifying: 1st, 1m 16.10s
Race result: 2nd, 1h 42m 19.7s (+1.3s)
Fastest lap: 2nd fastest, 1m 18.08s

Date: 28th March 1976
Circuit: Long Beach
Race: USA West Grand Prix
Car-engine: McLaren-Ford Cosworth
M23 (no.11)
Qualifying: 3rd, 1m 23.420s
Race result: retired (accident), 3 laps
Fastest lap: 16th fastest, 1m 27.985s

Date: 2nd May 1976
Circuit: Jarama
Race: Spanish Grand Prix
Car-engine: McLaren-Ford Cosworth
M23 (no.11)
Qualifying: 1st, 1m 18.52s
Race result: 1st, 1h 42m 20.43s
Fastest lap: 2nd fastest, 1m 21.07s

Date: 16th May 1976
Circuit: Zolder
Race: Belgian Grand Prix
Car-engine: McLaren-Ford Cosworth
M23 (no.11)
Qualifying: 3rd, 1m 26.74s
Race result: retired (transmission), 35
laps
Fastest lap: 14th fastest, 1m 29.00s

Date: 30th May 1976
Circuit: Monte-Carlo
Race: Monaco Grand Prix
Car-engine: McLaren-Ford Cosworth
M23 (no.11)
Qualifying: 14th, 1m 31.88s
Race result: retired (engine), 24 laps
Fastest lap: 8th fastest, 1m 32.13s
Date: 13th June 1976

Circuit: Anderstorp
Race: Swedish Grand Prix
Car-engine: McLaren-Ford Cosworth
M23 (no.11)
Qualifying: 8th, 1m 26.958s
Race result: 5th, 1h 47m 53.212s
(+59.483s)
Fastest lap: not recorded

Date: 4th July 1976
Circuit: Paul Ricard
Race: French Grand Prix
Car-engine: McLaren-Ford Cosworth
M23 (no.11)
Qualifying: 1st, 1m 47.89s
Race result: 1st, 1h 40m 58.60s
Fastest lap: 3rd fastest, 1m 51.3s

Date: 18th July 1976
Circuit: Brands Hatch
Race: British Grand Prix
Car-engine: McLaren-Ford Cosworth
M23 (no.11)
Qualifying: 2nd, 1m 19.41s
Race result: disqualified (used spare car
in restart), 76 laps
Fastest lap: - (set fastest lap in 1m
19.82s, but erased)

Date: 1st August 1976
Circuit: Nürburgring
Race: German Grand Prix
Car-engine: McLaren-Ford Cosworth
M23 (no.11)
Qualifying: 1st, 7m 06.5s
Race result: 1st, 1h 41m 42.7s
Fastest lap: joint 2nd fastest, 7m 11.1s

Date: 15th August 1976
Circuit: Österreichring
Race: Austrian Grand Prix
Car-engine: McLaren-Ford Cosworth
M23 (no.11)
Qualifying: 1st, 1m 35.02s

Race result: 4th, 1h 30m 20.30s
(+12.44s)
Fastest lap: fastest, 1m 35.91s

Date: 29th August 1976
Circuit: Zandvoort
Race: Dutch Grand Prix
Car-engine: McLaren-Ford Cosworth
M23 (no.11)
Qualifying: 2nd, 1m 21.39s
Race result: 1st, 1h 44m 52.09s
Fastest lap: 7th fastest, 1m 23.14s

Date: 12th September 1976
Circuit: Monza
Race: Italian Grand Prix
Car-engine: McLaren-Ford Cosworth
M23 (no.11)
Qualifying: 25th, 2m 08.76s
Race result: retired (spin), 11 laps
Fastest lap: joint 10th fastest, 1m 43.0s

Date: 3rd October 1976
Circuit: Mosport Park
Race: Canadian Grand Prix
Car-engine: McLaren-Ford Cosworth
M23 (no.11)
Qualifying: 1st, 1m 12.389s
Race result: 1st, 1h 40m 09.626s
Fastest lap: joint 3rd fastest, 1m 14.124s

Date: 10th October 1976
Circuit: Watkins Glen
Race: USA East Grand Prix
Car-engine: McLaren-Ford Cosworth
M23 (no.11)
Qualifying: 1st, 1m 43.622s
Race result: 1st, 1h 42m 40.741s
Fastest lap: fastest, 1m 42.851s

Date: 24th October 1976
Circuit: Fuji
Race: Japanese Grand Prix
Car-engine: McLaren-Ford Cosworth

M23 (no.11)
Qualifying: 2nd, 1m 12.80s
Race result: 3rd, 72 laps
Fastest lap: not recorded

1977

Date: 9th January 1977
Circuit: Buenos Aires No.15
Race: Argentinian Grand Prix
Car-engine: McLaren-Ford Cosworth
M23 (no.1)
Qualifying: 1st, 1m 48.68s
Race result: retired (rear suspension),
31 laps
Fastest lap: fastest, 1m 51.06s

Date: 23rd January 1977
Circuit: Interlagos
Race: Brazilian Grand Prix
Car-engine: McLaren-Ford Cosworth
M23 (no.1)
Qualifying: 1st, 2m 30.11s
Race result: 2nd, 1h 45m 18.43s
(+10.71s)
Fastest lap: fastest, 2m 34.55s

Date: 5th March 1977
Circuit: Kyalami
Race: South African Grand Prix
Car-engine: McLaren-Ford Cosworth
M23 (no.1)
Qualifying: 1st, 1m 15.96s
Race result: 4th, 1h 42m 31.10s (+9.5s)
Fastest lap: 3rd fastest, 1m 17.85s

Date: 3rd April 1977
Circuit: Long Beach
Race: USA West Grand Prix
Car-engine: McLaren-Ford Cosworth
M23 (no.1)
Qualifying: 8th, 1m 22.529s
Race result: 7th, 79 laps
Fastest lap: 4th fastest, 1m 22.928s
Date: 8th May 1977

Circuit: Jarama
Race: Spanish Grand Prix
Car-engine: McLaren-Ford Cosworth
M26 (no.1)
Qualifying: 7th, 1m 20.11s
Race result: retired (engine), 10 laps
Fastest lap: 8th fastest, 1m 22.20s

Date: 22nd May 1977
Circuit: Monte-Carlo
Race: Monaco Grand Prix
Car-engine: McLaren-Ford Cosworth
M23 (no.1)
Qualifying: 7th, 1m 30.85s
Race result: retired (dropped valve), 25
laps
Fastest lap: 8th fastest, 1m 31.93s

Date: 5th June 1977
Circuit: Zolder
Race: Belgian Grand Prix
Car-engine: McLaren-Ford Cosworth
M26 (M23 for qualifying) (no.1)
Qualifying: 9th, 1m 27.04s
Race result: 7th, 69 laps
Fastest lap: 8th fastest, 1m 28.94s

Date: 19th June 1977
Circuit: Anderstorp
Race: Swedish Grand Prix
Car-engine: McLaren-Ford Cosworth
M26 (no.1)
Qualifying: 3rd, 1m 25.626s
Race result: 12th, 71 laps
Fastest lap: 2nd fastest, 1m 27.615s

Date: 3rd July 1977
Circuit: Dijon-Prenois
Race: French Grand Prix
Car-engine: McLaren-Ford Cosworth
M26 (no.1)
Qualifying: 2nd, 1m 12.73s
Race result: 3rd, 1h 40m 14.00s
(+33.87s)

Fastest lap: 4th fastest, 1m 14.44s

Date: 16th July 1977
Circuit: Silverstone
Race: British Grand Prix
Car-engine: McLaren-Ford Cosworth M26 (no.1)
Qualifying: 1st, 1m 18.49s
Race result: 1st, 1h 31m 46.06s
Fastest lap: fastest, 1m 19.60s

Date: 31st July 1977
Circuit: Hockenheim
Race: German Grand Prix
Car-engine: McLaren-Ford Cosworth M26 (no.1)
Qualifying: 4th, 1m 53.68s
Race result: retired (fuel pump), 32 laps
Fastest lap: 3rd fastest, 1m 56.35s

Date: 14th August 1977
Circuit: Österreichring
Race: Austrian Grand Prix
Car-engine: McLaren-Ford Cosworth M26 (no.1)
Qualifying: 2nd, 1m 39.45s
Race result: retired (engine), 43 laps
Fastest lap: 6th fastest, 1m 42.23s

Date: 28th August 1977
Circuit: Zandvoort
Race: Dutch Grand Prix
Car-engine: McLaren-Ford Cosworth M26 (no.1)
Qualifying: 3rd, 1m 19.50s
Race result: retired (accident), 5 laps
Fastest lap: joint 9th fastest, 1m 21.74s

Date: 11th September 1977
Circuit: Monza
Race: Italian Grand Prix
Car-engine: McLaren-Ford Cosworth M26 (no.1)
Qualifying: 1st, 1m 38.08s

Race result: retired (brakes/ spin), 26 laps
Fastest lap: joint 8th fastest, 1m 40.5s

Date: 2nd October 1977
Circuit: Watkins Glen
Race: USA East Grand Prix
Car-engine: McLaren-Ford Cosworth M26 (no.1)
Qualifying: 1st, 1m 40.863s
Race result: 1st, 1h 58m 23.267s
Fastest lap: 2nd fastest, 1m 52.890s

Date: 9th October 1977
Circuit: Mosport Park
Race: Canadian Grand Prix
Car-engine: McLaren-Ford Cosworth M26 (no.1)
Qualifying: 2nd, 1m 11.942s
Race result: retired (accident), 61 laps
Fastest lap: 2nd fastest, 1m 13.549s

Date: 23rd October 1977
Circuit: Fuji
Race: Japanese Grand Prix
Car-engine: McLaren-Ford Cosworth M26 (no.1)
Qualifying: 2nd, 1m 12.39s
Race result: 1st, 1h 31m 51.68s
Fastest lap: not recorded

1978
Date: 15th January 1978
Circuit: Buenos Aires No.15
Race: Argentinian Grand Prix
Car-engine: McLaren-Ford Cosworth M26 (no.7)
Qualifying: 6th, 1m 48.72s
Race result: 4th, 1h 37m 20.52s (+16.05s)
Fastest lap: 3rd fastest, 1m 50.58s
Date: 29th January 1978
Circuit: Rio de Janeiro
Race: Brazilian Grand Prix

Car-engine: McLaren-Ford Cosworth
M26 (no.7)
Qualifying: 2nd, 1m 40.53s
Race result: retired (accident), 25 laps
Fastest lap: 11th fastest, 1m 44.61s

Date: 4th March 1978
Circuit: Kyalami
Race: South African Grand Prix
Car-engine: McLaren-Ford Cosworth
M26 (no.7)
Qualifying: 3rd, 1m 15.14s
Race result: retired (engine), 5 laps
Fastest lap: 8th fastest, 1m 17.49s

Date: 2nd April 1978
Circuit: Long Beach
Race: USA West Grand Prix
Car-engine: McLaren-Ford Cosworth
M26 (no.7)
Qualifying: 7th, 1m 21.738s
Race result: retired (accident), 5 laps
Fastest lap: 17th fastest, 1m 24.203s

Date: 7th May 1978
Circuit: Monte-Carlo
Race: Monaco Grand Prix
Car-engine: McLaren-Ford Cosworth
M26 (no.7)
Qualifying: 6th, 1m 29.22s
Race result: retired (rear anti-roll bar),
43 laps
Fastest lap: 9th fastest, 1m 31.47s

Date: 21st May 1978
Circuit: Zolder
Race: Belgian Grand Prix
Car-engine: McLaren-Ford Cosworth
M26 (no.7)
Qualifying: 6th, 1m 22.50s
Race result: retired (accident), 0 laps
Date: 4th June 1978
Circuit: Jarama
Race: Spanish Grand Prix

Car-engine: McLaren-Ford Cosworth
M26 (no.7)
Qualifying: 4th, 1m 17.66s
Race result: 6th, 74 laps
Fastest lap: 3rd fastest, 1m 20.44s

Date: 17th June 1978
Circuit: Anderstorp
Race: Swedish Grand Prix
Car-engine: McLaren-Ford Cosworth
M26 (no.7)
Qualifying: 14th, 1m 24.761s
Race result: 8th, 69 laps
Fastest lap: 14th fastest, 1m 27.271s

Date: 2nd July 1978
Circuit: Paul Ricard
Race: French Grand Prix
Car-engine: McLaren-Ford Cosworth
M26 (no.7)
Qualifying: 4th, 1m 44.92s
Race result: 3rd, 1h 39m 11.72s
(+19.80s)
Fastest lap: 2nd fastest, 1m 48.77s

Date: 16th July 1978
Circuit: Brands Hatch
Race: British Grand Prix
Car-engine: McLaren-Ford Cosworth
M26 (M26E for practice) (no.7)
Qualifying: 14th, 1m 19.05s
Race result: retired (accident), 8 laps
Fastest lap: 25th fastest, 1m 21.92s

Date: 30th July 1978
Circuit: Hockenheim
Race: German Grand Prix
Car-engine: McLaren-Ford Cosworth
M26 (no.7)
Qualifying: 8th, 1m 53.54s
Race result: disqualified (incorrect
route into pits), 34 laps
Fastest lap: - (set 3rd fastest time in 1m
55.84s, but erased)

Date: 13th August 1978
Circuit: Österreichring
Race: Austrian Grand Prix
Car-engine: McLaren-Ford Cosworth
M26 (no.7)
Qualifying: 8th, 1m 39.10s
Race result: retired (accident), 8 laps
Fastest lap: not recorded

Date: 27th August 1978
Circuit: Zandvoort
Race: Dutch Grand Prix
Car-engine: McLaren-Ford Cosworth
M26 (no.7)
Qualifying: 7th, 1m 17.67s
Race result: 10th, 74 laps
Fastest lap: 13th fastest, 1m 21.29s

Date: 10th September 1978
Circuit: Monza
Race: Italian Grand Prix
Car-engine: McLaren-Ford Cosworth
M26 (no.7)
Qualifying: 10th, 1m 38.938s
Race result: retired (distributor), 19 laps
Fastest lap: 15th fastest, 1m 40.86s

Date: 1st October 1978
Circuit: Watkins Glen
Race: USA East Grand Prix
Car-engine: McLaren-Ford Cosworth
M26 (no.7)
Qualifying: 6th, 1m 39.991s
Race result: 7th, 58 laps
Fastest lap: 8th fastest, 1m 41.477s

Date: 8th October 1978
Circuit: Montréal
Race: Canadian Grand Prix
Car-engine: McLaren-Ford Cosworth
M26 (no.7)
Qualifying: 19th, 1m 40.970s
Race result: retired (accident), 51 laps

Fastest lap: 16th fastest, 1m 40.617s

1979

Date: 21st January 1979
Circuit: Buenos Aires No.15
Race: Argentinian Grand Prix
Car-engine: Wolf-Ford Cosworth
WR7 (no.20)
Qualifying: 18th, 1m 48.77s
Race result: retired (electrics), 42 laps
Fastest lap: 15th fastest, 1m 51.21s

Date: 4th February 1979
Circuit: Interlagos
Race: Brazilian Grand Prix
Car-engine: Wolf-Ford Cosworth
WR7 (no.20)
Qualifying: 10th, 2m 26.37s
Race result: retired (steering rack), 7
laps
Fastest lap: 10th fastest, 2m 32.37s

Date: 3rd March 1979
Circuit: Kyalami
Race: South African Grand Prix
Car-engine: Wolf-Ford Cosworth
WR7 (no.20)
Qualifying: 13th, 1m 14.21s
Race result: 8th, 77 laps
Fastest lap: 11th fastest, 1m 16.18s

Date: 8th April 1979
Circuit: Long Beach
Race: USA West Grand Prix
Car-engine: Wolf-Ford Cosworth
WR8 (no.20)
Qualifying: 8th, 1m 19.643s
Race result: retired (driveshaft joint), 1 lap

Date: 29th April 1979
Circuit: Jarama
Race: Spanish Grand Prix
Car-engine: Wolf-Ford Cosworth
WR7 (WR8 for practice) (no.20)

Qualifying: 15th, 1m 16.88s
Race result: retired (brakes), 26 laps
Fastest lap: 21st fastest, 1m 20.46s

Date: 13th May 1979
Circuit: Zolder
Race: Belgian Grand Prix
Car-engine: Wolf-Ford Cosworth
WR8 (WR7 for practice) (no.20)
Qualifying: 9th, 1m 22.55s
Race result: retired (accident), 40 laps
Fastest lap: 6th fastest, 1m 24.07s

Date: 27th May 1979
Circuit: Monte-Carlo
Race: Monaco Grand Prix
Car-engine: Wolf-Ford Cosworth
WR7 (no.20)
Qualifying: 10th, 1m 27.96s
Race result: retired (cv joint), 4 laps
Fastest lap: 19th fastest, 1m 32.42s

APPENDIX VII
1973 to 1979 Non-Championship Formula One

Between 1973 and 1979, James Hunt raced in several non-championship Formula One races. He was a regular at Brands Hatch's Race of Champions and Silverstone's International Trophy, winning two events at each. He also participated at events in Brazil and France, and a sprint in memory of Gunnar Nilsson at Donington Park.

1973
Date: 18th March 1973
Circuit: Brands Hatch
Race: Daily Mail Race of Champions
Car-engine: Surtees-Ford Cosworth TS9B (no.24)
Qualifying: 13th, 1m 24.8s
Race result: 3rd, 57m 26.3s (+3.4s)

1974
Date: 3rd February 1974
Circuit: Brasilia, Brazil
Race: Grande Prêmio President Emilio Medici
Car-engine: March-Ford Cosworth 731 (no.24)
Qualifying: 12th, 2m 04.95s
Race result: retired (gear linkage), 4 laps

Date: 17th March 1974
Circuit: Brands Hatch
Race: Simoniz - Daily Mail Race of Champions
Car-engine: Hesketh-Ford Cosworth 308 (no.24)
Qualifying: 1st, 1m 21.5s
Race result: retired (accident damage), 20 laps

Date: 7th April 1974
Circuit: Silverstone

Race: Daily Express BRDC International Trophy
Car-engine: Hesketh-Ford Cosworth 308 (no.24)
Qualifying: 1st, 1m 16.7s
Race result: 1st, 52m 35.4s
Fastest lap: fastest, 1m 17.6s

1975
Date: 13th April 1975
Circuit: Silverstone
Race: Daily Express BRDC International Trophy
Car-engine: Hesketh-Ford Cosworth 308B (no.24)
Qualifying: 1st, 1m 17.3s
Race result: retired (engine), 25 laps
Fastest lap: joint fastest, 1m 17.7s

Date: 24th August 1975
Circuit: Dijon-Prenois, France
Race: Grand Prix de l'Automobile Club de Suisse
Car-engine: Hesketh-Ford Cosworth 308C (no.24)
Qualifying: 11th, 1m 00.47s
Race result: 8th, 59 laps
Fastest lap: 12th fastest, 1m 01.88s

1976
Date: 14th March 1976

Circuit: Brands Hatch
Race: Daily Mail Race of Champions
Car-engine: McLaren-Ford Cosworth
M23 (no.11)
Qualifying: 5th, 1m 23.80s
Race result: 1st, 58m 01.23s
Fastest lap: fastest, 1m 23.78s

Date: 11th April 1976
Circuit: Silverstone
Race: BRDC Graham Hill/
Daily Express International Trophy
Car-engine: McLaren-Ford Cosworth
M23 (no.11)
Qualifying: 1st, 1m 17.91s
Race result: 1st, 53m 04.57s
Fastest lap: fastest, 1m 18.81s

1977

Date: 20th March 1977
Circuit: Brands Hatch
Race: Marlboro - Daily Mail Race of
Champions
Car-engine: McLaren-Ford Cosworth
M23 (no.1)
Qualifying: 3rd, 1m 19.60s
Race result: 1st, 53m 54.35s
Fastest lap: fastest, 1m 19.48s

1978

Date: 19th March 1978
Circuit: Silverstone
Race: BRDC Daily Express
International Trophy
Car-engine: McLaren-Ford Cosworth
M26 (no.7)
Qualifying: 4th, 1m 16.85s
Race result: retired (spin), 0 laps

1979

Date: 3rd June 1979
Circuit: Donington Park
Race: Gunnar Nilsson Memorial
Trophy (Time Trial)

Car-engine: Wolf-Ford
Cosworth WR8
Race result: 2nd, 1m 02.54s (+1.17s)

APPENDIX VIII
1969 to 1978 Championship Tables

1969 MCD Lombank F3 Championship

1	Emerson Fittipaldi 57	
2	Alan Rollinson 49	
3	Bev Bond	39
4	Roy Pike	38
5	Richard Stott	36
6	Tim Schenken	33
7	Reine Wisell	27
8	Barrie Maskell	26
9	Morris Nunn	23
10	Keith Jupp	18
11	Dave Walker	14
12	Peter Deal	12
13	David Cole	10
14	Mike Watkins	9
15	**James Hunt**	**8**
16	Mike Beuttler	7
17	Howden Ganley	6
=	Cyd Williams	6
19	Mike Campbell	4
=	Norman Foulds	4
=	Bert Hawthorne	4
=	Roger Keele	4
=	Mike Keens	4
=	John Kendall	4
=	Terry McGrath	4
=	Wayne Mitchell	4
27	François Cevert	3
=	John Collings	3
=	Keith Holland	3
=	Brendan McInerney	3
31	Peter Gaydon	2
=	Jean-Pierre Jaussaud	2
=	Geoff Oliver	2
=	Andy Sutcliffe	2
35	Mike Beckwith	1
=	Ken Crook	1
=	Alan Harvey	1
=	Jim Morrison	1
=	Edward Reeves	1

1970 BRSCC MotorSport – Shell Super Oil British F3 Championship

1	Tony Trimmer	44 (+2)
2	Dave Walker	41
3	Mike Beuttler	32
4	Bev Bond	30
5	Carlos Pace	24
6	**James Hunt**	**24**
7	Gerry Birrell	21
8	Ulf Svensson	12
9	Jürg Dubler	12
10	Wilson Fittipaldi	7
11	Richard Scott	7
12	Ian Ashley	6
=	Jean-Pierre Cassegrain	6
=	Jean-Pierre Jaussaud	6
15	Cyd Williams	6
16	Keith Jupp	4
=	Dave Morgan	4
18	Peter Hanson	4
19	Sten Gunnarsson	2
=	Fritz Jordan	2
21	Jean-Pierre Jarier	1
=	Mike Keens	1
=	Freddy Hottulinsky	1
=	Colin Vandervell	1

1970 MCD Lombank F3 Championship

1	Dave Walker	48
2	Tony Trimmer	43
3	Carlos Pace	43
4	Bev Bond	35
5	Steve Matchett	15

6	Barrie Maskell	13
7	Wilson Fittipaldi	13
8	Bert Hawthorne	12
9	Dave Morgan	12
10	**James Hunt**	**10**
11	David Cole	9
=	Ulf Svensson	9
13	Richard Scott	7
14	Jean-Pierre Jaussaud	6
15	Roger Keele	6
16	Tom Walkinshaw	5
17	Chris Skeaping	4
18	Dick Barker	3
=	Gerry Birrell	3
20	Mike Beuttler	3
21	Sverrir Thorodsson	3
22	Allan McCully	3
23	Colin Vandervell	3
24	Cyd Williams	2
=	Brendan McInerney	2
=	Mike Watkins	2
=	Fritz Jordan	2
28	Andy Sutcliffe	1
=	Ken Bailey	1
=	Geoff Bremner	1
=	Peter Deal	1
=	Norman Foulds	1
=	John Buxton	1
=	David Purley	1

1970 BARC Forward Trust British F3 Championship

1	Carlos Pace	41
2	Dave Walker	37
3	Bev Bond	27
4	Wilson Fittipaldi	22
5	Cyd Williams	19
6	Mike Beuttler	16
7	Richard Scott	15
8	Dave Morgan	14
9	Steve Matchett	11
10	Chris Skeaping	10
11	Tony Trimmer	10
12	Norman Abbott	6

=	Jürg Dubler	6
14	Peter Hanson	6
15	Bert Hawthorne	4
=	**James Hunt**	**4**
17	Edward Reeves	4
18	Gerry Birrell	3
=	Barrie Maskell	3
=	Torsten Palm	3
21	Jean-Pierre Jarier	2
=	Allan McCully	2
=	Mike Keens	2
=	Andy Sutcliffe	2
25	Geoff Bremner	2
26	Roger Keele	1
=	Fritz Jordan	1
=	David Cole	1
=	Mike Tobitt	1

1971 BRSCC/MCD MotorSport Magazine Shell Super Oil British F3

1	Dave Walker	86
2	Roger Williamson	56
3	Bev Bond	48
4	Colin Vandervell	25
5	Barrie Maskell	16
6	Jochen Mass	16
7	Patrick Depailler	15
=	Jody Scheckter	15
9	Claude Bourgoignie	14
10	**James Hunt**	**12**
11	Steve Thompson	11
12	Pierre-François Rousselot	10
13	Alan Jones	8
=	Rikky von Opel	8
15	David Purley	7
16	Peter Hull	6
=	Jean-Pierre Jabouille	6
=	Manfred Mohr	6
19	Peter Lamplough	5
20	Ian Ashley	4
=	Gerry Birrell	4
=	Brendan McInerney	4
=	Giancarlo Naddeo	4
=	François Rabbione	4

=	Chris Skeaping	4
26	José Dolhem	3
=	Freddy Kottulinsky	3
=	Torsten Palm	3
=	Ronald Rossi	3
=	Mike Walker	3
=	Tom Walkinshaw	3
32	Willi Deutsch	2
=	Allan McCully	2
=	Andy Sutcliffe	2
35	John Bisignano	1
=	Wolfgang Bülow	1
=	Patrice Compain	1
=	Christian Ethuin	1
=	Lucien Guitteny	1
=	Sandy Shepard	1

1971 MCD Lombank F3 Championship

1	Roger Williamson	90
2	Colin Vandervell	63
3	Jody Scheckter	28
4	Alan Jones	21
5	David Purley	20
6	Brendan McInerney	13
=	Peter Hull	13
8	**James Hunt**	**12**
9	Steve Thompson	10
10	Bev Bond	9
=	Sonny Eade	9
=	Rikky von Opel	9
=	Dave Walker	9
14	John Bisignano	7
=	Peter Lamplough	7
=	Jochen Mass	7
17	Claude Bourgoignie	6
=	Andy Sutcliffe	6
19	José Ferreira	5
20	Gerry Birrell	4
=	Tony Brise	4
=	Ronald Rossi	4
23	Barrie Maskell	3
=	Tom Walkinshaw	3
25	Bob Evans	2

=	Allan McCully	2
=	Chris O'Brien	2
28	Patrice Compain	1
=	Tim Goss	1
=	Ray Mallock	1
=	Stan Matthews	1
=	Brian McGuire	1
=	Pierre-François Rousselot	1

1971 BARC Forward Trust British F3 Championship

1	Dave Walker	63
2	Roger Williamson	35
3	**James Hunt**	**19**
4	Sandy Shepard	13
=	Andy Sutcliffe	13
6	David Purley	12
7	Barrie Maskell	10
8	Brian McGuire	9
=	Dave Morgan	9
=	Rikky von Opel	9
=	Mike Walker	9
12	Tom Walkinshaw	7
13	Derek Lawrence	6
=	Allan McCully	6
=	Chris O'Brien	6
=	Ulf Svensson	6
17	Richard Longman	5
=	Steve Thompson	5
19	Brendan McInerney	4
=	Jody Scheckter	4
21	Conny Andersson	3
=	Tim Goss	3
=	Peter Lamplough	3
=	Alan Rollinson	3
25	Ian Ashley	2
=	Sonny Eade	2
=	Alan Joy	2
=	Ray Mallock	2
=	Ingvar Pettersson	2
30	John Bisignano	1
=	John Finch	1
=	Alan Jones	1

1972 BRSCC/MCD Shell Super Oil British F3 Championship

1	Roger Williamson	78
2	Colin Vandervell	44
3	Jacques Coulon	26
4	Mike Walker	25
5	Rikky von Opel	23
6	Tony Brise	18
7	Peter Hull	17
8	Barrie Maskell	16
9	Bob Evans	15
=	Tom Pryce	15
11	Jochen Mass	13
=	Andy Sutcliffe	13
13	Lucien Guitteny	11
14	Conny Andersson	10
15	**James Hunt**	**9**
16	Alan Jones	7
17	François Lacarrau	6
18	Pierre-François Rousselot	5
19	Bernard Beguin	4
=	Jean-Pierre Jarier	4
=	Stan Matthews	4
=	Allan McCully	4
23	Mike Wilds	2
=	Russell Wood	2
25	Willi Deutsch	1
=	Neil Ginn	1
=	Damien Magee	1
=	Torsten Palm	1

1972 MCD Lombard North Central British F3 Championship

1	Rikky von Opel	61
2	Tony Brise	55
3	Andy Sutcliffe	53
4	Roger Williamson	30
5	Damien Magee	24
6	Bob Evans	21
7	Masami Kuwashima	17
8	Mike Walker	15

9	Pierre-François Rousselot	11
=	Russell Wood	11
11	Alan Jones	9
12	Neil Ginn	8
13	Mo Harness	6
14	Tom Pryce	5
=	David Purley	5
16	Ian Ashley	4
=	Jochen Mass	4
=	Peter Hull	4
19	**James Hunt**	**3**
20	Brian McGuire	1
=	Chris Skeaping	1
=	Matt Spitzley	1
=	Mike Wilds	1

1972 European Formula 2 Championship

1	Mike Hailwood	55
2	Jean-Pierre Jaussaud	37
3	Patrick Depailler	27
4	Carlos Reutemann	26
5	Niki Lauda	25
6	Dave Morgan	23
7	Bob Wollek	21
8	Jody Scheckter	15
9	Mike Beuttler	12
=	Peter Gethin	12
11	Carlos Ruesch	11
12	Wilson Fittipaldi	10
13	Xavier Perrot	8
14	Jean-Pierre Jabouille	7
15	Patrick Dal Bo	6
=	Carlos Pace	6
17	**James Hunt**	**5**
=	Tom Belsø	5
19	Ernesto Brambilla	4
=	Andrea de Adamich	4
=	Claudio Francisci	4
=	David Purley	4
23	John Watson	4
24	Brett Lunger	3
=	Vic Elford	3
=	Hiroshi Kazato	3

27	José Dolhem	2
28	John Wingfield	1
=	Jochen Mass	1

**1972 John Player British
Formula 2 Championship**

1	Niki Lauda	31
2	Ronnie Peterson	27
3	Dave Morgan	14
4	Jody Scheckter	12
5	Gerry Birrell	10
6	**James Hunt**	**8**
7	François Cevert	8
=	Mike Hailwood	8
9	Carlos Reutemann	8
10	Richard Scott	6
11	Tim Schenken	4
12	Patrick Dal Bo	3
=	Vic Elford	3
14	John Wingfield	2
=	Claudio Francisci	2
16	Xavier Perrot	1
=	David Purley	1
=	Jean-Pierre Beltoise	1

**1972 Il Torneio Internacional
de Formula 2 do Brasil**

1	Emerson Fittipaldi	15
2	Mike Hailwood	13
3	Tim Schenken	12
4	Carlos Pace	9
5	Wilson Fittipaldi	8
6	**James Hunt**	**5**
7	Clay Regazzoni	4
8	Andrea de Adamich	3
9	Bob Wollek	2
=	Jean-Pierre Jaussaud	2
11	David Purley	1
=	José Dolhem	1

1973 Formula One World Championship

1	Jackie Stewart	Tyrrell-Ford Cosworth	71 points
2	Emerson Fittipaldi	JPS Lotus-Ford Cosworth	55 points
3	Ronnie Peterson	JPS Lotus-Ford Cosworth	52 points
4	François Cevert	Tyrrell-Ford Cosworth	47 points
5	Peter Revson	McLaren-Ford Cosworth	38 points
6	Denny Hulme	McLaren-Ford Cosworth	26 points
7	Carlos Reutemann	Brabham-Ford Cosworth	16 points
8	**James Hunt**	**March-Ford Cosworth**	**14 points**
9	Jacky Ickx	Ferrari/ McLaren-Ford Cosworth/ Iso Marlboro-Ford Cosworth	12 points
10	Jean-Pierre Beltoise	BRM	9 points
11	Carlos Pace	Surtees-Ford Cosworth	7 points
12	Arturo Merzario	Ferrari	6 points
13	George Follmer	Shadow-Ford Cosworth	5 points
14	Jackie Oliver	Shadow-Ford Cosworth	4 points
15	Andrea de Adamich	Surtees-Ford Cosworth/ Brabham-Ford Cosworth	3 points
16	Wilson Fittipaldi	Brabham-Ford Cosworth	3 points
17	Niki Lauda	BRM	2 points
18	Clay Regazzoni	BRM	2 points
19	Howden Ganley	Iso Marlboro-Ford Cosworth	1 point
20	Gijs van Lennep	Iso Marlboro-Ford Cosworth	1 point
21	Chris Amon	Tecno/Tyrrell-Ford Cosworth	1 point

Scoring system: 1st: 9 points; 2nd: 6; 3rd: 4; 4th: 3; 5th: 2; 6th: 1. Best 7 scores from first 8 races, best 6 from remaining 7 races.

1974 Formula One World Championship

1	Emerson Fittipaldi	McLaren-Ford Cosworth	55 points
2	Clay Regazzoni	Ferrari	52 points
3	Jody Scheckter	Tyrrell-Ford Cosworth	45 points
4	Niki Lauda	Ferrari	38 points
5	Ronnie Peterson	JPS Lotus-Ford Cosworth	35 points
6	Carlos Reutemann	Brabham-Ford Cosworth	32 points
7	Denny Hulme	McLaren-Ford Cosworth	20 points
8	**James Hunt**	**March-Ford Cosworth/ Hesketh-Ford Cosworth**	**15 points**
9	Patrick Depailler	Tyrrell-Ford Cosworth	14 points
10	Jacky Ickx	JPS Lotus-Ford Cosworth	12 points
11	Mike Hailwood	McLaren-Ford Cosworth	12 points
12	Carlos Pace	Surtees-Ford Cosworth/ Brabham-Ford Cosworth	11 points

13	Jean-Pierre Beltoise	BRM	10 points
14	Jean-Pierre Jarier	Shadow-Ford Cosworth	6 points
15	John Watson	Brabham-Ford Cosworth	6 points
16	Hans-Joachim Stuck	March-Ford Cosworth	5 points
17	Arturo Merzario	Iso Marlboro-Ford Cosworth	4 points
18	Graham Hill	Lola-Ford Cosworth	1 point
19	Tom Pryce	Token-Ford Cosworth/ Shadow-Ford Cosworth	1 point
20	Vittorio Brambilla	March-Ford Cosworth	1 point

Scoring system: 1st: 9 points; 2nd: 6; 3rd: 4; 4th: 3; 5th: 2; 6th: 1. Best 7 scores from first 8 races, best 6 from remaining 7 races.

1975 Formula One World Championship

1	Niki Lauda	Ferrari	64.5 points
2	Emerson Fittipaldi	McLaren-Ford Cosworth	45 points
3	Carlos Reutemann	Brabham-Ford Cosworth	37 points
4	**James Hunt**	**Hesketh-Ford Cosworth**	**33 points**
5	Clay Regazzoni	Ferrari	25 points
6	Carlos Pace	Brabham-Ford Cosworth	24 points
7	Jody Scheckter	Tyrrell-Ford Cosworth	20 points
8	Jochen Mass	McLaren-Ford Cosworth	20 points
9	Patrick Depailler	Tyrrell-Ford Cosworth	12 points
10	Tom Pryce	Shadow-Ford Cosworth	8 points
11	Vittorio Brambilla	March-Ford Cosworth	6.5 points
12	Jacques Laffite	Williams-Ford Cosworth	6 points
13	Ronnie Peterson	JPS Lotus-Ford Cosworth	6 points
14	Mario Andretti	Parnelli-Ford Cosworth	5 points
15	Mark Donohue	Penske-Ford Cosworth/ March-Ford Cosworth	4 points
16	Jacky Ickx	JPS Lotus-Ford Cosworth	3 points
17	Alan Jones	Hesketh-Ford Cosworth/ Hill-Ford Cosworth	2 points
18	Jean-Pierre Jarier	Shadow-Ford Cosworth/ Shadow-Matra	1.5 points
19	Tony Brise	Williams-Ford Cosworth/ Hill-Ford Cosworth	1 point
20	Gijs van Lennep	Ensign-Ford Cosworth	1 point
21	Lella Lombardi	March-Ford Cosworth/ Williams-Ford Cosworth	0.5 point

Scoring system: 1st: 9 points; 2nd: 6; 3rd: 4; 4th: 3; 5th: 2; 6th: 1. Best 7 scores from first 8 races, best 5 from remaining 6 races.
Half points were awarded in Spain and Austria where the races were stopped early.

1976 Formula One World Championship

1	**James Hunt**	**McLaren–Ford Cosworth**	**69 points**
2	Niki Lauda	Ferrari	68 points
3	Jody Scheckter	Tyrrell–Ford Cosworth	49 points
4	Patrick Depailler	Tyrrell–Ford Cosworth	39 points
5	Clay Regazzoni	Ferrari	31 points
6	Mario Andretti	JPS Lotus–Ford Cosworth/ Parnelli–Ford Cosworth	22 points
7	John Watson	Penske–Ford Cosworth	20 points
8	Jacques Laffite	Ligier–Matra	20 points
9	Jochen Mass	McLaren–Ford Cosworth	19 points
10	Gunnar Nilsson	JPS Lotus–Ford Cosworth	11 points
11	Ronnie Peterson	JPS Lotus–Ford Cosworth/ March–Ford Cosworth	10 points
12	Tom Pryce	Shadow–Ford Cosworth	10 points
13	Hans-Joachim Stuck	March–Ford Cosworth	8 points
14	Carlos Pace	Brabham–Alfa Romeo	7 points
15	Alan Jones	Surtees–Ford Cosworth	7 points
16	Carlos Reutemann	Brabham–Alfa Romeo/ Ferrari	3 points
17	Emerson Fittipaldi	Copersucar–Ford Cosworth	3 points
18	Chris Amon	Ensign–Ford Cosworth/ Wolf Williams–Ford Cosworth	2 points
19	Vittorio Brambilla	March–Ford Cosworth	1 point
20	Rolf Stommelen	Brabham–Alfa Romeo/ Hesketh–Ford Cosworth	1 point

Scoring system: 1st: 9 points; 2nd: 6; 3rd: 4; 4th: 3; 5th: 2; 6th: 1. Best 7 scores from first 8 races, best 7 from remaining 8 races.

1977 Formula One World Championship

1	Niki Lauda	Ferrari	72 points
2	Jody Scheckter	Wolf–Ford Cosworth	55 points
3	Mario Andretti	JPS Lotus–Ford Cosworth	47 points
4	Carlos Reutemann	Ferrari	42 points
5	**James Hunt**	**McLaren–Ford Cosworth**	**40 points**
6	Jochen Mass	McLaren–Ford Cosworth	25 points
7	Alan Jones	Shadow–Ford Cosworth	22 points
8	Gunnar Nilsson	JPS Lotus–Ford Cosworth	20 points
9	Patrick Depailler	Tyrrell–Ford Cosworth	20 points
10	Jacques Laffite	Ligier–Matra	18 points
11	Hans-Joachim Stuck	March–Ford Cosworth/ Brabham–Alfa Romeo	12 points

12	Emerson Fittipaldi	Copersucar-Ford Cosworth	11 points
13	John Watson	Brabham-Alfa Romeo	9 points
14	Ronnie Peterson	Tyrrell-Ford Cosworth	7 points
15	Carlos Pace	Brabham-Alfa Romeo	6 points
16	Vittorio Brambilla	Surtees-Ford Cosworth	
17	Clay Regazzoni	Ensign-Ford Cosworth	5 points
18	Patrick Tambay	Surtees-Ford Cosworth/	
		Ensign-Ford Cosworth	5 points
19	Jean-Pierre Jarier	Penske-Ford Cosworth/	
		Shadow-Ford Cosworth/	
		Ligier-Matra	1 point
20	Riccardo Patrese	Shadow-Ford Cosworth	1 point
21	Renzo Zorzi	Shadow-Ford Cosworth	1 point

Scoring system: 1st: 9 points; 2nd: 6; 3rd: 4; 4th: 3; 5th: 2; 6th: 1. Best 8 scores from first 9 races, best 7 from remaining 8 races.

1978 Formula One World Championship

1	Mario Andretti	JPS Lotus-Ford Cosworth	64 points
2	Ronnie Peterson	Lotus-Ford Cosworth	51 points
3	Carlos Reutemann	Ferrari	48 points
4	Niki Lauda	Brabham-Alfa Romeo	44 points
5	Patrick Depailler	Tyrrell-Ford Cosworth	34 points
6	John Watson	Brabham-Alfa Romeo	25 points
7	Jody Scheckter	Wolf-Ford Cosworth	24 points
8	Jacques Laffite	Ligier-Matra	19 points
9	Gilles Villeneuve	Ferrari	17 points
10	Emerson Fittipaldi	Copersucar-Ford Cosworth	17 points
11	Alan Jones	Williams-Ford Cosworth	11 points
12	Riccardo Patrese	Arrows-Ford Cosworth	11 points
13	**James Hunt**	**McLaren-Ford Cosworth**	**8 points**
14	Patrick Tambay	McLaren-Ford Cosworth	8 points
15	Didier Pironi	Tyrrell-Ford Cosworth	7 points
16	Clay Regazzoni	Shadow-Ford Cosworth	4 points
17	Jean-Pierre Jabouille	Renault	3 points
18	Hans-Joachim Stuck	Shadow-Ford Cosworth	2 points
19	Vittorio Brambilla	Surtees-Ford Cosworth	1 point
20	Derek Daly	Hesketh-Ford Cosworth/	
		Ensign-Ford Cosworth	1 point
21	Hector Rebaque	Lotus-Ford Cosworth	1 point

Scoring system: 1st: 9 points; 2nd: 6; 3rd: 4; 4th: 3; 5th: 2; 6th: 1. Best 7 scores from first 8 races, best 7 from remaining 8 races.

APPENDIX IX

1975 to 1977 Formula One Wins by Season

James Hunt spent 13 years as a race car driver from 1967 to 1979. It was a relatively short career by modern standards, when drivers can usually expect 19 years at the wheel before retirement. But he didn't discover motor racing until he was 18 and was too old for go-karting, which is where virtually every driver starts their career. When he got to Formula One, he was immediately accomplished and immediately competitive. Strangely, he performed better at the very highest level of the sport than he did in any other formulae. He spent three of his seven years in Formula One in uncompetitive cars and most of his success was achieved in just two years, 1976 and 1977.

1975 Hesketh–Ford Cosworth V8: one win
The most important win in James Hunt's career was the first win, and it made Hesketh racing a team that would never be forgotten. The win was made all the more memorable because the car was a dog and only became a winner because of Hunt's driving skills.

1976 McLaren–Ford Cosworth V8: six wins
In fact, it was seven wins after the British GP victory was taken away from him. In the end that didn't matter, as the dominant driver won the world championship in a car that was effectively obsolete. His one-point victory understated the superb performances he put in to beat a dominant Ferrari team.

1977 McLaren–Ford Cosworth V8: three wins
If only the team had stuck to its M23 model car and shelved the M28, Hunt could have won the championship again. But somehow Hunt took the unloved M28 to three race victories. It was a demonstration of mind over matter and a driver at the top of his form.

APPENDIX X
1975 to 1977
10 Formula One Wins

James Hunt had an even bigger problem with winning races, a problem he was very happy to talk about. His first win should have been in 1973 at the very last race of the year in the United States at Watkins Glen. He had a superior car and a tyre advantage but he wasn't psychologically equipped to do it. In truth, his first win in his third year of racing, in 1975, was fortuitous when the trye and weather conditions favoured him. But it gave him the taste for winning, and when he got to McLaren he was able to win frequently – ten times in all. But all his wins came in two of his seven years of racing. But it only happened after he had convinced himself he could do it.

1. 1975 Dutch Grand Prix: Zandvoort, 75 laps in 1h 46m 57.40s
Second: Niki Lauda, Ferrari, +1.06s
Third: Clay Regazzoni, Ferrari, +55.06s
Zandvoort's fluid, high-speed design suited the Ferraris perfectly. When it started raining before the start, Horsley knew the team had a chance from its third grid position. He looked up at the sky and saw a tiny patch of clear sky. Just as the mechanics had been about to change the dry weather set-up on the car, Horsley ordered that they leave it, believing the weather would clear up. Hunt started with wet grooved tyres and a dry set up – a severe disadvantage – while the rest of the grid did the opposite. Horsley told Hunt that the moment the track began to dry, he was to come into the pits to change to slick racing tyres. Hunt dropped down to 19th in the 22-car field. But as soon as all the others were forced to stop for dry tyres, the difference was crucial, as Hunt steeled himself and got right on the Ferrari's tail. On the 14th lap, Hunt took the lead. His tactics worked and Hunt crossed the line on the 75th lap – just one second ahead.

2. 1976 Spanish Grand Prix: Jarama, 75 laps in 1h 42m 20.43s
Second: Niki Lauda, Ferrari, +30.97s
Third: Gunnar Nilsson, Lotus, +48.02s
The start was delayed while King Juan Carlos, a keen Formula One fan, arrived in his helicopter. Once again, Hunt, fearful of his clutch, was slow to get away from the start while Lauda, high on painkillers, stormed into the lead for the first 31 laps. Hunt was again beaten off the line. But Lauda could feel his broken jagged rib-ends grinding together under the G-forces in hard cornering and, as the pain-killers wore off, he had increased difficulty controlling the car. Hunt was content to play a waiting game, knowing that Lauda's ribs simply wouldn't let him continue

at that pace for the entire race. Hunt recalled later: "Niki was motoring hard at the start and I was able to tuck in behind quite comfortably. I couldn't do anything about passing him, it was just a case of waiting until his ribs started to hurt and I'd be able to nip through." And so it proved, as Hunt went past on lap 32, followed by Mass a few laps later. Mass' engine failed with a few laps to go and Hunt crossed the line to take his first Grand Prix victory for McLaren. Lauda crawled in for second place, 31 seconds behind and in agony.

3. 1976 France Grand Prix: Paul Ricard, 54 laps in 1h 40m 58.60s
Second: Patrick Depailler, Tyrrell, +12.70s
Third: John Watson, Penske, +23.55s
Niki Lauda made the best of the start and disappeared into the distance. Hunt bided his time in second and started to close the gap gradually. On the eighth lap, Lauda coasted to a halt with a broken crankshaft. Eleven laps later, Regazzoni's Ferrari suffered its own crankshaft failure. Hunt led comfortably from Depailler in the Tyrrell-Ford but, by lap 40, Hunt began to feel ill and was sick inside his helmet. He barely made it to the chequered flag, with Depailler 12 seconds behind in second place. John Watson came home third.

4. 1976 German Grand Prix: Nürburgring, 14 laps in 1h 41m 42.70s
Second: Jody Scheckter, Tyrrell, +27.70s
Third: Jochen Mass, McLaren, +52.40s
Jochen Mass had made the right choice of tyres, established a big lead and was certain to win the race, but, after the restart, James
Hunt cleared his mind of everything but the task at hand and streaked into a lead that remained unthreatened. He called his first lap "probably the most aggressive piece of driving I did all year. I was absolutely determined to get as big a lead as possible, and everything turned out right." He was ten seconds clear at the end of the first restarted lap and was followed home by Jody Scheckter's Tyrrell-Ford, with Mass coming in third. He was half a minute ahead of Scheckter and called the victory: "One of my most satisfying drives."

5. 1976 Dutch Grand Prix: Zandvoort, 75 laps in 1h 44m 52.09s
Second: Clay Regazzoni, Ferrari, +0.92s
Third: Mario Andretti, Lotus, +2.09s
As usual, James Hunt botched his start, spinning his wheels and letting Ronnie Peterson pull away in the lead. To add to the ignominy, John Watson came through from the second row and overtook Hunt at the end of the pit straight in full view of everyone. Hunt bided his time in third as Peterson and Watson scrapped for the lead. His McLaren was understeering again as a braking air scoop worked loose. Despite that, Hunt overtook Watson on lap seven and Peterson for the lead on lap 12. Afterwards, he said he simply took advantage of mistakes by both drivers. Hunt had to drive as hard as ever to block Watson from getting past. In terms of car handling, the Ulsterman was easily faster, but Hunt was simply better at blocking

than Watson was at overtaking. In the end it didn't matter, as Watson coasted to a halt on lap 47 when his gearbox broke. Watson's demise was a signal for Clay Regazzoni to take up the chase in the lone Ferrari entered in the race. Hunt got in a panic because he feared Regazzoni might have instructions to punt him off if he couldn't get past. By the end, Hunt won the race barely a car's length ahead of the Ferrari.

6. 1976 Canadian Grand Prix: Mosport Park, 80 laps in 1h 40m 9.626s
Second: Patrick Depailler, Tyrrell, +6.331s
Third: Mario Andretti, Lotus, +10.366s
James Hunt was left behind at the start, bested by Ronnie Peterson, and for eight laps he trailed the Swede before moving into the lead. A few laps later, Depailler in the six-wheeled Tyrrell, nosed through into second place and moved closer to the McLaren. The Grand Prix had been enlivened by the duel between the two drivers, but in the closing laps Depailler began to drop back inexplicably and there were six seconds between them at the finish. It turned out that petrol fumes had been leaking into his Tyrrell cockpit, leaving Depailler feeling intoxicated in the last few laps. He said he felt as though he had consumed a bottle of whisky. The padded lining of his helmet was wet with fuel. But it was worse for Niki Lauda, who had fought an ill-handling car with a rear suspension problem for the whole race and could only manage eighth. He scored no points, a disaster for him.

7. 1976 USA East Grand Prix: Watkins Glen, 59 laps in 1h 42m 40.741s
Second: Jody Scheckter, Tyrrell, +8.030s
Third: Niki Lauda, Ferrari, +1m 02.324s
James Hunt was on pole eight times during 1976, but he had only led one first lap and this day would prove no exception. He was not good enough to prevent Jody Scheckter taking the lead. And that is how it stayed for many laps, with Hunt in station some three seconds behind him. Behind them was third place man Niki Lauda, five seconds back. But Hunt knew he had to win and started focusing hard on the physical act of driving the car, something which he confessed afterwards he did not often do. He called it a "self-administered driving lesson." On lap 36, Scheckter was delayed by another car slowing for a tight corner, and Hunt tucked his McLaren in behind the Tyrrell's rear wing. As they accelerated down the straight, Hunt darted out of Scheckter's slipstream and took the lead. But four laps later, Scheckter got in front again as they were lapping back markers: "Jody blasted past me on the straight. I really thought I'd blown it."
Within a lap, he was again within striking range. For several laps he waited to pounce and, finally, with 12 laps to go, Hunt forced his way alongside the Tyrrell coming into a slow corner. Hunt went across the line eight seconds ahead of Scheckter, and Lauda came in a minute behind in third.

8. 1977 British Grand Prix: Silverstone, 68 laps in 1h 31m 46.06s
Second: Niki Lauda, Ferrari, +18.31s
Third: Gunnar Nilsson, Lotus, +19.57s

SHUNT

James Hunt had trouble with his clutch on the start line and John Watson got ahead and stayed in the lead for 60 of the 68 laps. Then his car started to suffer from fuel starvation and he retired. Hunt inherited an easy lead and crossed the chequered flag in first place, cheered on by ecstatic British fans. It was his first victory of 1977. Afterwards, Hunt admitted that for the second race in succession Watson was the fastest man in Formula One. He said: "It was cruel luck and I really felt sorry for him." But, he added with a twinkle: "I was still very happy to see him go." The race was also marked by the Formula One debut of Canadian Gilles Villeneuve. Hunt had been directly responsible for putting Villeneuve into Formula One and the McLaren team. Villeneuve, driving Hunt's old M23, looked as though he would finish fourth in his first race. But a faulty engine temperature gauge meant an unnecessary pit stop after which he was 11th, where he stayed to the finish. Hunt was once again on top of the world and thought a good end-of-season run could still deliver him the world championship.

9. 1977 USA East Grand Prix: Watkins Glen, 59 laps in 1h 58m 23.267s
Second: Mario Andretti, Lotus, +2.026s
Third: Jody Scheckter, Wolf, +1m 18.679s
100,000 American fans poured into the circuit to see if Mario Andretti could win the race and if Lauda could clinch the championship, but James Hunt dominated the race on a favourite circuit as Niki Lauda just drove for points in his Ferrari. Andretti was well behind as the race drew to a close, but he drove the last laps like a demon. At the start of the penultimate lap, Andretti and Hunt were 6.5 seconds apart. At the start of the last lap, it was 1.5 seconds. Andretti had driven a lap five seconds faster than Hunt. That woke up Hunt, and in the end he cruised in over the line some two and a half seconds clear. As expected, Niki Lauda's fourth place was enough to see him crowned world champion for the second time. Lauda had only won three races all year but picked up six second-places along the way. In the absence of a dominant driver, Lauda's consistency won him the championship. In truth, Andretti, Reutemann, Watson, Scheckter or Hunt could just as easily have been champion had things gone their way.

10. 1977 Japanese Grand Prix: Fuji, 73 laps in 1h 31m 51.68s
Second: Carlos Reutemann, Ferrari, +1m 02.45s
Third: Patrick Depailler, Tyrrell, +1m 06.39s
Mario Andretti, by now the dominant driver in Formula One, was easily on pole position and James Hunt was once again second on the grid. The race would be between these two. But Andretti did not even last the first lap and Hunt drove an uneventful race to victory, leading from start to finish. Carlos Reutemann was second over a minute behind, and Patrick Depailler third. But the race was almost stopped when Gilles Villeneuve's Ferrari ran into Ronnie Peterson's Tyrrell-Ford and took off into a spectator's enclosure, killing two of them. It was a huge incident and there was little celebrating on the podium thereafter. The incident also caused the cancellation of the following year's race.

744

APPENDIX XI
1976 to 1977 Formula One Pole Positions by Season

1976 McLaren-Ford Cosworth V8 8 poles

James Hunt scored his first ever pole position in his first ever race for his new team at Interlagos and then went onto score another seven during the season. This performance mightily impressed team principal Teddy Mayer, who was minded to say: "I would say of all the drivers we've had, James has the greatest natural talent – by far, in fact. Possibly he makes more mistakes than, say, Emerson Fittipaldi but he certainly is quicker than Emerson ever was when he drove for us and I think James is as consistently fast a driver as anyone I've ever seen."

1977 McLaren-Ford Cosworth V8 6 poles

James Hunt had a lousy season in terms of reliability and race wins, but if the season had been decided on pole positions, he would have been champion again with six results to his name. His performance in 1977 was even more significant because he was driving, for the most part, a much less competitive car.

APPENDIX XII
1976 to 1977
14 Formula One Pole Positions

James Hunt proved all his qualifying detractors wrong when he went to McLaren in 1976. He had never scored a pole position before, and had only been on the first row twice and the second row five times. Considering how fast he was, particularly when he had the Firestone tyre advantage in 1973 and 1974, it was a poor performance. But all that changed at McLaren, when he planted his car on pole first time out in the dying minutes of qualifying. He scored a further eight poles that year out of 16 races and went on to take six poles in 1977 in a much less competitive car, and 14 in his career.

1. 1976 Brazilian Grand Prix: Interlagos   Gap: 0.02s
James Hunt knew he was in trouble if he qualified behind teammate Jochen Mass, so he couldn't have been more motivated to succeed. As he left the pit lane for his warm up lap, there were 20 minutes left in the session. In an extraordinary few minutes, Hunt landed pole on his first flying lap with a guessed set-up and a newly-rebuilt Ford Cosworth engine. He said: "It was my first-ever pole, which I was rather pleased about." The lap was arguably the most important of Hunt's career. Hunt had established undoubted number one status and felt it was one of the greatest days in his motor sport career.

2. 1976 South African Grand Prix: Kyalami   Gap: 0.10s
If James Hunt could do it once, he could do it again – and this time with no drama. It was a repeat of Interlagos and Hunt, now totally comfortable with his car and his team, effortlessly took pole once again alongside Niki Lauda on the front row of the grid. Alastair Caldwell and the McLaren mechanics were in awe of their new driver. It impressed everyone and demoralised Jochen Mass. Hunt was very much number one driver in the team.

3. 1976 Spanish Grand Prix: Jarama   Gap: 0.32s
The weekend began well, with James Hunt grabbing pole three-tenths of a second faster than Lauda in the Ferrari beside him. It was Hunt's third pole in four races. Mass was third as the two McLarens sandwiched Lauda's Ferrari on the front row of the starting grid. The Austrian, with Willy Dungl in attendance, seemed unaffected by the painful injury he had sustained when he damaged his ribs in a tractor accident a few days earlier.

4. 1976 France Grand Prix: Paul Ricard   Gap: 0.28s

In the first qualifying session, James Hunt was second fastest to Carlos Pace's Brabham-Alfa Romeo. In the second session, he was fastest ahead of Niki Lauda's Ferrari. The times were the fastest of qualifying and were carried through a slower final session to put Hunt on pole position. Ferrari was caught out, as it had been increasing the rev limit of its new engine in every session. Without that, Lauda and Regazzoni would undoubtedly have been sharing the front row. They also might have had some prior notice of the problems they would encounter the following day.

5. 1976 German Grand Prix: Nürburgring   Gap: 0.90s

When qualifying ended on Saturday afternoon, James Hunt was on pole position. Niki Lauda, with safety on his mind, admitted he was not driving as fast as he could. He was second on the grid and only a second slower than Hunt; over a seven minute lap, it was ridiculously close. Lauda summed it up: "My personal opinion is that the Nürburgring is just too dangerous to drive on nowadays." He would be proved right the following day.

6. 1976 Austrian Grand Prix: Österreichring   Gap: 0.82s

Despite the heat elsewhere in Europe, it rained for both qualifying days and, because the land was so dry, the water rolled off the hills and gathered in pools behind the circuit. But none of it affected James Hunt, who turned in a time that gave him his easiest pole position yet. The fast circuit suited him and his car perfectly. He would later set a new lap record at an average speed of 137.83 miles per hour.

7. 1976 Canadian Grand Prix: Mosport Park   Gap: 0.394s

Qualifying was fought out between James Hunt's McLaren-Ford and Ronnie Peterson's March-Ford. Peterson was now back on form. But that didn't stop Hunt taking pole position again, four-tenths of a second clear of Peterson; a huge margin. Vittorio Brambilla, also in a March-Ford, and Patrick Depailler's Tyrrell were on the second row. Lauda was only sixth fastest alongside an increasingly on-form Mario Andretti in a Lotus-Ford.

8. 1976 USA East Grand Prix: Watkins Glen   Gap: 0.248s

On track qualifying was uneventful round the 3.3-mile circuit, and for the eighth time in the season James Hunt seized pole position. This time he had Jody Scheckter alongside him in the six-wheel Tyrrell, which was proving very effective in its debut season.

9. 1977 Argentinian Grand Prix: Burnos Aires   Gap: 0.28s

As the 1977 season opened, James Hunt seemed to carry on where he had left off three months earlier: he was second fastest to Depailler's Tyrrell-Ford in the opening session of practice; fastest in the afternoon session; and faster still the following day, taking pole position – the ninth of his career. John Watson put himself alongside

Hunt on the front row of the grid in his first race with his new Brabham-Alfa Romeo. Surprisingly, Scheckter was a disappointing eleventh and Lauda fourth.

10. 1977 Brazilian Grand Prix: Interlagos   Gap: 0.07s
In the first session, James Hunt was really unwell and in no fit state to drive the car. By the final qualifying the following day, he had recovered and managed to secure pole position for the first race of the year. The McLaren-Ford, suited to long straights and fast bends, easily looked the best car on the São Paulo track.

11. 1977 South African Grand Prix: Kyalami   Gap: 0.05s
As if to emphasise his point, James Hunt scored yet another pole position; it was his third in a row in the old McLaren-Ford M23. Carlos Pace was second and Lauda third fastest, with Patrick Depailler making up the second row of the grid in fourth slot.

12. 1977 British Grand Prix: Silverstone   Gap: 0.28s
James Hunt had 30,000 cheering fans on the Saturday of qualifying, and he put his McLaren-Ford M26 on pole position for the first time. Inevitably, John Watson was alongside him in the Brabham-Alfa Romeo, and Niki Lauda lurked just behind them, with Scheckter fourth. Andretti was nowhere on a track where grip was not particularly at a premium. Jabouille qualified the turbo Renault 16th and impressed no one.

13. 1977 Italian Grand Prix: Monza   Gap: 0.07s
At Monza, after a supreme effort, Hunt put his car on pole in the final minute of qualifying, beating back Carlos Reutemann's Ferrari much to the chagrin of the partisan local crowd. It didn't receive any publicity but it was a supreme effort, as third on the grid Jody Scheckter would readily testify. He was nowhere near this battle.

14. 1977 USA East Grand Prix: Watkins Glen   Gap: 0.275s
James Hunt tried his very best right to the end of the 1977 season and wrung the neck of his McLaren-Ford M26 at Watkins Glen and put it on pole, beating out the ultra-quick pair of Brabham-Alfa Romeos of John Watson and the resurgent Hans Stuck who, aware his drive was up for grabs in 1978, was trying to impress the boss.

APPENDIX XIII
Top Pole Scorers of all Time

1	Michael Schumacher	68★
2	Ayrton Senna	65
3	Jim Clark	33
=	Alain Prost	33
5	Nigel Mansell	32
6	Juan Manuel Fangio	29
7	Mika Häkkinen	26
8	Niki Lauda	24
=	Nelson Piquet	24
10	Damon Hill	20
11	Fernando Alonso	19★
12	Mario Andretti	18
=	René Arnoux	18
=	Lewis Hamilton	18★
15	Jackie Stewart	17
16	Stirling Moss	16
=	Kimi Räikkönen	16
18	Felipe Massa	15★
19	Alberto Ascari	14
=	**James Hunt**	**14**
=	Ronnie Peterson	14
=	Rubens Barrichello	14

★Up to and including the 2010 Italian Grand Prix

APPENDIX XIV
Top Race Winners of All Time

1	Michael Schumacher	91★
2	Alain Prost	51
3	Ayrton Senna	41
4	Nigel Mansell	31
5	Jackie Stewart	27
6	Jim Clark	25
=	Niki Lauda	25
8	Juan Manuel Fangio	24
=	Fernando Alonso	24★
10	Nelson Piquet	23
11	Damon Hill	22
12	Mika Häkkinen	20
13	Kimi Räikkönen	18
14	Stirling Moss	16
15	Graham Hill	14
=	Jack Brabham	14
=	Emerson Fittipaldi	14
=	Lewis Hamilton	14★
19	Alberto Ascari	13
=	David Coulthard	13
21	Mario Andretti	12
=	Carlos Reutemann	12
=	Alan Jones	12
24	Jacques Villeneuve	11
=	Felipe Massa	11★
=	Rubens Barrichello	11★
27	**James Hunt**	**10**
=	Ronnie Peterson	10
=	Jody Scheckter	10
=	Gerhard Berger	10

★Up to and including the 2010 Italian Grand Prix

APPENDIX XV

James Hunt's Formula One Cars
1973 - 1979

March 731

Engine	Ford Cosworth DFV, 3 litre, 90° V8
Tyres	Firestone
Principal designers	Robin Herd/ Harvey Postlethwaite
Chassis	Aluminium monocoque
Gearbox	Hewland FG 400
Fuel/ Oil	Fina/ ?
Wheelbase	2438 mm
Track	Front : 1448 mm
	Rear : 1448 mm
Dry weight	576 kg
Power	460 bhp @ 10,500 rpm
Raced	1973 to 1974 (9 races + 1 practice only)

Hesketh 308

Engine	Ford Cosworth DFV, 3 litre, 90° V8
Tyres	Firestone
Principal designer	Harvey Postlethwaite
Chassis	Aluminium monocoque
Gearbox	Hewland FG 400
Fuel/ Oil	Shell/ Duckhams
Wheelbase	2540 mm
Track	Front : 1473 mm
	Rear : 1549 mm
Dry weight	589 kg
Power	465 bhp @ 10,500 rpm
Raced	1974 (13 races)

Hesketh 308B

Engine	Ford Cosworth DFV, 3 litre, 90° V8
Tyres	Goodyear
Principal designer	Harvey Postlethwaite
Chassis	Aluminium monocoque
Gearbox	Hewland FG 400
Fuel/ Oil	?/ Duckhams
Wheelbase	2540 mm

Track	Front : 1473 mm
	Rear : 1549 mm
Dry weight	589 kg
Power	485 bhp @ 10,600 rpm
Raced	1975 (12 races + 1 practice only)

Hesketh 308C

Engine	Ford Cosworth DFV, 3 litre, 90° V8
Tyres	Goodyear
Principal designers	Harvey Postlethwaite
Chassis	Aluminium monocoque
Gearbox	Hewland FGA 400
Fuel/ Oil	Fina /Duckhams
Wheelbase	2565 mm 99 in
Track	Front : 1397 mm
	Rear : 1422 mm
Dry weight	580 kg
Power	485 bhp @ 10,600 rpm
Raced	1975 (2 races)

McLaren M23

Engine	Ford Cosworth DFV, 3 litre, 90° V8
Tyres	Goodyear
Principal designer	Gordon Coppuck
Chassis	Aluminium monocoque
Gearbox	Hewland DG 400
Fuel/ Oil	Texaco
Wheelbase	2743 mm
Track	Front : 1651 mm
	Rear : 1626 mm
Dry weight	595 kg
Power	485 bhp @ 10,600 rpm
Raced	1976 to 77 (21 races + 1 practice only)

McLaren M26/M26E

Engine	Ford Cosworth DFV, 3 litre, 90° V8
Tyres	Goodyear
Principal designer	Gordon Coppuck
Chassis	Aluminium monocoque
Gearbox	Hewland DG 400
Fuel/ Oil	Texaco
Wheelbase	2743 mm
Track	Front : 1600 mm
	Rear : 1626 mm

APPENDIX XV

Dry weight	589 kg
Power	485 bhp @ 10,600 rpm
Raced	1977 to 1978 (28 races)

Wolf WR7/WR8

Engine	Ford Cosworth DFV, 3 litre, 90° V8
Tyres	Goodyear
Principal designer	Harvey Postlethwaite
Chassis	Aluminium monocoque
Gearbox	Hewland FGA 400
Fuel/ Oil	Texaco
Wheelbase	2667 mm
Track	Front : 1626 mm
	Rear : 1626 mm
Dry weight	585 kg
Power	485 bhp @ 10,600 rpm
Raced	1979 (7 races + 1 practice only)

Bibliography

Amburn, Ellis, *Elizabeth Taylor: The Obsessions, Passions and Courage of a Hollywood Legend (*Robson Books) 2000 Hardback 352 pages ISBN 1 86105 369 X

Benson, David, *Grand Prix Season 1976: Hunt v Lauda* (Beaverbrook Newspapers Ltd) 1976 Paperback 143 pages

Bragg, Melvyn, *Rich: The Life of Richard Burton* (Hodder & Stoughton) 1988 Hardback 533 pages ISBN 0 340 40537 6

Collings, Timothy, *The Piranha Club* (Virgin Books) 2001 Hardback 328 pages ISBN 1 85227 907 9

Donaldson, Gerald, *James Hunt: The Biography* (Collins Willow) 1994 Hardback 319 pages ISBN 0 00 218468 0

Ferris, Paul, *Richard Burton* (George Weidenfeld and Nicolson Ltd) 1981 Hardback 212 pages ISBN 0 297 77966 4

Hamilton, Maurice, *Ken Tyrrell – The Authorised Biography* (Collins Willow) 2002 Hardback 360 pages ISBN 0 00 714376 1

Hayhoe, David & Holland, David, *Grand Prix Data Book* (Haynes Publishing) 2006 Hardback 744 pages ISBN 1 84425 223 X

Heyman, C. David, *Liz – An Intimate Biography of Elizabeth Taylor* (William Heinemann) 1995 Hardback 516 pages ISBN 0 434 32938 X

Hill, Tim, *Formula One – Unseen Archives* (Atlantic Publishing/Parragon) 2001 Hardback 384 pages ISBN 0 75257 046 3

Hilton, Christopher, *James Hunt – Portrait of a Champion* (Patrick Stephens Ltd) 1993 Paperback 176 pages ISBN 1 85260 470 0

Hilton, Christopher, *Memories of James Hunt* (Haynes Publishing) 2006 Hardback 160 Pages ISBN 1 84425 215 9

Hilton, Christopher, *Murray Walker – The Very Last Word* (Haynes Publishing) 2002 Paperback 208 pages ISBN 1 85960 896 7

Hilton, Christopher, *Murray Walker – The Last Word* (Haynes) 2001 Hardback 144 pages ISBN 1 85960 851 5

Hotten, Russell, *Formula One – The People, Money and Profits that Power the World's Richest Sport* (Orion Business) 1999 Paperback 300 pages ISBN 0 75283 087 2

Jenkins, Graham, *Richard Burton, My Brother* (Michael Joseph Ltd) 1988 Hardback 247 pages ISBN 0 7181 3010 3

Junor, Penny, *Burton: The Man Behind the Myth* (Sidgwick & Jackson Ltd) 1985 Hardback 210 pages ISBN 0 283 99104 6

Kelley, Kitty, *Elizabeth Taylor: The Last Star* (Michael Joseph) 1981 Hardback 346 pages ISBN 0 7181 2075 2

Kerr, Phil, *To Finish First* (MRP Publishing) 2007 Hardback 384 pages
ISBN 978 1 899870 81 3

Lauda, Niki & Volker, Herbert, *To Hell and Back, An Autobiography* (Stanley Paul & Co. Ltd)
1986 Hardback 208 pages ISBN 0 09 164240 X

Lawrence, Mike, *Colin Chapman: Wayward Genius* (Breedon Books) 2002
Hardback 255 pages ISBN 1 85983 278 4

Lawrence, Mike, *March – The Rise and Fall of a Motor Racing Legend* (MRP Publishing)
2001 Hardback 272 pages ISBN 1 899870 54 7

Maddox, Brenda, *Who's Afraid of Elizabeth Taylor?* (Granada Publishing)
1977 Hardback 256 pages ISBN 0 246 10916 5

Mansell, Nigel, *My Autobiography* (HarperCollins)
1995 Hardback 351 pages ISBN 0 00 218497 4

Morrien, Alissa, *Nieuwe Revu Magazine,* Issue 27, 8th July 1977

Nye, Doug, *McLaren – The Grand Prix, Can-Am and Indy Cars* (Osprey)
1984 Hardback 309 pages ISBN 0 905138 54 6

Ramirez, Jo, *Jo Ramirez – Memoirs of a Racing Man* (Haynes)
2005 Hardback 352 pages ISBN 1 84425 238 8

Roebuck, Nigel, *Chasing the Title* (Haynes Publishing)
1999 Hardback 304 pages ISBN 1 85960 604 0

Rubython, Tom, *The Life of Senna* (BusinessF1 Books)
2004 Hardback 204 pages ISBN 0 9546857 3 3

Spoto, Donald, *Elizabeth Taylor* (Little, Brown and Company)
1995 Hardback 401 pages ISBN 0 316 91451 7

Stewart, Jackie, *The Autobiography – Winning is Not Enough* (Headline Publishing
Group) 2007 Hardback 548 pages ISBN 978 0 7553 1537 6

Tipler, Johnny, *Ronnie Peterson – Formula 1 – Super Swede* (Coterie Press)
2003 Hardback 231 pages ISBN 1 902351 07 X

Wheatcroft, Tom, *Thunder in the Park* (Live Wire Books)
2005 Hardback 280 pages ISBN 0 9542860 5 7

Walker, Alexander, *Elizabeth* (Weidenfeld & Nicolson)
1990 Hardback 423 pages ISBN 0 297 81079 0

Walker, Murray, *My Autobiography – Unless I'm Very Much Mistaken* (Collins Willow)
2002 Hardback 393 pages ISBN 0 00 712696 4

Young, Eoin, *James Hunt – Against All Odds* (Hamlyn Publishing Group)
1977 Hardback 176 pages ISBN 0 600 35250 1

Index

INDEX

INDEX

Pembrokeshire, UK 42
Penske 200, 201, 350, 369
Penske-Ford 350, 400
Penthouse 513
Perkins, Anthony 227
Perkins, Larry 405
Peterson, Barbro 520
Peterson, Ronnie 94, 125, 148, 151, 165, 172, 177,
178, 181, 182, 198, 201, 192, 195, 219, 248,
248, 249, 265, 282, 339, 351, 353, 354, 374,
383, 401, 461, 486, 490, 491, 497, 498, 500,
508, 512, 514, 519, 520, 521, 523, 524, 525,
527, 531, 534, 535, 539, 544, 550, 601, 645,
682
Pettet, Joanna 210
Philip Morris 170, 244, 266, 269, 271, 272, 273, 275,
276, 277, 352, 411, 415, 416, 417, 422, 424,
425, 428, 430, 431, 495, 698
Phillips, Ian 111, 118, 132, 152, 154, 157, 173, 211,
443, 477, 466, 609, 625, 643, 663, 699
Phipps, David 153, 419
Phipps, Priscilla 153
Piedale, Domingos 270
Piggot, Lester 461
Pincus, George 85
Piquet, Nelson 77, 541, 549, 552, 603
Pironi, Didier 541, 558
Playboy 210, 513
Plymouth Theatre 226
Pook, Chris 471, 501
Porsche 139, 183, 207, 245, 447, 616
Port Au Prince, Haiti 236, 240
Portrait of a Champion 700
Postlethwaite, Harvey 170, 171, 185, 186, 188, 189,
244, 257, 258, 266, 312, 546, 543, 549, 552,
553, 555, 566, 699
President Nixon 188
President Sadat 187
Presidente Medici Grand Prix 194
Presley, Elvis 210
Prince Alfonso of Hohenlohe-Langenburg 209
Prince Rainier 502, 503
Prost, Alain 5, 241, 583, 603, 610, 698
Pryce, Tom 198, 249, 255, 372, 373, 401, 467, 469,
471, 480
Puerto Vallarta, Mexico 238
Punjabi Times 230
Purley, David 178

R

Radley College 28
Rahal, Bobby 515
Raikkonen, Kimi 699
Ramirez, Jo 181
Rantzen, Esther 78
Reading, UK 270
Reagan, Ronald 623
Redman, Brian 150
Rees, Alan 126, 128
Regazzoni, Clay 191, 193, 198, 199, 200, 201, 202,
248, 251, 252, 257, 288, 296, 297, 306, 307,
313, 323, 324, 326, 328, 329, 336, 350, 355,
369, 375, 400, 401, 408, 411, 461, 502, 541,
552, 555, 556, 586, 616, 645
Reininghaus, Mariella von 292

Renault 475, 500, 525, 541, 555, 556
Reutemann, Carlos 150, 181, 195, 200, 201, 202, 248,
256, 257, 266, 309, 338, 344,366, 375, 461,
462, 470, 482, 486, 498, 499, 501, 502, 531,
541, 546, 547, 549
Revson, Peter 177, 180, 182, 192
Rich, Taormina 35, 50, 441, 632, 639, 695
Richardson, John 47, 54, 420, 516, 602, 698
Richardson, Mary 420, 421, 422
Ridge, Christopher 40
Ridge, Simon 47, 49
Rieck, Peter 100, 695
Rindt, Jochen 103, 140, 181, 294, 333, 424, 530
Rindt, Nina 294
Rivers, Alan 174
Robertson, General 24
Robertson, Liz 241
Roebuck, Nigel 12, 132, 410, 476, 547, 610, 639, 662,
672, 674, 700
Rolls Royce 139, 169, 152, 155, 197, 254, 429, 523,
524, 532
Rommel, General 23
Rosberg, Keke 500, 555, 556, 557
Rose Bearings 86, 87, 105
Rothmans cigarettes 32, 150, 276, 549
Rouen, France 101, 102
Rowe, Pam 419
Rowe, Pamela 699
Royal Albert Hall 175
Royal Automobile Club 54, 119, 120, 109, 314, 328,
426
Royal Gurkha Regiment 696
Royal Lancaster Hotel 96
Royal Marsden Hospital 51
Royal Scots Greys 593
Royal Swedish Automobile Club 537
Ryan, Dave 290

S

South African Broadcasting Corporation (SABC) 544
Salazar, Eliseo 596
Salomon, Jean-Luc 102
Salzburg, Austria 150, 298, 301
Sandhurst 21, 593
São Paulo 152, 154, 194, 225, 282, 283, 288, 465
São Paulo Times 465
Scheckter, Jody 110, 150, 151, 165, 176, 180, 191,
198, 199, 201, 202, 247, 248, 250, 251, 255,
257, 306, 307, 309, 310, 342, 351, 354, 387,
388, 400, 461, 464, 472, 474, 476, 482, 504,
506, 511, 526, 536, 542, 545, 556, 570, 580,
593, 603, 670
Schenken, Tim 89, 94
Schmidt, Gunter 495
Schumacher, Michael 5, 610, 698
Schuppan, Vern 165, 197
Scott, Mark 290
Sears, Jack 121
Segal, Abe 232, 499, 545
Sellers, Peter 210
Senna, Ayrton 504, 610, 670, 673, 698
Servoz-Gavin, Johnny 307
Sexton, Dave 173
Shadow-Ford 192, 198, 247, 249, 252, 255, 467
Shaffer, Peter 226

INDEX